UNIX®

TEXT PROCESSING

UNIX®
TEXT PROCESSING

DALE DOUGHERTY AND TIM O'REILLY

and the staff of O'Reilly & Associates, Inc.

CONSULTING EDITORS:

Stephen G. Kochan and Patrick H. Wood

HAYDEN BOOKS

A Division of Howard W. Sams & Company
4300 West 62nd Street
Indianapolis, Indiana 46268 USA

International Standard Book Number: 0-672-46291-5
Library of Congress Catalog Card Number: 87-60537

Acquisitions Editor: *Therese Zak*
Editor: *Susan Pink Bussiere*
Cover: *Visual Graphic Services, Indianapolis*
       Design by Jerry Bates
       Illustration by Patrick Sarles
Typesetting: *O'Reilly & Associates, Inc.*

Printed in the United States of America

Trademark Acknowledgements

C O N T E N T S

Preface   xi

1 **From Typewriters to Word Processors**   1

   A Workspace   2
   Tools for Editing   4
   Document Formatting   6
   Printing   8
   Other UNIX Text-Processing Tools .   .   .   10

2 **UNIX Fundamentals**   12

   The UNIX Shell   12
   Output Redirection   14
   Special Characters   19
   Environment Variables   20
   Pipes and Filters   21
   Shell Scripts   23

3 **Learning vi**   24

   Session 1: Basic Commands   25
   Opening a File   25
   Moving the Cursor   28
   Simple Edits   32
   Session 2: Moving around in a Hurry .   .   41
   Movement by Screens   42
   Movement by Text Blocks .   .   .   44
   Movement by Searches   45
   Movement by Line Numbers .   .   .   47
   Session 3: Beyond the Basics .   .   .   48
   Command-Line Options   49
   Customizing vi   50

Edits and Movement 53
More Ways to Insert Text 54
Using Buffers 54
Marking Your Place 57
Other Advanced Edits 57

4 **nroff and troff**   58

What the Formatter Does 59
Using **nroff** 63
Using **troff** 64
The Markup Language 67
Turning Filling On and Off 69
Controlling Justification 71
Hyphenation 73
Page Layout 75
Page Transitions 86
Changing Fonts 92
A First Look at Macros 99

5 **The ms Macros**   104

Formatting a Text File with **ms** 105
Page Layout 106
Paragraphs 106
Changing Font and Point Size 114
Displays 117
Headings 120
Cover Sheet Macros 122
Miscellaneous Features 123
Page Headers and Footers 126
Problems on the First Page 127
Extensions to **ms** 127

6 **The mm Macros**   128

Formatting a Text File 128
Page Layout 132
Justification 137
Word Hyphenation 137
Displays 138
Changing Font and Point Size 141
More About Displays 145
Forcing a Page Break 150
Formatting Lists 150

Headings 162
Table of Contents 168
Footnotes and References 170
Extensions to **mm** 173

7   **Advanced Editing**   177

The **ex** Editor 178
Using **ex** Commands in **vi** 180
Write Locally, Edit Globally 180
Pattern Matching 184
Writing and Quitting Files 190
Reading In a File · 192
Executing UNIX Commands 192
Editing Multiple Files 195
Word Abbreviation 198
Saving Commands with **map** 198

8   **Formatting with tbl**   203

Using **tbl** 204
Specifying Tables 205
A Simple Table Example 206
Laying Out a Table 207
Describing Column Formats 209
Changing the Format within a Table 219
Putting Text Blocks in a Column 221
Breaking Up Long Tables 224
Putting Titles on Tables 225
A **tbl** Checklist 226
Some Complex Tables 227

9   **Typesetting Equations with eqn**   232

A Simple **eqn** Example 233
Using **eqn** 233
Specifying Equations 234
Spaces in Equations 236
Using Braces for Grouping 238
Special Character Names 239
Special Symbols 241
Other Positional Notation 244
Diacritical Marks 246
Defining Terms 247
Quoted Text 248

Fine-Tuning the Document 248
Keywords and Precedence 250
Problem Checklist 251

10   Drawing Pictures   253

The **pic** Preprocessor 254
From Describing to Programming Drawings . . 281
pic Enhancements 291

11   A Miscellany of UNIX Commands   293

Managing Your Files 293
Viewing the Contents of a File 298
Searching for Information in a File 301
Proofing Documents 304
Comparing Versions of the Same Document . . 312
Manipulating Data 322
Cleaning Up and Backing Up 336
Compressing Files 338
Communications 339
Scripts of UNIX Sessions 341

12   Let the Computer Do the Dirty Work   342

Shell Programming 343
ex Scripts 354
Stream Editing (**sed**) 360
A Proofreading Tool You Can Build 380

13   The awk Programming Language   387

Invoking **awk** 388
Records and Fields 389
Testing Fields 390
Passing Parameters from a Shell Script . . . 390
Changing the Field Separator 391
System Variables 392
Looping 393
awk Applications 400
Testing Programs 410

14   Writing `nroff` and `troff` Macros   412

Comments   412
Defining Macros   413
Macro Names   414
Macro Arguments   416
Nested Macro Definitions   418
Conditional Execution   418
Interrupted Lines   423
Number Registers   424
Defining Strings   429
Diversions   431
Environment Switching   433
Redefining Control and Escape Characters   .   .   . 435
Debugging Your Macros   436
Error Handling   439
Macro Style   441

15   Figures and Special Effects   443

Formatter Escape Sequences   443
Local Vertical Motions   445
Local Horizontal Motions   447
Absolute Motions   448
Line Drawing   449
Talking Directly to the Printer   460
Marking a Vertical Position   461
Overstriking Words or Characters   462
Tabs, Leaders, and Fields   467
Constant Spacing   471
Pseudo-Fonts   473
Character Output Translations   473
Output Line Numbering   475
Change Bars   476
Form Letters   477
Reading in Other Files or Program Output   .   .   . 479

16   What's in a Macro Package?   481

Just What Is a Macro Package, Revisited   .   .   . 481
Building a Consistent Framework   484
Page Transitions   489
Page Transitions in **ms**   491
Some Extensions to the Basic Package   495
Other Exercises in Page Transition   500

17　**An Extended ms Macro Package**　　　　　　　509

    Creating a Custom Macro Package　.　　.　　.　　.　.510
    Structured Technical Documents　.　　.　　.　　.　.512
    Figure and Table Headings　.　　.　　.　　.　　.　.523
    Lists, Lists, and More Lists　.　　.　　.　　.　　.　.525
    Source Code and Other Examples　.　　.　　.　　.　.528
    Notes, Cautions, and Warnings　.　　.　　.　　.　.530
    Table of Contents, Index, and Other End Lists　.　　.　.532

18　**Putting It All Together**　　　　　　　　542

    Saving an External Table of Contents　.　　.　　.　.544
    Index Processing　.　　.　　.　　.　　.　　.　.548
    Let **make** Remember the Details　.　　.　　.　　.　.562
    Where to Go from Here　.　　.　　.　　.　　.　.567

A　**Editor Command Summary**　　　　　　　569

B　**Formatter Command Summary**　　　　　　593

C　**Shell Command Summary**　　　　　　　628

D　**Format of troff Width Tables**　　　　　　635

E　**Comparing mm and ms**　　　　　　　640

F　**The format Macros**　　　　　　　643

G　**Selected Readings**　　　　　　　646

    Index　　　　　　　647

Preface

Many people think of computers primarily as "number crunchers," and think of word processors as generating form letters and boilerplate proposals. That computers can be used productively by writers, not just research scientists, accountants, and secretaries, is not so widely recognized. Today, writers not only work with words, they work with computers and the software programs, printers, and terminals that are part of a computer system.

The computer has not simply replaced a typewriter; it has become a system for integrating many other technologies. As these technologies are made available at a reasonable cost, writers may begin to find themselves in new roles as computer programmers, systems integrators, data base managers, graphic designers, typesetters, printers, and archivists.

The writer functioning in these new roles is faced with additional responsibilities. Obviously, it is one thing to have a tool available and another thing to use it skillfully. Like a craftsman, the writer must develop a number of specialized skills, gaining control over the method of production as well as the product. The writer must look for ways to improve the process by integrating new technologies and designing new tools in software.

In this book, we want to show how computers can be used effectively in the preparation of written documents, especially in the process of producing book-length documents. Surely it is important to learn the tools of the trade, and we will demonstrate the tools available in the UNIX environment. However, it is also valuable to examine text processing in terms of problems and solutions: the problems faced by a writer undertaking a large writing project and the solutions offered by using the resources and power of a computer system.

In Chapter 1, we begin by outlining the general capabilities of word-processing systems. We describe in brief the kinds of things that a computer must be able to do for a writer, regardless of whether that writer is working on a UNIX system or on an IBM PC with a word-processing package such as WordStar or MultiMate. Then, having defined basic word-processing capabilities, we look at how a text-processing system includes and extends these capabilities and benefits. Last, we introduce the set of text-processing tools in the UNIX environment. These tools, used individually or in combination, provide the basic framework for a text-processing system, one that can be custom-tailored to supply additional capabilities.

Chapter 2 gives a brief review of UNIX fundamentals. We assume you are already somewhat acquainted with UNIX, but we included this information to make sure that you are familiar with basic concepts that we will be relying on later in the book.

Chapter 3 introduces the vi editor, a basic tool for entering and editing text. Although many other editors and word-processing programs are available with UNIX, vi has the advantage that it works, without modification, on almost every UNIX system and with almost every type of terminal. If you learn vi, you can be confident that your text editing skills will be completely transferable when you sit down at someone else's terminal or use someone else's system.

Chapter 4 introduces the nroff and troff formatting programs. Because vi is a text editor, not a word-processing program, it does only rudimentary formatting of the text you enter. You can enter special formatting codes to specify how you want the document to look, then format the text using either nroff or troff. (The nroff formatter is used for formatting documents to the screen or to typewriter-like printers; troff uses much the same formatting language, but has additional constructs that allow it to produce more elaborate effects on typesetters and laser printers.)

In this chapter, we also describe the different types of output devices for printing your finished documents. With the wider availability of laser printers, you need to become familiar with many typesetting terms and concepts to get the most out of troff's capabilities.

The formatting markup language required by nroff and troff is quite complex, because it allows detailed control over the placement of every character on the page, as well as a large number of programming constructs that you can use to define custom formatting requests or macros. A number of macro packages have been developed to make the markup language easier to use. These macro packages define commonly used formatting requests for different types of documents, set up default values for page layout, and so on.

Although someone working with the macro packages does not need to know about the underlying requests in the formatting language used by nroff and troff, we believe that the reader wants to go beyond the basics. As a result, Chapter 4 introduces additional basic requests that the casual user might not need. However, your understanding of what is going on should be considerably enhanced.

There are two principal macro packages in use today, ms and mm (named for the command-line options to nroff and troff used to invoke them). Both macro packages were available with most UNIX systems; now, however, ms is chiefly available on UNIX systems derived from Berkeley 4.x BSD, and mm is chiefly available on UNIX systems derived from AT&T System V. If you are lucky enough to have both macro packages on your system, you can choose which one you want to learn. Otherwise, you should read either Chapter 5, *The ms Macros*, or Chapter 6, *The mm Macros*, depending on which version you have available.

Chapter 7 returns to `vi` to consider its more advanced features. In addition, it takes a look at how some of these features can support easy entry of formatting codes used by `nroff` and `troff`.

Tables and mathematical equations provide special formatting problems. The low-level `nroff` and `troff` commands for typesetting a complex table or equation are extraordinarily complex. However, no one needs to learn or type these commands, because two preprocessors, `tbl` and `eqn`, take a high-level specification of the table or equation and do the dirty work for you. They produce a "script" of `nroff` or `troff` commands that can be piped to the formatter to lay out the table or equations. The `tbl` and `eqn` preprocessors are described in Chapters 8 and 9, respectively.

More recent versions of UNIX (those that include AT&T's separate *Documenter's Workbench* software) also support a preprocessor called `pic` that makes it easier to create simple line drawings with `troff` and include them in your text. We talk about `pic` in Chapter 10.

Chapter 11 introduces a range of other UNIX text-processing tools—programs for sorting, comparing, and in various ways examining the contents of text files. This chapter includes a discussion of the standard UNIX `spell` program and the *Writer's Workbench* programs `style` and `diction`.

This concludes the first part of the book, which covers the tools that the writer finds at hand in the UNIX environment. This material is not elementary. In places, it grows quite complex. However, we believe there is a fundamental difference between learning how to use an existing tool and developing skills that extend a tool's capabilities to achieve your own goals.

That is the real beauty of the UNIX environment. Nearly all the tools it provides are extensible, either because they have built-in constructs for self-extension, like `nroff` and `troff`'s macro capability, or because of the wonderful programming powers of the UNIX command interpreter, the shell.

The second part of the book begins with Chapter 12, on editing scripts. There are several editors in UNIX that allow you to write and save what essentially amount to programs for manipulating text. The `ex` editor can be used from within `vi` to make global changes or complex edits. The next step is to use `ex` on its own; and after you do that, it is a small step to the even more powerful global editor `sed`. After you have mastered these tools, you can build a library of special-purpose editing scripts that vastly extend your power over the recalcitrant words you have put down on paper and now wish to change.

Chapter 13 discusses another program—`awk`—that extends the concept of a text editor even further than the programs discussed in Chapter 12. The `awk` program is really a database programming language that is appropriate for performing certain kinds of text-processing tasks. In particular, we use it in this book to process output from `troff` for indexing.

The next five chapters turn to the details of writing `troff` macros, and show how to customize the formatting language to simplify formatting tasks. We start in Chapter 14 by looking at the basic requests used to build macros, then go on in Chapter 15 to the requests for achieving various types of special effects. In Chapters 16 and 17, we'll take a look at the basic structure of a macro package and focus on how to define the appearance /of large documents such as manuals. We'll show you how to define different styles of section headings, page headers, footers, and so on. We'll also talk about how to generate an automatic table of contents and index—two tasks that take you beyond `troff` into the world of shell programming and various UNIX text-processing utilities.

To complete these tasks, we need to return to the UNIX shell in Chapter 18 and examine in more detail the ways that it allows you to incorporate the many tools provided by UNIX into an integrated text-processing environment.

Numerous appendices summarize information that is spread throughout the text, or that couldn't be crammed into it.

* * *

Before we turn to the subject at hand, a few acknowledgements are in order. Though only two names appear on the cover of this book, it is in fact the work of many hands. In particular, Grace Todino wrote the chapters on `tbl` and `eqn` in their entirety, and the chapters on `vi` and `ex` are based on the O'Reilly & Associates' Nutshell Handbook, *Learning the Vi Editor*, written by Linda Lamb. Other members of the O'Reilly & Associates staff—Linda Mui, Valerie Quercia, and Donna Woonteiler—helped tirelessly with copyediting, proofreading, illustrations, typesetting, and indexing.

Donna was new to our staff when she took on responsibility for the job of copyfitting—that final stage in page layout made especially arduous by the many figures and examples in this book. She and Linda especially spent many long hours getting this book ready for the printer. Linda had the special job of doing the final consistency check on examples, making sure that copyediting changes or typesetting errors had not compromised the accuracy of the examples.

Special thanks go to Steve Talbott of Masscomp, who first introduced us to the power of `troff` and who wrote the first version of the extended `ms` macros, `format` shell script, and indexing mechanism described in the second half of this book. Steve's help and patience were invaluable during the long road to mastery of the UNIX text-processing environment.

We'd also like to thank Teri Zak, the acquisitions editor at Hayden Books, for her vision of the Hayden UNIX series, and this book's place in it.

In the course of this book's development, Hayden was acquired by Howard Sams, where Teri's role was taken over by Jim Hill. Thanks also to the excellent production editors at Sams, Wendy Ford, Lou Keglovitz, and especially Susan Pink Bussiere, whose copyediting was outstanding.

Through it all, we have had the help of Steve Kochan and Pat Wood of Pipeline Associates, Inc., consulting editors to the Hayden UNIX Series. We are grateful for their thoughtful and thorough review of this book for technical accuracy. (We must, of course, make the usual disclaimer: any errors that remain are our own.)

Steve and Pat also provided the macros to typeset the book. Our working drafts were printed on an HP LaserJet printer, using `ditroff` and TextWare International's `tplus` postprocessor. Final typeset output was prepared with Pipeline Associates' `devps`, which was used to convert `ditroff` output to PostScript, which was used in turn to drive a Linotronic L100 typesetter.

1

From Typewriters to Word Processors

Before we consider the special tools that the UNIX environment provides for text processing, we need to think about the underlying changes in the process of writing that are inevitable when you begin to use a computer.

The most important features of a computer program for writers are the ability to remember what is typed and the ability to allow incremental changes—no more retyping from scratch each time a draft is revised. For a writer first encountering word-processing software, no other features even begin to compare. The crudest command structure, the most elementary formatting capabilities, will be forgiven because of the immense labor savings that take place.

Writing is basically an iterative process. It is a rare writer who dashes out a finished piece; most of us work in circles, returning again and again to the same piece of prose, adding or deleting words, phrases, and sentences, changing the order of thoughts, and elaborating a single sentence into pages of text.

A writer working on paper periodically needs to clear the deck—to type a clean copy, free of elaboration. As the writer reads the new copy, the process of revision continues, a word here, a sentence there, until the new draft is as obscured by changes as the first. As Joyce Carol Oates is said to have remarked: ''No book is ever finished. It is abandoned.''

Word processing first took hold in the office as a tool to help secretaries prepare perfect letters, memos, and reports. As dedicated word processors were replaced with low-cost personal computers, writers were quick to see the value of this new tool. In a civilization obsessed with the written word, it is no accident that WordStar, a word-processing program, was one of the first best sellers of the personal computer revolution.

As you learn to write with a word processor, your working style changes. Because it is so easy to make revisions, it is much more forgivable to think with your fingers when you write, rather than to carefully outline your thoughts beforehand and polish each sentence as you create it.

If you do work from an outline, you can enter it first, then write your first draft by filling in the outline, section by section. If you are writing a structured document such as a technical manual, your outline points become the headings in your document; if you are writing a free-flowing work, they can be subsumed gradually in the text as you flesh them out. In either case, it is easy to write in small segments that can be moved as you reorganize your ideas.

Watching a writer at work on a word processor is very different from watching a writer at work on a typewriter. A typewriter tends to enforce a linear flow—you must write a passage and then go back later to revise it. On a word processor, revisions are constant—you type a sentence, then go back to change the sentence above. Perhaps you write a few words, change your mind, and back up to take a different tack; or you decide the paragraph you just wrote would make more sense if you put it ahead of the one you wrote before, and move it on the spot.

This is not to say that a written work is created on a word processor in a single smooth flow; in fact, the writer using a word processor tends to create many more drafts than a compatriot who still uses a pen or typewriter. Instead of three or four drafts, the writer may produce ten or twenty. There is still a certain editorial distance that comes only when you read a printed copy. This is especially true when that printed copy is nicely formatted and letter perfect.

This brings us to the second major benefit of word-processing programs: they help the writer with simple formatting of a document. For example, a word processor may automatically insert carriage returns at the end of each line and adjust the space between words so that all the lines are the same length. Even more importantly, the text is automatically readjusted when you make changes. There are probably commands for centering, underlining, and boldfacing text.

The rough formatting of a document can cover a multitude of sins. As you read through your scrawled markup of a preliminary typewritten draft, it is easy to lose track of the overall flow of the document. Not so when you have a clean copy—the flaws of organization and content stand out vividly against the crisp new sheets of paper.

However, the added capability to print a clean draft after each revision also puts an added burden on the writer. Where once you had only to worry about content, you may now find yourself fussing with consistency of margins, headings, boldface, italics, and all the other formerly superfluous impedimenta that have now become integral to your task.

As the writer gets increasingly involved in the formatting of a document, it becomes essential that the tools help revise the document's appearance as easily as its content. Given these changes imposed by the evolution from typewriters to word processors, let's take a look at what a word-processing system needs to offer to the writer.

▪ A Workspace ▪

One of the most important capabilities of a word processor is that it provides a space in which you can create documents. In one sense, the video display screen on your terminal, which echoes the characters you type, is analogous to a sheet of paper. But the workspace of a word processor is not so unambiguous as a sheet of paper wound into a typewriter, that may be added neatly to the stack of completed work when finished, or torn out and crumpled as a false start. From the computer's point of view, your workspace is a block of memory, called a *buffer*, that is allocated when you begin a word-processing session. This buffer is a temporary holding area for storing your work and is emptied at the end of each session.

To save your work, you have to write the contents of the buffer to a file. A file is a permanent storage area on a disk (a hard disk or a floppy disk). After you have saved your work in a file, you can retrieve it for use in another session.

When you begin a session editing a document that exists on file, a copy of the file is made and its contents are read into the buffer. You actually work on the copy, making changes to *it*, not the original. The file is not changed until you save your changes during or at the end of your work session. You can also discard changes made to the buffered copy, keeping the original file intact, or save multiple versions of a document in separate files.

Particularly when working with larger documents, the management of disk files can become a major effort. If, like most writers, you save multiple drafts, it is easy to lose track of which version of a file is the latest.

An ideal text-processing environment for serious writers should provide tools for saving and managing multiple drafts on disk, not just on paper. It should allow the writer to

- work on documents of any length;

- save multiple versions of a file;

- save part of the buffer into a file for later use;

- switch easily between multiple files;

- insert the contents of an existing file into the buffer;

- summarize the differences between two versions of a document.

Most word-processing programs for personal computers seem to work best for short documents such as the letters and memos that offices churn out by the millions each day. Although it is possible to create longer documents, many features that would help organize a large document such as a book or manual are missing from these programs.

However, long before word processors became popular, programmers were using another class of programs called *text editors*. Text editors were designed chiefly for entering computer programs, not text. Furthermore, they were designed for use by computer professionals, not computer novices. As a result, a text editor can be more difficult to learn, lacking many on-screen formatting features available with most word processors.

Nonetheless, the text editors used in program development environments can provide much better facilities for managing large writing projects than their office word-processing counterparts. Large programs, like large documents, are often contained in many separate files; furthermore, it is essential to track the differences between versions of a program.

UNIX is a pre-eminent program development environment and, as such, it is also a superb document development environment. Although its text editing tools at first may appear limited in contrast to sophisticated office word processors, they are in fact considerably more powerful.

▪ Tools for Editing ▪

For many, the ability to retrieve a document from a file and make multiple revisions painlessly makes it impossible to write at a typewriter again. However, before you can get the benefits of word processing, there is a lot to learn.

Editing operations are performed by issuing commands. Each word-processing system has its own unique set of commands. At a minimum, there are commands to

- move to a particular position in the document;
- insert new text;
- change or replace text;
- delete text;
- copy or move text.

To make changes to a document, you must be able to move to that place in the text where you want to make your edits. Most documents are too large to be displayed in their entirety on a single terminal screen, which generally displays 24 lines of text. Usually only a portion of a document is displayed. This partial view of your document is sometimes referred to as a *window*.* If you are entering new text and reach the bottom line in the window, the text on the screen automatically scrolls (rolls up) to reveal an additional line at the bottom. A cursor (an underline or block) marks your current position in the window.

There are basically two kinds of movement:

- scrolling new text into the window
- positioning the cursor within the window

When you begin a session, the first line of text is the first line in the window, and the cursor is positioned on the first character. Scrolling commands change which lines are displayed in the window by moving forward or backward through the document. Cursor-positioning commands allow you to move up and down to individual lines, and along lines to particular characters.

After you position the cursor, you must issue a command to make the desired edit. The command you choose indicates how much text will be affected: a character, a word, a line, or a sentence.

Because the same keyboard is used to enter both text and commands, there must be some way to distinguish between the two. Some word-processing programs assume that you are entering text unless you specify otherwise; newly entered text either

---

*Some editors, such as `emacs`, can split the terminal screen into multiple windows. In addition, many high-powered UNIX workstations with large bit-mapped screens have their own windowing software that allows multiple programs to be run simultaneously in separate windows. For purposes of this book, we assume you are using the `vi` editor and an alphanumeric terminal with only a single window.

replaces existing text or pushes it over to make room for the new text. Commands are entered by pressing special keys on the keyboard, or by combining a standard key with a special key, such as the *control key* (*CTRL*).

Other programs assume that you are issuing commands; you must enter a command before you can type any text at all. There are advantages and disadvantages to each approach. Starting out in text mode is more intuitive to those coming from a typewriter, but may be slower for experienced writers, because all commands must be entered by special key combinations that are often hard to reach and slow down typing. (We'll return to this topic when we discuss `vi`, a UNIX text editor.)

Far more significant than the style of command entry is the range and speed of commands. For example, though it is heaven for someone used to a typewriter to be able to delete a word and type in a replacement, it is even better to be able to issue a command that will replace every occurrence of that word in an entire document. And, after you start making such global changes, it is essential to have some way to undo them if you make a mistake.

A word processor that substitutes ease of learning for ease of use by having fewer commands will ultimately fail the serious writer, because the investment of time spent learning complex commands can easily be repaid when they simplify complex tasks.

And when you do issue a complex command, it is important that it works as quickly as possible, so that you aren't left waiting while the computer grinds away. The extra seconds add up when you spend hours or days at the keyboard, and, once having been given a taste of freedom from drudgery, writers want as much freedom as they can get.

Text editors were developed before word processors (in the rapid evolution of computers). Many of them were originally designed for printing terminals, rather than for the CRT-based terminals used by word processors. These programs tend to have commands that work with text on a line-by-line basis. These commands are often more obscure than the equivalent office word-processing commands.

However, though the commands used by text editors are sometimes more difficult to learn, they are usually very effective. (The commands designed for use with slow paper terminals were often extraordinarily powerful, to make up for the limited capabilities of the input and output device.)

There are two basic kinds of text editors, *line editors* and *screen editors*, and both are available in UNIX. The difference is simple: line editors display one line at a time, and screen editors can display approximately 24 lines or a full screen.

The line editors in UNIX include `ed`, `sed`, and `ex`. Although these line editors are obsolete for general-purpose use by writers, there are applications at which they excel, as we will see in Chapters 7 and 12.

The most common screen editor in UNIX is `vi`. Learning `vi` or some other suitable editor is the first step in mastering the UNIX text-processing environment. Most of your time will be spent using the editor.

UNIX screen editors such as `vi` and `emacs` (another editor available on many UNIX systems) lack ease-of-learning features common in many word processors—there are no menus and only primitive on-line help screens, and the commands are often complex and nonintuitive—but they are powerful and fast. What's more, UNIX line editors such as `ex` and `sed` give additional capabilities not found in word processors—the ability to write a script of editing commands that can be applied to multiple files. Such editing scripts open new ranges of capability to the writer.

· Document Formatting ·

Text editing is wonderful, but the object of the writing process is to produce a printed document for others to read. And a printed document is more than words on paper; it is an arrangement of text on a page. For instance, the elements of a business letter are arranged in a consistent format, which helps the person reading the letter identify those elements. Reports and more complex documents, such as technical manuals or books, require even greater attention to formatting. The format of a document conveys how information is organized, assisting in the presentation of ideas to a reader.

Most word-processing programs have built-in formatting capabilities. Formatting commands are intermixed with editing commands, so that you can shape your document on the screen. Such formatting commands are simple extensions of those available to someone working with a typewriter. For example, an automatic centering command saves the trouble of manually counting characters to center a title or other text. There may also be such features as automatic pagination and printing of headers or footers.

Text editors, by contrast, usually have few formatting capabilities. Because they were designed for entering programs, their formatting capabilities tend to be oriented toward the formats required by one or more programming languages.

Even programmers write reports, however. Especially at AT&T (where UNIX was developed), there was a great emphasis on document preparation tools to help the programmers and scientists of Bell Labs produce research reports, manuals, and other documents associated with their development work.

Word processing, with its emphasis on easy-to-use programs with simple on-screen formatting, was in its infancy. Computerized phototypesetting, on the other hand, was already a developed art. Until quite recently, it was not possible to represent on a video screen the variable type styles and sizes used in typeset documents. As a result, phototypesetting has long used a markup system that indicates formatting instructions with special codes. These formatting instructions to the computerized typesetter are often direct descendants of the instructions that were formerly given to a human typesetter—center the next line, indent five spaces, boldface this heading.

The text formatter most commonly used with the UNIX system is called `nroff`. To use it, you must intersperse formatting instructions (usually one- or two-letter codes preceded by a period) within your text, then pass the file through the formatter. The `nroff` program interprets the formatting codes and reformats the document "on the fly" while passing it on to the printer. The `nroff` formatter prepares documents for printing on line printers, dot-matrix printers, and letter-quality printers. Another program called `troff` uses an extended version of the same markup language used by `nroff`, but prepares documents for printing on laser printers and typesetters. We'll talk more about printing in a moment.

Although formatting with a markup language may seem to be a far inferior system to the "what you see is what you get" (*wysiwyg*) approach of most office word-processing programs, it actually has many advantages.

First, unless you are using a very sophisticated computer, with very sophisticated software (what has come to be called an electronic publishing system, rather than a mere word processor), it is not possible to display everything on the screen just as it will appear on the printed page. For example, the screen may not be able to represent boldfacing or underlining except with special formatting codes. WordStar, one of the grandfathers of word-processing programs for personal computers, represents underlining by surrounding the word or words to be underlined with the special control character ^S (the character generated by holding down the *control* key while typing the letter *S*). For example, the following title line would be underlined when the document is printed:

```
^SWord Processing with WordStar^S
```

Is this really superior to the following `nroff` construct?

```
.ul
Text Processing with vi and nroff
```

It is perhaps unfair to pick on WordStar, an older word-processing program, but very few word-processing programs can complete the illusion that what you see on the screen is what you will get on paper. There is usually some mix of control codes with on-screen formatting. More to the point, though, is the fact that most word processors are oriented toward the production of short documents. When you get beyond a letter, memo, or report, you start to understand that there is more to formatting than meets the eye.

Although "what you see is what you get" is fine for laying out a single page, it is much harder to enforce consistency across a large document. The design of a large document is often determined before writing is begun, just as a set of plans for a house are drawn up before anyone starts construction. The design is a plan for organizing a document, arranging various parts so that the same types of material are handled in the same way.

The parts of a document might be chapters, sections, or subsections. For instance, a technical manual is often organized into chapters and appendices. Within each chapter, there might be numbered sections that are further divided into three or four levels of subsections.

Document design seeks to accomplish across the entire document what is accomplished by the table of contents of a book. It presents the structure of a document and helps the reader locate information.

Each of the parts must be clearly identified. The design specifies how they will look, trying to achieve consistency throughout the document. The strategy might specify that major section headings will be all uppercase, underlined, with three blank lines above and two below, and secondary headings will be in uppercase and lowercase, underlined, with two blank lines above and one below.

If you have ever tried to format a large document using a word processor, you have probably found it difficult to enforce consistency in such formatting details as these. By contrast, a markup language—especially one like `nroff` that allows you to define repeated command sequences, or *macros*—makes it easy: the style of a heading is defined once, and a code used to reference it. For example, a top-level heading might be specified by the code `.H1`, and a secondary heading by `.H2`.

Even more significantly, if you later decide to change the design, you simply change the definition of the relevant design elements. If you have used a word processor to format the document as it was written, it is usually a painful task to go back and change the format.

Some word-processing programs, such as Microsoft WORD, include features for defining global document formats, but these features are not as widespread as they are in markup systems.

▪ Printing ▪

The formatting capabilities of a word-processing system are limited by what can be output on a printer. For example, some printers cannot backspace and therefore cannot underline. For this discussion, we are considering four different classes of printers: dot matrix, letter quality, phototypesetter, and laser.

A *dot-matrix* printer composes characters as a series of dots. It is usually suitable for preparing interoffice memos and obtaining fast printouts of large files.

```
This paragraph was printed with a dot-matrix printer. It uses a print
head containing 9 pins, which are adjusted to produce the shape of each
character. More sophicated dot-matrix printers have print heads
containing up to 24 pins. The greater the number of pins, the finer
the dots that are printed, and the more possible it is to fool the eye
into thinking it sees a solid character. Dot matrix printers are also
capable of printing out graphic displays.
```

A *letter-quality* printer is more expensive and slower. Its printing mechanism operates like a typewriter and achieves a similar result.

```
This paragraph was printed with a letter-
quality printer. It is essentially a
computer-controlled typewriter and, like a
typewriter, uses a print ball or wheel
containing fully formed characters.
```

A letter-quality printer produces clearer, easier-to-read copy than a dot-matrix printer. Letter-quality printers are generally used in offices for formal correspondence as well as for the final drafts of proposals and reports.

Until very recently, documents that needed a higher quality of printing than that available with letter-quality printers were sent out for typesetting. Even if draft copy was word-processed, the material was often re-entered by the typesetter, although many typesetting companies can read the files created by popular word-processing programs and use them as a starting point for typesetting.

> This paragraph, like the rest of this book, was phototypeset. In photo-typesetting, a photographic technique is used to print characters on film or photographic paper. There is a wide choice of type styles, and the characters are much more finely formed that those produced by a letter-quality printer. Characters are produced by an arrangement of tiny dots, much like a dot-matrix printer—but there are over 1000 dots per inch.

There are several major advantages to typesetting. The high resolution allows for the design of aesthetically pleasing type. The shape of the characters is much finer. In addition, where dot-matrix and letter-quality type is usually constant width (narrow letters like *i* take up the same amount of space as wide ones like *m*), typesetters use variable-width type, in which narrow letters take up less space than wide ones. In addition, it's possible to mix styles (for example, bold and italic) and sizes of type on the same page.

Most typesetting equipment uses a markup language rather than a *wysiwyg* approach to specify point sizes, type styles, leading, and so on. Until recently, the technology didn't even exist to represent on a screen the variable-width typefaces that appear in published books and magazines.

AT&T, a company with its own extensive internal publishing operation, developed its own typesetting markup language and typesetting program—a sister to `nroff` called `troff` (*typesetter-roff*). Although `troff` extends the capabilities of `nroff` in significant ways, it is almost totally compatible with it.

Until recently, unless you had access to a typesetter, you didn't have much use for `troff`. The development of low-cost laser printers that can produce near typeset-quality output at a fraction of the cost has changed all that.

> **This paragraph was produced on a laser printer. Laser printers produce high-resolution characters—300 to 500 dots per inch—though they are not quite as finely formed as phototypeset characters. Laser printers are not only cheaper to purchase than phototypesetters, they also print on plain paper, just like Xerox machines, and are therefore much cheaper to operate. However, as is always the case with computers, you need the proper software to take advantage of improved hardware capabilities.**

Word-processing software (particularly that developed for the Apple Macintosh, which has a high-resolution graphics screen capable of representing variable type fonts) is beginning to tap the capabilities of laser printers. However, most of the microcomputer-based packages still have many limitations. Nonetheless, a markup language such as that provided by `troff` still provides the easiest and lowest-cost access to the world of electronic publishing for many types of documents.

The point made previously, that markup languages are preferable to *wysiwyg* systems for large documents, is especially true when you begin to use variable size fonts, leading, and other advanced formatting features. It is easy to lose track of the overall format of your document and difficult to make overall changes after your formatted text is in place. Only the most expensive electronic publishing systems (most of them based on advanced UNIX workstations) give you both the capability to see what you will get on the screen and the ability to define and easily change overall document formats.

▪ Other UNIX Text-Processing Tools ▪

Document editing and formatting are the most important parts of text processing, but they are not the whole story. For instance, in writing many types of documents, such as technical manuals, the writer rarely starts from scratch. Something is already written, whether it be a first draft written by someone else, a product specification, or an outdated version of a manual. It would be useful to get a copy of that material to work with. If that material was produced with a word processor or has been entered on another system, UNIX's communications facilities can transfer the file from the remote system to your own.

Then you can use a number of custom-made programs to search through and extract useful information. Word-processing programs often store text in files with different internal formats. UNIX provides a number of useful analysis and translation tools that can help decipher files with nonstandard formats. Other tools allow you to "cut and paste" portions of a document into the one you are writing.

As the document is being written, there are programs to check spelling, style, and diction. The reports produced by those programs can help you see if there is any detectable pattern in syntax or structure that might make a document more difficult for the user than it needs to be.

Although many documents are written once and published or filed, there is also a large class of documents (manuals in particular) that are revised again and again. Documents such as these require special tools for managing revisions. UNIX program development tools such as SCCS (Source Code Control System) and `diff` can be used by writers to compare past versions with the current draft and print out reports of the differences, or generate printed copies with change bars in the margin marking the differences.

In addition to all of the individual tools it provides, UNIX is a particularly fertile environment for writers who aren't afraid of computers, because it is easy to write command files, or *shell scripts*, that combine individual programs into more complex tools to meet your specific needs. For example, automatic index generation is a complex task that is not handled by any of the standard UNIX text-processing tools. We will show you ways to perform this and other tasks by applying the tools available in the UNIX environment and a little ingenuity.

We have two different objectives in this book. The first objective is that you learn to use many of the tools available on most UNIX systems. The second objective is that you develop an understanding of how these different tools can work together in a document preparation system. We're not just presenting a UNIX user's manual, but suggesting applications for which the various programs can be used.

To take full advantage of the UNIX text-processing environment, you must do more than just learn a few programs. For the writer, the job includes establishing standards and conventions about how documents will be stored, in what format they should appear in print, and what kinds of programs are needed to help this process take place efficiently with the use of a computer. Another way of looking at it is that you have to make certain choices prior to beginning a project. We want to encourage you to make your own choices, set your own standards, and realize the many possibilities that are open to a diligent and creative person.

In the past, many of the steps in creating a finished book were out of the hands of the writer. Proofreaders and copyeditors went over the text for spelling and grammatical errors. It was generally the printer who did the typesetting (a service usually paid by the publisher). At the print shop, a typesetter (a person) retyped the text and specified the font sizes and styles. A graphic artist, performing layout and pasteup, made many of the decisions about the appearance of the printed page.

Although producing a high-quality book can still involve many people, UNIX provides the tools that allow a writer to control the process from start to finish. An analogy is the difference between an assembly worker on a production line who views only one step in the process and a craftsman who guides the product from beginning to end. The craftsman has his own system of putting together a product, whereas the assembly worker has the system imposed upon him.

After you are acquainted with the basic tools available in UNIX and have spent some time using them, you can design additional tools to perform work that you think is necessary and helpful. To create these tools, you will write shell scripts that use the resources of UNIX in special ways. We think there is a certain satisfaction that comes with accomplishing such tasks by computer. It seems to us to reward careful thought.

What programming means to us is that when we confront a problem that normally submits only to tedium or brute force, we think of a way to get the computer to solve the problem. Doing this often means looking at the problem in a more general way and solving it in a way that can be applied again and again.

One of the most important books on UNIX is *The UNIX Programming Environment* by Brian W. Kernighan and Rob Pike. They write that what makes UNIX effective "is an approach to programming, a philosophy of using the computer." At the heart of this philosophy "is the idea that the power of a system comes more from the relationships among programs than from the programs themselves."

When we talk about building a document preparation system, it is this philosophy that we are trying to apply. As a consequence, this is a system that has great flexibility and gives the builders a feeling of breaking new ground. The UNIX text-processing environment is a system that can be tailored to the specific tasks you want to accomplish. In many instances, it can let you do just what a word processor does. In many more instances, it lets you use more of the computer to do things that a word processor either can't do or can't do very well.

2

UNIX Fundamentals

The UNIX operating system is a collection of programs that controls and organizes the resources and activities of a computer system. These resources consist of hardware such as the computer's memory, various peripherals such as terminals, printers, and disk drives, and software utilities that perform specific tasks on the computer system. UNIX is a multiuser, multitasking operating system that allows the computer to perform a variety of functions for many users. It also provides users with an environment in which they can access the computer's resources and utilities. This environment is characterized by its command interpreter, the shell.

In this chapter, we review a set of basic concepts for users working in the UNIX environment. As we mentioned in the preface, this book does not replace a general introduction to UNIX. A complete overview is essential to anyone not familiar with the file system, input and output redirection, pipes and filters, and many basic utilities. In addition, there are different versions of UNIX, and not all commands are identical in each version. In writing this book, we've used System V Release 2 on a Convergent Technologies' Miniframe.

These disclaimers aside, if it has been a while since you tackled a general introduction, this chapter should help refresh your memory. If you are already familiar with UNIX, you can skip or skim this chapter.

As we explain these basic concepts, using a tutorial approach, we demonstrate the broad capabilities of UNIX as an applications environment for text-processing. What you learn about UNIX in general can be applied to performing specific tasks related to text-processing.

· The UNIX Shell ·

As an interactive computer system, UNIX provides a command interpreter called a shell. The shell accepts commands typed at your terminal, invokes a program to perform specific tasks on the computer, and handles the output or result of this program, normally directing it to the terminal's video display screen.

UNIX commands can be simple one-word entries like the `date` command:

```
$ date
Tue Apr  8 13:23:41 EST 1987
```

Or their usage can be more complex, requiring that you specify options and arguments, such as filenames. Although some commands have a peculiar syntax, many UNIX commands follow this general form:

command option(s) argument(s)

A *command* identifies a software program or utility. Commands are entered in lowercase letters. One typical command, `ls`, lists the files that are available in your immediate storage area, or *directory*.

An *option* modifies the way in which a command works. Usually options are indicated by a minus sign followed by a single letter. For example, `ls -l` modifies what information is displayed about a file. The set of possible options is particular to the command and generally only a few of them are regularly used. However, if you want to modify a command to perform in a special manner, be sure to consult a UNIX reference guide and examine the available options.

An *argument* can specify an expression or the name of a file on which the command is to act. Arguments may also be required when you specify certain options. In addition, if more than one filename is being specified, special *metacharacters* (such as `*` and `?`) can be used to represent the filenames. For instance, `ls -l ch*` will display information about all files that have names beginning with `ch`.

The UNIX shell is itself a program that is invoked as part of the login process. When you have properly identified yourself by logging in, the UNIX system prompt appears on your terminal screen.

The prompt that appears on your screen may be different from the one shown in the examples in this book. There are two widely used shells: the Bourne shell and the C shell. Traditionally, the Bourne shell uses a dollar sign (`$`) as a system prompt, and the C shell uses a percent sign (`%`). The two shells differ in the features they provide and in the syntax of their programming constructs. However, they are fundamentally very similar. In this book, we use the Bourne shell.

Your prompt may be different from either of these traditional prompts. This is because the UNIX environment can be customized and the prompt may have been changed by your system administrator. Whatever the prompt looks like, when it appears, the system is ready for you to enter a command.

When you type a command from the keyboard, the characters are echoed on the screen. The shell does not interpret the command until you press the *RETURN* key. This means that you can use the *erase character* (usually the *DEL* or *BACKSPACE* key) to correct typing mistakes. After you have entered a command line, the shell tries to identify and locate the program specified on the command line. If the command line that you entered is not valid, then an error message is returned.

When a program is invoked and processing begun, the output it produces is sent to your screen, unless otherwise directed. To interrupt and cancel a program before it has completed, you can press the *interrupt character* (usually *CTRL-C* or the *DEL* key). If the output of a command scrolls by the screen too fast, you can suspend the output by pressing the *suspend character* (usually *CTRL-S*) and resume it by pressing the *resume character* (usually *CTRL-Q*).

Some commands invoke utilities that offer their own environment—with a command interpreter and a set of special "internal" commands. A text editor is one such utility, the mail facility another. In both instances, you enter commands while you are "inside" the program. In these kinds of programs, you must use a command to exit and return to the system prompt.

The return of the system prompt signals that a command is finished and that you can enter another command. Familiarity with the power and flexibility of the UNIX shell is essential to working productively in the UNIX environment.

▪ **Output Redirection** ▪

Some programs do their work in silence, but most produce some kind of result, or output. There are generally two types of output: the expected result—referred to as *standard output*—and error messages—referred to as *standard error*. Both types of output are normally sent to the screen and appear to be indistinguishable. However, they can be manipulated separately—a feature we will later put to good use.

Let's look at some examples. The echo command is a simple command that displays a string of text on the screen.

```
$ echo my name
my name
```

In this case, the input echo my name is processed and its output is my name. The name of the command—echo—refers to a program that interprets the command-line arguments as a literal expression that is sent to standard output. Let's replace echo with a different command called cat:

```
$ cat my name
cat: Cannot open my
cat: Cannot open name
```

The cat program takes its arguments to be the names of files. If these files existed, their contents would be displayed on the screen. Because the arguments were not filenames in this example, an error message was printed instead.

The output from a command can be sent to a file instead of the screen by using the output redirection operator (>). In the next example, we redirect the output of the echo command to a file named reminders.

```
$ echo Call home at 3:00 > reminders
$
```

No output is sent to the screen, and the UNIX prompt returns when the program is finished. Now the cat command should work because we have created a file.

```
$ cat reminders
Call home at 3:00
```

The cat command displays the contents of the file named reminders on the screen. If we redirect again to the same filename, we overwrite its previous contents:

```
$ echo Pick up expense voucher > reminders
$ cat reminders
Pick up expense voucher
```

We can send another line to the file, but we have to use a different redirect operator to append (>>) the new line at the end of the file:

```
$ echo Call home at 3:00 > reminders
$ echo Pick up expense voucher >> reminders
$ cat reminders
Call home at 3:00
Pick up expense voucher
```

The cat command is useful not only for printing a file on the screen, but for con-*cat*enating existing files (printing them one after the other). For example:

```
$ cat reminders todolist
Call home at 3:00
Pick up expense voucher
Proofread Chapter 2
Discuss output redirection
```

The combined output can also be redirected:

```
$ cat reminders todolist > do_now
```

The contents of both reminders and todolist are combined into do_now. The original files remain intact.

If one of the files does not exist, an error message is printed, even though standard output is redirected:

```
$ rm todolist
$ cat reminders todolist > do_now
cat: todolist: not found
```

The files we've created are stored in our *current working directory*.

Files and Directories

The UNIX file system consists of files and directories. Because the file system can contain thousands of files, directories perform the same function as file drawers in a paper file system. They organize files into more manageable groupings. The file system is hierarchical. It can be represented as an inverted tree structure with the *root directory* at the top. The root directory contains other directories that in turn contain other directories.*

---

*In addition to subdirectories, the root directory can contain other *file systems*. A file system is the skeletal structure of a directory tree, which is built on a magnetic disk before any files or directories are stored on it. On a system containing more than one disk, or on a disk divided into several partitions, there are multiple file systems. However, this is generally invisible to the user, because the secondary file systems are *mounted* on the root directory, creating the illusion of a single file system.

On many UNIX systems, users store their files in the /usr file system. (As disk storage has become cheaper and larger, the placement of user directories is no longer standard. For example, on our system, /usr contains only UNIX software; user accounts are in a separate file system called /work.)

Fred's *home directory* is /usr/fred. It is the location of Fred's account on the system. When he logs in, his home directory is his current working directory. Your working directory is where you are currently located and changes as you move up and down the file system.

A *pathname* specifies the location of a directory or file on the UNIX file system. An *absolute pathname* specifies where a file or directory is located off the root file system. A *relative pathname* specifies the location of a file or directory in relation to the current working directory.

To find out the pathname of our current directory, enter pwd.

```
$ pwd
/usr/fred
```

The absolute pathname of the current working directory is /usr/fred. The ls command lists the contents of the current directory. Let's list the files and subdirectories in /usr/fred by entering the ls command with the −F option. This option prints a slash (/) following the names of subdirectories. In the following example, oldstuff is a directory, and notes and reminders are files.

```
$ ls −F
reminders
notes
oldstuff/
```

When you specify a filename with the ls command, it simply prints the name of the file, if the file exists. When you specify the name of directory, it prints the names of the files and subdirectories in that directory.

```
$ ls reminders
reminders
$ ls oldstuff
ch01_draft
letter.212
memo
```

In this example, a relative pathname is used to specify oldstuff. That is, its location is specified in relation to the current directory, /usr/fred. You could also enter an absolute pathname, as in the following example:

```
$ ls /usr/fred/oldstuff
ch01_draft
letter.212
memo
```

Similarly, you can use an absolute or relative pathname to change directories using the cd command. To move from /usr/fred to /usr/fred/oldstuff, you can enter a relative pathname:

```
$ cd oldstuff
$ pwd
/usr/fred/oldstuff
```

The directory `/usr/fred/oldstuff` becomes the current working directory.
     The `cd` command without an argument returns you to your home directory.

```
$ cd
```

When you log in, you are positioned in your home directory, which is thus your current working directory. The name of your home directory is stored in a shell variable that is accessible by prefacing the name of the variable (HOME) with a dollar sign ($). Thus:

```
$ echo $HOME
/usr/fred
```

You could also use this variable in pathnames to specify a file or directory in your home directory.

```
$ ls $HOME/oldstuff/memo
/usr/fred/oldstuff/memo
```

In this tutorial, `/usr/fred` is our home directory.
     The command to create a directory is `mkdir`. An absolute or relative pathname can be specified.

```
$ mkdir /usr/fred/reports
$ mkdir reports/monthly
```

Setting up directories is a convenient method of organizing your work on the system. For instance, in writing this book, we set up a directory `/work/textp` and, under that, subdirectories for each chapter in the book (`/work/textp/ch01`, `/work/textp/ch02`, etc.). In each of those subdirectories, there are files that divide the chapter into sections (`sect1`, `sect2`, etc.). There is also a subdirectory set up to hold old versions or drafts of these sections.

Copying and Moving Files

You can copy, move, and rename files within your current working directory or (by specifying the full pathname) within other directories on the file system. The `cp` command makes a copy of a file and the `mv` command can be used to move a file to a new directory or simply rename it. If you give the name of a new or existing file as the last argument to `cp` or `mv`, the file named in the first argument is copied, and the copy given the new name. (If the target file already exists, it will be overwritten by the copy. If you give the name of a directory as the last argument to `cp` or `mv`, the file or files named first will be copied to that directory, and will keep their original names.)
     Look at the following sequence of commands:

```
$ pwd                        Print working directory
/usr/fred
```

```
$ ls -F                      List contents of current directory
meeting
oldstuff/
notes
reports/
$ mv notes oldstuff          Move notes to oldstuff directory
$ ls                         List contents of current directory
meeting
oldstuff
reports/
$ mv meeting meet.306        Rename meeting
$ ls oldstuff                List contents of oldstuff subdirectory
ch01_draft
letter.212
memo
notes
```

In this example, the mv command was used to rename the file meeting and to move the file notes from /usr/fred to /usr/fred/oldstuff. You can also use the mv command to rename a directory itself.

Permissions

Access to UNIX files is governed by ownership and permissions. If you create a file, you are the owner of the file and can set the permissions for that file to give or deny access to other users of the system. There are three different levels of permission:

r   Read permission allows users to read a file or make a copy of it.

w   Write permission allows users to make changes to that file.

x   Execute permission signifies a program file and allows other users to execute this program.

File permissions can be set for three different levels of ownership:

owner   The user who created the file is its owner.

group   A group to which you are assigned, usually made up of those users engaged in similar activities and who need to share files among themselves.

other   All other users on the system, the public.

Thus, you can set read, write, and execute permissions for the three levels of ownership. This can be represented as:

```
rwxrwxrwx
 /   |   \
owner group other
```

HOWARD W. SAMS & COMPANY

Bookmark

DEAR VALUED CUSTOMER:

Howard W. Sams & Company is dedicated to bringing you timely and authoritative books for your personal and professional library. Our goal is to provide you with excellent technical books written by the most qualified authors. You can assist us in this endeavor by checking the box next to your particular areas of interest.

We appreciate your comments and will use the information to provide you with a more comprehensive selection of titles.

Thank you,

Vice President, Book Publishing
Howard W. Sams & Company

COMPUTER TITLES:

Hardware
- ☐ Apple 140   ☐ Macintosh I01
- ☐ Commodore I10
- ☐ IBM & Compatibles I14

Business Applications
- ☐ Word Processing J01
- ☐ Data Base J04
- ☐ Spreadsheets J02

Operating Systems
- ☐ MS-DOS K05   ☐ OS/2 K10
- ☐ CP/M K01   ☐ UNIX K03

Programming Languages
- ☐ C L03   ☐ Pascal L05
- ☐ Prolog L12   ☐ Assembly L01
- ☐ BASIC L02   ☐ HyperTalk L14

Troubleshooting & Repair
- ☐ Computers S05
- ☐ Peripherals S10

Other
- ☐ Communications/Networking M03
- ☐ AI/Expert Systems T18

ELECTRONICS TITLES:
- ☐ Amateur Radio T01
- ☐ Audio T03
- ☐ Basic Electronics T20
- ☐ Basic Electricity T21
- ☐ Electronics Design T12
- ☐ Electronics Projects T04
- ☐ Satellites T09

- ☐ Instrumentation T05
- ☐ Digital Electronics T11

Troubleshooting & Repair
- ☐ Audio S11   ☐ Television S04
- ☐ VCR S01   ☐ Compact Disc S02
- ☐ Automotive S06
- ☐ Microwave Oven S03

Other interests or comments: _____

_____

_____

Name_____

Title _____

Company _____

Address _____

City _____

State/Zip _____

Daytime Telephone No. _____

A Division of Macmillan, Inc.

4300 West 62nd Street   Indianapolis, Indiana 46268   **46291**

Bookmark

BUSINESS REPLY CARD

FIRST CLASS   PERMIT NO. 1076   INDIANAPOLIS, IND.

POSTAGE WILL BE PAID BY ADDRESSEE

HOWARD W. SAMS & CO.
ATTN: Public Relations Department
P.O. BOX 7092
Indianapolis, IN 46209-9921

*HOWARD W. SAMS
& COMPANY*

HOWARD W. SAMS & COMPANY
HAYDEN BOOKS

Topics in C Programming
*Stephen G. Kochan,
Patrick H. Wood*
ISBN: 0-672-46290-7, $24.95

UNIX® System Security
*Patrick H. Wood and
Stephen G. Kochan*
ISBN: 0-8104-6267-2, $34.95

Programming in C, Revised Edition
Stephen G. Kochan
ISBN: 0-672-48420-X, $24.95

Exploring the UNIX® System
*Stephen G. Kochan and
Patrick H. Wood*
ISBN: 0-8104-6268-0, $22.95

UNIX® System Administration
*David Fiedler and
Bruce H. Hunter*
ISBN: 0-8104-6289-3, $24.95

The Waite Group's UNIX® Communications
*Bart Anderson, Bryan Costales,
Harry Henderson*
ISBN: 0-672-22511-5, $26.95

The Waite Group's UNIX® Primer Plus
*Mitchell Waite, Donald Martin,
Stephen Prata*
ISBN: 0-672-22028-8, $22.95

The Waite Group's UNIX® System V Primer, Revised Edition
*Mitchell Waite, Donald Martin,
Stephen Prata*
ISBN: 0-672-22570-0, $22.95

The Waite Group's Tricks of the UNIX® Masters
Russell G. Sage
ISBN: 0-672-22449-6, $24.95

The Waite Group's UNIX® Papers
The Waite Group
ISBN: 0-672-22578-6, $26.95

The Waite Group's UNIX® System V Bible
Stephen Prata, Donald Martin
ISBN: 0-672-22562-X, $24.95

The Waite Group's Advanced UNIX®—A Programmer's Guide
Stephen Prata
ISBN: 0-672-22403-8, $24.95

The Waite Group's Inside XENIX®
Christopher L. Morgan
ISBN: 0-672-22445-3, $24.95

To order, return the card below, or call 1-800-428-SAMS. In Indiana call (317) 298-5699.

Please send me the books listed below.

Title	Quantity	ISBN #	Price

☐ Please add my name to your mailing list to receive more information on related titles.

Name (please print) _____

Company _____

City _____

State/Zip _____

Signature _____
(required for credit card purchase)

Telephone # _____

Subtotal _____

Standard Postage and Handling **$2.50**

All States Add Appropriate Sales Tax _____

TOTAL _____

Enclosed is My Check or Money Order for $_____

Charge my Credit Card: ☐ VISA   ☐ MC   ☐ AE

Account No.   Expiration Date _____

☐☐☐☐ ☐☐☐☐ ☐☐☐☐ ☐☐☐☐

46291

HOWARD W. SAMS & COMPANY

Dept. DM
4300 West 62nd Street
Indianapolis, IN 46268-2589

When you enter the command `ls -l`, information about the status of the file is displayed on the screen. You can determine what the file permissions are, who the owner of the file is, and with what group the file is associated.

```
$ ls -l meet.306
-rw-rw-r-- 1 fred   techpubs  126  March 6  10:32  meet.306
```

This file has read and write permissions set for the user `fred` and the group `techpubs`. All others can read the file, but they cannot modify it. Because `fred` is the owner of the file, he can change the permissions, making it available to others or denying them access to it. The `chmod` command is used to set permissions. For instance, if he wanted to make the file writeable by everyone, he would enter:

```
$ chmod o+w meet.306
$ ls -l meet.306
-rw-rw-rw- 1 fred   techpubs  126  March 6  10:32  meet.306
```

This translates to ''add write permission (+**w**) to others (o).'' If he wanted to remove write permission from a file, keeping anyone but himself from accidentally modifying a finished document, he might enter:

```
$ chmod go-w meet.306
$ ls -l meet.306
-rw-r--r-- 1 fred   techpubs  126  March 6  10:32  meet.306
```

This command removes write permission (−**w**) from group (**g**) and other (o).

File permissions are important in UNIX, especially when you start using a text editor to create and modify files. They can be used to protect information you have on the system.

▪ Special Characters ▪

As part of the shell environment, there are a few special characters (metacharacters) that make working in UNIX much easier. We won't review all the special characters, but enough of them to make sure you see how useful they are.

The *asterisk* (*) and the *question mark* (?) are filename generation metacharacters. The asterisk matches any or all characters in a string. By itself, the asterisk expands to all the names in the specified directory.

```
$ echo *
meet.306  oldstuff reports
```

In this example, the `echo` command displays in a row the names of all the files and directories in the current directory. The asterisk can also be used as a shorthand notation for specifying one or more files.

```
$ ls meet*
meet.306
$ ls /work/textp/ch*
/work/textp/ch01
/work/textp/ch02
```

```
/work/textp/ch03
/work/textp/chapter_make
```

The question mark matches any single character.

```
$ ls /work/textp/ch01/sect?
/work/textp/ch01/sect1
/work/textp/ch01/sect2
/work/textp/ch01/sect3
```

Besides filename metacharacters, there are other characters that have special meaning when placed in a command line. The *semicolon* (;) separates multiple commands on the same command line. Each command is executed in sequence from left to right, one before the other.

```
$ cd oldstuff;pwd;ls
/usr/fred/oldstuff
ch01_draft
letter.212
memo
notes
```

Another special character is the *ampersand* (&). The ampersand signifies that a command should be processed in the background, meaning that the shell does not wait for the program to finish before returning a system prompt. When a program takes a significant amount of processing time, it is best to have it run in the background so that you can do other work at your terminal in the meantime. We will demonstrate background processing in Chapter 4 when we look at the nroff/troff text formatter.

· Environment Variables ·

The shell stores useful information about who you are and what you are doing in *environment variables*. Entering the set command will display a list of the environment variables that are currently defined in your account.

```
$ set
PATH    .:bin:/usr/bin:/usr/local/bin:/etc
argv    ()
cwd     /work/textp/ch03
home    /usr/fred
shell   /bin/sh
status  0
TERM    wy50
```

These variables can be accessed from the command line by prefacing their name with a dollar sign:

```
$ echo $TERM
wy50
```

The TERM variable identifies what type of terminal you are using. It is important that you correctly define the TERM environment variable, especially because the vi text editor relies upon it. Shell variables can be reassigned from the command line. Some variables, such as TERM, need to be *exported* if they are reassigned, so that they are available to all shell processes.

> $ **TERM=tvi925; export TERM**   *Tell UNIX I'm using a Televideo 925*

You can also define your own environment variables for use in commands.

```
$ friends="alice ed ralph"
$ echo $friends
alice ed ralph
```

You could use this variable when sending mail.

```
$ mail $friends
A message to friends
<CTRL-D>
```

This command sends the mail message to three people whose names are defined in the friends environment variable. Pathnames can also be assigned to environment variables, shortening the amount of typing:

```
$ pwd
/usr/fred
$ book="/work/textp"
$ cd $book
$ pwd
/work/textp
```

▪ Pipes and Filters ▪

Earlier we demonstrated how you can redirect the output of a command to a file. Normally, command input is taken from the keyboard and command output is displayed on the terminal screen. A program can be thought of as processing a stream of input and producing a stream of output. As we have seen, this stream can be redirected to a file. In addition, it can originate from or be passed to another command.

A *pipe* is formed when the output of one command is sent as input to the next command. For example:

```
$ ls | wc
```

might produce:

```
   10      10      72
```

The ls command produces a list of filenames which is provided as input to wc. The wc command counts the number of lines, words, and characters.

Any program that takes its input from another program, performs some operation on that input, and writes the result to the standard output is referred to as a *filter*. Most UNIX programs are designed to work as filters. This is one reason why UNIX programs do not print "friendly" prompts or other extraneous information to the user.

Because all programs expect—and produce—only a data stream, that data stream can easily be processed by multiple programs in sequence.

One of the most common uses of filters is to process output from a command. Usually, the processing modifies it by rearranging it or reducing the amount of information it displays. For example:

```
$ who                              List who is on the system, and at which terminal
peter        tty001        Mar    6  17:12
walter       tty003        Mar    6  13:51
chris        tty004        Mar    6  15:53
val          tty020        Mar    6  15:48
tim          tty005        Mar    4  17:23
ruth         tty006        Mar    6  17:02
fred         tty000        Mar    6  10:34
dale         tty008        Mar    6  15:26
$ who | sort                       List the same information in alphabetic order
chris        tty004        Mar    6  15:53
dale         tty008        Mar    6  15:26
fred         tty000        Mar    6  10:34
peter        tty001        Mar    6  17:12
ruth         tty006        Mar    6  17:02
tim          tty005        Mar    4  17:23
val          tty020        Mar    6  15:48
walter       tty003        Mar    6  13:51
$
```

The sort program arranges lines of input in alphabetic or numeric order. It sorts lines alphabetically by default. Another frequently used filter, especially in text-processing environments, is grep, perhaps UNIX's most renowned program. The grep program selects lines containing a pattern:

```
$ who | grep tty001        Find out who is on terminal 1
peter        tty001        Mar    6  17:12
```

One of the beauties of UNIX is that almost any program can be used to filter the output of any other. The pipe is the master key to building command sequences that go beyond the capabilities provided by a single program and allow users to create custom ''programs'' of their own to meet specific needs.

If a command line gets too long to fit on a single screen line, simply type a backslash followed by a carriage return, or (if a pipe symbol comes at the appropriate place) a pipe symbol followed by a carriage return. Instead of executing the command, the shell will give you a secondary prompt (usually >) so you can continue the line:

```
$ echo This is a long line shown here as a demonstration |
>   wc
         1      10      49
```

This feature works in the Bourne shell only.

· Shell Scripts ·

A *shell script* is a file that contains a sequence of UNIX commands. Part of the flexibility of UNIX is that anything you enter from the terminal can be put in a file and executed. To give a simple example, we'll assume that the last command example (`grep`) has been stored in a file called `whoison`:

```
$ cat whoison
who | grep tty001
```

The permissions on this file must be changed to make it executable. After a file is made executable, its name can be entered as a command.

```
$ chmod +x whoison
$ ls -l whoison
-rwxrwxr-x   1 fred        doc          123 Mar   6 17:34 whois
$ whoison
peter          tty001          Mar   6 17:12
```

Shell scripts can do more than simply function as a batch command facility. The basic constructs of a programming language are available for use in a shell script, allowing users to perform a variety of complicated tasks with relatively simple programs.

The simple shell script shown above is not very useful because it is too specific. However, instead of specifying the name of a single terminal line in the file, we can read the name as an argument on the command line. In a shell script, `$1` represents the first argument on the command line.

```
$ cat whoison
who | grep $1
```

Now we can find who is logged on to any terminal:

```
$ whoison tty004
chris          tty004          Mar   6 15:53
```

Later in this book, we will look at shell scripts in detail. They are an important part of the writer's toolbox, because they provide the ''glue'' for users of the UNIX system—the mechanism by which all the other tools can be made to work together.

3

Learning `vi`

UNIX has a number of editors that can process the contents of readable files, whether those files contain data, source code, or text. There are line editors, such as `ed` and `ex`, which display a line of the file on the screen, and there are screen editors, such as `vi` and `emacs`, which display a part of the file on your terminal screen.

The most useful standard text editor on your system is `vi`. Unlike `emacs`, it is available in nearly identical form on almost every UNIX system, thus providing a kind of text editing *lingua franca*. The same might be said of `ed` and `ex`, but screen editors are generally much easier to use. With a screen editor you can scroll the page, move the cursor, delete lines, insert characters, and more, while seeing the results of your edits as you make them. Screen editors are very popular because they allow you to make changes as you read a file, much as you would edit a printed copy, only faster.

To many beginners, `vi` looks unintuitive and cumbersome—instead of letting you type normally and use special control keys for word-processing functions, it uses all of the regular keyboard keys for issuing commands. You must be in a special *insert mode* before you can type. In addition, there seem to be *so many* commands.

You can't learn `vi` by memorizing every single `vi` command. Begin by learning some basic commands. As you do, be aware of the patterns of usage that commands have in common. Be on the lookout for new ways to perform tasks, experimenting with new commands and combinations of commands.

As you become more familiar with `vi`, you will find that you need fewer keystrokes to tell `vi` what to do. You will learn shortcuts that transfer more and more of the editing work to the computer—where it belongs. Not as much memorization is required as first appears from a list of `vi` commands. Like any skill, the more editing you do, the more you know about it and the more you can accomplish.

This chapter has three sections, and each one corresponds to a set of material about `vi` that you should be able to tackle in a single session. After you have finished each session, put aside the book for a while and do some experimenting. When you feel comfortable with what you have learned, continue to the next session.

▪ Session 1: Basic Commands ▪

The first session contains the basic knowledge you need to operate the vi editor. After a general description of vi, you are shown some simple operations. You will learn how to

- open and close a file;

- give commands and insert text;

- move the cursor;

- edit text (change, delete, and copy).

You can use vi to edit any file that contains readable text, whether it is a report, a series of shell commands, or a program. The vi editor copies the file to be edited into a buffer (an area temporarily set aside in memory), displays as much of the buffer as possible on the screen, and lets you add, delete, and move text. When you save your edits, vi copies the buffer into a permanent file, overwriting the contents of the old file.

▪ Opening a File ▪

The syntax for the vi command is:

vi [*filename*]

where *filename* is the name of either an existing file or a new file. If you don't specify a filename, vi will open an unnamed buffer, and ask you to name it before you can save any edits you have made. Press *RETURN* to execute the command.

A filename must be unique inside its directory. On AT&T (System V) UNIX systems, it cannot exceed 14 characters. (Berkeley UNIX systems allow longer filenames.) A filename can include any ASCII character except /, which is reserved as the separator between files and directories in a pathname. You can even include spaces in a filename by "escaping" them with a backslash. In practice, though, filenames consist of any combination of uppercase and lowercase letters, numbers, and the characters . (dot) and _ (underscore). Remember that UNIX is case-sensitive: lowercase filenames are distinct from uppercase filenames, and, by convention, lowercase is preferred.

If you want to open a new file called notes in the current directory, enter:

$ **vi notes**

The vi command clears the screen and displays a new buffer for you to begin work. Because notes is a new file, the screen displays a column of *tildes* (~) to indicate that there is no text in the file, not even blank lines.

```
~
~
~
~
~
~
~
~
~
~
~
~
~
"notes"  [New file].
```

If you specify the name of a file that already exists, its contents will be displayed on the screen. For example:

   $ **vi letter**

might bring a copy of the existing file letter to the screen.

```
    Mr. John Fust
    Vice President, Research and Development
    Gutenberg Galaxy Software
    Waltham, Massachusetts 02154

    Dear Mr. Fust:

    In our conversation last Thursday, we discussed a
    documentation project that would produce a user's manual
    on the Alcuin product.  Yesterday, I received the product
    demo and other materials that you sent me.
    ~
    ~
    ~
    ~
    "letter" 11 lines, 250 characters
```

The prompt line at the bottom of the screen echoes the name and size of the file.

Sometimes when you invoke `vi`, you may get either of the following messages:

```
[using open mode]
```

or:

```
Visual needs addressable cursor or upline capability
```

In both cases, there is a problem identifying the type of terminal you are using. You can quit the editing session immediately by typing `:q`.

Although `vi` can run on almost any terminal, it must know what kind of terminal you are using. The terminal type is usually set as part of the UNIX login sequence. If you are not sure whether your terminal type is defined correctly, ask your system administrator or an experienced user to help you set up your terminal. If you know your terminal type (`wy50` for instance), you can set your TERM environment variable with the following command:

```
TERM=wy50; export TERM
```

`vi` Commands

The `vi` editor has two *modes*: command mode and insert mode. Unlike many word processors, `vi`'s command mode is the initial or *default* mode. To insert lines of text, you must give a command to enter insert mode and then type away.

Most commands consist of one or two characters. For example:

```
i            insert
c            change
```

Using letters as commands, you can edit a file quickly. You don't have to memorize banks of function keys or stretch your fingers to reach awkward combinations of keys.

In general, `vi` commands

- are case-sensitive (uppercase and lowercase keystrokes mean different things; e.g., *I* is different from *i*);

- are not echoed on the screen;

- do not require a *RETURN* after the command.

There is also a special group of commands that echo on the bottom line of the screen. Bottom-line commands are indicated by special symbols. The slash (`/`) and the question mark (`?`) begin search commands, which are discussed in session 2. A colon (`:`) indicates an `ex` command. You are introduced to one `ex` command (to quit a file without saving edits) in this chapter, and the `ex` line editor is discussed in detail in Chapter 7.

To tell `vi` that you want to begin insert mode, press `i`. Nothing appears on the screen, but you can now type any text at the cursor. To tell `vi` to stop inserting text, press *ESC* and you will return to command mode.

For example, suppose that you want to insert the word *introduction*. If you type the keystrokes `iintroduction`, what appears on the screen is

```
introduction
```

Because you are starting out in command mode, `vi` interprets the first keystroke (`i`) as the insert command. All keystrokes after that result in characters placed in the file, until you press *ESC*. If you need to correct a mistake while in insert mode, backspace and type over the error.

While you are inserting text, press *RETURN* to break the lines before the right margin. An autowrap option provides a carriage return automatically after you exceed the right margin. To move the right margin in ten spaces, for example, enter `:set wm=10`.

Sometimes you may not know if you are in insert mode or command mode. Whenever `vi` does not respond as you expect, press *ESC*. When you hear a beep, you are in command mode.

Saving a File

You can quit working on a file at any time, save the edits, and return to the UNIX prompt. The `vi` command to quit and save edits is `ZZ`. (Note that `ZZ` is capitalized.)

Let's assume that you create a file called `letter` to practice `vi` commands and that you type in 36 lines of text. To save the file, first check that you are in command mode by pressing *ESC*, and then give the write and save command, `ZZ`. Your file is saved as a regular file. The result is:

```
"letter" [New file] 36 lines, 1331 characters
```

You return to the UNIX prompt. If you check the list of files in the directory, by typing `ls` at the prompt, the new file is listed:

```
$ ls
ch01   ch02   letter
```

You now know enough to create a new file. As an exercise, create a file called `letter` and insert the text shown in Figure 3-1. When you have finished, type `ZZ` to save the file and return to the UNIX prompt.

▪ Moving the Cursor ▪

Only a small percentage of time in an editing session may be spent adding new text in insert mode. Much of the time, you will be editing existing text.

In command mode, you can position the cursor anywhere in the file. You start all basic edits (changing, deleting, and copying text) by placing the cursor at the text that you want to change. Thus, you want to be able to quickly move the cursor to that place.

                                        April 1, 1987

Mr. John Fust
Vice President, Research and Development
Gutenberg Galaxy Software
Waltham, Massachusetts 02159

Dear Mr. Fust:

In our conversation last Thursday, we discussed a
documentation project that would produce a user's
manual on the Alcuin product. Yesterday, I received
the product demo and other materials that you sent me.

Going through a demo session gave me a much better
understanding of the product. I confess to being
amazed by Alcuin. Some people around here, looking
over my shoulder, were also astounded by the
illustrated manuscript I produced with Alcuin. One
person, a student of calligraphy, was really impressed.

Today, I'll start putting together a written plan
that shows different strategies for documenting
the Alcuin product. After I submit this plan, and
you have had time to review it, let's arrange a
meeting at your company to discuss these strategies.

Thanks again for giving us the opportunity to bid on
this documentation project. I hope we can decide upon
a strategy and get started as soon as possible in order
to have the manual ready in time for the first customer
shipment. I look forward to meeting with you towards
the end of next week.

                                        Sincerely,

                                        Fred Caslon

Fig. 3-1. A sample letter entered with vi

There are vi commands to move

- up, down, left, or right, one *character* at a time;
- forward or backward by *blocks of text* such as words, sentences, or paragraphs;
- forward or backward through a file, one *screen* at a time.

To move the cursor, make sure you are in command mode by pressing *ESC*. Give the command for moving forward or backward in the file from the current cursor position. When you have gone as far in one direction as possible, you'll hear a beep and the cursor stops. You cannot move the cursor past the tildes (~) at the end of the file.

Single Movements

The keys h, j, k, and l, right under your fingertips, will move the cursor:

h	left one space
j	down one line
k	up one line
l	right one space

You *could* use the cursor arrow keys (↑, ↓, →, ←) or the *RETURN* and *BACK-SPACE* keys, but they are out of the way and are not supported on all terminals.

You can also combine the h, j, k, and l keys with numeric arguments and other vi commands.

Numeric Arguments

You can precede movement commands with numbers. The command 4l moves the cursor (shown as a small box around a letter) four spaces to the right, just like typing the letter l four times (llll).

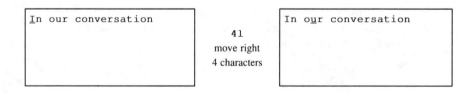

This one concept (being able to multiply commands) gives you more options (and power) for each command. Keep it in mind as you are introduced to additional commands.

Movement by Lines

When you saved the file letter, the editor displayed a message telling you how many lines were in that file. A *line* in the file is not necessarily the same length as a physical line (limited to 80 characters) that appears on the screen. A line is any text entered between carriage returns. If you type 200 characters before pressing *RETURN*, vi regards all 200 characters as a single line (even though those 200 characters look like several physical lines on the screen).

    Two useful commands in line movement are:

    0 <zero>   move to beginning of line
    $ move to end of line

In the following file, the line numbers are shown. To get line numbers on your screen, enter :set nu.

```
1   With the screen editor you can scroll the page,
2   move the cursor, delete lines, and insert characters,
    while seeing the results of edits as you make them.
3   Screen editors are very popular.
```

The number of logical lines (3) does not correspond to the number of physical lines (4) that you see on the screen. If you enter $, with the cursor positioned on the *d* in the word *delete*, the cursor would move to the period following the word *them*.

```
1   With the screen editor you can scroll the page,
2   move the cursor, delete lines, and insert characters,
    while seeing the results of edits as you make them.
3   Screen editors are very popular.
```

If you enter 0 (zero), the cursor would move back to the letter *t* in the word *the*, at the beginning of the line.

```
1   With the screen editor you can scroll the page,
2   move the cursor, delete lines, and insert characters,
    while seeing the results of edits as you make them.
3   Screen editors are very popular.
```

    If you do not use the automatic wraparound option (:set wm=10) in vi, you must break lines with carriage returns to keep the lines of manageable length.

Movement by Text Blocks

You can also move the cursor by blocks of text (words, sentences, or paragraphs).

    The command w moves the cursor forward one word at a time, treating symbols and punctuation marks as equivalent to words. The following line shows cursor movement caused by ten successive w commands:

    move the cursor, delete lines, and insert characters,

You can also move forward one word at a time, ignoring symbols and punctuation marks, using the command W (note the uppercase *W*). It causes the cursor to move to the first character following a blank space. Cursor movement using W looks like this:

    move the cursor, delete lines, and insert characters,

To move backward one word at a time, use the command b. The B command allows you to move backward one word at a time, ignoring punctuation.

With either the w, W, b, or B commands, you can multiply the movement with numbers. For example, 2w moves forward two words; 5B moves back five words, ignoring punctuation. Practice using the cursor movement commands, combining them with numeric multipliers.

▪ Simple Edits ▪

When you enter text in your file, it is rarely perfect. You find errors or want to improve a phrase. After you enter text, you have to be able to change it.

What are the components of editing? You want to *insert* text (a forgotten word or a missing sentence). And you want to *delete* text (a stray character or an entire paragraph). You also need to *change* letters and words (correct misspellings or reflect a change of mind). You want to *move* text from one place to another part of your file. And on occasion, you want to *copy* text to duplicate it in another part of your file.

There are four basic edit commands: i for *insert* (which you have already seen), c for *change*, d for *delete*, d then p for *move* (delete and put), and y for *yank* (copy). Each type of edit is described in this section. Table 3-1 gives a few simple examples.

TABLE 3-1. Basic Editing Commands

Object	Change	Delete	Copy (Yank)
One word	cw	dw	yw
Two words	2cW	2dW	2yW
Three words back	3cb	3db	3yb
One line	cc	dd	yy or Y
To end of line	c$ or C	d$ or D	y$
To beginning of line	c0	d0	y0
Single character	r	x	y1

Inserting New Text

You have already used the insert command to enter text into a new file. You also use the insert command while editing existing text to add characters, words, and sentences. Suppose you have to insert Today, at the beginning of a sentence. Enter the following sequence of commands and text:

```
┌─────────────────────┐                ┌─────────────────────┐
│ I'll start putting  │                │ I'll start putting  │
│ together a written  │      3k        │ together a written  │
│ plan that shows     │   move up 3    │ plan that shows     │
│ different strategies│     lines      │ different strategies│
└─────────────────────┘                └─────────────────────┘
```

```
┌─────────────────────┐                ┌─────────────────────┐
│ I'll start putting  │  iToday, <ESC> │Today, I'll start putting│
│ together a written  │                │ together a written  │
│ plan that shows     │     insert     │ plan that shows     │
│ different strategies│     Today,     │ different strategies│
└─────────────────────┘                └─────────────────────┘
```

In the previous example, vi moves existing text to the right as the new text is inserted. That is because we are showing vi on an "intelligent" terminal, which can adjust the screen with each character you type. An insert on a "dumb" terminal (such as an adm3a) will look different. The terminal itself cannot update the screen for each character typed (without a tremendous sacrifice of speed), so vi doesn't rewrite the screen until after you press *ESC*. Rather, when you type, the dumb terminal appears to overwrite the existing text. When you press *ESC*, the line is adjusted immediately so that the missing characters reappear. Thus, on a dumb terminal, the same insert would appear as follows:

```
┌─────────────────────┐                ┌─────────────────────┐
│ I'll start putting  │     iToday     │ Today, art putting  │
│ together a written  │     insert     │ together a written  │
│ plan that shows     │     Today,     │ plan that shows     │
│ different strategies│                │ different strategies│
└─────────────────────┘                └─────────────────────┘
```

```
┌─────────────────────┐                ┌─────────────────────┐
│ Today, art putting  │     <ESC>      │Today, I'll start putting│
│ together a written  │     leave      │ together a written  │
│ plan that shows     │  insert mode   │ plan that shows     │
│ different strategies│                │ different strategies│
└─────────────────────┘                └─────────────────────┘
```

Changing Text

You can replace any text in your file with the change command, c. To identify the amount of text that you want replaced, combine the change command with a movement command. For example, c can be used to change text from the cursor

cw	to the end of a word
2cb	back two words
c$	to the end of a line

Then you can replace the identified text with any amount of new text: no characters at all, one word, or hundreds of lines. The c command leaves you in insert mode until you press the *ESC* key.

Words

You can replace a word (cw) with a longer word, a shorter word, or any amount of text. The cw command can be thought of as "delete the word marked and insert new text until *ESC* is pressed."

Suppose that you have the following lines in your file letter and want to change *designing* to *putting together*. You only need to change one word.

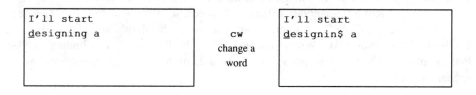

Note that the cw command places a $ at the last character of the word to be changed.

The cw command also works on a portion of a word. For example, to change *putting* to *puts*, position the cursor on the second *t*, enter cw, then type *s* and press *ESC*. By using numeric prefixes, you can change multiple words or characters immediately. For example:

3cw	change three words to the right of the cursor
5cl	change five letters to the right of the cursor

You don't need to replace the specified number of words, characters, or lines with a like amount of text. For example:

```
┌─────────────────────────────┐                    ┌─────────────────────────────┐
│ I'll start                  │                    │ I'll start                  │
│ putting together a          │       2cw          │ designing a                 │
│                             │    designing       │                             │
│                             │      <ESC>         │                             │
│                             │                    │                             │
└─────────────────────────────┘                    └─────────────────────────────┘
```

Lines

To replace the entire current line, there is the special change command cc. This command changes an entire line, replacing that line with the text entered before an *ESC*. The cc command replaces the entire line of text, regardless of where the cursor is located on the line.

The C command replaces characters from the current cursor position to the end of the line. It has the same effect as combining c with the special end-of-line indicator, $ (as in c$).

Characters

One other replacement edit is performed with the r command. This command replaces a single character with another single character. One of its uses is to correct misspellings. You probably don't want to use cw in such an instance, because you would have to retype the entire word. Use r to replace a single character at the cursor:

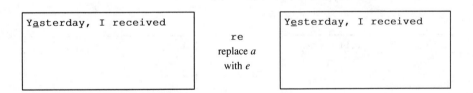

```
┌─────────────────────────────┐                    ┌─────────────────────────────┐
│ Yasterday, I received       │                    │ Yesterday, I received       │
│                             │        re          │                             │
│                             │    replace a       │                             │
│                             │     with e         │                             │
│                             │                    │                             │
└─────────────────────────────┘                    └─────────────────────────────┘
```

The r command makes only a single character replacement. You do *not* have to press *ESC* to finish the edit. Following an r command, you are automatically returned to command mode.

Deleting Text

You can also delete any text in your file with the delete command, d. Like the change command, the delete command requires an argument (the amount of text to be operated on). You can delete by word (dw), by line (dd and D), or by other movement commands that you will learn later.

With all deletions, you move to where you want the edit to take place and enter the delete command (d) followed by the amount of text to be deleted (such as a text object, w for *word*).

Words

Suppose that in the following text you want to delete one instance of the word *start* in the first line.

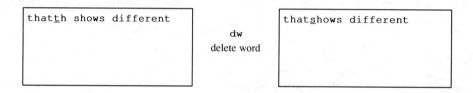

```
Today, I'll start               dw         Today, I'll_
start putting together       delete word   start putting together
a written plan                             a written plan
thatth shows different                     thatth shows different
```

The `dw` command deletes from the cursor's position to the end of a word. Thus, `dw` can be used to delete a portion of a word.

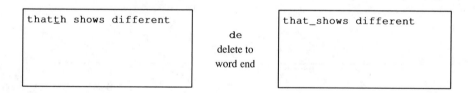

```
thatth shows different           dw        thatshows different
                              delete word
```

As you can see, `dw` deleted not only the remainder of the word, but also the space before any subsequent word on the same line. To retain the space between words, use `de`, which will delete only to the end of the word.

```
thatth shows different           de        that_shows different
                             delete to
                             word end
```

You can also delete backwards (`db`) or to the end or beginning of a line (`d$` or `d0`).

Lines

The `dd` command deletes the entire line that the cursor is on. Using the same text as in the previous example, with the cursor positioned on the first line as shown, you can delete the first two lines:

```
┌─────────────────────────────┐                    ┌─────────────────────────────┐
│ Today, I'll_                │                    │ a written plan              │
│ start putting together      │      2dd           │ that shows different        │
│ a written plan              │   delete first     │                             │
│ that shows different        │    2 lines         │                             │
│                             │                    │                             │
└─────────────────────────────┘                    └─────────────────────────────┘
```

If you are using a dumb terminal or one working at less than 1200 baud, line deletions look different. The dumb or slow terminal will not redraw the screen until you scroll past the bottom of the screen. Instead the deletion appears as:

```
┌─────────────────────────────┐
│ @                           │
│ @                           │
│ a written plan              │
│ that shows different        │
│                             │
└─────────────────────────────┘
```

An @ symbol "holds the place" of the deleted line, until the terminal redraws the entire screen. (You can force vi to redraw the screen immediately by pressing either *CTRL-L* or *CTRL-R*, depending on the terminal you're using.)

The D command deletes from the cursor position to the end of the line:

```
┌─────────────────────────────┐                    ┌─────────────────────────────┐
│ Today, I'll start           │                    │ Today, I'll start           │
│ putting together a          │      D             │ putting together a          │
│ written plan                │   delete to        │ written plan that           │
│ that shows different        │  end of line       │ that_                       │
│                             │                    │                             │
└─────────────────────────────┘                    └─────────────────────────────┘
```

You cannot use numeric prefixes with the D command.

Characters

Often, while editing a file, you want to delete a single character or two. Just as r changes one character, x deletes a single character. The x command deletes any character the cursor is on. In the following line, you can delete the letter *l* by pressing x.

```
┌─────────────────────────────┐                    ┌─────────────────────────────┐
│ Today, I'lll start          │                    │ Today, I'll start           │
│ putting                     │      x             │ putting                     │
│                             │   delete           │                             │
│                             │  character         │                             │
│                             │                    │                             │
└─────────────────────────────┘                    └─────────────────────────────┘
```

The X command deletes the character before the cursor. Prefix either of these commands with a number to delete that number of characters. For example, 5X will delete the five characters to the left of the cursor.

Moving Text

You can move text by deleting it and then placing that deleted text elsewhere in the file, like a "cut and paste." Each time you delete a text block, that deletion is temporarily saved in a buffer. You can move to another position in the file and use the put command to place the text in a new position. Although you can move any block of text, this command sequence is more useful with lines than with words.

The put command, p, places saved or deleted text (in the buffer) *after* the cursor position. The uppercase version of the command, P, puts the text *before* the cursor. If you delete one or more lines, p puts the deleted text on a new line(s) below the cursor. If you delete a word, p puts the deleted text on the same line after the cursor.

Suppose that in your file letter you have the following lines and you want to move the fourth line of text. Using delete, you can make this edit. First delete the line in question:

```
Today, I'll start
putting together a
plan for documenting
the Alcuin product
that shows
```

dd
delete line

```
Today, I'll start
putting together a
plan for documenting
that shows
```

Then use p to restore the deleted line at the next line below the cursor:

```
Today, I'll start
putting together a
plan for documenting
that shows
```

p
restore deleted
line

```
Today, I'll start
putting together a
plan for documenting
that shows
the Alcuin product
```

You can also use xp (delete character and put after cursor) to transpose two letters. For example, in the word *mvoe*, the letters *vo* are transposed (reversed). To correct this, place the cursor on *v* and press x then p.

After you delete the text, you must restore it before the next change or delete command. If you make another edit that affects the buffer, your deleted text will be lost. You can repeat the put command over and over, as long as you don't make a new edit. In the advanced vi chapter, you will learn how to retrieve text from named and numbered buffers.

Copying Text

Often, you can save editing time (and keystrokes) by copying part of your file to another place. You can copy any amount of existing text and place that copied text elsewhere in the file with the two commands y *(yank)* and p *(put)*. The yank command is used to get a copy of text into the buffer without altering the original text. This copy can then be placed elsewhere in the file with the put command.

Yank can be combined with any movement command (for example, yw, y$, or 4yy). Yank is most frequently used with a line (or more) of text, because to yank and put a word generally takes longer than simply inserting the word. For example, to yank five lines of text:

```
on the Alcuin product.           on the Alcuin product.
Yesterday, I received    5yy     Yesterday, I received
the product demo         yank 5  the product demo
and other materials      lines   and other materials
that you sent me.                that you sent me.
~                                ~
~                                ~
~                                5 lines yanked
```

To place the yanked text, move the cursor to where you want to put the text, and use the p command to insert it below the current line, or P to insert it above the current line.

```
that you sent me.                that you sent me.
~                                on the Alcuin product.
~                  p             Yesterday, I received
~            place yanked        the product demo
~                text            and other materials
~                                that you sent me.

                                 5 more lines
```

The yanked text will appear on the line below the cursor. Deleting uses the same buffer as yanking. Delete and put can be used in much the same way as yank and put. Each new deletion or yank replaces the previous contents of the yank buffer. As we'll see later, up to nine previous yanks or deletions can be recalled with put commands.

Using Your Last Command

Each command that you give is stored in a temporary buffer until you give the next command. If you insert *the* after a word in your file, the command used to insert the text, along with the text that you entered, is temporarily saved. Anytime you are making the same editing command repeatedly, you can save time by duplicating the command with . (dot). To duplicate a command, position the cursor anywhere on the screen, and press . to repeat your last command (such as an insertion or deletion) in the buffer. You can also use numeric arguments (as in 2.) to repeat the previous command more than once.

Suppose that you have the following lines in your file letter. Place the cursor on the line you want to delete:

```
Yesterday, I received
the product demo.
Yesterday, I received
other materials
```
         dd
     delete line
```
Yesterday, I received
the product demo.
other materials
```

```
Yesterday, I received
the product demo.
other materials
```
         .
     repeat last
     command (dd)
```
Yesterday, I received
the product demo.
```

In some versions of vi, the command CTRL-@ (^@) repeats the last insert (or append) command. This is in contrast to the . command, which repeats the last command that changed the text, including delete or change commands.

You can also *undo* your last command if you make an error. To undo a command, the cursor can be anywhere on the screen. Simply press u to undo the last command (such as an insertion or deletion).

To continue the previous example:

```
Yesterday, I received
the product demo.
```
         u
     undo last
     command
```
Yesterday, I received
the product demo.
other materials
```

The uppercase version of u (U) undoes all edits on a single line, as long as the cursor remains on that line. After you move off a line, you can no longer use U.

Joining Two Lines with J

Sometimes while editing a file, you will end up with a series of short lines that are difficult to read. When you want to merge two lines, position the cursor anywhere on the first line and press J to join the two lines.

```
Yesterday,
I received
the product demo.
```

J
join lines

```
Yesterday, I received
the product demo.
```

A numeric argument joins that number of consecutive lines.

Quitting without Saving Edits

When you are first learning vi, especially if you are an intrepid experimenter, there is one other command that is handy for getting out of any mess that you might create. You already know how to save your edits with ZZ, but what if you want to wipe out all the edits you have made in a session and return to the original file?

You can quit vi without saving edits with a special bottom-line command based on the ex line editor. The ex commands are explained fully in the advanced vi chapter, but for basic vi editing you should just memorize this command:

```
:q!    <RETURN>
```

The q! command quits the file you are in. All edits made since the last time you saved the file are lost.

You can get by in vi using only the commands you have learned in this session. However, to harness the real power of vi (and increase your own productivity) you will want to continue to the next session.

▪ Session 2: Moving Around in a Hurry ▪

You use vi not only to create new files but also to edit existing files. You rarely open to the first line in the file and move through it line by line. You want to get to a specific place in a file and start work.

All edits begin with moving the cursor to where the edit begins (or, with ex line editor commands, identifying the line numbers to be edited). This chapter shows you how to think about movement in a variety of ways (by screens, text, patterns, or line numbers). There are many ways to move in vi, because editing speed depends on getting to your destination with only a few keystrokes.

In this session, you will learn how to move around in a file by

- screens;

- text blocks;

- searches for patterns;

- lines.

▪ Movement by Screens ▪

When you read a book you think of "places" in the book by page: the page where you stopped reading or the page number in an index. Some `vi` files take up only a few lines, and you can see the whole file at once. But many files have hundreds of lines.

You can think of a `vi` file as text on a long roll of paper. The screen is a window of (usually) 24 lines of text on that long roll. In insert mode, as you fill up the screen with text, you will end up typing on the bottom line of the screen. When you reach the end and press *RETURN*, the top line rolls out of sight, and a blank line for new text appears on the bottom of the screen. This is called *scrolling*. You can move through a file by scrolling the screen ahead or back to see any text in the file.

Scrolling the Screen

There are `vi` commands to scroll forward and backward through the file by full and half screens:

^F	forward one screen
^B	backward one screen
^D	forward half screen
^U	backward half screen

(The `^` symbol represents the *CTRL* key. `^F` means to simultaneously press the *CTRL* key and the *F* key.)

```
In our conversation last Thursday, we
discussed a documentation project that would
produce a user's manual on the Alcuin product.
Yesterday, I received the product demo and
other materials that you sent me.

Going through a demo session gave me a
much better understanding of the product.   I
confess to being amazed by Alcuin.   Some
```

If you press ^F, the screen appears as follows:

```
better understanding of the product.   I
confess to being amazed by Alcuin.   Some
people around here, looking over my shoulder,
were also astounded by the illustrated
manuscript I produced with Alcuin.   One
person, a student of calligraphy, was really
impressed.


Today, I'll start putting together a written
```

There are also commands to scroll the screen up one line (^E) and down one line (^Y). (These commands are not available on small systems, such as the PDP-11 or Xenix for the PC-XT.)

Movement within a Screen

You can also keep your current screen or view of the file and move around within the screen using:

H	home—top line on screen
M	middle line on screen
L	last line on screen
nH	to n lines below top line
nL	to n lines above last line

The H command moves the cursor from anywhere on the screen to the first, or *home*, line. The M command moves to the middle line, L to the last. To move to the line below the first line, use 2H.

```
Today, I'll start              Today, I'll start
putting together a      2H     putting together a
written plan that    move to   written plan that
shows the different  second line  shows the different
strategies for the             strategies for the
```

These screen movement commands can also be used for editing. For example, dH deletes to the top line shown on the screen.

Movement within Lines

Within the current screen there are also commands to move by line. You have already learned the line movement commands $ and 0.

RETURN	beginning of next line
^	to first character of current line
+	beginning of next line
−	beginning of previous line

Going through a demo session gave me a much better understanding of the product.	− go to start of previous line	Going through a demo session gave me a much better understanding of the product.

The ^ command moves to the first *character* of the line, ignoring any spaces or tabs. (0, by contrast, moves to the first *position* of the line, even if that position is blank.)

• Movement by Text Blocks •

Another way that you can think of moving through a vi file is by text blocks—words, sentences, or paragraphs. You have already learned to move forward and backward by word (w or b).

e	end of word
E	end of word (ignore punctuation)
(	beginning of previous sentence
)	beginning of next sentence
{	beginning of previous paragraph
}	beginning of next paragraph

The vi program locates the end of a sentence by finding a period followed by at least two spaces, or a period as the last nonblank character on a line. If you have left only a single space following a period, the sentence won't be recognized.

A *paragraph* is defined as text up to the next blank line, or up to one of the default paragraph macros (.IP, .P, .PP, or .QP) in the mm or ms macro packages. The macros that are recognized as paragraph separators can be customized with the :set command, as described in Chapter 7.

In our conversation last Thursday, we . . . Going through a demo session gave me . . .	{ go to start of previous paragraph	In our conversation last Thursday, we . . . Going through a demo session gave me . . .

Most people find it easier to visualize moving ahead, so the forward commands are generally more useful.

Remember that you can combine numbers with movement. For example, 3) moves ahead three sentences. Also remember that you can edit using movement commands: d) deletes to the end of the current sentence, 2y} copies (yanks) two paragraphs ahead.

▪ Movement by Searches ▪

One of the most useful ways to move around quickly in a large file is by searching for text, or, more properly, for a *pattern* of characters. The pattern can include a "wildcard" shorthand that lets you match more than one character. For example, you can search for a misspelled word or each occurrence of a variable in a program.

The search command is the *slash* character (/). When you enter a slash, it appears on the bottom line of the screen; then type in the pattern (a word or other string of characters) that you want to find:

/*text*<RETURN>   search forward for *text*

A space before or after *text* will be included in the search. As with all bottom-line commands, press *RETURN* to finish.

The search begins at the cursor and moves forward, wrapping around to the start of the file if necessary. The cursor will move to the first occurrence of the pattern (or the message "Pattern not found" will be shown on the status line if there is no match).

If you wanted to search for the pattern *shows*:

```
Today, I'll start
putting together a
written plan that
shows the different
~
~
~
```
/shows<CR>
search for
shows
```
Today, I'll start
putting together a
written plan that
shows the different
~
~
/shows
```

```
Today, I'll start
putting together a
written plan that
shows the different
~
~
~
```
/th<CR>
search for
th
```
Today, I'll start
putting together a
written plan that
shows the different
~
~
/th
```

The search proceeds forward from the present position in the file. You can give any combination of characters; a search does not have to be for a complete word.

You can also search backwards using the ? command:

?*text*<RETURN>   search backward for *text*

The last pattern that you searched for remains available throughout your editing session. After a search, instead of repeating your original keystrokes, you can use a command to search again for the last pattern.

n	repeat search in same direction
N	repeat search in opposite direction
/<RETURN>	repeat search in forward direction
?<RETURN>	repeat search in backward direction

Because the last pattern remains available, you can search for a pattern, do some work, and then search again for the pattern without retyping by using n, N, /, or ?. The direction of your search (/=forwards, ?=backwards) is displayed at the bottom left of the screen.

Continuing the previous example, the pattern *th* is still available to search for:

```
Today, I'll start
putting together a
written plan that
shows the different
```

n
search for
next *th*

```
Today, I'll start
putting together a
written plan that
shows the different
```

```
Today, I'll start
putting together a
written plan that
shows the different
~
~
~
```

?<CR>
search back
for *th*

```
Today, I'll start
putting together a
written plan that
shows the different
~
~
?the
```

```
Today, I'll start
putting together a
written plan that
shows the different
```

N
repeat search
in opposite
direction

```
Today, I'll start
putting together a
written plan that
shows the different
```

This section has given only the barest introduction to searching for patterns. Chapter 7 will teach more about pattern matching and its use in making global changes to a file.

Current Line Searches

There is also a miniature version of the search command that operates within the current line. The command f moves the cursor to the next instance of the character you name. Semicolons can then be used to repeat the "find." Note, however, that the f command will not move the cursor to the next line.

f*x*	find (move cursor to) next occurrence of *x* in the line, where *x* can be any character
;	repeat previous find command

Suppose that you are editing on this line:

Today, I'll start	f' find first ' in line	Today, I'll start

Use df' to delete up to and including the named character (in this instance '). This command is useful in deleting or copying partial lines.

The t command works just like f, except it positions the cursor just before the character searched for. As with f and b, a numeric prefix will locate the *n*th occurrence. For example:

Today, I'll start	2ta place cursor before 2nd *a* in line	Today, I'll start

▪ Movement by Line Numbers ▪

A file contains sequentially numbered lines, and you can move through a file by specifying line numbers. Line numbers are useful for identifying the beginning and end of large blocks of text you want to edit. Line numbers are also useful for programmers because compiler error messages refer to line numbers. Line numbers are also used by ex commands, as you will learn in Chapter 7.

If you are going to move by line numbers, you need a way to identify line numbers. Line numbers can be displayed on the screen using the `:set nu` option described in Chapter 7. In `vi`, you can also display the current line number on the bottom of the screen.

The command `^G` displays the following on the bottom of your screen: the current line number, the total number of lines in the file, and what percentage of the total the present line number represents. For example, for the file `letter`, `^G` might display:

```
"letter" line 10 of 40 --25%--
```

`^G` is used to display the line number to use in a command, or to orient yourself if you have been distracted from your editing session.

The `G` (*go to*) command uses a line number as a numeric argument, and moves to the first position on that line. For instance, `44G` moves the cursor to the beginning of line 44. The `G` command without a line number moves the cursor to the last line of the file.

Two single quotes (`´´`) return you to the beginning of the line you were originally on. Two backquotes (```` `` ````) return you to your original position exactly. If you have issued a search command (`/` or `?`), ```` `` ```` will return the cursor to its position when you started the search.

The total number of lines shown with `^G` can be used to give yourself a rough idea of how many lines to move. If you are on line 10 of a 1000-line file:

```
"ch01" line 10 of 1000 --1%--
```

and know that you want to begin editing near the end of that file, you could give an approximation of your destination with:

```
800G
```

Movement by line number can get you around quickly in a large file.

▪ Session 3: Beyond the Basics ▪

You have already been introduced to the basic `vi` editing commands, `i`, `c`, `d`, and `y`. This session expands on what you already know about editing. You will learn

- additional ways to enter `vi`;

- how to customize `vi`;

- how to combine all edits with movement commands;

- additional ways to enter insert mode;

- how to use buffers that store deletions, yanks, and your last command;

- how to mark your place in a file.

▪ **Command-Line Options** ▪

There are other options to the vi command that can be helpful. You can open a file directly to a specific line number or pattern. You can also open a file in read-only mode. Another option recovers all changes to a file that you were editing when the system crashes.

Advancing to a Specific Place

When you begin editing an existing file, you can load the file and then move to the first occurrence of a pattern or to a specific line number. You can also combine the open command, vi, with your first movement by search or by line number. For example:

```
$ vi +n letter
```

opens letter at line number *n*. The following:

```
$ vi + letter
```

opens letter at the last line. And:

```
$ vi +/pattern letter
```

opens letter at the first occurrence of *pattern*.

To open the file letter and advance directly to the line containing *Alcuin*, enter:

```
$ vi +/Alcuin letter
```

```
Today I'll start putting together a
written plan that presents the different
strategies for the Alcuin
~
~
~
~
~
~
~
~
~
```

There can be no spaces in the pattern because characters after a space are interpreted as filenames.

If you have to leave an editing session before you are finished, you can mark your place by inserting a pattern such as ZZZ or HERE. Then when you return to the file, all you have to remember is /ZZZ or /HERE.

Read-Only Mode

There will be times that you want to look at a file, but you want to protect that file from inadvertent keystrokes and changes. (You might want to call in a lengthy file to practice `vi` movements, or you might want to scroll through a command file or program.) If you enter a file in read-only mode, you can use all the `vi` movement commands, but you cannot change the file with any edits. To look at your file `letter` in read-only mode, you can enter either:

    $ **vi -R letter**

or:

    $ **view letter**

Recovering a Buffer

Occasionally, there will be a system failure while you are editing a file. Ordinarily, any edits made after your last write (save) are lost. However, there is an option, `-r`, which lets you recover the edited buffer at the time of a system crash. (A system program called `preserve` saves the buffer as the system is going down.)

When you first log in after the system is running again, you will receive a mail message stating that your buffer is saved. The first time that you call in the file, use the `-r` option to recover the edited buffer. For example, to recover the edited buffer of the file `letter` after a system crash, enter:

    $ **vi -r letter**

If you first call in the file *without* using the `-r` option, your buffered edits are lost.

You can force the system to preserve your buffer even when there is not a crash by using the command `:pre`. You may find this useful if you have made edits to a file, then discover you can't save your edits because you don't have write permission. (You could also just write a copy of the file out under another name or in a directory where you do have write permission.)

· Customizing `vi` ·

A number of options that you can set as part of your editing environment affect how `vi` operates. For example, you can set a right margin that will cause `vi` to wrap lines automatically, so you don't need to insert carriage returns.

You can change options from within `vi` by using the `:set` command. In addition, `vi` reads an initialization file in your home directory called `.exrc` for further operating instructions. By placing `set` commands in this file, you can modify the way `vi` acts whenever you use it.

You can also set up `.exrc` files in local directories to initialize various options that you want to use in different environments. For example, you might define one set of options for editing text, but another set for editing source programs. The `.exrc` file in your home directory will be executed first, then the one on your current directory.

Finally, if the shell variable EXINIT is set in your environment (with the Bourne shell export command, or the C shell setenv command), any commands it contains will be executed by vi on startup. If EXINIT is set, it will be used instead of .exrc; vi will not take commands from both.

The set Command

There are two types of options that can be changed with the set command: toggle options, which are either on or off, and options that take a numeric or string value (such as the location of a margin or the name of a file).

Toggle options may be on or off by default. To turn a toggle option on, the command is:

    :set *option*

To turn a toggle option off, the command is:

    :set no*option*

For example, to specify that pattern searches should ignore case, you type:

    :set ic

If you want vi to return to being case-sensitive in searches, give the command:

    :set noic

Some options have values. For example, the option window sets the number of lines shown in the screen "window." You set values for these options with an equals sign (=). For example:

    set window=20

During a vi session, you can check what options are available. The command:

    :set all

displays the complete list of options, including options that you have set and defaults that vi has chosen. The display will look something like this:

```
noautoindent       open              tabstop=8
autoprint          prompt            taglength=0
noautowrite        noreadonly        term=wy50
nobeautify         redraw            noterse
directory=/tmp     /remap            timeout
noedcompatible     report=5          ttytype=wy50
noerrorbells       scrolls=11        warn
hardtabs=8         sections=AhBhChDh window=20
noignorecase       shell=/bin/csh    wrapscan
nolisp             shiftwidth=8      wrapmargin=10
nolist             noshowmatch       nowriteany
magic              noslowopen
mesg               paragraphs=IPLPPPQP LIpplpipbb
number             tags=tags /usr/lib/tags
nooptimize
```

You can also ask about the setting for any individual option by name, using the command:

```
:set option?
```

The command :set shows options that you have specifically changed, or set, either in your .exrc file or during the current session. For example, the display might look like this:

```
number  window=20  wrapmargin=10
```

See Appendix A for a description of what these options mean.

The .exrc File

The .exrc file that controls the vi environment for you is in your home directory. Enter into this file the set options that you want to have in effect whenever you use vi or ex.

The .exrc file can be modified with the vi editor, like any other file. A sample .exrc file might look like this:

```
set  wrapmargin=10  window=20
```

Because the file is actually read by ex before it enters visual mode (vi), commands in .exrc should not have a preceding colon.

Alternate Environments

You can define alternate vi environments by saving option settings in an .exrc file that is placed in a local directory. If you enter vi from that directory, the local .exrc file will be read in. If it does not exist, the one in your home directory will be read in.

For example, you might want to have one set of options for programming:

```
set number lisp autoindent sw=4 tags=/usr/lib/tags terse
```

and another set of options for text editing:

```
set wrapmargin=15  ignorecase
```

Local .exrc files are especially useful when you define abbreviations, which are described in Chapter 7.

Some Useful Options

As you can see when you type :set all, there are many options. Most options are used internally by vi and aren't usually changed. Others are important in certain cases, but not in others (for example, noredraw and window can be useful on a dialup line at a low baud rate). Appendix A contains a brief description of each option. We recommend that you take some time to play with option setting—if an option looks interesting, try setting it (or unsetting it) and watch what happens while you edit. You may find some surprisingly useful tools.

There is one option that is almost essential for editing nonprogram text. The wrapmargin option specifies the size of the right margin that will be used to autowrap text as you type. (This saves manually typing carriage returns.) This option is in effect if its value is set to greater than 0. A typical value is 10 or 15:

```
set  wrapmargin=15
```

There are also three options that control how vi acts in conducting a search. By default, it differentiates between uppercase and lowercase (*foo* does not match *Foo*), wraps around to the beginning of the file during a search (this means you can begin your search anywhere in the file and still find all occurrences), and recognizes wildcard characters when matching patterns. The default settings that control these options are noignorecase, wrapscan, and magic, respectively. To change any of these defaults, set the opposite toggles: ignorecase, nowrapscan, or nomagic.

Another useful option is shiftwidth. This option was designed to help programmers properly indent their programs, but it can also be useful to writers. The >> and << commands can be used to indent (or un-indent) text by shiftwidth characters. The position of the cursor on the line doesn't matter—the entire line will be shifted. The shiftwidth option is set to 8 by default, but you can use :set to change this value.

Give the >> or << command a numeric prefix to affect more than on line. For example:

```
10>>
```

will indent the next 10 lines by shiftwidth.

▪ Edits and Movement ▪

You have learned the edit commands c, d, and y, and how to combine them with movements and numbers (such as 2cw or 4dd). Since that point, you have added many more movement commands to your repertoire. Although the fact that you can combine edit commands with movement is not a "new" concept to you, Table 3-2 gives you a feel for the many editing options you now have.

TABLE 3-2. Combining vi Commands

From Cursor to	Change	Delete	Copy
Bottom of screen	cL	dL	yL
Next line	c+	d+	y+
Next sentence	c)	d)	y)
Next paragraph	c}	d}	y}
Pattern	c/*pattern*	d/*pattern*	y/*pattern*
End of file	cG	dG	yG
Line number 13	c13G	d13G	y13G

You can also combine numbers with any of the commands in Table 3-2 to multiply them. For example, 2c) changes the next two sentences. Although this table may seem forbidding, experiment with combinations and try to understand the patterns. When you find how much time and effort you can save, combinations of change and movement keys will no longer seem obscure, but will readily come to mind.

· More Ways to Insert Text ·

You have inserted text before the cursor with the sequence:

i *text* <ESC>

There are many insert commands. The difference between them is that they insert text at different positions relative to the cursor:

a	append text after cursor
A	append text to end of current line
i	insert text before cursor
I	insert text at beginning of line
o	open new line below cursor for text
O	open new line above cursor for text
R	overstrike existing characters with new characters

All these commands leave you in insert mode. After inserting text, remember to press *ESC* to escape back to command mode.

The A (*append*) and I (*insert*) commands save you from having to move the cursor to the end or beginning of the line before invoking insert mode. For example, A saves one keystroke over $a. Although one keystroke might not seem like a timesaver, as you become a more adept (and impatient) editor, you'll want to omit any unnecessary keystrokes.

There are other combinations of commands that work together naturally. For example, ea is useful for appending new text to the end of a word. (It sometimes helps to train yourself to recognize such frequent combinations so that invoking them becomes automatic.)

· Using Buffers ·

While you are editing, you have seen that your last deletion (d or x) or yank (y) is saved in a buffer (a place in stored memory). You can access the contents of that buffer and put the saved text back in your file with the put command (p or P).

The last nine deletions are stored by vi in *numbered* buffers. You can access any of these numbered buffers to restore any (or all) of the last nine deletions. You can also place yanks (copied text) in buffers identified by *letters*. You can fill up to 26 buffers (*a* through *z*) with yanked text and restore that text with a put command any time in your editing session.

The vi program also saves your last edit command (insert, change, delete, or yank) in a buffer. Your last command is available to repeat or undo with a single keystroke.

Recovering Deletions

Being able to delete large blocks of text at a single bound is all well and good, but what if you mistakenly delete 53 lines that you need? There is a way to recover any of your past nine deletions, which are saved in numbered buffers. The last deletion is saved in buffer 1; the second-to-last in buffer 2, and so on.

To recover a deletion, type " (quotation mark), identify the buffered text by number, and then give the put command. For example, to recover your second-to-last deletion from buffer 2, type:

    `"2p`

Sometimes it's hard to remember what's in the last nine buffers. Here's a trick that can help.

The `.` command (repeat last command) has a special meaning when used with `p` and `u`. The `p` command will print the last deletion or change, but `2p` will print the last two. By combining `p`, `.` (dot), and `u` (undo), you can step back through the numbered buffers.

The `"1p` command will put the last deletion, now stored in buffer 1, back into your text. If you then type `u`, it will go away. But when you type the `.` command, instead of repeating the last command (`"1p`), it will show the next buffer as if you'd typed `"2p`. You can thus step back through the buffers. For example, the sequence:

    `"1pu.u.u.u.`

will show you, in sequence, the contents of the last six numbered buffers.

Yanking to Named Buffers

With unnamed buffers, you have seen that you must put (p or P) the contents of the buffer before making any other edit, or the buffer is overwritten. You can also use `y` with a set of 26 named buffers (*a* through *z*), which are specifically for copying and moving text. If you name a buffer to store the yanked text, you can place the contents of the named buffer at any time during your editing session.

To yank into a named buffer, precede the yank command with a quotation mark (") and the character for the name of the buffer you want to load. For example:

    `"dyy`   yank current line into buffer *d*
    `"a6yy`   yank next six lines into buffer *a*

After loading the named buffers and moving to the new position, use `p` or `P` to put the text back.

    `"dP`   put buffer *d* before cursor
    `"ap`   put buffer *a* after cursor

```
In our conversation last                In our conversation last
Thursday, we discussed a      "a6yy      Thursday, we discussed a
documentation project       yank 6 lines documentation project
that would produce a         to buffer a that would produce a
user's manual on the                     user's manual on the
Alcuin product.                          Alcuin product.


                                         6 lines yanked
```

```
Alcuin product.                          Alcuin product.
                               "ap       In our conversation last
                            put buffer a Thursday, we discussed a
                            after cursor documentation project
                                         that would produce a
                                         user's manual on the
                                         Alcuin product.
```

There is no way to put part of a buffer into the text—it is all or nothing.

Named buffers allow you to make other edits before placing the buffer with p.
After you know how to travel between files without leaving vi, you can use named
buffers to selectively transfer text between files.

You can also delete text into named buffers, using much the same procedure. For
example:

    "a5dd   delete five lines into buffer *a*

If you specify the buffer name with a capital latter, yanked or deleted text will be
appended to the current contents of the buffer. For example:

    "byy   yank current line into buffer *b*
    "B5dd   delete five lines and append to buffer *b*
    3}   move down three paragraphs
    "bP   insert the six lines from buffer *b* above the cursor

When you put text from a named buffer, a copy still remains in that buffer; you can
repeat the put as often as you like until you quit your editing session or replace the text
in the buffer.

For example, suppose you were preparing a document with some repetitive elements, such as the skeleton for each page of the reference section in a manual. You
could store the skeleton in a named buffer, put it into your file, fill in the blanks, then
put the skeleton in again each time you need it.

▪ **Marking Your Place** ▪

During a vi session, you can mark your place in the file with an invisible "book-mark," perform edits elsewhere, then return to your marked place. In the command mode:

"m*x*	marks current position with *x* (*x* can be any letter)
" ´*x*	moves cursor to beginning of line marked by *x*
"` *x*	moves cursor to character marked by *x*
"` `	returns to previous mark or context after a move

```
Today, I'll start
putting together a
written plan that
```
mxG
mark and move
to end of file
```
Sincerely,



Fred Caslon
```

```
Sincerely,



Fred Caslon
```
`x
return to mark
```
Today, I'll start
putting together a
written plan that
```

Place markers are set only during the current vi session; they are not stored in the file.

▪ **Other Advanced Edits** ▪

You may wonder why we haven't discussed global changes, moving text between files, or other advanced ex topics. The reason is that, to use these tools, it helps to learn more about ex and a set of UNIX pattern-matching tools that we discuss together in Chapter 7.

4

nroff and troff

The `vi` editor lets you edit text, but it is not much good at formatting. A text file such as program source code might be formatted with a simple program like `pr`, which inserts a header at the top of every page and handles pagination, but otherwise prints the document exactly as it appears in the file. But for any application requiring the preparation of neatly formatted text, you will use the `nroff` ("en-roff") or `troff` ("tee-roff") formatting program.

These programs are used to process an input text file, usually coded or "marked up" with formatting instructions. When you use a *wysiwyg* program like most word processors, you use commands to lay out the text on the screen as it will be laid out on the page. With a markup language like that used by `nroff` and `troff`, you enter commands into the text that tell the formatting program what to do.

Our purpose in this chapter is twofold. We want to introduce the basic formatting codes that you will find useful. But at the same time, we want to present them in the context of what the formatter is doing and how it works. If you find this chapter rough-going—especially if this is your first exposure to `nroff/troff`—skip ahead to either Chapter 5 or Chapter 6 and become familiar with one of the macro packages, `ms` or `mm`; then come back and resume this chapter. We assume that you are reading this book because you would like more than the basics, that you intend to master the complexities of `nroff/troff`. As a result, this chapter is somewhat longer and more complex than it would be if the book were an introductory user's guide.

Conventions

To distinguish input text and requests shown in examples from formatter output, we have adopted the convention of showing "page corners" around output from `nroff` or `troff`. Output from `nroff` is shown in the same constant-width typeface as other examples:

```
Here is an example of nroff output.
```

Output from `troff` is shown in the same typeface as the text, but with the size of the type reduced by one point, unless the example calls for an explicit type size:

Here is an example of troff output.

In representing output, compromises sometimes had to be made. For example, when showing `nroff` output, we have processed the example separately with `nroff`, and read the results back into the source file. However, from there, they have been typeset in a constant-width font by `troff`. As a result, there might be slight differences from true `nroff` output, particularly in line length or page size. However, the context should always make clear just what is being demonstrated.

▪ **What the Formatter Does** ▪

Take a moment to think about the things you do when you format a page on a *wysiwyg* device such as a typewriter:

- You set aside part of the page as the text area. This requires setting top, bottom, left, and right margins.

- You adjust the lines that you type so they are all approximately the same length and fit into the designated text area.

- You break the text into syntactic units such as paragraphs.

- You switch to a new page when you reach the bottom of the text area.

Left to themselves, `nroff` or `troff` will do only one of these tasks: they will adjust the length of the lines in the input file so that they come out even in the output file. To do so, they make two assumptions:

- They assume that the line length is 6.5 inches.

- They assume that a blank line in the input signals the start of a new paragraph. The last line of the preceding text is not adjusted, and a blank line is placed in the output.

The process of filling and adjusting is intuitively obvious—we've all done much the same thing manually when using a typewriter or had it done for us by a *wysiwyg* word processor. However, especially when it comes to a typesetting program like `troff`, there are ramifications to the process of line adjustment that are not obvious. Having a clear idea of what is going on will be very useful later. For this reason, we'll examine the process in detail.

Line Adjustment

There are three parts to line adjustment: *filling*, *justification*, and *hyphenation*. Filling is the process of making all lines of text approximately equal in length. When working on a typewriter, you do this automatically, simply by typing a carriage return when the line is full. Most word-processing programs automatically insert a carriage return at the end of a line, and we have seen how to set up `vi` to do so as well.

However, `nroff` and `troff` ignore carriage returns in the input except in a special ''no fill'' mode. They reformat the input text, collecting all input lines into even-length output lines, stopping only when they reach a blank line or (as we shall see shortly) a formatting instruction that tells them to stop. Lines that begin with one or more blank spaces are not filled, but trailing blank spaces are trimmed. Extra blank spaces between words on the input line are preserved, and the formatter adds an extra blank space after each period, question mark, or exclamation point.

Justification is a closely related feature that should not be confused with filling. Filling simply tries to keep lines approximately the same length; justification adjusts the space between words so that the ends of the lines match exactly.

By default, `nroff` and `troff` both fill and justify text. Justification implies filling, but it is possible to have filling without justification. Let's look at some examples. First, we'll look at a paragraph entered in `vi`. Here's a paragraph from the letter you entered in the last chapter, modified so that it offers to prepare not just a user's guide for the Alcuin illuminated lettering software, but a reference manual as well. In the course of making the changes, we've left a short line in the middle of the paragraph.

```
In our conversation last Thursday, we discussed a
documentation project that would produce a user's guide
and reference manual
for the Alcuin product. Yesterday, I received the product
demo and other materials that you sent me.
```

Now, let's look at the paragraph after processing by `nroff`:

```
In our   conversation   last Thursday, we discussed   a
documentation project   that   would   produce a user's
guide and reference manual   for the Alcuin   product.
Yesterday, I   received   the   product   demo and other
materials that you sent me.
```

The paragraph has been both filled and justified. If the formatter were told to fill, but not to justify, the paragraph would look like this:

```
In our conversation last Thursday, we discussed a
documentation project that would produce a user's guide
and reference manual for the Alcuin product. Yesterday,
I received the product demo and other materials that
you sent me.
```

As you can see, `nroff` justified the text in the first example by adding extra space between words.

Most typewritten material is filled but not justified. In printer's terms, it is typed *ragged right*. Books, magazines, and other typeset materials, by contrast, are usually *right justified*. Occasionally, you will see printed material (such as ad copy) in which the right end of each line is justified, but the left end is ragged. It is for this reason that we usually say that text is *right* or *left justified*, rather than simply *justified*.

When it is difficult to perform filling or justification or both because a long word falls at the end of a line, the formatter has another trick to fall back on (one we are all familiar with)—hyphenation.

The `nroff` and `troff` programs perform filling, justification, and hyphenation in much the same way as a human typesetter used to set cold lead type. Human typesetters used to assemble a line of type by placing individual letters in a tray until each line was filled. There were several options for filling as the typesetter reached the end of the line:

- The next word might fit exactly.

- The next word might fit if the typesetter squeezed the words a little closer together.

- The next word could be hyphenated, with part put on the current line and part on the next line.

If, in addition to being filled, the text was to be justified, there was one additional issue: after the line was approximately the right length, space needed to be added between each word so that the line length came out even.

Just like the human typesetter they replace, `nroff` and `troff` assemble one line of text at a time, measuring the length of the line and making adjustments to the spacing to make the line come out even (assuming that the line is to be justified). Input lines are collected into a temporary storage area, or *buffer*, until enough text has been collected for a single output line. Then that line is output, and the next line collected.

It is in the process of justification that you see the first significant difference between the two programs. The `nroff` program was designed for use with typewriter-like printers; `troff` was designed for use with phototypesetters.

A typewriter-style printer has characters all of the same size—an *i* takes up the same amount of space as an *m*. (Typical widths are 1/10 or 1/12 inch per character.) And although some printers (such as daisywheel printers) allow you to change the style of type by changing the daisywheel or thimble, you can usually have only one typeface at a time.

A typesetter, by contrast, uses typefaces in which each letter takes up an amount of space proportional to its outline. The space allotted for an *i* is quite definitely narrower than the space allotted for an *m*. The use of variable-width characters makes the job of filling and justification much more difficult for `troff` than for `nroff`. Where `nroff` only needs to count characters, `troff` has to add up the width of each character as it assembles the line. (Character widths are defined by a ''box'' around the character, rather than by its natural, somewhat irregular shape.)

The `troff` program also justifies by adding space between words, but because the variable-width fonts it uses are much more compact, it fits more on a line and generally does a much better job of justification.*

There's another difference as well. Left to itself, `nroff` will insert only full spaces between words—that is, it might put two spaces between one pair of words, and three between another, to fill the line. If you call `nroff` with the `-e` option, it will attempt to make all interword spaces the same size (using fractional spaces if possible). But even then, `nroff` will only succeed if the output device allows fractional spacing. The `troff` program always uses even interword spacing.

Here's the same paragraph filled and justified by `troff`:

In our conversation last Thursday, we discussed a documentation project that would produce a user's guide and reference manual for the Alcuin product. Yesterday, I received the product demo and other materials that you sent me.

To make matters still more difficult, typeset characters come in a variety of different designs, or *fonts*. A font is a set of alphabetic, numeric, and punctuation characters that share certain design elements. Typically, fonts come in families of several related typefaces. For example, this book is typeset for the most part in the Times Roman family of typefaces. There are three separate fonts:

roman
bold
italic

Typesetting allows for the use of multiple fonts on the same page, as you can see from the mixture of fonts throughout this book. Sometimes the fonts are from the same family, as with the Times Roman, Times Bold, and Times Italic just shown. However, you can see other fonts, such as Helvetica, in the running headers on each page. Bold and italic fonts are generally used for emphasis; in computer books such as this, a constant-width typewriter font is used for examples and other "computer voice" statements.

Even within the same font family, the width of the same character varies from font to font. For example, a bold "**m**" is slightly wider than a Roman "m."

To make things still more complicated, the same font comes in different sizes. If you look at this book, you will notice that the section headings within each chapter are slightly larger for emphasis. Type sizes are measured in units called *points*. We'll talk more about this later, but to get a rough idea of what type sizes mean, simply look at the current page. The body type of the book is 10-point Times Roman; the next heading is 12-point Times Bold. The spacing between lines is generally proportional to the point size, instead of fixed, as it is with `nroff`.

---

*The very best typesetting programs have the capability to adjust the space between individual characters as well. This process is called *kerning*. SoftQuad Publishing Software in Toronto sells an enhanced version of `troff` called `SQroff` that does support kerning.

The `troff` program gets information about the widths of the various characters in each font from tables stored on the system in the directory `/usr/lib/font`. These tables tell `troff` how far to move over after it has output each character on the line.

We'll talk more about `troff` later. For the moment, you should be aware that the job of the formatting program is much more complicated when typesetting than it is when preparing text for typewriter-style printers.

▪ Using `nroff` ▪

As mentioned previously, left to themselves, `nroff` and `troff` perform only rudimentary formatting. They will fill and justify the text, using a default line length of 6.5 inches, but they leave no margins, other than the implicit right margin caused by the line length. To make this clearer, let's look at the sample letter from the last chapter (including the edit we made in this chapter) as it appears after formatting with `nroff`.

First, let's look at how to invoke the formatter. The `nroff` program takes as an argument the name of a file to be formatted:

```
$ nroff letter
```

Alternatively, it can take standard input, allowing you to preprocess the text with some other program before formatting it:

```
$ tbl report | nroff
```

There are numerous options to `nroff`. They are described at various points in this book (as appropriate to the topic) and summarized in Appendix B.

One basic option is −T, which specifies the terminal (printer) type for which output should be prepared. Although `nroff` output is fairly straightforward, some differences between printers can significantly affect the output. (For example, one printer may perform underlining by backspacing and printing an underscore under each underlined letter, and another may do it by suppressing a newline and printing the underscores in a second pass over the line.) The default device is the Teletype Model 37 terminal—a fairly obsolete device. Other devices are listed in Appendix B. If you don't recognize any of the printers or terminals, the safest type is probably `lp`:

```
$ nroff −Tlp file
```

In examples in this book, we will leave off the −T option, but you may want to experiment, and use whichever type gives the best results with your equipment.

Like most UNIX programs, `nroff` prints its results on standard output. So, assuming that the text is stored in a file called `letter`, all you need to do is type:

```
$ nroff letter
```

A few moments later, you should see the results on the screen. Because the letter will scroll by quickly, you should pipe the output of `nroff` to a paging program such as `pg` or `more`:

```
$ nroff letter | pg
```

or out to a printer using `lp` or `lpr`:

```
$ nroff letter | lp
```

▪ Using `troff` ▪

The chief advantage of `troff` over `nroff` is that it allows different types of character sets, or fonts, and so lets you take full advantage of the higher-quality printing available with typesetters and laser printers. There are a number of requests, useful only in `troff`, for specifying fonts, type sizes, and the vertical spacing between lines. Before we describe the actual requests though, we need to look at a bit of history.

The `troff` program was originally designed for a specific typesetter, the Wang C/A/T. Later, it was modified to work with a wide range of output devices. We'll discuss the original version of `troff` (which is still in use at many sites) first, before discussing the newer versions. The C/A/T typesetter was designed in such a way that it could use only four fonts at one time.

(Early phototypesetters worked by projecting light through a film containing the outline of the various characters. The film was often mounted on a wheel that rotated to position the desired character in front of the light source as it flashed, thus photographing the character onto photographic paper or negative film. Lenses enlarged and reduced the characters to produce various type sizes. The C/A/T typesetter had a wheel divided into four quadrants, onto which one could mount four different typefaces.)

Typically, the four fonts were the standard (roman), bold, and italic fonts of the same family, plus a ''special'' font that contained additional punctuation characters, Greek characters (for equations), bullets, rules, and other nonstandard characters. Figure 4-1 shows the characters available in these standard fonts.

The Coming of `ditroff`

Later, `troff` was modified to support other typesetters and, more importantly (at least from the perspective of many readers of this book), laser printers. The later version of `troff` is often called `ditroff` (for device-independent `troff`), but many UNIX systems have changed the name of the original `troff` to `otroff` and simply call `ditroff` by the original name, `troff`.

The `ditroff` program has not been universally available because, when it was developed, it was ''unbundled'' from the basic UNIX distribution and made part of a separate product called *Documenter's Workbench* or *DWB*. UNIX system manufacturers have the option not to include this package, although increasingly, they have been doing so. Versions of DWB are also available separately from third party vendors.

The newer version of `troff` allows you to specify any number of different fonts. (You can mount fonts at up to ten imaginary ''positions'' with `.fp` and can request additional fonts by name).

Times Roman

abcdefghijklmnopqrstuvwxyz
ABCDEFGHIJKLMNOPQRSTUVWXYZ
1234567890
! $ % & ( ) ' ' * + - . , / : ; = ? [ ] |
• ◻ — - _ ¹/₄ ¹/₂ ³/₄ fi fl   ° † ´ ¢ ® ©

Times Italic

abcdefghijklmnopqrstuvwxyz
ABCDEFGHIJKLMNOPQRSTUVWXYZ
1234567890
*! $ % & ( ) ' ' * + - . , / : ; = ? [ ] |*
• ◻ — - _ ¹/₄ ¹/₂ ³/₄ fi fl   ° † ´ ¢ ® ©

Times Bold

abcdefghijklmnopqrstuvwxyz
ABCDEFGHIJKLMNOPQRSTUVWXYZ
1234567890
! $ % & ( ) ' ' * + - . , / : ; = ? [ ] |
• ◻ — - _ ¹/₄ ¹/₂ ³/₄ fi fl   ° † ´ ¢ ® ©

Special Mathematical Font

" ´ \ ^ _ ` ~ / < > { } # @ + - = *
α β γ δ ε ζ η θ ι κ λ μ ν ξ ο π ρ σ ς τ υ φ χ ψ ω
Γ Δ Θ Λ Ξ Π Σ Υ Φ Ψ Ω
√ ‾ ≥ ≤ ≡ ∼ ≠ → ← ↑ ↓ × ÷ ± ∪ ∩ ⊂ ⊃ ⊆ ⊇ ∞ ∂
§ ∇ ¬ ∫ ∝ ∅ ∈ ‡ ☛ ☚ | ○ ⌈ ⌊ ⌋ ⌉ { } | ⌊ ⌋ ⌈ ⌉ |

Fig. 4-1. The Four Standard Fonts

There may also be different font sizes available, and there are some additional commands for line drawing (ditroff can draw curves as well as straight lines). For the most part, though, ditroff is very similar to the original program, except in the greater flexibility it offers to use different output devices.

One way to find out which version of troff you have on your system (unless you have a program explicitly called ditroff) is to list the contents of the directory /usr/lib/font:

```
$ls -F /usr/lib/font
devlj/
devps/
ftB
ftI
ftR
ftS
```

If there are one or more subdirectories whose name begins with the letters `dev`, your system is using `ditroff`. Our system supports both `ditroff` and `otroff`, so we have both a device subdirectory (for `ditroff`) and font files (for `otroff`) directly in `/usr/lib/font`.

We'll talk more about font files later. For the moment, all you need to know is that they contain information about the widths of the characters in various fonts for a specific output device.

Contrary to what a novice might expect, font files do not contain outlines of the characters themselves. For a proper typesetter, character outlines reside in the typesetter itself. All `troff` sends out to the typesetter are character codes and size and position information.

However, `troff` has increasingly come to be used with laser printers, many of which use *downloadable fonts*. An electronic image of each character is loaded from the computer into the printer's memory, typically at the start of each printing job. There may be additional "font files" containing character outlines in this case, but these files are used by the software that controls the printer, and have nothing to do with `troff` itself. In other cases, font images are stored in ROM (read-only memory) in the printer.

If you are using a laser printer, it is important to remember that `troff` itself has nothing to do with the actual drawing of characters or images on the printed page. In a case like this, `troff` simply formats the page, using tables describing the widths of the characters used by the printer, and generates instructions about page layout, spacing, and so on. The actual job of driving the printer is handled by another program, generally referred to as a *printer driver* or `troff` *postprocessor*.

To use `troff` with such a postprocessor, you will generally need to pipe the output of `troff` to the postprocessor and from there to the print spooler:

$ **troff** *file* | *postprocessor* | **lp**

If you are using the old version of `troff`, which expects to send its output directly to the C/A/T typesetter, you need to specify the `-t` option, which tells `troff` to use standard output. If you don't, you will get the message:

```
Typesetter busy.
```

(Of course, if by any chance you *are* connected to a C/A/T typesetter, you don't need this option. There are several other options listed in Appendix B that you may find useful.) When you use `ditroff`, on the other hand, you will need to specify the `-T` command-line option that tells it what device you are using. The postprocessor will then translate the device-independent `troff` output into instructions for that particular type of laser printer or typesetter. For example, at our site, we use `troff` with an

Apple LaserWriter and Pipeline Associates' `devps` postprocessor, which translates `troff` output for the LaserWriter. Our command line looks something like this:

```
$ ditroff -Tps files | devps | lp
```

You can print the same file on different devices, simply by changing the −T option and the postprocessor. For example, you can print drafts on a laser printer, then switch to a typesetter for final output without making extensive changes to your files. (To actually direct output to different printers, you will also have to specify a printer name as an option to the `lp` command. In our generic example, we simply use `lp` without any options, assuming that the appropriate printer is connected as the *default* printer.)

Like all things in life, this is not always as easy as it sounds. Because the fonts used by different output devices have different widths even when the nominal font names and sizes are the same, pagination and line breaks may be different when you switch from one device to another.

The job of interfacing `ditroff` to a wide variety of output devices is becoming easier because of the recent development of industry-wide *page description languages* like Adobe Systems' PostScript, Xerox's Interpress, and Imagen's DDL. These page description languages reside in the printer, not the host computer, and provide a device-independent way of describing placement of characters and graphics on the page.

Rather than using a separate postprocessor for each output device, you can now simply use a postprocessor to convert `troff` output to the desired page description language. For example, you can use Adobe Systems' TranScript postprocessor (or an equivalent postprocessor like `devps` from Pipeline Associates) to convert `troff` output to PostScript, and can then send the PostScript output to any one of a number of typesetters or laser printers.

From this point, whenever we say `troff`, we are generally referring to `ditroff`. In addition, although we will continue to discuss `nroff` as it differs from `troff`, our emphasis is on the more capable program. It is our opinion that the growing availability of laser printers will make `troff` the program of choice for almost all users in the not too distant future.

However, you can submit a document coded for `troff` to `nroff` with entirely reasonable results. For the most part, formatting requests that cannot be handled by `nroff` are simply ignored. And you can submit documents coded for `nroff` to `troff`, though you will then be failing to use many of the characteristics that make `troff` desirable.

▪ The Markup Language ▪

The `nroff` and `troff` markup commands (often called *requests*) typically consist of one or two lowercase letters and stand on their own line, following a period or apostrophe in column one. Most requests are reasonably mnemonic. For example, the request to leave space is:

```
.sp
```

There are also requests that can be embedded anywhere in the text. These requests are commonly called *escape sequences*. Escape sequences usually begin with a backslash

(\). For example, the escape sequence \l will draw a horizontal line. Especially in troff, escape sequences are used for line drawing or for printing various special characters that do not appear in the standard ASCII character set. For instance, you enter \(bu to get •, a bullet.

There are three classes of formatting instructions:

- Instructions that have an immediate one-time effect, such as a request to space down an inch before outputting the next line of text.

- Instructions that have a persistent effect, such as requests to set the line length or to enable or disable justification.

- Instructions that are useful for writing *macros*. There is a "programming language" built into the formatter that allows you to build up complex requests from sequences of simpler ones. As part of this language there are requests for storing values into variables called *strings* and *number registers*, for testing conditions and acting on the result, and so on.

For the most part, we will discuss the requests used to define macros, strings, and number registers later in this book.

At this point, we want to focus on understanding the basic requests that control the basic actions of the formatter. We will also learn many of the most useful requests with immediate, one-time effects. Table 4-1 summarizes the requests that you will use most often.

TABLE 4-1. Basic nroff/troff Requests

Request	Meaning	Request	Meaning
.ad	Enable line adjustment	.na	No justification of lines
.br	Line break	.ne	Need lines to end of page
.bp	Page break	.nf	No filling of lines
.ce	Center next line	.nr	Define and set number register
.de	Define macro	.po	Set page offset
.ds	Define string	.ps	Set point size
.fi	Fill output lines	.so	Switch to source file and return
.ft	Set current font	.sp	Space
.in	Set indent	.ta	Set tab stop positions
.ls	Set double or triple spacing	.ti	Set temporary indent
.ll	Specify line length	.vs	Set vertical line spacing

Looking at nroff Output

When we discussed the basic operations of the text formatter, we saw that nroff and troff perform rudimentary formatting. They will fill and justify the text, using a default line length of 6.5 inches, but they leave no margins, other than the implicit right margin caused by the line length.

To make this clearer, let's look at the sample letter from the last chapter as it appears after formatting with `nroff`, without any embedded requests, and without using any macro package. From Figure 4-2, you can see immediately that the formatter has adjusted all of the lines, so that they are all the same length—even in the address block of the letter, where we would have preferred them to be left as they were. Blank lines in the input produce blank lines in the output, and the partial lines at the ends of paragraphs are not adjusted.

The most noticeable aspect of the raw formatting is a little difficult to reproduce here, though we've tried. No top or left margin is automatically allocated by `nroff`.

▪ Turning Filling On and Off ▪

Even though filling of uneven text lines resulting from editing is probably the most basic action we want from the formatter, it is not always desirable. For example, in our letter, we don't want the address block to be filled. There are two requests we could use to correct the problem: `.br` (*break*) and `.nf` (*no fill*).

A `.br` request following a line outputs the current contents of the line buffer and starts the next line, even though the buffer is not yet full. To produce a properly formatted address block, we could enter the following requests in the file:

```
Mr. John Fust
.br
Vice President, Research and Development
.br
Gutenberg Galaxy Software
.br
Waltham, Massachusetts 02159
```

Each individual input line will be output without filling or justification. We could also use the `.nf` request, which tells `nroff` to stop filling altogether. Text following this request will be printed by the formatter exactly as it appears in the input file. Use this request when you want text to be laid out as it was typed in.

Because we do want the body of the letter to be filled, we must turn filling back on with the `.fi` (*fill*) request:

```
                                        April 1, 1987

.nf
Mr. John Fust
Vice President, Research and Development
Gutenberg Galaxy Software
Waltham, Massachusetts 02159
.fi
Dear Mr. Fust:
```

April 1, 1987

Mr. John Fust Vice President, Research and
Development Gutenberg Galaxy Software Waltham,
Massachusetts 02159

Dear Mr. Fust:

In our conversation last Thursday, we discussed a
documentation project that would produce a user's
guide and reference manual for the Alcuin product.
Yesterday, I received the product demo and other
materials that you sent me. After studying them,
I want to clarify a couple of points:

Going through a demo session gave me a much better
understanding of the product. I confess to being
amazed by Alcuin. Some people around here,
looking over my shoulder, were also astounded by
the illustrated manuscript I produced with Alcuin.
One person, a student of calligraphy, was really
impressed.

Tomorrow, I'll start putting together a written
plan that presents different strategies for
documenting the Alcuin product. After I submit
this plan, and you have had time to review it,
let's arrange a meeting at your company to discuss
these stratgies.

Thanks again for giving us the opportunity to bid
on this documentation project. I hope we can
decide upon a strategy and get started as soon as
possible in order to have the manual ready in time
for first customer ship. I look forward to meeting
with you towards the end of next week.

Sincerely,

Fred Caslon

Fig. 4-2. A Raw nroff-formatted File

If you look carefully at the previous example, you will probably notice that we entered the two formatting requests on blank lines in the letter. If we were to format the letter now, here is what we'd get:

```
                                          April 1, 1987

    Mr. John Fust
    Vice President, Research and Development
    Gutenberg Galaxy Software
    Waltham, Massachusetts 02159
    Dear Mr. Fust:
```

As you may notice, we've lost the blank lines that used to separate the date from the address block, and the address block from the salutation. Lines containing formatting requests do not result in any space being output (unless they are spacing requests), so you should be sure not to inadvertently replace blank lines when entering formatting codes.

▪ Controlling Justification ▪

Justification can be controlled separately from filling by the `.ad` (*adjust*) request. (However, filling must be on for justification to work at all.) You can adjust text at either margin or at both margins.

Unlike the `.br` and `.nf` requests introduced, `.ad` takes an *argument*, which specifies the type of justification you want:

l	adjust left margin only
r	adjust right margin only
b	adjust both margins
c	center filled line between margins

There is another related request, `.na` (*no adjust*). Because the text entered in a file is usually left justified to begin with, turning justification off entirely with `.na` produces similar results to `.ad l` in most cases.

However, there is an important difference. Normally, if no argument is given to the `.ad` request, both margins will be adjusted. That is, `.ad` is the same as `.ad b`. However, following an `.na` request, `.ad` reverts to the value last specified. That is, the sequence:

```
.ad r
```
Some text
```
.ad l
```
Some text
```
.ad
```
Some text

will adjust both margins in the third block of text. However, the sequence:

```
.ad  r
```
Some text
```
.na
```
Some text
```
.ad
```
Some text

will adjust only the right margin in the third block of text.

It's easy to see where you would use `.ad  b` or `.ad  l`. Let's suppose that you would like a ragged margin for the body of your letter, to make it look more like it was prepared on a typewriter. Simply follow the `.fi` request we entered previously with `.ad  l`.

Right-only justification may seem a little harder to find a use for. Occasionally, you've probably seen ragged-left copy in advertising, but that's about it. However, if you think for a moment, you'll realize that it is also a good way to get a single line over to the right margin.

For example, in our sample letter, instead of typing all those leading spaces before the date (and having it fail to come out flush with the margin anyway), we could enter the lines:

```
.ad  r
April 1, 1987
.ad  b
```

As it turns out, this construct won't *quite* work. If you remember, when filling is enabled, `nroff` and `troff` collect input in a one-line buffer and only output the saved text when the line has been filled. There are some non-obvious consequences of this that will ripple all through your use of `nroff` and `troff`. If you issue a request that temporarily sets a formatting condition, then reset it before the line is output, your original setting may have no effect. *The result will be controlled by the request that is in effect at the time the line is output, not at the time that it is first collected in the line buffer.*

Certain requests cause implicit line breaks (the equivalent of carriage returns on a typewriter) in the output, but others do not. The `.ad` request does not cause a break. Therefore, a construction like:

```
.ad  r
April 1, 1987
.ad  b
Mr. John Fust
```

will result in the following output:

```
    April 1, 1987 Mr. John Fust
```

and not:

```
                                              April 1, 1987
    Mr. John Fust
```

To make sure that you get the desired result from a temporary setting like this, be sure to follow the line to be affected with a condition that will cause a break.* For instance, in the previous example, you would probably follow the date with a blank line or an .sp request, either of which will normally cause a break. If you don't, you should put in an explicit break, as follows:

```
.ad r
April 1, 1987
.br
.ad b
Mr. John Fust
```

A final point about justification: the formatter adjusts a line by widening the blank space between words. If you do not want the space between two words adjusted or split across output lines, precede the space with a backslash. This is called an *unpaddable space*.

There are many obscure applications for unpaddable spaces; we will mention them as appropriate. Here's a simple one that may come in handy: nroff and troff normally add two blank spaces after a period, question mark, or exclamation point. The formatter can't distinguish between the end of a sentence and an abbreviation, so if you find the extra spacing unaesthetic, you might follow an abbreviation like Mr. with an unpaddable space: Mr.\ John Fust.

▪ Hyphenation ▪

As pointed out previously, hyphenation is closely related to filling and justification, in that it gives nroff and troff some additional power to produce filled and justified lines without large gaps.

The nroff and troff programs perform hyphenation according to a general set of rules. Occasionally, you need to control the hyphenation of particular words. You can specify either that a word not be hyphenated or that it be hyphenated in a certain way. You can also turn hyphenation off entirely.

Specifying Hyphenation for Individual Words

There are two ways to specify that a word be hyphenated a specific way: with the .hw request and with the special hyphenation indicator \%.

The .hw (*hyphenate word*) request allows you to specify a small list of words that should be hyphenated a specific way. The space available for the word list is small (about 128 characters), so you should use this request only for words you use frequently, and that nroff and troff hyphenate badly.

---

*The following requests cause a break:

   .bp .br .ce .fi .nf .sp .in .ti

All other requests can be interspersed with text without causing a break. In addition, as discussed later, even these requests can be introduced with a special "no break" control character (′ instead of .) so that they too will not cause a break.

To use `.hw`, simply specify the word or words that constitute the exception list, typing a hyphen at the point or points in the word where you would like it to be hyphenated:

```
.hw hy-phen-a-tion
```

You can specify multiple words with one `.hw` request, or you can issue multiple `.hw` requests as you need them.

However, if it is just a matter of making sure that a particular instance of a word is hyphenated the way you want, you can use the hyphenation indication character sequence `\%`. As you type the word in your text, simply type the two characters `\%` at each acceptable hyphenation point, or at the front of the word if you don't want the word to be hyphenated at all:

`\%acknowledge`	the word *acknowledge* will not be hyphenated
`ac\%know\%ledge`	the word *acknowledge* can be hyphenated only at the specified points

This character sequence is the first instance we have seen of a formatting request that does not consist of a request name following a period in column one. We will see many more of these later. This sequence is embedded right in the text but does not print out.

In general, `nroff` and `troff` do a reasonable job with hyphenation. You will need to set specific hyphenation points only in rare instances. In general, you shouldn't even worry about hyphenation points, unless you notice a bad break. Then use either `.hw` or `\%` to correct it.

The UNIX `hyphen` command can be used to print out all of the hyphenation points in a file formatted with `nroff` or `troff -a`.

$ **nroff** *options files* | **hyphen**

or:

$ **troff** *options* **-a** *files* | **hyphen**

If your system doesn't have the `hyphen` command, you can use `grep` instead:

$ **nroff** *options files* | **grep** `'-$'`

(The single quotation marks are important because they keep `grep` from interpreting the − as the beginning of an option.)

Turning Hyphenation Off and On

If you don't want any hyphenation, use the `.nh` (*no hyphenation*) request. Even if you do this, though, you should be aware that words already containing embedded hyphens, em dashes (—), or hyphen indication characters (`\%`) will still be subject to hyphenation.

After you've turned hyphenation off, you can turn it back on with the `.hy` (*hyphenate*) request. This request has a few twists. Not only does it allow you to turn hyphenation on, it also allows you to adjust the hyphenation rules that `nroff` and `troff` use. It takes the following numeric arguments:

0	turn hyphenation off
1	turn hyphenation on
2	do not hyphenate the last line on a page
4	do not hyphenate after the first two characters of a word
8	do not hyphenate before the last two characters of a word

Specifying .hy with no argument is the same as specifying .hy 1. The other numeric values are additive. For example, .hy 12 (.hy 4 plus .hy 8) will keep nroff and troff from breaking short syllables at the beginning or end of words, and .hy 14 will put all three hyphenation restrictions into effect.

▪ Page Layout ▪

Apart from the adjusted address block, the biggest formatting drawback that you probably noticed when we formatted the sample letter is that there was no left or top margin. Furthermore, though it is not apparent from our one-page example, there is no bottom margin either. If there were enough text in the input file to run onto a second page, you would see that the text ran continuously across the page boundary.

In normal use, these layout problems would be handled automatically by either the ms or mm macro packages (described later). Here, though, we want to understand how the formatter itself works.

Let's continue our investigation of the nroff and troff markup language with some basic page layout commands. These commands allow you to affect the placement of text on the page. Some of them (those whose descriptions begin with the word *set*) specify conditions that will remain in effect until they are explicitly changed by another instance of the same request. Others have a one-time effect.

As shown in Table 4-2, there are two groups of page layout commands, those that affect horizontal placement of text on the page and those that affect vertical placement. A moment's glance at these requests will tell you that, before anything else, we need to talk about units.

TABLE 4-2. Layout Commands

	.ll *n*	Set the line length to *n*
	.po *n*	Set the left margin (page offset) to *n*
Horizontal Layout	.in *n*	Indent the left margin to *n*
	.ti *n*	Temporarily indent the left margin to *n*
	.ce *n*	Center the following *n* lines
	.pl *n*	Set the page length to *n*
	.sp *n*	Insert *n* spaces
Vertical Layout	.bp *n*	Start a new page
	.wh *n*	Specify *when* (at what vertical position on the page) to execute a command

Units of Measure

By default, most `nroff` and `troff` commands that measure vertical distance (such as `.sp`) do so in terms of a number of "lines" (also referred to as vertical spaces, or vs). The `nroff` program has constant, device-dependent line spacing; `troff` has variable line spacing, which is generally proportional to the point size. However, both programs do allow you to use a variety of other units as well. You can specify spacing in terms of inches and centimeters, as well as the standard printer's measures *picas* and *points*. (A pica is 1/6 of an inch; a point is about 1/72 of an inch. These units were originally developed to measure the size of type, and the relationship between these two units is not as arbitrary as it might seem. A standard 12-point type is 1 pica high.)

Horizontal measures, such as the depth of an indent, can also be specified using any of these measures, as well as the printer's measures *ems* and *ens*. These are relative measures, originally based on the size of the letters *m* and *n* in the current type size and typeface. By default, horizontal measures are always taken to be in ems.

There is also a relationship between these units and points and picas. An em is always equivalent in width to the height of the character specified by the point size. In other words, an em in a 12-point type is 12 points wide. An en is always half the size of an em, or half of the current point size. The advantage of using these units is that they are relative to the size of the type being used. This is unimportant in `nroff`, but using these units in `troff` gives increased flexiblility to change the appearance of the document without recoding.

The `nroff` and `troff` programs measure not in any of these units, but in device-dependent basic units. Any measures you specify are converted to basic units before they are used. Typically, `nroff` measures in horizontal units of 1/240 of an inch and `otroff` uses a unit of 1/432 inch. These units too are not as arbitrary as they may seem. According to Joseph Osanna's *Nroff/Troff User's Manual*—the original, dense, and authoritative documentation on `troff` published by AT&T as part of the *UNIX Programmer's Manual*—the `nroff` units were chosen as "the least common multiple of the horizontal and vertical resolutions of various typewriter-like output devices." The units for `otroff` were based on the C/A/T typesetter (the device for which `troff` was originally designed), which could move in horizontal increments of 1/432 of an inch and in vertical increments of exactly one-third that, or 1/144 inch. Units for `ditroff` depend on the resolution of the output device. For example, units for a 300 dot-per-inch (dpi) laser printer will be 1/300 of an inch in either a vertical or a horizontal direction. See Appendix D for more information on `ditroff` device units.

You don't need to remember the details of all these measures now. You can generally use the units that are most familiar to you, and we'll come back to the others when we need them.

To specify units, you simply need to add the appropriate scale indicator from Table 4-3 to the numeric value you supply to a formatting request. For example, to space down 3 inches rather than 3 lines, enter the request:

```
.sp 3i
```

The numeric part of any scale indicator can include decimal fractions. Before the specified value is used, `nroff` and `troff` will round the value to the nearest number of device units.

TABLE 4-3. Units of Measure

Indicator	Units
c	Centimeters
i	Inches
m	Ems
n	Ens
p	Points
P	Picas
u	Device Units
v	Vertical spaces (lines)
none	Default

In fact, you can use any reasonable numeric expression with any request that expects a numeric argument. However, when using arithmetic expressions, you have to be careful about what units you specify. All of the horizontally oriented requests—.ll, .in, .ti, .ta, .po, .lt, and .mc—assume you mean ems unless you specify otherwise.

Vertically oriented requests like .sp assume v's unless otherwise specified. The only exceptions to this rule are .ps and .vs, which assume points by default—but these are not really motion requests anyway.

As a result, if you make a request like:

```
.ll 7i/2
```

what you are really requesting is:

```
.ll 7i/2m
```

The request:

```
.ll 7i/2i
```

is not what you want either. In performing arithmetic, as with fractions, the formatter converts scaled values to device units. In otroff, this means the previous expression is really evaluated as:

```
.ll (7*432u)/(2*432u)
```

If you really want half of 7 inches, you should specify the expression like this:

```
.ll 7i/2u
```

You could easily divide 7 by 2 yourself and simply specify 3.5i. The point of this example is that when you are doing arithmetic—usually with values stored in variables called number registers (more on these later)—you will need to pay attention to the interaction between units. Furthermore, because fractional device units are always rounded down, you should avoid expressions like 7i/2.5u because this is equivalent to 7i/2u.

In addition to absolute values, many `nroff` and `troff` requests allow you to specify relative values, by adding a + or a − before the value. For example:

```
.ll -.5i
```

will subtract ½ inch from the current line length, whatever it is.

Setting Margins

In `nroff` and `troff`, margins are set by the combination of the `.po` (*page offset*) and `.ll` (*line length*) requests. The `.po` request defines the left margin. The `.ll` request defines how long each line will be after filling, and so implicitly defines the right margin:

po	ll	*right margin*

The `nroff` program's default line length of 6.5 inches is fairly standard for an 8½-by-11 page—it allows for 1-inch margins on either side.

Assuming that we'd like 1¼-inch margins on either side of the page, we would issue the following requests:

```
.ll 6i
.po 1.25i
```

This will give us 1¼ inches for both the right and left margins. The `.po` request specifies a left margin, or page offset, of 1¼ inches. When the 6-inch line length is added to this, it will leave a similar margin on the right side of the page.

Let's take a look at how our sample letter will format now. One paragraph of the output should give you the idea.

```
In   our   conversation   last   Thursday,   we
discussed   a   documentation   project   that would
produce a user's guide and reference   manual   for
the   Alcuin   product.   Yesterday,   I received the
product demo and other materials that you sent me.
```

As we saw earlier, `nroff` assumes a default page offset of 0. Either you or the macro package you are using must set the page offset. In `troff`, though, there is a default page offset of 26/27 inch, so you can get away without setting this value.

(Keep in mind that all `nroff` output examples are actually simulated with `troff`, and are reduced to fit on our own 5-inch wide printed page. As a result, the widths shown in our example output are not exact, but are suggestive of what the actual result would be on an 8½-by-11 inch page.)

Setting Indents

In addition to the basic page offset, or left margin, you may want to set an indent, either for a single line or an entire block of text. You may also want to center one or more lines of text.

To do a single-line indent, as is commonly used to introduce a paragraph, use the `.ti` (*temporary indent*) request. For example, if you followed the blank lines between paragraphs in the sample letter with the request `.ti 5`, you'd get a result like this from `nroff`:

```
        ...Yesterday, I received the product demo and other
     materials that you sent me.

        Going  through  a  demo  session  gave  me  a
     much  better  understanding  of  the  product.  I
     confess  to being  amazed by  Alcuin...
```

The `.in` request, by contrast, sets an indent that remains in effect until it is changed. For example, if you had entered the line `.in 5` between the paragraphs, (instead of `.ti 5`), the result would have looked like this:

```
        ...Yesterday, I received the product demo and other
     materials that you sent me.

        Going  through  a  demo  session  gave  me  a
        much better  understanding  of  the  product.
        I confess  to being  amazed by  Alcuin...
```

All succeeding paragraphs will continue to be indented, until the indent is reset. The default indent (the value at the left margin) is 0.

These two indent requests can be combined to give a "hanging indent." Remember that you can specify negative values to many requests that take numeric arguments. Here is the first case where this makes sense. Let's say we would like to modify the letter so that it numbers the points and indents the body of the numbered paragraph:

```
     ...Yesterday, I received the product demo and other materials
     that you sent me.  After studying them, I want to clarify
     a couple of points:

     .in 4
     .ti -4
     1.  Going through a demo session gave me a much better
     understanding of the product.  I confess to being amazed by
     Alcuin...
```

The first line will start at the margin, and subsequent lines will be indented:

```
        ...Yesterday, I received the product demo and other
        materials that you sent me.      After studying them,
        I want to clarify a couple of points:

        1.   Going through  a demo session  gave  me  a much
             better understanding of the product.  I confess
             to   being   amazed   by   Alcuin...
```

To line up an indented paragraph like this in `nroff`, just count the number of characters you want to space over, then use that number as the size of the indent. But this
trick is not so simple in `troff`. Because characters, and even spaces, are not of constant width, it is more difficult to create a hanging indent. Ens are a good unit to use
for indents. Like ems, they are relative to the point size, but they are much closer to the
average character width than an em. As a result, they are relatively intuitive to work
with. An indent of `5n` is about where you expect a 5-character indent to be from familiarity with a typewriter.

Centering Output Lines

Centering is another useful layout tool. To center the next line, use the `.ce` request:

```
.ce
This line will be centered.
```

Here's the result:

```
                         This line will be centered.
```

Centering takes into account any indents that are in effect. That is, if you have used
`.in` to specify an indent of 1 inch, and the line length is 5 inches, text will be centered
within the 4-inch span following the indent.

To center multiple lines, specify a number as an argument to the request:

```
.ce 3
Documentation for the Alcuin Product

A Proposal Prepared by
Fred Caslon
```

Here's the result:

Documentation for the Alcuin Product

A Proposal Prepared by
Fred Caslon

Notice that .ce centered all three *text* lines, ignoring the blank line between.

To center an indeterminately large number of lines, specify a very large number with the .ce request, then turn it off by entering .ce 0:

```
.ce 1000
```
Many lines of text here.
```
.ce 0
```

In looking at the examples, you probably noticed that centering automatically disables filling and justification. Each line is centered individually. However, there is also the case in which you would like to center an entire filled and justified paragraph. (This paragraph style is often used to set off quoted material in a book or paper.) You can do this by using both the .in and .ll requests:

```
I was particularly interested by one comment that I
read in your company literature:

.in +5n
.ll −5n
The development of Alcuin can be traced back to our
founder's early interest in medieval manuscripts.
He spent several years in the seminary before
becoming interested in computers.  After he became
an expert on typesetting software, he resolved to
put his two interests together.
.in −5n
.ll +5n
```

Here's the result:

```
I  was  particularly  interested  by  one  comment  that  I
read in your company literature:

    The  development  of Alcuin  can  be  traced  back  to
    our    founder's    early    interest    in    medieval
    manuscripts.   He  spent  several  years  in  the
    seminary  before  becoming  interested  in  comput-
    ers.   After  he  became  an  expert  on  typesetting
    software,  he  resolved  to  put  his  two  interests
    together.
```

Remember that a line centered with `.ce` takes into account any indents in effect at the time. You can visualize the relationship between page offset, line length, indents, and centering as follows:

po	in	ce
	ll	

Setting Tabs

No discussion of how to align text would be complete without a discussion of tabs. A tab, as anyone who has used a typewriter well knows, is a horizontal motion to a predefined position on the line.

The problem with using tabs in `nroff` and `troff` is that what you see on the screen is very different from what you get on the page. Unlike a typewriter or a *wysiwyg* word processor, the editor/formatter combination presents you with two different tab settings. You can set tabs in `vi`, and you can set them in `nroff` and `troff`, but the settings are likely to be different, and the results on the screen definitely unaesthetic.

However, after you get used to the fact that tabs will not line up on the screen in the same way as they will on the printed page, you can use tabs quite effectively.

By default, tab stops are set every .8 inches in `nroff` and every .5 inches in `troff`. To set your own tab stops in `nroff` or `troff`, use the `.ta` request. For example:

```
.ta 1i 2.5i 3i
```

will set three tab stops, at 1 inch, 2½ inches, and 3 inches, respectively. Any previous or default settings are now no longer in effect.

You can also set incremental tab stops. The request:

```
.ta 1i +1.5i +.5i
```

will set tabs at the same positions as the previous example. Values preceded with a plus sign are added to the value of the last tab stop.

You can also specify the alignment of text at a tab stop. Settings made with a numeric value alone are left adjusted, just as they are on a typewriter. However, by adding either the letter `R` or `C` to the definition of a tab stop, you can make text right adjusted or centered on the stop.

For example, the following input lines (where a tab character is shown by the symbol |⸺|):

```
.nf
.ta 1i 2.5i 3.5i
|⸺|First|⸺|Second|⸺|Third
.fi
```

will produce the following output:

```
                          First              Second      Third
```

But:

```
.nf
.ta 1i 2.5iR 3.5iC
|———|First|———|Second|———|Third
.fi
```

will produce:

```
                    First        Second        Third
```

Right-adjusted tabs can be useful for aligning numeric data. This is especially true in troff, where all characters (including blank spaces) have different sizes, and, as a result, you can't just line things up by eye. If the numbers you want to align have an uneven number of decimal positions, you can manually force right adjustment of numeric data using the special escape sequence \0, which will produce a blank space exactly the same width as a digit. For example:

```
.ta 1iR
|———|500.2\0
|———|125.35
|———|50.\0\0
```

will produce:

```
        500.2
        125.35
        50.
```

As on a typewriter, if you have already spaced past a tab position (either by printing characters, or with an indent or other horizontal motion), a tab in the input will push text over to the next available tab stop. If you have passed the last tab stop, any tabs present in the input will be ignored.

You must be in no-fill mode for tabs to work correctly. This is not just because filling will override the effect of the tabs. Using .nf when specifying tabs is an important rule of thumb; we'll look at the reasoning behind it in Chapter 15.

Underlining

We haven't yet described how to underline text, a primary type of emphasis in nroff, which lacks the troff ability to switch fonts for emphasis.

There are two underlining requests: .ul (*underline*) and .cu (*continuous underline*). The .ul request underlines only printable characters (the words, but not the spaces), and .cu underlines the entire text string.

These requests are used just like `.ce`. Without an argument, they underline the text on the following input line. You can use a numeric argument to specify that more than one line should be underlined.

Both of these requests produce italics instead of underlines in `troff`. Although there is a request, `.uf`, that allows you to reset the underline font to some other font than italics,* there is no way to have these requests produce underlining even in `troff`. (The `ms` and `mm` macro packages both include a *macro* to do underlining in `troff`, but this uses an entirely different mechanism, which is not explained until Chapter 15.)

Inserting Vertical Space

As you have seen, a blank line in the input text results in a blank line in the output. You can leave blank space on the page (for example, between the closing of a letter and the signature) by inserting a number of blank lines in the input text.

However, particularly when you are entering formatting codes as you write, rather than going back to code an existing file like our sample letter, it is often more convenient to specify the spacing with the `.sp` request.

For example, you could type:

```
Sincerely,
.sp 3
Fred Caslon
```

In `troff`, the `.sp` request is even more important, because `troff` can space in much finer increments.

For example, if we were formatting the letter with `troff`, a full space between paragraphs would look like this:

In our conversation last Thursday, we discussed a documentation project that would produce a user's guide and reference manual for the Alcuin product. Yesterday, I received the product demo and other materials that you sent me.

Going through a demo session gave me a better understanding of the product. I confess to being amazed by Alcuin. Some people around here, looking over my shoulder, were also astounded by the illuminated manuscript I produced with Alcuin. One person, a student of calligraphy, was really impressed.

The output would probably look better if there was a smaller amount of space between the lines. If we replace the line between the paragraphs with the request `.sp .5`, here is what we will get:

---

*This request is generally used when the document is being typeset in a font family other than Times Roman. It might be used to set the ''underline font'' to Helvetica Italic, rather than the standard Italic.

> In our conversation last Thursday, we discussed a documentation project that would produce a user's guide and reference manual for the Alcuin product. Yesterday, I received the product demo and other materials that you sent me.
>
> Going through a demo session gave me a much better understanding of the product. I confess to being amazed by Alcuin. Some people around here, looking over my shoulder, were also astounded by the illuminated manuscript I produced with Alcuin. One person, a student of calligraphy, was really impressed.

Although it may not yet be apparent how this will be useful, you can also space to an absolute position on the page, by inserting a vertical bar before the distance. The following:

```
.sp |3i
```

will space down to a position 3 inches from the top of the page, rather than 3 inches from the current position.

You can also use negative values with ordinary relative spacing requests. For example:

```
.sp -3
```

will move back up the page three lines. Of course, when you use any of these requests, you have to know what you are doing. If you tell nroff or troff to put one line on top of another, that's exactly what you'll get. For example:

```
This is the first line.
.sp -2
This is the second line.
.br
This is the third line.
```

will result in:

> ```
> This is the second line.
> This is the first line.
> ```

Sure enough, the second line is printed above the first, but because we haven't restored the original position, the third line is then printed on top of the first.

When you make negative vertical motions, you should always make compensatory positive motions, so that you end up at the correct position for future output. The previous example would have avoided disaster if it had been coded:

```
This is the first line.
.sp -2
This is the second line.
.sp
This is the third line.
```

(Notice that you need to space down one less line than you have spaced up because, in this case, printing the second line "uses up" one of the spaces you went back on.)

These kind of vertical motions are generally used for line drawing (e.g., for drawing boxes around tables), in which all of the text is output, and the formatter then goes back up the page to draw in the lines. At this stage, it is unlikely that you will find an immediate use for this capability. Nonetheless, we are sure that a creative person, knowing that it is there, will find it just the right tool for a job. (We'll show a few creative uses of our own later.)

You probably aren't surprised that a typesetter can go back up the page. But you may wonder how a typewriter-like printer can go back up the page like this. The answer is that it can't. If you do any reverse line motions (and you do when you use certain macros in the standard packages, or the `tbl` and `eqn` preprocessors), you must pass the `nroff` output through a special filter program called `col` to get all of the motions sorted out beforehand, so that the page will be printed in the desired order:

```
$   nroff files | col | lp
```

Double or Triple Spacing

Both `nroff` and `troff` provide a request to produce double- or triple-spaced output without individually adjusting the space between each line. For example:

```
.ls 2
```

Putting this at the top of the file produces double-spaced lines. An argument of 3 specifies triple-spaced lines.

· Page Transitions ·

If we want space at the top of our one-page letter, it is easy enough to insert the command:

```
.sp 1i
```

before the first line of the text. However, `nroff` and `troff` do not provide an easy way of handling page transitions in multipage documents.

By default, `nroff` and `troff` assume that the page length is 11 inches. However, neither program makes immediate use of this information. There is no default top and bottom margin, so text output begins on the first line, and goes to the end of the page.

The `.bp` (*break page*) request allows you to force a page break. If you do this, the remainder of the current page will be filled with blank lines, and output will start again at the top of the second page. If you care to test this, insert a `.bp` anywhere in the text of our sample letter, then process the letter with `nroff`. If you save the resulting output in a file:

```
$ nroff letter > letter.out
```

you will find that the text following the .bp begins on line 67 (11 inches at 6 lines per inch equals 66 lines per page).

To automatically leave space at the top and bottom of each page, you need to use the .wh (*when*) request. In nroff and troff parlance, this request sets a *trap*—a position on the page at which a given macro will be executed.

You'll notice that we said *macro*, not *request*. There's the rub. To use .wh, you need to know how to define a macro. It doesn't work with single requests.

There's not all that much to defining macros, though. A macro is simply a sequence of stored requests that can be executed all at once with a single command. We'll come back to this later, after we've looked at the process of macro definition.

For the moment, let's assume that we've defined two macros, one containing the commands that will handle the top margin, and another for the bottom margin. The first macro will be called .TM, and the second .BM. (By convention, macros are often given names consisting of uppercase letters, to distinguish them from the basic nroff and troff requests. However, this is a convention only, and one that is not always followed.)

To set traps that will execute these macros, we would use the .wh request as follows:

```
.wh 0 TM
.wh -1i BM
```

The first argument to .wh specifies the vertical position on the page at which to execute the macro. An argument of 0 always stands for the top of the page, and a negative value is always counted from the bottom of the page, as defined by the page length.

In its simplest form, the .TM macro need only contain the single request to space down 1 inch, and .BM need only contain the single request to break to a new page. If .wh allowed you to specify a single request rather than a macro, this would be equivalent to:

```
.wh 0 .sp 1i
.wh -1i .bp
```

With an 11-inch page length, this would result in an effective 9-inch text area, because on every page, the formatter's first act would be to space down 1 inch, and it would break to a new page when it reached 1 inch from the bottom.

You might wonder why nroff and troff have made the business of page transition more complicated than any of the other essential page layout tasks. There are two reasons:

- The nroff and troff programs were designed with the typesetting heritage in mind. Until fairly recently, most typesetters produced continuous output on rolls of photographic paper or film. This output was manually cut and pasted up onto pages.

- Especially in troff, page transition is inherently more complex than the other tasks we've described. For example, books often contain headers and footers that are set in different type sizes or styles. At every page transition, the software must automatically save information about the current type style, switch to the style used by the header or footer, and then revert to the original style when it returns to the main text. Or consider the matter of footnotes—the position at which the page ends is different when a footnote is on the page. The page transition trap must make some allowance for this.

In short, what you might like the formatter to do during page transitions can vary. For this reason, the developers of `nroff` and `troff` have allowed users to define their own macros for handling this area.

When you start out with `nroff` or `troff`, we advise you to use one of the ready-made macro packages, `ms` or `mm`. The standard macro package for UNIX systems based on System V is `mm`; the standard on Berkeley UNIX systems is `ms`. Berkeley UNIX systems also support a third macro package called `me`. In addition, there are specialized macro packages for formatting viewgraphs, standard UNIX reference manual pages (`man`), and UNIX permuted indexes (`mptx`). Only the `ms` and `mm` packages are described in this book. The macro packages have already taken into account many of the complexities in page transition (and other advanced formatting problems), and provide many capabilities that would take considerable time and effort to design yourself.

Of course, it is quite possible to design your own macro package, and we will go into all of the details later. (In fact, this book is coded with neither of the standard macro packages, but with one developed by Steve Kochan and Pat Wood of Pipeline Associates, the consulting editors of this series, for use specifically with the Hayden UNIX library.)

Page Length Revisited

Before we take a closer look at macros, let's take a moment to make a few more points about page length, page breaks, and the like.

Assuming that some provision has been made for handling page transitions, there are several wrinkles to the requests we have already introduced, plus several new requests that you will probably find useful.

First, let's talk about page length. It's important to remember that the printing area is defined by the interaction of the page length and the location of the traps you define. For example, you could define a text area 7.5 inches high (as we did in preparing copy for this book) either by

- changing the page length to 9.5 inches, and setting 1-inch margins at the top and bottom;

- leaving the page length at 11 inches, and setting 1.75-inch margins at the top and bottom.

In general, we prefer to think of `.pl` as setting the *paper length*, and use the page transition traps to set larger or smaller margins.

However, there are cases where you really are working with a different paper size. A good example of this is printing addresses on envelopes: the physical paper height is about 4 inches (24 lines on a typewriter-like printer printing 6 lines per inch), and we want to print in a narrow window consisting of four or five lines. A good set of definitions for this case would be:

```
.pl 4i
.wh 0 TM
.wh −9v BM
```

with `.TM` containing the request `.sp 9v`, and with `.BM`, as before, containing `.bp`.

There is more to say about traps, but it will make more sense later, so we'll leave the subject for now.

Page Breaks without Line Breaks

Page breaks—we've talked about their use in page transition traps, but they also have a common use on their own. Often, you will want to break a page before it would normally end. For example, if the page breaks right after the first line of a paragraph, you will probably want to force the line onto the next page, rather than leaving an "orphaned" line. Or you might want to leave blank space at the bottom of a page for an illustration. To do this, simply enter a `.bp` at the desired point. A new page will be started immediately.

However, consider the case in which you need to force a break in the middle of a paragraph to prevent a "widowed" line at the top of the next page. If you do this:

```
The medieval masters of calligraphy and illumination
are largely unknown to us.  We thankfully have examples
of their work, and even
.bp
marginal notes by the copyists of some manuscripts,
but the men who produced these minute masterpieces
are anonymous.
```

the `.bp` request will also cause a line break, and the text will not be filled properly:

```
The  medieval  masters  of  calligraphy  and  illumination
are  largely  unknown  to  us.   We  thankfully  have  examples
of their work, and even


New page begins here


marginal  notes  by  the  copyists  of  some  manuscripts,  but
the  men  who  produced  these  minute  masterpieces  are
anonymous.
```

Fortunately, there is a way around this problem. If you begin a request with an apostrophe instead of a period, the request will not cause a break.

```
The medieval masters of calligraphy and illumination
are largely unknown to us.  We thankfully have examples
of their work, and even
'bp
marginal notes by the copyists of some manuscripts,
but the men who produced these minute masterpieces
are anonymous.
```

Now we have the desired result:

```
The  medieval  masters  of  calligraphy  and  illumination
are  largely  unknown  to  us.   We  thankfully  have  examples
```

New page begins here

```
of  their  work,  and  even  marginal  notes  by  the  copyists
of  some  manuscripts,  but  the  men  who  produced  these
minute  masterpieces  are  anonymous.
```

(In fact, most page transition macros use this feature to make paragraphs continue across page boundaries. We'll take a closer look at this in later chapters.)

Another very useful request is the conditional page break, or `.ne` (*need*) request. If you want to make sure an entire block of text appears on the same page, you can use this request to force a page break if there isn't enough space left. If there is sufficient space, the request is ignored.

For example, the two requests:

```
.ne 3.2i
.sp 3i
```

might be used to reserve blank space to paste in an illustration that is 3 inches high.

The `.ne` request does not cause a break, so you should be sure to precede it with `.br` or another request that causes a break if you don't want the remnants of the current line buffer carried to the next page if the `.ne` is triggered.

It is often better to use `.ne` instead of `.bp`, unless you're absolutely sure that you will *always* want a page break at a particular point. If, in the course of editing, an `.ne` request moves away from the bottom of the page, it will have no effect. But a `.bp` will always start a new page, sometimes leaving a page nearly blank when the text in a file has been changed significantly.

There are other special spacing requests that can be used for this purpose. (Depending on the macro package, these may have to be used.) For example, `.sv` (*save space*) requests a block of contiguous space. If the remainder of the page does not contain the requested amount of space, no space is output. Instead, the amount of space requested is remembered and is output when an `.os` (*output saved space*) request is encountered.

These are advanced requests, but you may need to know about them because most macro packages include two other spacing requests in their page transition macros: `.ns` (*no space*) and `.rs` (*restore space*). An `.ns` inhibits the effect of spacing requests; `.rs` restores the effectiveness of such requests.

Both the `ms` and `mm` macros include an `.ns` request in their page transition macros. As a result, if you issue a request like:

```
.sp 3i
```

with 1 inch remaining before the bottom of the page, you will not get 1 inch at the bottom, plus 2 inches at the top of the next page, but only whatever remains at the bottom. The next page will start right at the top. However, both macro packages also include an `.os` request in their page top macro, so if you truly want 3 inches, use `.sv 3i`, and you will get the expected result.

However, if you use `.sv`, you will also have another unexpected result: text following the spacing request will "float" ahead of it to fill up the remainder of the current page.

We'll talk more about this later. We introduced it now to prevent confusion when spacing requests don't always act the way you expect.

Page Numbering

The `nroff` and `troff` programs keep track of page numbers and make the current page number available to be printed out (usually by a page transition macro). You can artificially set the page number with the `.pn` request:

`.pn 5`	Set the current page number to 5
`.pn +5`	Increment the current page number by 5
`.pn -5`	Decrement the current page number by 5

You can also artificially set the number for the *next* page whenever you issue a `.bp` request, simply by adding a numeric argument:

`.bp 5`	Break the page and set the next page number to 5
`.bp +5`	Break the page and increment the next page number by 5
`.bp -5`	Break the page and decrement the next page number by 5

In addition to inhibiting `.sp`, the `.ns` request inhibits the action of `.bp`, *unless* a page number is specified. This means (at least in the existing macro packages), that the sequence:

```
.bp
.bp
```

will not result in a blank page being output. You will get the same effect as if you had specified only a simple `.bp`. Instead, you should specify:

```
.bp +1
```

The starting page number (usually 1) can also be set from the command line, using the −n option. For example:

```
$ nroff -ms -n10 file
```

will start numbering *file* at page number 10. In addition, there is a command-line option to print only selected pages of the output. The −o option takes a list of page numbers as its argument. The entire file (up to the last page number in the list) is processed, but only the specified pages are output. The list can include single pages separated by commas, or a range of pages separated by a hyphen, or both. A number followed by a trailing hyphen means to output from that page to the end. For example:

```
$ nroff -ms -o1,5,7-9,13- file
```

will output pages 1, 5, 7 through 9, and from 13 to the end of the file. There should be no spaces anywhere in the list.

▪ **Changing Fonts** ▪

In old troff (otroff), you were limited to four fonts at a time, because the fonts had to be physically mounted on the C/A/T typesetter. With ditroff and a laser printer or a modem typesetter, you can use a virtually unlimited number of fonts in the same document.

In otroff you needed to specify the basic fonts that are in use with the .fp (*font position*) request. Normally, at the front of a file (or, more likely, in the macro package), you would use this request to specify which fonts are mounted in each of the four quadrants (positions) of the typesetter wheel. By default, the roman font is mounted in position 1, the italic font in position 2, the bold font in position 3, and the special font in position 4. That is, troff acts as though you had included the lines:

```
.fp 1 R
.fp 2 I
.fp 3 B
.fp 4 S
```

In ditroff, up to ten fonts are automatically mounted, with the special font in position 10. Which fonts are mounted, and in which positions, depends on the output device. See Appendix D for details. The font that is mounted in position 1 will be used for the body type of the text—it is the font that will be used if no other specification is given. The special font is also used without any intervention on your part when a character not in the normal character set is requested.

To request one of the other fonts, you can use either the .ft request, or the inline font-switch escape sequence \f.

For example:

```
.ft B
This line will be set in bold type.
.br
.ft R
This line will again be set in roman type.
```

will produce:

> **This line will be set in bold type.**
> This line will again be set in roman type.

You can also change fonts using an inline font *escape sequence*. For example, the preceding sentence was coded like this:

```
...an inline font \fIescape sequence\fP.
```

You may wonder at the `\fP` at the end, rather than `\fR`. The `P` command is a special code that can be used with either the `.ft` request or the `\f` escape sequence. It means "return to the previous font, whatever it was." This is often preferable to an explicit font request, because it is more general.

All of this begs the question of fonts different than Times Roman, Bold, and Italic. There are two issues: first, which fonts are available on the output device, and second, which fonts does `troff` have width tables for. (As described previously, `troff` uses these tables to determine how far to space over after it outputs each character.) For `otroff` these width tables are in the directory `/usr/lib/font`, in files whose names begin with `ft`. If you list the contents of this directory, you might see something like this for `otroff`:

```
$ ls /usr/lib/font
ftB     ftBC    ftC     ftCE    ftCI
ftCK    ftCS    ftCW    ftFD    ftG
ftGI    ftGM    ftGR    ftH     ftHB
ftHI    ftI     ftL     ftLI    ftPA
ftPB    ftPI    ftR     ftS     ftSB
ftSI    ftSM    ftUD
```

You can pick out the familiar R, I, B, and S fonts, and may guess that `ftH`, `ftHI`, and `ftHB` refer to Helvetica, Helvetica Italic, and Helvetica Bold fonts. However, unless you are familiar with typesetting, the other names might as well be Greek to you. In any event, these width tables, normally supplied with `troff`, are for fonts that are commonly used with the C/A/T typesetter. *If you are using a different device, they may be of no use to you.*

The point is that if you are using a different typesetting device, you will need to get information about the font names for your system from whoever set up the equipment to work with `troff`. The contents of `/usr/lib/font` will vary from installation to installation, depending on what fonts are supported.

For `ditroff`, there is a separate subdirectory in `/usr/lib/font` for each supported output device. For example:

```
$ ls /usr/lib/font
devlj     devps
$ ls /usr/lib/font/devps
B.out     BI.out    CB.out    CI.out    CW.out    CX.out
DESC.out  H.out     HB.out    HI.out    HK.out    HO.out
HX.out    I.out     LI.out    PA.out    PB.out    PI.out
PX.out    R.out     O.out     RS.out    S.out     S1.out
```

Here, the font name is followed by the string `.out`.

Again, the font names themselves are probably Greek to you. However, with `ditroff`, you can actually use any of these names, and see what results they give you, because all fonts should be available at any time.

For the sake of argument, let's assume that your typesetter or other `troff`-compatible equipment supports the Helvetica font family shown in Figure 4-3, with the names `H`, `HI`, and `HB`. (This is a fairly reasonable assumption, because Helvetica is probably the most widely available font family after Times.)

Helvetica

abcdefghijklmnopqrstuvwxyz
ABCDEFGHIJKLMNOPQRSTUVWXYZ
1234567890
! $ % & ( ) ' ' * + - . , / : ; = ? [ ] |
• □ — - _ ¼ ½ ¾ fi fl   ° † ´ ® ©

Helvetica Italic

abcdefghijklmnopqrstuvwxyz
ABCDEFGHIJKLMNOPQRSTUVWXYZ
1234567890
*! $ % & ( ) ' ' * + - . , / : ; = ? [ ] |*
• □ — - _ ¼ ½ ¾ fi fl   ° † ´ ® ©

Helvetica   Bold

abcdefghijklmnopqrstuvwxyz
ABCDEFGHIJKLMNOPQRSTUVWXYZ
1234567890
! $ % & ( ) ' ' * + - . , / : ; = ? [ ] |
• □ — - _ ¼ ½ ¾ fi fl   ° † ´ ® ©

Special Mathematical Font

" ´ \ ^ _ ` ~ / < > { } # @ + - = *
α β γ δ ε ζ η θ ι κ λ μ ν ξ ο π ρ σ ς τ υ φ χ ψ ω
Γ Δ Θ Λ Ξ Π Σ Υ Φ Ψ Ω
√ ̄ ≥ ≤ ≡ ~ ⊭ → ← ↑ ↓ × ÷ ± ∪ ∩ ⊂ ⊃ ⊆ ⊇ ∞ ∂
§ ∇ ¬ ∫ ∝ ∅ ∈ ‡ ☛ ☜ | ○ ⌈ ⌊ ⌉ ⌋ | ⌞ ⌠⌡|

Fig. 4-3. Helvetica Fonts

When specifying two-character font names with the `\f` escape sequence, you must add the `(` prefix as well. For example, you would specify Helvetica Italic by the inline sequence `\f(HI`, and Helvetica Bold by `\f(HB`.

There is another issue when you are using fonts other than the Times Roman family. Assume that you decide to typeset your document in Helvetica rather than Roman. You reset your initial font position settings to read:

```
.fp 1 H
.fp 2 HI
.fp 3 HB
.fp 4 S
```

However, throughout the text, you have requests of the form:

```
.ft B
```

or:

```
\fB
```

You will need to make a set of global replacements throughout your file. To insulate yourself in a broader way from overall font change decisions, `troff` allows you to specify fonts by position, even within `.ft` and `\f` requests:

`.ft 1`	or	`\f1`	Use the font mounted in position 1
`.ft 2`	or	`\f2`	Use the font mounted in position 2
`.ft 3`	or	`\f3`	Use the font mounted in position 3
`.ft 4`	or	`\f4`	Use the font mounted in position 4

Because you don't need to use the `.fp` request to set font positions with `ditroff`, and the range of fonts is much greater, you may have a problem knowing which fonts are mounted in which positions. A quick way to find out which fonts are mounted is to run `ditroff` on a short file, sending the output to the screen. For example:

```
$ ditroff -Tps junk | more
x T ps
x res 720 1 1
x init
x font 1 R
x font 2 I
x font 3 B
x font 4 BI
x font 5 CW
x font 6 CB
x font 7 H
x font 8 HB
x font 9 HI
x font 10 S
...
```

The font positions should appear at the top of the file. In this example, you see the following fonts: (Times) Roman, (Times) Bold, (Times) Italic, (Times) Bold Italic, Constant Width, Constant Bold, Helvetica, Helvetica Bold, Helvetica Italic, and Special. Which font is mounted in which position is controlled by the file `DESC.out` in the device subdirectory of `/usr/lib/font`. See Appendix D for details.

Special Characters

A variety of special characters that are not part of the standard ASCII character set are supported by `nroff` and `troff`. These include Greek letters, mathematical symbols, and graphic characters. Some of these characters are part of the font referred to earlier as the *special font*. Others are part of the standard typesetter fonts.

Regardless of the font in which they are contained, special characters are included in a file by means of special four-character escape sequences beginning with \ (.

Appendix B gives a complete list of special characters. However, some of the most useful are listed in Table 4-4, because even as a beginner you may want to include them in your text. Although `nroff` makes a valiant effort to produce some of these characters, they are really best suited for `troff`.

TABLE 4-4. Special Characters

Name	Escape Sequence	Output Character
em dash	\(em	—
bullet	\(bu	•
square	\(sq	□
baseline rule	\(ru	_
underrule	\(ul	_
1/4	\(14	¼
1/2	\(12	½
3/4	\(34	¾
degrees	\(de	°
dagger	\(dg	†
double dagger	\(dd	‡
registered mark	\rg	®
copyright symbol	\(co	©
section mark	\(sc	§
square root	\(sq	√
greater than or equal	\(>=	≥
less than or equal	\(<=	≤
not equal	\(!=	≠
multiply	\(mu	×
divide	\(di	÷
plus or minus	\(+-	±
right arrow	\(->	→
left arrow	\(<-	←
up arrow	\(ua	↑
down arrow	\(da	↓

We'll talk more about some of these special characters as we use them. Some are used internally by `eqn` for producing mathematical equations. The use of symbols such as the copyright, registered trademark, and dagger is fairly obvious.

However, you shouldn't limit yourself to the obvious. Many of these special characters can be put to innovative use. For example, the square root symbol can be used to simulate a check mark, and the square can become an alternate type of bullet. As we'll show in Chapter 15, you can create additional, effective character combinations, such as a checkmark in a box, with overstriking.

The point is to add these symbols to your repertoire, where they can wait until need and imagination provide a use for them.

Type Size Specification

Typesetting also allows for different overall sizes of characters. Typesetting character sizes are described by units called *points*. A point is approximately 1/72 of an inch. Typical type sizes range from 6 to 72 points. A few different sizes follow:

This line is set in 6-point type.

This line is set in 8-point type.

This line is set in 10-point type.

This line is set in 12-point type.

This line is set in 14-point type.

This line is set in 18-point type.

(The exact size of a typeface does not always match its official size designation.. For example, 12-point type is not always 1/6 inch high, nor is 72-point type 1 inch high. The precise size will vary with the typeface.)

As with font changes, there are two ways to make size changes: with a request and with an inline escape sequence. The `.ps` request sets the point size. For example:

    `.ps 10`   Set the point size to 10 points

A `.ps` request that does not specify any point size reverts to the previous point size setting, whatever it was:

    `.ps 10`

    Some text here

    `.ps`   Revert to the point size before we changed it

To switch point size in the middle of the line, use the `\s` escape sequence. For example, many books reduce the point size when they print the word UNIX in the middle of a line. The preceding sentence was produced by these input lines:

```
For example, many books reduce the point size when
they print the word \s8UNIX\s0 in the middle of a line.
```

As you can probably guess from the example, \s0 does not mean to use a point size of 0, but to revert to the previous size.

In addition, you can use relative values when specifying point sizes. Knowing that the body of the book is set in 10-point type, we could have achieved the same result by entering:

```
For example, many books reduce the point size when
they print the word \s-2UNIX\s0 in the middle of a line.
```

You can increment or decrement point sizes only using a single digit; that is, you can't increment or decrement the size by more than 9 points.

Only certain sizes may be available on the typesetter. (Legal point sizes in otroff are 6, 7, 8, 9, 10, 11, 12, 14, 16, 18, 20, 22, 24, 28, and 36. Legal point sizes in ditroff depend upon the output device, but there will generally be more sizes available.) If you request a point size between two legal sizes, otroff will round up to the next legal point size; ditroff will round to the nearest available size.

Vertical Spacing

In addition to its ability to change typefaces and type sizes on the same page, a typesetter allows you to change the amount of vertical space between lines. This spacing is sometimes referred to as the *baseline spacing* because it is the distance between the base of characters on successive lines. (The difference between the point size and the baseline spacing is referred to as *leading*, from the old days when a human compositor inserted thin strips of lead between successive lines of type.)

A typewriter or typewriter-style printer usually spaces vertically in 1/6-inch increments (i.e., 6 lines per inch). A typesetter usually adjusts the space according to the point size. For example, the type samples shown previously were all set with 20 points of vertical space. More typically, the vertical space will vary along with the type size, like this:

This line is set in 6-point type and 8-point spacing.
This line is set in 8-point type and 10-point spacing.
This line is set in 10-point type and 12-point spacing.
This line is set in 12-point type and 14-point spacing.
This line is set in 14-point type and 16-point spacing.
This line is set in 18-point type and 20-poi

Typically, the body of a book is set with a single size of type (usually 9 or 10 point, with vertical spacing set to 11 or 12 points, respectively). Larger sizes are used occasionally for emphasis, for example, in chapter or section headings. When the type size is changed, the vertical spacing needs to be changed too, or the type will overrun the previous line, as follows, where 14-point type is shown with only 10-point spacing.

> Here is type larger than
> the space allotted for it.

Vertical spacing is changed with the `.vs` request. A vertical space request will typically be paired with a point size request:

```
.ps 10
.vs 12
```

After you set the vertical spacing with `.vs`, this becomes the basis of the `v` unit for `troff`. For example, if you enter `.vs 12`, the request `.sp` will space down 12 points; the request:

```
.sp 0.5v
```

will space down 6 points, or half the current vertical line spacing. However, if you change the baseline vertical spacing to 16, the `.sp` request will space down 16 points. Spacing specified in any other units will be unaffected. What all this adds up to is the commonsense observation that a blank line takes up the same amount of space as one containing text.

When you use double and triple spacing, it applies a multiplication factor to the baseline spacing. The request `.ls 2` will double the baseline spacing. You can specify any multiplication factor you like, though 2 and 3 are the most reasonable values.

The `.ls` request will only affect the spacing between output lines of text. It does not change the definition of `v` or affect vertical spacing requests.

▪ A First Look at Macros ▪

Although we won't go into all the details of macro design until we have discussed the existing macro packages in the next two chapters, we'll cover some of the basic concepts here. This will help you understand what the macro packages are doing and how they work.

To define a macro, you use the `.de` request, followed by the sequence of requests that you want to execute when the macro is invoked. The macro definition is terminated by the request `..` (two dots). The name to be assigned to the macro is given as an argument to the `.de` request.

You should consider defining a macro whenever you find yourself issuing a repetitive sequence of requests. If you are not using one of the existing macro packages (which have already taken care of this kind of thing), paragraphing is a good example of the kind of formatting that lends itself to macros.

Although it is certainly adequate to separate paragraphs simply by a blank line, you might instead want to separate them with a blank line and a temporary indent. What's more, to prevent "orphaned" lines, you would like to be sure that at least two lines of each paragraph appear at the bottom of the page. So you might define the following macro:

```
.de P
.sp
.ne 2
.ti 5n
..
```

This is the simplest kind of macro—a straightforward sequence of stored commands. However, macros can take arguments, take different actions depending on the presence or absence of various conditions, and do many other interesting and wonderful things.

We'll talk more about the enormous range of potential in macros in later chapters. For the moment, let's just consider one or two points that you will need to understand in order to use the existing macro packages.

Macro Arguments

Most basic `troff` requests take simple arguments—single characters or letters. Many macros take more complex arguments, such as character strings. There are a few simple pointers you need to keep in mind through the discussion of macro packages in the next two chapters.

First, a space is taken by default as the separator between arguments. If a single macro argument is a string that contains spaces, you need to quote the entire string to keep it from being treated as a series of separate arguments.

For example, imagine a macro to print the title of a chapter in this book. The macro call looks like this:

```
.CH 4 "Nroff and Troff"
```

A second point: to skip an argument that you want to ignore, supply a null string (`""`). For example:

```
.CH "" "Preface"
```

As you can see, it does no harm to quote a string argument that doesn't contain spaces (`"Preface"`), and it is probably a good habit to quote all strings.

Number Registers

When you use a specific value in a macro definition, you are limited to that value when you use the macro. For example, in the paragraph macro definition shown previously, the space will always be 1, and the indent always 5n.

However, `nroff` and `troff` allow you to save numeric values in special variables known as *number registers*. If you use the value of a register in a macro definition, the action of the macro can be changed just by placing a new value in the register. For example, in `ms`, the size of the top and bottom margins is not specified with an absolute value, but with a number register. As a result, you don't need to change the macro definition to change these margins; you simply reset the value of the appropriate number register. Just as importantly, the contents of number registers can be used as *flags* (a kind of message between macros). There are conditional statements in the markup language of `nroff` and `troff`, so that a macro can say: "If number register

Y has the value *x*, then do thus-and-so. Otherwise, do this.'' For example, in the mm macros, hyphenation is turned off by default. To turn it on, you set the value of a certain number register to 1. Various macros test the value of this register, and use it as a signal to re-enable hyphenation.

To store a value into a number register, use the `.nr` request. This request takes two arguments: the name of a number register,* and the value to be placed into it.

For example, in the ms macros, the size of the top and bottom margins is stored in the registers HM (*header margin*) and FM (*footer margin*). To reset these margins from their default value of 1 inch to 1.75 inches (thus producing a shorter page like the one used in this book), all you would need to do is to issue the requests:

```
.nr HM 1.75i
.nr FM 1.75i
```

You can also set number registers with single-character names from the command line by using the −r option. (The mm macros make heavy use of this capability.) For example:

```
$ nroff -mm -rN1 file
```

will format *file* using the mm macros, with number register N set to the value 1. We will talk more about using number registers later, when we describe how to write your own macros. For the moment, all you need to know is how to put new values into existing registers. The next two chapters will describe the particular number registers that you may find useful with the mm and ms macro packages.

Predefined Strings

The mm and ms macro packages also make use of some predefined text strings. The nroff and troff programs allow you to associate a text string with a one- or two-character string name. When the formatter encounters a special escape sequence including the string name, the complete string is substituted in the output.

To define a string, use the `.ds` request. This request takes two arguments, the string name and the string itself. For example:

```
.ds nt Nroff and Troff
```

The string should *not* be quoted. It can optionally begin with a quotation mark, but it should not end with one, or the concluding quotation mark will appear in the output. If you want to *start* a string with one or more blank spaces, though, you should begin the definition with a quotation mark. Even in this case, there is no concluding quotation mark. As always, the string is terminated by a newline.

---

*Number register names can consist of either one or two characters, just like macro names. However, they are distinct—that is, a number register and a macro can be given the same name without conflict.

You can define a multiline string by hiding the newlines with a backslash. For example:

```
.ds LS This is a very long string that goes over \
more than one line.
```

When the string is interpolated, it will be subject to filling (unless no-fill mode is in effect) and may not be broken into lines at the same points as you've specified in the definition. To interpolate the string in the output, you use one of the following escape sequences:

```
\*a
\*(ab
```

where *a* is a one-character string name, and *ab* is a two-character string name.

To use the *nt* string we defined earlier, you would type:

```
\*(nt
```

It would be replaced in the output by the words *Nroff and Troff.*

Strings use the same pool of names as macros. Defining a string with the same name as an existing macro will make the macro inoperable, so it is not advisable to go around wildly defining shorthand strings. The vi editor's abbreviation facility (described in Chapter 7) is a more effective way to save yourself work typing.

Strings are useful in macro design in much the same way number registers are— they allow a macro to be defined in a more general way. For example, consider this book, which prints the title of the chapter in the header on each odd-numbered page. The chapter title is not coded into the page top macro. Instead, a predefined string is interpolated there. The same macro that describes the format of the chapter title on the first page of the chapter also defines the string that will appear in the header.

In using each of the existing macro packages, you may be asked to define or interpolate the contents of an existing string. For the most part, though, string definitions are hidden inside macro definitions, so you may not run across them. However, there are a couple of handy predefined strings you may find yourself using, such as:

```
\*(DY
```

which always contains the current date in the ms macro package. (The equivalent string in mm is *(DT.) For example, if you wanted a form letter to contain the date that it was formatted and printed rather than the date it was written, you could interpolate this string.

Just What Is a Macro Package?

Before leaving the topic of macros, we ought to take a moment to treat a subject we have skirted up to this point: just what is a macro package?

As the name suggests, a macro package is simply a collection of macro definitions. The fact that there are command-line options for using the existing packages may seem to give them a special status, but they are text files that you can read and modify (assuming that your system has the UNIX file permissions set up so you can do so).

There is no magic to the options −ms and −mm. The actual option to nroff and troff is −m*x*, which tells the program to look in the directory /usr/lib/tmac for a file with a name of the form tmac.*x*. As you might expect, this means that there is a file in that directory called tmac.s or tmac.m (depending on which package you have on your system). It also means that you can invoke a macro package of your own from the command line simply by storing the macro definitions in a file with the appropriate pathname. This file will be added to any other files in the formatting run. This means that if you are using the ms macros you could achieve the same result by including the line:

```
.so /usr/lib/tmac/tmac.s
```

at the start of each source file, and omitting the command-line switch −ms. (The .so request reads another file into the input stream, and when its contents have been exhausted, returns to the current file. Multiple .so requests can be nested, not just to read in macro definitions, but also to read in additional text files.)

The macros in the standard macro packages are no different (other than in complexity) than the macros you might write yourself. In fact, you can print out and study the contents of the existing macro packages to learn how they work. We'll be looking in detail at the actions of the existing macro packages, but for copyright reasons we can't actually show their internal design. We'll come back to all this later. For now, all you need to know is that macros aren't magic—just an assemblage of simple commands working together.

The ms Macros

The UNIX shell is a user interface for the kernel, the actual heart of the operating system. You can choose the C shell or Korn shell instead of the Bourne shell, without worrying about its effects on the low-level operations of the kernel. Likewise, a macro package is a user interface for accessing the capabilities of the `nroff/troff` formatter. Users can select either the `ms` or `mm` macro packages (as well as other packages that are available on some systems) to use with `nroff/troff`.

The `ms` package was the original Bell Labs macro package, and is available on many UNIX systems, but it is no longer officially supported by AT&T. Our main reason for giving `ms` equal time is that many Berkeley UNIX systems ship `ms` instead of `mm`. In addition, it is a less complex package, so it is much easier to learn the principles of macro design by studying `ms` than by studying `mm`.

A third general-purpose package, called `me`, is also distributed with Berkeley UNIX systems. It was written by Eric Allman and is comparable to `ms` and `mm`. (Mark Horton writes us: I think of `ms` as the FORTRAN of `nroff`, `mm` as the PL/I, and `me` as the Pascal.) The `me` package is not described in this book.

In addition, there are specialized packages—`mv`, for formatting viewgraphs, `mptx`, for formatting the permuted index found in the *UNIX Reference Manual*, and `man`, for formatting the reference pages in that same manual. These packages are simple and are covered in the standard UNIX documentation.

Regardless of which macro package you choose, the formatter knows only to replace each call of a macro with its definition. The macro definition contains the set of requests that the formatter executes. Whether a definition is supplied with the text in the input file or found in a macro package is irrelevant to `nroff/troff`. The formatter can be said to be oblivious to the idea of a macro package.

You might not expect this rather freely structured arrangement between a macro package and `nroff/troff`. Macros are application programs of sorts. They organize the types of functions that you need to be able to do. However, the actual work is accomplished by `nroff/troff` requests.

In other words, the basic formatting capabilities are inherent in `nroff` and `troff`; the user implementation of these capabilities to achieve particular formats is accomplished with a macro package. If a macro doesn't work the way you expect, its definition may have been modified. It doesn't mean that nroff/troff works differently on your system. It is one thing to say "nroff/troff won't let me do it," and another to say "I don't have the macro to do it (but I could do it, perhaps)."

A general-purpose macro package like ms provides a way of describing the format of various kinds of documents. Each document presents its own specific problems, and macros help to provide a simple and flexible solution. The ms macro package is designed to help you format letters, proposals, memos, technical papers, and reports.

For simple documents such as letters, ms offers few advantages to the basic format requests described in Chapter 4. But as you begin to format more complex documents, you will quickly see the advantage of working with a macro package, which provides specialized tools for so many of the formatting tasks you will encounter.

A text file that contains ms macros can be processed by either nroff or troff, and the output can be displayed on a terminal screen or printed on a line printer, a laser printer, or a typesetter.

▪ Formatting a Text File with ms ▪

If you want to format an ms document for a line printer or for a terminal screen, enter this command line:

    $ **nroff −ms** *file(s)*

To format for a laser printer or typesetter, enter this command line:

    $ **troff −ms** *file(s)* **|** *device postprocessor*

Be sure to redirect the output to a file or pipe it to the printer; if you do not, the output will be sent to your terminal screen.

Problems in Getting Formatted Output

There are two ways for a program to handle errors. One is to have the program terminate and issue an error message. The other way is to have it keep going in hopes that the problems won't affect the rest of the output. The ms macros take this second approach.

In general, ms does its best to carry on no matter how scrambled the output looks. Sometimes the problems do get corrected within a page or two; other times the problem continues, making the remaining pages worthless. Usually, this is because the formatter had a problem executing the codes as they were entered in the input file. Most of the time input errors are caused by not including one of the macros that must be used in pairs.

Because ms allows formatting to continue unless the error is a "fatal" one, error correction is characteristic of the ms macro definitions. Apart from the main function of the macro, some of them, such as the paragraph macro, also invoke another macro called .RT to restore certain default values.

Thus, if you forget to reset the point size or indentation, you might notice that the problem continues for a while and then stops.

▪ Page Layout ▪

As suggested in the last chapter, one of the most important functions of a macro package is that it provides basic page layout defaults. This feature makes it worthwhile to use a macro package even if you don't enter a single macro into your source file.

At the beginning of Chapter 4, we showed how `nroff` alone formatted a sample letter. If we format the same letter with `ms`, the text will be adjusted on a page that has a default top and bottom margin of 1 inch, a default left margin, or page offset, of about 1 inch, and a default line length of 6 inches.

All of these default values are stored in number registers so that you can easily change them:

LL	Line Length
HM	Header (top) Margin
FM	Footer (bottom) Margin
PO	Page offset (left margin)

For example, if you like larger top and bottom margins, all you need to do is insert the following requests at the top of your file:

```
.nr HM 1.5i
.nr FM 1.5i
```

Registers such as these are used internally by a number of `ms` macros to reset the formatter to its default state. They will not take effect until one of those "reset" macros is encountered. In the case of `HM` and `FM`, they will not take effect until the next page unless they are specified at the very beginning of the file.*

▪ Paragraphs ▪

As we saw in the last chapter, paragraph transitions are natural candidates for macros because each paragraph generally will require several requests (spacing, indentation,) for proper formatting.

There are four paragraph macros in `ms`:

---

*These "reset" macros (those that call the internal macro `.RT`) include `.LP`, `.PP`, `.IP`, `.QP`, `.SH`, `.NH`, `.RS`, `.RE`, `.TS`, and `.TE`. The very first reset macro calls a special initialization macro called `.BG` that is used only once, on the first page. This macro prints the cover sheet, if any (see "Cover Sheet Macros" later in this chapter), as well as performing some special first-page initialization.

.LP	Block paragraph
.PP	First line of paragraph indented
.QP	Paragraph indented from both margins
.IP	Paragraph with hanging indent (list item)

The `.LP` macro produces a justified, block paragraph. This is the type of paragraph used for most technical documentation. The `.PP` macro produces a paragraph with a temporary indent for the first line. This paragraph type is commonly used in published books and magazines, as well as in typewritten correspondence.

Let's use the same letter to illustrate the use of these macros. In the original example (in Chapter 4), we left blank lines between paragraphs, producing an effect similar to that produced by the `.LP` macro.

In contrast, `.PP` produces a standard indented paragraph. Let's code the letter using `.PP` macros. Because this is a letter, let's also disable justification with an `.na` request. And of course, we want to print the address block in no-fill mode, as shown in Chapter 4. Figure 5-1 shows the coded letter and Figure 5-2 shows the formatted output.

Spacing between Paragraphs

With `nroff`, all of the paragraph macros produce a full space between paragraphs. However, with `troff`, the paragraph macros output a blank space of 0.3v. Basically, this means that a blank line will output one full space and the paragraph macros will output about a third of that space.

The amount of spacing between paragraphs is contained in the number register PD (*paragraph distance*). If you want to change the amount of space generated by any of the paragraph macros, simply change the contents of this register.

For example, if you don't want to leave any space between paragraphs in the letter, you could put the following line at the start of your file:

```
.nr PD 0
```

This flexibility afforded by macro packages is a major advantage. It is often possible to completely change the appearance of a coded document by resetting only a few number registers at the start of a file. (As we'll see, this statement is even more true of of mm than of ms.)

Quoted Paragraphs

A paragraph that is indented equally from the left and right margins is typically used to display quoted material. It is produced by `.QP`. For example:

```
.QP
In the next couple of days, I'll be putting together a ...
```

```
.ad r
April 1, 1987
.sp 2
.ad
.nf
Mr. John Fust
Vice President, Research and Development
Gutenberg Galaxy Software
Waltham, Massachusetts 02159
.fi
.sp
.na
Dear Mr. Fust:
.PP
In our conversation last Thursday, we discussed a documentation
project that would produce a user's manual on the Alcuin
product.  Yesterday, I received the product demo and other
materials that you sent me.
.PP
Going through a demo session gave me a much better understanding
of the product.  I confess to being amazed by Alcuin.
Some people around here, looking over my shoulder, were also
astounded by the illustrated manuscript I produced with Alcuin.
One person, a student of calligraphy, was really impressed.
.PP
In the next couple of days, I'll be putting together a written
plan that presents different strategies for documenting the
Alcuin product. After I submit this plan, and you have had time
to review it, let's arrange a meeting at your company to discuss
these strategies.
.PP
Thanks again for giving us the opportunity to bid on this
documentation project.  I hope we can decide upon a strategy
and get started as soon as possible in order to have the manual
ready in time for the first customer shipment. I look forward to
meeting with you towards the end of next week.
.sp
Sincerely,
.sp 3
Fred Caslon
```

Fig. 5-1. Letter Coded with ms Macros

April 1, 1987

Mr. John Fust
Vice President, Research and Development
Gutenberg Galaxy Software
Waltham, Massachusetts 02159

Dear Mr. Fust:

In our conversation last Thursday, we discussed a documentation project that would produce a user's manual on the Alcuin product. Yesterday, I received the product demo and other materials that you sent me.

Going through a demo session gave me a much better understanding of the product. I confess to being amazed by Alcuin. Some people around here, looking over my shoulder, were also astounded by the illustrated manuscript I produced with Alcuin. One person, a student of calligraphy, was really impressed.

In the next couple of days, I'll be putting together a written plan that presents different strategies for documenting the Alcuin product. After I submit this plan, and you have had time to review it, let's arrange a meeting at your company to discuss these strategies.

Thanks again for giving us the opportunity to bid on this documentation project. I hope we can decide upon a strategy and get started as soon as possible in order to have the manual ready in time for the first customer shipment. I look forward to meeting with you towards the end of next week.

Sincerely,

Fred Caslon

Fig. 5-2. Formatted Output

The .QP macro produces a paragraph indented on both sides. The pair of macros .QS and .QE can be used to mark a section longer than one paragraph that is indented. This is useful in reports and proposals that quote at length from another source.

```
.LP
I was particularly interested in the following comment
found in the product specification:
.QS
Users first need a brief introduction to what
the product does.  Sometimes this is more for the
benefit of people who haven't yet bought the
product, and are just looking at the manual.
However, it also serves to put the rest of the
manual, and the product itself, in
the proper context.
.QE
```

The result of formatting is:

```
I was particularly interested in the following comment
found in the product specification:

    Users first need a brief introduction to what the
    product does.  Sometimes this is more for the bene-
    fit of people who haven't yet bought the product,
    and are just looking at the manual.  However, it
    also serves to put the rest of the manual, and the
    product itself, in the proper context.
```

Use the .QP macro inside a .QS/.QE block to break up paragraphs.

Indented Paragraphs

The .IP macro produces an entire paragraph indented from the left margin. This is especially useful for constructing lists, in which a mark of some kind (e.g., a letter or number) extends into the left margin. We call these *labeled item lists*.

The .IP macro takes three arguments. The first argument is a text label; if the label contains spaces, it should be enclosed within quotation marks. The second argument is optional and specifies the amount of indentation; a default of 5 is used if the second argument is not specified. A third argument of 0 inhibits spacing before the indented paragraph.

Item lists are useful in preparing command reference pages that describe various syntax items, and in glossaries that present a term in one column and its definition in the other. The following example shows a portion of the input file for a reference page:

```
.IP figure 10
is the name of a cataloged figure.  If
a figure has not been cataloged, you need to use
the LOCATE command.
.IP f:p 10
is the scale of the
figure in relation to the page.
.IP font 10
is the two-character abbreviation or
full name of one of the available fonts
from the Alcuin library.
```

The following item list is produced:

```
figure      is the name of a cataloged figure.  If a figure
            has not been   cataloged,   you   need  to use the
            LOCATE command.

f:p         is the scale of the figure in relation  to  the
            page.

font        is the two-character abbreviation or full  name
            of one of the available fonts from  the  Alcuin
            library.
```

An `.LP` or `.PP` should be specified after the last item so that the text following the list is not also indented.

If you want to indent the label as well as the paragraph, you can use the `.in` request around the list. The following example:

```
.in 10
.IP figure 10
is the name of a cataloged figure.  If
a figure has not been cataloged, you need to use
the LOCATE command.
.in 0
```

will produce:

```
        figure      is the name of a  cataloged  figure.   If a
                    figure has not been cataloged,  you need to
                    use the LOCATE command.
```

You can specify an absolute or relative indent. To achieve the effect of a nested list, you can use the `.RS` (you can think of this as either *relative start* or *right shift*) and `.RE` (*relative end* or *retreat*) macros:

```
.IP font 10
is the two-character abbreviation or
full name of one of the available fonts
from the Alcuin library.
.RS
.IP CU
Cursive
.IP RS
Slanted
.RS
.IP LH 5 0
Left handed
.IP RH 5 0
Right handed
.RE
.IP BL
Block
.RE
```

The labels on the second level are aligned with the indented left margin of paragraphs
on the first level.

```
    font    is the two-character abbreviation or full name  of
            one   of  the  available  fonts  from  the  Alcuin
            library.

    CU     Cursive

    RS     Slanted

           LH    Left handed
           RH    Right handed

    BL     Block
```

One thing you need to watch out for in using the .IP macro is not to include space in
the label argument. Because of the way the macro is coded, the space may be expanded
when the finished line is adjusted. The first line will not be aligned with the rest. For
example:

```
.IP "font name" 10
is the two-character abbreviation or full name . . .
```

might produce the following:

```
    font name    is the two-character  abbreviation  or full
                 name of one of the  available  fonts from the
                 Alcuin library.
```

To avoid this problem, always use an unpaddable space (a backslash followed by a space) to separate words in the label argument to .IP. This caution applies to many other formatting situations as well.

Automatically numbered and alphabetized lists are not provided for in ms. (Chapter 16 shows how to write your own macros for this.) However, by specifying the number or letter as a label, you can make do with the .IP macro. For example:

```
User-oriented documentation recognizes three things:
.in +3n
.IP 1) 5n
that a new user needs
to learn the system in stages, getting a sense of the
system as a whole while becoming proficient in performing
particular tasks;
.IP 2) 5n
that there are different levels of users, and not
every user needs to learn all the capabilities
of the system in order to be productive;
.IP 3) 5n
that an experienced user must be able to rely on
the documentation for accurate and thorough reference
information.
.in -3n
```

This produces:

```
    User-oriented documentation recognizes three things:

        1)    that a new   user   needs to   learn the   system in
              stages, getting   a   sense   of   the   system   as a
              whole   while   becoming   proficient in performing
              particular tasks;

        2)    that there are different levels   of   users,   and
              not every user needs to   learn   all the capabil-
              ities of the system in   order   to be productive;

        3)    that an experienced user must be able to rely on
              the   documentation   for   accurate   and   thorough
              reference information.
```

The number is indented three ens and the text is indented five more ens. (Note: If you are using nroff, you don't need to specify units on the indents. However, if you are using troff, the default scaling for both the .IP macro and the .in requests shown in the previous example is ems. Remember that you can append a scaling indicator to the numeric arguments of most macros and troff requests.)

▪ **Changing Font and Point Size** ▪

When you format with `nroff` and print on a line printer, you can put emphasis on individual words or phrases by underlining or overstriking. When you are use `troff` and send your output to a laser printer or typesetter, you can specify variations of type, font, and point size based on the capabilities of the output devices.

Roman, Italic, and Bold Fonts

Most typefaces have at least three fonts available: roman, **bold**, and *italic*. Normal body copy is printed in the roman font. You can change temporarily to a bold or italic font for emphasis. In Chapter 4, you learned how to specify font changes using the `.ft` request and inline `\f` requests. The `ms` package provides a set of mnemonic macros for changing fonts:

```
.B        bold
.I        italic
.R        roman
```

Each macro prints a single argument in a particular font. You might code a single sentence as follows:

```
.B Alcuin
revitalizes an
.I age-old
tradition.
```

The printed sentence has one word in bold and one in italic.

Alcuin revitalizes an *age-old* tradition.

If no argument is specified, the selected font is current until it is explicitly changed:

```
The art of
.B
calligraphy
.R
is, quite simply,
.I
beautiful
.R
handwriting;
```

The example produces:

The art of **calligraphy** is, quite simply, *beautiful* handwriting;

You've already seen that the first argument is changed to the selected font. If you supply a second argument, it is printed in the previous font. (You are limited to two arguments, set off by a space; a phrase must be enclosed within quotation marks to be taken as a single argument.) A good use for the alternate argument is to supply punctuation, especially because of the restriction that you cannot begin a line with a period.

```
its opposite is
.B cacography .
```

This example produces:

its opposite is **cacography**.

If the second argument is a word or phrase, you must supply the spacing:

```
The ink pen has been replaced by a
.I light " pen."
```

This produces:

The ink pen has been replaced by a *light* pen.

If you are using `nroff`, specifying a bold font results in character overstrike; specifying an italic font results in an underline for each character (not a continuous rule). Overstriking and underlining can cause problems on some printers and terminals.

The chief advantage of these macros over the corresponding `troff` constructs is the ease of entry. It is easier to type:

```
.B calligraphy
```

than:

```
\fBcalligraphy\fP
```

However, you'll notice that using these macros changes the style of your input considerably. As shown in the examples on the preceding pages, these macros require you to code your input file using short lines that do not resemble the resulting filled output text.

This style, which clearly divorces the form of the input from the form of the output, is recommended by many `nroff` and `troff` users. They recommend that you use macros like these rather than inline codes, and that you begin each sentence or clause on a new line. There are advantages in speed of editing. However, there are others (one of the authors included) who find this style of input unreadable on the screen, and prefer to use inline codes, and to keep the input file as readable as possible. (There is no difference in the output file.)

Underlining

If you want to underline a single word, regardless of whether you are using `nroff` or `troff`, use the `.UL` macro:

```
the
.UL art
of calligraphy.
```

It will print a continuous rule beneath the word.   You cannot specify more than a single word with this macro.

Changing Point Size

As discussed in Chapter 4, you can change the point size and vertical spacing with the `.ps` and `.vs` requests. However, if you do this in `ms`, you will find that the point size and vertical spacing revert to 10 and 12 points, respectively, after the next paragraph macro. This is because the paragraph macro, in addition to other tasks, resets the point size and vertical spacing (along with various other values) to default values stored in number registers.

The default point size and vertical spacing for a document are kept in the registers `PS` and `VS`, respectively. If you want to change the overall point size or vertical spacing, change the value in these registers. (The default values are 10 and 12, respectively.) For example, to change the body type to 8 points and the spacing to 10 points, enter the following requests at the top of your document:

```
.nr PS 8
.nr VS 12
```

At the top of a document, these settings will take effect immediately. Otherwise, you must wait for the next paragraph macro for the new values to be recognized. If you need both immediate and long-lasting effects, you may need a construct like:

```
.ps 8
.nr PS 8
.vs 12
.nr VS 12
```

There are also several macros for making local point size changes. The `.LG` macro increases the current point size by 2 points; the `.SM` macro decreases the point size by 2 points. The new point size remains in effect until you change it. The `.NL` macro changes the point size back to its default or normal setting. For example:

```
.LG
Alcuin
.NL
is a graphic arts product for
.SM
UNIX
.NL
systems.
```

The following line is produced:

> Alcuin is a graphic arts product for UNIX systems.

The `.LG` and `.SM` macros simply increment or decrement the current point size by 2 points. Because you change the point size relative to the current setting, repeating a macro adds or subtracts 2 more points. If you are going to change the point size by more than 2, it makes more sense to use the `.ps` request. The `.NL` macro uses the value of the number register `PS` to reset the normal point size. Its default value is 10.

In the following example, the `.ps` request changes the point size to 12. The `.LG` and `.SM` macros increase and decrease the point size relative to 12 points. The `.NL` macro is not used until the end because it changes the point size back to 10.

```
.ps 12
.LG
Alcuin
.SM
is a graphic arts product for
.SM
UNIX
.LG
systems.
.NL
```

It produces the following line:

> Alcuin is a graphic arts product for UNIX systems.

A change in the point size affects how much vertical space is needed for the larger or smaller characters. Vertical spacing is usually 2 points larger than the point size (10 on 12). Use the vertical spacing request to temporarily change the vertical spacing, if necessary.

▪ Displays ▪

A document often includes material—such as tables, figures, or equations—that are not a part of the running text, and must be kept together on the page. In ᴍs and ᴍᴍ, such document elements are referred to generically as *displays*.

The macros `.DS`, `.DE`, `.ID`, `.CD`, and `.LD` are used to handle displays in ᴍs. The display macros can be relied upon to provide

- adequate spacing before and after the display;

- horizontal positioning of the display as a left-justified, indented, or centered block;

- proper page breaks, keeping the entire display together.

The default action of the `.DS` macro is to indent the block of text without filling lines:

```
Some of the typefaces that are currently available are:
.DS
Roman
Caslon
Baskerville
Helvetica
.DE
```

This produces:

```
Some of the typefaces that are currently available are:


    Roman
    Caslon
    Baskerville
    Helvetica
```

You can select a different format for a display by specifying a left-justified or centered display with one of the following arguments:

I	Indented (default)
L	Left-justified
C	Center each line
B	Block (center entire display)

The `L` argument can be used for formatting an address block in a letter:

```
.DS L
Mr. John Fust
Vice President, Research and Development
Gutenberg Galaxy Software
Waltham, Massachusetts 02154
.DE
```

The display macro prevents these lines from being filled; it "protects" the carriage returns as they were entered in the file.

A display can be centered in two ways: either each individual line in the display is centered (C), or the entire display is centered as a block (B) based on the longest line of the display.

The use of tabs often presents a problem outside of displays. Material that has been entered with tabs in the input file should be formatted in no-fill mode, the default setting of the display macros. The following table was designed using tabs to provide the spacing.

```
.DS L
Dates              Description of Task

June 30            Submit audience analysis
July 2             Meeting to review audience analysis
July 15            Submit detailed outline
August 1           Submit first draft
August 5           Return of first draft
August 8           Meeting to review comments
                   and establish revisions
.DE
```

This table appears in the output just as it looks in the file. If this material had not been processed inside a display, the columns would be improperly aligned.

Static and Floating Displays

One of the basic functions of a display is to make sure the displayed material stays together on one page. If the display is longer than the distance to the bottom of the page, there is a page break.

    If the display is large, causing a page break can leave a large block of white space at the bottom of the page. To avoid this problem, ms provides a set of macros for *floating displays*, as well as macros for the *static displays* we've already discussed. If a floating display doesn't fit on the page, the formatter doesn't force a page break. Instead, it simply holds the displayed text in reserve while it fills up the remainder of the page with the text following the display. It prints the display at the top of the next page, then continues where it left off.

    We have already used .DS and .DE to mark the beginning and end of a static display. To specify a floating display, the closing mark is the same but the beginning is marked by a different macro:

.ID	Same as .DS I (indented) but floating
.LD	Same as .DS L (left justified) but floating
.CD	Same as .DS C (center each line) but floating
.BD	Same as .DS B (center display) but floating

    In the following example of an input file, numbers are used instead of actual lines of text to make the placement of the display more obvious:

```
1
2
3
4
5
.LD
```
Long Display
```
.DE
6
```

```
7
8
9
10
```

The following two formatted pages might be produced, assuming that there are a sufficient number of lines to cause a page break:

```
┌─────────────────────┐     ┌─────────────────────┐
│        -1-          │     │        -2-          │
│                     │     │                     │
│  1                  │     │  Long Display       │
│  2                  │     │                     │
│  3                  │     │  8                  │
│  4                  │     │  9                  │
│  5                  │     │  10                 │
│  6                  │     │                     │
│  7                  │     │                     │
│                     │     │                     │
└─────────────────────┘     └─────────────────────┘
```

If there had been room on page 1 to fit the display, it would have been placed there, and lines 6 and 7 would have followed the display, as they did in the input file.

If a static display had been specified in the previous example, the display would be placed in the same position on the second page, and lines 6 and 7 would have followed it, leaving extra space at the bottom of page 1. A floating display attempts to make the best use of the available space on a page.

The formatter maintains a queue to hold floating displays that it has not yet output. When the top of a page is encountered, the next display in the queue is output. The queue is emptied in the order in which it was filled (first in, first out).

The macros called by the display macros to control output of a block of text are available for other uses. They are known as "keep and release" macros. The pair `.KS/.KE` keep a block together and output it on the next available page. The pair `.KF/.KE` specify a floating keep; the block saved by the keep can float and lines of text following the block may appear before it in the text.

▪ Headings ▪

In ms, you can have numbered and unnumbered headings. There are two heading macros: `.NH` for numbered headings and `.SH` for unnumbered section headings.

Let's first look at how to produce numbered headings. The syntax for the `.NH` macro is:

```
.NH  [level]
[heading text]
.LP
```

(The brackets indicate optional arguments.) You can supply a numerical value indicating the *level* of the heading. If no value is provided for *level*, then a top-level heading is assumed. The *heading text* begins on the line following the macro and can extend over several lines. You have to use one of the paragraph macros, either `.LP` or `.PP`, after the last line of the heading. For example:

```
.NH
Quick Tour of Alcuin
.LP
```

The result is a heading preceded by a first-level heading number:

```
1.   Quick Tour of Alcuin
```

The next time you use this macro the heading number will be incremented to 2, and after that, to 3.

You can add levels by specifying a numeric argument. A second-level heading is indicated by 2:

```
.NH 2
Introduction to Calligraphy
.LP
```

The first second-level heading number is printed:

```
1.1   Introduction to Calligraphy
```

When another heading is specified at the same level, the heading number is automatically incremented. If the next heading is at the second level:

```
.NH 2
Digest of Alcuin Commands
.LP
```

`ms` produces:

```
1.2  Digest of Alcuin Commands
```

Each time you go to a new level, `.1` is appended to the number representing the existing level. That number is incremented for each call at the same level. When you back out of a level (for instance, when you go from level 5 to 4) the counter for the level (in this case level 5) is reset to 0.

The macro for unnumbered headings is `.SH`:

```
.SH
Introduction to Calligraphy
.LP
```

Unnumbered headings and numbered headings can be intermixed without affecting the numbering scheme:

```
1.   Quick Tour of Alcuin

Introduction to Calligraphy

1.1  Digest of Alcuin Commands
```

Headings are visible keys to your document's structure. Their appearance can contribute significantly to a reader recognizing that organization. If you are using unnumbered headings, it becomes even more important to make headings stand out. A simple thing you can do is use uppercase letters for a first-level heading.

▪ Cover Sheet Macros ▪

In their original incarnation at Bell Laboratories, the `ms` macros were called on to format many internal AT&T documents. Accordingly, it is not surprising that there were quite a few macros that controlled the format of specific internal document types. What is surprising is that these macros are still present in copies of the `ms` macros distributed outside of AT&T.

You have the option of specifying that your document contains Engineer's Notes (`.EG`), an Internal Memorandum (`.IM`), a Memorandum for Record (`.MR`), a Memorandum for File (`.MF`), a Released Paper (`.RP`), a Technical Reprint (`.TR`), or a letter (`.LT`).

Many of these formats are quite useless outside of AT&T, unless you customize them heavily for other institutions. We prefer simply to ignore them.

In general, what these document type macros control is the appearance of the document's cover sheet. The content of that cover sheet is specified using the following macros:

`.TL`	Title
`.AU`	Author
`.AI`	Author's Institution
`.AB`	Abstract Start
`.AE`	Abstract End

These macros are general enough that you can still use them even if you aren't from Bell Laboratories.

Each macro takes its data from the following line(s) rather than from an argument. They are typically used together. For example:

```
.TL
UNIX Text Processing
.AU
Dale Dougherty
.AU
Tim O'Reilly
```

```
.AI
O'Reilly & Associates, Inc.
.AB
This book provides a comprehensive introduction to the major
UNIX text-processing tools.  It includes a discussion of
vi, ex, nroff, and troff, as
well as many other text-processing programs.
.AE
.LP
```

Exactly how the output will look depends on which document types you have selected. If you don't specify any of the formats, you will get something like this:

UNIX Text Processing

Dale Dougherty

Tim O'Reilly

O'Reilly & Associates, Inc.

ABSTRACT

This book provides a comprehensive introduction to the major UNIX text-processing tools. It includes a discussion of `vi`, `ex`, `nroff`, and `troff`, as well as many other text-processing programs.

You can specify as many title lines as you want following `.TL`. The macro will be terminated by any of the other cover sheet macros, or by any paragraph macro. For multiple authors, `.AU` and `.AI` can be repeated up to nine times.

The cover sheet isn't actually printed until a reset (such as that caused by any of the paragraph macros) is encountered, so if you want to print only a cover page, you should conclude it with a paragraph macro even if there is no following text.

In addition, if you use these macros without one of the overall document type macros like `.RP`, the cover sheet will not be printed separately. Instead, the text will immediately follow. Insert a `.bp` if you want a separate cover sheet.

· Miscellaneous Features ·

Putting Information in a Box

Another way of handling special information is to place it in a box. Individual words can be boxed for emphasis using the `.BX` command:

```
To move to the next menu, press the
.BX RETURN
key.
```

This draws a box around the word RETURN.

```
To move to the next menu, press the
RETURN
key.
```

As you can see, it might be a good idea to reduce the point size of the boxed word.

You can enclose a block of material within a box by using the pair of macros .B1 and .B2:

```
.B1
.B
.ce
Note to Reviewers
.R
.LP
Can you get a copy of a manuscript without annotations?
It seems to me that you should be
able to mark up a page with comments or
other scribbles while in Annotation Mode and
still obtain a printed copy without these marks.
Any ideas?
.sp
.B2
```

This example produces the following boxed section in troff:

> **Note to Reviewers**
>
> Can you get a copy of a manuscript without annotations? It seems to me that you should be able to mark up a page with comments or other scribbles while in Annotation Mode and still obtain a printed copy without these marks. Any ideas?

You may want to place boxed information inside a pair of keep or display macros. This will prevent the box macro from breaking if it crosses a page boundary. If you use these macros with nroff, you must also pipe your output through the col postprocessor as described in Chapter 4.

Footnotes

Footnotes present special problems—the main is printing the text at the bottom of the page. The .FS macro indicates the start of the text for the footnote, and .FE indicates the end of the text for the footnote. These macros surround the footnote text that will appear at the bottom of the page. The .FS macro is put on the line immediately following some kind of marker, such as an asterisk, that you supply in the text and in the footnote.

```
... in an article on desktop publishing.*
.FS
* "Publish or Perish: Start-up grabs early page language
lead," Computerworld, April 21, 1986, p. 1.
.FE
```

All the footnotes are collected and output at the bottom of each page underneath a short rule. The footnote text is printed in smaller type, with a slightly shorter line length then the body text. However, you can change these if you want.

Footnotes in ms use an nroff/troff feature called *environments* (see Chapter 14), so that parameters like line length or font that are set inside a footnote are saved independently of the body text. So, for example, if you issued the requests:

```
.FS
.ft B
.ll -5n
.in +5n
```
Some text
```
~

~

~

.FE
```

the text within the footnote would be printed in boldface, with a 5-en indent, and the line length would be shortened by 5 ens. The text following the footnote would be unaffected by those formatting requests. However, the next time a footnote was called, that special formatting would again be in effect.

---

*"Publish or Perish: Start-up grabs early page language lead," *Computerworld*, **April 21, 1986, p. 1.**

If a footnote is too long to fit on one page, it will be continued at the bottom of the next page.

Two-Column Processing

One of the nice features of the ms macros is the ease with which you can create multiple columns and format documents, such as newsletters or data sheets, that are best suited to a multicolumn format.

To switch to two-column mode, simply insert the .2C macro. To return to single-column mode, use .1C. Because of the way two-column processing works in ms, you can switch to two-column mode in the middle of a page, but switching back to a single column forces a page break. (You'll understand the reason for this when we return to two-column processing in Chapter 16.)

The default column width for two-column processing is 7/15th of the line length. It is stored in the register CW (*column width*). The gutter between the columns is

1/15th of the line length, and is stored in the register GW (*gutter width*). By changing the values in these registers, you can change the column and gutter width.

For more than two columns, you can use the .MC macro. This macro takes two arguments, the column width and the gutter width, and creates as many columns as will fit in the line length. For example, if the line lengths are 7 inches, the request:

```
.MC 2i .3i
```

would create three columns 2 inches wide, with a gutter of .3 inches between the columns.

Again, .1C can be used to return to single-column mode. In some versions of ms, the .RC macro can be used to break columns. If you are in the left column, following text will go to the top of the next column. If you are in the right column, .RC will start a new page.

▪ **Page Headers and Footers** ▪

When you format a page with ms, the formatter is instructed to provide several lines at the top and the bottom of the page for a header and a footer. Beginning with the second page, a page number appears on a single line in the header and only blank lines are printed for the footer.

The ms package allows you to define strings that appear in the header or footer. You can place text in three locations in the header or footer: left justified, centered, and right justified. For example, we could place the name of the client, the title of the document, and the date in the page header and we could place the page number in the footer.

```
.ds LH GGS
.ds CH Alcuin Project Proposal
.ds RH \*(DY
.ds CF Page %
```

You may notice that we use the string DY to supply today's date in the header. In the footer, we use a special symbol (%) to access the current page number. Here are the resulting header and footer:

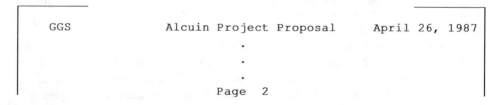

```
GGS                  Alcuin Project Proposal      April 26, 1987
                              .
                              .
                              .
                            Page  2
```

Normally, you would define the header and footer strings at the start of the document, so they would take effect throughout. However, note that there is nothing to prevent you from changing one or more of them from page to page. (Changes to a footer string will take effect on the same page; changes to a header string will take effect at the top of the next page.)

• **Problems on the First Page** •

Because ms was originally designed to work with the cover sheet macros and one of the standard Bell document types, there are a number of problems that can occur on the first page of a document that doesn't use these macros.*

First, headers are not printed on the first page, nor is it apparent how to get them printed there if you want them. The trick is to invoke the internal .NP (*new page*) macro at the top of your text. This will not actually start a new page, but will execute the various internal goings-on that normally take place at the top of a page.

Second, it is not evident how to space down from the top if you want to start your text at some distance down the page. For example, if you want to create your own title page, the sequence:

```
.sp 3i
.ce
\s16The Invention of Movable Type\s0
```

will not work.

The page top macro includes an .ns request, designed to ensure that all leftover space from the bottom of one page doesn't carry over to the next, so that all pages start evenly. To circumvent this on all pages after the first one, precede your spacing request with an .rs (*restore spacing*) request. On the first page, a .fl request must precede a .rs request.

• **Extensions to ms** •

In many ways, ms can be used to give you a head start on defining your own macro package. Many of the features that are missing in ms can be supplied by user-defined macros. Many of these features are covered in Chapters 14 through 18, where, for example, we show macros for formatting numbered lists.

---

*This problem actually can occur on any page, but is most frequently encountered on the first page.

The mm Macros

A macro package provides a way of describing the format of various kinds of documents. Each document presents its own specific problems, and macros help to provide a simple and flexible solution. The mm macro package is designed to help you format letters, proposals, memos, technical papers, and reports. A text file that contains mm macros can be processed by either `nroff` or `troff`, the two text formatting programs in UNIX. The output from these programs can be displayed on a terminal screen or printed on a line printer, a laser printer, or a typesetter.

Some users of the mm macro package learn only a few macros and work productively. Others choose from a variety of macros to produce a number of different formats. More advanced users modify the macro definitions and extend the capabilities of the package by defining their own special-purpose macros.

Macros are the *words* that make up a format description language. Like words, the result of a macro is often determined by context. That is, you may not always understand your output by looking up an individual macro, just like you may not understand the meaning of an entire sentence by looking up a particular word. Without examining the macro definition, you may find it hard to figure out which macro is causing a particular result. Macros are interrelated; some macros call other macros, like a subroutine in a program, to perform a particular function.

After finding out what the macro package allows you to do, you will probably decide upon a particular format that you like (or one that has evolved according to the decisions of a group of people). To describe that format, you are likely to use only a few of the macros, those that do the job. In everyday use, you want to minimize the number of codes you need to format documents in a consistent manner.

· Formatting a Text File ·

To figure out the role of a macro package such as mm, it may help to consider the distinction between *formatting* and *format*. Formatting is an operation, a process of supplying and executing instructions. You can achieve a variety of results, some pleasing, some not, by any combination of formatting instructions. A format is a consistent product, achieved by a selected set of formatting instructions. A macro package makes it possible for a format to be recreated again and again with minimal difficulty. It encourages the user to concentrate more on the requirements of a document and less on the operations of the text formatter.

Working with a macro package will help reduce the number of formatting instructions you need to supply. This means that a macro package will take care of many things automatically. However, you should gradually become familiar with the operations of the `nroff`/`troff` formatter and the additional flexibility it offers to define new formats. If you have a basic understanding of how the formatter works, as described in Chapter 4, you will find it easier to learn the intricacies of a macro package.

Invoking `nroff`/`troff` with `mm`

The `mm` command is a shell script that invokes the `nroff` formatter and reads in the files that contain the `mm` macro definitions before processing the text file(s) specified on the command line.

     $ **mm** *option(s) filename(s)*

If more than one file is specified on the command line, the files are concatenated before processing. There are a variety of *options* for invoking preprocessors and postprocessors, naming an output device, and setting various number registers to alter default values for a document. Using the `mm` command is the same as invoking `nroff` explicitly with the −mm option.

Unless you specify otherwise, the `mm` command sets `nroff`'s −T option to the terminal type set in your login environment. By default, output is sent to the terminal screen. If you have problems viewing your output, or if you have a graphics terminal, you may want to specify another device name using the −T option. For a list of available devices, see Appendix B. The `mm` command also has a −c option, which invokes the `col` filter to remove reverse linefeeds, and options to invoke `tbl` (−t) and `eqn` (−e).

When you format a file to the screen, the output usually streams by too swiftly to read, just as when you `cat` a file to the screen. Pipe the output of the `mm` command through either of the paging programs, `pg` or `more`, to view one screenful at a time. This will give you a general indication that the formatting commands achieved the results you had expected. To print a file formatted with `mm`, simply pipe the output to the print spooler (e.g., `lp`) instead of to a screen paging program.

Many of the actions that a text formatter performs are dependent upon how the document is going to be printed. If you want your document to be formatted with `troff` instead of `nroff`, use the `mmt` command (another shell script) or invoke `troff` directly, using the −mm option. The `mmt` command prepares output for laser printers and typesetters. The formatted output should be piped directly to the print spooler (e.g., `lp`) or directed to a file and printed separately. You will probably need to check at your site for the proper invocation of `mmt` if your site supports more than one type of laser printer or typesetter.

If you are using `otroff`, be sure you don't let `troff` send the output to your terminal because, in all probability, it will cause your terminal to hang, or at least to scream and holler.

In this chapter, we will generally show the results of the `mm` command, rather than `mmt`—that is, we'll be showing `nroff` rather than `troff`. Where the subject under discussion is better demonstrated by `troff`, we will show `troff` output instead. We assume that by now, you will be able to tell which of the programs has been used, without our mentioning the actual commands.

Problems in Getting Formatted Output

When you format an `mm`-coded document, you may only get a portion of your format-ted document. Or you may get none of it. Usually, this is because the formatter has had a problem executing the codes as they were entered in the input file. Most of the time it is caused by omitting one of the macros that must be used in pairs.

When formatting stops like this, one or more error messages might appear on your screen, helping you to diagnose the problems. These messages refer to the line numbers in the input file where the problems appear to be, and try to tell you what is missing:

> **ERROR**:(*filename*) *line number*
> *Error message*

Sometimes, you won't get error messages, but your output will break midway. Gen-erally, you have to go in the file at the point where it broke, or before that point, and examine the macros or a sequence of macros. You can also run a program on the input file to examine the code you have entered. This program, available at most sites, is called `checkmm`.

Default Formatting

In Chapter 4, we looked at a sample letter formatted by `nroff`. It might be interest-ing, before putting any macros in the file, to see what happens if we format `letter` as it is, this time using the `mm` command to read in the `mm` macro package.

Refer to Figure 6-1 and note that

- a page number appears in a header at the top of the page;

- the address block still forms two long lines;

- lines of input text have been filled, forming block paragraphs;

- the right margin is ragged, not justified as with `nroff`;

- the text is not hyphenated;

- space has been allocated for a page with top, bottom, left, and right margins.

- 1 -

April 1, 1987

Mr. John Fust Vice President, Research and
Development Gutenberg Galaxy Software Waltham,
Massachusetts 02159

Dear Mr. Fust:

In our conversation last Thursday, we discussed a
documentation project that would produce a user's
manual on the Alcuin product. Yesterday, I
received the product demo and other materials that
you sent me.

Going through a demo session gave me a much better
understanding of the product. I confess to being
amazed by Alcuin. Some people around here,
looking over my shoulder, were also astounded by
the illustrated manuscript I produced with Alcuin.
One person, a student of calligraphy, was really
impressed.

In the next couple of days, I'll be putting
together a written plan that presents different
strategies for documenting the Alcuin product.
After I submit this plan, and you have had time to
review it, let's arrange a meeting at your company
to discuss these strategies.

Thanks again for giving us the opportunity to bid
on this documentation project. I hope we can
decide upon a strategy and get started as soon as
possible in order to have the manual ready in time
for the first customer shipment. I look forward to
meeting with you towards the end of next week.

Sincerely,

Fred Caslon

Fig. 6-1. A Raw mm-formatted File

▪ Page Layout ▪

When you format a page with mm, the formatter is instructed to provide several lines at the top and the bottom of the page for a header and a footer. By default, a page number appears on a single line in the header and only blank lines are printed for the footer.

There are basically two different ways to change the default header and footer. The first way is to specify a command-line parameter with the mm or mmt commands to set the number register N. This allows you to affect how pages are numbered and where the page number appears. The second way is to specify in the input file a macro that places text in the header or footer. Let's look at both of these techniques.

Setting Page Numbering Style

When you format a document, pages are numbered in sequence up to the end of the document. This page number is usually printed in the header, set off by dashes.

```
-1-
```

Another style of page numbering, used in documents such as technical manuals, numbers pages specific to a section. The first page of the second section would be printed as:

```
2-1
```

The other type of change affects whether or not the page number is printed in the header at the top of the first page.

The number register N controls these actions. This register has a default setting of 0 and can take values from 0 through 5. Table 6-1 shows the effect of these values.

TABLE 6-1. Page Number Styles, Register N

Value	Action
0	The page number prints in the header on all pages. This is the default page numbering style.
1	On page 1, the page number is printed in place of the footer.
2	On page 1, the page number in not printed.
3	All pages are numbered by section, and the page number appears in the footer. This setting affects the defaults of several section-related registers and macros. It causes a page break for a top-level heading (Ej=1), and invokes both the .FD and .RP macros to reset footnote and reference numbering.

TABLE 6-1. —(Cont'd)

Value	Action
4	The default header containing the page number is suppressed, but it has no effect on a header supplied by a page header macro.
5	All pages are numbered by section, and the page number appears in the footer. In addition, labeled displays (.FC, .TB, .EX, and .EC) are also numbered by section.

The register N can be set from the command line using the −r option. If we set it to 2, no page number will appear at the top of page 1 when we print the sample letter:

```
$ mm -rN2 letter | lp
```

Header and Footer Macros

The mm package has a pair of macros for defining what should appear in a page header (.PH) and a page footer (.PF). There is also a set of related macros for specifying page headers and footers for odd-numbered pages (.OH and .OF) or for even-numbered pages (.EH and .EF). All of these macros have the same form, allowing you to place text in three places in the header or footer: left justified, centered, and right justified. This is specified as a single argument in double quotation marks, consisting of three parts delimited by single quotation marks.

' left' center' right'

For example, we could place the name of a client, the title of the document, and the date in the page header, and we could place the page number in the footer:

```
.PH "'GGS'Alcuin Project Proposal'\*(DT'"
.PF "''Page % ''"
```

You may notice that we use the string DT to supply today's date in the header. The following header appears at the top of the page.

```
   GGS          Alcuin Project Proposal    April 26, 1987
```

In the footer, we use a special symbol (%) to access the current page number. Only text to be centered was specified; however, the four delimiters were still required to place the text correctly. This footer appears at the bottom of the page:

⋮

_____   Page   2

The header and footer macros override the default header and footer.

Setting Other Page Control Registers

The mm package uses number registers to supply the values that control line length, page offset, point size, and page length, as shown in Table 6-2.

TABLE 6-2. Number Registers

Register	Contains	`troff` Default	`nroff` Default
O	Page offset (left margin)	.75i	.5i
N	Page numbering style	0	0
P	Page length	66v	66 lines
S	Point size (`troff` only)	10	NA
W	Line length or width	6i	60

These registers must be defined before the mm macro package is read by `nroff` or `troff`. Thus, they can be set from the command line using the −r option, as we showed when we gave a new value for register N. Values of registers O and W for `nroff` must be given in character positions (depending on the character size of the output device for `nroff`, .5i might translate as either 5 or 6 character positions), but `troff` can accept any of the units descibed in Chapter 4. For example:

$ **mm −rN2 −rW65 −r10** _file_

but:

$ **mmt −rN2 −rW6.5i −rO1i** _file_

Or the page control registers can be set at the top of your file, using the .so request to read in the mm macro package, as follows:

```
.nr N 2
.nr W 65
.nr O 10
.so /usr/lib/tmac/tmac.m
```

If you do it this way, you cannot use the mm command. Use `nroff` or `troff` without the −mm option. Specifying −mm would cause the mm macro package to be read twice; mm would trap that error and bail out.

Paragraphs

The `.P` macro marks the beginning of a paragraph.

```
.P
In our conversation last Thursday, we discussed a
```

This macro produces a left-justified, block paragraph. A blank line in the input file also results in a left-justified, block paragraph, as you saw when we formatted an uncoded file.

However, the paragraph macro controls a number of actions in the formatter, many of which can be changed by overriding the default values of several number registers. The `.P` macro takes a numeric argument that overrides the default paragraph type, which is a block paragraph. Specifying 1 results in an indented paragraph:

```
.P 1
Going through a demo session gave me a much better
```

The first three paragraphs formatted for the screen follow:

```
    In our conversation last Thursday, we discussed a
    documentation project that would produce a user's manual
    on the Alcuin product.  Yesterday, I received the product
    demo and other materials that you sent me.

        Going through a demo session gave me a much better
    understanding of the product.  I confess to being amazed
    by Alcuin.  Some people around here, looking over my
    shoulder, were also astounded by the illustrated
    manuscript I produced with Alcuin.  One person, a student
    of calligraphy, was really impressed.

    In the next couple of days, I'll be putting together a
    written plan that presents different strategies for
    documenting the Alcuin product. After I submit this plan,
    and you have had time to review it, let's arrange a
    meeting at your company to discuss these strategies.
```

The first line of the second paragraph is indented five spaces. (In `troff` the default indent is three ens.) Notice that the paragraph type specification changes only the second paragraph. The third paragraph, which is preceded in the input file by `.P` without an argument, is a block paragraph.

If you want to create a document in which all the paragraphs are indented, you can change the number register that specifies the default paragraph type. The value of `Pt` is 0 by default, producing block paragraphs. For indented paragraphs, set the value of `Pt` to 1. Now the `.P` macro will produce indented paragraphs.

```
.nr Pt 1
```

If you want to obtain a block paragraph after you have changed the default type, specify an argument of 0:

```
.P  0
```

When you specify a type argument, it overrides whatever paragraph type is in effect.

There is a third paragraph type that produces an indented paragraph with some exceptions. If Pt is set to 2, paragraphs are indented except those following section headings, lists, and displays. It is the paragraph type used in this book.

The following list summarizes the three default paragraph types:

0	Block
1	Indented
2	Indented with exceptions

Vertical Spacing

The paragraph macro also controls the spacing between paragraphs. The amount of space is specified in the number register Ps. This amount differs between nroff and troff.

With nroff, the .P macro has the same effect as a blank line, producing a full space between paragraphs. However, with troff, the .P macro outputs a blank space that is equal to one-half of the current vertical spacing setting. Basically, this means that a blank line will cause one full space to be output, and the .P macro will output half that space.

The .P macro invokes the .SP macro for vertical spacing. This macro take a numeric argument requesting that many lines of space.

```
Sincerely,
.SP 3
Fred Caslon
```

Three lines of space will be provided between the salutation and the signature lines.

You do not achieve the same effect if you enter .SP macros on three consecutive lines. The vertical space does not accumulate and one line of space is output, not three.

Two or more consecutive .SP macros with numeric arguments results in the spacing specified by the greatest argument. The other arguments are ignored.

```
.SP 5
.SP
.SP 2
```

In this example, five lines are output, not eight.

Because the .P macro calls the .SP macro, it means that two or more consecutive paragraph macros will have the same effect as one.

The `.SP` Macro versus the `.sp` Request

There are several differences between the `.SP` macro and the `.sp` request. A series of `.sp` requests does cause vertical spacing to accumulate. The following three requests produce eight blank lines:

```
.sp 5
.sp
.sp 2
```

The argument specified with the `.SP` macro cannot be scaled nor can it be a negative number. The `.SP` macro automatically works in the scale (v) of the current vertical spacing. However, both `.SP` and `.sp` accept fractions, so that each of the following codes has the same result:

```
.sp .3v    .SP .3    .sp .3
```

▪ Justification ▪

A document formatted by `nroff` with `mm` produces, by default, unjustified text (an uneven or ragged-right margin). When formatted by `troff`, the same document is automatically justified (the right margin is even).

If you are using both `nroff` and `troff`, it is probably a good idea to explicitly set justification on or off rather than depend upon the default chosen by the formatter. Use the `.SA` macro (*set adjustment*) to set document-wide justification. An argument of 0 specifies no justification; 1 specifies justification.

If you insert this macro at the top of your file:

```
.SA 1
```

both `nroff` and `troff` will produce right-justified paragraphs like the following:

```
      In  our  conversation  last Thursday,  we  discussed
a documentation  project  that  would produce  a  user's
manual on the Alcuin product.  Yesterday, I received the
product demo and other materials that you sent me.
```

▪ Word Hyphenation ▪

One way to achieve better line breaks and more evenly filled lines is to instruct the formatter to perform word hyphenation.

Hyphenation is turned off in the `mm` macro package. This means that the formatter does not try to hyphenate words to make them fit on a line unless you request it by setting the number register `Hy` to 1. If you want the formatter to automatically hyphenate words, insert the following line at the top of your file:

```
.nr Hy 1
```

Most of the time, the formatter breaks up a word correctly when hyphenating. Some-times, however, it does not and you have to explicitly tell the formatter either how to split a word (using the `.hy` request) or not to hyphenate at all (using the `.nh` request).

· Displays ·

When we format a text file, the line breaks caused by carriage returns are ignored by `nroff/troff`. How text is entered on lines in the input file does not affect how lines are formed in the output. It doesn't really matter whether information is typed on three lines or four; it appears the same after formatting.

You probably noticed that the name and address at the beginning of our sample file did not come out in block form. The four lines of input ran together and produced two filled lines of output:

```
Mr. John Fust Vice President, Research and Development
Gutenberg Galaxy Software Waltham, Massachusetts 02159
```

The formatter, instead of paying attention to carriage returns, acts on specific macros or requests that cause a break, such as `.P`, `.SP`, or a blank line. The formatter request `.br` is probably the simplest way to break a line:

```
Mr. John Fust
.br
Vice President, Research and Development
```

The `.br` request is most appropriate when you are forcing a break of a single line. For larger blocks of text, the mm macro package provides a pair of macros for indicating that a block of text should be output just as it was entered in the input file. The `.DS` (*display start*) macro is placed at the start of the text, and the `.DE` (*display end*) macro is placed at the end:

```
.DS
Mr. John Fust
Vice President, Research and Development
Gutenberg Galaxy Software
Waltham, Massachusetts 02159
.DE
```

The formatter does not fill these lines, so the address block is output on four lines, just as it was typed. In addition, the `.DE` macro provides a line of space following the display.

Our Coding Efforts, So Far

We have pretty much exhausted what we can do using the sample letter. Before going on to larger documents, you may want to compare the coded file in Figure 6-2 with the `nroff`-formatted output in Figure 6-3. Look them over and make sure you understand what the different macros are accomplishing.

```
.nr Pt 1
.SA 1
```
                                        April 1, 1987
```
.SP 2
.DS
```
Mr. John Fust
Vice President, Research and Development
Gutenberg Galaxy Software
Waltham, Massachusetts 02159
```
.DE
```
Dear Mr. Fust:
```
.P
```
In our conversation last Thursday, we discussed a
documentation project that would produce a user's manual
on the Alcuin product. Yesterday, I received the product
demo and other materials that you sent me.
```
.P
```
Going through a demo session gave me a much better
understanding of the product. I confess to being amazed
by Alcuin. Some people around here, looking over my
shoulder, were also astounded by the illustrated
manuscript I produced with Alcuin. One person, a student
of calligraphy, was really impressed.
```
.P
```
In the next couple of days, I'll be putting together a
written plan that presents different strategies for
documenting the Alcuin product. After I submit this plan,
and you have had time to review it, let's arrange a
meeting at your company to discuss these strategies.
```
.P
```
Thanks again for giving us the opportunity to bid on this
documentation project. I hope we can decide upon a
strategy and get started as soon as possible in order to
have the manual ready in time for the first customer
shipment. I look forward to meeting with you towards the
end of next week.
```
.SP
```
                                        Sincerely,
```
.SP 2
```
                                        Fred Caslon

Fig. 6-2. Coded File

```
                              - 1 -


                                        April 1, 1987


     Mr. John Fust
     Vice President, Research and Development
     Gutenberg Galaxy Software
     Waltham, Massachusetts 02159

     Dear Mr. Fust:

         In  our  conversation  last  Thursday,  we
     discussed  a  documentation  project  that  would
     produce a user's manual  on  the  Alcuin  product.
     Yesterday,  I  received the product demo and other
     materials that you sent me.

         Going through a demo session gave me  a  much
     better understanding of the product.  I confess to
     being amazed by Alcuin.  Some people around  here,
     looking  over  my shoulder, were also astounded by
     the illustrated manuscript I produced with Alcuin.
     One  person,  a student of calligraphy, was really
     impressed.

         In the next couple of days, I'll  be  putting
     together  a  written  plan that presents different
     strategies for  documenting  the  Alcuin  product.
     After I submit this plan, and you have had time to
     review it, let's arrange a meeting at your company
     to discuss these strategies.

         Thanks again for giving us the opportunity to
     bid  on this documentation project.  I hope we can
     decide upon a strategy and get started as soon  as
     possible in order to have the manual ready in time
     for the first customer shipment. I look forward to
     meeting with you towards the end of next week.

                                        Sincerely,


                                        Fred Caslon
```

Fig. 6-3. Formatted Output

We have worked through some of the problems presented by a very simple one-page letter. As we move on, we will be describing specialized macros that address the problems of multiple page documents, such as proposals and reports. In many ways, the macros for more complex documents are the feature performers in a macro package, the ones that really convince you that a markup language is worth learning.

▪ Changing Font and Point Size ▪

When you format with `nroff` and print on a line printer, you can put emphasis on individual words or phrases by underlining or overstriking. When you are using `troff` and send your output to a laser printer or typesetter, you can specify variations of type, font, and point size based on the capabilities of the output device.

Roman, Italic, and Bold Fonts

Most typefaces have at least three fonts available: roman, **bold**, and *italic*. Normal body copy is printed in the roman font. You can change temporarily to a bold or italic font for emphasis. In Chapter 4, you learned how to specify font changes using the `.ft` request and inline `\f` requests. The mm package provides a set of mnemonic macros for changing fonts:

```
.B          Bold
.I          Italic
.R          Roman
```

Each macro prints a single argument in a particular font. You might code a single sentence as follows:

```
.B Alcuin
revitalizes an
.I age-old
tradition.
```

The printed sentence has a word in bold and one in italic. (In `nroff`, bold space is simulated by overstriking, and italics by underlining.)

Alcuin revitalizes an *age-old* tradition.

If no argument is specified, the selected font is current until it is explicitly changed:

```
The art of
.B
calligraphy
.R
is, quite simply,
.I
beautiful
.R
handwriting;
```

The previous example produces:

The art of **calligraphy** is, quite simply, *beautiful* handwriting;

You've already seen that the first argument is changed to the selected font. If you supply a second argument, it is printed in the previous font. Each macro takes up to six arguments for alternating font changes. (An argument is set off by a space; a phrase must be enclosed within quotation marks to be taken as a single argument.) A good use for the alternate argument is to supply punctuation, especially because of the restriction that you cannot begin an input line with a period.

```
its opposite is
.B cacography .
```

This example produces:

---

its opposite is **cacography**.

If you specify alternate arguments consisting of words or phrases, you must supply the spacing:

```
The ink pen has been replaced by a
.I light " pen."
```

This produces:

The ink pen has been replaced by a *light* pen.

Here's an example using all six arguments:

```
Alcuin uses three input devices, a
.B "light pen" ", a " "mouse" ", and a " "graphics tablet."
```

This produces:

Alcuin uses three input devices, a **light pen**, a **mouse**, and a **graphics tablet**.

There are additional macros for selecting other main and alternate fonts. These macros also take up to six arguments, displayed in alternate fonts:

.BR	Alternate bold and roman
.IB	Alternate italic and bold
.RI	Alternate roman and italic
.BI	Alternate bold and italic
.IR	Alternate italic and roman
.RB	Alternate roman and bold

If you are using nroff, specifying a bold font results in character overstrike; specifying an italic font results in an underline for each character (not a continuous rule). Overstriking and underlining can cause problems on some printers and terminals.

Changing Point Size

When formatting with troff, you can request a larger or smaller point size for the type. A change in the point size affects how much vertical space is needed for the larger or smaller characters. Normal body copy is set in 10-point type with the vertical spacing 2 points larger.

You learned about the .ps (*point size*) and .vs (*vertical spacing*) requests in Chapter 4. These will work in mm; however, mm also has a single macro for changing both the point size and vertical space:

.S [*point size*] [*vertical spacing*]

The values for *point size* and *vertical spacing* can be set in relation to the current setting: + increments and − decrements the current value. For example, you could specify relative point size changes:

.S +2 +2

or absolute ones:

.S 12 14

By default, if you don't specify vertical spacing, a relation of 2 points greater than the point size will be maintained. A null value ("") does not change the current setting.

The new point size and vertical spacing remain in effect until you change them. Simply entering the .S macro without arguments restores the previous settings:

.S

The mm package keeps track of the default, previous, and current values, making it easy to switch between different settings using one of these three arguments:

D	Default
P	Previous
C	Current

To restore the default values, enter:

```
.S D
```

The point size returns to 10 points and the vertical spacing is automatically reset to 12 points. To increase the vertical space to 16 points while keeping the point size the same, enter:

```
.S C 16
```

In the following example for a letterhead, the company name is specified in 18-point type and a tag line in 12-point type; then the default settings are restored:

```
.S 18
Caslon Inc.
.S 12
Communicating Expertise
.S D
```

The result is:

Caslon Inc.
Communicating Expertise

You can also change the font along with the point size, using the `.I` macro described previously. Following is the tag line in 12-point italic.

Communicating Expertise

A special-purpose macro in mm reduces by 1 point the point size of a specified string. The `.SM` macro can be followed by one, two, or three strings. Only one argument is reduced; which one depends upon how many arguments are given. If you specify one or two arguments, the first argument will be reduced by 1 point:

```
using
.SM UNIX ,
you will find
```

The second argument is concatenated to the first argument, so that the comma immediately follows the word *UNIX*:

using UNIX, you will find

If you specify three arguments:

```
.SM [ UNIX ]
```

The second argument is reduced by one point, but the first and third arguments are printed in the current point size, and all three are concatenated:

[UNIX]

▪ **More about Displays** ▪

Broadly speaking, a display is any kind of information in the body of a document that cannot be set as a normal paragraph. Displays can be figures, quotations, examples, tables, lists, equations, or diagrams.

The display macros position the display on the page. Inside the display, you might use other macros or preprocessors such as `tbl` or `eqn`. You might simply have a block of text that deserves special treatment.

The display macros can be relied upon to provide

- adequate spacing before and after the display;

- horizontal positioning of the display as a left justified, indented, or centered block;

- proper page breaks by keeping the entire display together.

The default action of the `.DS` macro is to left justify the text block in no-fill mode. It provides no indentation from the current margins.

You can specify a different format for a display by specifying up to three arguments with the `.DS` macro. The syntax is:

> `.DS` [*format*] [*fill mode*] [*right indent*]

The *format* argument allows you to specify an indented or centered display. The argument can be set by a numeric value or a letter corresponding to the following options:

0	L	No indent (default)
1	I	Indented
2	C	Center each line
3	CB	Center entire display

For consistency, the indent of displays is initially set to be the same as indented paragraphs (five spaces in `nroff` and three ens in `troff`), although these values are maintained independently in two different number registers, `Pi` and `Si`. (To change the defaults, simply use the `.nr` request to put the desired value in the appropriate register.)

A display can be centered in two ways: either each individual line in the display is centered (C) or the entire display is centered as a block based on the longest line of the display (CB).

For instance, the preceding list was formatted using `tbl`, but its placement was controlled by the display macro.

```
.DS  CB
.TS
```
table specifications
```
.TE
.DE
```

The *fill mode* argument is represented by either a number or a letter.

0	N	No-fill mode (default)
1	F	Fill mode

The *right indent* argument is a numeric value that is subtracted from the right margin. In `nroff`, this value is automatically scaled in ens. In `troff`, you can specify a scaled number; otherwise, the default is ems.

The use of fill mode, along with other indented display options, can provide a paragraph indented on both sides. This is often used in reports and proposals that quote at length from another source. For example:

```
.P
I was particularly interested in the following comment
found in the product specification:
.DS I F 5
Users first need a brief introduction to what the product
does.  Sometimes this is more for the benefit of people
who haven't yet bought the product, and
are just looking at the manual.
However, it also serves to put the rest of
the manual, and the product itself, in the proper context.
.DE
```

The result of formatting is:

```
I was particularly interested in the following comment
found in the the product specification:

        Users  first   need   a   brief   introduction to
        what the product  does.   Sometimes   this  is
        more for the  benefit of people  who haven't
        yet bought the product, and are  just looking
        at the manual.  However, it   also   serves to
        put the rest of the manual,   and the product
        itself, in the proper context.
```

The use of tabs often presents a problem outside of displays. Material that has been entered with tabs in the input file should be formatted in no-fill mode, the default setting of the display macros. The following table was designed using tabs to provide the spacing:

```
.DF I
Dates                   Description of Task

June 30                 Submit audience analysis
July 2                  Meeting to review audience analysis
July 15                 Submit detailed outline
August 1                Submit first draft
August 5                Return of first draft
August 8                Meeting to review comments
.DE
```

This table appears in the output just as it looks in the file. If this material had not been processed inside a display in no-fill mode, the columns would be improperly aligned.

Static and Floating Displays

There are two types of displays, *static* and *floating*. The difference between them has to do with what happens when a display cannot fit in its entirety on the current page. Both the static and the floating display output the block at the top of the next page if it doesn't fit on the current page; however, only the floating display allows text that follows the display to be used to fill up the preceding page. A static display maintains the order in which a display was placed in the input file.

We have already used `.DS` and `.DE` to mark the beginning and end of a static display. To specify a floating display, the closing mark is the same, but the beginning is marked by the `.DF` macro. The options are the same as for the `.DS` macro.

In the following example of an input file, numbers are used instead of actual lines of text:

```
1
2
3
4
5
.DF
```
Long Display
```
.DE
6
7
8
9
10
```

The following two formatted pages might be produced, assuming that there are a sufficient number of lines in the display to cause a page break:

```
┌─────────────────────────┐      ┌─────────────────────────┐
│           -1-           │      │           -2-           │
│                         │      │                         │
│  1                      │      │  Long Display           │
│  2                      │      │                         │
│  3                      │      │  8                      │
│  4                      │      │  9                      │
│  5                      │      │  10                     │
│  6                      │      │                         │
│  7                      │      │                         │
│                         │      │                         │
└─────────────────────────┘      └─────────────────────────┘
```

If there had been room on page 1 to fit the display, it would have been placed there, and lines 6 and 7 would have followed the display, as they did in the input file.

If a static display had been specified, the display would be placed in the same position on page 2, and lines 6 and 7 would have to follow it, leaving extra space at the bottom of page 1. A floating display attempts to make the best use of the available space on a page.

The formatter maintains a queue to hold floating displays that it has not yet output. When the top of a page is encountered, the next display in the queue is output. The queue is emptied in the order in which it was filled, (first in, first out). Two number registers, De and Df, allow you to control when displays are removed from the queue and placed in position.

At the end of a section, as indicated by the section macros .H and .HU (which we will see shortly), or at the end of the input file, any floating displays that remain in the queue will be placed in the document.

Display Labels

You can provide a title or caption for tables, equations, exhibits, and figures. In addition, the display can be labeled and numbered in sequence, as well as printed in a table of contents at the end of the file. The following group of macros are available:

.EC	Equation
.EX	Exhibit
.FG	Figure

All of these macros work the same way and are usually specified within a pair of .DS/.DE macros, so that the title and the display appear on the same page. Each macro can be followed by a title. If the title contains spaces, it should be enclosed within quotation marks. The title of a table usually appears at the top of a table, so it must be specified before the .TS macro that signals to tbl the presence of a table (see Chapter 8).

```
.TB "List of Required Resources"
.TS
```

The label is centered:

Table 1. List of Required Resources

If the title exceeds the line length, then it will be broken onto several lines. Additional lines are indented and begin at the first character of the title.

Table 1. List of Required Resources
Provided by Gutenberg Galaxy
Software

The label for equations, exhibits, and figures usually follows the display. The following:

```
.FG "Drawing with a Light Pen"
```

produces a centered line:

Figure 1. Drawing with a Light Pen

The default format of the label can be changed slightly by setting the number register `Of` to 1. This replaces the period with a dash.

Figure 1 — Drawing with a Light Pen

Second and third arguments, specified with the label macros, can be used to modify or override the default numbering of displays. Basically, the second argument is a literal and the third argument a numeric value that specifies what the literal means.

If the third argument is

0   then the second argument will be treated as a prefix;

1   then the second argument will be treated as a suffix;

2   then the second argument replaces the normal table number.

Thus, a pair of related tables could be specified as 1a and 1b using the following labels:

```
.TB "Estimated Hours: June, July, and August" a 1
.TB "Estimated Hours: September and November," 1b 2
```

(These labels show two different uses of the third argument. Usually, you would consistently use one technique or the other for a given set of tables.)

For `tbl`, the delimiters for tables are `.TS/.TE`. For `eqn`, the delimiters for equations are `.EQ/.EN`. For `pic`, the delimiters for pictures or diagrams are `.PS/.PE`. These pairs of delimiters indicate a block to be processed by a specific preprocessor. You will find the information about each of the preprocessors in Chapters 8 through 10. As mentioned, the preprocessor creates the display, the display macros position it, and the label macros add titles and a number.

Although it may seem a minor point, each of these steps is independent, and because they are not fully integrated, there is some overlap.

The label macros, being independent of the preprocessors, do not make sure that a display exists or check whether a table has been created with `tbl`. You can create a two-column table using tabs or create a figure using character symbols and still give it a label. Or you can create a table heading as the first line of your table and let `tbl` process it (`tbl` won't provide a number and the table won't be collected for the table of contents).

In `tbl`, you can specify a centered table and not use the `.DS`/`.DE` macros. But, as a consequence, `nroff`/`troff` won't make a very good attempt at keeping the table together on one page, and you may have to manually break the page. It is recommended that you use the display macros throughout a document, regardless of whether you can get the same effect another way, because if nothing else you will achieve consistency.

▪ Forcing a Page Break ▪

Occasionally, you may want to force a page break, whether to ensure that a block of related material is kept together or to allow several pages for material that will be manually pasted in, such as a figure. The `.SK` (*skip*) macro forces a page break. The text following this macro is output at the top of the next page. If supplied with an argument greater than 0, it causes that number of pages to be skipped before resuming the output of text. The "blank" pages are printed, and they have the normal header and footer.

```
On the next page, you will find a sample page from an
Alcuin manuscript printed with a 16-color plotter.
.SK 1
```

▪ Formatting Lists ▪

The mm macro package provides a variety of different formats for presenting a list of items. You can select from four standard list types:

- bulleted
- dashed
- numbered
- alphabetized

In addition, you have the flexibility to create lists with nonstandard marks or text labels. The list macros can also be used to produce paragraphs with a hanging indent.

Each list item consists of a special mark, letter, number, or label in a left-hand column with a paragraph of text indented in a right-hand column.

Structuring a List

The list macros help to simplify what could be a much larger and tedious formatting task. Here's the coding for the bulleted list just shown:

```
.BL
.LI
bulleted
.LI
dashed
.LI
numbered
.LI
alphabetized
.LE
```

The structure of text in the input file has three parts: a list-initialization macro (`.BL`), an item-mark macro (`.LI`), and a list-end macro (`.LE`).

First, you initialize the list, specifying the particular macro for the type of list that you want. For instance, `BL` initializes a bulleted list.

You can specify arguments with the list-initialization macro that change the indentation of the text and turn off the automatic spacing between items in the list. We will examine these arguments when we look at the list-initialization macros in more detail later.

Next, you specify each of the items in the list. The item-mark macro, `.LI`, is placed before each item. You can enter one or more lines of text following the macro.

```
.BL
.LI
Item 1
.LI
Item 2
.LI
Item 3
```

When the list is formatted, the `.LI` macro provides a line of space before each item. (This line can be omitted through an argument to the list-initialization macro if you want to produce a more compact list. We'll be talking more about this in a moment.)

The `.LI` macro can also be used to override or prefix the current mark. If a mark is supplied as the only argument, it replaces the current mark. For example:

```
.LI  o
Item 4
```

If a mark is supplied as the first argument, followed by a second argument of 1 , then the specified mark is prefixed to the current mark. The following:

```
.LI  - 1
Item 5
```

would produce:

-•   Item 5

A text label can also be supplied in place of the mark, but it presents some additional problems for the proper alignment of the list. We will look at text labels for variable-item lists.

The .LI macro does not automatically provide spacing after each list item. An argument of 1 can be specified if a line of space is desired.

The end of the list is marked by the list-end macro .LE. It restores page formatting settings that were in effect prior to the invocation of the last list-initialization macro. The .LE macro does not output any space following the list unless you specify an argument of 1. (Don't specify this argument when the list is immediately followed by a macro that outputs space, such as the paragraph macro.)

Be sure you are familiar with the basic structure of a list. A common problem is not closing the list with .LE. Most of the time, this error causes the formatter to quit at this point in the file. A less serious, but nonetheless frequent, oversight is omitting the first .LI between the list-initialization macro and the first item in the list. The list is output but the first item will be askew.

Here is a sample list:

```
.BL
.LI
Item 1
.LI
Item 2
.LI
Item 3
.LI  o
Item 4
.LI  - 1
Item 5
.LE
```

The `troff` output produced by the sample list is:

```
•      Item 1

•      Item 2

•      Item 3

o      Item 4

-•     Item 5
```

Complete list structures can be nested within other lists up to six levels. Different types of lists can be nested, making it possible to produce indented outline structures. But, like nested if-then structures in a program, make sure you know which level you are at and remember to close each list.

For instance, we could nest the bulleted list inside a numbered list. The list-initialization macro `.AL` generates alphabetized and numbered lists.

```
.AL
.LI
Don't worry, we'll get to the list-initialization macro .AL.
You can specify five different variations of
alphabetic and numbered lists.
.BL
.LI
Item 1
.LI
Item 2
.LI
Item 3
.LE
.LI
We'll also look at variable-item lists.
.LE
```

This input produces the following formatted list from `troff`:

1.   Don't worry, we'll get to the list-initialization macro `.AL`. You can specify five different variations of alphabetic and numbered lists.

 - Item 1

 - Item 2

 - Item 3

2.   We'll also look at variable-item lists.

You may already realize the ease with which you can make changes to a list. The items in a list can be easily put in a new order. New items can be added to a numbered list without readjusting the numbering scheme. A bulleted list can be changed to an alphabetized list by simply changing the list-initialization macro. And you normally don't have to be concerned with a variety of specific formatting requests, such as setting indentation levels or specifying spacing between items.

On the other hand, because the structure of the list is not as easy to recognize in the input file as it is in the formatted output, you may find it difficult to interpret complicated lists, in particular ones that have been nested to several levels. The code-checking program, `checkmm`, can help; in addition, you may want to format and print repeatedly to examine and correct problems with lists.

Marked Lists

Long a standby of technical documents, a marked list clearly organizes a group of related items and sets them apart for easy reading. A list of items marked by a bullet (•) is perhaps the most common type of list. Another type of marked list uses a dash (—). A third type of list allows the user to specify a mark, such as a square (□). The list-initialization macros for these lists are:

```
.BL     [text indent] [1]
.DL     [text indent] [1]
.ML     [mark] [text indent] [1]
```

With the `.BL` macro, the text is indented the same amount as the first line of an indented paragraph. A single space is maintained between the bullet and the text. The bullet is right justified, causing an indent of several spaces from the left margin.

As you can see from this `nroff`-formatted output, the bullet is simulated in `nroff` by a + overstriking an o:

```
        Currently, the following internal documentation is
    available on the Alcuin product:

        ⏀ GGS Technical Memo 3200

        ⏀ GGS Product Marketing Spec

        ⏀ Alcuin/UNIX interface definition

        ⏀ Programmer's documentation for Alcuin
```

If you specify a *text indent*, the first character of the text will start at that position. The position of the bullet is relative to the text, always one space to its left.

If the last argument is 1, the blank line of space separating items is omitted. If you want to specify only this argument, you must specify either a value or a null value ("") for a *text indent*.

```
    .BL "" 1
```

It produces a much more compact list:

```
        ⏀ GGS Technical Memo 3200
        ⏀ GGS Product Marketing Spec
        ⏀ Alcuin/UNIX interface definition
        ⏀ Programmer's documentation for Alcuin
```

Because the bullets produced by `nroff` are not always appropriate due to the overstriking, a dashed list provides a suitable alternative. With the `.DL` macro, the dash is placed in the same position as a bullet in a bulleted list. A single space is maintained between the dash and the text, which, like the text with a bulleted list, is indented by the amount specified in the number register for indented paragraphs (`Pi`).

The `nroff` formatter supplies a dash that is a single hyphen, and `troff` supplies an em dash. Because the em dash is longer, and the dash is right justified, the alignment with the left margin is noticeably different. It appears left justified in `troff`; in `nroff`, the dash appears indented several spaces because it is smaller.

```
        The third chapter on the principles of computerized
    font design should cover the following topics:

        - Building a Font Dictionary

        - Loading a Font

        - Scaling a Font
```

You can specify a *text indent* and a second argument of 1 to inhibit spacing between items.

With the .ML macro, you have to supply the mark for the list. Some possible candidates are the square (enter \(sq to get □), the square root (enter \(sr to get √), which resembles a check mark, and the gradient symbol (enter \(gr to get ∇). The user-specified mark is the first argument.

```
.ML \(sq
```

Not all of the characters or symbols that you can use in troff will have the same effect in nroff.

Unlike bulleted and dashed lists, text is not automatically indented after a user-specified mark. However, a space is added after the mark. The following example of an indented paragraph and a list, which specifies a square as a mark, has been formatted using nroff. The square appears as a pair of brackets.

```
[] Remove old initialization files.

[] Run install program.

[] Exit to main menu and choose selection 3.
```

The user-supplied mark can be followed by a second argument that specifies a *text indent* and a third argument of 1 to omit spacing between items.

The following example was produced using the list-initialization command:

```
.ML \(sq 5 1
```

The specified indent of 5 aligns the text with an indented paragraph:

```
     Check to see that you have completed the following
steps:

   [] Remove old initialization files.
   [] Run install program.
   [] Exit to main menu and choose selection 3.
```

Numbered and Alphabetic Lists

The .AL macro is used to initialize automatically numbered or alphabetized lists. The syntax for this macro is:

```
.AL    [type] [text indent] [1]
```

If no arguments are specified, the .AL macro produces a numbered list. For instance, we can code the following paragraph with the list-initialization macro .AL:

```
User-oriented documentation recognizes three things:
.AL
.LI
that a new user needs to learn the system in stages,
getting a sense of the system as a whole while becoming
proficient in performing particular tasks;
.LI
that there are different levels of users, and not every
user needs to learn all the capabilities of the system
in order to be productive;
.LI
that an experienced user must be able to rely on the
documentation for accurate and thorough reference
information.
.LE
```

to produce a numbered list:

```
User-oriented documentation recognizes three things:

   1.   that a new user needs to learn the system in stages,
        getting a sense of the system as a whole while
        becoming proficient in performing particular tasks;

   2.   that there are different levels of users, and not
        every user needs to learn all the capabilities of
        the system in order to be productive;

   3.   that an experienced user must be able to rely on the
        documentation for accurate and thorough reference
        information.
```

The number is followed by a period, and two spaces are maintained between the period and the first character of text.

The level of *text indent*, specified in the number register `Li`, is 6 in `nroff` and 5 in `troff`. This value is added to the current indent. If a *text indent* is specified, that value is added to the current indent, but it does not change the value of `Li`.

The third argument inhibits spacing between items in the list. Additionally, the number register `Ls` can be set to a value from 0 to 6 indicating a nesting level. Lists after this level will not have spacing between items. The default is 6, the maximum nesting depth. If `Ls` were set to 2, lists only up to the second level would have a blank line of space between items.

Other types of lists can be specified with `.AL`, using the first argument to specify the list type, as follows:

Value	Sequence	Description
1	1, 2, 3	Numbered
A	A, B, C	Alphabetic (uppercase)
a	a, b, c	Alphabetic (lowercase)
I	I, II, III	Roman numerals (uppercase)
i	i, ii, iii	Roman numerals (lowercase)

You can produce various list types by simply changing the *type* argument. You can create a very useful outline format by nesting different types of lists. The example we show of such an outline is one that is nested to four levels using I, A, 1, and a, in that order. The rather complicated looking input file is shown in Figure 6-4 (indented for easier viewing of each list, although it could not be formatted this way), and the nroff-formatted output is shown in Figure 6-5.

Another list-initialization macro that produces a numbered list is .RL (*reference list*). The only difference is that the reference number is surrounded by brackets ([ ]).

.RL [*text indent*] [1]

The arguments have the same effect as those specified with the .AL macro. To initialize a reference list with no spacing between items, use:

.RL "" 1

It produces the following reference list:

```
    [1]  The Main Menu
    [2]  Menus or Commands?
    [3]  Error Handling
    [4]  Getting Help
    [5]  Escaping to UNIX
```

Variable-Item Lists

With a variable-item list, you do not supply a mark; instead, you specify a text label with each .LI. One or more lines of text following .LI are used to form a block paragraph indented from the label. If no label is specified, a paragraph with a hanging indent is produced. The syntax is:

.VL *text indent* [*label indent*] [1]

Unlike the other list-initialization macros, a *text indent* is required. By default, the label is left justified, unless a *label indent* is given. If you specify both a *text indent* and a *label indent*, the indent for the text will be added to the *label indent*.

```
.AL I
.LI
Quick Tour of Alcuin
      .AL A
      .LI
      Introduction to Calligraphy
      .LI
      Digest of Alcuin Commands
            .AL 1
            .LI
            Three Methods of Command Entry
                  .AL a
                  .LI
                  Mouse
                  .LI
                  Keyboard
                  .LI
                  Light Pen
                  .LE
            .LI
            Starting a Page
            .LI
            Drawing Characters
                  .AL a
                  .LI
                  Choosing a Font
                  .LI
                  Switching Fonts
                  .LE
            .LI
            Creating Figures
            .LI
            Printing
            .LE
      .LI
      Sample Illuminated Manuscripts
      .LE
.LI
Using Graphic Characters
      .AL A
      .LI
      Modifying Font Style
      .LI
      Drawing Your Own Font
      .LE
.LI
Library of Hand-Lettered Fonts
.LE
```

Fig. 6-4. Input for a Complex List

– 1 –

I. Quick Tour of Alcuin

    A. Introduction to Calligraphy

    B. Digest of Alcuin Commands

        1. Three Methods of Command Entry

            a. Mouse

            b. Keyboard

            c. Light Pen

        2. Starting a Page

        3. Drawing Characters

            a. Choosing a Font

            b. Switching Fonts

        4. Creating Figures

        5. Printing

    C. Sample Illuminated Manuscripts

II. Using Graphic Characters

    A. Modifying Font Style

    B. Drawing Your Own Font

III. Library of Hand-Lettered Fonts

Fig. 6-5. Output of a Complex List

Variable-item lists are useful in preparing command reference pages, which describe various syntax items, and glossaries, which present a term in one column and its definition in the other. The text label should be a single word or phrase. The following example shows a portion of the input file for a reference page:

```
.VL 15 5
.LI figure
is the name of a cataloged figure.  If
a figure has not been cataloged, you need to use
the LOCATE command.
.LI f:p
is the scale of the
figure in relation to the page.
.LI font
is the two-character abbreviation or
full name of one of the available fonts
from the Alcuin library.
.LE
```

The following variable-item list is produced:

```
        figure      is the name of a cataloged figure.  If a
                    figure has not been cataloged, you need to
                    use the LOCATE command.

        f:p         is the scale of the figure in relation to
                    the page.

        font        is the two-character abbreviation or full
                    name of one of the available fonts from the
                    Alcuin library.
```

If you don't provide a text label with `.LI` or give a null argument (`""`), you will get a paragraph with a hanging indent. If you want to print an item without a label, specify a backslash followed by a space (`\ `) or `\0` after `.LI`. Similarly, if you want to specify a label that contains a space, you should also precede the space with a backslash and enclose the label within quotation marks:

```
.LI "point\ size"
```

or simply substitute a `\0` for a space:

```
.LI point\0size
```

The first line of text is left justified (or indented by the amount specified in *label indent*) and the remaining lines will be indented by the amount specified by *text indent*. This produces a paragraph with a hanging indent:

```
.VL 15
.LI
There are currently 16 font dictionaries in the Alcuin
library.  Any application may have up to 12 dictionaries
resident in memory at the same time.
.LE
```

When formatted, this item has a hanging indent of 15:

```
There are currently 16 font dictionaries in the Alcuin
                library.  Any application may have up to
                12 dictionaries resident in memory at the
                same time.
```

▪ Headings ▪

Earlier we used the list macros to produce an indented outline. That outline, indented to four levels, is a visual representation of the structure of a document. Headings perform a related function, showing how the document is organized into sections and subsections. In technical documentation and book-length manuscripts, having a structure that is easily recognized by the reader is very important.

Numbered and Unnumbered Headings

Using mm, you can have up to seven levels of numbered and unnumbered headings, with variable styles. There are two heading macros: .H for numbered headings and .HU for unnumbered headings. A different style for each level of heading can be specified by setting various number registers and defining strings.

Let's first look at how to produce numbered headings. The syntax for the .H macro is:

.H   *level* [*heading text*] [*heading suffix*]

The simplest use of the .H macro is to specify the *level* as a number between 1 and 7 followed by the text that is printed as a heading. If the *heading text* contains spaces, you should enclose it within quotation marks. A heading that is longer than a single line will be wrapped on to the next line. A multiline heading will be kept together in case of a page break.

If you specify a *heading suffix*, this text or mark will appear in the heading but will not be collected for a table of contents.

A top-level heading is indicated by an argument of 1:

```
.H 1 "Quick Tour of Alcuin"
```

The result is a heading preceded by a heading-level number. The first-level heading has the number 1.

```
     1.   Quick Tour of Alcuin
```

A second-level heading is indicated by an argument of 2:

```
     .H 2 "Introduction to Calligraphy"
```

The first second-level heading number is printed:

```
     1.1  Introduction to Calligraphy
```

When another heading is specified at the same level, the heading-level number is automatically incremented. If the next heading is at the second level:

```
     .H 2 "Digest of Alcuin Commands"
```

it produces:

```
     1.2  Digest of Alcuin Commands
```

Each time you go to a new (higher-numbered) level, .1 is appended to the number representing the existing level. That number is incremented for each call at the same level. When you back out of a level (for instance, from level 5 to 4), the counter for the level (in this case level 5), is reset to 0.

An unnumbered heading is really a zero-level heading:

```
     .H 0 "Introduction to Calligraphy"
```

A separate macro, .HU, has been developed for unnumbered headings, although its effect is the same.

```
     .HU "Introduction to Calligraphy"
```

Even though an unnumbered heading does not display a number, it increments the counter for second-level headings. Thus, in the following example, the heading "Introduction to Calligraphy" is unnumbered, but it has the same effect on the numbering scheme as if it had been a second-level heading (1.1).

```
     1.   Quick Tour of Alcuin


     Introduction to Calligraphy


     1.2  Digest of Alcuin Commands
```

If you are going to intermix numbered and unnumbered headings, you can change the number register Hu to the lowest-level heading that is in the document. By changing Hu from 2 to a higher number:

```
     .nr Hu 5
     .H 1 "Quick Tour of Alcuin"
     .HU "Introduction to Calligraphy"
     .H 2 "Digest of Alcuin Commands"
```

the numbering sequence is preserved for the numbered heading following an unnumbered heading:

```
1.   Quick Tour of Alcuin

Introduction to Calligraphy

1.1  Digest of Alcuin Commands
```

Headings are meant to be visible keys to your document's structure. If you are using unnumbered headings, it becomes even more important to make headings stand out. A simple thing you can do is use uppercase letters for a first-level heading.

Here is a list of some of the other things you can do to affect the appearance of headings, although some of the items depend upon whether you are formatting with `nroff` or `troff`:

- change to roman, italic, or bold font

- change the point size of the heading

- adjust spacing after the heading

- center or left justify the heading

- change the numbering scheme

- select a different heading mark

The basic issue in designing a heading style is to help the reader distinguish between different levels of headings. For instance, in an outline form, different levels of indent show whether a topic is a section or subsection. Using numbered headings is an effective way to accomplish this. If you use unnumbered headings, you probably want to vary the heading style for each level, although, for practical purposes, you should limit yourself to two or three levels.

First, let's look at what happens if we use the default heading style.

The first two levels of headings are set up to produce italicized text in `troff` and underlined text in `nroff`. After the heading, there is a blank line before the first paragraph of text. In addition, a top-level heading has two blank lines before the heading; all the other levels have a single line of space.

```
         1.2  Introduction to Calligraphy


Alcuin revitalizes an age-old tradition.  Calligraphy, quite simply, is the art of
beautiful handwriting.
```

Levels three through seven all have the same appearance. The text is italicized or underlined and no line break occurs. Two blank lines are maintained before and after the text of the heading. For example:

1.2.1.3 *Light Pen* The copyist's pen and ink has been replaced by a light pen.

To change the normal appearance of headings in a document, you specify new values for the two strings:

HF   Heading font
HP   Heading point size

You can specify individual settings for each level, up to seven values.

The font for each level of heading can be set by the string HF. The following codes are used to select a font:

1   Roman
2   Italic
3   Bold

By default, the arguments for all seven levels are set to 2, resulting in italicized headings in `troff` and underlining in `nroff`. Here the .HF string specifies bold for the top three levels followed by two italic levels:

```
.ds HF 3 3 3 2 2
```

If you do not specify a level, it defaults to 1. Thus, in the previous example, level 6 and 7 headings would be printed in a roman font.

The point size is set by the string HP. Normally, headings are printed in the same size as the body copy, except for bold headings. A bold heading is reduced by 1 point when it is a standalone heading, as are the top-level headings. The HP string can take up to seven arguments, setting the point size for each level.

```
.ds HP 14 14 12
```

If an argument is not given, or a null value or 0 is given, the default setting of 10 points is used for that level. Point size can also be given relative to the current point size:

```
.ds HP +4 +4 +2
```

A group of number registers control other default formats of headings:

Ej   Eject page
Hb   Break follows heading
Hc   Center headings
Hi   Align text after heading
Hs   Vertical spacing after heading

For each of these number registers, you specify the number of the level at which some action is to be turned on or off.

The Ej register is set to the highest-level heading, usually 1, that should start on a new page. Its default setting is 0. This ensures that the major sections of a document will begin on their own page.

```
.nr Ej 1
```

The Hb register determines if a line break occurs after the heading. The Hs register determines if a blank line is output after the heading. Both are set to 2 by default. Settings of 2 mean that, for levels 1 and 2, the section heading is printed, followed by a line break and a blank line separating the heading from the first paragraph of text. For lower-level headings (an argument greater than 2), the first paragraph follows immediately on the same line.

The Hc register is set to the highest-level heading that you want centered. Normally, this is not used with numbered headings and its default value is 0. However, unnumbered heads are often centered. A setting of 2 will center first- and second-level headings:

```
.nr Hc 2
```

With unnumbered headings, you also have to keep in mind that the value of Hc must be greater than or equal to Hb and Hu. The heading must be on a line by itself; therefore a break must be set in Hb for that level. The Hu register sets the level of an unnumbered heading to 2, requiring that Hc be at least 2 to have an effect on unnumbered headings.

There really is no way, using these registers, to get the first and second levels left justified and have the rest of the headings centered.

The number register Hi determines the paragraph type for a heading that causes a line break (Hb). It can be set to one of three values:

0	Left justified
1	Paragraph type determined by Pt
2	Indented to align with first character in heading

If you want to improve the visibility of numbered headings, set Hi to 2:

```
.nr Hi 2
```

It produces the following results:

```
4.1  Generating Output

An  Alcuin manuscript  is a computer  representation
that has to be converted for output on various kinds
of devices, including plotters and laser printers.
```

Changing the Heading Mark

Remember how the list-initialization macro `.AL` allowed you to change the mark used for a list, producing an alphabetic list instead of a numbered list? These same options are available for headings using the `.HM` macro.

The `.HM` macro takes up to seven arguments specifying the mark for each level. The following codes can be specified:

1	Arabic
001	Arabic with leading zeros
A	Uppercase alphabetic
a	Lowercase alphabetic
I	Uppercase roman
i	Lowercase roman

If no mark is specified, the default numbering system (arabic) is used. Uppercase alphabetic marks can be used in putting together a series of appendices. You can specify A for the top level:

```
.HM A
```

and retain the default section numbering for the rest of the headings. This could produce sections in the following series:

A, A.1, A.2, A.2.1, etc.

Marks can be mixed for an outline style similar to the one we produced using the list macros:

```
.HM I A 1 a i
```

Roman numerals can be used to indicate sections or parts. If you specify:

```
.HM I i
```

the headings for the first two levels are marked by roman numerals. A third-level heading is shown to demonstrate that the heading mark reverted to arabic by default:

```
    I.   Quick Tour of Alcuin

    I.i   Introduction to Calligraphy

    I.ii   Digest of Alcuin Commands

    I.ii.1   Three Methods of Command Entry
```

When you use marks consisting of roman numerals or alphabetic characters, you might not want the mark of the current level to be concatenated to the mark of the previous level. Concatenation can be suppressed by setting the number register `Ht` to 1:

```
.HM I i
.nr Ht 1
```

Now, each heading in the list has only the mark representing that level:

```
    I.   Quick Tour of Alcuin

    i.   Introduction to Calligraphy

   ii.   Digest of Alcuin Commands

    1.   Three Methods of Command Entry
```

▪ Table of Contents ▪

Getting a table of contents easily and automatically is almost reason enough to justify all the energy, yours and the computer's, that goes into text processing. You realize that this is something that the computer was really meant to do.

When the table of contents page comes out of the printer, a writer attains a state of happiness known only to a statistician who can give the computer a simple instruction to tabulate vast amounts of data and, in an instant, get a single piece of paper listing the results.

The reason that producing a table of contents seems so easy is that most of the work is performed in coding the document. That means entering codes to mark each level of heading and all the figures, tables, exhibits, and equations. Processing a table of contents is simply a matter of telling the formatter to collect the information that's already in the file.

There are only two simple codes to put in a file, one at the beginning and one at the end, to generate a table of contents automatically.

At the beginning of the file, you have to set the number register `Cl` to the level of headings that you want collected for a table of contents. For example, setting `Cl` to 2 saves first- and second-level headings.

Place the `.TC` macro at the end of the file. This macro actually does the processing and formatting of the table of contents. The table of contents page is output at the end of a document.

A sample table of contents page follows. The header "CONTENTS" is printed at the top of the page. At the bottom of the page, lowercase roman numerals are used as page numbers.

CONTENTS

1. Quick Tour of Alcuin... 1
   1.1 Introduction to Calligraphy 3
   1.2 Digest of Alcuin Commands...................................... 8
   1.3 Sample Illuminated Manuscripts................................ 21

2. Using Graphic Characters 31
   2.1 Scaling a Font.. 33
   2.2 Modifying Font Style 37
   2.3 Drawing Your Own Font.. 41

3. Library of Hand-Lettered Fonts 51

- i -

One blank line is output before each first-level heading. All first-level headings are left justified. Lower-level headings are indented so that they line up with the start of text for the previous level.

If you have included various displays in your document, and used the macros `.FG`, `.TB`, and `.EX` to specify captions and headings for the displays, this information is collected and output when the `.TC` macro is invoked. A separate page is printed for each accumulated list of figures, tables, and exhibits. For example:

LIST OF TABLES

TABLE 1. List of Required Resources..................... 7

TABLE 2. List of Available Resources................... 16

If you want the lists of displays to be printed immediately following the table of contents (no page breaks), you can set the number register `Cp` to 1.

If you want to suppress the printing of individual lists, you can set the following number registers to 0:

`Lf`	If 0, no figures
`Lt`	If 0, no tables
`Lx`	If 0, no exhibits

In addition, there is a number register for equations that is set to 0 by default. If you want equations marked by .EC to be listed, specify:

```
.nr Le 1
```

There are a set of strings, using the same names as the number registers, that define the titles used for the top of the lists:

Lf	LIST OF FIGURES
Lt	LIST OF TABLES
Lx	LIST OF EXHIBITS
Le	LIST OF EQUATIONS

You can redefine a string using the .ds (*define string*) request. For instance, we can redefine the title for figures as follows:

```
.ds Lf LIST OF ALCUIN DRAWINGS
```

▪ Footnotes and References ▪

Footnotes and references present special problems, as anyone who has ever typed a term paper knows. Fortunately, mm has two pairs of specialized macros. Both of them follow a marker in the text and cause lines of delimited text to be saved and output either at the bottom of the page, as a footnote, or at end of the document, as a reference.

Footnotes

A footnote is marked in the body of a document by the string *F. It follows immediately after the text (no spaces).

```
in an article on desktop publishing.\*F
```

The string F supplies the number for the footnote. It is printed (using troff) as a superscript in the text and its value is incremented with each use.

The .FS macro indicates the start, and .FE the end, of the text for the footnote. These macros surround the footnote text that will appear at the bottom of the page. The .FS macro is put on the line immediately following the marker.

```
.FS
"Publish or Perish: Start-up grabs early page language lead,"
\fIComputerworld\fR, April 21, 1986, p. 1.
.FE
```

You can use labels instead of numbers to mark footnotes. The label must be specified as a mark in the text and as an argument with .FS.

```
...in accord with the internal specs.[APS]
.FS [APS]
"Alcuin Product Specification," March 1986
.FE
```

You can use both numbered and labeled footnotes in the same document. All the foot-notes are collected and output at the bottom of each page underneath a short line rule. If you are using `troff`, the footnote text will be set in a type size 2 points less than the body copy.

If you want to change the standard format of footnotes, you can specify the `.FD` macro. It controls hyphenation, text adjustment, indentation, and justification of the label.

Normally, the text of a footnote is indented from the left margin and the mark or label is left justified in relation to the start of the text. It is possible that a long footnote could run over to the next page. Hyphenation is turned off so that a word will not be broken at a page break. These specifications can be changed by giving a value between 0 and 11 as the first argument with `.FD`, as shown in Table 6-3.

TABLE 6-3. `.FD` Argument Values

Argument	Hyphenation	Adjust	Text Indent	Label Justification
0	no	yes	yes	left
1	yes	yes	yes	left
2	no	no	yes	left
3	yes	no	yes	left
4	no	yes	no	left
5	yes	yes	no	left
6	no	no	no	left
7	yes	no	no	left
8	no	yes	yes	right
9	yes	yes	yes	right
10	no	no	yes	right
11	yes	no	yes	right

The second argument for `.FD`, if 1, resets the footnote numbering counter to 1. This can be invoked at the end of a section or paragraph to initiate a new numbering sequence. If specified by itself, the first argument must be null:

```
.FD "" 1
```

References

A reference differs from a footnote in that all references are collected and printed on a single page at the end of the document. In addition, you can label a reference so that you can refer to it later.

A reference is marked where it occurs in the text with *(Rf. The formatter converts the string into a value printed in brackets, such as [1]. The mark is followed by a pair of macros surrounding the reference text. The .RS macro indicates the start, and .RF the end, of the text for the reference.

```
You will find information on this page description language
in their reference manual, which has been published
as a book.\*(Rf
.RS
Adobe Systems, Inc. PostScript Reference Manual.
Reading, Massachusetts: Addison-Wesley; 1985.
.RF
```

You can also give as a *string label* argument to .RS the name of a string that will be assigned the current reference number. This string can be referenced later in the document. For instance, if we had specified a *string label* in the previous example:

```
.RS As
```

We could refer back to the first reference in another place:

```
The output itself is a readable file which you can interpret
with the aid of the PostScript manual.\*(As
```

At the end of the document, a reference page is printed. The title printed on the reference page is defined in the string Rp. You can replace ''REFERENCES'' with another title simply by redefining this string with .ds.

REFERENCES

1. Adobe Systems, Inc.; PostScript Reference Manual.
   Reading, Massachusetts: Addison-Wesley; 1985.

In a large document, you might want to print a list of references at the end of a chapter or a long section. You can invoke the .RP macro anywhere in a document.

```
.RP
.H 1 "Detailed Outline of User Guide"
```

It will print the list of references on a separate page and reset the reference counter to 0. A *reset* argument and a *paging* argument can be supplied to change these actions. The *reset* argument is the first value specified with the .RP macro. It is normally 0, resetting the reference counter to 1 so that each section is numbered independently. If reference numbering should be maintained in sequence for the entire document, specify a value of 1.

The *paging* argument is the second value specified. It controls whether or not a page break occurs before and after the list. It is normally set to 0, putting the list on a new page. Specifying a value of 3 suppresses the page break before and after the list; the result is that the list of references is printed following the end of the section and the next section begins immediately after the list. A value of 1 will suppress only the page break that occurs after the list and a value of 2 will suppress only the page break that occurs before the list.

If you want an effect opposite that of the default settings, specify:

```
.RP 1 3
```

The first argument of 1 saves the current reference number for use in the next section or chapter. The second argument of 3 inhibits page breaks before and after the list of references.

▪ **Extensions to mm** ▪

So far, we have covered most but not all of the features of the mm macro package.

We have not covered the Technical Memorandum macros, a set of specialized macros for formatting technical memos and reports. Like the ones in the ms macro package, these macros were designed for internal use at AT&T's Bell Laboratories, reflecting a company-wide set of standards. Anyone outside of Bell Labs will want to make some modifications to the macros before using them. The Technical Memorandum macros are a good example of employing a limited set of user macros to produce a standard format. Seeing how they work will be especially important to those who are responsible for implementing documentation standards for a group of people, some of whom understand the basics of formatting and some of whom do not.

Writing or rewriting macros is only one part of the process of customizing mm. The mm macros were designed as a comprehensive formatting system. As we've seen, there are even macros to replace common primitive requests, like .sp. The developers of mm recommend, in fact, that you not use nroff or troff requests unless absolutely necessary, lest you interfere with the action of the macros.

Furthermore, as you will see if you print out the mm macros, the internal code of mm is extraordinarily dense, and uses extremely un-mnemonic register names. This makes it very difficult for all but the most experienced user to modify the basic structure of the package. You can always add your own macros, as long as they don't conflict with existing macro and number register names, but you can't easily go in and change the basic macros that make up the mm package.

At the same time, the developers of mm have made it possible for the user to make selective modifications—those which mm has allowed mechanisms for in advance. There are two such mechanisms:

- mm's use of number registers to control all aspects of document formatting

- mm's invocation of undefined (and therefore user-definable) macros at various places in the mm code

The mm package is very heavily parameterized. Almost every feature of the formatting system—from the fonts in which different levels of heading are printed to the size of indents and the amount of space above and below displays—is controlled by values in number registers. By learning and modifying these number registers, you can make significant changes to the overall appearance of your documents.

In addition, there are a number of values stored in strings. These strings are used like number registers to supply default values to various macros.

The registers you are most likely to want to change follow. Registers marked with a dagger can only be changed on the comand line with the $-r$ option (e.g., $-rN4$).

Cl	Level of headings saved for table of contents. See .TC macro. Default is 2.
Cp	If set to 1, lists of figures and tables appear on same page as table of contents. Otherwise, they start on a new page. Default is 1.
Ds	Sets the pre- and post-space used for static displays.
Fs	Vertical spacing between footnotes.
Hb	Level of heading for which break occurs before output of body text. Default is 2 lines.
Hc	Level of heading for which centering occurs. Default is 0.
Hi	Indent type after heading. Default is 1 (paragraph indent). Legal values are: 0=left justified (default); 1=indented; 2=indented except after .H, .LC, .DE.
Hs	Level of heading for which space after heading occurs. Default is 2, i.e., space will occur after first- and second-level headings.
Hy	Sets hyphenation. If set to 1, enables hyphenation. Default is 0.
L†	Sets length of page. Default is 66v.
Li	Default indent of lists. Default is 5.
Ls	List spacing between items by level. Default is 6, which is spacing between all levels of list.
N†	Page numbering style. 0=all pages get header; 1=header printed as footer on page 1; 2=no header on page 1; 3=section page as footer; 4=no header unless .PH defined; 5=section page and section figure as footer. Default is 0.
Np	Numbering style for paragraphs. 0=unnumbered; 1=numbered.
O	Offset of page. For nroff, this value is an unscaled number representing character positions. (Default is 9 characters; about .75i.) For troff, this value is scaled (.5i).

`Of`	Figure caption style. 0=period separator; 1=hyphen separator. Default is 0.
`Pi`	Amount of indent for paragraph. Default is 5 for `nroff`, 3n for `troff`.
`Ps`	Amount of spacing between paragraphs. Default is 3v.
`Pt`	Paragraph type. Default is 0.
`S†`	Default point size for `troff`. Default is 10. Vertical spacing is `\nS+2`.
`Si`	Standard indent for displays. Default is 5 for `nroff`, 3 for `troff`.
`W`	Width of page (line and title length). Default is 6 in `troff`, 60 characters in `nroff`.

There are also some values that you would expect to be kept in number registers that are actually kept in strings:

`HF`	Fonts used for each level of heading (1=roman, 2=italic, 3=bold)
`HP`	Point size used for each level of heading

For example, placing the following register settings at the start of your document:

```
.nr Hc 1
.nr Hs 3
.nr Hb 4
.nr Hi 2
.ds HF 3 3 3 3 2 2 2
.ds HP 16 14 12 10 10 10 10
```

will have the following effects:

- Top-level headings (generated by `.H1`) will be centered.

- The first three levels of heading will be followed by a blank line.

- The fourth-level heading will be followed by a break.

- Fifth- through seventh-level headings will be run-in with the text.

- All headings will have the following text indented under the first word of the heading, so that the section number hangs in the margin.

- The first five levels of heading will be in bold type; the sixth and seventh will be italic.

- A first-level heading will be printed in 16-point type; a second-level heading in 14-point type; a third-level heading in 12-point type; and all subsequent levels in 10-point type.

There isn't space in this book for a comprehensive discussion of this topic. However, a complete list of user-settable mm number registers is given in Appendix B. Study this list, along with the discussion of the relevant macros, and you will begin to get a picture of just how many facets of mm you can modify by changing the values in number registers and strings.

The second feature—the provision of so-called "user exit macros" at various points—is almost as ingenious. The following macros are available for user definition:

```
.HX    .HY    .HZ    .PX    .TX    .TY
```

The .HX, .HY, and .HZ macros are associated with headings. The .HX macro is executed at the start of each heading macro, .HY in the middle (to allow you to respecify any settings, such as temporary indents, that were lost because of mm's own processing), and .HZ at the end.

By default, these macros are undefined. And, when troff encounters an undefined macro name, it simply ignores it. These macros thus lie hidden in the code until you define them. By defining these macros, you can supplement the processing of headings without actually modifying the mm code. Before you define these macros, be sure to study the mm documentation for details of how to use them.

Similarly, .PX is executed at the top of each page, just after .PH. Accordingly, it allows you to perform additional top-of-page processing. (In addition, you can redefine the .TP macro, which prints the standard header, because this macro is relatively self-contained.)

There is a slightly different mechanism for generalized bottom-of-page processing. The .BS/.BE macro pair can be used to enclose text that will be printed at the bottom of each page, after any footnotes but before the footer. To remove this text after you have defined it, simply specify an empty block.

The .VM (*vertical margins*) macro allows you to specify additional space at the top of the page, bottom of the page, or both. For example:

```
.VM 3 3
```

will add three lines each to the top and bottom margins. The arguments to this macro should be unscaled. The first argument applies to the top margin, the second to the bottom.

The .TX and .TY macros allow you to control the appearance of the table of contents pages. The .TX macro is executed at the top of the first page of the table of contents, above the title; .TY is executed in place of the standard title ("CONTENTS").

In Chapter 14, you will learn about writing macro definitions, which should give you the information you need to write these supplementary "user exit macros."

7

Advanced Editing

Sometimes, in order to advance, you have to go backward. In this chapter, we are
going to demonstrate how you can improve your text-editing skills by understanding
how line editors work. This doesn't mean you'll have to abandon full-screen editing.
The vi editor was constructed on top of a line editor named ex, which was an
improved version of another line editor named ed. So in one sense we'll be looking at
the ancestors of vi. We'll look at many of the ways line editors attack certain problems and how that applies to those of us who use full-screen editors.

Line editors came into existence for use on "paper terminals," which were basically printers. This was before the time of video display terminals. A programmer, or
some other person of great patience, worked somewhat interactively on a printer. Typically, you saw a line of your file by printing it out on paper; you entered commands
that would affect just that line; then you printed out the edited line again. Line editors
were designed for this kind of process, editing one line at a time.

People rarely edit files on paper terminals any more, but there are diehards who
still prefer line editors. For one thing, it imposes less of a burden on the computer.
Line editors display the current line; they don't update the entire screen.

On some occasions, a line editor is simpler and faster than a full-screen editor.
Sometimes, a system's response can be so slow that it is less frustrating to work if you
switch to a line editor. Or you may have occasion to work remotely over a dial-up line
operating at a baud rate that is too slow to work productively with a full-screen editor.
In these situations, a line editor can be a way to improve your efficiency. It can reduce
the amount of time you are waiting for the computer to respond to your commands.

The truth is, however, that after you switch from a screen editor to a line editor,
you are likely to feel deprived. But you shouldn't skip this chapter just because you
won't be using a line editor. The purpose of learning ex is to extend what you can do
in vi.

· The **ex** Editor ·

The ex editor is a line editor with its own complete set of editing commands. Although it is simpler to make most edits with vi, the line orientation of ex is an advantage when you are making large-scale changes to more than one part of a file. With ex, you can move easily between files and transfer text from one file to another in a variety of ways. You can search and replace text on a line-by-line basis, or globally. You can also save a series of editing commands as a macro and access them with a single keystroke.

Seeing how ex works when it is invoked directly will help take some of the "mystery" out of line editors and make it more apparent to you how many ex commands work.

Let's open a file and try a few ex commands. After you invoke ex on a file, you will see a message about the total number of lines in the file, and a colon command prompt. For example:

```
$ ex intro
 "intro" 20 lines, 731 characters
 :
```

You won't see any lines in the file, unless you give an ex command that causes one or more lines to be printed.

All ex commands consist of a line address, which can simply be a line number, and a command. You complete the command with a carriage return. A line number by itself is equivalent to a print command for that line. So, for example, if you type the numeral 1 at the prompt, you will see the first line of the file:

```
 :1
 Sometimes, to advance,
 :
```

To print more than one line, you can specify a range of lines. Two line numbers are specified, separated by commas, with no spaces in between them:

```
 :1,3
 Sometimes, to advance,
 you have to go backward.
 Alcuin is a computer graphics tool
```

The current line is the last line affected by a command. For instance, before we issued the command 1,3, line 1 was the current line; after that command, line 3 became the current line. It can be represented by a special symbol, a dot (.).

```
 :.,+3
 that lets you design and create hand-lettered, illuminated
 manuscripts, such as were created in the Middle Ages.
```

The previous command results in three more lines being printed, starting with the current line. A + or − specifies a positive or negative offset from the current line.

The ex editor has a command mode and an insert mode. To put text in a file, you can enter the append or a command to place text on the line following the current line. The insert or i command places text on the line above the current line. Type in your text and when you are finished, enter a dot (.) on a line by itself:

```
:a
Monks, skilled in calligraphy,
labored to make copies of ancient
documents and preserve in a
library the works of many Greek and
Roman authors.
.
:
```

Entering the dot takes you out of insert mode and puts you back in command mode.

A line editor does not have a cursor, and you cannot move along a line of text to a particular word. Apart from not seeing more of your file, the lack of a cursor (and therefore cursor motion keys) is probably the most difficult thing to get used to. After using a line editor, you long to get back to using the cw command in vi.

If you want to change a word, you have to move to the line that contains the word, tell the editor which word on the line you want to change, and then provide its replacement. You have to think this way to use the substitute or s command. It allows you to substitute one word for another.

We can change the last word on the first line from *tool* to *environment*:

```
:1
Alcuin is a computer graphics tool
:s/tool/environment/
Alcuin is a computer graphics environment
:
```

The word you want to change and its replacement are separated by slashes (/). As a result of the substitute command, the line you changed is printed.

With a line editor, the commands that you enter affect the current line. Thus, we made sure that the first line was our current line. We could also make the same change by specifying the line number with the command:

```
:1s/environment/tool/
Alcuin is a computer graphics tool
```

If you specify an *address*, such as a range of line numbers, then the command will affect the lines that you specify:

```
:1,20s/Alcuin/ALCUIN/
ALCUIN is named after an English scholar
```

The last line on which a substitution was made is printed.

Remember, when using a line editor, you have to tell the editor which line (or lines) to work on as well as which command to execute.

Another reason that knowing ex is useful is that sometimes when you are working in vi, you might unexpectedly find yourself using "open mode." For instance, if you press Q while in vi, you will be dropped into the ex editor. You can switch to vi by entering the command vi at the colon prompt:

```
:vi
```

After you are in vi, you can execute any ex command by first typing a : (colon). The colon appears on the bottom of the screen and what you type will be echoed there. Enter an ex command and press *RETURN* to execute it.

▪ Using ex Commands in vi ▪

Many ex commands that perform normal editing operations have equivalent vi commands that do the job in a simpler manner. Obviously, you will use dw or dd to delete a single word or line rather than using the delete command in ex. However, when you want to make changes that affect numerous lines, you will find that the ex commands are very useful. They allow you to modify large blocks of text with a single command.

Some of these commands and their abbreviations follow. You can use the full command name or the abbreviation, whichever is easier to remember.

delete	d	Delete lines
move	m	Move lines
copy	co	Copy lines
substitute	s	Substitute one string for another

The substitute command best exemplifies the ex editor's ability to make editing easier. It gives you the ability to change any string of text every place it occurs in the file. To perform edits on a global replacement basis requires a good deal of confidence in, as well as full knowledge of, the use of pattern matching or "regular expressions." Although somewhat arcane, learning to do global replacements can be one of the most rewarding experiences of working in the UNIX text-processing environment.

Other ex commands give you additional editing capabilities. For all practical purposes, they can be seen as an integrated part of vi. Examples of these capabilities are the commands for editing multiple files and executing UNIX commands. We will look at these after we look at pattern-matching and global replacements.

▪ Write Locally, Edit Globally ▪

Sometimes, halfway through a document or at the end of a draft, you recognize inconsistencies in the way that you refer to certain things. Or, in a manual, some product that you called by name is suddenly renamed (marketing!). Often enough, you have to go back and change what you've already written in several places.

The way to make these changes is with the search and replace commands in ex. You can automatically replace a word (or string of characters) wherever it occurs in the file. You have already seen one example of this use of the substitute command, when we replaced *Alcuin* with *ALCUIN*:

```
:1,20s/Alcuin/ALCUIN/
```

There are really two steps in using a search and replace command. The first step is to define the area in which a search will take place. The search can be specified locally to cover a block of text or globally to cover the entire file. The second step is to specify, using the substitute command, the text that will be removed and the text that will replace it.

At first, the syntax for specifying a search and replace command may strike you as difficult to learn, especially when we introduce pattern matching. Try to keep in mind that this is a very powerful tool, one that can save you a lot of drudgery. Besides, you will congratulate yourself when you succeed, and everyone else will think you are very clever.

Searching Text Blocks

To define a search area, you need to be more familiar with how line addressing works in ex. A line address simply indicates which line or range of lines an ex command will operate on. If you don't specify a line address, the command only affects the current line. You already know that you can indicate any individual line by specifying its number. What we want to look at now are the various ways of indicating a block of text in a file.

You can use absolute or relative line numbers to define a range of lines. Identify the line number of the start of a block of text and the line number of the end of the block. In vi, you can use ^G to find the current line number.

There are also special symbols for addressing particular places in the file:

.	Current line
$	Last line
%	All lines (same as 1,$)

The following are examples that define the block of text that the substitute command will act upon:

:.,$s	Search from the current line to the end of the file
:20,.s	Search from line 20 through the current line
:.,.+20s	Search from the current line through the next 20 lines
:100,$s	Search from line 100 through the end of the file
:%s	Search all lines in the file

Within the search area, as defined in these examples, the substitute command will look for one string of text and replace it with another string.

You can also use pattern matching to specify a place in the text. A pattern is delimited by a slash both *before* and *after* it.

/pattern1/,/pattern2/ s	Search from the first line containing *pattern1* through the first line containing *pattern2*
:.,*/pattern/* s	Search from the current line through the line containing *pattern*

It is important to note that the action takes place on the entire line containing the pattern, not simply the text up to the pattern.

Search and Replace

You've already seen the substitute command used to replace one string with another one. A slash is used as a delimiter separating the old string and the new. By prefixing the s command with an address, you can extend its range beyond a single line:

```
:1,20s/Alcuin/ALCUIN/
```

Combined with a line address, this command searches all the lines within the block of text. But it only replaces the first occurrence of the pattern on each line. For instance, if we specified a substitute command replacing *roman* with *Roman* in the following line:

```
after the roman hand.  In teaching the roman script
```

only the first, not the second, occurrence of the word would be changed.

To specify each occurrence on the line, you have to add a g at the end of the command:

```
:s/roman/Roman/g
```

This command changes *every* occurrence of *roman* to *Roman* on the current line.

Using search and replace is much faster than finding each instance of a string and replacing it individually. It has many applications, especially if you are a poor speller.

So far, we have replaced one word with another word. Usually, it's not that easy. A word may have a prefix or suffix that throws things off. In a while, we will look at pattern matching. This will really expand what you are able to do. But first, we want to look at how to specify that a search and replace take place globally in a file.

Confirming Substitutions

It is understandable if you are over-careful when using a search and replace command. It does happen that what you get is not what you expected. You can undo any search and replacement command by entering u. But you don't always catch undesired changes until it is too late to undo them. Another way to protect your edited file is to save the file with :w before performing a replacement. Then, at least you can quit the file without saving your edits and go back to where you were before the change was made. You can also use :e! to read in the previous version of the buffer.

It may be best to be cautious and know exactly what is going to be changed in your file. If you'd like to see what the search turns up and confirm each replacement before it is made, add a c at the end of the substitute command:

```
:1,30s/his/the/gc
```

It will display the entire line where the string has been located and the string itself will be marked by a series of carets (^^^).

```
copyists at his school
             ^^^
```

If you want to make the replacement, you must enter y and press *RETURN*.
   If you don't want to make a change, simply press *RETURN*.

```
this can be used for invitations, signs, and menus.
 ^^^
```

The combination of the vi commands // (repeat last search) and . (repeat last command) is also an extraordinarily useful (and quick) way to page through a file and make repetitive changes that require a judgment call rather than an absolute global replacement.

Global Search and Replace

When we looked at line addressing symbols, the percent symbol, %, was introduced. If you specify it with the substitute command, the search and replace command will affect all lines in the file:

```
:%s/Alcuin/ALCUIN/g
```

This command searches all lines and replaces each occurrence on a line.
   There is another way to do this, which is slightly more complex but has other benefits. The pattern is specified as part of the address, preceded by a g indicating that the search is global:

```
:g/Alcuin/s//ALCUIN/g
```

It selects all lines containing the pattern *Alcuin* and replaces every occurrence of that pattern with *ALCUIN*. Because the search pattern is the same as the word you want to change, you don't have to repeat it in the substitute command.
   The extra benefit that this gives is the ability to search for a pattern and then make a different substitution. We call this context-sensitive replacement.
   The gist of this command is globally search for a pattern:

```
:g/pattern/
```

Replace it:

```
:g/pattern/s//
```

or replace another string on that line:

```
:g/pattern/s/string/
```

with a new string:

```
:g/pattern/s/string/new/
```

and do this for every occurrence on the line:

```
:g/pattern/s/string/new/g
```

For example, we use the macro .BX to draw a box around the name of a special key. To show an *ESCAPE* key in a manual, we enter:

```
.BX Esc
```

Suppose we had to change *Esc* to *ESC*, but we didn't want to change any references to *Escape* in the text. We could use the following command to make the change:

```
:g/BX/s/Esc/ESC/
```

This command might be phrased: "Globally search for each instance of BX and on those lines substitute the Esc with ESC". We didn't specify g at the end of the command because we would not expect more than one occurrence per line.

Actually, after you get used to this syntax, and admit that it is a little awkward, you may begin to like it.

▪ Pattern Matching ▪

If you are familiar with grep, then you know something about regular expressions. In making global replacements, you can search not just for fixed strings of characters, but also for patterns of words, referred to as *regular expressions.*

When you specify a literal string of characters, the search might turn up other occurrences that you didn't want to match. The problem with searching for words in a file is that a word can be used in many different ways. Regular expressions help you conduct a search for words in context.

Regular expressions are made up by combining normal characters with a number of special characters. The special characters and their use follow.*

.   Matches any single character except newline.

*   Matches any number (including 0) of the single character (including a character specified by a regular expression) that immediately precedes it. For example, because . (dot) means any character, .* means match any number of any character.

---

*\(and \), and \{*n,m*\} are not supported in all versions of vi. \<, \>, \u, \U, \l, and \L are supported only in vi/ex, and not in other programs using regular expressions.

[...]	Matches any one of the characters enclosed between the brackets. For example, [AB] matches either A or B. A range of consecutive characters can be specified by separating the first and last characters in the range with a hyphen. For example, [A-Z] will match any uppercase letter from A to Z and [0-9] will match any digit from 0 to 9.
\{n,m}\	Matches a range of occurrences of the single character (including a character specified by a regular expression) that immediately precedes it. The n and m are integers between 0 and 256 that specify how many occurrences to match. \{n\} will match exactly n occurrences, \{n,\} will match at least n occurrences, and \{n,m\} will match any number of occurrences between n and m. For example, A\{2,3\} will match either AA (as in AARDVARK or AAA but will not match the single letter A).
^	Requires that the following regular expression be found at the beginning of the line.
$	Requires that the preceding regular expression be found at the end of the line.
\	Treats the following special character as an ordinary character. For example, \. stands for a period and * for an asterisk.
\(	Saves the pattern enclosed between \(and \) in a special holding space. Up to nine patterns can be saved in this way on a single line. They can be ''replayed'' in substitutions by the escape sequences \1 to \9.
\n	Matches the nth pattern previously saved by \(and \), where n is a number from 0 to 9 and previously saved patterns are counted from the left on the line.
\< \>	Matches characters at the beginning (\<) or at the end (\>) of a word. The expression \<ac would only match words that begin with ac, such as action but not react.
&	Prints the entire search pattern when used in a replacement string.
\u	Converts the first character of the replacement string to uppercase.
\U	Converts the replacement string to uppercase as in :/Unix/\U&/.
\l	Converts the first character of the replacement string to lowercase, as in :s/ Act/\l&/.
\L	Converts the replacement string to lowercase.

Unless you are already familiar with UNIX's wildcard characters, this list of special characters probably looks complex. A few examples should make things clearer. In the examples that follow, a square (▫) is used to mark a blank space.

Let's follow how you might use some special characters in a replacement. Suppose you have a long file and you want to substitute the word *balls* for the word *ball* throughout that file. You first save the edited buffer with `:w`, then try the global replacement:

```
:g/ball/s//balls/g
```

When you continue editing, you notice occurrences of words such as *ballsoon*, *globallsy*, and *ballss*. Returning to the last saved buffer with `:e!`, you now try specifying a space after *ball* to limit the search:

```
:g/ball□/s//balls□/g
```

But this command misses the occurrences *ball.*, *ball,*, *ball:*, and so on.

```
:g/\<ball\>/s//balls/g
```

By surrounding the search pattern with `\<` and `\>`, we specify that the pattern should only match entire words, with or without a subsequent punctuation mark. Thus, it does not match the word *balls* if it already exists.

Because the `\<` and `\>` are only available in `ex` (and thus `vi`), you may have occasions to use a longer form:

```
:g/ball\([□,.;:!?]\)/s//balls\1/g
```

This searches for and replaces *ball* followed by either a space (indicated by □) or any one of the punctuation characters `,.;:!?`. Additionally, the character that is matched is saved using `\(` and `\)` and restored on the right-hand side with `\1`. The syntax may seem complicated, but this command sequence can save you a lot of work in a similar replacement situation.

Search for General Classes of Words

The special character `&` is used in the replacement portion of a substitution command to represent the pattern that was matched. It can be useful in searching for and changing similar but different words and phrases.

For instance, a manufacturer decides to make a minor change to the names of their computer models, necessitating a change in a marketing brochure. The *HX5000* model has been renamed the *Series HX5000*, along with the *HX6000* and *HX8500* models. Here's a way to do this using the `&` character:

```
:g/HX[568][05]00/s//Series &/g
```

This changes *HX8500* to *Series HX8500*. The `&` character is useful when you want to replay the entire search pattern and add to it. If you want to capture only part of the search pattern, you must use `\(` and `\)` and replay the saved pattern with `\1 . . . \n.`)

For instance, the same computer manufacturer decides to drop the *HX* from the model numbers and place *Series* after that number. We could make the change using the following command:

```
:g/\(Series\) HX\([568])[05]00\)/s//\2 \1/g
```

This command replaces *Series HX8500* with *8500 Series*.

    Suppose you have subroutine names beginning with the prefixes `mgi`, `mgr`, and `mga`.

```
mgibox routine
mgrbox routine
mgabox routine
```

If you want to save the prefixes, but want to change the name *box* to *square*, either of the following replacement commands will do the trick:

```
:g/mg([iar])box/s//mg\1square/
```

The global replacement keeps track of whether an `i`, `a`, or `r` is saved, so that only *box* is changed to *square*. This has the same effect as the previous command:

```
:g/mg[iar]box/s/box/square/g
```

The result is:

```
mgisquare routine
mgrsquare routine
mgasquare routine
```

Block Move by Patterns

You can edit blocks of text delimited by patterns. For example, assume you have a 150 page reference manual. All references pages are organized in the same way: a paragraph with the heading *SYNTAX*, followed by *DESCRIPTION*, followed by *PARAMETERS*. A sample of one reference page follows:

```
.Rh 0 "Get status of named file" "STAT"
.Rh "SYNTAX"
.nf
integer*4 stat, retval
integer*4 status(11)
character*123 filename
...
retval = stat (filename, status)
.fi
.Rh "DESCRIPTION"
Writes the fields of a system data structure into the
status array.  These fields contain (among other
things) information about the file's location, access
privileges, owner, and time of last modification.
.Rh "PARAMETERS"
.IP "filename" 15n
```

```
A character string variable or constant containing
the UNIX pathname for the file whose status you want
to retrieve.  You can give the...
```

Suppose that you decide to move *DESCRIPTION* above the *SYNTAX* paragraph. With pattern matching, you can move blocks of text on all 150 pages with one command!

```
:g/SYNTAX/,/DESCRIPTION/-1,mo/PARAMETERS/-1
```

This command moves the block of text between the line containing the word *SYNTAX* and the line just before the word *DESCRIPTION* (/DESCRIPTION/-1) to the line just before *PARAMETERS*. In a case like this, one command literally saves hours of work.

This applies equally well to other ex commands. For example, if you wanted to delete all *DESCRIPTION* paragraphs in the reference chapter, you could enter:

```
:g/SYNTAX/,/DESCRIPTION/-1,d
```

This very powerful kind of change is implicit in the ex editor's line addressing syntax, but is not readily apparent. For this reason, whenever you are faced with a complex, repetitive editing task, take the time to analyze the problem and find out if you can apply pattern-matching tools to do the job.

More Examples

Because the best way to learn pattern matching is by example, the following section gives a list of examples with brief explanations. Study the syntax carefully, so that you understand the principles at work. You should then be able to adapt them to your situation.

1. Delete all blank lines:

    ```
    :g/^$/d
    ```

    What you are matching is the beginning of the line followed by the end of the line, with nothing in between.

2. Put troff italic codes around the word *RETURN*:

    ```
    :g/RETURN/s//\\fIRETURN\\fR/g
    ```

    Notice that two backslashes (\\) are needed in the replacement, because the backslash in the troff italic code will be interpreted as a special character. (\fI alone would be interpreted as fI; it takes \\fI to get \fI.)

3. Modify a list of pathnames in a file:

    ```
    :g/\/usr\/tim/s//\/usr\/linda/g
    ```

    A slash (used as a delimiter in the global replacement sequence) must be escaped with a backslash when it is part of the pattern or replacement; use \/ to get /. Another way to achieve this same effect is to use a different character as the pattern delimiter. For example, you could make the previous replacement as follows:

```
:g:/usr/tim:s::/usr/linda:g
```

4. Change all periods to semicolons in lines 1 to 10:

    ```
    :1,10g/\./s//;/g
    ```

    A period is a special character and must be escaped with a backslash.

5. Reverse the order of all hyphen-separated items in a list:

    ```
    :g/\(.*\)□-□\(.*\)/s//\2□-□\1/
    ```

    The effect of this command on several items is:

    ```
    more-display files becomes display files-more
    lp-print files becomes print files-lp
    ```

6. Standardize various uses of a word or heading:

    ```
    :g/^Example[□s:]/s//Examples:□/g
    ```

    Note that the brackets enclose three characters: a space (represented in the example by □), a colon, and the letter s. Therefore, this command searches for *Example□*, *Examples*, or *Example:* at the beginning of a line and replaces it with *Examples:*. (If you don't include the space, *Examples* would be replaced with *Exampless:*.)

    As another similar example, change all occurrences of the word *help* (or *Help*) to *HELP*:

    ```
    :g/[Hh]elp/s//HELP/g
    ```

7. Replace *one or more* spaces with a single space:

    ```
    :g/□□*/s//□/g
    ```

    Make sure you understand how the asterisk works as a special character. An asterisk following any character (or any regular expression that matches a single character, such as . or [a-z]) matches *zero or more* instances of that character. Therefore, you must specify *two* spaces followed by an asterisk to match one or more spaces (one plus zero or more).

8. Replace one or more spaces following a colon with two spaces:

    ```
    :g/:□□*/s//:□□/g
    ```

9. Replace one or more spaces following a period *or* a colon with two spaces:

    ```
    :g/\([:.]\)□□*/s//\1□□/g
    ```

    Either of the two characters within brackets can be matched. This character is saved, using parentheses, and restored on the right-hand side as 1. Note that a special character such as a period does not need to be escaped within brackets.

10. Delete all leading blanks on a line:

    `:g/^□□*\(.*\)/s//\1/g`

    Search for one or more blanks at the beginning of a line; save the rest of the line and replace it without any leading blanks.

11. Delete all trailing blanks:

    `:g/□□*$/s///`

12. Remove manual numbering from section headings (e.g., *1.1 Introduction*) in a document:

    `:g/[1-9]\.[1-9]*\(.*\)/s//\1/g`

    A hyphen-separated pair of letters or digits enclosed in square brackets (e.g, `[1-9]`) specifies a range of characters.

13. Change manually numbered section heads (e.g., *1.1, 1.2*) to a `troff` macro (e.g., `.Ah` for an *A-level heading*):

    `:g/^[1-9]\.[1-9]/s//\.Ah/`

14. Show macros in the output by protecting them from interpretation. Putting `\&` in front of a macro prevents `troff` from expanding them. This command was used frequently throughout this book to print an example that contained macros. Three backslashes are needed in the replacement pattern: two to print a backslash and one to have the first ampersand interpreted literally.

    `:g/^\./s//\\\&&/`

▪ Writing and Quitting Files ▪

You have learned the `vi` command `ZZ` to quit and write (save) your file. But you will usually want to exit a file using `ex` commands, because these commands give you greater control.

`:w`   Writes (saves) the buffer to the file but does not exit. You can use `:w` throughout your editing session to protect your edits against system failure or a major editing error.

`:q`   Quits the file (and returns to the UNIX prompt).

`:wq`   Both writes and quits the file.

The `vi` editor protects existing files and your edits in the buffer. For example, if you want to write your buffer to an existing file, `vi` will give you a warning, because this would delete the original file. Likewise, if you have invoked `vi` on a file, made edits, and want to quit *without* saving the edits, vi will give you an error message such as:

```
No write since last change.
```

These warnings can prevent costly mistakes, but sometimes you want to proceed with the command anyway. An exclamation mark (!) after your command overrides this warning:

```
:w! filename
:q!
```

The :q! command is an essential editing command that allows you to quit without affecting the original file, regardless of any changes you made in the session. The contents of the buffer are discarded.

Renaming the Buffer

You can also use :w to save the entire buffer (the copy of the file you are editing) under a new filename.

Suppose that you have a file letter that contains 600 lines. You call in a copy and make extensive edits. You want to quit and save *both* the old version of letter and your new edits for comparison. To rename your buffer letter.new, give the command:

```
:wq letter.new
```

Saving Part of a File

In an editing session, you will sometimes want to save just part of your file as a separate, new file. For example, you might have entered formatting codes and text that you want to use as a header for several files.

You can combine ex line addressing with the write command, w, to save part of a file. For example, if you are in the file letter and want to save part of letter as the file newfile, you could enter:

```
:230,$w newfile
```

which saves from line 230 to the end of the file, or:

```
:.,600w newfile
```

which saves from the current line to line 600 in newfile.

Appending to a Saved File

You can use the UNIX redirect and append operator (>>) with w to append the contents of the buffer to an existing file. For example:

```
:1,10w newfile
:340,$w>>newfile
```

The existing file, `newfile`, will contain lines 1 through 10, and from line 340 to the end of the buffer.

• Reading In a File •

Sometimes you want to copy text or data already entered on the system into the file you are editing. In `vi`, you can read in the contents of another file with the `ex` command:

   :read *filename*

or:

   :r *filename*

This reads in the contents of *filename* on the line after the cursor position in the file.

Let's suppose that you are editing the file `letter`, and want to read in data from a file in another directory called `/work/alcuin/ch01`. Position the cursor just above the line where you want the new data inserted, and enter:

   :r /work/alcuin/ch01

The entire contents of `/work/alcuin/ch01` are read into `letter`, beginning below your cursor position.

• Executing UNIX Commands •

You can also display or read in the results of any UNIX command while you are editing in `vi`. An exclamation mark (`!`) tells `ex` to create a shell and regard what follows as a UNIX command.

   :!*command*

So, if you are editing and want to check the time or date without exiting `vi`, you can enter:

   :!date

The time and date will appear on your screen; press *RETURN* to continue editing at the same place in your file. If you want to give several UNIX commands in a row, without returning to `vi` in between, you can create a shell with the `ex` command:

   :sh

When you want to exit the shell and return to `vi`, press `^D`.

You can combine `:read` with a call to UNIX, to read the results of a UNIX command into your file. As a very simple example:

```
:r !date
```

This will read in the system's date information into the text of your file.

Suppose that you are editing a file, and want to read in four phone numbers from a file called `phone`, but in alphabetical order. The `phone` file is in the following order:

```
Willing, Sue   333-4444
Walsh, Linda   555-6666
Quercia, Valerie  777-8888
Dougherty, Nancy  999-0000
```

The command:

```
:r !sort phone
```

reads in the contents of `phone` after they have been passed through the `sort` filter:

```
Dougherty, Nancy  999-0000
Quercia, Valerie  777-8888
Walsh, Linda   555-6666
Willing, Sue   333-4444
```

Suppose that you are editing a file and want to insert text from another file in the directory, but you can't remember the new file's name.

You *could* perform this task the long way: exit your file, give the `ls` command, note the correct filename, reenter your file, and search for your place.

Or, you could do the task in fewer steps. The command `:!ls` will display a list of files in the directory. Note the correct filename. Press *RETURN* to continue editing.

```
file1
file2
letter
newfile
```

The command:

```
:r newfile
```

will read in the new file:

```
"newfile" 35 lines, 949 characters
```

Filtering Text through a Command

You can also send a block of text as standard input to a UNIX command. The output from this command replaces the block of text in the buffer. Filtering text through a command can be done either from `ex` or `vi`. The main difference between the two methods is that the block of text is indicated with line addresses in `ex` and with text objects in `vi`.

The first example demonstrates how to do this with `ex`. Assume that instead of being contained in a separate file called `phone`, the list of names in the preceding example was already contained in the current file, on lines 96 to 99.

You simply type the addresses of the lines you want affected, followed by an exclamation mark and the UNIX command line to be executed. For example, the command:

```
:96,99!sort
```

will pass lines 96 to 99 through the sort filter, and replace those lines with the output of sort.

In vi, this sequence is invoked by typing an exclamation mark followed by any vi objects that indicate a block of text, and then the UNIX command line to be executed. For example:

```
!)command
```

will pass the next sentence through *command*.

There are some unusual features about how vi acts when you use this feature. First, the exclamation mark that you type is not echoed right away. When you type the symbol for the text object to be affected, the exclamation mark appears at the bottom of the screen, *but the symbol you type to reference the object does not*.

Second, only objects that refer to more than one line of text (G, {}, (), []) can be used. A number may precede either the exclamation mark or the object to repeat the effect. Objects such as w do not not work unless enough of them are specified so as to exceed a single line. A slash (/) followed by a pattern and a *RETURN* can also be specified, taking the text up to the pattern as input to the command.

Third, there is a special object that is used only with this command syntax. The current line can be specified by entering a second exclamation mark:

```
!!command
```

Either the entire sequence or the text object can be preceded by a number to repeat the effect. For instance, to change the same lines as in the previous example, you could position the cursor on line 96, and enter:

```
4!!sort
```

or:

```
!4!sort
```

As another example, assume you have a portion of text in a file that you want to change from lowercase to uppercase letters. You could process that portion with the tr command. In these examples, the second sentence is the block of text that will be filtered to the command. An exclamation mark appears on the last line to prompt you for the UNIX command:

```
of the product.                              of the product.
I confess to being          !)               I confess to being
amazed by Alcuin.        ! appears on         amazed by Alcuin.
Some people around         last line          Some people around
                                              !_
```

Enter the UNIX command and press *RETURN*. The input is replaced by the output.

```
of the product.                              of the product.
I confess to being       tr`[a-z]'           I CONFESS TO BEING
amazed by Alcuin.          `[A-Z]'           AMAZED BY ALCUIN.
Some people around      input replaced        Some people around
                          by output
```

To repeat the previous command, the syntax is:

> ! *block* !

It is sometimes useful to send sections of a coded document to `nroff` to be replaced by formatted output. However, remember that the "original" input is replaced by the output.

If there is a mistake, such as an error message being sent instead of the expected output, you can undo the command and restore the lines.

▪ **Editing Multiple Files** ▪

The `ex` commands enable you to edit multiple files. The advantage to editing multiple files is speed. When you are sharing the system with other users, it takes time to exit and reenter `vi` for each file you want to edit. Staying in the same editing session and traveling between files is not only faster in access time: you save abbreviations and command sequences you have defined and keep named buffers so that you can copy text from one file to another.

Invoking **vi** on Multiple Files

When you first invoke `vi`, you can name more than one file to edit files sequentially, and then use `ex` commands to travel between the files. The following:

```
$ vi file1 file2
```

invokes *file1* first. After you have finished editing the first file, the `ex` command `:w` writes (saves) *file1*, and `:n` calls in the next file (*file2*).

Suppose that you know you want to edit two files, `letter` and `note`. Open the two files by typing:

```
$ vi letter note
```

The message:

```
Two files to edit
```

appears on the screen. The first named file, `letter`, appears. Perform your edits to `letter`, and then save it with the `ex` command `:w`. Call in the next file, `note`, with the `ex` command `:n` and press *RETURN*. Perform any edits and use `:wq` to quit the editing session.

There is no practical limit to the number of files you can invoke `vi` on at one time. You can use any of the shell's pattern-matching characters, or even more complex constructions. Suppose you were writing a program, and wanted to change the name of a function call, for example, `getcursor`. The command:

```
$ vi `grep -l getcursor *`
```

would invoke `vi` on all of the files in the current directory containing the string `getcursor`. The command:

```
$ grep -l
```

prints the names of all files containing a string; using a command enclosed in backquotes (``) as an argument to another command causes the shell to use the *output* of the command in backquotes as the argument list for the first command.

The `vi` editor will print a message similar to:

```
5 files to edit
```

before displaying the first file.

If you try to quit without editing all of the files, `vi` will issue a warning message:

```
4 more files to edit
```

You must type `:q!` if you want to exit without editing all of the files.

Calling In New Files

You don't have to call in multiple files at the beginning of your editing session. Any time in `vi`, you can switch to another file with the `ex` command `:e`. If you want to edit another file within `vi`, first save your current file (:w), then give the command:

```
:e filename
```

Suppose that you are editing the file `letter`, and want to edit the file `note` and then return to `letter`.

Save `letter` with `w` and press *RETURN*. The file `letter` is saved and remains on the screen. You can now switch to another file, because your edits are saved. Call in the file `letter` with `:e` and press *RETURN*.

The `vi` editor "remembers" two filenames at a time as the current and alternate filenames. These can be referred to by the symbols `%` (current filename) and `#` (alternate filename). The `#` symbol is particularly useful with `:e`, because it allows you to switch easily back and forth between files. In the example just given, you could return to the first file, `letter`, by typing the command `:e#`.

If you have not first saved the current file, `vi` will not allow you to switch files with `:e` or `:n` unless you tell it imperatively to do so by adding an exclamation mark after the command. For example, if after making some edits to `note`, you wanted to discard the edits and return to `letter`, you could type `:e!#`.

The command:

```
e!
```

is also useful. It discards your edits and returns to the last saved version of the current file. The `%` symbol, by contrast, is useful mainly when writing out the contents of the buffer to a new file. For example, a few pages earlier we showed how to save a second version of the file `letter` with the command:

```
:w letter.new
```

This could also have been typed:

```
:w %.new
```

Edits between Files

Named buffers provide one convenient way to move text from one file to another. Named buffers are not cleared when a new file is loaded into the `vi` buffer with the `:e` command. Thus, by yanking text in one file (into multiple named buffers if necessary), reading in a new file with `:e`, and putting the named buffer into the new file, material can be transferred selectively between files.

The following example illustrates transferring text from one file to another.

```
In our conversation
last Thursday, we
discussed a
documentation project
that would produce a
user's manual on the...
```

`"f6yy`
yank 6 lines
to buffer *f*

```
In our conversation
last Thursday, we
discussed a
documentation project
that would produce a
user's manual on the...

6 lines yanked
```

Save the file with the `:w` command. Enter the file `note` with `:e`, and move the cursor to where the copied text will be placed.

```
Dear Mr. Caslon,                              Dear Mr. Caslon,
Thank you for...              "fp             In our conversation
                     put yanked text          last Thursday, we dis-
                        below cursor          cussed a documentation
                                              project that would
                                              produce a user's
                                              manual on the...
                                              Thank you for...
```

▪ Word Abbreviation ▪

Often, you will type the same long phrases over and over in a file. You can define abbreviations that `vi` will automatically expand into the full text whenever you type the abbreviation in insert mode. To define an abbreviation, use the `ex` command:

> :ab *abbr phrase*

Where *abbr* is an abbreviation for the specified *phrase*. The sequence of characters that make up the abbreviation will be expanded in insert mode only if you type it as a full word; *abbr* will not be expanded within a word.

Suppose that in the file `letter` you want to enter text that contains a frequently recurring phrase, such as a difficult product or company name. The command:

> :ab IMRC International Materials Research Center

abbreviates *International Materials Research Center* to the initials IMRC.

Now when you type IMRC in insert mode:

> i the IMRC

IMRC expands to the full text:

> the International Materials Research Center

When you are choosing abbreviations, select combinations of characters that don't ordinarily occur while you are typing text.

▪ Saving Commands with map ▪

While you are editing, you may use a particular command sequence frequently, or you may occasionally use a very complex command sequence. To save keystrokes, or the time that it takes to remember the sequence, you can assign the sequence to an unused key.

The `map` command acts a lot like `ab` except that you define a macro for command mode instead of insert mode.

:map *x sequence*	Define character *x* as a *sequence* of editing commands
:unmap *x*	Disable the *sequence* defined for *x*
:map	List the characters that are currently mapped

Before you can start creating your own maps, you need to know the keys not used in command mode that are available for user-defined commands:

```
^A      g       K       ^K
^O      q       ^T      v
V       ^W      ^X      ^Z
*       \       _  (underscore)
```

Depending on your terminal, you may also be able to associate map sequences with special function keys. With maps, you can create simple or complex command sequences. As a simple example, you could define a command to reverse the order of words. In vi, with the cursor as shown:

```
you can the scroll page
```

the sequence to put *the* after *scroll* would be dwelp: delete word, dw; move to the end of next word, e; move one space to the right, 1; put the deleted word there, p. Saving this sequence:

```
:map v dwelp
```

enables you to reverse the order of two words anytime in the editing session with the single keystroke v.

Note that when defining a map, you cannot simply type certain keys, such as *RETURN, ESC, TAB, BACKSPACE,* and *DELETE,* as part of the map command. If you want to include one of these keys as part of the command sequence, preface that key with a ^V. The keystroke ^V appears in the map as the ^ character. Characters following the ^V also do not appear as you expect. For example, a carriage return appears as ^M, escape as ^[, tab as ^I, and so on.

You can undo the effect of any map sequence with the u command. Fortunately, the undo restores the file as it was before you executed the map sequence, treating the series of commands as though it were a single vi command.

Unless you use unmap to remove a mapped key, its special meaning is in effect for as long as your current session, even if you move between files. It can therefore be a convenient way of making the same edits in a number of files.

All the vi and ex commands can be used in map sequences, with the exception that the p or put command cannot be used to replace entire lines yanked in the same mapping. If you try to yank and then put back a deleted line within a map, you will get the error message:

```
Cannot put inside global macro.
```

If you want to move lines from one place to another within a mapping, you can usually get around this restriction using the ex editor's copy or co command.

Complex Mapping Example

Assume that you have a glossary with entries like this:

```
map - an ex command that allows you to associate
a complex command sequence with a single key.
```

You would like to convert this glossary list to `nroff` format, so that it looks like this:

```
.IP "map" 10n
An ex command...
```

The best way to do this is to perform the edit on one of the entries and write down the sequence of commands. You want to:

1. Insert the macro for an indented paragraph at the beginning of the line.

2. Press *ESC* to terminate insert mode.

3. Move to the end of the word and add the size of the indent.

4. Press *RETURN* to insert a new line.

5. Press *ESC* to terminate insert mode.

6. Remove the hyphen and capitalize the next word.

That's quite an editing chore if you have to repeat it more than a few times! With `:map`, you can save the entire sequence so that it can be re-executed with a single keystroke:

```
:map z I.IP "^[ea" 10n^M^[3x~
```

The sequence `^[` appears when you type `^V` followed by *ESC*. The sequence `^M` is shown when you type `^V` *RETURN*.

Now, simply typing z will perform the entire series of edits. On a slow terminal, you can actually see the edits happening individually. On a fast terminal, it will seem to happen by magic.

Don't be discouraged if your first attempt at key mapping fails. A small error in defining the map can give you very different results than you expect. Simply type u to undo the edit, and try again.

Remember, the best way to define a complex map is to do the edit once manually, writing down each keystroke that you must type.

Mapping Keys for Insert Mode

Normally, maps apply only to command mode—after all, in insert mode, keys stand for themselves, and shouldn't be mapped as commands.

However, by adding an exclamation mark (!) to the `map` command, you can force it to override the ordinary meaning of a key and produce the map in insert mode. You may find this feature appropriate for tying character strings to special keys that you wouldn't otherwise use. It is especially useful with programmable function keys, as we'll see in a minute. Many terminals have programmable function keys. You can usually set up these keys to print whatever character or characters you want using a special setup mode on the terminal. But this will limit you to a particular terminal, and may limit the actions of programs that want to set up those function keys themselves.

The `ex` editor allows you to map function keys by number, using the syntax:

```
:map #1 commands
```

for function key number 1, and so on. (It can do this because the editor has access to the entry for that terminal found in either the `termcap` or `terminfo` database and knows the escape sequence normally output by the function key.)

As with other keys, maps apply by default to command mode, but by using the `map!` commands as well, you can define two separate values for a function key—one to use in command mode, the other in insert mode. For example, if you are a `troff` user, you might want to put font-switch codes on function keys. For example:

```
:map #1 i\f(CW^[
:map! #1 \fI
```

If you are in command mode, the first function key will enter insert mode, type in the three characters `\fI`, and return to command mode. If you are already in insert mode, the key will simply type the three-character `troff` code.

Note: If function keys have been redefined in the terminal's setup mode, the #*n* syntax might not work because the function keys no longer put out the expected control or escape sequence as described in the terminal database entry. You will need to examine the `termcap` entry (or `terminfo` source) for your terminal and check the definitions for the function keys. The terminal capabilties `k1`, `k2` through `k9`, `k0` describe the first ten function keys. The capabilities `l1`,`l2` through `l9`, `l0` describe the remaining function keys. Using your terminal's setup mode, you can change the control or escape sequence output by the function key to correspond with the `termcap` or `terminfo` entry. (If the sequence contains `^M`, which is a carriage return, press `^M`, not the *RETURN* key.) For instance, to have function key 1 available for mapping, the terminal database entry for your terminal must have a definition of `k1`, such as `k1=^A@`. In turn, the definition `^A@` must be what is output when you press that key. To test what the function key puts out, press the key at the UNIX prompt, followed by a *RETURN* if necessary. The shell should display the sequence output by the function key after trying unsuccessfully to execute it as a command.

@ Functions

Named buffers provide yet another way to create macros—complex command sequences that you can repeat with only a few keystrokes.

If you type a command line in your text (either a `vi` sequence or an `ex` command *preceded by a colon*), then yank or delete it into a named buffer, you can execute the contents of that buffer with the `@` command. It works in the same way as a `map` sequence, except that you enter the command line in the file instead of at the colon prompt; this is helpful if the command sequence is long and might need editing to work properly. Let's look at a simple but not very useful example of an `@` function. In your file, enter this key sequence:

```
cw\fIgadfly\fR^VESC
```

This will appear on your screen as:

```
cw\fIgadfly\fR^[
```

Then delete your command line into buffer *g* by typing `"gdd`. Now, whenever you place the cursor at the beginning of a word and type `@g`, that word in your text will be changed to *gadfly*. Because `@` is interpreted as a `vi` command, `.` will repeat the entire sequence, even if it is an `ex` command. The command `@@` repeats the last `@`, and `u` or `U` can be used to undo the effect of `@`. The `@` function is useful because you can create very specific commands. It is especially useful when you are making specific editing commands between files, because you can store the commands in named buffers and access them in any file you edit.

8

Formatting with `tbl`

Some information is best presented in tabular format, that is, displayed in rows and columns. You can structure data in columns using tabs, but that can be difficult, especially if the table consists of long lines of text. The `tbl` preprocessor was designed to make it easier to prepare complicated tables, such as the following.

Production of Audio Equipment (units: 1000 sets)		
Product	1984	1985
General radio	8,895	8,770
Clock radio	5,467	6,500
Radio/cassette	29,734	27,523
Tape deck	11,788	14,300
Car radio	9,450	10,398
Car stereo	15,670	17,456

With `tbl`, you can center, left justify, and right justify columns of data or align numeric data within a column. You can put headings that span one or more columns or rows, and draw horizontal and vertical lines to box individual entries or the whole table. An entry may contain equations or consist of several lines of text, as is usually the case with descriptive tables. A table can have as many as 35 columns and essentially an unlimited number of rows.

When you use `tbl`, you should have an idea or, better still, a written design of the table. Then, using a few `tbl` specifications, you can define how a formatted table should look. The data is entered row by row; each column is separated by ordinary tabs.

For example, the `tbl` description for the previous table looks like this:

```
.TS
center,box;
c s s
c s s
c c c
l r r.
Production of Audio Equipment
(units:1000 sets)
_
Product           1984         1985
_
General radio     8,895        8,770
Clock radio       5,467        6,500
Radio/cassette    29,734 27,523
Tape deck         11,788 14,300
Car radio         9,450        10,398
Car stereo        15,670 17,456
.TE
```

When tbl processes the specifications, it calculates all the values needed to produce the table and passes these values to nroff or troff, which formats or outputs the final table.

In this chapter, we will show you how to use tbl to specify the general appearance of a table. We begin with some very simple examples, then gradually work up to more complicated ones to show all of tbl's capabilities.

▪ Using tbl ▪

The tbl description can be written in a file or as part of a larger file that contains other tables and text. You can format a table in a file using the tbl command as in the following:

```
$ tbl file | troff
$ tbl file | nroff
```

The tbl command writes its results to standard output. Because you will probably not be interested in the generated formatting requests, you would normally pipe the output to nroff or troff and then to a printer.

The tbl command also accepts a list of filenames as input and processes them one by one in the order in which they are named on the command line. If you don't give any filenames, tbl reads from standard input. The standard input may also be read in the middle of a list of files by typing a minus sign at the desired place.

If you're using a line printer that doesn't have fractional or reverse line motions, use the −T option of nroff and give the type of output device you're using. This is important when you're using nroff together with tbl to create boxed tables. For example, if you're using a regular line printer, the option should read −Tlp. You must also pipe the `nroff` output to a program called `col`, which filters the reverse linefeeds. The command line for a table with boxes would then read:

$ **tbl** *file* **| nroff -Tlp | col**

`tbl` with `eqn`

When you have equations within your table and you use the `eqn` preprocessor to format them, invoke `tbl` before `eqn`. The `tbl` command usually executes faster because `eqn` normally produces a larger amount of output. To use `eqn` with `tbl`, use the following command line:

$ **tbl** *file* **| eqn | troff**

There is a possible complication that can occur with any of the preprocessors (`tbl`, `eqn`, or `pic`). If you read in subsidiary files with the `.so` request, those files will never be passed through the preprocessor, since the `.so` request has not been encountered yet by the preprocessor. Some UNIX systems support a program called `soelim`, which works just like `cat`, except that it reads in files called by `.so` requests. If any subsidiary files contain data that must be processed, start your command line with `soelim`:

$ **soelim** *file* **| tbl | eqn ... | nroff**

▪ Specifying Tables ▪

A table is always indicated by a `.TS` (*table start*) at the beginning of the table description and a `.TE` (*table end*) at the end. The general format of each table looks like this:

```
.TS
```
global options line;
format section.
data
```
.TE
```

These delimiters serve two functions. First, they signal to `tbl` the beginning and end of the table description. The `tbl` program processes the table, and enables formatting requests into the text of the table. The `.TS` and `.TE` lines remain after processing by `tbl`. This allows them to be used as macro calls by `nroff` and `troff`. Both `ms` and `mm` define these macros; however, an enterprising user can redefine them, and surround a table with consistent formatting effects. If the macros are undefined, `tbl` will not suffer in any way because the use of `.TS/.TE` as delimiters is separate from their secondary use as macros.

As you can see from the general format, `tbl` sees a table in terms of three distinct parts:

1. The overall layout of the table described in the *global options line*. For example, this line describes whether the table is to be centered on the page or made as wide as the rest of the document. The global options line is optional.

2. The layout of each column in the table described in the *format section*. For example, in this section, you specify whether a column is to be left or right justified. The format section is required and may contain one or more format lines.

3. The actual text or numbers, *data*, to be entered in the table.

▪ A Simple Table Example ▪

Let's start with a simple table like the following to show the different parts of the `tbl` description:

```
1    User console
2    Monochromatic graphics terminal
3    Color graphics terminal
4    Line printer
5    Digitizer
6    Laser printer
7    Unallocated
```

You can lay out this table using the following `tbl` requests:

`.TS`	*Table Start macro*
`tab (@);`	*Options line*
`c l.`	*Format line*
`1@User console`	
`2@Monochromatic graphics terminal`	
`3@Color graphics terminal`	
`4@Line printer`	
`5@Digitizer`	*Table entries*
`6@Laser printer`	
`7@Unallocated`	
`.TE`	*Table End macro*

Now let's see what these lines mean:

1. The `.TS` at the beginning says that a table follows.

2. The options line applies to the layout of the table as a whole. The option `tab(@)` means that you will be using the @ character as a tab character when you input data to the table. Normally, `tbl` expects the columns in

the table to be separated by actual tabs. But it is much easier to figure out whether you have the right number of columns if you use a visible character that is not part of the data. This is useful in debugging a table error when the formatted data doesn't appear in the proper columns. The options line *always* ends with a semicolon (;).

3. The format section applies to the lines of data in the table. Each format line contains a *key letter* for each column of the table. The layout of the key letters resembles the layout of actual data in the table.

    Each format line corresponds to a single line in the table. However, you can have fewer format lines than lines in the table. In this case, the *last* line of the description applies to all remaining lines of data. In our example, we have only one format line, so all lines in the table will follow this format. For example:

    ```
    c l.
    ```

    means that there are two columns in each line. The first column will be centered (c), and the second left justified (l). The format section ends with a period at the end of the last format line.

4. The data itself. Each line of data corresponds to one line in the table. If you have very long input lines, they can be broken into smaller line segments. A backslash (\) at the end of a line segment means that it continues to the next line and is part of a longer input line. Each of the columns in our table is separated by an @ sign, which we are using in place of a tab character, as we have specified in the options line.

5. A `.TE` signals the end of the table description.

▪ Laying Out a Table ▪

The global options line is an optional line that controls the overall appearance of the table. Normally, a table is positioned on the left-hand side of the page. Because the table is probably part of a larger document, you may want to center the table and enclose it in a box to make it stand out. Let's modify the options line in our example to produce this new layout:

```
.TS
center,box,tab(@);   New options line
c l.
1@User console
2@Monochromatic graphics terminal
3@Color graphics terminal
        etc.
```

When formatted, the table looks like this:

1	User console
2	Monochromatic graphics terminal
3	Color graphics terminal
4	Line printer
5	Digitizer
6	Laser printer
7	Unallocated
8	Pen plotter
9	Raster plotter
10, 11, 12	Unallocated

Now you know how to use three of the option names: `center`, `box`, and `tab()`. If you use one or more option names, they must be separated by spaces, tabs, or commas. The options line, if present, must *immediately follow* the `.TS` line. There are other options that you can use:

expand	Make the table as wide as the current line length
allbox	Enclose each item in the table in a box
doublebox	Box the whole table with a double line
linesize (*n*)	Set lines (for `box`, `allbox`, and `doublebox`) in *n*-point type
delim (*xy*)	Set *x* and *y* as eqn delimiters. See Chapter 9 for information on the equation preprocessor eqn.

The difference between a table that is centered or left justified and one that is expanded is the amount of space between columns. If you specify `center` or the default, the width between columns will be three ens. If you specify `expand`, tbl will expand the width of the overall columns until the table is as wide as the current margins.

If the overall width of the table calculated by `tbl` is greater than the width of the text, `nroff/troff` will ignore any positioning option you specify. The table will be printed as is necessary to fit everything, even if the table runs to the edge of the paper.

The `linesize` option changes the width of the lines used in enclosing tables to a given point size. Normally, the lines are 10 point. You can specify an absolute line size, such as `linesize (24)`, to print thicker box lines, or a relative size, such as `linesize (+14)`, to produce the same effect.

Let's try one more example by enclosing all the data entries in boxes. The options line for the table now reads:

```
center,allbox,tab(@);
```

The new table would look like this:

1	User console
2	Monochromatic graphics terminal
3	Color graphics terminal
4	Line printer
5	Digitizer
6	Laser printer
7	Unallocated
8	Pen plotter
9	Raster plotter
10, 11, 12	Unallocated

The `tbl` program isn't very good at keeping boxed tables on one page. If you have a long table, `tbl` may break it up at an awkward point (for example, placing the last line of a table on another page). To keep a boxed table together on one page, enclose it in a `.DS/.DE` macro pair (in either `ms` or `mm`). Alternatively, you can give `tbl` the latitude to split a table and print each section with its own table heading using the `.TS H` macro, as you will see later.

▪ Describing Column Formats ▪

Each column in the table is described by a key letter in the format section. Key letters are separated from each other by spaces or tabs for readability. The basic set of key letters includes:

L or l	Left justify the data within a column.
R or r	Right justify the data within a column.
C or c	Center the data within a column.
S or s	Extend data in the previous column to this column (horizontal span).
N or n	Align numbers by their decimal points. If there are no decimal points, align them by the units digit.
A or a	Indent characters in the column from the standard left alignment by one em.
^	Extend entry from previous row down through this row (vertical span). Text will be centered between the specified rows.
T or t	Also vertical span, but text will appear at the top of the column instead of midway within the specified area.

If all columns of the table follow the same format, you need only one format line for the entire table. However, not all tables contain the same number of columns throughout. For example, you might have a table where the upper half consists of three columns, and the lower half contains only two.

The rule in writing format lines is to specify key letters for the largest number of columns in the table and carry that number for all format lines. That way, if you specify three columns, and you're using only two, you can use two consecutive tab characters (with nothing in between) to denote an empty field for the unused column. The longest format line defines the number of columns in the table.

Suppose you defined four columns in the first format line, and then defined only three columns in the succeeding lines. The `tbl` program will still format your table, but it assumes that the undefined column is left justified.

In the following sections, we will show some typical applications of these and other key letters to format table headings and columns of data.

Tables with Headers

You can think of a table header as an extra row of data that may or may not have the same format as the actual data. If the format of the header is different, you must add another line at the beginning of your format section to describe the header.

For example, we'll change the first column in the previous table to have the header *Port* and the second to have the header *Device*, so that we get the following table.

Port	Device
1	User console
2	Monochromatic graphics terminal
3	Color graphics terminal
4	Line printer
5	Digitizer
6	Laser printer
7	Unallocated
8	Pen plotter
9	Raster plotter
10, 11, 12	Unallocated

The relevant lines that produced this table follow:

```
.TS
center, box, tab(@);
c c
c l.
Port@Device
.sp
1@User console
```

```
2@Monochromatic graphics terminal
```
        etc.

The first line of the format description (c c) says that there are two columns of data, each one centered within each column. (Note that there is no period at the end of this line.) Because this is the first line of the format description, it applies to the first line of our data, which happens to be the table heading. This means that the words *Port* and *Device* will be centered in each column. The second (and last) format line is the same as in the previous example and applies to the rest of the table. Note the period at the end of this line.

    We used `.sp` to produce a blank line after the table header. The `tbl` command assumes that any non-numeric string preceded by a dot is a `troff` or `nroff` request and passes it unchanged to the formatter. Thus, you can vary spacing between rows, or use other `nroff`/`troff` commands within a table.

Tables with Spanned Headers

Our previous table now contains a header for each column. We now want to have an overall title or header that spans the width of the table. As before, you can think of the spanned header as an extra data line with its own format description.

    We want the header to be only one column, centered across the whole table like the following.

Output Device Configuration	
Port	Device
1	User console
2	Monochromatic graphics terminal
3	Color graphics terminal
4	Line printer
5	Digitizer
6	Laser printer
7	Unallocated
8	Pen plotter
9	Raster plotter
10, 11, 12	Unallocated

Because we should keep the number of columns the same throughout the table, we use the *span* format option (s) to tell `tbl` that the entry in a preceding column continues on to the other columns. The relevant portion of our table description contains the following lines:

```
.TS
center, box, tab (@);
c s
c c
c l.
```

```
Output Device Configuration
.sp .5v
Port@Device
.sp .5v
1@User console
        etc.
```

We now have three format lines: the first describes the main header, the second describes each column header, and the third applies to the rest of the data in the table.

Numeric and Alphabetic Columns

You can align numeric data by the decimal point or the units digit using the key letter n in the format line. When you use n, numbers in a column will be aligned as follows:

$$
\begin{array}{r}
23.6 \\
155 \\
98.08.6 \\
5.26 \\
12798 \\
0.2365 \\
980.
\end{array}
$$

You should never enter non-numeric data in a column that is designated as n. On the other hand, you can enter numbers in columns that are aligned using any of the other key letters. The numbers will just be treated as if they were ordinary alphabetic characters. Thus, a column of numbers might also be centered, left justified, or right justified.

You should also avoid putting equations in numeric columns because tbl attempts to split numeric format items into two parts. To prevent this from happening, use the delim *(xy)* global option. For example, if the eqn delimiters are $$, a delim ($$) option causes a numeric column such as:

```
79.909 $+- .157$
```

to be divided after 79.909 and not after .157.

Columns designated as a are always slightly indented relative to left-justified columns. If necessary, tbl increases the column width to force this. Data in an a format is positioned so that the widest entry is centered within the column.

A note about n and a: when you have several command lines, do not use both n and a to format different rows in the same column. For example, the format lines:

```
r n r
r a r
```

are not allowed. This is because n and a share the same number register location in nroff/troff's memory.

The special nonprinting character string `\&` may be used to override the normal alignment of numeric or alphabetic data. For example, if you use `\&` before a digit, then the digit will line up with the decimal point and `\&` will not appear in the output. The effect of `\&` is as follows.

Input Form	Output
`9.65`	`9.65`
`12.4.8`	`12.4.8`
`15.\&7.32`	`15.7.32`
`2\&0.9.19`	`20.9.19`
`processor`	`processor`
`half`	`half`
`half\&`	`half`

Vertically Spanned Columns

Let's see how the vertical span key (`^`) is used in a table like the following.

Fuel	Substance	kcal/ gram mol. wt.
	Hydrogen	68.4
Gases	Methane	211
	Butane	680
	Ethane	368
	Benzene	782
Liquids	Ethyl alcohol	328
	Methyl alcohol	171

The `tbl` description for this table is:

```
.TS
tab(@);
c c c
^ ^ c
l l n.
Fuel@Substance@kcal/
@@gram mol. wt.
.sp
Gases@Hydrogen@68.4
\^@Methane@211
\^@Butane@680
\^@Ethane@368
.sp
```

```
Liquids@Benzene@82
\^@Ethyl alcohol@328
\^@Methyl alcohol@171
.TE
```

There are three lines in the format section: the first two describe the column headings, and the last describes the format of the data.

We can imagine the first line of the header as consisting of the words *Fuel Substance kcal/* and the second line as *Fuel Substance gram mol. wt.* The words *Fuel Substance* don't actually appear twice, but are centered relative to the two lines that form the third column header. We use the caret key (^) in the second format line to tell `tbl` that these two column names vertically span their respective columns. Note the first two data lines that correspond to the first two format lines.

We could have also used the same approach to describe the rest of the data, but this would mean writing seven more format lines, one for each of the lines of data. The table really has three columns with the same format throughout, so you can use just one format line to describe all of them. Then you can enter the characters `\^` in place of a column entry to tell `tbl` that the entry in the previous row for that column vertically spans this row also.

You can use the ^ key letter in the format section and at the same time enter `\^` in the data section as we did previously. You don't lose anything by doing this and `tbl` doesn't complain.

Another way of describing a vertically spanned column is by using the key letter `t` (or `T`) in the format line. Any corresponding vertically spanned item will begin at the top of its range. Thus, if we specify `t` instead of ^ in the format line, the words *Fuel and Substance* will be in line with *kcal/*.

Drawing Lines in Tables

Horizontal rules are specified by underscores and by equal signs entered between the appropriate lines of data. An underscore on a line by itself entered between two rows of data produces a single rule running the whole width of the table. An equal sign on a line by itself produces a double rule.

If you want a horizontal rule to be only as wide as the contents of the column, enter an underscore or equal sign in that column as part of the data. The underscore or equal sign must be separated from the other columns by tabs or the tab character we've specified in the options line. To print these characters explicitly, they should be preceded by a `\&` or followed by a space before the usual tab or newline character.

You can also use these two characters in place of a key letter in the format line. If an adjacent column contains a horizontal or vertical line, the horizontal line is extended to meet nearby lines. If you enter any data in this column, the data will be ignored and you will get a warning message. The following table has a fairly complicated heading:

	1984 (Jan.-July)	
Items	Units	1984/1983 (%)
TV	3,889,543	145.7
Color	2,766,004	110.7
B/W	1,123,539	12.5

The `tbl` description for this table looks like this:

```
.TS
center,box,tab(@);
c s s
c c _
^ ^ | c
^ ^ | c
l r n.
1984 (Jan.-July)
Items@Units
@@1984/1983
@@(%)

_
TV@3,889,543@145.7
Color@2,766,004@110.7
B/W@1,123,539@12.5
.TE
```

As you can see from the preceding description, vertical lines are drawn by specifying bars *within the format lines*. A single vertical bar between two key letters draws a single vertical line between those two columns in the table. You can enter the bar after the first key letter or before the second key letter. A vertical bar to the left of the first key letter or to the right of the last one produces a vertical line at the edge of the table. Two vertical bars (∣ ∣) draw a double rule.

These characters are really more useful for drawing lines inside the table rather than for manually enclosing a table in a box because there are global options that automatically do this. To draw vertical and horizontal lines in our table "Fuels," we modify the relevant format and data lines as follows:

```
c  | |c  |c
^  | |^  |c
l  | |l  |n.
Fuel@Substance@kcal/
@@gram mol. wt.
=
Gases@Hydrogen@68.4
    etc.
```

```
Liquids@Benzene@782
        etc.
```

This input produces the following table:

Fuel	Substance	kcal/ gram mol. wt.
Gases	Hydrogen	68.4
	Methane	211
	Butane	680
	Ethane	368
Liquids	Benzene	782
	Ethyl alcohol	328
	Methyl alcohol	171

Changing Fonts and Sizes

The `tbl` program assumes that the table is always set in roman type. However, you can always change the typeface of all entries in a column to italic or boldface. You can add one of the following letters after the column key letter:

```
fb      fB      b       B       Boldface
fi      fI      i       I       Italic
fcw     fCW     cw      CW      Constant width
```

If you want to change the font of only some of the entries, you should use explicit `nroff`/`troff` requests rather than specifying the font in the format line. For example, let's change the headers in the previous table to boldface and the words *Gases* and *Liquids* to italic. The format lines would look like this:

```
c   |  |cB   |cB
^   |  |^    |cB
l   |  |l    |n.
```

Gases will be written as `\fIGases\fR` and *Liquids* as `\fILiquids\fR`. The effect would be as follows:

Fuel	Substance	kcal/ gram mol. wt.
Gases	Hydrogen	68.4
	Methane	211
	Butane	680
	Ethane	368
Liquids	Benzene	782
	Ethyl alcohol	328
	Methyl alcohol	171

The type size in which headings and data are printed is normally 10 points. You can also change the size of the type by using the key letter p and an absolute or relative point size. To specify a change in size relative to the existing point size, use a + or − before the value. For example, a column specification of cp12 or cp+2 will both result in a centered column using 12-point type.

Changing the Column Width

When you're not using the expand option, the normal spacing between any two columns is three ens. You can change the spacing by specifying a numeric value between the key letters representing those columns. The number specifies the separation in ens. When you're using the expand option and you specify a column space, the number is multiplied by a constant such that the table is as wide as the current line length.

If you don't want any spaces between the columns, simply write 0, as in:

```
r0 l
```

which yields:

Hydrogen68.4

Methane211

Butane680

These spacings are only nominal spacings. The data may be so irregular in length that no two columns will actually appear to be separated by the specified distance. However, varying the amount of separation between two columns still leaves tbl free to make each column as wide or as narrow as is necessary.

You can specify a minimum width for any column by entering the letter w (or W) after the key letter, followed by the desired width in parentheses. You can use any unit of measurement recognized by nroff/troff when specifying a width dimension. You can also enter a value without a unit of measurement, in which case tbl assumes the value is in ens. Thus, the format:

```
rw(15)
```

specifies a column that is 15 ens wide with the text right justified within the column, and:

```
lw(2.25i)
```

specifies a left-justified column that is 2.25 inches wide.

You can also force `tbl` to make the width of particular columns equal by using the letter `e` (or `E`) after the key letter for those columns. This allows a group of regularly spaced columns.

To show that `tbl` can be used for any text that needs to be laid out in columns (as opposed to tables), we can print the following text:

Signature		
August 31, 1987	J. White	K. Kimura

using this `tbl` description:

```
.TS
expand, tab(@);
c c c
cew(1.3i) ce ce.
Signature@@
\_@\_@\_
August 31,@J. White@K. Kimura
1987@@
.TE
```

In the last format line, we specified that all three columns be 1.3 inches wide. Because all columns will be of equal width, we need to specify the width only once.

Other Key Letters

We already showed you some of the more widely used key letters. Additional features that can be used with the basic set of key letters are:

V or v   Used with a number to indicate the vertical line spacing used within a table entry. Used only with text blocks (discussed in a later section).

U or u   Move the corresponding entry up by one-half line to produce staggered columns. This doesn't work with the `allbox` global option.

Z or z   Ignore the data entry in calculating column width. This is use-
                     ful in allowing headings to run across adjacent columns where
                     spanned headings might be inappropriate.

Key letters for a column can be written in any order. They do not need to be
separated, except when you specify both a point size (p) and a column separation
number. Thus, a numeric column entered in bold 18-point type with a minimum
column width of 1.5 inches and separated from the next column by 12 ens can be written as:

```
np18w(1.5i)B 12
```

Two or more format lines can also be written on one line by separating them with commas. For example, the format lines:

```
c c c
l l n.
```

can be written as:

```
c c c, l l n.
```

▪ Changing the Format within a Table ▪

All our examples so far have shown tables that consist of somewhat complicated headings followed by identical rows of data. Thus, we can keep the number of format lines
comparatively small. This may not be the case when a table is divided into sections,
each of which has its own heading. Let's look at the following table (from AT&T's
Documenter's Workbench Text Formatter's Reference):

Horizontal Local Motions		
Function	*Effect in*	
	troff	*nroff*
\h'N'	Move distance N	
\(space)	Unpaddable space-size space	
\0	Digit-size space	
|	1/6 em space	ignored
\^	1/12 em space	ignored

It has both a main header and column headers. The body of the table is divided
into two parts. The upper part contains two columns, and the lower part contains three.
To format each part correctly, we must enter a command line for each row of data so
that `tbl` can keep track of which rows of the table have which format. This process is
tedious and prone to error. Fortunately, `tbl` has a way around this.

To change the format of columns within a table, `tbl` has the table continue
request `.T&`. We can change the format of a table at any time by entering `.T&` fol-

lowed by the new format line(s) and the additional data. The general format for the `tbl` description is as follows:

```
.TS
option line;
format section.
data
.T&
new format section.
data
.T&
another new format section.
data
.TE
```

There are two things we cannot change after a `.T&` request: the global options line and the number of columns specified. Our original options line holds for the entire table.

Let's see how we can use the `.T&` request to produce the previous table:

```
.TS
center,box,linesize (6),tab(@);
cB s s.
Horizontal Local Motions
_
.T&
cI | cI s
cI | cI s
cI | cI | cI
c | l s.
Function@Effect in
\e^@_
\e^@troff@nroff
_
\eh'N'@Move distance N
\e(space)@Unpaddable space-size space
\e0@Digit-size space
_
.T&
c | l | l.
\e|@1/6 em space@ignored
\e^@1/12 em space@ignored
.TE
```

We take the largest number of columns in the table, which is three. We have two `.T&` requests to break up the table into three parts with their own format sections. The first part applies to the main header only. The second describes the column headers and the three-column segment of the table. Finally, the lower part applies to the last part of the table.

Although you can have hundreds of lines in a table, `tbl` uses only the first 200 lines to set up the table. Any format changes you make after the 200th column will not be processed by `tbl`. In this case, you should break up the table into smaller table segments.

Should you specify `.TS H` but forget to follow it with `.TH`, some strange things will happen. One recent instance of this caused the table to be output in a nearly endless succession of pages. (In `troff` terms, a diversion created to capture the table heading filled up with the table instead; this caused the first page break that triggered the output of the diversion at the top of the next page; each time the diversion was output, it caused a new page break and the diversion was output again.)

▪ **Putting Text Blocks in a Column** ▪

Some tables consist of column entries that cannot be conveniently typed as a simple string between tabs. Descriptive tables, for example, require ordinary flowing text justified between the margins of the specific column in which it appears in the table. These sections of flowing text are called *text blocks*.

Each block of text is preceded by a `T{` and followed by a `T}`. The `T{` marker must be at the end of a line, and the `T}` must be at the start of a line:

```
...T{
Block of
text
T}...
```

When a text block is included in a row that contains other columns of data or text, the `T{` that marks the beginning of the text block must appear at the end of the line in the text. Even a single blank space following the `T{` will cause the table to fail. Likewise, the `T}` symbol must always begin the line:

```
... Data@T{
Block of
text
T}@data ...
```

This makes it easy for you to revise text when necessary and also allows you to insert any special `nroff/troff` commands before or after the text block.

Let's lay out the following table:

Some Pattern-Matching Characters in *vi*	
Special Characters	*Usage*
.	Matches any single character except *newline*.
*	Matches any number (including zero) of the single character (including a character specified by a regular expression) that immediately precedes it.
[. . .]	Matches any *one* of the characters enclosed between the brackets. A range of consecutive characters can be specified by separating the first and last characters in the range with a hyphen.
$	Requires that the preceding regular expression be found at the end of the line.
\{*n,m*\}	Matches a range of occurrences of the single character (including a character specified by a regular expression) that immediately precedes it. *n* and *m* are integers between 0 and 256 that specify how many occurrences to match.

The `tbl` description of this table is:

```
.TS
box,tab(@);
cb s
cI| cI
cw(1.25i)| lw(3.25i).
Some Pattern-Matching Characters in \fIvi\fR

_
Special Characters@Usage

_
\fI.\fR@Matches any single character\
except \fInewline\fR.

*@T{
Matches any number (including zero) of the
single character (including
a character specified by a regular expression)
that immediately precedes it.
T}
```

```
[...]@T{
Matches any \fIone\fR of the characters enclosed
between the brackets.
A range of consecutive characters can be
specified by separating the
first and last characters in the range with a hyphen.
T}

$@T{
Requires that the preceding regular
expression be found at the end of the line.
T}

\{\fIn,m\fR\}@T{
Matches a range of occurrences of the
single character (including a
character specified by a regular expression)
that immediately precedes
it.  n and m are integers between
0 and 256 that specify how many occurrences to match.
T}
.TE
```

What might confuse you about this source text is that each block of text occupies two or more lines. Just think of everything that comes between a `T{` and a `T}` as a single entry that occupies a single column in that row. It is separated from its neighbors by tabs. If you keep track of the tabs, you will be able to sort out quite easily the sequence of columns.

In the previous description, we specified a minimum width for each column. If a width is not given, `tbl` uses the default:

$L * C/(N+1)$

where L is the current line length, C is the number of table columns spanned by the text, and N is the total number of columns in the table. It is sometimes better to define a column width because `tbl` might make the table too narrow by default.

You can also use the `nroff/troff` commands `.na` and `.ad` to left justify text blocks if the output doesn't come out fully justified. The `tbl` description would be:

```
... T{
.na
Block of
text
.ad
T}
```

The `nroff` and `troff` formatters can accept only about twenty or thirty small text blocks in a table without exceeding certain internal limits. If the limits are exceeded, you will get error messages like "too many string/macro names" or "too many number registers."

In this case, you should divide the table into two or more independent tables, each with its own `.TS` and `.TE` requests. The final formatted sections can be "joined" and made to appear as one table by inserting minus `.sp` requests (such as `.sp -12p`) between the sections. This will cause the formatter to draw them together.

You can also change the vertical line spacing within a text block using a key letter followed by `v` (or `V`) and a number. The number may be a signed digit and is taken as an increase or decrease from the current vertical spacing.

▪ Breaking Up Long Tables ▪

If you have a very long table that will fill many pages, it might be helpful to break up the table into several smaller ones, with the main heading reproduced at the top of each page. Then the reader doesn't have to keep returning to the first page to see what the columns indicate. The `tbl` program also automatically breaks a boxed table if it runs over one page.

You can use the `.TS H` and `.TH` macros to reproduce the original heading at the top of each page of the table:

```
.TS H
options;
format section.
main header
.TH
data
.TE
```

The `.TH` (*table header*) macro is a feature of the `ms` macro package (not `tbl`). This macro can take the letter `N` as an argument; this causes the table header to be printed *only if it is the first table header on a page*. This is useful when you have to build a long table from smaller `.TS H`/`.TE` segments. For example:

```
.TS  H
```
global options;
format section.
main header
```
.TH
```
data
```
.TE
.TS  H
```
global options;
format section.
main header
```
.TH  N
```
data
```
.TE
```

This causes the table header to appear at the top of the first table segment. The header will not appear on top of the second segment when both segments appear on the same page. If the table continues to another page, the heading will still appear at the top of the new page. This feature is useful when breaking a long complex table into segments.

▪ **Putting Titles on Tables** ▪

The mm macro `.TB` can be used to automatically number and title a table. All tables with `.TB` are numbered consecutively. The title is centered above the table if it can fit on one line. If the title is longer than one line, all succeeding lines of the title are indented to line up with the first character of the title. The `.TB` macro is normally used inside a `.DS`/`.DE` pair.

The `.TB` macro is not part of `tbl`. Thus, it can be used to generate titles or headers for tables that are created using only tabs and none of the `tbl` commands. The general format of the `.TB` macro is:

    `.TB` [*title*] [*n*] [*flag*]

where *n* is used to override the normal numbering. The *flag* option can take one of the following values:

0   *n* is used as a prefix to the normal table number

1   *n* is used as a suffix to the normal table number

2   *n* replaces the normal table number

If you put the `.TB` macro before the `.TS` macro, the title is placed above the table. You can also put the title below the table by using the `.TB` macro after `.TE`.

For example, we can modify one of our tables by adding a title and labeling it as *Table 5*. We add the following lines before the `.TS`:

```
.DS
.TB "Horizontal Local Motions" "5" "2"
.sp
```

And we add a `.DE` after the `.TE`. The table now looks like this.

Table 5. Horizontal Local Motions

Function	Effect in	
	troff	*nroff*
\h'N'	Move distance N	
\(space)	Unpaddable space-size space	
\0	Digit-size space	
|	1/6 em space	ignored
\^	1/12 em space	ignored

Another useful mm macro is the `.TC` macro. The `.TC` macro is placed at the end of the file. When the file is formatted, `.TC` collects the titles of tables that were generated using `.TB` for the table of contents. Thus, if we had used `.TB` to put headers in our examples, the table of contents might look like this:

LIST OF TABLES

TABLE 1. Production of Audio Equipment 2

TABLE 2. Output Device Configuration 14

TABLE 3. Heating Value of Fuels 17

▪ A **tbl** Checklist ▪

Most table formatting errors come from specifying too few columns in the format section, forgetting a tab character between column entries in a table, or omitting one or more of the characters that `tbl` expects in a table description. After you've finished laying out a table, check that you have the following:

- a `.TS` with a `.TE`

- a `.TH` with a `.TS H`

- a semicolon at the end of the options line (if there is one)

- a period at the end of the last format line (including format sections with a `.T&`)

- in the format section, an item for each column and a format line for each line of the table

- a tab symbol for each column in each line of the table, except for the first column when horizontally spanning, and within text blocks

- for text blocks, a `T{` with every `T}`

- no extra blanks after:

    > any `.TS`, `.TE`, `.TS H`, `.TH`, or `.T&`

    > the end of the options and format lines

    > any `T{` or `T}`

- no periods at the beginning of any ''data'' text lines (add a `\&` before the period, if necessary)

- a space after each table entry of `_` and `=` unless you want the lines to extend across the column

▪ Some Complex Tables ▪

Surely, the best way to learn more about `tbl` is to study tables of greater complexity than the ones we've look at so far. The `tbl` article by M.E. Lesk in the *UNIX Programmer's Manual* provides many fine examples of difficult tables. Look at the formatted tables and try to ''break'' the code that produced them. In this section, you'll find two complicated tables followed by the `tbl` input for you to decipher.

The weight table shown in Figure 8-1 is taken from a manual that describes the safe operation of mobile cranes. This table was coded by an associate, Daniel Gilly, over several hours. The code is listed in Figure 8-2. Look at how the vertical line indicator (|) is used between entries to draw a line at the end of each column. Note also the use of the alphabetic (a) format specification to produce indented text.

The financial table shown in Figure 8-3 is adapted from a prospectus prepared by `troff` users at a large New York law firm. The code for this table is listed in Figure 8-4. Note the use of a leader character (\a) in the first entry, coupled with a fixed width specification for the first column, to produce leaders that fill out the column. Also, notice how the table headings are printed in a smaller point size than the rest of the table, using the format specification (p8).

WEIGHTS OF MATERIALS (Based On Volume)			
Material	Approx. Weight, Lbs. Per Cubic Foot	Material	Approx. Weight, Lbs. Per Cubic Foot
METALS		**TIMBER, AIR-DRY**	
Aluminum	165	Cedar	22
Brass	535	Fir, Douglas, seasoned	34
Bronze	500	Fir, Douglas, unseasoned	40
Copper	560	Fir, Douglas, wet	50
Iron	480	Fir, Douglas, glue	
Lead	710	laminated	34
Steel	490	Hemlock	30
Tin	460	Pine	30
MASONRY		Poplar	30
Ashlar masonry	140-160	Spruce	28
Brick masonry, soft	110	**LIQUIDS**	
Brick masonry, com-		Alcohol, pure	49
mon (about 3 tons		Gasoline	42
per thousand)	125	Oil	58
Brick masonry, pressed	140	Water	62
Clay tile masonry,		**EARTH**	
average	60	Earth, wet	100
Rubble masonry	130-155	Earth, dry (about 2050	
Concrete, cinder,		lbs. per cu. yd.)	75
haydite	100-110	Sand and gravel, wet	120
Concrete, slag	130	Sand and gravel, dry	105
Concrete, stone	144	River sand (about 3240	
Concrete, stone,		lbs. per cu. yd.)	120
reinforced (4050 lbs.		**VARIOUS BUILDING**	
per cu. yd.)	150	**MATERIALS**	
ICE AND SNOW		Cement, Portland, loose	94
Ice	56	Cement, Portland, set	183
Snow, dry, fresh fallen	8	Lime, gypsum, loose	53-64
Snow, dry, packed	12-25	Mortar, cement-lime,	
Snow, wet	27-40	set	103
MISCELLANEOUS		Crushed rock (about	
Asphalt	80	2565 lbs. per	
Tar	75	cu. yd.)	90-110
Glass	160		
Paper	60		

Fig. 8-1. A Complex Table

```
.ps 8
.vs 10
.TS
center,box,tab(@);
cb s s s
c|c|c|c
^|c|^|c
^|c|^|c
^|c|^|c.
WEIGHTS OF MATERIALS (Based On Volume)
_
Material@Approx.@Material@Approx.
@Weight,@@Weight,
@Lbs. Per@@Lbs. Per
@Cubic Foot@@Cubic Foot
_
.sp .5
.T&
lb|c|lb|c.
METALS@@TIMBER, AIR-DRY@
.T&
a|c|a|c.
Aluminum@165@Cedar@\022
Brass@535@Fir, Douglas, seasoned@\034
Bronze@500@Fir, Douglas, unseasoned@\040
Copper@560@Fir, Douglas, wet@\050
Iron@480@Fir, Douglas, glue@
Lead@710@\0\0laminated@\034
Steel@490@Hemlock@\030
Tin@460@Pine@\030
.T&
lb|c|a|c.
MASONRY@@Poplar@\030
.T&
a|c|a|c.
Ashlar masonry@140-160@Spruce@\028
.T&
a|c|lb|c.
Brick masonry, soft@110@LIQUIDS@
.T&
a|c|a|c.
Brick masonry, com-@@Alcohol, pure@\049
\0\0mon (about 3 tons@@Gasoline@\042
\0\0per thousand)@125@Oil@\058
Brick masonry, pressed@140@Water@\062
.T&
a|c|lb|a.
Clay tile masonry,@@EARTH@
.T&
a|c|a|c.
\0\0average@\060@Earth, wet@100
Rubble masonry@130-155@Earth, dry (about 2050@
```

Fig. 8-2. Input for Figure 8-1

```
Concrete, cinder,@@\0\0lbs. per cu. yd.)@\075
\0\0haydite@100-110@Sand and gravel, wet@120
Concrete, slag@130@Sand and gravel, dry@105
Concrete, stone@144@River sand (about 3240@
Concrete, stone,@@\0\0lbs. per cu. yd.)@120
.T&
a|c|lb|c.
\0\0reinforced (4050 lbs.@@VARIOUS BUILDING@
\0\0per cu. yd.)@150@\0\0MATERIALS@
.T&
lb|c|a|c.
ICE AND SNOW@@Cement, Portland, loose@\094
.T&
a|c|a|c.
Ice@\056@Cement, Portland, set@183
Snow, dry, fresh fallen@\0\08@Lime, gypsum, loose@53-64
Snow, dry, packed@12-25@Mortar, cement-lime,@
Snow, wet@27-40@\0\0set@103
.T&
lb|c|a|c.
MISCELLANEOUS@@Crushed rock (about@
.T&
a|c|a|c.
Asphalt@\080@\0\02565 lbs. per@
Tar@\075@\0\0cu. yd.)@90-110
Glass@160@@
Paper@\060@@
.sp .5
.TE
```

Fig. 8-2. —(Cont'd)

	Year Ending December 31			
	1986	1985	1984	1983
	(Dollars in millions)			
Premiums..	$ 10,922.7	$ 10,330.7	$ 9,252.4	$ 9,071.8
Investment income	3,671.7	3,146.0	2,749.7	2,308.9
Federal income taxes...........................	24.4	91.6	71.9	20.8
Operating income................................	359.8	346.1	342.6	309.6
Realized gains (losses)........................	15.4	27.0	(30.2)	(15.2)
Net income	375.2	373.1	312.4	295.8
Cash provided by operations	4,123.2	3,560.8	3,514.9	3,067.4
Assets	41,645.8	34,434.7	32,876.6	27,987.6

Fig. 8-3. Financial Table

```
.TS
expand, tab(@);
lw(13P) cbp8 s s s
lw(13P) c s s s
lw(13P) cbp8 cbp8 cbp8 cbp8
lw(13P) cbp8 s s s
lw(13P) n n n n.
@Year Ending December 31
.sp .2v
@_
@1986@1985@1984@1983
@(Dollars in millions)
.sp .5v
Premiums\a@$\010,922.7@$\010,330.7@$\0\09,252.4@$\0\09,071.8
Investment income\a@3,671.7@3,146.0@2,749.7@2,308.9
Federal income taxes\a@24.4@91.6@71.9@20.8
Operating income\a@359.8@346.1@342.6@309.6
Realized gains (losses)\a@15.4@27.0@(30.2)@(15.2)
Net income\a@375.2@373.1@312.4@295.8
Cash provided by operations\a@4,123.2@3,560.8@3,514.9@3,067.4
Assets\a@41,645.8@34,434.7@32,876.6@27,987.6
.TE
```

Fig. 8-4. Input for Figure 8-3

9

Typesetting Equations with eqn

Typesetting mathematical equations has always been a problem for users who have a limited knowledge of mathematics or typesetting. This is because mathematical expressions are often a mixture of standard text and special characters in different point sizes. For example, the equation:

$$\sum_{i=0}^{\infty} c^i = \lim_{m \to \infty} \sum_{i=0}^{m} c^i$$

requires three special characters (Σ, ∞, and $\to$) and roman and italic characters in two different sizes. Expressions also may require horizontal and vertical printing motions (as in subscripts and superscripts).

You could code this example using `troff` requests, but the syntax for describing the printing motions, sizes, and fonts are difficult to learn and difficult to type in correctly. UNIX has formatting tools specifically designed for documents containing mathematical symbols—the programs `eqn` and `neqn`. The `eqn` program is a preprocessor for `troff`; `neqn` is a preprocessor for `nroff`.

With `eqn` you can typeset both inline equations and equations that are set off from the body of the text like the example shown. It takes an English-like description of a mathematical equation and generates a `troff` script. You don't need to understand what you are typing.

The `eqn` preprocessor was designed to be easy to learn and even easier to use. This implies that normal mathematical conventions such as operator precedence and parentheses cannot be used. Nor does `eqn` assume that parentheses are always balanced, or that an expression is better written in another form. There are only a few rules, keywords, special symbols, and operators to remember. If something works in one situation, it should work everywhere.

This section shows you how to typeset mathematical equations using a set of special words that belong to the `eqn` vocabulary. With `eqn`, you can format the following quite easily:

- the Greek alphabet

- special symbols, such as summations (Σ), products (Π) integrals ($\int$), and square roots ($\sqrt{}$)

- positional notation, such as subscripts and superscripts, fractions, matrices, and vertical piles

- diacritical marks

- sizes and fonts

- horizontal and vertical spacing

You can even define a string that appears repeatedly throughout the document so that you do not need to type it in each time it appears.

▪ A Simple eqn Example ▪

To best illustrate how eqn works and how easy it is to learn the syntax, let's take a simple example:

$$\frac{a_2}{b}$$

If you were to read this mathematical expression aloud to another person, you might say "a sub 2 over b." This is exactly how you would describe the expression to eqn. The word sub denotes a *sub*script; the word over denotes a fraction. You will see the other words that eqn treats as special (i.e., that belong to the eqn vocabulary) as we move along in this section.

When you use eqn, it assumes that you have a two-dimensional picture of how the equation should appear in the document. The key in writing the eqn decription is to familiarize yourself with the special words used by eqn in printing mathematical characters. Then, describe the equation as if you were reading it aloud to another person.

The eqn preprocessor takes care of the standard things that you would expect to happen automatically, such as printing superscripts and subscripts in an appropriately smaller size, and adjusting the length and size of fraction bars. Following mathematical convention, variables are made italic, parentheses, operators, and digits are made roman, and normal spacing is automatically adjusted to make the expression look better.

▪ Using eqn ▪

The eqn preprocessor is used not only for typesetting equations, but also for typesetting nontechnical documents. For example, many documents contain subscripted or superscripted words. Using eqn can be easier than formatting the subscript or super-script using troff commands.

To format a document with `eqn`, you would enter:

```
$ eqn /usr/pub/eqnchar files | troff [options]
```

You can then pipe the output to the desired printer. The file `/usr/pub/eqnchar` contains definitions of additional special characters that can be used by `eqn`. It is not essential that you use it, but you may get better results with certain equations if you do.

If you use `eqn` with the `tbl` preprocessor to print tables containing mathematical expressions, invoke `tbl` before `eqn` to mimimize the data passed through the pipe:

```
$ tbl /usr/pub/eqnchar file | eqn | troff
```

If you are using `nroff` instead of `troff`, you can get a reasonable approximation of `eqn` output by using `neqn`. However, printers used with `nroff` may be unable to print many of the special characters used in equations.

▪ Specifying Equations ▪

Mathematical documents contain both displayed equations and standard text mixed with mathematical expressions. The `eqn` preprocessor allows you to typeset both forms.

Displayed Equations

For equations that appear outside the body of the text, mark the beginning of each equation with an `.EQ` and the end with an `.EN`. Note that these delimiters may or may not also be defined as macros. They are recognized by `eqn` as flags to begin and end processing.

If they are not defined as macros by the package you are using, you can define them yourself, or can simply supplement them with `troff` requests (such as `.ce` to center the equation) as desired.

If you are using the `ms` macro package, `.EQ` and `.EN` are defined as macros, and the equation is centered by default. Thus, if you type:

```
.EQ
C=Ax+By
.EN
```

the output will be:

$$C = Ax + By$$

In `ms`, you can also left justify the equation using `.EQ L` or indent it using `.EQ I`. You can further specify an arbitrary equation number or label that will be printed at the right margin. For example, the lines:

```
.EQ I (13a)
C=Ax+By
.EN
```

produce the following:

$$C=Ax+By \tag{13a}$$

The mathematical symbols +, −, =, and ( ) are typed in just as they appear in the equation.

If you're using the mm macro package, put the .EQ/.EN pair inside a .DS/.DE pair so that the format looks like this:

```
.DS
.EQ
equation
.EN
.DE
```

This automatically centers the displayed equation. You can also use a break producing request (such as .br or .sp) immediately following the .DS macro but before the .EQ macro to display the equation at the left margin of the text.

Inline Expressions

If you are using ms or mm, .EQ and .EN imply a displayed equation and so cannot be used for short inline expressions. But eqn provides a shorthand notation for displaying this type of expression. You can define any two characters as delimiters to mark the beginning and end of an inline equation, and then type the expression right in the middle of the text. To do this, define the equation delimiters within an .EQ and an .EN at the beginning of your file.

For example, to set both delimiters to #, add the following lines:

```
.EQ
delim ##
.EN
```

If you're using mm, do not use the .DS/.DE pair to enclose a .EQ/.EN pair that only defines the delimiters for inline equations. If you do, extra blank lines will appear in the output.

Do *not* use braces ({ }), a circumflex (^), a tilde (~), or double quotation marks ('') as delimiters because these have a special meaning to eqn. Choose characters that you are unlikely to use within any equation in the document. After you have defined your delimiter, you can begin using it within a line of text as in the following example:

```
The possible prices of an ice cream cone in cents are
#y sub 1 = 75#, #y sub 2 = 85#, and #y sub 3 = 95#.
```

This produces the line:

Assume that the possible prices of an ice cream cone in cents are y_1=76, y_2=85, and y_3=95.

The eqn program leaves enough room before and after a line containing inline expressions with fractions or large characters so that they don't interfere with the surrounding lines.

To turn off the delimiters, use:

```
.EQ
delim off
.EN
```

Throughout this section, we will use the delimiters ## in our eqn examples. However, we will typically show the results as a displayed equation.

· Spaces in Equations ·

You may have noticed in the previous example that the word sub is surrounded by blanks, and the subscript is separated from the = sign with a blank. Spaces and new lines are used to tell eqn that certain words belong to the eqn vocabulary and deserve special treatment. The spaces and new lines that you type in the input equation do *not* appear in the printed output.

For example, all of the following equations:

```
#C=Ax+By#
#C = Ax + By#
#C= A x +
    By#
```

produce the same output:

$$C = Ax + By$$

Note that the spaces and newlines were ignored by eqn.

You should use spaces as freely as possible to break up more complex equations and make your input more readable and easier to edit. Remember that any spaces or newlines you enter within an equation are *not* printed out. This is often a point of confusion for new users. If your equation doesn't turn out the way it should, chances are you missed typing in a space somewhere. A useful rule of thumb is: when in doubt, use a space.

Printing Spaces in the Output

You may want to fine-tune the printed appearance of an equation by adding spaces between groups of terms. If you want to print spaces in the output, use a tilde (~) for each space. A circumflex (^) gives a space half the width of a tilde. For example:

```
#C~=~Ax~+~By#
```

yields:

$$C = Ax + By$$

and:

```
#C^=^Ax^+^By#
```

yields:

$$C = Ax + By$$

You can also use tabs to separate parts of an equation, but the tab stops must set by the `troff` `.ta` request. For example:

```
.ta 1i 1.5i 2i 2.5i
.EQ
x sub 1
+x sub 2
+s sub 1
=10
.EN
.EQ
-2x sub 1
+s sub 1
=42
.EN
```

yields:

$$x_1 \qquad\qquad +x_2 \qquad +s_1 \qquad =10$$
$$-2x_1 \qquad\qquad\qquad\qquad +s_1 \qquad =42$$

(Note that each equation must have its own pair of `.EQ`/`.EN` delimiters.) Another way of aligning equations uses the eqn words `mark` and `lineup`, as you will see later.

Subscripts and Superscripts: A Common Use

Perhaps the most common application of eqn is in generating subscripts and superscripts within a line of text or a table. As you have seen in previous examples, subscripts are denoted by the word `sub`. Superscripts are designated by `sup`. For example:

```
#y sub 1 = x sup 2^+^1#
```

yields:

$$y_1 = x^2 + 1$$

There are two simple rules to remember in writing subscripts and superscripts:

1. Put at least one space or space delimiter (such as ^ or ~) before *and* after the words sup and sub.

2. Leave at least one space or space delimiter after the subscript or superscript.

Let's see the effect on the output when you omit necessary spaces. For example:

```
#y sub 1 =x sup2^+^1#
```

yields:

$$y_{1=x} \, sup \, 2 + 1$$

and:

```
#y sub 1 =x sup 2+^1#
```

yields:

$$y_{1=x}^{2+} 1$$

If you don't leave a space after `sub` or `sup` (as in the first example), `eqn` will not recognize them as special words, and so will not produce a subscript or superscript. Also, if you don't leave a space after the subscript or superscript, `eqn` thinks that the character(s) following it are still part of the subscript or superscript. This is a very common mistake made by new users.

You can also write subscripted subscripts and superscripted superscripts. If a superscript and subscript both appear for the same item, `sub` should come before `sup`. Therefore:

```
#a sub k sup 2#
```

yields:

$$a_k^2$$

Reversing the order of the words:

```
#a sup 2 sub k#
```

yields:

$$a^{2_k}$$

Some equations also require you to type chemical symbols like:

$$2He_4$$

Because `sup` technically means a superscript on something, you must use a place-holder (a pair of double quotation marks) before the word `sup` and write this expression as:

```
#"" sup 2 He sub 4#
```

▪ Using Braces for Grouping ▪

Normally, you would use a blank or a space delimiter to signal the end of a subscript or superscript. But if your subscript or superscript consists of two or more characters or words separated by blanks, or if you are writing nested subscripts or superscripts, this will not work. In this case, use braces to mark the beginning and end of your subscript or superscript.

For example, the line:

```
#r sub {i=5;t=10^years}#
```

yields:

$$r_{i=5;t=10\,years}$$

In contrast, this line without the braces:

```
#r sub i=5;t=10^years#
```

yields:

$$r_{i=5;t=10}\,years$$

In the first example, we used braces to force eqn to treat the string:

```
i=5;t=10 years
```

as a subscript. Use braces to make your intent perfectly clear whenever you are unsure of how eqn will treat the equation. You can also use braces within braces, as in the line:

```
#e sup {i sup {k+1}}#
```

which yields:

$$e^{i^{k+1}}$$

Make sure that a left brace always has a corresponding right brace.

If you have to print braces in your document, enclose them in double quotation marks like "{" and "}".

▪ Special Character Names ▪

In many mathematical equations, you use the Greek alphabet to define variables. To print Greek letters, spell them out in the case that you want. For example, delta produces δ, and DELTA gives Δ. Thus, you only need to spell out the character π, as in:

```
#pi r sup 2#
```

to print:

$$\pi r^2$$

Note that special names don't exist for all uppercase Greek letters, such as ALPHA or ETA, because they are identical to the equivalent English letters. See Table 9-1 for a list of Greek letters.

TABLE 9-1. Names for Greek Letters

Name	Character	Name	Character
DELTA	Δ	iota	ι
GAMMA	Γ	kappa	κ
LAMBDA	Λ	lambda	λ
OMEGA	Ω	mu	μ
PHI	Φ	nu	ν
PI	Π	omega	ω
PSI	Ψ	omicron	o
SIGMA	Σ	phi	φ
THETA	Θ	pi	π
UPSILON	Υ	psi	ψ
XI	Ξ	rho	ρ
alpha	α	sigma	σ
beta	β	tau	τ
chi	χ	theta	θ
delta	δ	upsilon	υ
epsilon	ε	xi	ξ
eta	η	zeta	ζ
gamma	γ		

A common mistake is to forget to put a space around the Greek name. For example, typing:

```
#f(theta)#
```

yields:

$f(theta)$

and not:

$f(\theta)$

which is what we want. Because there are no spaces surrounding the word `theta`, `eqn` doesn't recognize it as a special word.

You can also use `troff` four-character names for characters, as in the description:

```
#c = a \(pl b#
```

which yields:

$c = a + b$

▪ **Special Symbols** ▪

The eqn program recognizes the sequences in Table 9-2 as belonging to the eqn vocabulary, and translates them to the appropriate symbols.

TABLE 9-2. eqn Special Symbols

Sequence	Symbol	Sequence	Symbol
>=	$\geq$	approx	$\approx$
<=	$\leq$	nothing	
==	$\equiv$	cdot	$\cdot$
!=	$\neq$	times	$\times$
+-	$\pm$	del	∇
->	$\rightarrow$	grad	∇
w<-	$\leftarrow$	...	$\cdots$
<<	$\ll$	,...,	$,\cdots,$
>>	$\gg$	sum	$\sum$
inf	∞	int	$\int$
partial	∂	prod	$\prod$
half	$\frac{1}{2}$	union	$\cup$
prime	$'$	inter	$\cap$

The following examples illustrate the use of these character sequences.

```
#C sub O prime
```

yields:

$$C_O{}'$$

and:

```
#0 <= a <= 1#
```

yields:

$$0 \leq a \leq 1$$

and:

```
#del y / del x#
```

yields:

$$\nabla y / \nabla x$$

and:

```
#partial x / partial t#
```

yields:

$$\partial x / \partial t$$

Digits, parentheses, brackets, punctuation marks, and the following mathematical words are converted into roman font instead of the italic font used for other text:

```
sin   cos   tan   sinh  cosh  tanh  arc
max   min   lim   log   ln    exp
Re    Im    and   if    for   det
```

Summations, Integrals, Products, and Limits

Summations, integrals, products, and limits often require an upper and lower part around the symbol. The word `from` indicates the character sequence to be entered at the lower part; the word `to` indicates the upper part. These parts are both optional, but if they are used, they should appear in that order. For example, you would type:

```
#Expected~Value~=~sum from {i=1} to inf pi sub 1 X sub i#
```

to print the following expression:

$$Expected\ Value\ =\ \sum_{i=1}^{\infty}\pi_i X_i$$

Notice that we used braces around the `from` part although this was not neccessary because there were no imbedded blanks in the string `i=1`. But if the `from` and `to` parts contain any blanks to separate special words, you must use braces around them.

A `from` does not necessarily need an accompanying `to`, as you will see in the following example:

```
#lim from {m -> inf} sum from i=0 to m c sup i#
```

which yields:

$$\lim_{m \to \infty} \sum_{i=0}^{m} c^i$$

Square Root Signs

To draw a square root sign, use the word `sqrt`. For example:

```
#sqrt {b sup 2 - 4ac}#
```

yields:

$$\sqrt{b^2-4ac}$$

Square roots of tall quantities appear too dark and heavy. Big square root quantities are better written to the power $1/2$, as in:

$$2C_O/D^{1/2}$$

Creating a cube root or a higher root sign requires a little imagination. You can think of a cube root sign, for example, as consisting of two parts: a superscript 3 (with nothing before it) and a square root sign. However, you can't type:

```
#sup 3 sqrt x#
```

because a sup is a superscript on something. You must use a pair of double quotation marks as a placeholder for sup. For example:

```
#"" sup 3 sqrt x#
```

yields:

$$\sqrt[3]{x}$$

Enclosing Braces and Brackets

You can generate big brackets [], braces {}, parentheses (), and bars | around quantities by using the words left and right, followed by the desired character. For example:

```
#P~=~R~left [ 1^-^{1+i sup n } over i right ]#
```

yields:

$$P = R \left[\frac{1 - 1 + i^n}{i} \right]$$

The resulting brackets (and any character you specify) are made big enough to enclose the quantity. (Braces are typically bigger than brackets and parentheses.) Note the spaces surrounding the words left and right and the character to be expanded.

Two other characters that you can use are the floor and ceiling characters shown in the following example:

```
#left floor a over b right floor !=
left ceiling x over y right ceiling#
```

which yields:

$$\left\lfloor \frac{a}{b} \right\rfloor \neq \left\lceil \frac{x}{y} \right\rceil$$

A left does not need a corresponding right. If the right part is omitted, use braces to enclose the quantity that you want the left bracket to cover. This is useful when you are making piles, as you will see in the next section.

You can also omit the left part, although technically you can't have a right without an accompanying left. To get around this, you must type:

```
#left "" expression right )#
```

The left "" in this equation means a "left nothing."

▪ Other Positional Notation ▪

In addition to subscripts and superscripts, eqn lets you format expressions containing fractions, matrices, and vertical piles.

Fractions

Making a fraction, such as one-third, is as simple as typing "1 over 3." For more complex fractions, eqn automatically positions the fraction bar and adjusts its length. Thus, the line:

```
#Income over Capital~=~Income over Sales~times~Sales
over Capital#
```

yields:

$$\frac{Income}{Capital} = \frac{Income}{Sales} \times \frac{Sales}{Capital}$$

When you have both a sup and an over in the same equation, eqn does sup before over. However, you can always use braces to tell eqn what part goes with what. For example, you would type:

```
#e sup {k over t}#
```

to yield:

$$e^{\frac{k}{t}}$$

You would *not* type:

```
#e sup k over t#
```

The latter form produces:

$$\frac{e^k}{t}$$

which is not what we want.

Arrays and Matrices

To make an array or a matrix, use the word matrix , and the words lcol, ccol, and rcol to denote the position of the columns. For example:

```
.EQ
matrix {
    lcol {1 above 0}
    rcol {half above -1}
}
.EN
```

yields:

$$1 \quad {}^1\!/_2$$
$$0 \quad -1$$

This produces a matrix with the first column left justified and the second column right justified. Each item is separated from the item below it by the word `above`. You can also center the columns using `ccol`. You can adjust each column separately and use as many columns as you like. However, each column must have the *same* number of items in it as the other columns.

A matrix should be used when the items in the columns don't all have the same height (for example, when you have fractions mixed with whole numbers). This forces the items to line up because `matrix` looks at the entire structure before deciding what spacing to use.

Vertical Piles

To make vertical piles or columns of items, use the word `pile` before the equation description and the keyword `above` to separate the items. You can also enclose the piles in big braces or big brackets. For example:

```
.EQ
P~=~left [
    pile { nu sub 1 above nu sub 2 above cdot
    above cdot above cdot above nu sub N }
right ]
.EN
```

yields:

$$P = \begin{bmatrix} v_1 \\ v_2 \\ \cdot \\ \cdot \\ \cdot \\ v_N \end{bmatrix}$$

The items are centered one above the other and separated by the word `above`. Braces enclose the entire pile list. The items in the pile can themselves contain piles.

You can left justify (`lpile`), right justify (`rpile`), or center (`cpile`) the elements of the pile. (A `cpile` is the same as a regular pile.) However, the vertical spacing you get using these three forms will be somewhat larger than the normal pile. For example:

```
.EQ
f sub X (x)^=^left {
   rpile { 0 above 2x above 0 }
   ~~lpile { x < 0 above 0 <= x <= 1 above x > 1}
.EN
```

yields:

$$f_X(x) = \begin{cases} 0 & x<0 \\ 2x & 0\le x\le 1 \\ 0 & x>1 \end{cases}$$

Note that in this example, we have a left brace without a corresponding right brace.

▪ **Diacritical Marks** ▪

With eqn, writing diacritical marks on top of letters is straightforward. The words known by eqn follow, with examples of how they appear on top of the letter x:

```
bar        x̄
under      x
dot        ẋ
dotdot     ẍ
hat        x̂
tilde      x̃
vec        x⃗
dyad       x⃡
```

The following examples show how these keywords are used:

```
#cr e hat pes#
```

yields:

$$cr\hat{e}pes$$

and:

```
#Citr o dotdot en#
```

yields:

$$Citr\ddot{o}en$$

and:

```
#a vec + b vec#
```

yields:

$$\vec{a}+\vec{b}$$

and:

```
#X bar sub st#
```

yields:

$$\bar{X}_{st}$$

The eqn program positions the diacritical marks at the appropriate height. It also makes bar and under the right length to cover the entire item. Other marks are centered above the character(s).

Typing words with diacritical marks may seem confusing at first because you have to leave spaces around the letter and its corresponding mark. Just remember that eqn doesn't print the spaces you type in.

▪ Defining Terms ▪

In some documents, you type a string of characters often, either within the text or within several equations. If you notice a string that is frequently used, you can name it using a define statement within an .EQ and .EN. Then you can use the name within an expression instead of typing the whole string.

Suppose you notice that the string 2 sup i appears repeatedly in equations. You can avoid retyping by naming it 2i, for example, as in the following commands:

```
.EQ
define 2i '2 sup i'
.EN
```

You should enclose the string between single quotation marks or between any two characters that don't appear inside the definition. After you've defined a term, you can use it as a convenient shorthand in other equations, just as if it were one of eqn's special keywords.

A note about using definitions: although a definition can use a previous definition, do *not* define something in terms of itself. Thus:

```
.EQ
define 2i '2 sup i'
define 1/2i '1 over 2i'
.EN
```

is acceptable, but:

```
.EQ
define X 'X bar'
.EN
```

is not because X is defined in terms of itself. If you want to do this, protect the X in the definition with double quotation marks, as in:

```
.EQ
define X ' "X" bar '
.EN
```

You can also redefine eqn keywords. For example, you can make / mean over by typing:

```
.EQ
define / 'over'
.EN
```

▪ Quoted Text ▪

You have seen the use of double quotation marks as placeholders (in the `sup`, `sqrt`, and `define` examples) when `eqn` needs something grammatically but you don't want anything in the output. Quotation marks are also used to get braces and other `eqn` keywords printed in the output. For example:

```
#"{ size beta }"#
```

prints the words:

> { *size beta* }

instead of looking up the two words `size` and `beta` in the `eqn` vocabulary and converting them. (The word `size` is used to change the size of the characters from the 10-point default.)

Any string entirely within quotation marks is not subject to font changes and spacing adjustments normally done by `troff` or `nroff` on the equation. This provides for individual spacing and adjusting, if needed. Thus, the line:

```
#italic "cos(x)" + cos (x)#
```

yields:

> *cos(x)* +cos(*x*)

To print a literal quotation mark, you must escape it with a backslash character in the form \".

▪ Fine-Tuning the Document ▪

Typesetting a technical document is not only a matter of getting the `eqn` vocabulary right so you can print the appropriate mathematical expressions. Although `eqn` tries to make some actions automatic and puts items in the proper places, some fine-tuning is occasionally needed. With `eqn`, you can line up equations, define font sizes and types, and vary horizontal and vertical spacing.

Lining Up Equations

Earlier we showed you how to line up pieces of an equation using tabs. Another method of doing this is to use the commands `mark` and `lineup`. This is useful when you have to line up a series of equations at some horizontal position, often at an equal sign.

For example, you would type in:

```
.EQ
mu~mark =~lambda t
.EN
.EQ
lineup =~int from 0 to t lambda dz
.EN
```

to line up the two equations:

$$\mu = \lambda t$$

$$= \int_0^t \lambda dz$$

The word `mark` can appear *only once* at any place in an equation. Successive equations should also contain `lineup` only once. Thus, when you have a series of equations that require you to line up items in more than one position, like the following:

$a_1 + a_2$	$+ x_1 + x_2$	$= 34$
$2a_1$	$+ 4a_2$	$= 28$
$3a_1$	$+4x_2$	$= 56$

it might be better to line up the pieces of the equation on the left-hand side using tabs, and those on the right-hand side using `mark` and `lineup`.

If at all possible, you should type in the longest expression first to serve as the marking point. If you type in shorter expressions first, `mark` will not have enough room to line up successive longer expressions.

Changing Fonts and Sizes

In `eqn`, equations are automatically set in 10-point type, with standard mathematical conventions to write some characters as roman or italic. To change sizes and fonts, use the following keywords:

`size`	Change to any of the following legal sizes:
	12, 14, 16, 18, 20, 22, 24, 28, 36
	You can also change the size by a relative amount, such as `size +2` to make a character 2 points bigger, or `size -2` to make it 2 points smaller.
`bold`	Change to bold.
`fat`	Widen the current font by overstriking.

```
italic              Change to italic.

roman               Change to roman.
```

Like `sup` and `sub`, these keywords only apply to the character(s) immediately following them, and revert to the original size and font at the next space. To affect more complex or longer strings (such as a whole equation), use braces. Consider the following examples:

```
#bold qP#                qP
#roman alpha~beta#       α β
#fat half#               ½
#size +3 x =y#           x=y
#size 8 {A + B}#         A +B
```

If the entire paper is to be typeset in a nonstandard size or format, you can avoid redefining each and every character sequence by setting a global size (`gsize`) or font (`gfont`) that will affect the whole document. You can set this up at the top of your file (or wherever the font and size changes begin) within an `.EQ` and `.EN`.

For example, to change the fonts to roman and the size to 12, you could enter:

```
.EQ
gfont R
gsize 12
.EN
```

The rest of the equations in the document (up to another `gfont` or `gsize`) will be set in 12-point roman type. You can use any other `troff` font names in place of `R`.

Horizontal and Vertical Motions

You have already learned how to obtain small extra horizontal spaces in the output using `~` and `^`. To move terms at some arbitrary length backward or forward, use the commands `back` *n* and `fwd` *n*, where *n* denotes how far you want to move, in 1/100s of an em. (An em is about the width of the letter *m*).

You can also move items up or down using `up` *n* or `down` *n*, where *n* is the same unit of measure as described. These local horizontal and vertical motions affect only the character(s) next to the keyword. To move larger strings or whole expressions, enclose them in braces.

▪ Keywords and Precedence ▪

Braces are used to group items or change the precedence of operations if you are unsure of how `eqn` will treat multiple keywords in a single expression. If you don't use braces, `eqn` performs the operations in the following order:

```
dyad vec under bar tilde hat dot dotdot
fwd back down up
fat roman italic bold size
sub sup sqrt over
from to
```

All operations group to the right, except for the following, which group to the left:

```
over sqrt left right
```

· Problem Checklist ·

The eqn program usually displays self-explanatory messages when it encounters a syntax error or any other formatting error. To check a document before printing, type:

$ **eqn** *files* **> /dev/null**

This discards the output but prints the error message. Some of the error messages you might encounter are:

```
eqn: syntax error between lines 14 and 42, file book
```

A syntax error (such as leaving out a brace, having one too many braces, having a sup with nothing before it, or using a wrong delimiter) has occurred between lines 14 and 42, approximately, in the file book. These line numbers are not accurate, so you have to look at nearby lines as well. If the following message is displayed:

```
word overflow
```

you have exceeded the limits of troff's internal buffer. If you print the equation as a displayed equation, this message will usually go away. If the message is line overflow, the only solution is to break up the equation across multiple lines, marking each with a separate .EQ and .EN. The eqn program does not warn about equations that are too long for one line. If the following message is displayed:

```
eqn: fatal error: Unexpected end of input at 2 sub a
```

you forgot to put a closing quotation mark after the string 2 sub a when you named it in the define statement.

It is also easy to leave out an ending delimiter in an equation. In this case, eqn thinks that successive character sequences (which may run to hundreds of lines) are still part of the inline expression. You may then get an overflow error or a garbled document. The checkeq program checks for misplaced or missing inline delimiters and similar problems.

For example, when run on a draft of this chapter, checkeq produced the following report:

```
$ checkeq sect1
sect1:
    New delims ##, line 6
    2 line ##, lines 618-619
```

```
2 line ##, lines 619-620
2 line ##, lines 620-621
               .

               .

               .

EQ in ##, line 689
EN in ##, line 691
13 line ##, lines 709-721
               .

               .

               .

2 line ##, lines 1300-1301
2 line ##, lines 1301-1302
Unfinished ##
```

This report (which ran to 66 lines) was telling us that somewhere before line 618 there was an unclosed inline equation using the delimeter #. Sure enough, the following error was found:

```
B#f( theta )
```

Because there was only one delimiter, eqn gets "out of phase" and all subsequent delimiters are misplaced. After we fixed this one error, checkeq printed the following "null" report:

```
$ checkeq sect1
sect1:
```

Because a simple problem like the one shown here can cause every subsequent equation in the file to be garbled, and can waste an entire formatting run, it makes sense to run checkeq before you format any files containing equations.

10

Drawing Pictures

If you are one of those who can't draw a straight line, let alone a decent picture or graph, you probably replace pictures with verbal descriptions. Perhaps you know what it is like to describe a drawing to a person who knows how to draw. The `pic` preprocessor requires you to follow the process of using ''words'' to describe something pictorial.

The `pic` preprocessor has a dual purpose. The first is to provide a ''natural language'' method of describing simple pictures and graphs in your documents. The second is to offer a ''programming language'' for generating pictures and graphs with minimal user input. Learning `pic` is an iterative process: describe what you want and then look at what you get. We have included many examples that show both the description and the resulting picture or graph. Take the time to create variations of these descriptions, making modifications and improvements.

The `pic` preprocessor was designed to produce output on a typesetter, which makes `pic` expensive and difficult to learn. Fortunately, some graphics terminals and most laser printers can be set up to display or print `pic` drawings. Access to one or the other is essential if you are going to get enough practice to know how `pic` responds.

As a preprocessor, `pic` is a program that processes a specific portion of an input file before the whole document goes to the `troff` formatter. (The `nroff` formatter cannot produce `pic` output for terminals or line printers.) The preprocessors translate your description into low-level formatter requests for `troff`.

Just like with `tbl` and `eqn`, a pair of macros in the input file mark the beginning and end of input to be processed by `pic`. The delimiters for `pic` are:

```
.PS
pic description
.PE
```

When you format a document that contains `pic` descriptions, you must invoke the `pic` preprocessor as follows:

```
$ pic file | troff | device
```

▪ The `pic` Preprocessor ▪

Imagine that you have to describe over the telephone the following picture:

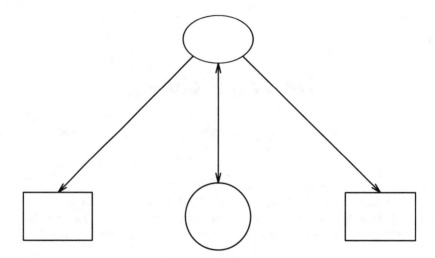

You might say: "There's an ellipse at the top. Arrows are connected to two boxes and a circle below it." Now, think about describing this picture to someone who is attempting to draw it. No matter how careful you are, you realize that it is difficult to translate a drawing into words.

> "First, draw an ellipse. Move down and draw a circle below it. Then draw one box to the left and draw another box of the same size to the right. Then draw an arrow from the bottom of the ellipse to the top of the left-hand box. Then draw a line from the bottom of the ellipse to the top of the right-hand box. The last thing to do is draw a line between the circle and the ellipse and put arrowheads on both ends."

Here's what the actual `pic` description looks like:

```
.PS
down
ellipse
move down 1.25
circle radius .35
move left 1i from left of last circle; box
move right 1i from right of last circle; box
arrow from lower left of last ellipse to top of 1st box
arrow from lower right of last ellipse to top of 2nd box
arrow <-> from bottom of last ellipse to top of last circle
.PE
```

Even though you may know nothing about `pic`, you should be able to make some sense out of this description. It names several objects: an ellipse, two boxes, a circle, and three arrows. It specifies motion in inches as well as changes in direction. It also arranges some objects in relation to others, locating the boxes to the left and right of the circle and drawing arrows between the ellipse and the circle.

Having seen a full description of a `pic` drawing in this example, you should be able to get something of the flavor of `pic`. The simpler the drawing, the less explaining you have to do. We won't go into any more detail about this `pic` description right now. We'll look at it later in this chapter after we've covered the basics of the `pic` language.

Naming Objects

The `pic` program is easy to use if you are describing only a single box or a circle. To draw a circle, you name that object within the `.PS`/`.PE` macros:

```
.PS
circle
.PE
```

When this description is processed by `pic` it produces:

There are seven graphics primitives: `arc`, `arrow`, `box`, `circle`, `ellipse`, `line`, and `spline`. We will show these primitives in examples that present additional aspects of `pic`.

In using a computer language, you have to be precise, using as few words as possible to get the picture you want. This means that you allow the program to make as many of the decisions about the drawing as is practical. After you understand `pic`'s normal behavior, you will know what `pic` will do on its own.

For instance, we didn't specify the size of the circle in the last example. By default, `pic` draws a circle with a diameter of $1/2$ inch (or a radius of .25 inch). You can get a circle of a different size, but you have to specify the size.

```
.PS
circle radius .5
.PE
```

The `pic` program understands any number to be in inches. You specify the size of a circle by giving its `radius`, which can be abbreviated as `rad`, or its `diameter`, which can be abbreviated as `diam`. The previous input produces a circle twice the size of the standard circle:

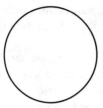

Similarly, if you specify `box`, you will get a box with a height of .5 inch and a width of .75 inch. You can get a larger or smaller box by changing its dimensions:

```
.PS
box height 1i width .5
.PE
```

The output for this example is a box twice as high as it is wide:

You can also use the abbreviations `ht` and `wid` for these attributes. The order in which you specify the dimensions does not matter, and you can change one attribute without changing the other. That is how we can draw a square:

```
.PS
box ht .75
.PE
```

The default width is already .75 inch, so this `pic` description produces:

With the attribute `same`, you can reuse the dimensions specified for a previous object of the same type. For instance, after you had described the square box, `box same` would duplicate a square of the same size.

Labeling Objects

To provide a label for any object, specify the text within double quotation marks after the name of the object. The label is placed at the center of the object.

```
.PS
box ht .75 "Square One"
.PE
```

This `pic` description produces:

Even if a label does not contain blank spaces, you must enclose it within double quotation marks. Each individually quoted item will be output on a new line.

```
box wid .5 "Second" "Square"
```

This description produces:

Because `troff`, not `pic`, actually handles the text, `pic` doesn't really try to fit a label inside an object. You must determine the amount of text that will fit. The `pic` program ignores lines beginning with a period, permitting you to use `troff` requests to change the point size, font, or typeface. It is best to avoid spacing requests, and be sure to reset any change in point size.

When you specify a single text label with a `line`, `pic` centers it on the line. For instance, inline `troff` requests can be used to print a label in 14-point italic (i.e., 4 points larger than the current point size).

```
.PS
line "\fI\s14pic\s10\fR"
.PE
```

It produces:

pic

Because the standard placement of labels is not always useful, you can specify the attributes `above` or `below`. In the following example, the point size is specified using the following `.ps` request:

```
.ps +2
line "\fIPIC\fR" above
.ps -2
```

It produces:

PIC

If you supply two quoted arguments with `line`, the first will be printed above the line and the second printed below.

You can also select a `line` or `box` that is `dotted` or `dashed`, as you can see in the next example:

```
box dotted "\f(CWbox dotted\fP" above
```

Note the inline request to invoke the constant-width font for the label. The `above` keyword places the label above the center line of the box. This description produces:

The box, composed of dots, contains a label printed in constant-width font. It is obvious here that `pic` made no attempt to fit the label "inside" the box. The `above` attribute does not place text above the box, but rather above the center of the box. The description:

```
line dashed "sign here" below
```

produces a dashed line:

sign here

If the attributes of texture are followed by a value, `pic` will try to keep that amount of spacing between the dashes or dots. The description `dashed .1` will result in dashes spaced .1 inch apart.

`pic`'s Drawing Motion

After you have named an object and determined its size, you have to think about where `pic` is going to draw it. (Indentation and other matters concerning the placement of the drawing on the page are supplied by either the `.PS/.PE` or `.DS/.DE` macros. The `pic` program places a single object at the left margin. If you name three objects in the same description, where will `pic` draw them?

```
.PS
circle "A"
line "1" "2"
box "B"
.PE
```

The following output is produced:

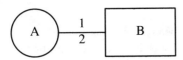

Objects are placed one after another from left to right. The `pic` program assumes that objects should be connected, as in the following example:

```
.PS
box ht 1.25
box ht 1
box ht .75
box ht .5
.PE
```

This description produces a row of boxes of decreasing size:

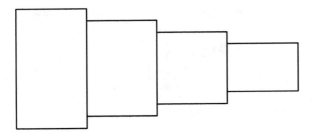

If you don't want objects to be connected, you can `move` before specifying the next object. In the next example, `move` places a `box` to the right of a `circle`:

```
.PS
circle "A" ; move; box "B"
.PE
```

As shown in this example, `pic` commands can be entered on the same line, separated by semicolons, instead of on separate lines. This description produces:

Changing Direction

As you have seen, pic places objects in a continuous motion from left to right. You can also get pic to change direction using the attributes left, right, up, or down. We'll see examples of their use shortly.

The distance of a move is the same length as a line (.5 inch). If you want to change the distance of a move or the length of a line, then the change must be accompanied by an attribute of direction. Although it seems natural to write:

```
line 2; move 1; arrow 1    Wrong
```

pic does not accept this command unless you specify directions for all three cases. When pic objects to your choice of words, it will display the offending line, using a caret (^) to mark the error.

```
pic: syntax error near line 1, file test
 context is
        line 2 ^; move 1
```

Only the first error on the line is marked. (It is acceptable to write line; move, using the standard length and distance.) The next example shows how to draw a line of a specified length and how to move a specified distance. The pic program assumes that any value is in inches; thus you can say 2i or simply 2 to indicate 2 inches.

```
line up 2; move down 1; arrow right 1
```

Note that the attribute of direction precedes the distance. The preceding description produces:

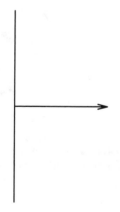

You cannot specify down 1 or right 1 without also specifying either a line or move. These attributes change the direction of the motion used to draw objects. They do not cause movement. The attributes of direction affect the position of the objects that follow it, as shown in the next example.

```
.PS
down; circle "A"; line; box "B"
.PE
```

These objects are drawn from top to bottom:

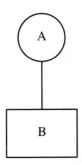

If you describe a change of motion, it affects the points where objects are connected. Look what happens if we specify the attribute down *after* the circle:

```
.PS
circle "A"; down; line; box "B"
.PE
```

Now the line begins at a different position:

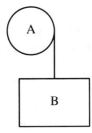

The pic program keeps track of the start and end points for each object, and
their relationship to the direction in which objects are being drawn. The next object is
drawn from the exit point of the previous object. Entry and exit points may seem obvious for a line, but not so obvious with circles. When the motion is from left to right, a
circle's entry point is at 9 o'clock and its exit point is at 3 o'clock. When we specified
down after the circle in the first example, the exit point of the circle did not
change; only the direction in which the line was drawn from that point changed. Entry
and exit points are reversed when the motion is from right to left, as specified by the
left attribute.

```
left; arrow; circle "A"; arrow; box "B"
```

This description produces:

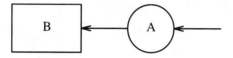

You can draw a diagonal line by applying two changes in direction. Look at how we describe a right triangle:

```
.PS
line down 1i
line right 1i
line up 1i left 1i
.PE
```

This description produces:

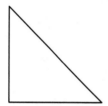

The diagonal line is drawn by combining two attributes of direction, up and left. You can describe a continuous line using then. In the next example we use arrow to demonstrate that we are describing a single object.

```
.PS
arrow down 1i then right 1i then up 1i left 1i
.PE
```

When using then, you have to define the motion on a single line or escape the end of the line with a backslash (\). It produces:

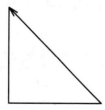

If the description ended with:

```
then up 1i then left 1i
```

we would have a 1-inch square instead of a right triangle.

An `arc` is a portion of a circle. Naming four arcs consecutively will draw a circle. An arc is drawn counterclockwise from the current position (from 6 o'clock to 3 o'clock, for instance). The next example uses arcs to produce a box with rounded corners:

```
line right 1; arc; line up ; arc
line left 1; arc; line down; arc
```

This description starts with the bottom line of the curved box. The motion is counter-clockwise.

The attribute `cw` draws an arc in a clockwise direction:

```
arc "A"; arc "B" cw
```

This description produces:

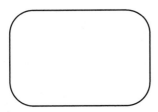

Note that text is placed at what `pic` considers to be the center of the arc, which is the center of the corresponding circle.

A `spline` is a cross between an `arc` and a `line`. It is used to draw smoothed curves. In this example, a spline traces a path between two circles.

```
circle rad .25
spline right 1 then down .5 left 1 then right 1
circle same
```

This description produces:

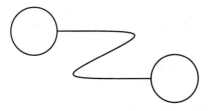

A `spline` is used in the same way as a `line`. When drawn continuously using `then`, a `spline` that changes direction draws a curve. (Similarly, a `line` would produce an angle.) We'll see more examples of `spline` later.

Placing Objects

It isn't always useful to place objects in a continuous motion. Look at the following example, which seems like it ought to work but doesn't:

```
.PS
down; arrow; box
right; arrow; ellipse; arrow
.PE
```

This `pic` description produces:

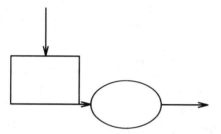

Note the short arrow, drawn from the box to the circle. What happened? The end point of the box was not on the right, but on the bottom, because the motion in effect where the box is drawn is `down`. Changing direction (`right`) affects only the direction in which the arrow is drawn; it does not change where the arrow begins. Thus, the arrow is drawn along the bottom line of the box.

Sometimes, it is best to place an object in relation to previously placed objects. The `pic` program provides a natural way to locate objects that have been drawn. For example, the attribute `first` locates the first occurrence of an object, and the attribute `from` specifies that the object serves as a starting point for the next object drawn.

```
.PS
circle ; move; circle ; arrow up from first circle
.PE
```

It produces:

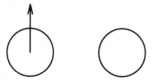

You can reference each type of object using an ordinal number. Referring to the order in which an object is drawn, you can say `first box` (`1st box` is also acceptable) or `2nd circle`. You can also work back from the last object, specifying the `last box` or `2nd last box`.

The center of each object is used as the reference point. In the last example, the arrow was drawn from the center of the circle. The attribute `chop` can be used to chop off the part of the line that would extend to the center of each circle. In the next example, a chopped line is drawn between the first and third circles:

```
.PS
circle "1" ; move down from last circle
circle "2"; move right from last circle; circle "3"
line from 1st circle to last circle chop
.PE
```

This description produces:

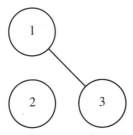

The amount that is chopped is by default equal to the radius of the circle. You can specify how much of the line is chopped, for use with other objects or text, by supplying either one or two values after the attribute. If a single value is given, then both ends of the line are chopped by that amount. If two values are given, the start of the line is chopped by the first amount and the end of the line chopped by the second amount.

It is important to remember that movement `from` a referenced object is measured from its center, unless otherwise specified. Look at these four circles:

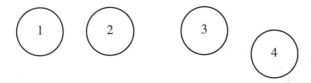

The second circle is produced by the description:

```
move right from last circle; circle "2"
```

Because the distance (.5 inch by default) is measured from the center of the circle, there is only .25 inch between the two circles. The third circle is produced by the description:

```
move right from right of last circle; circle "3"
```

Now the distance is measured from the right of the second circle. There is twice as much space between the second and third circle as between the first and second. The fourth circle is produced by the description:

```
move right from bottom of last circle; circle "4"
```

The starting point of the fourth circle (its left "side") is .5 inch right from the bottom of the previous circle.

Using bottom, top, right, and left, you can locate specific points on any object. In the next example, we solve the problem of turning a corner by specifying the place from which the arrow will be drawn:

```
.PS
down; arrow; box
right; arrow from right of last box; ellipse; arrow ; box
up; arrow from top of last box
.PE
```

In our earlier example, the arrow was drawn from the bottom of the box; now we change the starting point of the arrow to the right of the previous box. This description produces:

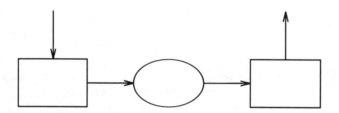

With boxes and ellipses, you can refer to an upper or lower position:

```
.PS
box; arrow from upper right of last box;
arrow down from lower left of last box
.PE
```

This description produces:

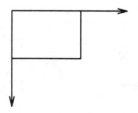

With objects like lines and arcs, it is more useful to refer to the start and end of the object. For example, here's another way to draw a triangle:

```
.PS
line down 1i
line right
line from start of 1st line to end of 2nd line
.PE
```

The last line could also be written:

```
line to start of 1st line
```

The pic description produces:

You now know enough of the basic features of pic to benefit from a second look at the pic description shown at the beginning of this chapter. The only thing we haven't covered is how to get a double-headed arrow. Because an arrow can also be specified as line -> or line <-, you can get a double-headed arrow with line <->.

```
     .PS
1    down
2    ellipse
3    move down 1.25
4    circle radius .35
5    move left 1i from left of last circle; box
6    move right 1i from right of last circle; box
7    arrow from lower left of last ellipse to top of \
     1st box
8    arrow from lower right of last ellipse to top of \
     2nd box
9    line <-> from bottom of last ellipse to top of last \
     circle
     .PE
```

The lines in this description are numbered for easy reference in the following exercise.

As is true with almost anything you describe, a pic description could be written in several different ways. In fact, you will learn a lot about pic by making even minor changes and checking the results. See if you can answer these questions:

- Why is down specified before the ellipse? If you removed down, would the circle be centered underneath the ellipse?

- down changes direction of movement. Does pic allow you to say move 1.25 as well as move down 1.25?

- Where is the exit point of the circle when it is drawn with a downward motion in effect? If lines 5 and 6 were replaced by:

```
move left 1i; box
move right 2i; box
```

where would the boxes be drawn?

- There is 1 inch between the circle and each box. How much space would there be if lines 5 and 6 were replaced by:

```
move left from last circle; box
move right from last circle; box
```

Hint: The distance of a move is .5 inch, and this would be measured from the center of the circle, which has a radius of .35 inch.

- Line 8 draws an arrow from the lower right of the ellipse to the top of the right-hand box. If it were simplified to:

```
arrow from last ellipse to 2nd box
```

where would the beginning and ending of the arrow be?

- This drawing can present an interesting problem if the circle is omitted. How would you draw the two boxes if the circle was not there as a reference point?

Fortunately, there is a simple way to deal with the problem presented in the last question. Lacking a reference object, you can create an invisible one using the invis attribute. This lets you specify a circle that is not drawn but still holds a place that you can reference.

```
.PS
down
ellipse
move down 1.25
circle radius .35 invis
move left 1i from left of last circle; box
move right 1i from right of last circle; box
arrow from lower left of last ellipse to top of 1st box
arrow from lower right of last ellipse to top of 2nd box
.PE
```

This `pic` description produces:

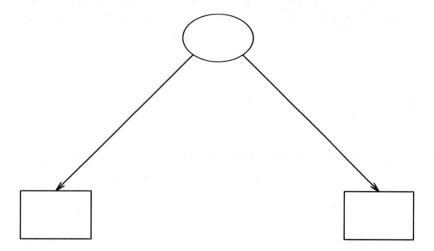

One thing that seems hard to get used to is that your current position always changes after an object is drawn, based on the motion in effect. This means you have to keep in mind the location of the starting point for the next object that you are going to draw.

You can use braces to enclose an object (or a series of objects or motions) so that the starting point is unchanged. In the last drawing, if the `invis` attribute didn't solve the problem so easily, we could have used braces to maintain a central point below the ellipse from which you can move to draw the boxes. Here's a different example that illustrates how braces can be used to control your position:

```
.PS
{arrow down}
{arrow up}
{arrow left}
arrow right
.PE
```

Each object, except the last, is enclosed in braces; all objects share the same starting point. This description produces:

Placing Text

Text can be placed in a drawing just like an object. You have to take care in placing text, as in the next example, where we specify a move so that the compass points are not drawn on top of the arrowheads:

```
.PS
{arrow down; move; "S" }
{arrow up; move; "N" }
{arrow left; move; "W" }
{arrow right; move; "E" }
.PE
```

Notice that the attributes of direction cause the object to be drawn in that direction and establish a new motion for successive objects. This description produces:

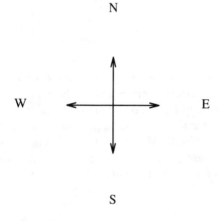

As mentioned, `pic` does not really handle text, allowing `troff` to do the work. In some ways, this is unfortunate. The thing to remember is that `pic` does not know where the text begins or ends. (You can use the attributes `ljust` or `rjust` to have the text left justified—the first character is positioned at that point—or right justified—the last character is at that point. These attributes can also be used with text labels.)

The `pic` program does not keep track of the start and the end of a text object. It only knows a single point which is the point where `troff` centers the text. In other words, a text item does not cause a change in position. Two consecutive quoted items of text (not used as labels to another object) will overwrite one another. Objects are drawn without regard to where the text item is, as shown in the next example:

```
"Start"; line;arrow;line; "Finish"
```

This description produces:

Start────────────➤────────Finish

This example can be improved by right justifying the first text item (`"Start"` `rjust`) and left justifying the last text item (`"Finish"` `ljust`). As you'll notice, though, the picture starts at the margin, and the label is forced out where it doesn't belong.

StartFinish

The location of the point that `pic` knows about is unchanged. Most of the time, you will have to use the `move` command before and after inserting text.

Because `pic` works better with objects than text, the `invis` attribute can be used to disguise the object behind the text, and give you a way to place text where you can point to it.

```
.PS
down
ellipse invis "DECISION?"
move down 1.25
circle rad .35 invis "Maybe"
move left 1i from left of last circle; box invis "Yes"
move right 1i from right of last circle; box invis "No"
arrow from lower left of last ellipse to top of 1st box
arrow from lower right of last ellipse to top of 2nd box
line <-> from bottom of last ellipse to top of last circle
.PE
```

This description produces:

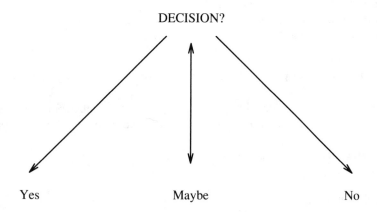

You may have recognized that the description for this drawing is basically the same one that produced the drawing at the beginning of this chapter. The `invis` attribute makes text labels, not objects, the subject of this picture. This should lead you to the idea that `pic` descriptions can be reused. Try to think of the form of a drawing separately from its content. Most drawings contain forms that can be reworked in the service of new material.

Place and Position Notation

Can you locate the starting points of the arrows on this ellipse?

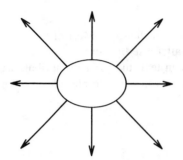

To write the description for this example is a test of patience and thoroughness, if nothing else. We start at the `upper left` of the ellipse and move clockwise around the ellipse.

```
.PS
ellipse
arrow up left from upper left of last ellipse
arrow up from top of last ellipse
arrow up right from upper right of last ellipse
arrow right from right of last ellipse
arrow right down from lower right of last ellipse
arrow down from bottom of last ellipse
arrow left down from lower left of last ellipse
arrow left from left of last ellipse
.PE
```

Although you can say `upper left` or `lower left`, you cannot say `top left` or `bottom right`.

Sometimes `pic`'s English-like input can get to be cumbersome. Fortunately, `pic` supports several different kinds of place and position notations that shorten descriptions.

You can reduce the phrase:

```
from bottom of last ellipse
```

to either of the following:

```
from .b of last ellipse
from last ellipse.b
```

You can use this notation for the primary points of any object. You can also refer to the compass points of an object, which provides a way to specify corners. Table 10-1 lists the placename notations.

TABLE 10-1. `pic` Placename Notation

Value	Position
t	Top
b	Bottom
l	Left
r	Right
n	North
e	East
w	West
s	South
nw	Northwest
sw	Southwest
ne	Northeast
se	Southeast

Instead of writing:

```
from lower left of last ellipse
```

you might write:

```
from last ellipse.sw
```

Another simple way to shorten a description is to give an object its own name. The name must begin with an uppercase letter. If we assign the placename `Elp` to the ellipse:

```
Elp: ellipse
```

then we have either of the following ways to refer to specific points:

```
arrow up left from upper left of Elp
arrow up left from Elp.nw
```

Here's the condensed version of the description for the previous example:

```
.PS
Elp: ellipse
arrow up left from Elp.nw
arrow up from Elp.n
arrow up right from Elp.ne
arrow right from Elp.e
arrow right down from Elp.se
arrow down from Elp.s
arrow left down from Elp.sw
arrow left from Elp.w
.PE
```

At least it helps to keep you from confusing the placement of the arrow with the drawing motion.

If you want to specify a point that is not at one of the compass points, you can indicate a point somewhere in between two places. You can use the following kind of construction:

fraction of the way between *first.position* and *second.position*

or use the following notation:

fraction < *first.position, second.position* >

The following example shows both forms:

```
box
arrow down left from 1/2 of the way between last box.sw \
and last box.w
arrow down right from 1/2 < last box.se, last box.e >
```

Although you may not want to intermix different forms for the sake of someone reading the description, `pic` does allow it. The preceding description produces:

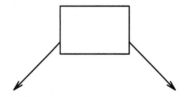

The `at` attribute can be used to position objects in a drawing.

```
box "A"; box with .se at last box.nw "B"
box with .sw at last box.ne "C"
```

This description produces:

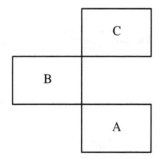

The next example illustrates again the problem of placing text. This time we want to position callouts above and below the text.

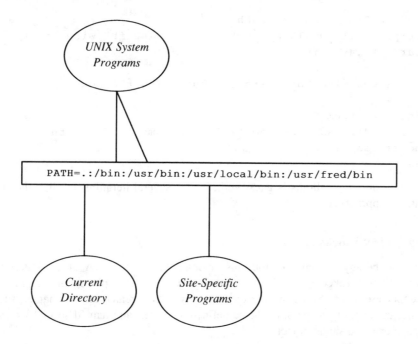

We position the text inside a long box. Because the callout lines will point to the box that surrounds the text rather than to the text itself, we try to specify approximately where to draw the lines.

```
.PS
        #     "#" introduces a comment
        #
        # Describe box; escape end of line to include
        # text on separate line
        #
Path: box ht .25 wid 4 \
"\f(CWPATH=.:/bin:/usr/bin:/usr/local/bin:/usr/fred/bin\fR"
        #
        # Describe line down from box and put top of ellipse
        # at end of last line; label will be printed
        # in 9-point italic.
        #
line down from 1/3 <Path.sw, Path.s>
ellipse "\fI\s9Current" "Directory\s0\fP" with .t at \
end of last line
        #
        # Describe two lines, one up from box
        # and a second down to the point right of it.
        #
line up from 1/2 <Path.nw, Path.n>
```

```
line to 2/3 <Path.nw, Path.n>
ellipse "\fI\s9UNIX System" "Programs\s0\fP" with .b at \
start of last line
    #
    # Describe the third callout below the box.
    #
line down from Path.s
ellipse "\fI\s9Site-Specific" "Programs\s0\fP" with .t at \
end of last line
.PE
```

Admittedly, positioning callouts is guesswork; it took several iterations to align the callouts with the appropriate text.

Defining Object Blocks

You can describe any sequence of motions or objects as a block. A block is defined between a pair of brackets ([ ]). You can also give the block a placename, beginning with an uppercase letter. Some of the objects that we have created in this chapter, such as a square, triangle, or compass, could be defined as blocks and named so that we can refer to each one as a single object.

```
Rtriangle: [
        linewid = 1
        line down then right then up left
        ]
.ps 18
.ft I
"1" at Rtriangle.w
"2" at Rtriangle.s
"3" at Rtriangle
.ft R
.ps 10
```

This description produces:

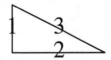

We are able to refer to the compass points of the block, although these points may not always be where you expect. The number 3 is printed at the center of Rtriangle according to pic. But in fact its position is the side opposite the right angle. The "center" of this block is at the center of a box that shares the bottom and left sides of the right triangle.

You can also refer to positions for a single block using brackets. The reference [].w is a position at the west end of the block.

In this example, instead of specifying individual line lengths, we redefined the variable `linewid`. This is the variable that `pic` accesses to determine how long a line should be. Shortly, we'll look at all the variables preset by `pic`. Generally, what you describe within a block remains local to the block. Thus, `linewid` would not affect other lines outside the block. Otherwise, resetting a variable has an effect not only on other objects in that drawing but also on other drawings in that file.

The best use of blocks in a drawing is to define significant portions so that you can position them accurately. Blocks usually relate to the content of a drawing. In the next example, we describe a two-dimensional box to represent a modem.

```
MOD: [
BOXA: box wid 1 ht .25 " \(bu    \(bu    \(bu    \(bu    \(bu "
line from BOXA.nw up 1 right .5 x
then right 1 then down 1 left .5 to BOXA.ne
line from BOXA.se up 1 right .5 then up .25
]
```

The block, named MOD, consists of a box followed by a series of lines. The box is given a name, BOXA. The special character sequence \(bu represents a bullet (interpreted by `troff`, not `pic`). This description produces:

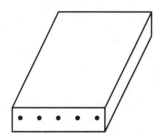

The next block, named WALL, describes a drawing of a telephone wall socket. It contains two objects, a box named BOXB and a circle inside the box named CIR.

```
WALL: [
BOXB: box wid .25 ht .5
CIR: circle at center of BOXB radius .05
]  with .s at MOD.ne + (.5,1)
```

To position this block in relation to MOD, we describe a position 1 inch up and .5 inch to the left of the top right-hand corner of MOD. Then we draw a spline from the modem to the wall socket. This introduces us to the fact that no matter how we specify an object, `pic` locates that object in a Cartesian coordinate system. We'll look at this in more detail in a later section. For now, it is sufficent to note how we change position by adding or subtracting from the position on the x-axis and y-axis. MOD.ne+(.5,1) adds .5 to the x-axis (moving to the right) and 1 to the y-axis (moving up) from the coordinates of MOD.ne.

```
spline from MOD.n up .25 right .5 then right 1 to center \
of WALL.CIR
```

Notice that we can refer to objects inside a block. If we had not named the circle, we could still refer to it as `WALL.circle`.

The last thing to do is to position the text:

```
move right 1 from WALL.e; " Telephone Line"
move down .5 from MOD.s "Modem"
```

This entire description produces the following drawing:

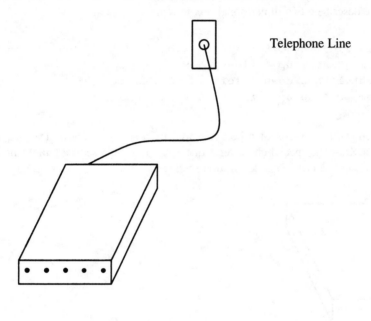

Telephone Line

Modem

Resetting Standard Dimensions

The `pic` program has a number of built-in variables that define the values used to draw standard `pic` objects.

Refer to Table 10-2. You can redefine these variables anywhere in a `pic` description. A variable set inside one `pic` description will remain in effect for other descriptions within the same file. One exception is a variable defined within a block; that definition is local to the block.

TABLE 10-2. `pic` System Variables

Variable	Default Value	Meaning
arcrad	.25	Radius of arc
arrowwid	.05	Width or thickness of arrowhead
arrowht	.1	Height or length of arrowhead
boxwid	.75	Width of box
boxht	.5	Height of box
circlerad	.25	Radius of circle
dashwid	.05	Width of dash
ellipseht	.5	Height of ellipse
linewid	.5	Length of horizontal line
lineht	.5	Length of vertical line
movewid	.5	Distance of horizontal motion
moveht	.5	Distance of vertical motion
scale	1	Scale dimensions
textwid	0	Width of area used for drawing
textht	0	Height of area used for drawing

For instance, we can specify an oversize arrow by changing the following variables:

```
arrowwid = 1
arrowht = 1
linewid = 2
arrow
```

It produces the following `pic` drawing:

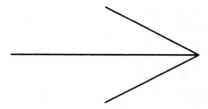

Controlling the Dimensions of a Drawing

The `textwid` and `textht` variables control the width and height respectively, of the area used by `pic` on a page. (It doesn't refer to the amount of space occupied by an item of text.) These values can also be set as arguments to the `.PS` macro.

`.PS` *width height*

When you specify the width or height or both, `pic` scales the drawing to that size regardless of the absolute dimensions that are specified within the drawing. The only thing it doesn't scale adequately is text. It can be easier to describe a drawing with simple units and have them scaled more precisely to fit on the page than to work with exact sizes.

A good example of scaling is turning the rounded box described previously in this chapter into a representation of a terminal screen.

```
.PS 2 4
line right 1; arc; line up ; arc
line left 1; arc; line down; arc
.PE
```

Although the `pic` description is made up of 1-inch lines, the actual screen produced by `pic` will be 4 inches wide and 2 inches high.

Normally, you want `troff` to output the regular lines of text on lines that follow the `pic` drawing. If the `.PF` (*F* for *flyback*) macro is used in place of `.PE`, `troff` will return to the position it held before the `pic` drawing was output. This feature is useful if we want to put formatted text within our large screen.

```
.PS 2 4
line right 1; arc; line up ; arc
line left 1; arc; line down; arc
.PE
.ft CW
.sp 2
Alcuin Development System          5/31/87
.sp
Please login:
.sp 6
```

This description produces:

```
Alcuin Development System          5/31/87

Please login:
```

You have to remember to provide the space after the text to push the current position past the end of the screen. Otherwise subsequent text will also appear within the box.

Debugging `pic` Descriptions

You can invoke the `pic` preprocessor on its own to have it check through your file and report any syntax errors. This can save a lot of time, especially if your file contains other text that will be sent to `troff`, assuming that you wouldn't want the file processed unless the `pic` descriptions succeeded. If you have the file `circles`, for example, that contains a `pic` description, you can invoke `pic` as:

```
$ pic circles
```

If processing is successful, `pic` output will stream past on your terminal screen. If `pic` finds an error in your description, it will print the error message.

If you have several `pic` descriptions in a file, or you have regular text surrounding a `pic` description, you can send the output to `/dev/null`, and only the error messages will be displayed on your screen.

You may want to invoke `pic` on its own simply to look at the output `pic` produces. For a discussion of the output that `pic` sends to `troff`, read about line drawing in Chapter 14.

• From Describing to Programming Drawings •

As we look at more advanced examples of `pic`, you may begin to question the amount of description that is required to produce a drawing. You may be amazed that drawings that look so simple require so many words. After you realize that you are approaching the limits of what can be described using an English-like syntax, you may want to look at `pic` from another perspective. You can view `pic` as a programming language for generating graphics.

Looking at this other side of `pic`, you will find that the descriptions are perhaps more difficult to read but much easier to write. The purpose of a "programmed" `pic` description is not to imitate a verbal description, but to minimize user input, to provide structures that can be used to produce several kinds of drawings, and to make it easier to change a drawing.

The focus of the rest of this chapter will be to introduce many of these special features of `pic`, including variables, expressions, and macros. But there are more possibilities than we can attempt to describe. The `pic` program follows the general UNIX philosophy that any program should be able to accept input from any program and direct its output to another program, `troff`. Thus, `pic` descriptions can be built by other UNIX utilities. For instance, you might develop an `awk` program specifically designed for creating flow charts.

Locating Objects Using Cartesian Coordinates

For more exact positioning of objects and text, pic uses a standard Cartesian coordinate system. The first object drawn, including a move, starts at position 0,0. The x and y position of a circle, an ellipse, or a box is at the center of the object. For lines, this position refers to the beginning. For arcs, this position is at the center point of the related circle. You can position objects using the at attribute:

```
circle "0,0" at 0,0
circle "1,1" at 1,1
circle "1,0" at 1,0
circle "2,1" at 2,1
```

This description produces:

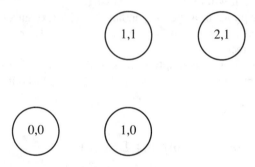

The center of the circle is placed at the specified coordinates. You could also write:

```
circle with .t at 1,1
```

and it would place the top of the circle at that position. A reference to last circle would still locate the center of the circle, but a line drawn from 1,1 would begin at the top of the circle.

Note that the position of 0,0 will not always be the same place on the page. The first object drawn is the point of reference; movement to the left of that point will cause 0,0 to be moved over towards the center of the page.

```
box ht 0.3 wid 0.3 "0,0"
move to 1,0
box "1,0" same
move to -1,0
box "-1,0" same
```

This description produces:

It may be helpful to sketch a drawing on graph paper and then translate it into a pic description. Standard graph paper is divided into quarter-inch squares. When you use graph paper, you might find it useful to set the `scale` variable to 4. All dimensions and positions will be divided by the value of `scale`, which is 1 by default.

It is much easier to describe a drawing in full units rather than fractions. Look at the following description:

```
scale=4
line from 0,0 to 0,3 then to 6,3 then to 6,0 then to 0,0
line from 6,0 to 8,1 then to 8,4 then to 2,4 then to 0,3
line from 6,3 to 8,4
```

The distance between 0 and 1 is normally 1 inch. Because we are scaling this drawing by 4, the actual distance is ¼ inch. It seems easier to describe a point as 2,3 rather than 5,.75. This description produces a two-dimensional box:

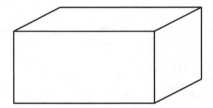

Although `pic` scales the location of text, it is your responsibility to reduce the size of the text to fit a scaled object. You can also use `scale` to change the basic unit of measurement from inches to any other unit. For instance, setting `scale` to 6 will cause all dimensions and coordinates to be interpreted in picas (6 picas to the inch).

Splines and arcs are much easier to draw using coordinates. In the following example, we use a spline to draw a smooth curve between several points on a crude graph.

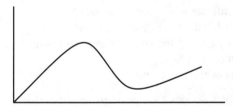

This graph is produced by the following description:

```
scale=4
line from 0,0 to 0,4
line from 0,0 to 9,0
spline from 0,0 to 3,3 then to 5,.25 then to 8,1.5
```

You can also specify relative coordinates as an expression within parentheses. It has the effect of adding or subtracting from the absolute coordinates of a particular place.

```
circle rad .5
circle same at last circle+(.25,0)
```

The `same` attribute allows us to duplicate the size of a previous object. The expression `circle same` means "the same size as the last circle." This description produces:

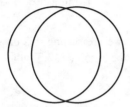

Similarly, you can achieve finer control over positioning by moving from a compass point:

```
box with .sw at last box.ne+(.05,-.05)
```

Expressions and User-Defined Variables

An expression can be used to supply the dimensions or the position of an object. Any of the following operators can be used in an expression: +, −, *, /, and % (modulo)." Expressions can be used to manipulate the built-in variables as follows:

```
circle rad circlerad/2
```

This will draw a circle with a radius that is half the size of the default radius. An expression can also refer to the value of placenames. The coordinates of any object can be specified as `.x` and `.y`. Here's a list of some of the possibilities:

`BoxA.x`	The x-coordinate of the center of `BoxA`
`last box.y`	The y-coordinate of the center of the last box
`BoxA.s.y`	The y-coordinate of the southern compass point of `BoxA`
`BoxA.wid`	The width of `BoxA`
`last circle.rad`	The radius of the last circle

The next description defines a box and then divides the specified height and width of that box to produce a second box half that size.

```
Boxa: box ht 2 wid 3; arrow
box ht Boxa.ht/2 wid Boxa.wid/2
```

The `pic` program also has a number of functions that can be evaluated in an expression, as shown in Table 10-3:

TABLE 10-3. pic Functions

Function	Description
sin (a)	Sine of a
cos (a)	Cosine of a
atan2 (a,b)	Arctangent of a/b
log (a)	Natural logarithm of a
sqrt (a)	Square root of a
int (a)	Integer a
max (a,b)	Maximum value of a,b
min (a,b)	Minimum value of a,b
rand (a)	Random number generator

In giving the size or length of an object, you can name and define your own variables. A variable is any lowercase name that is not reserved as part of the pic language. A variable can be defined as a constant or an expression.

```
a=ellipsewid*3
b=ellipseht/2
ellipse wid a ht b
```

This description produces:

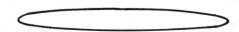

Defining Macros

With macros, you can predefine a series of objects or motions that will be included in the description each time you refer to the macro by name.

```
define name %
    definition
            %
```

A percent sign (%) is used here as the delimiter but any character not in the definition can be used. The format of the define statement is shown on three lines for readability only; a simple macro could be put on a single line. The definition can extend across as many lines as necessary.

When you refer to *name* in your description, The pic program will replace it with the definition.

Macros can also take arguments. These arguments are specified in the definition as $1 thru $9. They will be replaced by the arguments supplied when the macro is invoked.

```
name(arg1, arg2, arg3)
```

A macro does not exist as a place or position as far as `pic` is concerned. The `pic` program simply replaces the macro name with the lines defined in the macro. You cannot refer to the macro as you would refer to a block. However, you can set positions from within a macro.

In the following example, the "tail" hanging down from the box and the list of items drawn to the right of it were produced by a macro.

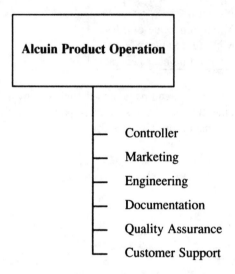

In the `pic` description that produced this drawing, the box is drawn explicitly and a short line is started down from the bottom of the box. Then a macro named `dept` is invoked to produce each item on the list.

```
define dept %
        line down .25
        { line right .15; move right .2; "$1" ljust }
        %
```

In this macro, after a line down is described, the rest of the description is put within braces to reserve the starting position for the next macro call. A short line is drawn, followed by a move to place the text in the correct position. Quotation marks are placed around the argument because the argument will contain a text label.

This macro is invoked for the first item as:

```
dept(Controller)
```

`Controller` is supplied as the first argument, which the macro inserts as a text object. Notice that the argument in the definition is quoted (`"$1"`) so that the actual text when specified does not have to be quoted.

The previous drawing was modeled after an example shown in *Estimating Illustration Costs: A Guide* published by the Society for Technical Communication. The guide considered this drawing to be of medium difficulty and estimated that it would require an hour of an illustrator's time. It took ten to fifteen minutes to design and execute this description for pic, including correcting some syntax errors and formatting for the laser printer. Here's the complete description of the drawing:

```
.PS
box ht .75 wid 1.75 "Alcuin Product Operation"
line down .25 from bottom of last box
define dept %
            line down .25
            { line right .15; move right .2; "$1" ljust }
            %
dept(Controller)
dept(Marketing)
dept(Engineering)
dept(Documentation)
dept(Quality Assurance)
dept(Customer Support)
.PE
```

The second example of macro use is probably harder to read than it is to write. Let's look at it in portions. The purpose of the drawing is to represent a network of computers. We decided to use three types of objects to represent each type of computer: a square, a triangle, and small circle. These objects will appear in a hierarchy and lines will be drawn to connect an object on one level with an object on the level below it. Before starting to describe it in pic terms, we prepared a rough sketch of the drawing on graph paper. This made us realize that we could easily determine the coordinate points of objects; thus, all the macros are set up to accept coordinate positions.

Comments, beginning with #, describe the user-supplied arguments. Following are the definitions for three macros: backbone (a box), local (a triangle), and endpt (a small circle).

```
scale = 4
top = 10
define backbone %
            #  $1 = x coordinate ; $2 = label
            ycoord = top-2
            BB$1: box wid 1 ht 1 with .sw at $1,ycoord
            "$2" at ($1,ycoord)+(2,1) ljust
            %
define local %
            #  $1 = x coordinate; $2 = label
            ycoord = top-5
            LO$1: move to $1,ycoord
            line down 1 left 1 then right 2 then up 1 left 1
```

```
        "$2" at ($1,ycoord)-(0,.7)
        %
define endpt %
        # $1 = x coordinate
        ycoord = top-8
        circle rad .125 with .n at $1,ycoord
        EP$1: last circle.n
        %
```

Because each type of object maintained the same height (or position on the y-axis), a variable ycoord was set up to supply that position from the top of the drawing. (The top of the drawing is defined by another variable.)

Each of these macros requires that you supply an x-axis coordinate as the first argument. This argument is also used to assign a unique placename that is used later when we draw lines between objects.

The backbone and local macros also take a second argument for a label. Handling text inside a macro definition is especially convenient if you are going to change the font and point size.

The next task is to connect the backbone systems to the local systems and the local systems to endpoints. Although we know which types of objects are connected, not all objects are connected in the same way. We decided that the macros require two arguments to supply the x-coordinate for each of the two objects.

```
define BtoL %
        # $1 = x coord of backbone; $2 = x coord of
        # local
        line from BB$1-(0,.5) to LO$2
        %
define LtoE %
        # $1 = x coord of local; $2 = x coord of endpt
        line from LO$1-(0,1) to EP$2
        %
```

The BtoL and LtoE macros draw lines between the placenames set up by the backbone, local, and endpt macros.

Here are the actual macro calls:

```
backbone(10,IBM/370)
backbone(18,DEC VAX)
local(8,68K-1)
local(13,68K-2)
local(17,68K-3)
endpt(7)
endpt(9)
endpt(12)
endpt(13)
endpt(14)
endpt(16)
endpt(18)
```

```
BtoL(10,8)
BtoL(10,13)
BtoL(18,17)
LtoE(8,7);  LtoE(8,9)
LtoE(13,12);  LtoE(13,13);  LtoE(13,14)
LtoE(17,16);  LtoE(17,18)
line from LO13 to LO17
"\s8Personal Computers\s0" at 13,1
"\s12\fBA Network of Computers\s0\fR" ljust at 10,top
```

Notice that arguments supplied to a macro are separated by commas and that an argument may contain a space. Here's what the description produces:

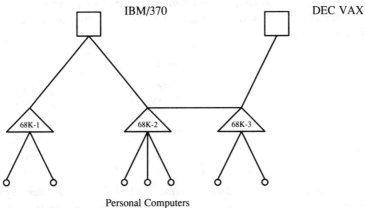

A Network of Computers

Twelve objects are specified and eleven lines are drawn between the objects. One line is explicitly drawn connecting the second triangle to the third triangle. It didn't make sense to define a macro for this single instance. But if you were setting this up for others to use, such a macro would be necessary.

Shortly, we will be looking at several relatively new features that make `pic` even more powerful for generating pictures. In particular, these features allow us to improve our effort to generate a diagram of a computer network.

pic's Copy Facility

The `pic` program provides an interesting copy facility that has two different uses: it allows you to read a `pic` description from a remote file, and it allows you to read lines of data and pass them as individual arguments to a macro.

If you are going to use `pic` regularly, you should think about maintaining a macro library. You might define frequently used objects, such as triangles, and place

them in their own file. You can include the file in your description with the following
line:

```
copy "usr/lib/macros/pic/triangles"
```

Putting the filename in double quotation marks is required. Any `.PS`/`.PE` macros that
are found in the remote file are ignored.

You might also define a set of related macros for a particular type of drawing,
such as an organizational chart or a flow diagram. After you have taken the time to
create and test a description, you should consider structuring it so that the forms can be
easily used in other drawings.

This copy facility replaces an older construct that allowed you to redirect input
from another file through the `.PS` macro.

```
.PS < triangles
```

A second use of the copy facility is to read data through a macro. We'll show
how the `endpt` macro from our last example can be designed to use this facility. In a
file where we had already defined a macro named `endpt`, we could invoke this macro
with the following command:

```
copy thru endpt
7
9
12
13
14
16
18
```

The `pic` program reads each line of data up to the `.PE` and replaces each argument
in the macro definition with the corresponding field from each line. In this example,
the macro is executed seven times, once for each line of data.

We could put the data in a separate file, named `endpt.d`, for example. Then
you enter this version of the `copy` command:

```
copy "endpt.d" thru endpt
```

The double quotation marks are required. Now the `endpt` macro will be executed for
each line in the file `endpt.d`. (The filename suffix `.d` is optional and signifies that
the file contains data for a macro call.)

You can specify a string that `pic` will recognize in the remote file as a signal to
stop reading input. Used with `copy thru`, `until` is followed by the string. In
the following example, the word *STOP* is used as the string:

```
copy "endpt.d" thru endpt until STOP
```

You can also use `until` when you are taking input from the same file:

```
copy thru local until STOP
8 68K-1
13 68K-2
```

```
17 68K-3
STOP
```

In both cases, `pic` will read lines of data until it comes across the string *STOP*.

Another way to use `copy thru` is to supply the macro definition. This is a compact, single-step method:

```
copy "endpt.d" thru %
        # $1 = x coordinate
        ycoord = top-8
        circle rad .125 with .n at $1,ycoord
        EP$1: last circle.n
                    %
```

Although the percent sign is used as the delimiter, any character not found in the definition could be used. The `copy thru` statement with the macro definition can be put on a single line, which is helpful for short definitions.

```
copy thru % box at $1,$2 %
1 1
1 2
1 3
1 4
```

Because you can get a description down to this level, basically consisting of functions, you could have a standard description file associated with independent data files. You could write a program to build the data files from user input or from some other source.

Executing UNIX Commands

You can execute any UNIX command from `pic`, using the following syntax:

```
sh % command %
```

Again, the percent sign represents any valid delimiter character. The `pic` program submits this command to the shell for execution and then returns to interpret the next line of the description. You could issue a command to obtain data from another file:

```
sh % awk -F: {print$1} /etc/passwd %
```

▪ pic Enhancements ▪

Most of the enhancements found in new versions of `pic` are aimed at developing `pic` as a graphics programming language. Additional capabilities include `for` loops and `if` conditional statements. A `for` loop allows one or more `pic` commands to be executed as long as a condition is met.

```
for i=1 to 3 by .05
do%
box ht i;move
%
```

Each time through the loop the value of the variable i is incremented by .05, producing five boxes of increasing height. The by clause specifies the amount that the variable is incremented each time through the loop. If the by clause is omitted, then the variable is incremented by 1. The % is used as the delimiter marking the commands to be executed on each pass.

The if statement evaluates an expression to determine if it is true or false. If true, then specified pic commands are executed. If false, the then clause is not acted upon; instead, an else clause, if specified, is read and commands specified inside it are executed.

```
if x > y then % x = y % else % x = x + 1%
```

This conditional statement evaluates the expression x > y. If true, x is set to y; if false, the value of x is incremented by 1. The % is a delimiter marking the beginning and end of the commands specified for both then and else clauses. The expression inside an if statement can use any of the relational operators that are shown in Table 10-4.

TABLE 10-4. pic Relational Operators

Operator	Meaning
==	Equal to
!=	Not equal to
>	Greater than
>=	Greater than or equal to
<	Less than
<=	Less than or equal to
&&	And
|	Or
!	Not

In addition to enhancements that add more graphics programming features to pic, progress has been made in allowing input to be taken from bit-mapped graphic terminals and translated into pic output. A separate program called cip, available on some systems, allows users to create drawings using a mouse (a la MacDraw for the Macintosh). The cip program generates a pic description of a drawing that can be included in any file to be processed by troff.

11

A Miscellany of UNIX Commands

In this chapter, we present a miscellany of UNIX programs with text-processing applications. In addition, we introduce several UNIX utilities for communications and for reading and writing to tapes and floppy disks. These utilities are not specifically designed for text processing, but we have found them necessary for working in the UNIX environment. Although you can find more detailed information on these utilities in books aimed at a general audience, we've included brief discussions of them to encourage you to learn them.

UNIX has many standard programs, as a run-down of the table of contents for the *UNIX Reference Manual* will demonstrate. The challenge of UNIX is knowing which programs are appropriate for a specific situation. No one learns all the commands, but becoming familiar with a great number of them can be helpful. It is rather like those of us who collect far more books on our shelves than are ''needed,'' knowing the reward of finding the right book for the right occasion.

At times, you will be surprised when you discover a program with rather unusual or specialized capabilities; at other times, you may be frustrated by a demanding program or confused by inconsistencies from one program to the next. These qualities seem to originate from the open design of UNIX, and serve to distinguish this text-processing environment from the closed systems of most word processors.

In some ways, what we are trying to do in this chapter is to address problems that arise in typical documentation projects and show how one or more UNIX programs can be applied as solutions to these problems. The emphasis is on the interactive use of these programs, although many of them can be used effectively in shell scripts or as parts of other programs. (In the next chapter, we go into more detail about shell scripts.) The commands are presented in sections, grouped by function.

· Managing Your Files ·

One of the realities of using a computer is that you begin to think of a document in terms of files, rather than chapters or sections. You edit and print files; create and copy files; delete files accidentally and lose your edits; and look through files to find the information that is contained in them. Increasingly, files contain the goods that you trade. You exchange not only printed copies of documents, but using floppy disks, tapes, or modems, you take files off one system and put them on another system. Learning to organize and maintain files is essential to working on a computer.

Using the File System to Your Advantage

One obvious feature of UNIX that makes it easy to handle large numbers of files is the hierarchical file system. With carefully named files and directories, the pathname, which specifies a file's unique place in the file system hierarchy, can tell a lot about not only how to get at the file, but its contents as well.

For example, on our system, we keep all source files for various books in progress on a file system called `/work`; work for a given client is kept in a directory named for the client, with a subdirectory for each separate manual. Within each manual's subdirectory, individual chapters are named consistently, `ch01`, `ch02`, and so on. As a result, it is easy both to locate a file (Chapter 1 of the FORTRAN manual for ABC Corp. can predictably be found in `/work/abc/fortran/ch01`) and to guess its contents.

If you are using the C shell, you can create an `alias` that provides a shorthand way of entering a command. In the following example, the alias allows you to think in terms of manuals instead of directories:

```
% alias fortran "cd /work/abc/fortran; pwd"
% pwd
 /work/fred
% fortran
 /work/abc/fortran
```

You can place an `alias` definition in your `.cshrc` file so that it becomes part of your environment.

In the Bourne shell, you achieve a similar result by using an environment variable called `CDPATH` to define a search path for the `cd` command. For example:

```
$ CDPATH=/work/abc:/work/textp:/usr
$ cd fortran
/work/abc/fortran
$ cd jane
/usr/jane
$ cd ch03
/work/textp/ch03
```

When you issue a `cd` command, the shell searches for a subdirectory with that name under any of the directories in the path, changes to it, and prints the full directory name.

The search directories in `CDPATH` are specified between colons. Directories listed in `CDPATH` are searched in order from left to right.

Shell Filename Metacharacters

Even with files organized into directories, you can still accumulate a lot of files. Developing some consistent naming conventions that take advantage of shell metacharacters (wildcards) can save you a lot of trouble. Most users are familiar with metacharacters but many don't make full use of them.

In UNIX, you can match any part of a filename with a wildcard. Remember that * matches *zero* or more characters. This gives you more power to select a specific group of files out of a directory. In the following example, assume that you want to delete the files lock, filelocks, and lock.release, but ignore the files filelist, lecture, and stocks.c.

```
$ ls
filelist
filelocks
lecture
lock
lock.release
stocks.c
$ rm *lock*
```

Because * can match zero characters, *lock* will match lock as well as filelocks.

The shell interprets the pattern-matching character ? to match any single character, and the construct [*m-n*] to match a range of consecutive characters.

If you name your files consistently, you can use these characters to select groups of files. For example, in a directory containing a BASIC manual, you might have the following list of files:

```
$ ls
appa
appb
changes
ch01
ch01.old
ch02
ch03
ch03.examples
ch03.out
ch04
ch04.examples
ch05
letter.613
```

As usual in any directory, there are a number of auxiliary files. Some of these files apply to the work on this project, but they are not actually part of the book. If you've carefully chosen the names of related files, you can use metacharacters to select only the files in a particular group. For example:

```
$ ls ch0?
ch01
ch02
ch03
ch04
ch05
```

You could select a range of files, using brackets:

```
$ ls ch0[3-5]
ch03
ch04
ch05
```

If you had entered ch0*, miscellaneous files such as ch01.old would have been included. (Note that whenever you use numbers in filenames, as shown here, to consistently name a group of related files, you should begin the numbering sequence with 01, 02 . . . rather than 1, 2. . . . This will cause ls to list the files in proper alphabetical order. Otherwise, ls will list ch1, then ch11, ch12 . . . ch2, ch20 . . . and so on.)

Metacharacters have broader applications than for simply listing files. Look at this example of running spell on an entire book:

```
$ spell ch0? app? > spell.out
```

(We'll be looking at the spell command later in the section "Proofing Documents.") This command is run on the seven files that match one of the two patterns specified on the command line.

Metacharacters are also useful in moving and copying files from one directory to another:

```
$ cp basic/ch0? /work/backup
```

Locating Files

Although a hierarchical file system with consistent naming conventions helps a lot, it is still easy to lose track of files, or just to have difficulty specifying the ones you want to manipulate. The number of files contained on even a small hard disk can be enormous, and complex directory hierarchies can be difficult to work with.

It is possible to lose a file on the file system when you have forgotten in which directory you put it. To look through an entire file system or a large directory hierarchy, you need a utility called find. The find utility looks at the external characteristics of a file—who created it, when it was last accessed, its name, and so on.

The find utility probably wins top honors for having the most cumbersome command-line syntax in UNIX. It's not that find is a difficult command; its syntax is simply difficult to recall. You might expect that all you have to enter is find and the name of the file that you want to look for. This is not the way it works, however, which is a nuisance to new users. The find command requires repeated trips to the *UNIX Reference Manual* before you grasp its atypical format.

To use find, specify the pathnames of the directories that you want to search; then place one or more conditions upon the search. The name of a particular file that you want to search for is considered one of these conditions. It is expressed as:

−name *filename*

To obtain a listing of the pathnames of files that are found, you have to specify the −print condition as well (−name must precede −print).

If you wanted to find any file named notes on the /work file system, here's the command to enter:

```
$ find /work -name notes -print
/work/alcuin/notes
/work/textp/ch02/notes
```

The output is the pathname (starting with the specified file system or directory) of each file that is found. More than one pathname can be supplied. A slash (/) represents the root directory and thus is used if you want to search the entire file system. Note that the search can take some time, and that if you do not have read permissions to a directory you will get a message saying that it cannot be opened.

In the next example, we add another condition, −user, and limit the search to files named memo that are owned by the user fred. This is helpful when you are searching for a file that has a fairly common name and might exist in several users' accounts. Filename metacharacters can be used but they must be protected from the shell using backslashes or single quotation marks. (If you don't do this, the metacharacters will be interpreted by the shell as referring to files in the current directory, and will not be passed to the find command.)

```
$ find /work /usr -name 'memo*' -user fred -print
/usr/fred/alcuin/memo
/work/alcuin/memo.523
/work/caslon/memo.214
```

Two directory hierarchies are searched, /work and /usr. If you did not specify the −name condition, this command would locate all the files owned by fred in these two file systems.

Many find conditions have uses for other tasks besides locating files. For instance, it can be useful to descend a directory hierarchy, using find to print the complete pathname of each file, as in the following example:

```
$ find /work/alcuin -print
/work/alcuin
/work/alcuin/ch01
/work/alcuin/ch01.old
/work/alcuin/commands/open
/work/alcuin/commands/stop
    . . .
```

This usage provides a kind of super ls that will list all files under a given directory, not just those at the current directory level. As you'll see, this becomes very useful when it comes time to back up your files.

The longer you work with a UNIX system, the more you will come to appreciate find. Don't be put off by its awkward syntax and many options. The time you spend studying this command will be well repaid.

File Characteristics

Most of us are concerned only with the contents of a file. However, to look at files from UNIX's point of view, files are labeled containers that are retrieved from storage and soon put back in the same place. It might be said that the operating system reads (and writes) the label but doesn't really care to look inside the container. The label describes a set of physical or external characteristics for each file. This information is displayed when the ls command produces a long listing.

```
$ ls -l /work/textp/ch01
total 20
-rw-rw-r--   1 fred    doc    9496 Jun 10 15:18 ch01
```

To the operating system, the file (ch01) contains a certain number of *bytes* (9496), each representing a character. The date and time (Jun 10 15:18) refer to the last time the file was modified. The file has an *owner* (fred), who is usually the person who created the file. The owner belongs to a *group* of users (doc) who can be given different permissions from all *other* users. The operating system keeps track of the file permissions (-rw-rw-r--) for the owner, group, and other users—determining who can read, write, or execute the file.

All of these characteristics can be modified either by use of the file or by commands such chmod (change permissions) and chown (change owner). You may need to become a super-user to change these characteristics.

There are some options for ls that allow you to make use of this information. For instance, if you had recently made some changes to a set of files, but couldn't remember which ones, you could use the -t option to sort a list of files with the most recently modified files first. The -r option reverses that order, so that ls -rt produces a list with the oldest files first.

In addition, find has a number of options that make use of external file characteristics. As we've seen, you can look for files that belong to a particular user. You can also look for files that are larger than a particular size, or have been modified more recently than a certain date.

Don't get stuck thinking that the only handle you can pick a file up with is the file's name.

▪ Viewing the Contents of a File ▪

You are probably familiar with a number of UNIX commands that let you view the contents of a file. The cat command streams a file to the screen at a rate that is usually too swift. The pg and more commands display a file one page at a time. They are frequently used as *filters*, for instance, to supply paging for nroff output.

```
$ nroff -mm ch01 | pg
```

You can also use these commands to examine unformatted files, proofing formatting codes as well as text. Although these are frequently used commands, not everyone is aware that they have interactive subcommands, too. You can search for a pattern; execute a UNIX command; move to another file specified on the command line; or go to the end of the file.

You can list these subcommands by entering h when the program pauses at the bottom of a page. Here's the help screen pg provides:

```
----------------------------------------------------------
   h                     help
   q or Q                quit
   <blank> or \n         next page
   l                     next line
   d or ^D               display half a page more
   . or ^L               redisplay current page
   f                     skip the next page forward
   n                     next file
   p                     previous file
   $                     last page
   w or z                set window size and display next page
   s savefile            save current file in savefile
   /pattern/             search forward for pattern
   ?pattern? or
   ^pattern^             search backward for pattern
   !command              execute command
Most commands can be preceded by a number, as in:
+1\n (next page); -1\n (previous page); 1\n (page 1).
See the manual page for more detail.
----------------------------------------------------------
```

One advantage of pg is that you can move backward as well as forward when going through a file. A special feature of more is the ability to invoke vi at the current point in the file. When you quit vi, more resumes paging through the rest of the file.

Another command used for examining a file is pr. Its most common use is to perform minor page formatting for a file on the way to a line printer. It breaks the input file into pages (66 lines to a page) and supplies a header that contains the date, the name of the file, and the current page number. Top, bottom, and side margins are also added.

The pr command also has many options that can be used to perform some odd-ball tasks. For example, the -n option adds line numbers:

```
$ pr -n test
```

The following is displayed:

```
Jul   4 14:27 1987   test Page 1


    1     apples
    2     oranges
    3     walnuts
    4     chestnuts
```

You can adjust the page length using the −l option. If you are printing to a terminal, the −p option specifies a pause at the beginning of each page. You can also display an input file in *-n* columns.

The −m option simultaneously merges two or more files and prints each of them, one per column:

```
$ pr -m -t test*
```

In this example, we display four files side-by-side:

```
apples         apples         apples         oranges
oranges        oranges        oranges        walnuts
walnuts        walnuts        grapes         chestnuts
chestnuts
```

The test* file specification is expanded to four filenames: test, test1, test2, and test3. The −t option suppresses the heading and does not print linefeeds to fill a page, which is especially useful when you are sending the output of pr to a file or the terminal.

We found a use for pr when working on this book. We wanted to include nroff-formatted examples in the text. We had difficulty because nroff inserts tabs, instead of spaces, to optimize horizontal positioning on printers. To remove the tabs, we used pr with the −e option to expand the tabs to their equivalent in blank spaces. The following shell script implements this process so that it can be invoked as a single command:

```
$ nroff -mm -rO0 examples/$1 | pr -e -t
```

The pr command works as a filter for nroff. The −r option is used with nroff to set register O (page offset or left margin) to zero.

Sometimes it can be useful to examine just the beginning or the end of a file. Two commands, head and tail, print the first or last ten lines of a file. The head command can be used to look at the initial settings of number registers and strings that are often set at the top of a file.

```
$ head ch02
.nr W 65
.nr P 3
.nr L 60
.so /usr/lib/tmac/tmac.m
.nr Pt 2
.ds Ux \s-2UNIX\s0
.ds HP 3321
```

```
.H1 "Product Overview"
.ds HM 11A
.
```

This output could be redirected to a file as a way of starting a new chapter. The `tail` command has the same syntax; it can save time when you want to check the end of a large file.

▪ Searching for Information in a File ▪

The many benefits provided by `grep` to the user who doesn't remember what his or her files contain are well known. Even users of non-UNIX systems who make fun of its obscure name wish they had a utility with its power to search through a set of files for an arbitrary text pattern, known as a *regular expression*. We have already discussed regular expressions and their use in search and replace commands in `vi` (see Chapter 7). In this section, we show some of the ways to perform pattern-matching searches using `grep` and its siblings, `egrep` and `fgrep`.

The main function of `grep` is to look for strings matching a regular expression and print only those lines that are found. Use `grep` when you want to look at how a particular word is used in one or more files.

```
$ grep "run[- ]time" ch04
This procedure avoids run-time errors for not-assigned
and a run-time error message is produced.
run-time error message is produced.
program aborts and a run-time error message is produced.
DIMENSION statement in  BASIC is executable at run time.
This means that arrays can be redimensioned at run time.
accessible or not open, the program aborts and a run-time
```

This example lists the lines in the file `ch04` that contain either `run-time` or `run time`.

Another common use is to look for a specific macro in a file. In a file coded with mm macros, the following command will list top-level and second-level headings:

```
$ grep "^\.H[12]" ch0[12]
ch01:.H1 "Introduction"
ch01:.H1 "Windows, Screens, and Images"
ch01:.H2 "The Standard Screen-stdscr"
ch01:.H2 "Adding Characters"
...
ch02:.H1 "Introduction"
ch02:.H1 "What Is Terminal Independence?"
ch02:.H2 "Termcap"
ch02:.H2 "Terminfo"
```

In effect, it produces a quick outline of the contents of these files. When more than one file is specified, the name of the file appears with each line. Note that we use brackets as metacharacters both in the regular expression and when specifying the filename. Because metacharacters (and spaces) have meaning to the shell, they will be interpreted as such unless the regular expression is placed within quotation marks.

There are several options commonly used with `grep`. The `-i` option specifies that the search ignore the distinction between uppercase and lowercase. The `-c` option tells `grep` to return only a count of the number of lines matched. The `-l` option returns only the name of the file when `grep` finds a match. This can be used to prepare a list of files for another command.

The shell construct *command1* `command2` causes the output of *command2* to be used as an argument to *command1*. For example, assume that you wanted to edit any file that has a reference to a function call named `getcursor`. The command:

```
$ vi `grep -l getcursor *`
```

would invoke `vi` on all of the files in the current directory containing the string `getcursor`. Because the `grep` command is enclosed in single backquotes (` `), its output becomes the list of files to be edited.

The `grep` command can work on the results of a `find` command. You can use `find` to supply a list of filenames and `grep` to search for a pattern in those files. For example, consider the following command, which uses `find` to look for all files in the specified directory hierarchy and passes the resulting names to `grep` to scan for a particular pattern:

```
$ find /work/docbook -exec grep "[aA]lcuin" {} \;
Alcuin product. Yesterday, I received the product   demo
Alcuin.  Some people around here, looking over my shoulder,
with Alcuin. One  person,  a  student  of  calligraphy,
presents different strategies for documenting the Alcuin
The development of Alcuin can be traced to our founder's
the installation file "alcuin.install"> and the font
configuration file "alcuin.ftables."
```

The `-exec` condition allows you to specify a command that is executed upon each file that is found (`{}` indicates the pathname of the file). The command must end with an escaped semicolon.

Although this is a good way to introduce the very useful `-exec` option to `find`, it is actually not the best way to solve the problem. You'll notice that even though `grep` is working on more than one file, the filenames are not printed because the data is actually passed to `grep` from a pipe. The reason is that `grep` is being invoked many times (once for each file that is found), and is not really working on many files at once. If you wanted to produce a list of the selected files, you could use the `-l` option with `grep`. But more to the point, this is a very inefficient way to do the job.

In this case, it would be preferable to write:

```
$ grep "[aA]lcuin" `find /work/docbook -print`
```

Because `grep` is invoked only once, this command will run much faster.

There is a potential danger in this approach. If the list of files is long, you may exceed the total allowable length of a command line. The best approach uses a command we haven't shown yet—`xargs`. This command provides an extended version of the same function the shell provides with backquotes. It converts its input into a form that can be used as an argument list by another command. The command to which the argument list is passed is specified as the first argument to `xargs`. So, you would write:

```
$ find /work/docbook -print | xargs grep "[aA]lcuin"
```

Or you could generalize this useful tool and save it as the following shell script, which could be called `mfgrep` (*multifile* `grep`). This script takes the pathname for `find` as the first argument and the pattern for `grep` as the second. The list of files found is passed to `grep` by `xargs`:

```
find $1 | xargs grep "$2"
```

The `fgrep` (*fast* `grep`)* command performs the same function as `grep`, except it searches for a fixed string rather than a regular expression. Because it doesn't interpret metacharacters, it often does a search faster than `grep`. For interactive use, you may not find enough difference to keep this command in your active repertoire. However, it may be of more benefit inside shell scripts.

The `egrep` command is yet another version of `grep`, one that extends the syntax of regular expressions. A `+` following a regular expression matches one or more occurrences of the regular expression; a `?` matches zero or one occurrences. In addition, regular expressions can be nested within parentheses.

```
$ egrep "Lab(oratorie)?s" name.list
AT&T Bell Laboratories
AT&T Bell Labs
```

Parentheses surround a second regular expression and `?` modifies this expression. The nesting helps to eliminate unwanted matches; for instance, the word *Labors* or *oratories* would not be matched.

Another special feature of `egrep` is the vertical bar (|), which serves as an *or* operator between two expressions. Lines matching either expression are printed, as in the next example:

```
$ egrep "stdscr|curscr" ch03
into the stdscr, a character array.
When stdscr is refreshed, the
stdscr is refreshed.
curscr.
initscr() creates two windows: stdscr
and curscr.
```

---

*Despite what the documentation says, `egrep` is usually the fastest of the three `grep` programs.

Remember to put the expression inside quotation marks to protect the vertical bar from being interpreted by the shell as a pipe symbol. Look at the next example:

```
$ egrep "Alcuin (User|Programmer)('s)? Guide" docguide
Alcuin Programmer's Guide is a thorough
refer to the Alcuin User Guide.
Alcuin User's Guide introduces new users to
```

You can see the flexibility that `egrep`'s syntax can give you, matching either *User* or *Programmer* and matching them if they had an *'s* or not.

Both `egrep` and `fgrep` can read search patterns from a file using the `-f` option.

▪ Proofing Documents ▪

There are no computer tools that completely replace the close examination of final printed copy by the human eye. However, UNIX does include a number of proofing aids, ranging from a simple spelling checker to programs for checking style and diction, and even sexist usage.

We'll look at some of these programs in this section. Not all of the programs we'll discuss are available on all UNIX systems. Keep in mind, though, that `grep` is also a very powerful proofing aid, which you can use to check for consistent usage of words and phrases.

Looking for Spelling Errors

The `spell` command reads one or more files and prints a list of words that are possibly misspelled. You can redirect the output to a file, then use `grep` to locate each of the words, and `vi` or `ex` to make the edits. In the next chapter, though, we introduce a shell script named `proof` for running `spell` interactively and correcting spelling errors in place in a file. You will probably prefer to use `spell` in that manner rather than invoking it manually.

Even if you do build that script, you can use `spell` on its own if you are unsure about which of two possible spellings is right. Type the name of the command, followed by a *RETURN*, then type the alternative spellings you are considering. Press `^D` (on a line by itself) to end the list. The `spell` command will echo back the word(s) in the list that it considers to be in error.

```
$ spell
misspelling
mispelling
^D
mispelling
```

You can invoke `spell` in this way from within `vi`, by typing the `ex` colon prompt, an exclamation point, and the name of the `spell` command.

When you run `spell` on a file, the list of words it produces usually includes a number of legitimate words or terms that the program does not recognize. You must cull out the proper nouns and other words `spell` doesn't know about to arrive at a list of true misspellings. For instance, look at the results on this sample sentence:

```
$ cat sample
Alcuin uses TranScript to convert ditroff into
PostScript output for the LaserWriter printerr.
$ spell sample
Alcuin
ditroff
printerr
LaserWriter
PostScript
TranScript
```

Only one word in this list is actually misspelled.

On many UNIX systems, you can supply a local dictionary file so that `spell` recognizes special words and terms specific to your site or application. After you have run `spell` and looked through the word list, you can create a file containing the words that were not actual misspellings. The `spell` command will check this list after it has gone through its own dictionary.

If you added the special terms in a file named `dict`, you could specify that file on the command line using the `+` option:

```
$ spell +dict sample
printerr
```

The output is reduced to the single misspelling.

The `spell` command will also miss words specified as arguments to `nroff` or `troff` macros, and, like any spelling checker, will make some errors based on incorrect derivation of spellings from the root words contained in its dictionary. If you understand how `spell` works, you may be less surprised by some of these errors.

The directory `/usr/lib/spell` contains the main program invoked by the `spell` command along with auxiliary programs and data files.

```
$ ls -l /usr/lib/spell
total 604
-rwxr-xr-x   1 bin    bin     20176 Mar   9  1985 hashcheck
-rwxr-xr-x   1 bin    bin     14352 Mar   9  1985 hashmake
-rw-r--r--   1 bin    bin     53872 Mar   9  1985 hlista
-rw-r--r--   1 bin    bin     53840 Mar   9  1985 hlistb
-rw-r--r--   1 bin    bin      6328 Mar   9  1985 hstop
-rw-rw-rw-   1 root   root   102892 Jul  12 16:10 spellhist
-rwxr-xr-x   1 bin    bin     23498 Mar   9  1985 spellin
-rwxr-xr-x   1 bin    bin     27064 Mar   9  1985 spellprog
```

The `spell` command pipes its input through `deroff -w` and `sort -u` to remove formatting codes and prepare a sorted word list, one word per line. (The `deroff` and `sort` commands are discussed later in this chapter.) Two separate spelling lists are maintained, one for American usage and one for British usage (invoked with the −b option to spell). These lists, hlista and hlistb, cannot be read or updated directly. They are compressed files, compiled from a list of words represented as nine-digit hash codes. (Hash-coding is a special technique for quick search of information.)

The main program invoked by spell is spellprog. It loads the list of hash codes from either hlista or hlistb into a table, and looks for the hash code corresponding to each word on the sorted word list. This eliminates all words (or hash codes) actually found in the spelling list. For the remaining words, spellprog tries to see if it can derive a recognizable word by performing various operations on the word stem, based on suffix and prefix rules. A few of these manipulations follow:

```
-y+iness
+ness
-y+i+less
+less
-y+ies
-t+ce
-t+cy
```

The new words created as a result of these manipulations will be checked once more against the spell table. However, before the stem-derivative rules are applied, the remaining words are checked against a table of hash codes built from the file hstop. The stop list contains typical misspellings that stem-derivative operations might allow to pass. For instance, the misspelled word *thier* would be converted into *thy* using the suffix rule -y+ier. The hstop file accounts for as many cases of this type of error as possible.

The final output consists of words not found in the spell list, even after the program tried to search for their stems, and words that were found in the stop list.

You can get a better sense of these rules in action by using the −v or −x option.

The −v option eliminates the last lookup in the table, and produces a list of words that are not actually in the spelling list along with possible derivatives. It allows you to see which words were found as a result of stem-derivative operations, and prints the rule used.

```
$ spell -v sample
Alcuin
ditroff
LaserWriter
PostScript
printerr
TranScript
+out    output
+s      uses
```

The −x option makes spell begin at the stem-derivative stage, and prints the various attempts it makes to find the word stem of each word.

```
$ spell -x sample
...
=into
=LaserWriter
=LaserWrite
=LaserWrit
=laserWriter
=laserWrite
=laserWrit
=output
=put
...
LaserWriter
...
```

The stem is preceded by an equals sign. At the end of the output are the words whose stem does not appear in the spell list.

One other file you should know about is `spellhist`. Each time you run `spell`, the output is appended through a command called `tee` into `spellhist`, in effect creating a list of all the misspelled or unrecognized words for your site. The `spellhist` file is something of a ''garbage'' file that keeps on growing. You will want to reduce it or remove it periodically. To extract useful information from this `spellhist`, you might use the `sort` and `uniq -c` commands shown later in this chapter to compile a list of misspelled words or special terms that occur most frequently. It is possible to add these words back into the basic spelling dictionary, but this is too complex a process to describe here.

Checking Hyphenation

The `hyphen` command is used on `nroff`-formatted files to print a list of words that have been hyphenated at the end of a line. You can check that `nroff` has correctly hyphenated words.

```
$ hyphen ch03.out
ch03.out:
applica-tion
pro-gram
charac-ter
```

If you disagree with the hyphenation of a word, you can go back into your source file and use either the `.hw` request to specify hyphenation points or the `.nh` request to inhibit hyphenation of the word.

If you don't have the `hyphen` command on your system, you can print the lines ending in hyphens using `grep`:

```
$ grep '-$' ch03.out
```

This will not display the second half of the hyphenated word on the following line, but it should give you enough of an idea. Alternatively, you could use `awk` or `sed`, described in the next chapter, to create a version of this command that would print both lines.

Counting Words

In the past, writers were paid by the word. The `wc` command will count words for you:

```
$ wc ch01
    180    1529    9496 ch01
```

The three numbers printed represent the number of lines, words, and characters, respectively. (The presence of formatting commands in the input file will make this measurement somewhat inaccurate.)

Writer's Workbench

No book on UNIX text processing can avoid some discussion of Writer's Workbench (WWB), a collection of programs for the analysis of writing style.

Unfortunately, unlike most of the programs described in this book, the Writer's Workbench is not available on all UNIX systems. It was originally developed for internal use at Bell Labs, and was available in early releases of UNIX to the academic community. But it was made into a separate product when UNIX was commercially released.

The three original programs, `style`, `diction`, and `explain`, are available in Berkeley UNIX systems and in Xenix, but not in System V.

AT&T has released a greatly improved and expanded version, including additional programs for proofreading, that is controlled from a master program called `wwb`. However, this version is only available as a separately priced package for 3B2 and 3B5 computers. The unfortunate result is that one of UNIX's most unusual contributions to text processing is not officially part of UNIX and has never been ported to many UNIX systems.

In this section, we'll describe the original `style` and `diction` programs, with a brief discussion of `wwb`.

The `style` program analyzes a document's style and computes readability indexes based on several algorithms widely accepted in the academic community. For example, when run on a draft of this section, `style` gave the following report:

```
readability grades:
        (Kincaid) 11.1  (auto) 11.6  (Coleman-Liau) 11.0
        (Flesch) 11.5 (52.7)
sentence info:
        no. sent 53 no. wds 1110
        av sent leng 20.9 av word leng 4.79
        no. questions 0 no. imperatives 0
        no. nonfunc wds 624   56.2%   av leng 6.25
        short sent (<16) 34% (18) long sent (>31)   17% (9)
        longest sent 46 wds at sent 4;
```

```
              shortest sent 5 wds at sent 47
    sentence types:
          simple   32% (17) complex  47% (25)
          compound   4% (2) compound-complex  17% (9)
    word usage:
          verb types as % of total verbs
          tobe  29% (33) aux  28% (32) inf  15% (17)
          passives as % of non-inf verbs   9% (9)
          types as % of total
          prep 12.0% (133) conj 3.6% (40) adv 5.0% (56)
          noun 26.8% (298) adj 15.5% (172) pron 7.3% (81)
          nominalizations   3 % (30)
    sentence beginnings:
          subject opener: noun (22) pron (5) pos (1) adj (2)
                            art (4) tot  64%
          prep  17% (9) adv   9% (5)
          verb  0% (0)  sub_conj  6% (3) conj  0% (0)
          expletives   4% (2)
```

Even if you aren't an English teacher and don't know the Kincaid algorithm from the Flesch, this report can be very useful.

First, regardless of the differences between the algorithms, they all give you a general idea of the required reading level for what you have written. It is up to you to adjust your style according to the audience level you want to reach. This may not be a trivial task; however, it may be a vital one if you are writing a book for a specific audience. For example, if you were writing an instruction manual for heavy equipment to be used by people reading at the sixth-grade level, a `style` report like the one shown would be a dire warning that the manual would not be successful.

In general, to lower the reading level of a document, use shorter sentences and simpler constructions. (Incidentally, most writing in newspapers and general circulation magazines is at the sixth-grade level. But you shouldn't get the impression that text written for a lower reading level is *better*. Writing can be clear and effective at any level of complexity. At the same time, each of us must recognize, and adjust for, the skills of our intended reader.)

The analysis of reading level is only a small part of what `style` offers. The detailed analysis of sentence length and type, word usage, and sentence beginnings can give you considerable insight into your writing. If you take the time to read the report carefully at the same time as you reread your text, you will begin to see patterns and can make intelligent decisions about editorial changes.

As an exercise, run `style` on a short passage you have written, read the report carefully, then rewrite your work based on the report. See what difference this makes to the `style` report. You will eventually get a feel for what the program provides.

In some cases, `diction`, the other major program in the Writer's Workbench, can also help you find areas to change.

The `diction` program relies on a library of frequently misused words and phrases. It relentlessly searches out these words and flags them as inappropriate by enclosing them in brackets. For example, when run on a previous draft of this section, `diction` made the following recommendations:

```
wwb
    style performs stylistic analysis of a document  and
    computes readability indexes based on a[ number of ]
    algorithms widely accepted in the academic community.

    this may not be a trivial  task  however it may be a
    [ vital ] one if you are writing a book  with a specific
    target audience.

    for example  if you were  writing an instruction manual
    for heavy equipment to be used by  people reading at the
    sixth grade level a style report like the one shown above
    would be a dire warning that the manual would not be
    [ very ]successful.

    [ in some cases ] diction  the other  major program in the
    writer s workbench can help you  to find possible areas to
    change.

    in the latest official release of wwb there are a
    [ number of ] additional programs  including  .

    morestyle  which looks for abstract words as well as
    listing the  frequency with which each word is used
    and the word diversity the[ number of ]different words
    divided by the total[ number of ] words .

    morestyle also gives a count of the[ number of ]negative
    constructions contained in your writing.

    spellwwb  which lists possible spelling errors in a
    slightly more  usable format than the standard spell
    program  and spelladd  which allows you to build a local
    dictionary word of spelling  exceptions  words that spell
    regards as errors  but[ which ]you  know to be correct .

    you can run these programs individually  or using one of
    several [ overall ]control programs.

    running wwb will run[ all of ]these programs.

    number of sentences 37 number of hits 10
```

The diction program lists "problem" sentences from your source file, with words or phrases it has taken exception to enclosed in brackets. You can redirect this output to a file, or page through it on the screen. Punctuation and macros are first stripped by the `deroff` program, which explains the odd appearance of the text.

We find that we ignore `diction`'s advice much of the time—the exception list is applied across the board, without regard for context. For example, you'll notice that it flagged the phrase *number of* several times, though that was exactly what we meant in all but one case. However, the twenty percent of its recommendations that we agree with are worth the effort of running the program.

If you don't understand why `diction` complains about a phrase, you can use `explain` to ask for help. For example:

```
$ explain
phrase?
which
use "that" when clause is restrictive" for "which"
use "when" for "at which time"
phrase?
number of
use "many" for "a large number of"
use "several, many, some" for "a number of"
use "usually" for "except in a small number of cases"
use "some" for "in a number of cases"
use "enough" for "sufficient number of"
use "often" for "in a considerable number of cases"
phrase?
perform
use "do" for "perform"
use "measure" for "perform a measurement"
phrase?
^D
```

The official release of WWB for 3B computers contains improved versions of `style` and `diction`, as well as many additional programs. These programs include

- `abst`, which evaluates the abstractness of your writing.

- `acro`, which looks for acronyms (any word printed in all capital letters) so you can check that they have been properly defined.

- `dictadd`, which allows you to add to the dictionaries used by `diction`, `spell`, and `sexist`.

- `double`, which looks for double words.

- `findbe`, which looks for syntax that may be difficult to understand.

- `morestyle`, which looks for abstract words and lists the frequency with which each word is used and the word diversity (the number of different words divided by the total number of words). The `morestyle` program also gives a count of the number of negative constructions contained in your writing.

- org, which prints the first and last sentence of each paragraph, so you can analyze paragraph transitions and the flow of ideas within your writing.

- punct, which checks punctuation (e.g., the placement of commas and periods with quotation marks).

- sexist, which checks your writing against a dictionary of sexist words and phrases.

- spellwwb, which lists possible spelling errors in a slightly more usable format than the standard spell program, and spelladd, which allows you to build a local dictionary of spelling exceptions (words that spell regards as errors, but that you know to be correct).

- splitrules, which finds split infinitives.

- syl, which prints the average number of syllables in the words you use.

You can run these programs individually or use one of several control programs. The wwb program will run just about everything. The proofr program will run those programs that help you proofread (such as spell, double, punct, and diction). The prose program will run those that analyze style (such as style and sexist).

There is also an interactive version of proofr called proofvi, which stores its output in a temporary file and then allows you to edit your original, stepping through each flagged problem.

· Comparing Versions of the Same Document ·

UNIX provides a number of useful programs for keeping track of different versions of documents contained in two or more files:

- the diff family of programs, which print out lines that are different between two or more files

- the SCCS system, which lets you keep a compact history of differences between files, so that you can go back and reconstruct any previous version

- the make program, which keeps track of a predefined list of dependencies between files

Checking Differences

The diff command displays different versions of lines that are found when comparing two files. It prints a message that uses ed-like notation (a for append, c for change, and d for delete) to describe how a set of lines has changed. This is followed by the lines themselves. The < character precedes lines from the first file and > precedes lines from the second file.

Let's create an example to explain the output produced by diff. Look at the contents of three sample files:

TEST1	TEST2	TEST3
apples	apples	oranges
oranges	oranges	walnuts
walnuts	grapes	chestnuts

When you run diff on these files, the following output is produced:

```
$ diff test1 test2
3c3
< walnuts
---
> grapes
```

The diff command displays the only line that differs between the two files. To understand the report, remember that diff is prescriptive, describing what changes need to made to the first file to make it the same as the second file. This report specifies that only the third line is affected, exchanging walnuts for grapes. This is more apparent if you use the −e option, which produces an editing script that can be submitted to ed, the UNIX line editor. (You must redirect standard output to capture this script in a file.)

```
$ diff −e test1 test2
3c
grapes
.
```

This script, if run on test1, will bring test1 into agreement with test2. (Later in this section, we'll look at how to get ed to execute this script.) If you compare the first and third files, you find more differences:

```
$ diff test1 test3
1d0
< apples
3a3
> chestnuts
```

To make test1 the same as test3, you'd have to delete the first line (*apples*) and append the third line from test3 after the third line in test1. Again, this can be seen more clearly in the editing script produced by the −e option. Notice that the script specifies editing lines in reverse order; otherwise, changing the first line would alter all succeeding line numbers.

```
$ diff -e test1 test3
3a
chestnuts
.
1d
```

You can use the `diff3` command to look at differences between three files. For each set of differences, it displays a row of equals signs (====) followed by 1, 2, or 3, indicating which file is different; if no number is specified, then all three files differ. Then, using ed-like notation, the differences are described for each file.

```
$ diff3 test1 test2 test3
====3
1:1c
2:1c
  apples
3:0a
====3
1:3c
2:3c
  grapes
3:2,3c
  walnuts
  chestnuts
```

With the output of `diff3`, it is easy to keep track of which file is which; however, the prescription given is a little harder to decipher. To bring these files into agreement, you would have to add apples at the beginning of the third file; change line 3 of the second file to line 3 of the first file; and change lines 2 and 3 of the third file, effectively dropping the last line.

The `diff3` command also has a −e option for creating an editing script for ed. It doesn't quite work the way you might think. Basically, it creates a script for building the first file from the second and third files.

```
$ diff3 -e test1 test2 test3
3c
walnuts
chestnuts
.
1c
.
w
q
```

If you reverse the second and third files, a different script is produced:

```
$ diff3 -e test1 test3 test2
3c
grapes
.
```

```
    w
    q
```

As you might guess, this is basically the same output as doing
a `diff` on the first and third files. (The only difference in the output is the result of a
rather errant inconsistency between `diff` and `diff3`. The latter produces an `ed`
script that ends with the commands that save the edited version of the file; `diff`
requires that you supply them.)

    Another useful program is `sdiff` (*side-by-side* `diff`). Its most straightfor-
ward use is to display two files in two columns on the screen. In a gutter between the
two columns, the program displays a `<` if the line is unique to the first file, a `>` if the
line is unique to the second file, and a `|` if the line is different in both files. Because
the default line length of this program (130 characters) is too wide for most terminals, it
is best to use the `-w` option to specify a smaller width. Here are the results of running
`sdiff` on two different pairs of files:

```
$ sdiff -w60 test1 test2
apples                              apples
oranges                             oranges
walnuts                         |   grapes
$ sdiff -w60 test1 test3
apples                          <
oranges                             oranges
walnuts                             walnuts
                                >   chestnuts
```

The `-s` option to the `sdiff` command only shows the differences between the two
files. Identical lines are suppressed. One of the most powerful uses of `sdiff` is
interactive, building an output file by choosing between different versions of two files.
You have to specify the `-o` option and the name of an output file to be created. The
`sdiff` command then displays a `%` prompt after each set of differences. You can
compare the different versions and select the one that will be sent to the output file.
Some of the possible responses are `l` to choose the left column, `r` to choose the right
column, and `q` to exit the program.

```
$ sdiff -w60 -o test test1 test3
apples                          <
% l
oranges                             oranges
walnuts                             walnuts
                                >   chestnuts

% r
$ cat test
apples
oranges
walnuts
chestnuts
```

Having looked at these commands in simplified examples, let's now consider some practical applications for comparing documents.

When working on a document, it is not an uncommon practice to make a copy of a file and edit the copy rather than the original. This might be done, for example, if someone other than the writer is inputting edits from a written copy. The `diff` command can be used to compare the two versions of a document. A writer could use it to proof an edited copy against the original.

```
$ diff brochure brochure.edits
49c43,44
< environment for program development and communications,
---
> environment for multiprocessing, program development
> and communications, programmers
56c51
< offering even more power and productivity for commericial
---
> offering even more power and productivity for commercial
76c69
< Languages such as FORTRAN, COBOL, Pascal, and C can be
---
> Additional languages such as FORTRAN, COBOL, Pascal, and
```

Using `diff` in this manner is a simple way for a writer to examine changes without reading the entire document. By capturing `diff` output in a file, you can keep a record of changes made to any document.

As another example, suppose a company has a number of text files that comprise its help facility. These files are shipped with the product and maintained online by the customer. When there is a documentation update, these files also need to be updated. One way to accomplish this is to replace each text file in its entirety, but that involves distributing a lot of material that remains unchanged. Another way is to use `diff` and simply send a record of changes between the old and the new. The −e option creates an editing script for `ed` that can be used to recreate the second file from the first.

```
$ diff -e help.txt help.new > help.chgs
$ cat help.chgs
153,199d
65c
$INCLUDE {filename} program.name
.
56a
.Rh 0 "" "$CHAIN Statement"
.Rh "Syntax"
.in 5n
.nf
$CHAIN {filename} program.name
.fi
.in 0
```

```
.Rh "Description"
Use the $CHAIN statement to direct the compiler to read
source code from program.name and compile it along
....
```

The company could ship the file `help.chgs` with instructions on how to input this editing script to `ed`. You'd want to create a shell script to automate this process, but that is really an extension of knowing how it might be done from the command line. The following command pipes the editing script to `ed`:

```
$ (cat help.chgs; echo 'w' ) | ed - help.txt
```

To save the changes, a `w` command is submitted through `echo`. (In fact, if you have any concern about sparing the original file, you could change the `w` to `1,$p`, which will cause the edited contents to be printed to standard output, but not saved in the file. Redirect standard output to a new file to keep both copies.)

As a further example, let's take the instance where two people have made copies of a file and made changes to their own copies, and now you want to compare them both against the original. In this example, `ch01` is the original; `ch01.tom` contains edits made by Tom; and `ch01.ann` contains changes made by Ann.

```
$ diff3 ch01 ch01.ann ch01.tom
====3
1:56a
2:56a
3:57,103c
  .mc |
  .Rh 0 "" "$CHAIN Statement"
  .XX "BASIC statements, $CHAIN"
  .XX "$CHAIN statement"
  .Rh "Syntax"
  .UN
  .in 5n
  .nf
  $CHAIN {file} program.name
  .fi
  .in 0
  .Rh "Description"
  Use the $CHAIN statement to direct the compiler to read
  source code from program.name and compile it along
  ....
====3
1:65c
2:65c
  $INCLUDE {file}
3:112c
  $INCLUDE {file} program.name
====2
1:136c
```

```
2:136c
  Nesting of $INSERT statements is not permitted.
3:183c
  Nesting of $INSERT statements is permitted.
====
1:143,144c
  program.name is converted to a valid UNIX filename.
  .LP
2:143,152c
  program.name is converted to a valid UNIX filename using
  the following conversion rules:
  .TS
  center, tab(@);
  c l c.
  /@is converted to@?
  ?@is converted to@??
  Null@is converted to@?0
  An initial .@is converted to@?.
  .TE
3:190,191c
  program.name is converted to a valid UNIX filename using
  a set of conversion rules.
```

You often find that one version has some things right and another version has other things right. What if you wanted to compile a single version of this document that reflects the changes made to each copy? You want to select which version is correct for each set of differences. One effective way to do this would be to use sdiff.

We'll use the −s option to suppress the printing of identical lines. To make the example fit on the printed page, we specify a 45-character line length. (You would generally use an 80-character line length for the screen.) Because the total line length is limited to 45 characters, sdiff will be able to display only the first 15 or so characters of the line for each file; the rest of the line will be truncated.

```
$ sdiff -w45 -s -o ch01.new ch01.ann ch01.tom
56a57,103
                          >   .Rh 0 "" "$CHAIN Statement"
                          >   .XX "BASIC statements, $CHAIN"
                          >   .XX "$CHAIN statement"
                          >   .Rh "Syntax"
                          >   .UN
                          >   .in 5n
                          >   .nf
                          >   $CHAIN {\fIfile\fP} \fI
                          >   .fi
                          >   .in 0
                          >   .Rh "Description"
                          >   Use the $CHAIN statement to de
```

```
                              >   code from \fIprogram.name\fP
                   . . . . . . .
    % r
    65c112
    $ INCLUDE {\fIfile\fP}    |   $INCLUDE {\fIfile\fP}
    % r
    % 143,152c190,191
    \fIprogram.name\fP is     |   \fIprogram.name\fP is
    following rules.          |   following rules.
    .TS                       <
    center, tab(@);           <
    c l c.                    <
    /@is converted to@?       <
    ?@is converted to@??      <
    Null@is converted to@?0   <
    An initial .@is converted<
    .TE                       <
    % 1
```

The file `ch01.new` contains the portions of each file that were selected along with all the lines that both files have in common.

Another program worth mentioning is `bdiff` (*big file* `diff`). It is used on files too large for `diff`. This program breaks up a large file into smaller segments and then passes each one through `diff`. It maintains line numbering as though `diff` were operating on one large file.

SCCS

We've shown an example using `diff` to produce a file that described the changes made to a text file for a help facility. It allowed the distribution of a smaller file describing changes instead of a wholly new version of the file. This indicates a potential application for `diff`, which is fully realized in the Source Code Control System or SCCS. SCCS is a facility for keeping track of the changes to files that take place at different stages of a software development or documentation project.

Suppose you have a first draft of a manual. (This is referred to as a *delta* when it is saved in a special SCCS format.) The second draft, of course, is based on changes to the first draft.

When you make the delta for the second draft, SCCS, instead of keeping a separate copy for each draft, uses `diff` to record the changes to the first draft that resulted in the second draft. Only the changes, and the instructions for having an editor make them, need to be maintained. SCCS allows you to regenerate earlier drafts, which saves disk space.

SCCS is quite complex—too complex to describe here—but we seriously suggest that you investigate it if you are working on a large, frequently-revised or multiple-author writing project.

Using make

The make program is a UNIX facility for describing dependencies among a group of related files, usually ones that are part of the same project. This facility has enjoyed widespread use in software development projects. Programmers use make to describe how to ''make'' a program—what source files need to be compiled, what libraries must be included, and which object files need to be linked. By keeping track of these relationships in a single place, individual members of a software development team can make changes to a single module, run make, and be assured that the program reflects the latest changes made by others on the team.

We group make with the other commands for keeping track of differences between files only by a leap of the imagination. However, although it does not compare two versions of the same source file, it can be used to compare versions such as a source file and the formatted output.

Part of what makes UNIX a productive environment for text processing is discovering other uses for standard programs. The make utility has many possible applications for a documentation project. One such use is to maintain up-to-date copies of formatted files that make up a single manual and provide users with a way of obtaining a printed copy of the entire manual without having to know which preprocessors or nroff/troff options need to be invoked.

The basic operation that make performs is to compare two sets of files, for example, formatted files and unformatted files, and determine if any members of one set, the unformatted files, are more recent than their counterpart in the other set, the formatted files. This is accomplished by simply comparing the date or time stamp of pairs of files. If the unformatted source file has been modified since the formatted file was made, make executes the specified command to ''remake'' the formatted file.

To use make, you have to write a description file, usually named makefile (or Makefile), that resides in the working directory for the project. The makefile specifies a hierarchy of dependencies among individual files, called *components*. At the top of this hierarchy is a *target*. For our purposes, you can think of the target as a printed copy of a book; the components are formatted files generated by processing an unformatted file with nroff.

Here's the makefile that reflects these dependencies.

```
manual: ch01.fmt ch02.fmt ch03.fmt
        lp ch0[1-3].fmt
ch01.fmt: ch01
        nroff -mm ch01 > ch01.fmt
ch02.fmt: ch02
        tbl ch02 | nroff -mm > ch01.fmt
ch03.fmt: ch03a ch03b ch03c
        nroff -mm ch03? > ch03.fmt
```

This hierarchy can be represented in a diagram:

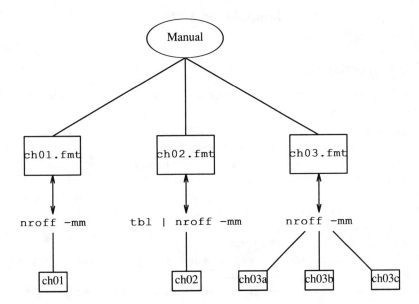

The target is `manual` and it is made up of three formatted files whose names appear after the colon. Each of these components has its own dependency line. For instance, `ch01.fmt` is dependent upon a coded file named `ch01`. Underneath the dependency line is the command that generates `ch01.fmt`. Each command line *must* begin with a tab.

When you enter the command `make`, the end result is that the three formatted files are spooled to the printer. However, a sequence of operations is performed before this final action. The dependency line for each component is evaluated, determining if the coded file has been modified since the last time the formatted file was made. The formatting command will be executed only if the coded file is more recent. After all the components are made, the `lp` command is executed.

As an example of this process, we'll assume that all the formatted files are up-to-date. Then by editing the source file `ch03a`, we change the modification time. When you execute the `make` command, any output files dependent on `ch03a` are reformatted.

```
$ make
nroff -mm ch03? > ch03.fmt
lp ch0[1-3].fmt
```

Only `ch03.fmt` needs to be remade. As soon as that formatting command finishes, the command underneath the target `manual` is executed, spooling the files to the printer.

Although this example has actually made only limited use of `make`'s facilities, we hope it suggests more ways to use `make` in a documentation project. You can keep your `makefiles` just this simple, or you can go on to learn additional notation, such as internal macros and suffixes, in an effort to generalize the description file for increased usefulness. We'll return to `make` in Chapter 18.

• Manipulating Data •

Removing Formatting Codes

The `deroff` command removes `nroff/troff` requests, macros, inline backslash sequences, and `eqn` and `tbl` specifications.

```
$ cat temp
.CH 11 "A Miscellany of UNIX Commands"
In this chapter, we present a miscellany of \s-2UNIX\s0
programs with text-processing applications.
.P
In addition, we introduce several \s-2UNIX\s0 utilities
$ deroff temp
    Miscellany  UNIX Programs
In this chapter, we present a miscellany of UNIX programs
with text-processing applications.
In addition, we introduce several UNIX utilities
```

Special rules are applied to text specified as arguments to a macro so that they are not passed through `deroff`. A word in a macro call must contain at least three letters. Thus, *A* and *of* are omitted.

The `deroff -w` command is used by `spell` to remove `troff` requests and place each word on a separate line. You can use `deroff` in a similar manner to prepare a word list.

```
$ deroff -w temp
Miscellany
UNIX
Programs
In
this
chapter
we
present
miscellany
of
UNIX
programs
with
text
processing
applications
In
addition
```

Again, not all "words" are recognized as words. The `deroff` command requires that a word consist of at least two characters, which may be letters, numerals, ampersands, or apostrophes. (As mentioned above, it applies slightly different rules to text specified as an argument to a macro.)

We had hoped `deroff` might be useful for our clients who wanted online copies of a document but used a word processor. Because `deroff` drops words, it was not practical for stripping out `troff`-specific constructs. Perhaps the best way to do this is to use `nroff` to process the file, and then use a combination of terminal filters to strip out tabs, backspaces (overstrikes), and reverse linefeeds.

The `sort` and `uniq` Commands

The `sort` command puts lines of a file in alphabetic or numeric order. The `uniq` command eliminates duplicate lines in a file.

The `sort` command works on each line of a text file. Normally, it is used to order the contents of files containing data such as names, addresses, and phone numbers. In the following example, we use `grep` to search for index entries, coded with the macro `.XX` or `.XN`, and sort the output in alphabetic order.

```
$ grep ".X[XN]" ch04 | sort -df
.XX "ABORT statement"
.XX "ASSIGNMENT statement"
.XX "BASIC statements, ABORT"
.XX "BASIC statements, ASSIGNMENT"
.XX "BASIC statements, BEGIN CASE"
```

The `-f` option folds uppercase and lowercase words together (that is, it ignores case when performing the sort). The `-d` option sorts in dictionary order, ignoring any special characters.

The `uniq` command works only on sorted files, comparing each adjacent line. The `sort` command has a `-u` option for removing all but one indentical set of lines. Usually this is sufficient, but `uniq` does have several options, which gives you additional flexibility. For example, here's the sorted output of four files:

```
$ sort test*
apples
apples
apples
chestnuts
chestnuts
grapes
oranges
oranges
oranges
oranges
walnuts
walnuts
walnuts
```

The `-d` option prints one line for each duplicate line, but does not print lines that are unique.

```
$ sort test* | uniq -d
apples
chestnuts
oranges
walnuts
```

In this example, *grapes* has been filtered out. The −u option prints only unique lines. If we used the −u option, only *grapes* would appear.

You wouldn't expect sort to be useful on a document containing long lines of text. However, if you bothered to start sentences on a new line when creating the input file (as we recommended in Chapter 3), scanning a sorted file can produce some interesting things. The following command sorts the contents of ch03 and pipes the output through pg:

```
$ sort -u ch03 | pg
```

Looking at the results gives you a slightly turned about view of your document. For instance, you might notice inconsistencies among arguments to formatter requests:

```
.sp
.sp .2i
.sp .3v
.sp .5
```

Or you could check the frequency with which sentences begin in the same manner:

```
It is dangerous to use mvcur()
It is designed so that each piece of code
It is possible that some programs
```

In the next example, we use deroff to create a word list. Then we sort it and use uniq to remove duplicates. The −c option with uniq provides a count of the occurrences of identical lines. (It overrides −u and −d.)

```
$ deroff -w ch03 | sort -fd | uniq -c
      1 abort
      1 aborted
      3 about
      4 above
      1 absolute
      1 absorb
      1 accepting
      1 accomplishes
      1 active
      2 actual
      5 actually
      2 Add
      7 add
    ...
     68 you
      3 Your
```

```
 13 your
  2 zero
```

In the next example, we repeat the previous command, this time adding another sort at the end to order the words by frequency. The −r option is used to *reverse* the comparison, putting the greatest number first.

```
$ deroff -w ch03 | sort -fd | uniq -c | sort -rfd
666 the
234 to
219 is
158 window
156 of
148 and
114 in
111 screen
105 that
 83 character
 76 are
...
  1 aborted
  1 abort
```

You will find other examples of sort in the next section, where we look at sorting particular fields. Be sure to read the UNIX command pages for sort and uniq and experiment using different options.

The join Command

The join command compares lines contained in separate files and joins lines that have the same key. (When you use sort or join, each line is separated into *fields* by blanks or tabs. Normally, the first field is the key field, on which the sort or join is performed. However, there are options that allow you to change the key field.) The file must be sorted in ascending ASCII sequence before being processed by join.

```
$ cat 85
jan    19
feb    05
mar    14
apr    15
may    15
jun    18
jul    19
aug    20
sep    19
nov    18
dec    18
$ cat 86
```

```
jan    09
feb    15
mar    04
apr    06
may    14
jun    13
jul    13
aug    10
sep    14
nov    13
dec    12
$ sort 85 > 85.temp; sort 86 > 86.temp
```

First we sort both of these files, creating temporary files. Then we perform the `join`, followed by a `sort` with the `-M` option, to reorder them by month.

```
$ join 85.temp 86.temp | sort -M > joiner
$ cat joiner
jan 19 09
feb 05 15
mar 14 04
apr 15 06
may 15 14
jun 18 13
jul 19 13
aug 20 10
sep 19 14
nov 18 13
dec 18 12
$
```

After the data is joined in this manner, it can be sorted by field. Fields are separated by blank spaces or tabs. The sort can be performed on specific fields, using + to indicate the first sort field and - to indicate the last sort field. The first field is +0. To sort on the second field, use +1.

```
$ sort +1 joiner
feb 05 15
mar 14 04
apr 15 06
may 15 14
dec 18 12
jun 18 13
nov 18 13
jan 19 09
jul 19 13
sep 19 14
aug 20 10
```

The comm Command

The comm command reads the contents of two sorted files and produces for output a three-column listing of lines that are found

- only in the first file;
- only in the second file;
- in both the first and second files.

For example, let's suppose that we had generated a list of UNIX commands found in Berkeley 4.2 and another list of commands found in AT&T System V.2. We can use comm to produce a compact listing of commands found exclusively in one version and commands common to both. For obvious reasons, this example uses only the beginning of the list.

```
$ cat bsd4.2
adb
addbib
apply
apropos
ar
as
at
awk

$ cat attV.2
adb
admin
ar
as
asa
at
awk
```

Note that both files have already been sorted.

```
$ comm bsd4.2 attV.2
                                adb
addbib
                admin
apply
apropos
                                ar
                                as
                asa
                                at
                                awk
```

Commands found only on systems running Berkeley 4.2 are in the left-hand column, and those found only on AT&T System V.2 are in the center column. Commands found in both versions are listed in the right-hand column.

You can also suppress the display of one or more columns. For instance, if you wanted to display only the commands that were found on both systems, you'd enter:

```
$ comm -12 bsd4.2 attV.2
```

Only the third column would be shown.

By specifying – instead of a filename, you can also use standard input. In the next example, we produce a listing of filenames from two directories on the system, sort them, and compare them against the commands named in the bsd4.2 file. This allows us to compare commands found on our system with those on the list of Berkeley commands.

```
$ ( cd /bin ; ls ; cd /usr/bin ; ls ) | sort | comm - bsd4.2
acctcom
                adb
                addbib
admin
apnum
                apply
                apropos
                                ar
                                as
asa
                at
                                awk
```

Parentheses are used to group a series of commands, combining their output into a single stream; we want a list of command names without pathnames from several directories. Because a new shell is created to execute these commands, notice that we do not change our current working directory when the commands in parentheses have finished executing.

The cut and paste Commands

The cut and paste commands modify a table or any other data in fields or columns. You can extract specific columns of data using cut, and join them horizontally using paste.

For our examples, we'll make use of a portion of a table of ASCII characters that specifies their decimal and hexadecimal values. (This example is probably unnecessarily complex; you can use cut and paste for much simpler jobs than this!) Here's what the table looks like to begin with:

```
$ cat appc
.TS
center, box;
cb cb cb
```

```
n n l.
Decimal      Hexadecimal  ASCII
=
000    00      NUL
001    01      SO
002    02      STX
003    03      ETX
004    04      EOT
005    05      ENQ
006    06      ACK
007    07      BEL
008    08      BS
009    09      HT
.TE
```

Each column is separated by a tab. A tab is the default field delimiter for cut; the −d option can be used to change it. The −c option allows you to specify character positions or ranges. The command cut −c6−80 would print characters beginning at position 6 through 80, truncating the first five characters. The −f option is used to specify one or more fields that are passed to standard output. (Given the name of the command, one might reasonably think you'd specify the fields or column position you wanted *cut* out, but...)

In the next example we extract the third field, which contains the ASCII names:

```
$ cut -f3 -s appc
ASCII
NUL
SO
STX
ETX
EOT
ENQ
ACK
BEL
BS
HT
```

We use the −s option to remove all lines that do not have any delimiters, thus dropping the tbl constructs from the output. Normally, cut passes lines without delimiters straight through, and that is what we really want for our next feat. We are going to reorder the table so that it can be referenced by the ASCII name rather than by decimal number. All of this can be done from the command line, with only a brief entry into the editor at the end.

We'll look at this in stages. First, we extract the third column and send it along to paste:

```
$ cut -f3 appc | paste - appc
.TS     .TS
center, box; center, box;
cb cb cb     cb cb cb
n n l.n n l.
ASCII Decimal     Hexadecimal ASCII
=       =
NUL    000    00    NUL
SO     001    01    SO
STX    002    02    STX
ETX    003    03    ETX
EOT    004    04    EOT
ENQ    005    05    ENQ
ACK    006    06    ACK
BEL    007    07    BEL
BS     008    08    BS
HT     009    09    HT
.TE     .TE
```

The paste command reads one or more files or standard input (the − option) and replaces the newline with a tab in all but the last file. This gives us four columns. (Yes, it doubled the tbl specifications, but we have an editor.) Now, all we have to do is extract the first three columns from the output. Only cut −f1,2,3 has been added to the previous command, and the output is redirected to a file.

```
$ cut -f3 appc | paste - appc | cut -f1,2,3 > ascii.table
$ cat ascii.table
.TS     .TS
center, box; center, box;
cb cb cb     cb cb cb
n n l.n n l.
ASCII Decimal     Hexadecimal
=       =
NUL    000    00
SO     001    01
STX    002    02
ETX    003    03
EOT    004    04
ENQ    005    05
ACK    006    06
BEL    007    07
BS     008    08
HT     009    09
.TE     .TE
```

This gives us three columns in the correct order. We can go into vi to rearrange the tbl constructs and execute a sort command on just the data portion of the table to bring it all together.

```
$ cat ascii.table
.TS
center, box;
cb cb cb
n n l.
ASCII  Decimal      Hexadecimal
=
ACK    006    06
BEL    007    07
BS     008    08
ENQ    005    05
EOT    004    04
ETX    003    03
HT     009    09
NUL    000    00
SO     001    01
STX    002    02
.TE
```

The `paste` command can be used in several interesting ways. Normally, in order to merge two files, `paste` replaces the newline in the first file with a tab. The `-d` option allows you to specify a substitute for the tab. This can be any single character or a list of characters. Special characters can be represented as follows: newline (\n), tab (\t), backslash (\\), and empty string (\0). Each character in the list is assigned in sequence to replace a newline, and the list is recycled as many times as necessary. We can use `paste` to present our three-column table in six columns:

```
$ paste -s -d"\t\n" appci
.TS    center, box;
cb cb cb    n n l.
Decimal     Hexadecimal ASCII =
000    00   NUL    001    01   SO
002    02   STX    003    03   ETX
004    04   EOT    005    05   ENQ
006    06   ACK    007    07   BEL
008    08   BS     009    09   HT
.TE
```

The `-s` option is used when only a single file is specified. It tells `paste` to merge subsequent lines in the same file rather than to merge one line at a time from several files. In this example, the first line's newline is replaced by a tab while the second line retains the newline. To get nine columns out of three-column input, you'd specify -d"\t\t\n".

A little work needs to be done to the `tbl` specifications. You could also execute the `paste` command from within `vi` so that it only affects the data portion.

You would probably want to go to this much trouble for a large table (or many small tables) rather than the small examples shown here. A more practical example that uses `paste` alone would be to construct a multi-column table from a single long list of words. Simply split the list into equal-sized chunks, then paste them together side by side.

The `tr` Command

The `tr` command is a character translation filter, reading standard input and either deleting specific characters or substituting one character for another.

The most common use of `tr` is to change each character in one string to the corresponding character in a second string. (A string of consecutive ASCII characters can be represented as a hyphen-separated range.)

For example, the command:

```
$ tr "A-Z" "a-z" < file
```

will convert all uppercase characters in *file* to the equivalent lowercase characters. The result is printed on standard output.

As described in Chapter 7, this translation (and the reverse) can be useful from within `vi` for changing the case of a string. You can also delete specific characters. The `-d` option deletes from the input each occurrence of one or more characters specified in a string (special characters should be placed within quotation marks to protect them from the shell). For instance, the following command passes to standard output the contents of *file* with all punctuation deleted:

```
$ cat file | tr -d ",.!?;:"
```

The `-s` (*squeeze*) option of `tr` removes multiple consecutive occurrences of the same character. For example, the command:

```
$ tr -s " " < file
```

will print on standard output a copy of *file* in which multiple spaces in sequence have been replaced with a single space.

We've also found `tr` useful when converting documents created on other systems for use under UNIX. For example, one of our writers created some files using an IBM PC word processor. When we uploaded the files to our system, and tried to edit them with `vi`, we got the message:

```
Not an ascii file
```

and a blank screen. The `vi` editor could not read the file. However, using a programming utility that lists the actual binary values that make up the contents of a file (od, or *octal dump*), we were able to determine that the word processor used nulls (octal 000) instead of newlines (octal 012) to terminate each line.

The `tr` command allows you to specify characters as octal values by preceding the value with a backslash, so the command:

```
$ tr '\000' '\012'
```

was what we needed to convert the file into a form that could be edited with `vi`.

Splitting Large Files

Splitting a single large file into smaller files can be done out of necessity—when you come across a program that can't handle a large file—or as a matter of preference—when you find it easier to work with smaller files. UNIX offers two different programs for breaking up files, `split` and `csplit`.

The `split` command divides a file into chunks, consisting of the same number of lines. This is 1000 lines, unless specified differently. In the following example of `split`, we break up a 1700-line file into 500-line chunks. The `wc` command supplies a summary of the number of lines, words, and characters in a text file.

```
$ wc ch03
1708    8962    59815 ch03
$ split -500 ch03
$ wc ch03*
500     2462    16918 ch03aa
500     2501    16731 ch03ab
500     2976    19350 ch03ac
208     1023     6816 ch03ad
1708    8962    59815 ch03
```

The `split` command created four files. It appended `aa`, `ab`, `ac`, etc. to the end of the original filename to create a unique filename for each file. You can also specify, as a third argument, a different filename to be used instead of the original filename.

Look at the end of one of these files:

```
$ tail ch03ac
.Bh "Miscellaneous Functions"
.in 5n
.TS
tab(@);
l l l.
```

Unfortunately, the file breaks in the middle of a table. The `split` command pays no attention to content, making it inadequate for breaking a file into manageable, but complete, sections.

The `csplit` command offers an alternative, allowing you to break a file in context. There are two ways to use it. The first is to supply one or more line numbers. You could enter the following command:

```
$ csplit ch03 100 145 200
```

Four files would be created (0-99, 100-144, 145-199, 200-end). The naming convention for files created by `csplit` is different than `split`. Files are named `xx00`, `xx01`, `xx02`, and so on. If you want to specify a prefix that is different than `xx`, you can do so with the `-f` option.

Because we do not know in advance which line numbers to specify, we can use `grep` to get this information. The `-n` option to `grep` causes line numbers to be returned. In this example, we specify a pattern to match the section header macros, `Ah` and `Bh`:

```
$ grep -n ".[AB]h" ch03
```

It produces the following listing:

```
   5:.Ah "Introduction"
  30:.Ah "Using the Curses Library"
 175:.Ah "The Curses Functions"
 398:.Bh "Adding Characters to the Screen Image"
 638:.Bh "Standout Mode"
 702:.Bh "Getting Characters from the Terminal"
 777:.Bh "Input Modes"
 958:.Bh "Erasing and Clearing"
1133:.Bh "Creating and Removing Multiple Windows"
1255:.Bh "Window-Specific Functions"
1301:.Bh "Manipulating Multiple Windows"
1654:.Bh "Terminal Manipulation"
```

From this listing, we select the appropriate places at which to split the file and supply these numbers to split. The -f option is used to supply a filename prefix.

```
$ csplit -f ch03. ch03 175 1133
6803                              Number of bytes in each segment
32544
20468
$ ls ch03.*
ch03.00
ch03.01
ch03.02
```

The csplit command prints a character count for each of the three files it created. (This count can be suppressed using the -s option.)

The second way to use csplit is to supply a list of patterns. For instance, if you had prepared an outline that you wanted to break into files correponding to sections I, II, and III, you could specify:

```
$ csplit -s -f sect. outline /I./ /II./ /III./
$ ls sect.*
sect.01
sect.02
sect.03
```

You can also repeat a pattern. In one project we were working on, one large file contained a number of commands in reference page format. We decided it would be easier if we put each command in its own file. The beginning of a reference header was marked by the macro .Rh 0. First, we used grep to determine the number of times this macro occurred.

```
$ grep -c ".Rh 0" ch04
43
```

We reduce this number by 1 and surround it with braces:

```
$ csplit -s -f ch04. ch04 "/.Rh 0/" {42}
```

The pattern is enclosed within double quotation marks because it contains a space. (If you use the C shell, you must protect the braces from being interpreted by placing them in double quotation marks as well.) This command creates 43 files:

```
$ ls ch04*
ch04
ch04.00
ch04.01
ch04.02
ch04.03
...
ch04.39
ch04.40
ch04.41
ch04.42
ch04.43
```

The only task remaining is to rename the files, using the name of the command listed as the first argument to the `.Rh` macro. (We'd have to write an `awk` or `shell` script to do this automatically.)

After you have divided a large file into a number of smaller files, you might organize them in a subdirectory. Let's look at a small example of this:

```
$ mkdir ch04.files
$ mv ch04.?? ch04.files
```

Again, the usefulness of filename metacharacters is apparent, giving us the ability to move 43 files without typing 43 filenames.

Encryption

The cloak-and-dagger set and the security conscious will find uses for the encryption facilities of UNIX. (These facilities are not available on UNIX systems sold outside the United States.) The `crypt` command reads a file from standard input, asks you to supply a *key* for encoding the file, and passes to standard output an encrypted version of the file. You should redirect standard output to a new file because the encrypted file is not readable text.

```
$ cat message | crypt > encrypted.msg
Enter key:alabaster
```

Just as when you enter a password, the key does not appear on the screen as you enter it. If you prefer, you can enter the key as an argument to `crypt`. To decode an encrypted file, you simply `cat` the file to `crypt` and supply the key.

The UNIX editors `ed`, `ex`, and `vi`, can be invoked with the `-x` option to read or edit an encrypted file. (Some versions of these programs recognize this option but do not support the encryption feature.) Of course, you have to supply the correct key.

▪ Cleaning Up and Backing Up ▪

In this section, we show some procedures for backing up active files to some other medium such as tape or floppy disk. At many sites, backups are the responsibility of one person, who performs these tasks on a regular basis to ensure that users can recover much of their data in case there is a serious system crash. At other sites, individual users might be responsible for doing their own backups, especially if there are only a few users on the system. Whoever does it must ensure that backups of important files are made periodically.

A second reason for learning a backup procedure is to enable you to store files on an off-line medium. For users of PCs, this is the standard method of operation (and therefore much simpler to do), but all UNIX systems have hard disks as the primary storage medium. No matter how large a disk drive is, sooner or later, users will fill it to capacity. Frequently, there are useless files that can be deleted. Other inactive files, such as an early draft of a document, might be removed from the system after you have made a copy on floppy disk or tape. After a project is finished, you probably want to make several copies of all important files. At a later time, should you need files that have been stored off-line, you can easily restore them to the system.

We are going to describe how to use the cpio command for backing up one or more working directories. There are other UNIX commands that might be used as well (tar and dd, for instance). At your site, you may even have simpler shell scripts that prevent you from having to deal with cpio directly. Ask an expert user at your site about backup procedures and go through it once or twice. Apart from learning about cpio, you will need:

1.   The UNIX filename of the device (/dev/*xxxx*) to which you are directing the output of the cpio command.

2.   Familiarity with operating the device, such as being able to load a tape in the tape drive and knowing how to format a floppy disk prior to use.

You can use cpio in two basic ways, either to back up or to restore files. You use cpio with the −o option and > to redirect output to the device for backup, or with the −i option and < to redirect input from the device to restore files.

Unlike many of the commands we've looked at, cpio depends exclusively on reading a list of filenames from standard input. This list identifies the files that will be backed up. For practical purposes, this involves doing an ls command on the directory you want backed up and piping the results to cpio.

You need to know the UNIX filename for the backup device. This name is site specific, so you need to check with a knowledgeable user. At our site, we have a floppy disk drive named /dev/rfp021. A tape drive might be named /dev/mt0.

After you have loaded the tape in the tape drive or placed the floppy disk in the disk drive, you can perform the backup using your own version of this command:

```
$ ls /work/docbook/ch13 | cpio -ov > /dev/rfp021
sect3
dict
shellstuff
...
384 blocks
```

The −v (*verbose*) option prints a list of filenames on the screen.

The −i option to cpio reads or restores files from a tape or floppy disk device. Sometimes, before you actually restore files, you want to list the contents of the tape or disk. The −t option prints a table of contents but does not actually read these files onto the system.

```
$ cpio -it < /dev/rfp021
384 blocks
sect3
dict
shellstuff
...
```

Using the −v option along with the −t option produces a long (verbose) listing of files, as if you had entered ls −l.

You don't have to extract all the files from disk or tape. You can specify certain files, using filename metacharacters to specify a pattern.

```
$ cpio -iv "sect?" < /dev/rfp021
No match.
```

Remember to refer to the full pathname if the files were saved using a complete pathname, and to put pathnames that include metacharacters within double quotation marks.

```
$ cpio -i "/work/docbook/ch13/sect?" < /dev/rfp021
384 blocks
sect3
sect2
sect1
```

Before restoring a file, cpio checks to see that it won't overwrite an existing file of the same name that has been modified more recently than the file being read.

You can also use the find command with the −cpio condition to do a back up. The advantage of using find is that it descends all the way down a directory hierarchy.

```
$ find /work/docbook/ch13 -cpio /dev/rfp021
```

To restore a directory hierarchy, use the −d option to cpio. Administrators frequently use find to generate a list of files that have been modified within a certain time period. The conditions −mtime (*modification time*) and −atime (*access time*) can be followed by a number indicating a number of days. This number can be preceded by a plus sign, indicating *more than* that number of days, or a minus sign, indicating *less than* that many days. If there is no sign, the condition indicates exactly that number of days.

This example uses `find` to produce a list of files that have been modified within the last seven days. These active files are good candidates for backups.

```
$ find /work/docbook -mtime -7 -print
/work/docbook
/work/docbook/oshell
/work/docbook/ch01
...
```

Don't forget you have to specify `-print` to see the results of a `find` command.

You could work up your own version of this command to look for your own files that have not been accessed in the last 21 days. Add the option `-atime` with an argument of `+21` to list the files and directories that have not been accessed in over 21 days. Add the `-user` option to look only for your own files, the `-cpio` option to backup these files, and the `-ok` option to execute an `rm` command to delete them from the system after they've been backed up.

```
$ find /work -atime +21 -user -cpio /dev/rfp021 -ok rm {} \;
```

The `-ok` option is the same as the `-exec` option; however, instead of executing the command specified within parentheses on all files selected by `find`, it prompts you first to approve the command for each file.

▪ Compressing Files ▪

You can conserve the amount of disk space that text files take up by storing some of your files in a compressed form. The `pack` command can be used to compress a file. It generally reduces a text file by 25 to 40 percent.

```
$ ls -l ch04/sect1
-rw-rw-rw-   1 fred    doc     29350 Jun 10 15:22 ch04/sect1
$ pack ch04/sect1
pack: ch04/sect1: 39.9% Compression
```

The original file is replaced by a packed file with a `.z` appended to the original filename.

```
$ ls -l ch04/sect1.z
-rw-rw-rw-   1 fred    doc     17648 Jun 10 15:29 ch04/sect1.z
```

The `pack` command reduced the size of this file from 29K to 17K bytes. If used system-wide, it could save a significant amount of disk space, although the amount of compression will vary from file to file. Obviously, there is less benefit in packing small files.

To expand a packed file, use the `unpack` command. You can specify the name of the file with or without the `.z` suffix.

```
$ unpack ch04/sect1
unpack: ch04/sect1: unpacked
```

Another way to temporarily unpack a file is to use a special version of cat for packed files, called pcat. Use this command to view a packed file (pipe it through more or pg) or send it as input to another command, as in the following example:

```
$ pcat ch04/sect1 | nroff -mm
```

▪ Communications ▪

More and more, we find that our projects require us to work on several different computer systems, some of them UNIX systems, some not. Given this situation, the ability to work remotely on other systems and to transfer files has been essential. Fortunately, a number of useful communications programs are part of the standard UNIX shipment.

Two basic types of connections between computer systems are a *dial-up* line, using a modem to communicate across phone lines, and a *direct* line, when two computer systems are in close proximity and can be connected by a single cable. The uucp and cu commands establish communication links using both types of connections.

The cu command (Berkeley's version is called tip) is a UNIX program for conducting a login session on a remote computer system. UUCP (UNIX-to-UNIX copy) is a series of related programs for transferring files between UNIX systems. Its main program is called uucp.

We cannot provide full descriptions of these facilities here. A good way to learn is to ask an expert user to help you transfer files or begin a remote login session. Keep notes on the procedure and when following it, if things don't work as expected, get more help.

The UUCP programs are quite straightforward and easy to use after you are accustomed to the conventions. Each system on the UUCP network has a file that describes the other systems linked to it and what types of links are available. This file is created by the system administrator of each system. You can find out the names of these remote systems by entering the uuname command. If your system is properly configured and you have a login on a remote system, such as boston, you can begin a remote session by entering:

```
$ cu boston
```

After you are connected to the remote system, you should get a login message. To quit a remote session, log out and then enter ~. (tilde dot) to return to your own machine.

There are a number of commands you can enter while under the control of cu, permitting, for instance, the execution of commands on the local system while you are still logged in to the remote system. Check the reference page in your UNIX documentation.

You can also *dial direct* to a non-UNIX system by specifying a telephone number on the command line (providing, of course, that the files accessed by these communications programs have been properly configured by the system administrator).

You can send mail to users on these remote systems and transfer files. Generally, file transfers take place between *public directories* on both systems, usually /usr/spool/uucppublic. File transfers between other directories will contend with file and directory access permissions as well as uucp permissions set by the system administrator. The character ~ serves as a shorthand for the public directory.

For instance, when working on site for a client, we often create files that we want to send to our own system. If we are logged in on their system, we can send the file outline to our system named ora by entering:

```
$ uucp -m outline ora!~/fred/
```

The UUCP facility is batch oriented, accepting requests and acting upon them in the order in which they are received. Although it may execute your request immediately, if it is busy or encounters difficulty making the connection, UUCP will carry out the request at a later time.

The −m option is used so that we are sent mail when the copy is actually completed. The system name is followed by an exclamation mark (if you use the C shell, escape ! with a backslash). Then you specify a tilde (~) followed by the user's name. Putting a slash after the user name (fred) ensures that the user name will be interpreted as a directory (or a directory will be created if one does not exist).

Occasionally, you will need to transfer a large number of files or, perhaps, an entire directory hierarchy. There are some simple tricks you can use to combine multiple files into a single file, making it easier to transmit to another system. They are especially helpful when you transfer between public directories.

You must first create a list of the files to be included. (You can do this either manually or with a command like ls or find.) Then use cpio to create what we can call a file *archive* on standard output rather than on a backup device. Redirect standard output to a file, then use UUCP to send the archive. Use the same backup program on the target system to restore the archive. For example, if you had a book made up of files ch01, ch02, etc., you could "package" that book for transfer to another system using cpio:

```
boston$ cd /usr/proj/book
boston$ find . -name 'ch0?' -print | cpio -oc > book.archive
```

or using a manually generated list of filenames:

```
boston$ ls ch0? > filelist
boston$ cpio -oc < filelist > book.archive
```

Then, after transferring book.archive (instead of numerous individual files) to the remote system with UUCP, a user can restore the archive:

```
calif$ mkdir /usr/proj/book
calif$ mv /usr/spool/uucppublic/book.archive /usr/proj/book
calif$ cd /usr/proj/book
calif$ cpio -icd < book.archive
```

(The −c option of cpio writes header information in ASCII for portability; −d tells cpio to create directories if needed when doing the restore.)

(On Berkeley UNIX systems, you can do something similar with `tar`. See your UNIX manual for details.)

▪ Scripts of UNIX Sessions ▪

Throughout this chapter, we have provided examples of UNIX commands. These examples were made using a command called `script` (which is not a standard System V command). The `script` command allows you to make a file copy of a UNIX session. Without this facility, we'd have to simulate the examples by hand.

After you invoke `script`, your input and output is copied to a file. By default, the name of this file is `typescript`, but you can supply a different name on the command line.

```
$ script
Script started on Thu Jul 10 12:49:57 1987
$ echo hello
hello
$
```

To quit, you enter *CTRL-D*.

```
$ cat typescript
Script started on Thu Jul 10 12:49:57 1987
$ echo hello
hello
$
script done on Thu Jul 10 12:50:11 1987
```

After we make a script, we simply read the file into our text using `vi`.

Keeping a script of a procedure is also a good start for building a shell script that performs a routine task automatically.

12

Let the Computer Do the Dirty Work

Computers are very good at doing the same thing repeatedly, or doing a series of very similar things one after another. These are just the kinds of things that people hate to do, so it makes sense to learn how to let the computer do the dirty work.

As we discussed in Chapter 7, you can save `ex` commands in a *script*, and execute the script from within `vi` with the `:so` command. It is also possible to apply such a script to a file from the outside—without opening the file with `vi`. As you can imagine, when you apply the same series of edits to many different files, you can work very quickly using a script.

In addition, there is a special UNIX editor, called `sed` (*stream editor*), that *only* works with scripts. Although `sed` can be used to edit files (and we will show many useful applications in this chapter), it has a unique place in the UNIX editing pantheon not as a file editor, but as a filter that performs editing operations on the fly, while data is passed from one program to another through a pipe.

The `sed` editor uses an editing syntax that is similar to that used by `ex`, so it should not be difficult to learn the basics.

The `awk` program, which is discussed in the next chapter, is yet another text-processing program. It is similar to `sed`, in that it works from the outside and can be used as a filter, but there the resemblance ends. It is really not an editor at all, but a database manipulation program that can be turned into an editor. Its syntax goes beyond the global substitution/regular expression syntax we've already seen, and so `awk` may be the last thing that many writers learn. Nonetheless, it has some important capabilities that you may want to be familiar with.

Finally, to make best use of these tools, you need to know a bit about shell programming. In fact, because the shell provides a framework that you can use to put all these other tools together, we need to discuss it first.

If you are a programmer, and have already worked with the shell, this discussion may be too elementary; however, we are assuming that many of our readers are writers with only minimal exposure to programming. They, like us when we started working with UNIX, need encouragement to branch out into these untried waters that have so little apparent connection to the task at hand.

This chapter is different from those in the first part of the book in that it not only teaches the basics of some new programs, but also puts them to work building some useful text-processing tools. At times, material is organized according to what is needed to build the tools, rather than as a comprehensive attempt to teach the program itself. As a result, the material presented on `sed`, for example, is less complete than our earlier treatment of `vi`. We cover the most important points, but in many ways this chapter is suggestive. If you come away with a sense of possibility, it has done its job.

• Shell Programming •

A shell script, or shell program, can be no more than a sequence of stored commands, entered in a file just as you would type them yourself to the shell.

There are two shells in common use in the UNIX system, the Bourne shell (`sh`), championed by AT&T, and the C shell (`csh`), developed at the University of California at Berkeley. Although the C shell has many features that make it preferable for interactive use, the Bourne shell is much faster, so it is the tool of choice for writing shell scripts. (Even if you use the C shell, scripts written using Bourne shell syntax will be executed in the Bourne shell.)

We discuss the Bourne shell exclusively in this chapter, although we make reference to differences from the C shell on occasion. This should pose no problem to C shell users, however, because the basic method of issuing commands is identical. The differences lie in more advanced programming constructs, which we will not introduce in detail here.

Stored Commands

The `.profile` (or `.login` if you use the C shell) file in your home directory is a good example of a shell program consisting only of stored commands. A simple `.profile` might look like this:

```
stty erase '^H' echoe kill '^X' intr '^C'
PATH=/bin:/usr/bin:/usr/local/bin:.;export PATH
umask 2
date
mail
```

This file does some automatic housekeeping to set up your account environment every time you log in. Even if you aren't familiar with the commands it contains, you can get the basic idea. The commands are executed one line at a time; it is a tremendous time-saving to be able to type one command instead of five.

You can probably think of many other repetitive sequences of commands that you'd rather not type one at a time. For example, let's suppose you were accustomed to working on an MS-DOS system, and wanted to create a `dir` command that would print out the current directory and the names and sizes of all of your files, rather than just the names. You could save the following two commands in a file called `dir`:

```
pwd
ls -l
```

To execute the commands saved in a file, you can simply give its name as an argument
to the sh command. For example:

```
$ sh dir
/work/docbook/ch13
total 21
-rw-rw-r--    3 fred        doc          263 Apr 12 09:17 abbrevs
-rw-rw-r--    1 fred        doc           10 May  1 14:01 dir
-rw-rw-r--    1 fred        doc         6430 Apr 12 15:00 sect1
-rw-rw-r--    1 fred        doc        14509 Apr 15 16:29 sect2
-rw-rw-r--    1 fred        doc         1024 Apr 28 10:35 stuff
-rw-rw-r--    1 fred        doc         1758 Apr 28 10:00 tmp
```

Or you can make a file *executable* by changing its file permissions with the chmod
command:

```
$ ls -l dir
-rw-rw-r--    1 fred        doc           10 May  1 14:01 dir
$ chmod +x dir
$ ls -l dir
-rwxrwxr-x    1 fred        doc           10 May  1 14:01 dir
```

After a file has executable permission, all you need to do to execute the commands it
contains is to type the file's name:

```
$ dir
/work/docbook/ch13
total 21
-rw-rw-r--    3 fred        doc          263 Apr 12 09:17 abbrevs
-rwxrwxr-x    1 fred        doc           10 May  1 14:01 dir
-rw-rw-r--    1 fred        doc         6430 Apr 12 15:00 sect1
-rw-rw-r--    1 fred        doc        14509 Apr 15 16:29 sect2
-rw-rw-r--    1 fred        doc         1024 Apr 28 10:35 stuff
-rw-rw-r--    1 fred        doc         1758 Apr 28 10:00 tmp
```

The next step is to make the shell script accessible from whatever directory you happen
to be working in. The Bourne shell maintains a variable called PATH, which is set up
during the login process, and contains a list of directories in which the shell should look
for executable commands. This list is usually referred to as your *search path*.

To use the value of a variable, simply precede its name with a dollar sign ($).
This makes it easy to check the value of a variable like PATH—simply use the echo
command:

```
$ echo $PATH
/bin:/usr/bin:/usr/local/bin:.
```

The Bourne shell expects the list of directory names contained in the PATH variable to
be separated by colons. If your search path is defined as shown, the following directories will be searched, in order, whenever you type the name of a command:

```
/bin
/usr/bin
/usr/local/bin
```
. (shorthand for the current directory)

The allocation of system commands to the three `bin` directories is historical and somewhat arbitrary, although `/usr/local/bin` tends to contain commands that are local to a specific implementation of UNIX. It is sometimes called `/usr/lbin` or some other name.

To ensure that any shell scripts you create are automatically found whenever you type their names, you can do one of two things:

1.   You can add shell scripts to one of the directories already in your search path. However, in most cases, these directories are only writable by the super-user, so this option is not available to all users.

2.   You can create a special ''tools'' directory of your own, and add the name of that directory to your search path. This directory might be a subdirectory of your own home directory, or could be a more globally available directory used by a group of people.

For example, you could put the following line in your `.profile`:

```
PATH=/usr/fred/tools:.:/bin:/usr/bin:/usr/local/bin:
```

The `/usr/fred/tools` directory would be searched before any of the standard search directories. (This means that you can define an alternate command with the same name as an existing command. The version found first in the search path is executed, and the search is stopped at that point. You should not put local directories before the standard directories if you are concerned at all with system security, because doing so creates a loophole that can be exploited by an intruder.)

If you are using the C shell, the search path is stored in a variable called `path`, and has a different format; see your UNIX documentation for details. In addition, you must use the `rehash` command whenever you add a command to one of the search directories.

Passing Arguments to Shell Scripts

The previous example is very simple; the commands it used took no arguments. In contrast, consider a case in which you want to save a single complex command line in a file. For example, if you use `tbl` and `eqn` with `nroff`, your typical command line might look like this:

```
$ tbl file | eqn | nroff -ms | col | lp
```

How much easier it would be to save that whole line in a single file called `format`, and simply type:

```
$ format file
```

The question then becomes: how do you tell your `format` script where in the command line to insert the *file* argument?

Because all of the programs in the script are designed to read standard input as well as take a filename argument, we could avoid the problem by writing the script thus:

```
tbl | eqn | nroff -ms | col | lp
```

and using it like this:

```
$ cat file | format
```

or like this:

```
$ format < file
```

But this still begs the question of how to pass an argument to a shell script.

Up to nine arguments can be represented by positional notation. The first argument is represented in the shell script by the symbol $1, the second by $2, and so on.

So, for example, we could write our script:

```
tbl $1 | eqn | nroff -ms | col | lp
```

When specified as an argument to the `format` command:

```
$ format ch01
```

the filename would be substituted in the script for the symbol $1.

But what if you want to specify several files at once? The symbol $* means "use all arguments," so the script:

```
tbl $* | eqn | nroff -ms | col | lp
```

will allow us to write:

```
$ format file1 file2...
```

Now consider the slightly more complex case in which you'd like to support either the `ms` or the `mm` macros. You could write the script like this:

```
tbl $2 | eqn | nroff $1 | col | lp
```

The first argument will now follow the invocation of `nroff`, and the second will represent the filename:

```
$ format -ms file
```

However, at this point we have lost the ability to specify "all arguments," because the first argument is used differently than all the rest. There are several ways to handle this situation, but we need to learn a few things first.

Conditional Execution

Commands in a shell script can be executed conditionally using either the `if...then...else` or `case` command built into the shell. However, any conditional commands require the ability to test a value and make a choice based on the result. As its name might suggest, the `test` command does the trick.

There are different kinds of things you can test, using various options to the command. The general form of the command is:

$ **test** *condition*

Condition is constructed from one or more options; some of the most useful are listed in Table 12-1.

TABLE 12-1. Useful `test` Options

Option	Meaning
−d *file*	True if *file* exists and is a directory
−f *file*	True if *file* exists and is a regular file
−n *s1*	True if the length of string *s1* is nonzero
−r *file*	True if *file* exists and is readable
−s *file*	True if *file* exists and has a size greater than zero
−w *file*	True if *file* exists and is writable
−x *file*	True if *file* exists and is executable
−z *s1*	True if the length of string *s1* is zero
str1 = *str2*	True if strings *str1* and *str2* are identical
str1 != *str2*	True if strings *str1* and *str2* are not identical
str1	True if string *str1* is not the null string
n1 −eq *n2*	True if the integers *n1* and *n2* are algebraically equal (any of the comparisons −ne, −gt, −ge, −lt, and −le may be used in place of −eq)

The `test` command has a special form just for use in shell scripts. Instead of using the word *test*, you can simply enclose *condition* in square brackets. The expression must be separated from the enclosing brackets by spaces.

So, for example, to return to our `format` script, we could write:

```
if [ "$1" = "-mm" ]
then
     tbl $2 | eqn | nroff -mm | col | lp
else
     tbl $2 | eqn | nroff -ms | col | lp
fi
```

We've simply used the `test` command to compare the value of two strings—the first argument, and the string `"-mm"`—and executed the appropriate command line as a result. If the strings are equal, the first command line is executed; if they are not equal, the second line is executed instead. (Notice that there are spaces surrounding the equals sign in the test.)

The syntax of if...then...else clauses can get confusing. One trick is to think of each keyword (if, then, and else) as a separate command that can take other commands as its argument. The else clause is optional. (That is, you can say, "if the condition is met, do this," and give no alternatives. If the condition is not met, the script will simply go on to the next line, or exit if there is no next line.) The entire sequence is terminated with the fi keyword.

After you realize that each part of the sequence is really just a separate command, like other UNIX commands, the abbreviated form, which uses semicolons rather than newlines to separate the commands, will also make sense:

```
if condition; then command; fi
```

An if...then...else clause allows you to make a choice between at most two options. There is also an elif statement that allows you to create a sequence of if clauses to deal with more conditions. For example, suppose your system supports a third macro package—one you've written yourself, and called mS because it's a super-set of ms. (More on this in Chapter 17!) You could write the script like this:

```
if [ "$1" = "-mm" ]
then tbl $2 | eqn | nroff -mm | col | lp
elif [ "$1" = "-ms" ]
then tbl $2 | eqn | nroff -ms | col | lp
elif [ "$1" = "-mS" ]
then tbl $2 | eqn | nroff -mS | col | lp
fi
```

This syntax can get awkward for more than a few conditions. Fortunately, the shell provides a more compact way to handle multiple conditions: the case statement. The syntax of this statement looks complex (even in the slightly simplified form given here):

```
case value in
pattern) command;;
..
pattern) command;;
esac
```

In fact, the statement is quite easy to use, and is most easily shown by example. We could rewrite the previous script as follows:

```
case $1 in
    -mm) tbl $2 | eqn | nroff -mm | col | lp;;
    -ms) tbl $2 | eqn | nroff -ms | col | lp;;
    -mS) tbl $2 | eqn | nroff -mS | col | lp;;
esac
```

This form is considerably more compact, especially as the number of conditions grows. (Be sure to note the ;; at the end of each line. This is an important part of the syntax.)

Here's how the `case` statement works. Each *value* in turn is compared (using standard shell metacharacters like * and ?, if present) against the *pattern* before the close parenthesis at the start of each line. If the pattern matches, the line is executed. If not, the script tries again with the next line in the `case` statement. After the value has been compared against each case, the process starts over with the next value (if more than one has been specified).

Discarding Used Arguments

All of the conditions we've tested for so far are mutually exclusive. What if you want to include more than one potentially true condition in your script? The trick to dealing with this situation requires two more shell commands: `while` and `shift`.

Consider the following example. You realize that it is inefficient to pass your files through `eqn` every time you use `format`. In addition, you sometimes use `pic`. You want to add options to your `format` shell script to handle these cases as well.

You could decree that the macro package will always be the first argument to your script, the name of the preprocessor the second, and the file to be formatted the third. To delay execution of the command until all of the options have been assembled, you can use the `case` statement to set shell variables, which are evaluated later to make up the actual command line. Here's a script that makes these assumptions:

```
case $1 in
    -mm) macros="-mm";;
    -ms) macros="-ms";;
    -mS) macros="-mS";;
esac
case $2 in
    -E) pre="| eqn"
    -P) pre="| pic"
esac
tbl $3 $pre | nroff $macros | col | lp
```

But what if you don't want either preprocessor, or want both `eqn` and `pic`? The whole system breaks down. We need a more general approach.

There are several ways to deal with this. For example, there is a program called `getopt` that can be used for interpreting command-line options. However, we will use another technique—discarding an argument after it is used, and *shifting* the remaining arguments. This is the function of the `shift` command.

This command finds its most elementary use when a command needs to take more than nine arguments. There is no `$10`, so a script to echo ten arguments might be written:

```
echo The first nine arguments: $1 $2 $3 $4 $5 $6 $7 $8 $9
shift
echo The tenth argument: $9
```

After the `shift` command, the old `$1` has disappeared, as far as the shell is concerned, and the remaining arguments are all shifted one position to the left. (The old `$2` is the current `$1`, and so on.) Take a moment to experiment with this if you want.

Shifting works well with conditional statements, because it allows you to test for a condition, discard the first argument, and go on to test the next argument, without requiring the arguments to be in a specific order. However, we still can't quite get the job done, because we have to establish a *loop*, and repeat the `case` statement until all of the arguments are used up.

Repetitive Execution

As we suggested at the start of this chapter, the real secret of programming is to get the computer to do all the repetitive, boring tasks. The basic mechanism for doing this is the loop—an instruction or series of instructions that cause a program to do the same thing over and over again as long as some condition is true.

The `while` command is used like this:

```
while condition
do
commands
done
```

In the script we're trying to write, we want to repeatedly test for command-line arguments *as long as there are arguments*, build up a command line using shell variables, and then go ahead and issue the command. Here's how:

```
while [ $# -gt 0 ]
do
    case $1 in
      -E) eqn="| eqn";;
      -P) pic="| pic";;
      -*) options="$options $1";;
      *)  files="$files $1";;
    esac
    shift
done
tbl $files $eqn $pic | nroff $options | col | lp
```

The special shell variable `$#` always contains the number of arguments given to a command. What this script is saying in English is: As long as there is at least one argument

- test the first argument against the following list of possibilities; if there is a match, set the variable as instructed;

- throw away the argument now that you've used it, and shift the remaining arguments over one place;

- decrement the shell variable `$#`, which contains the number of arguments;

- go back to the first line following the `do` statement, and start over.

The loop will continue as long as the condition specified in the `while` statement is met—that is, until all the arguments have been used up and shifted out of existence.

As you've no doubt noticed, to make this work, we had to account for *all* of the arguments. We couldn't leave any to be interpreted in the command line because we had to use them all up to satisfy the `while` statement. That meant we needed to think about what other kinds of arguments there might be and include them in the `case` statement. We came up with two possibilities: additional `nroff` options and files.

In addition, because of the pattern-matching flexibility in the `case` statement, we don't need to call out each of the macro packages separately, but can just treat them as part of a more general case. Any argument beginning with a minus sign is simply assumed to be an `nroff` option.

You'll notice that we used a somewhat different syntax for assigning these last two potential groups of arguments to variables:

variable="$variable additional_value"

Or, as shown in the script:

```
options="$options $1"
files="$files $1"
```

This syntax is used to *add* a value to a variable. We know that we can expect at least one option to `nroff`, so we simply add any other options to the same variable. Similarly, there may be more than one filename argument. The `*)` case can be executed any number of times, each time adding one more filename to the variable.

If you want to become more familiar with how this works, you can simulate it on the command line:

```
$ files=sect1
$ files="$files sect2"
$ echo $files
sect1 sect2
```

As you've seen, in the script we used the standard shell metacharacter `*`, which means "any number of any characters," right in the pattern-matching part of the `case` statement. You can use any of the shell metacharacters that you can type on the command line equally well in a shell script. However, be sure you realize that when you do this, you're making *assumptions*—that any option not explicitly tested for in the `case` statement is an `nroff` option, and that any argument not beginning with a minus sign is a filename.

This last assumption may not be a safe one—for example, one of the filenames may be mistyped, or you may not be in the directory you expect, and the file will not be found. We may therefore want to do a little defensive programming, using another of the capabilities provided by the `test` command:

```
*) if [ -f $1 ]
   then
   files="$files $1"
   else echo "format: $1: file not found"; exit
   fi;;
```

The [-f] test checks to see whether the argument is the name of an existing file. If it is not, the script prints an informative message and exits. (The exit command is used to break out of a script. After this error occurs, we don't want to continue with the loop, or go on to execute any commands.)

This example is also instructive in that it shows how each element in the case statement's condition list does not need to be on a single line. A line can contain a complex sequence of commands, separated by semicolons or newlines or both, and is not terminated till the concluding ;; is encountered.

Setting Default Values

We've considered the case where multiple values are stored in the same variable. What about the other extreme, where no value is stored?

If an option, such as −E for eqn, is not specified on the command line, the variable will not be defined. That is, the variable will have no value, and the variable substitution $eqn on the final line of the script will have no effect—it is as if it isn't there at all.

On the other hand, it is possible to export a variable, so that it will be recognized not just in the shell that created it, but in any subshell. This means that the commands:

```
$ eqn="| eqn"; export eqn
$ format -ms myfile
```

will have the same effect as:

```
$ format -ms -E myfile
```

Although there are occasions where you might want to do this sort of thing, you don't want it to happen unexpectedly. For this reason, it is considered good programming practice to *initialize* your variables—that is, to set them to a predefined value (or in many cases, a null value) to minimize random effects due to interaction with other programs.

To set a shell variable to a null value, simply equate it to a pair of quotation marks with nothing in between. For example, it would be a good idea to start off the format script with the line:

```
eqn="";pic="";options=""
```

In addition to setting arguments to null values, we can also set them to *default values*—that is, we can give them values that will be used unless the user explicitly requests otherwise. Let's suppose that we want the script to invoke troff by default, but also provide an option to select nroff. We could rewrite the entire script like this:

```
eqn="";pic="";roff="ditroff -Tps";post="| devps"
lp="lp -dlaser"
while [ $# -gt 0 ]
do
    case $1 in
      -E) eqn="| eqn";;
      -P) pic="| pic";;
      -N) roff="nroff"; post="| col";lp="lp -dline";;
      -*) options="$options $1";;
       *) if [ -f $1 ]; then
          files="$files $1"
          else echo "format: $1: file not found"; exit
          fi;;
    esac
    shift
done
eval "tbl $files $eqn $pic | $roff $options $post | $lp"
```

The `troff` output needs to be passed through a postprocessor before it can be sent to a printer. (We use `devps`, but there are almost as many different postprocessors as there are possible output devices.) The `nroff` output, for some printers, needs to be passed through `col`, which is a special filter used to remove reverse linefeeds. Likewise, the `lp` command will need a "destination" option. We're assuming that the system has a printer called `laser` for `troff` output, and one called `line` for line-printer output from `nroff`. The default case (`troff`) for both the postprocessor and destination printer is set in the variables at the start of the file. The `-N` option resets them to alternate values if `nroff` is being used. The `eval` command is necessary in order for the pipes to be evaluated correctly inside a variable substitution.

What We've Accomplished

You might wonder if this script really saved you any time. After all, it took a while to write, and it seems almost as complex to use as just typing the appropriate command line. After all, was it worth all that work, just so that we can type:

```
$ format -ms -E -P -N myfile
```

instead of:

```
$ tbl myfile | eqn | pic | nroff -ms | lp
```

There are two answers to that question. First, many of the programs used to format a file may take options of their own—options that are always the same, but always need to be specified—and, especially if you're using `troff`, a postprocessor may also be involved. So your actual command line might work out to be something like this:

```
$ tbl myfile | eqn | pic -T720 -D | ditroff -ms -Tps |
> devps | lp
```

That's considerably more to type! You could just save your most frequently used combinations of commands into individual shell scripts. But if you build a general tool, you'll find that it gives you a base to build from, and opens up additional possibilities as you go on. For example, later in this book we'll show how to incorporate some fairly complex indexing scripts into format—something that would be very difficult to do from the command line. That is the far more important second reason for taking the time to build a solid shell script when the occasion warrants.

As this chapter goes on, we'll show you many other useful tools you can build for yourself using shell scripts. Many of them will use the features of the shell we introduced in this section, although a few will rely on additional features we've yet to learn.

▪ ex Scripts ▪

We've discussed ex already in Chapter 7. As we pointed out, any command, or sequence of commands, that you can type at ex's colon prompt can also be saved in a file and executed with ex's :so command.

This section discusses a further extension of this concept—how to execute ex scripts from outside a file and on multiple files. There are certain ex commands that you might save in scripts for use from within vi that will be of no use from the outside—maps, abbreviations, and so on. For the most part, you'll be using substitute commands in external scripts.

A very useful application of editing scripts for a writer is to ensure consistency of terminology—or even of spelling—across a document set. For the sake of example, let's assume that you've run spell, and it has printed out the following list of misspellings:

```
$ spell sect1 sect2
chmod
ditroff
myfile
thier
writeable
```

As is often the case, spell has flagged a few technical terms and special cases it doesn't recognize, but it has also identified two genuine spelling errors.

Because we checked two files at once, we don't know which files the errors occurred in, or where in the files they are. Although there are ways to find this out, and the job wouldn't be too hard for only two errors in two files, you can easily imagine how the job could grow time consuming for a poor speller or typist proofing many files at once.

We can write an ex script containing the following commands:

```
g/thier/s//their/g
g/writeable/s//writable/g
wq
```

Then we can edit the files as follows:

```
$ ex - sect1 < exscript
$ ex - sect2 < exscript
```

(The minus sign following the invocation of ex tells it to accept its commands from standard input.)

If the script were longer than the one in our simple example, we would already have saved a fair amount of time. However, given our earlier remarks about letting the computer do the dirty work, you might wonder if there isn't some way to avoid repeating the process for each file to be edited. Sure enough, we can write a shell script that includes the invocation of ex, but generalizes it, so that it can be used on any number of files.

Looping in a Shell Script

One piece of shell programming we haven't discussed yet is the for loop. This command sequence allows you to apply a sequence of commands for each argument given to the script. (And, even though we aren't introducing it until this late in the game, it is probably the single most useful piece of shell programming for beginners. You will want to remember it even if you don't write any other shell programs.)

Here's the syntax of a for loop:

```
for variable in list
do
commands
done
```

For example:

```
for file in $*
do
    ex - $file < exscript
done
```

(The command doesn't need to be indented; we indented for clarity.) Now (assuming this shell script is saved in a file called correct), we can simply type:

```
$ correct sect1 sect2
```

The for loop in correct will assign each argument (each file in $*) to the variable file and execute the ex script on the contents of that variable.

It may be easier to grasp how the for loop works with an example whose output is more visible. Let's look at a script to rename files:

```
for file in $*
do
   mv $file $file.x
done
```

Assuming this script is in an executable file called move, here's what we can do:

```
$ ls
ch01      ch02      ch03      move
$ move ch??
$ ls
ch01.x     ch02.x      ch03.x      move
```

With a little creativity, you could rewrite the script to rename the files more specifically:

```
for nn in $*
do
   mv ch$nn sect$nn
done
```

With the script written this way, you'd specify numbers instead of filenames on the command line:

```
$ ls
ch01      ch02      ch03      move
$ move 01 02 03
$ ls
sect01      sect02      sect03      move
```

The `for` loop need not take `$*` (all arguments) as the list of values to be substituted. You can specify an explicit list as well, or substitute the output of a command. For example:

```
for variable in a b c d
```

will assign `variable` to a, b, c, and d in turn. And:

```
for variable in `grep -l "Alcuin"`
```

will assign `variable` in turn to the name of each file in which `grep` finds the string *Alcuin*.

If no list is specified:

```
for variable
```

the variable will be assigned to each command-line argument in turn, much as it was in our initial example. This is actually not equivalent to `for variable in $*` but to `for variable in $@`, which has a slightly different meaning. The symbols `$*` expand to `$1`, `$2`, `$3`, etc., but `$@` expands to `"$1"`, `"$2"`, `"$3"`, etc. Quotation marks prevent further interpretation of special characters.

Let's return to our main point, and our original script:

```
for file in $*
do
   ex - $file < exscript
done
```

It may seem a little inelegant to have to use two scripts—the shell script and the ex script. And in fact, the shell does provide a way to include an editing script directly into a shell script.

Here Documents

The operator << means to take the following lines, up to a specified string, as input to a command. (This is often called a *here document*.) Using this syntax, we could include our editing commands in correct like this:

```
for file in $*
do
ex - $file << end-of-script
g/thier/s//their/g
g/writeable/s//writable/g
wq
end-of-script
done
```

The string end-of-script is entirely arbitrary—it just needs to be a string that won't otherwise appear in the input and can be used by the shell to recognize when the here document is finished. By convention, many users specify the end of a here document with the string EOF, or E-O-F, to indicate *end of file*.

There are advantages and disadvantages to each approach shown. If you want to make a one-time series of edits and don't mind rewriting the script each time, the here document provides an effective way to do the job.

However, writing the editing commands in a separate file from the shell script is more general. For example, you could establish the convention that you will always put editing commands in a file called exscript. Then, you only need to write the correct script once. You can store it away in your personal "tools" directory (which you've added to your search path), and use it whenever you like.

ex Scripts Built by diff

A further example of the use of ex scripts is built into a program we've already looked at—diff. The −e option to diff produces an editing script usable with either ed or ex, instead of the usual output. This script consists of a sequence of a (add), c (change), and d (delete) commands necessary to recreate *file1* from *file2* (the first and second files specified on the diff command line).

Obviously, there is no need to completely recreate the first file from the second, because you could do that easily with cp. However, by editing the script produced by diff, you can come up with some desired combination of the two versions.

It might take you a moment to think of a case in which you might have use for this feature. Consider this one: two people have unknowingly made edits to different copies of a file, and you need the two versions merged. (This can happen especially easily in a networked environment, in which people copy files between machines. Poor coordination can easily result in this kind of problem.)

To make this situation concrete, let's take a look at two versions of the same paragraph, which we want to combine:

Version 1:

```
The Book of Kells, now one of the treasures of the Trinity
College Library in Dublin, was found in the ancient
monastery at Ceannanus Mor, now called Kells.  It is a
beautifully illustrated manuscript of the Latin Gospels,
and also contains notes on local history.
It was written in the eighth century.
The manuscript is generally regarded as the finest example
of Celtic illumination.
```

Version 2:

```
The Book of Kells was found in the ancient
monastery at Ceannanus Mor, now called Kells.  It is a
beautifully illustrated manuscript of the Latin Gospels,
and also contains notes on local history.
It is believed to have been written in the eighth century.
The manuscript is generally regarded as the finest example
of Celtic illumination.
```

As you can see, there is one additional phrase in each of the two files. We would like to merge them into one file that incorporates both edits.

Typing:

```
$ diff -e version1 version2 > exscript
```

will yield the following output in the file `exscript`:

```
6c
It is believed to have been written in the eighth century.
.
1,2c
The Book of Kells was found in the ancient
.
```

You'll notice that the script appears in reverse order, with the changes later in the file appearing first. This is essential whenever you're making changes based on line numbers; otherwise, changes made earlier in the file may change the numbering, rendering the later parts of the script ineffective.

You'll also notice that, as mentioned, this script will simply recreate version 1, which is not what we want. We want the change to line 5, but not the change to lines 1 and 2. We want to edit the script so that it looks like this:

```
6c
It is believed to have been written in the eighth century.
.
w
```

(Notice that we had to add the w command to write the results of the edit back into the file.) Now we can type:

```
$ ex - version1 < exscript
```

to get the resulting merged file:

```
The Book of Kells, now one of the treasures of the Trinity
College Library in Dublin, was found in the ancient
monastery at Ceannanus Mor, now called Kells.   It is a
beautifully illustrated manuscript of the Latin Gospels,
and also contains notes on local history.
It is believed to have been written in the eighth century.
The manuscript is generally regarded as the finest example
of Celtic illumination.
```

Using diff like this can get confusing, especially when there are many changes. It is very easy to get the direction of changes confused, or to make the wrong edits. Just remember to do the following:

- Specify the file that is closest in content to your eventual target as the first file on the diff command line. This will minimize the size of the editing script that is produced.

- After you have corrected the editing script so that it makes only the changes that you want, apply it to that same file (the first file).

Nonetheless, because there is so much room for error, it is better not to have your script write the changes back directly into one of your source files. Instead of adding a w command at the end of the script, add the command 1,$p to write the results to standard output. This is almost always preferable when you are using a complex editing script.

If we use this command in the editing script, the command line to actually make the edits would look like this:

```
$ ex - version1 < exscript > version3
```

The diff manual page also points out another application of this feature of the program. Often, as a writer, you find yourself making extensive changes, and then wishing you could go back and recover some part of an earlier version. Obviously, frequent backups will help. However, if backup storage space is at a premium, it is possible (though a little awkward) to save only some older version of a file, and then keep incremental diff −e scripts to mark the differences between each successive version.

To apply multiple scripts to a single file, you can simply pipe them to ex rather than redirecting input:

```
cat script1 script2 script3 | ex - oldfile
```

But wait! How do you get your w (or 1,$p) command into the pipeline? You could edit the last script to include one of these commands. But, there's another trick that we ought to look at because it illustrates another useful feature of the shell that many people are unaware of.

If you enclose a semicolon-separated list of commands in parentheses, the standard output of all of the commands are combined, and can be redirected together. The immediate application is that, if you type:

```
cat script1 script2 script3; echo '1,$p' | ex - oldfile
```

the results of the `cat` command will be sent, as usual, to standard output, and only the results of `echo` will be piped to `ex`. However, if you type:

```
(cat script1 script2 script3; echo '1,$p') | ex - oldfile
```

the output of the entire sequence will make it into the pipeline, which is what we want.

▪ Stream Editing ▪

We haven't seen the `sed` program yet. Not only is it a line editor rather than a screen editor, but it takes the process one step further: it is a "noninteractive" line editor. It can only be used with editing scripts. It was developed in 1978 as an extension to `ed` for three specific cases (according to the original documentation):

- to edit files too large for comfortable interactive editing

- to edit any size file when the sequence of editing commands is too complicated to be comfortably typed in interactive mode

- to perform multiple "global" editing functions efficiently in one pass through the input

All of these are still good reasons for using `sed`. But these cases can be solved by the scripting ability of `ex` that we have already looked at. Why learn yet another editor?

One answer lies in the third point. Because it was specifically designed to work with scripts, `sed` is considerably faster than `ex` when used with a comparable script.

The other answer lies in `sed`'s unique capability to be used as an editing *filter*—a program that makes edits on the fly as data is being passed through a pipe on its way to other programs.

The `sed` program uses a syntax that is very similar to that used by `ex`, so it is not very difficult to learn. However, there are some critical differences, which make it inadvisable for an experienced `ed` or `ex` user to just blindly jump in.

We're going to take a close look at `sed`, not as a general-purpose editor, but as a tool to accomplish specific tasks. As a result, we won't cover every command, but only those that differ significantly from their `ex` equivalents or offer specific benefits that we want to utilize.

First, a brief note on usage. The `sed` command has two forms:

```
sed -e  command editfiles
sed -f  scriptfile editfiles
```

The first form, using −e, allows you to specify an editing command right on the command line. Multiple −e options can be specified on the same line.

The second form, using −f, takes the name of a script containing editing commands. We prefer this form for using sed.

In addition, you can specify an entire multiline editing script as an argument to sed, like this:

```
sed '
```
Editing script begins here

.

.

.

Editing script ends here' *editfiles*

This last form is especially useful in shell scripts, as we shall see shortly. However, it can also be used interactively. The Bourne shell will prompt for continuation lines after it sees the first single quotation mark.

You can also combine several commands on the same line, separating them with semicolons:

```
sed −e 'command1; command2; ...' editfiles
```

One last point: when using sed −e, you should enclose the expression in quotation marks. Although this is not absolutely essential, it can save you from serious trouble later.

Consider the following example:

```
$ sed −e s/thier/their own/g myfile
```

The expression s/thier/their own/g will work correctly in a sed script used with the −f option. But from the command line it will result in the message ''Command garbled,'' because the shell interprets the space as a separator between arguments, and will parse the command expression as s/thier/their and treat the remainder of the line as two filenames, own/g and myfile. Lacking a closing / for the s command, sed will complain and quit.

Differences between ex and sed

The first difference between sed and interactive line editors like ed and ex is the way lines are addressed. In ex, the default is to affect only a specifically addressed line; therefore, commands like g exist to address multiple lines. The sed program, on the other hand, works by default on all lines, so it needs commands that allow it to bypass selected lines. The sed program is implicitly global. In ex, the default is to edit the current line, and you must explicitly request global edits, or address particular lines that you want to have edited. In sed, the default is to edit every line, and line addresses are used to restrict the operation of the edit.

For example, consider the difference between ex and sed in how they interpret a command of the form:

/pattern/s/oldstring/newstring/

In ex, this means to locate the first line matching *pattern* and, on that line, perform the specified substitution. In sed, the same command matches every line containing *pattern*, and makes the specified edits. In other words, this command in sed works the same as ex's global flag:

g/*pattern*/s/*oldstring*/*newstring*/

In both sed and ex, a command of the form:

/*pattern1*/, /*pattern2*/*command*

means to make the specified edits on all lines between *pattern1* and *pattern2*.

Although you can use absolute line number addresses in sed scripts, you have to remember that sed has the capability to edit multiple files at once in a stream. And in such cases, line numbers are consecutive throughout the entire stream, rather than restarted with each new file.

Besides its addressing peculiarities, you also need to get used to the fact that sed automatically writes to standard output. You don't need to issue any special commands to make it print the results of its edits; in fact, you need to use a command-line option to make it stop.

To make this point clear, let's consider the following admittedly artificial example. Your file contains the following three lines:

```
The files were writeable by thier owner, not by all.
The files were writeable by thier owner, not by all.
The files were writeable by thier owner, not by all.
```

You use the following editing script (in a file called edscript):

```
/thier/s//their/
/writeable/s//writable/
1,$p
```

Here are the very different results with ex and sed:

```
$ ex - junk < edscript
The files were writeable by their owner, not by all.
The files were writable by thier owner, not by all.
The files were writeable by thier owner, not by all.
```

```
$ sed -f edscript junk
The files were writable by their owner, not by all.
The files were writable by their owner, not by all.
The files were writable by their owner, not by all.
The files were writable by their owner, not by all.
The files were writable by their owner, not by all.
The files were writable by their owner, not by all.
```

The ex command, lacking the g prefix to make the edits global, applies the first line in the script to the first line in the file, and then goes to the second line, to which it applies the second line in the script. No edits are performed on the third line. The contents of the buffer are printed to standard output by the final line in the script. This is analogous to what would happen if you issued the same commands manually in ex.

The sed command, in contrast, applies each line in the script to every line in the file, and then sends the results to standard output. A second copy of the input is printed to standard output by the final line in the script.

Although the same script almost works for ex and sed, the sed script can be written more simply as:

```
s/thier/their/
s/writeable/writable/
```

Because edits are applied by default to every line, we can skip the initial pattern address and simply give the s command. And we want to omit the print command, which gave us the annoying second copy of the input.

There are also some special added commands that support sed's noninteractive operation. We will get to these commands in due course. However, in some ways, the special commands are easier to learn than the familiar ones. The cautionary example shown was intended to underline the fact that there is a potential for confusion when commands that look identical produce very different results.

Some Shell Scripts Using sed

The sed command you are most likely to start with is s (or substitute) because you can put it to work without knowing anything about sed's advanced control structures. Even if you learn no other sed commands, you should read this section, because this command is easy to learn and will greatly extend your editing power.

Within the constraints just outlined, the s command works similarly to its ex equivalent. Let's look at several shell scripts that use sed.

First, because speed is definitely a factor when you're making large edits to a lot of files, we might want to rewrite the correct script shown previously with ex as follows:

```
for file in $*
do
    sed -f sedscr $file > $file.tmp
    mv $file.tmp $file
done
```

This script will always look for a local editing script called sedscr, and will apply its edits to each file in the argument list given to correct. Because sed sends the result of its work to standard output, we capture that output in a temporary file, then move it back to the original file.

As it turns out, there is a real danger in this approach! If there is an error in the sed script, sed will abort without producing any output. As a result, the temporary file will be empty and, when copied back onto the original file, will effectively delete the original.

To avoid this problem, we need to include a test in the correct shell script:

```
for file in $*
do
    sed -f sedscr $file > $file.tmp
    if [ -s $file.tmp ]
    then
        mv $file.tmp $file
    else
        echo "Sed produced an empty file."
    fi
done
```

The [-s] test checks to see whether or not a file is empty—a very useful thing indeed when you are using editing scripts.

You might want to create another simple shell script that uses sed to correct simple errors. We'll call this one change:

```
sed -e "s/$1/$2/g" $3 > $3.tmp
if [ -s $3.tmp ]
then
    mv $3.tmp $3
else
    echo "Possible error using regular expression syntax."
```

This script will simply change the first argument to the second in the file specified by the third argument:

$ **change mispeling misspelling myfile**

(Because we control the actual editing script, the most likely errors could come from faulty regular expression syntax in one of the first two arguments; thus, we changed the wording of the error message.)

Integrating sed into format

Let's consider a brief application that shows sed in its role as a true stream editor, making edits in a pipeline—edits that are never written back into a file.

To set the stage for this script, we need to turn back briefly to typesetting. On a typewriter-like device (including a CRT), an em dash is typically typed as a pair of hyphens (--). In typesetting, it is printed as a single, long dash (—). The troff program provides a special character name for the em dash, but it is inconvenient to type \ (em in your file whenever you want an em dash.

Suppose we create a sed script like this:

```
s/--/\\(em/g
```

and incorporate it directly into our format script? We would never need to worry about em dashes—sed would automatically insert them for us. (Note that we need to double the backslash in the string \ (em because the backslash has meaning to sed as well at to troff, and will be stripped off by sed.)

The `format` script might now look like this:

```
eqn="";pic="";macros="ms";col="";roff="ditroff -Tlj"
sed="| sed -e 's/--/\\(em/g'"
while [ $# -gt 0 ]
do
    case $1 in
      -E) eqn="| eqn";;
      -P) pic="| pic";;
      -N) roff="nroff";col="| col";sed="";;
      -*) options="$options $1";;
       *) if [ -f $1 ]; then
          files="$files $1"
          else echo "format: $1: file not found"; exit
          fi;;
    esac
    shift
done
eval "cat $files $sed|tbl $eqn $pic|$roff $options $col|lp"
```

(Notice that we've set up the −N option for `nroff` so that it sets the `sed` variable to null, because we only want to make this change if we are using `troff`.)

Excluding Lines from Editing

Before we go any further, let's take a moment to be sure the script is complete.

What about the case in which someone is using hyphens to draw a horizontal line? We want to exclude from the edit any lines containing three or more hyphens together. To do this, we use the `!` (*don't!*) command:

```
/---/!s/--/\(em/g
```

It may take a moment to understand this syntax. It says, simply, "If you find a line containing three hyphens together, don't make the edit." The `sed` program will treat all other lines as fair game. (It's important to realize that the `!` command applies to the pattern match, not to the `s` command itself. Although, in this case, the effect might seem to be the same whether you read the command as "Don't match a line containing `---`" or "Match a line containing `---`, and don't substitute it," there are other cases in which it will be very confusing if you don't read the line the same way that `sed` does.)

We might also take the opportunity to improve the aesthetics even further, by putting in a very small space between the ends of the dash and the preceding and following words, using the `troff` construct `\^`, which produces a 1/12-em space:

```
/---/!s/--/\\^\\(em\\^/g
```

As it turns out, changing hyphens to em dashes is not the only "prettying up" edit we might want to make when typesetting. For example, some laser printers do not have a true typeset quotation mark ('' and '' as opposed to " and "). If you are using an output device with this limitation, you could use `sed` to change each double quotation mark character to a pair of single open or close quotation marks (depending on context), which, when typeset, will produce the appearance of a proper double quotation mark.

This is a considerably more difficult edit to make because there are many separate cases that we need to account for using regular expression syntax. Our script might need to look like this:

```
s/^"/``/
s/"$/´´/
s/"? /´´? /g
s/"?$/´´?/g
s/ "/ ``/g
s/" /´´ /g
s/|————|"/|————|``/g
s/"|————|/´´|————|/g
s/")/´´)/g
s/"]/´´]/g
s/("/(``/g
s/\["/\[``/g
s/";/´´;/g
s/":/´´:/g
s/,"/,´´/g
s/",/´´,/g
s/\."/.\\\&´´/g
s/"\./´´.\\\&/g
s/"\\^\\(em/´´\\(em/g
s/\\(em\\^"/\\(em``/g
s/"\\(em/´´\\(em/g
s/\\(em"/\\(em``/g
```

(This list could be shortened by judicious application of \ ([. . .] \ ) regular expression syntax, but it is shown in its long form for effect. Note that the symbol |————| represents a tab.)

Branching to Selective Parts of a Script

In technical books like this, it is usually desirable to show examples in a constant-width font that clearly shows each character as it actually appears. A pair of single quotation marks in a constant-width font will not appear at all similar to a proper typeset double quotation mark in a variable-width font. In short, it is not always desirable to make the substitutions shown previously.

However, we can assume that examples will be set off by some sort of macro pair (in this book, we used .ES and .EE, for *example start* and *example end*), and we can use those as the basis for exclusion. There are two ways to do this:

- Use the ! command, as we did before.

- Use the b (*branch*) command to skip portions of the editing script.

Let's look at how we'd use the ! command first.

We could apply the ! command to each individual line:

```
/^\.ES/,/^\.EE/!s/^"/``/
/^\.ES/,/^\.EE/!s/"$/''/
/^\.ES/,/^\.EE/!s/"? /''? /g
        .
        .
        .
```

But there has to be a better way, and there is. The sed program supports the flow control symbols { and } for grouping commands. So we simply need to write:

```
/^\.ES/,/^\.EE/!{
s/^"/``/
s/"$/''/
s/"? /''? /g
        .
        .
        .
s/\\(em\\^"/\\(em``/g
s/"\\(em/''\\(em/g
s/\\(em"/\\(em``/g
}
```

All commands enclosed in braces will be subject to the initial pattern address.

There is another way we can do the same thing. The sed program's b (*branch*) command allows you to transfer control to another line in the script that is marked with an optional label. Using this feature, we could write the previous script like this:

```
/^\.ES/,/^\.EE/bend
s/^"/``/
s/"$/''/
s/"? /''? /g
        .
        .
        .
s/\\(em\\^"/\\(em``/g
s/"\\(em/''\\(em/g
s/\\(em"/\\(em``/g
:end
```

A label consists of a colon, followed by up to eight characters. If the label is missing, the b command branches to the end of the script. (Because we don't have anything past this point at the moment, we don't actually need the label in this case. That is the form we will use from now on.)

The b command is designed for flow control within the script. It allows you to create subscripts that will only be applied to lines matching certain patterns and will not be applied elsewhere. However, as in this case, it also gives you a powerful way to exempt part of the text from the action of a single-level script.

The advantage of b over ! for our application is that we can more easily specify multiple conditions to avoid. The ! symbol can apply to a single command, or can apply to a set of commands enclosed in braces that immediately follows. The b command, on the other hand, gives you almost unlimited control over movement around the script.

For example, if we are using multiple macro packages, there may be other macro pairs besides .ES and .EE that enclose text that we don't want to apply the sed script to. So, for example, we can write:

```
/^.ES/,/^.EE/b
/^.PS/,/^.PE/b
/^.G1/,/^.G2/b
```

In addition, the quotation mark is used as part of troff's own comment syntax (\" begins a comment), so we don't want to change quotation marks on lines beginning with either a . or a ':

```
/^[.']/b
```

It may be a little difficult to grasp how these branches work unless you keep in mind how sed does its work:

1. It reads each line in the file into its buffer one line at a time.

2. It then applies all commands in the script to that one line, then goes to the next line.

When a branch dependent on a pattern match is encountered, it means that if a line that matches the pattern is read into the buffer, the branch command will cause the relevant portion of the script to be skipped *for that line*. If a label is used, the script will continue at the label; if no label is used, the script is effectively finished for that line. The next line is read into the buffer, and the script starts over.

The previous example shows how to exempt a small, clearly delineated portion of a file from the action of a sed script. To achieve the opposite effect—that is, to make a sed script affect only a small part of a file and ignore the rest—we can simply anchor the desired edits to the enclosing pattern.

For example, if there were some edits we wanted to make only within the confines of our .ES and .EE macros, and not elsewhere, we could do it like this:

```
/^\.ES/,/^\.EE/{
Editing commands here
}
```

If the script is sufficiently complex that you'd rather have a more global method of exclusion, you can reverse the sense of a branch by combining it with !:

```
/^\.ES/,/^\.EE/!b
```

When the first line in the script is applied to each line in the input, it says: "Does the line match the pattern? No? Branch to the end of the script. (That is, start over on the next line of the input.) Yes? Go on to the next line in the script, and make the edits."

Back to `format`

The edits we've shown using `sed` are very useful, so we want to be sure to properly integrate them with `format`. Because we are now making a large series of edits rather than just one, we need to use `sed` with a script file rather than a single-line script using `-e`. As a result, we'll change the variable assignment in `format` to:

```
sed="| sed -f /usr/local/cleanup.sed"
```

where `cleanup.sed` is the name of the script containing the editing commands, and `/usr/local` could be any generally accessible directory. We'll add additional formatting cleanup commands to this file later.

Inserting Lines of Text

The `sed` program, like `ex` and `vi`, has commands for inserting new lines of text. The `i` (insert) command adds text before the current line; `a` (append) adds text *after* the current line. In `ex`, after you enter insert mode, you can type as long as you like, breaking lines with carriage returns.* Insert mode is terminated by typing a period at the start of a line, followed immediately by a carriage return. In `sed`, you must instead type a backslash at the end of each inserted line. Insert mode is terminated by the first newline that is not "escaped" with a backslash in this way. For example, the `sed` script:

```
1a\
The backslash is a ubiquitous escape character used by\
many UNIX programs.  Perhaps its most confusing appearance\
is at the end of a line, when it is used to "hide a\
newline." It appears to stand alone, when in fact it is\
followed by a nonprinting character—a newline.
```

---

*The terms "carriage return" and "newline" are used somewhat loosely here. They are actually distinct characters in the ASCII character set—equivalent to ^M (carriage return) and ^J (linefeed). The confusion arises because UNIX changes the carriage return (^M) generated by the carriage return key to a linefeed (^J) on input. (That is, when you type a carriage return when editing a file, what is actually stored is a linefeed.) On output, the linefeed is mapped to both characters—that is, a ^J in a file actually is output to the terminal as a carriage return/linefeed pair (^M^J).

will append the five lines shown in the example following line 1 in the file to which the sed script is applied. The insert ends on the fifth line, when sed encounters a newline that is not preceded by a backslash.

A sed Script for Extracting Information from a File

The −n option to sed suppresses normal output and causes sed to print only the output you explicitly ask for using the p command.

There are two forms of the p command:

- As an absolute print command. For example:

  /*pattern*/p

  will always print the line(s) matched by *pattern*.

- In combination with a substitute command, in which case the line will only be printed if a substitution is actually made. For example:

  /*pattern*/s/*oldstring*/newstring/gp

  will not be printed if a line containing *pattern* is found but *oldstring* was not replaced with *newstring*.

This becomes much clearer if you realize that a line of the form:

s/*oldstring*/*newstring*/p

is unrestricted—it matches every line in the file—but you only want to print the result of successful substitutions.

Using sed −n with the p command gives you a grep-like facility with the ability to select not just single lines but larger blocks of text.

For example, you could create a simple online quick-reference document, in which topics are delineated by an initial heading and a distinct terminating string, as in the following abbreviated example:

```
$ cat alcuin_online
        .
        .
        .

Output Devices

Alcuin requires the use of a graphics device with at least
300 dpi resolution, and the ability to store at least
one-half page of graphics at that resolution...
%%%%
        .
        .
        .

Type Styles
```

```
There are a number of ornamental type styles available on
many typesetters.  For example, many have an Old English
font.  But no typesetter currently on the market has the
capability of Alcuin to create unique characters in the
style of medieval illuminated manuscripts.
%%%%
        .
        .
        .
   $
```

A shell program like the following is all you need to display entries from this "full text database":

```
pattern=$*
sed -n "/$pattern/,/%%%%/p" alcuin_online
```

(The entire argument list supplied to the command ($*) is assigned to the variable pattern, so that the user can type a string including spaces without having to type quotation marks.)

We'll give an example that is perhaps a bit more realistic. Consider that when you are developing macros for use with an existing package, you may often need to consult macros in the package you are either using or worried about affecting. Of course, you can simply read in the entire file with the editor. However, to make things easier, you can use a simple shell script that uses sed to print out the definition of the desired macro. We use a version of this script on our own system, where we call it getmac:

```
mac="$2"
case $1 in
 -ms) file="/usr/lib/macros/tmac.s";;
 -mm) file="/usr/lib/macros/mmt";;
 -man) file="/usr/lib/macros/an";;
esac
sed -n -e "/^\.de *$mac/,/^\.\.$/p" $file
done
```

There are a couple of things about this script that bear mention. First, the name of a macro does not need to be separated from the .de request by a space. The ms package uses a space, but mm and man do not. This is the reason the search pattern includes a space followed by an asterisk (this pattern matches zero or more spaces).

Second, we use the −n option of sed to keep it from printing out the entire file. It will now print out only the lines that match: the lines from the start of the specified macro definition (.de *$mac) to the .. that ends the definition.

(If you are new to regular expressions, it may be a little difficult to separate the regular expression syntax from troff and shell special characters, but do make the effort, because this is a good application of sed and you should add it to your repertoire.)

The script prints the result on standard output, but it can easily be redirected into a file, where it can become the basis for your own redefinition. We'll find good use for this script in later chapters.

Yet another example of how we can use sed to extract (and manipulate) information from a file is provided by the following script, which we use to check the structure of documents we are writing.

The script assumes that troff macros (in this case, the macros used to format this book) are used to delineate sections, and prints out the headings. To make the structure more apparent, the script removes the section macros themselves, and prints the headings in an indented outline format.

There are three things that sed must accomplish:

1. Find lines that begin with the macro for chapter (.CH) or section headings (.H1 or .H2).

2. Make substitutions on those lines, replacing macros with text.

3. Print only those lines.

The sed command, do.outline, operates on all files specified on the command line ($*). It prints the result to standard output (without making any changes within the files themselves).

```
sed -n  '/^\.[CH][H12]/ {
        s/"//g
        s/^\.CH /\
CHAPTER  /
        s/^\.H1/      A. /
        s/^\.H2/           B. /
        p
}' $*
```

The sed command is invoked with the −n option, which suppresses the automatic printing of lines. Then we specify a pattern that selects the lines we want to operate on, followed by an opening brace ({). This signifies that the group of commands up to the closing brace (}) are applied only to lines matching the pattern. This construct isn't as unfamiliar as it may look. The global regular expression of ex could work here if we only wanted to make one substitution (g/^\.[CH][H12]/s/"//g). The sed command performs several operations:

1. It removes double quotation marks.

2. It replaces the macro for chapter headings with a newline (to create a blank line) followed by the word *CHAPTER*.

3. It replaces the section heading with an appropriate letter and tabbed indent.

4. It prints the line.

The result of do.outline is as follows:

```
$ do.outline ch13/sect1
CHAPTER  13 Let the Computer Do the Dirty Work
        A.   Shell Programming
             B.   Stored Commands
             B.   Passing Arguments to Shell Scripts
             B.   Conditional Execution
             B.   Discarding Used Arguments
             B.   Repetitive Execution
             B.   Setting Default Values
             B.   What We've Accomplished
```

Because the command can be run on a series of files or "chapters," an outline for an entire book can be produced in a matter of seconds. We could easily adapt this script for ms or mm section heading macros, or to include a C-level heading.

The Quit Command

The q command causes sed to stop reading new input lines (and to stop sending them to the output). So, for example, if you only want some initial portion of your file to be edited, you can select a pattern that uniquely matches the last line you want affected, and include the following command as the last line of your script:

```
/pattern/q
```

After the line matching *pattern* is reached, the script will be terminated.*

This command is not really useful for protecting portions of a file. But, when used with a complex sed script, it is useful for improving the performance of the script. Even though sed is quite fast, in an application like getmac there is some inefficiency in continuing to scan through a large file after sed has found what it is looking for.

So, for example, we could rewrite getmac as follows:

```
mac="$2"
case $1 in
 -ms) file="/usr/lib/macros/tmac.s";;
 -mm) file="/usr/lib/macros/mmt";;
 -man) file="/usr/lib/macros/an";;
esac
shift
sed -n "
/^\.de *$mac/,/^\.\.\./{
```

---

*You need to be very careful not to use q in any program that writes its edits back to the original file (like our correct shell script shown previously). After q is executed, no further output is produced. It should not be used in any case where you want to edit the front of the file and pass the remainder through unchanged. Using q in this case is a very dangerous beginner's mistake.

```
p
/^\.\./q
}" $file
done
```

The grouping of commands keeps the line:

```
/^\.\./q
```

from being executed until sed reaches the end of the macro we're looking for. (This line by itself would terminate the script at the conclusion of the first macro definition.) The sed program quits on the spot, and doesn't continue through the rest of the file looking for other possible matches.

Because the macro definition files are not that long, and the script itself not that complex, the actual time saved from this version of the script is negligible. However, with a very large file, or a complex, multiline script that needs to be applied to only a small part of the file, this script could be a significant timesaver.

For example, the following simple shell program uses sed to print out the top ten lines of a file (much like the standard UNIX head program):

```
for file
do
sed 10q $file
done
```

This example shows a dramatic performance gain over the same script written as follows:

```
for file
do
sed -n 1,10p $file
done
```

Matching Patterns across Two Lines

One of the great weaknesses of line-oriented editors is their helplessness in the face of global changes in which the pattern to be affected crosses more than one line.

Let me give you an example from a recent manual one of our writers was working on. He was using the ms .BX macro (incorrectly, it turns out) to box the first letter in a menu item, thus graphically highlighting the sequence of menu selections a user would select to reach a given command. For example:

M̲ain menu
    P̲ortfolio commands
        E̲valuate portfolios
        S̲hock factors

He had created a menu reference divided into numerous files, with hundreds of commands coded like this:

```
.in 5n
.BX "\s-2M\s0"\c
ain menu
.in +5n
.BX "\s-2P\s0"\c
ortfolio commands
.in +5n
.BX "\s-2E\s0"\c
valuate portfolios
.in +5n
.BX "\s-2S\s0"\c
hock factors
.in 0
```

Suddenly, the writer realized that the *M* in *Main Menu* should not be boxed because the user did not need to press this key. He needed a way to remove the box around the *M* if—and only if—the next line contained the string *ain menu*.

(A `troff` aside: The `\c` escape sequence brings text from the following line onto the current line. You would use this, for example, when you don't want the argument to a macro to be separated from the first word on the next line by the space that would normally be introduced by the process of filling. The fact that the `.BX` macro already makes provision for this case, and allows you to supply continued text in a second optional argument, is somewhat irrelevant to this example. The files had been coded as shown here, the mistake had been made, and there were hundreds, perhaps thousands, of instances to correct.)

The `N` command allows you to deal with this kind of problem using `sed`. This command temporarily "joins" the current line with the next for purposes of a pattern match. The position of the newline in the combined line can be indicated by the escape sequence `\n`. In this case, then, we could solve the problem with the following two-line `sed` script:

```
/.BX "\s-2M\s0"/N
s/.BX "\s-2M\s0"\c\nain Menu/Main Menu/
```

We search for a particular pattern and, after we find it, "add on" the next line using `N`. The next substitution will now apply to the combined line.

Useful as this solution was, the number of cases in which you know exactly where in the input a newline will fall are limited. Fortunately, `sed` goes even further, providing commands that allow you to manipulate multiline patterns in which the newline may occur at any point. Let's take a look at these commands.

The Hold Space and the Pattern Space

The next set of commands—hold (h or H), get (g or G), and exchange (x)—can be difficult to understand, especially if you have read the obscure documentation provided with most UNIX systems. It may help to provide an analogy that reviews some of the points we've already made about how `sed` works.

The operations of sed can be explained, somewhat fancifully, in terms of an extremely deliberate scrivener or amanuensis toiling to make a copy of a manuscript. His work is bound by several spacial restrictions: the original manuscript is displayed in one room; the set of instructions for copying the manuscript are stored in a middle room; and the quill, ink, and folio are set up in yet another room. The original manuscript as well as the set of instructions are written in stone and cannot be moved about. The dutiful scrivener, being sounder of body than mind, is able to make a copy by going from room to room, working on only one line at a time. Entering the room where the original manuscript is, he removes from his robes a scrap of paper to take down the first line of the manuscript. Then he moves to the room containing the list of editing instructions. He reads each instruction to see if it applies to the single line he has scribbled down.

Each instruction, written in special notation, consists of two parts: a *pattern* and a *procedure*. The scrivener reads the first instruction and checks the pattern against his line. If there is no match, he doesn't have to worry about the procedure, so he goes to the next instruction. If he finds a match, then the scrivener follows the action or actions specified in the *procedure*.

He makes the edit on his piece of paper before trying to match the pattern in the next instruction. Remember, the scrivener has to read through a series of instructions, and he reads all of them, not just the first instruction that matches the pattern. Because he makes his edits as he goes, he is always trying to match the latest version against the next pattern; he doesn't remember the original line.

When he gets to the bottom of the list of instructions, and has made any edits that were necessary on his piece of paper, he goes into the next room to copy out the line. (He doesn't need to be told to print out the line.) After that is done, he returns to the first room and takes down the next line on a new scrap of paper. When he goes to the second room, once again he reads every instruction from first to last before leaving.

This is what he normally does, that is, unless he is told otherwise. For instance, before he starts, he can be told *not* to write out every line (the −n option). In this case, he must wait for an instruction that tells him to print (p). If he does not get that instruction, he throws away his piece of paper and starts over. By the way, regardless of whether or not he is told to write out the line, he always gets to the last instruction on the list.

Let's look at other kinds of instructions the scrivener has to interpret. First of all, an instruction can have zero, one, or two patterns specified:

- If no pattern is specified, then the same procedure is followed for each line.

- If there is only one pattern, he will follow the procedure for any line matching the pattern.

- If a pattern is followed by a !, then the procedure is followed for all lines that do *not* match the pattern.

- If two patterns are specified, the actions described in the procedure are performed on the first matching line and all succeeding lines until a line matches the second pattern.

The scrivener can work only one line at a time, so you might wonder how he handles a range of lines. Each time he goes through the instructions, he only tries to match the first of two patterns. Now, after he has found a line that matches the first pattern, each time through with a new line he tries to match the second pattern. He interprets the second pattern as pattern!, so that the procedure is followed only if there is no match. When the second pattern is matched, he starts looking again for the first pattern.

Each procedure contains one or more commands or *actions*. Remember, if a pattern is specified with a procedure, the pattern must be matched before the procedure is executed. We have already shown many of the usual commands that are similar to other editing commands. However, there are several highly unusual commands.

For instance, the N command tells the scrivener to go, right now, and get another line, adding it to the same piece of paper. The scrivener can be instructed to "hold" onto a single piece of scrap paper. The h command tells him to make a copy of the line on another piece of paper and put it in his pocket. The x command tells him to exchange the extra piece of paper in his pocket with the one in his hand. The g command tells him to throw out the paper in his hand and replace it with the one in his pocket. The G command tells him to append the line he is holding to the paper in front of him. If he encounters a d command, he throws out the scrap of paper and begins again at the top of the list of instructions. A D command has effect when he has been instructed to append two lines on his piece of paper. The D command tells him to delete the first of those lines.

If you want the analogy converted back to computers, the first and last rooms in this medieval manor are standard input and standard output. Thus, the original file is never changed. The line on the scrivener's piece of scrap paper is in the *pattern space*; the line on the piece of paper that he holds in his pocket is in the *hold space*. The hold space allows you to retain a duplicate of a line while you change the original in the pattern space. Let's look at a practical application, a sed program that searches for a particular phrase that might be split across two lines.

As powerful as regular expressions are, there is a limitation: a phrase split across two lines will not be matched. As we've shown, even though you can specify a newline, you have to know between which two words the newline might be found. Using sed, we can write instructions for general-purpose pattern matching across two lines.

```
N
h
s/ *\n/ /
/pattern-matching syntax/{
g
p
d
}
g
D
```

This sed script will recognize the phrase *pattern-matching syntax* even when it's in the input file on two lines. Let's see how the pattern space and hold space allow this to be done.

At the start, there is one line in the pattern space. The first action (N) is to get another line and append it to the first. This gives us two lines to examine, but there is an embedded newline that we have to remove (otherwise we'd have to know where the newline would fall in the pattern). Before that, we copy (h) the contents of the pattern space into the hold space so that we can have a copy that retains the newline. Then we replace the embedded newline (\n), and any blank spaces that might precede it, with a single blank. (The sed command does not remove a newline when it terminates the line in the pattern space.) Now we try to match the phrase against the contents of the pattern space. If there is a match, the duplicate copy that still contains the newline is retrieved from the hold space (g) and printed (p). The d command sends control back to the top of the list of instructions so that another line is read into the pattern space, because no further editing is attempted ''on the corpse of a deleted line'' (to use the phrasing of the original sed documentation). If, on the other hand, there is no match, then the contents of the hold buffer are replaced (g) with the contents of the pattern space. Now we have our original two lines in the pattern space, separated by a newline. We want to discard the first of these lines, and retain the second in order to pair it up with the next line. The D command deletes the pattern space up to the newline and sends us back to the top to append the next line.

This script demonstrates the limits of flow control in sed. After the first line of input is read, the action N is responsible for all input. And, using d and D to avoid ever reaching the bottom of the instruction list, sed does not print the line automatically or clear the pattern space (regardless of the −n option). To return to our analogy, after the scrivener enters the second room, an instruction is always telling him which room to go to next and whether to get another line or to write it out, for as long as there are lines to be read from the manuscript.

As we have emphasized, you can always refine a script, perfecting the way it behaves or adding features. There are three problems with the way this script works. First and most important, it is not general enough because it has been set up to search for a specific string. Building a shell script around this sed program will take care of that. Second, the program does not ''go with the flow'' of sed. We can rewrite it, using the b (*branch*) command, to make use of sed's default action when it reaches the bottom of its instruction list. Last, this program always prints matching lines in pairs, even when the search string is found in its entirety on a single line of input. We need to match the pattern before each new line of input is paired with the previous line.

Here's a generalized version of this sed script, called phrase, which allows you to specify the search string as a quoted first argument. Additional command-line arguments represent filenames.

```
search=$1
shift
for file
do
    sed '
/'"$search"'/b
N
h
s/.*\n//
```

```
        /'"$search"'/b
        g
        s/ *\n/ /
        /'"$search"'/{
        g
        b
        }
        g
        D' $file
    done
```

A shell variable defines the search string as the first argument on the command line. Now the sed program tries to match the search string at three different points. If the search string is found in a new line read from standard input, that line is printed. We use the b command to drop to the bottom of the list; sed prints the line and clears the pattern space. If the single line does not contain the pattern, the next input line is appended to the pattern space. Now it is possible that this line, by itself, matches the search string. We test this (after copying the pattern space to the hold space) by removing the previous line up to the embedded newline. If we find a match, control drops to the bottom of the list and the line is printed. If no match is made, then we get a copy of the duplicate that was put in the hold space. Now, just as in the earlier version, we remove the embedded newline and test for the pattern. If the match is made, we want to print the pair of lines. So we get another copy of the duplicate because it has the newline, and control passes to the bottom of the script. If no match is found, we also retrieve the duplicate and remove the first portion of it. The delete action causes control to be passed back to the top, where the N command causes the next line to be appended to the previous line.

Here's the result when the program is run on this section:

```
$ phrase "the procedure is followed" sect3
If a pattern is followed by a \f(CW!\fP, then the procedure
is followed for all lines that do \fInot\fP match the
so that the procedure is followed only if there is
```

In Conclusion

The examples given here only begin to touch on the power of sed's advanced commands. For example, a variant of the hold command (H) appends matched lines to the hold space, rather than overwriting the initial contents of the hold space. Likewise, the G variant of the get command appends the contents of the hold space to the current line, instead of replacing it. The X command swaps the contents of the pattern space with the contents of the hold space. As you can imagine, these commands give you a great deal of power to make complex edits.

However, it's important to remember that you don't need to understand everything about sed to use it. As we've shown, it is a versatile editor, fast enough to recommend to beginners for making simple global edits to a large set of files, yet complex enough to tackle tasks that you'd never think to accomplish with an editor.

Although the syntax is convoluted even for experienced computer users, sed does have flow control mechanisms that, given some thought and experimentation, allow you to devise editing programs. It is easy to imagine (though more difficult to execute) a sed script that contains editing "subroutines," branched to by label, that perform different actions on parts of a file and quit when some condition has been met.

Few of us will go that far, but it is important to understand the scope of the tool. You never know when, faced with some thorny task that would take endless repetitive hours to accomplish, you'll find yourself saying: "Wait! I bet I could do that with sed."*

▪ A Proofreading Tool You Can Build ▪

Now let's look at a more complex script that makes minimal use of sed but extensive use of shell programming. It is the first example of a full-fledged tool built with the shell that offers significantly greater functionality than any of the individual tools that make it up.

We call this script proof. It uses spell to check for misspelled words in a file, shows the offending lines in context, and then uses sed to make the corrections. Because many documents contain technical terms, proper names, and so on that will be flagged as errors, the script also creates and maintains a local dictionary file of exceptions that should not be flagged as spelling errors.

This script was originally published with the name spellproofer in Rebecca Thomas's column in the June 1985 issue of *UNIX World*, to which it was submitted by Mike Elola. The script as originally published contained several errors, for which we submitted corrections. The following script, which incorporates those corrections, was published in the January 1986 issue, and is reprinted with permission of *UNIX World*. (Actually, we've added a few further refinements since then, so the script is not exactly as published.)

Because the contents of the script will become clearer after you see it in action, let's work backward this time, and show you the results of the script before we look at what it contains. The following example shows a sample run on an early draft of Chapter 2. In this example, <CR> indicates that the user has typed a carriage return in response to a prompt.

```
$ proof sect1
Do you want to use a local dictionary?  If so, enter
the name or press RETURN for the default dictionary: <CR>

Using local dictionary file dict
working ...
```

---

*The preceding sections have not covered all sed commands. See Appendix A for a complete list of sed commands.

The word Calisthentics appears to be misspelled.
Do you want to see it in context (y or n)?
n

Press RETURN for no change or replace "Calisthentics" with:
Calisthenics

.H1 "UNIX Calisthenics"
Save corrections in "sect1" file (y or n)?
y

The word metachacters appears to be misspelled.
Do you want to see it in context (y or n)?
n

Press RETURN for no change or replace "metachacters" with:
metacharacters

generation metacharacters.   The asterisk matches any or all
Save corrections in "sect1" file (y or n)?
y

The word textp appears to be misspelled.
Do you want to see it in context (y or n)?
y
a directory "/work/textp" and under that directories for
each of the chapters in the book, "/work/textp/ch01",
$ cp notes /work/textp/ch01
name in the directory /work/textp/ch01.
$ ls /work/textp/ch*
$ ls /work/textp/ch01/sect?
cwd   /work/textp/ch03
$ book="/work/textp"
/work/textp

Press RETURN for no change or replace 'textp' with: **<CR>**

You left the following words unchanged
textp

Do you wish to have any of the above words entered
into a local dictionary file (y/n)?
y
Append to dict (y/n)?
y

```
Do you wish to be selective (y/n)?
y
Include textp (y/n)?
y

Done.
$
```

Now let's look at the script. Because it is more complex than anything we have looked at so far, we have printed line numbers in the margin. These numbers are not part of the script but are used as a reference in the commentary that follows. You will find that the indentation of nested loops and so forth will make the program much easier to read.

```
1    echo "Do you want to use a local dictionary? If so, enter"
2    echo "the name or press RETURN for the default dictionary: "
3    read localfile
4    if [ -z "$localfile" ]; then
5      localfile=dict
6      echo Using local dictionary file $localfile
7    fi
8    echo "working ..."
9    touch $localfile
10   filelist="$*"; excused=""
11   if [ -z "$filelist" ]; then
12     echo 'Usage: proof file...'
13     exit 1
14   fi
15   for word in `spell $filelist`
16   do
17     found=`grep "^$word$" $localfile`
18     if [ -z "$found" ] ; then
19       echo
20       echo "The word $word appears to be misspelled."
21       echo "Do you want to see it in context (y or n)? "
22       read context
23       if [ "$context" = y ]; then
24         grep $word $filelist
25       fi
26       echo
27       echo "Press RETURN for no change or replace \"$word\" with:"
28       read correction
29       if [ -n "$correction" ]; then
30         hitlist="`grep -l $word $filelist`"
31         for file in $hitlist
32         do
33           echo
```

```
34              sed -n -e "s/$word/$correction/gp" <$file
35              echo "Save corrections in \"$file\" file (y or n)? "
36              read response
37              if [ "$response" = y ]; then
38                sed -e "s/$word/$correction/g" <$file>/usr/tmp/$file
39                if test -s /usr/tmp/$file; then
40                 mv /usr/tmp/$file $file
41                fi
42              fi
43            done
44        else
45            excused="$excused $word"
46        fi
47    fi
48 done
49 echo;echo;echo
50 if [ -n "$excused" ]; then
51   echo "You left the following words unchanged"
52   echo $excused | tr "\ " "\012" | pr -5 -t
53   echo
54   echo "Do you wish to have any of the above words entered"
55   echo "into a local dictionary file (y/n)? "
56   read response
57   if [ "$response" = "y" ]; then
58     if [ -n "$localfile" ]; then
59         echo "Append to $localfile (y/n)? "
60         read response
61         if [ "$response" != y ]; then
62         echo "Enter new/alternate local dictionary file: "
63         read localfile
64         fi
65     fi
66     echo
67     echo "Do you wish to be selective (y/n)? "
68     read select
69     for word in $excused
70     do
71        if [ "$select" = y ]; then
72           echo "Include $word (y/n)? "
73          read response
74          if test "$response" = y; then
75             echo $word >>$localfile
76          fi
77        else
78          echo $word >>$localfile
79        fi
```

```
80      done
81    fi
82  fi
83  echo
84  echo "Done."
```

1-8   The UNIX programming philosophy is to create small programs as general-purpose tools that can be joined in pipelines. Because of this, programs generally don't do prompting, or other "user-friendly" things that will limit the program to interactive operation. However, there are times, even in UNIX (!), when this is appropriate.

The shell has commands to handle prompting and reading the resulting responses into the file, as demonstrated here. The echo command prints the prompt, and read assigns whatever is typed in response (up to a carriage return) to a variable. This variable can then be used in the script.

The lines shown here prompt for the name of the local dictionary file, and, if none is supplied, use a default dictionary in the current directory called dict. In the sample run, we simply typed a carriage return, so the variable localfile is set to dict.

9   If this is the first time the script has been run, there is probably no local dictionary file, and one must be created. The touch command is a good way to do this because if a file already exists, it will merely update the access time that is associated with the file (as listed by ls -l). If the file does not exist, however, the touch command will create one.

Although this line is included in the script as a sanity check, so that the script will work correctly the first time, it is preferable to create the local dictionary manually, at least for large files. The spell program tends to flag as errors many words that you want to use in your document. The proof script handles the job of adding these words to a local dictionary, but doing this interactively can be quite time-consuming. It is much quicker to create a base dictionary for a document by redirecting the output of spell to the dictionary, then editing the dictionary to *remove* authentic spelling errors and leave only the exception list. The errors can then be corrected with proof without the tedium of endlessly repeating n for words that are really not errors.

If you use this script, you should run spell rather than proof on the first draft of a document, and create the dictionary at that time. Subsequent runs of proof for later drafts will be short and to the point.

10-14   In these lines, the script sets up some variables, in much the same way as we've seen before. The lines:

```
filelist="$*"
if [ -z "$filelist" ]; then
    echo "Usage:  proof file..."
    exit 1
fi
```

have much the same effect as the test of the number of arguments greater than zero that we used in earlier scripts. If `filelist` is a null string, no arguments have been specified, and so it is time to display an error message and end the program, using the shell's `exit` command.

15   This line shows a feature of the shell we've seen before, but it is still worthy of note because it may take a while to remember. The output of a command enclosed in backquotes (``` `` ```) can be substituted for the argument list of another command. That is what is happening here; the output of the `spell` command is used as the pattern list of a `for` loop.

17-18   You'll notice that `spell` still flags all of the words it finds as errors. But the `for` loop then uses `grep` to compare each word in the list generated by `spell` with the contents of the dictionary. Only those words *not* found in the dictionary are submitted for correction.

The pattern given to `grep` is "anchored" by the special pattern-matching characters `^` and `$` (beginning and end of line, respectively), so that only whole words in the dictionary are matched. Without these anchors, the presence of the word `ditroff` in the list would prevent the discovery of misspellings like `trof`.

20-25   Sometimes it is difficult to tell beforehand whether an apparent misspelling is really an error, or if it is correct in context. For example, in our sample run, the word `textp` appeared to be an error, but was in fact part of a pathname, and so correct. Accordingly, `proof` (again using `grep`) gives you the opportunity to look at each line containing the error before you decide to change it or not.

As an aside, you'll notice a limitation of the script. If, as is the case in our example, there are multiple occurrences of a string, they must all be changed or left alone as a set. There is no provision for making individual edits.

26-48   After a word is offered as an error, you have the option to correct it or leave it alone. The script needs to keep track of which words fall into each category, because words that are not corrected may need to be added to the dictionary.

If you do want to make a correction, you type it in. The variable `correction` will now be nonzero and can be used as the basis of a test (`test -n`). If you've typed in a correction, `proof` first checks the files on the command line to see which ones (there can be more than one) can be corrected. (`grep -l` just gives the names of files in which the string is found into the variable `hitlist`, and the script stores the names.) The edit is then applied to each one of these files.

35 Just to be on the safe side, the script prints the correction first, rather than making any edits. (The `-n` option causes `sed` not to print the entire file on standard output, but only to print lines that are explicitly requested for printing with a `p` command. Used like this, `sed` performs much the same function as `grep`, only we are making an edit at the same time.

37-42 If the user approves the correction, `sed` is used once again, this time to actually make the edit. You should recognize this part of the script. Remember, it is essential in this application to enclose the expression used by `sed` in quotation marks.

50-84 If you've understood the previous part of the shell script, you should be able to decipher this part, which adds words to the local dictionary. The `tr` command converts the spaces separating each word in the `excused` list into carriage returns. They can then be printed in five tab-separated columns by `pr`. Study this section of the program until you do, because it is an excellent example of how UNIX programs that appear to have a single, cut-and-dry function (or no clear function at all to the uninitiated) can be used in unexpected but effective ways.

C H A P T E R

13

The awk Programming Language

A program is a solution to a problem, formulated in the syntax of a particular language. It is a small step from writing complex editing scripts with sed to writing programs with awk, but it is a step that many writers may fear to take. "Script" is less loaded a term than "program" for many people, but an editing script is still a program.

Each programming language has its own "style" that lends itself to performing certain tasks better than other languages. Anyone can scan a reference page and quickly learn a language's syntax, but a close examination of programs written in that language is usually required before you understand how to apply this knowledge. In this sense, a programming language is simply another tool; you need to know not only how to use it but also when and why it is used.

We recommend that you learn more than one programming language. We have already looked at a number of different programs or scripts written for and executed by the shell, ex, and sed. As you learn the awk programming language, you will notice similarities and differences. Not insignificantly, an awk script looks different from a shell script. The awk language shares many of the same basic constructs as the shell's programming language, yet awk requires a slightly different syntax. The awk program's basic operations are not much different from sed's: reading standard input one line at a time, executing instructions that consist of two parts, *pattern* and *procedure*, and writing to standard output.

More importantly, awk has capabilities that make it the tool of choice for certain tasks. A programming language is itself a program that was written to solve certain kinds of problems for which adequate tools did not exist. The awk program was designed for text-processing applications, particularly those in which information is structured in records and fields. The major capabilities of awk that we will demonstrate in upcoming pages are as follows:

- definable record and field structure
- conditional and looping constructs

- assignment, arithmetic, relational, and logical operators
- numeric and associative arrays
- formatted print statements
- built-in functions

A quick comparison of a single feature will show you how one programming language can differ from another. You will find it much easier to perform arithmetic operations in awk than in the shell. To increment the value of x by 1 using the shell, you'd use the following line:

```
x=`expr $x + 1`
```

The expr command is a UNIX program that is executed as a separate process returning the value of its arguments. In awk, you only have to write:

```
++x
```

This is the same as x = x + 1. (This form could also be used in awk.)

▪ Invoking awk ▪

The awk program itself is a program that, like sed, runs a specified program on lines of input. You can enter awk from the command line, or from inside a shell script.

$ **awk** *'program'* *files*

Input is read a line at a time from one or more *files*. The *program*, enclosed in single quotation marks to protect it from the shell, consists of *pattern* and *procedure* sections. If the pattern is missing, the procedure is performed on all input lines:

$ **awk '{print}' sample**   *Prints all lines in* sample *file*

The procedure is placed within braces. If the procedure is missing, lines matching the pattern are printed:

$ **awk '/programmer's guide/' sample**   *Prints lines matching pattern*
                                              in sample *file*

The awk program allows you to specify zero, one, or two pattern addresses, just like sed. Regular expressions are placed inside a pair of slashes (/). In awk, patterns can also be made up of expressions. An expression (or a primary expression so as not to confuse it with a regular expression) can be a string or numeric constant (for example, *red* or *1*), a variable (whose value is a string or numeric), or a function (which we'll look at later).

You can associate a pattern with a specific procedure as follows:

```
/pattern1/ {
        procedure 1
     }
/pattern2/ {
```

```
            procedure 2
        }
    { procedure 3 }
```

Like sed, only the lines matching the particular pattern are the object of a procedure, and a line can match more than one pattern. In this example, the third procedure is performed on all input lines. Usually, multiline awk scripts are placed in a separate file and invoked using the −f option:

```
$ awk −f awkscript sample
```

▪ Records and Fields ▪

Perhaps the most important feature of awk is that it divides each line of input into fields. In the simplest case, each field contains a single word, delimited by a blank space. The awk program allows you to reference these fields by their position in the input line, either in patterns or procedures. The symbol $0 represents the entire input line. $1, $2, ... refer, by their position in the input line, to individual fields.

We'll demonstrate some of these capabilities by building an awk program to search through a list of acronyms in a file. Each acronym is listed along with its meaning. If we print the first field of each line, we'll get the name of the acronym:

```
$ awk '{print $1}' sample
BASIC
CICS
COBOL
DBMS
GIGO
GIRL
```

We can construct a useful program that would allow you to specify an acronym and get its description. We could use awk just like grep:

```
$ awk '/BASIC/' sample
BASIC Beginner's All−Purpose Symbolic Instruction Code
```

However, there are three things we'd like to do to improve this program and make better use of awk's capabilities:

1. Limit the pattern-matching search.

2. Make the program more general and not dependent on the particular acronym that is the subject of the search.

3. Print only the description.

· Testing Fields ·

The pattern as specified will match the word *BASIC* anywhere on the line. That is, it might match *BASIC* used in a description. To see if the first field (`$1`) matches the pattern, we write:

```
$1 == "BASIC"
```

The symbol `==` is a relational operator meaning "equal to" and is used to compare the first field of each line with the string *BASIC*. You could also construct this test using a given regular expression that looks for the acronym at the beginning of the line.

```
$1 ~ /^BASIC/
```

The pattern-matching operator `~` evaluates as true if an expression (`$1`) matches a regular expression. Its opposite, `!~`, evaluates true if the expression does not match the regular expression.

Although these two examples look very similar, they achieve very different results. The relational operator `==` evaluates true if the first field is *BASIC* but false if the first field is *BASIC,* (note the comma). The pattern-matching operator `~` locates both occurrences.

Pattern-matching operations must be performed on a regular expression (a string surrounded by slashes). Variables cannot be used inside a regular expression with the exception of shell variables, as shown in the next section. Constants cannot be evaluated using the pattern-matching operator.

· Passing Parameters from a Shell Script ·

Our program is too specific and requires too much typing. We can put the `awk` script in a file and invoke it with the `-f` option. Or we can put the command inside a shell script, named for the function it performs. This shell script should be able to read the first argument from the command line (the name of the acronym) and pass it as a parameter to `awk`. We'll call the shell script `awkronym` and set it up to read a file named `acronyms`. Here's the simplest way to pass an argument into an `awk` procedure:

```
$ cat awkronym
awk '$1 == search' search=$1 acronyms
```

Parameters passed to an `awk` program are specified *after* the program. The `search` variable is set up to pass the first argument on the command line to the `awk` program. Even this gets confusing, because `$1` inside the `awk` program represents the first field of each input line, while `$1` in the shell represents the first argument supplied on the command line. Here's how this version of the program works:

```
$ awkronym CICS
CICS Customer Information Control System
```

By replacing the search string `BASIC` with a variable (which could be set to the string `CICS` or `BASIC`), we have a program that is fairly generalized.

Notice that we had to test the parameter as a string ($1 == search). This is because we can't pass the parameter inside a regular expression. Thus, the expressions "$1 ~ /search/" or "$1 ~ search" will produce syntax errors.

As an aside, let's look at another way to import a shell variable into an awk program that even works inside a regular expression. However, it looks complicated:

```
search=$1
awk '$1 ~ /'"$search"'/' acronyms
```

This program works the same as the prior version (with the exception that the argument is evaluated inside a regular expression.) Note that the first line of the script makes the variable assignment before awk is invoked. In the awk program, the shell variable is enclosed within single, then double, quotation marks. These quotes cause the shell to insert the value of $search inside the regular expression before it is interpreted by awk. Therefore, awk never sees the shell variable and evaluates it as a constant string.

You will come upon situations when you wish it were possible to place awk variables within regular expressions. As mentioned in the previous section, pattern matching allows us to search for a variety of occurences. For instance, a field might also include incidental punctuation marks and would not match a fixed string unless the string included the specific punctuation mark. Perhaps there is some undocumented way of getting an awk variable interpreted inside a regular expression, or maybe there is a convoluted work-around waiting to be figured out.

• Changing the Field Separator •

The awk program is oriented toward data arranged in fields and records. A record is normally a single line of input, consisting of one or more fields. The field separator is a blank space or tab and the record separator is a newline. For example, here's one record with five fields:

```
CICS Customer Information Control System
```

Field three or $3 is the string *Information*. In our program, we like to be able to print the description as a field. It is obvious that we can't just say print $2 and get the entire description. But that is what we'd like to be able to do.

This will require that we change the input file using another character (other than a blank) to delimit fields. A tab is frequently used as a field separator. We'll have to insert a tab between the first and second fields:

```
$ cat acronyms
awk    Aho, Weinstein & Kernighan
BASIC  Beginner's All-Purpose Symbolic Instruction Code
CICS   Customer Information Control System
COBOL  Common Business Orientated Language
DBMS   Data Base Management System
GIGO   Garbage In, Garbage Out
GIRL   Generalized Information Retrieval Language
```

You can change the field separator from the command line using the −F option:

```
$ awk -F"|————|" '$1 == search {print $2}' search=$1 acronyms
```

Note that |————| is entered by typing a double quotation mark, pressing the *TAB* key, and typing a double quotation mark. This makes the tab character (represented in the example as |————|) the exclusive field separator; spaces no longer serve to separate fields. Now that we've implemented all three enhancements, let's see how the program works:

```
$ awkronym GIGO
Garbage In, Garbage Out
```

▪ System Variables ▪

The awk program defines a number of special variables that can be referenced or reset inside a program. See Table 13-1.

TABLE 13-1. awk System Variables

System Variable	Meaning
FILENAME	Current filename
FS	Field separator (a blank)
NF	Number of fields in the current record
NR	Number of the current record
OFS	Output field separator (a blank)
ORS	Output record separator (a newline)
RS	Record separator (a newline)

The system variable FS defines the field separator used by awk. You can set FS inside the program as well as from the command line.

Typically, if you redefine the field or record separator, it is done as part of a BEGIN procedure. The BEGIN procedure allows you to specify an action that is performed before the first input line is read.

```
BEGIN { FS = "|————|" }
```

You can also specify actions that are performed after all input is read by defining an END procedure.

The awk command sets the variable NF to the number of fields on the current line. Try running the following awk command on any text file:

```
$ awk '{print $NF}' test
```

If there are five fields in the current record, NF will be set to five; $NF refers to the fifth and last field. Shortly, we'll look at a program, double, that makes good use of this variable.

▪ **Looping** ▪

The awkronym program can print field two because we restructured the input file and redefined the field separator. Sometimes, this isn't practical, and you need another method to read or print a number of fields for each record. If the field separator is a blank or tab, the two records would have six and five fields, respectively.

```
BASIC Beginner's All-Purpose Symbolic Instruction Code
CICS Customer Information Control System
```

It is not unusual for records to have a variable number of fields. To print all but the first field, our program would require a loop that would be repeated as many times as there are fields remaining. In many awk programs, a loop is a commonly used procedure.

The while statement can be employed to build a loop. For instance, if we want to perform a procedure three times, we keep track of how many times we go through the loop by incrementing a variable at the bottom of the loop, then we check at the top of the loop to see if that variable is greater than 3. Let's take an example in which we print the input line three times.

```
{       i = 1
        while(i <= 3) {
                print
                ++i
                }
}
```

Braces are required inside the loop to describe a procedure consisting of more than a single action. Three operators are used in this program: = assigns the value 1 to the variable i; <= compares the value of i to the constant 3; and ++ increments the variable by 1. The first time the while statement is encountered, i is equal to 1. Because the expression i <= 3 is true, the procedure is performed. The last action of the procedure is to increment the variable i. The while expression is true after the end of the second loop has incremented i to 3. However, the end of the third loop increments i to 4 and the expression evaluates as false.

A for loop serves the same purpose as a while loop, but its syntax is more compact and easier to remember and use. Here's how the previous while statement is restructured as a for loop:

```
for (i = 1; i <= 3; i++)
        print
```

The for statement consists of three expressions within parentheses. The first expression, i = 1, sets the initial value for the counter variable. The second expression states a condition that is tested at the top of the loop. (The while statement tested the condition at the bottom of the loop.) The third expression increments the counter.

Now, to loop through remaining fields on the line, we have to determine how many times we need to execute the loop. The system variable NF contains the number of fields on the current input record. If we compare our counter (i) against NF each time through the loop, we'll be able to tell when all fields have been read:

```
for (i = 1; i <= NF; i++)
```

We will print out each field ($i), one to a line. Just to show how awk works, we'll print the record and field number before each field.

```
awk '{ for (i = 1; i <= NF; i++)
        print NR":"i, $i } ' $*
```

Notice that the print statement concatenates NR, a colon, and i. The comma produces an output field separator, which is a blank by default.

This program produces the following results on a sample file:

```
1:1 awk
1:2 Aho,
1:3 Weinstein
1:4 &
1:5 Kernighan
2:1 BASIC
2:2 Beginner's
2:3 All-Purpose
2:4 Symbolic
2:5 Instruction
2:6 Code
```

Symbolic is the fourth field of the second record. You might note that the sample file is acronyms, the one in which we inserted a tab character between the first and second fields. Because we did not change the default field separator, awk interpreted the tab or blank as a field separator. This allows you to write programs in which the special value of the tab is ignored.

Conditional Statements

Now let's change our example so that when given an argument, the program returns the record and field number where that argument appears.

Essentially, we want to test each field to see if it matches the argument; if it does, we want to print the record and field number. We need to introduce another flow control construct, the if statement. The if statement evaluates an expression—if true, it performs the procedure; if false, it does not.

In the next example, we use the if statement to test whether the current field is equal to the argument. If it is, the current record and field number are printed.

```
awk '{ for (i = 1; i <= NF; i++){
        if ($i == search) {
            print NR":"i
            }
        }
} ' search=$1 acronyms
```

This new procedure prints *2:1* or *3:4* and isn't very useful by itself, but it demonstrates that you can retrieve and test any single field from any record.

The next program, double, checks if the first word on a line is a duplicate of the last word on the previous line. We use double in proofing documents and it catches a surprisingly common typing mistake.

```
awk '
NF > 0 {
      if ($1 == lastword){
            print NR ": double " $1
            }
            lastword = $NF
}' $1
```

When the first line of input is read, if the number of fields is greater than 0, then the expression in the if statement is evaluated. Because the variable lastword has not been set, it evaluates to false. The final action assigns the value of $NF to the variable lastword. ($NF refers to the last field; the value of NF is the number of the last field.) When the next input line is read, the first word is compared against the value of lastword. If they are the same, a message is printed.

```
double sect1
15: double the
32: double a
```

This version of double is based on the program presented by Kernighan and Pike in *The UNIX Programming Environment*. (Writer's Workbench now includes this program.) Kernighan and Pike's program also checks for duplicate words, side-by-side, in the same line. You might try implementing this enhancement, using a for loop and checking the current field against the previous field. Another feature of Kernighan and Pike's double is that you can run the program on more than one file. To allow for additional files, you can change the shell variable from $1 to $* but the record or line number printed by NR will correspond to consecutive input lines. Can you write a procedure to reset NR to 0 before reading input from a new file?

Arrays

The double program shows us how we can retain data by assigning it to a variable. In awk, unlike several other programming languages, variables do not have to be initialized before they are referenced in a program. In the previous program, we evaluated lastword at the top, although it was not actually assigned a value until the bottom of the program. The awk program initialized the variable, setting it to the null string or 0, depending upon whether the variable is referenced as a string or numeric value.

An array is a variable that allows you to store a list of items or elements. An array is analogous to a restaurant menu. Each item on this menu is numbered:

#1   tuna noodle casserole

#2   roast beef and gravy

#3   pork and beans

One way of ordering roast beef is to say simply "Number 2." Using ordinary variables, you would have had to define a variable *two* and assign it the value *roast beef and gravy*. An array is a way of referencing a group of related values. This might be written:

```
menu[choice]
```

where `menu` is the name of the array and `choice` is the *subscript* used to reference items in the array. Thus, `menu[1]` is equal to *tuna noodle casserole*. In `awk`, you don't have to declare the size of the array; you only have to load the array (before referencing it). If we put our three menu choices on separate lines in a file, we could load the array with the following statement:

```
menu[NR] = $0
```

The variable `NR`, or record number, is used as the subscript for the array. Each input line is read into the next element in the array. We can print an individual element by referring to the value of the subscript (not the variable that set this value).

```
print menu[3]
```

This statement prints the third element in the array, which is *pork and beans*. If we want to refer to all the elements of this array, we can use a special version of the `for` loop. It has the following syntax:

```
for (element in array)
```

This statement can be used to descend the array to print all of the elements:

```
for (choice in menu)
        print menu[choice]
```

Each time through the loop, the variable `choice` is set to the next element in the array. The `menu` array is an example of an array that uses a numeric subscript as an index to the elements.

Now, let's use arrays to increase the functionality of `awkronym`. Our new version will read acronyms from a file and load them into an array; then we'll read a second file and search for the acronyms. Basically, we're reading one input file and defining keywords that we want to search for in other files. A similar program that reads a list of terms in a glossary might show where the words appear in a chapter. Let's see how it works first:

```
$ awkronym sect1
exposure to BASIC programming.
in COBOL and take advantage of a DBMS environment.
in COBOL and take advantage of a DBMS environment.
Of the high-level languages, BASIC is probably
```

Let's look at the program carefully.

```
awk ' {
if ( FILENAME == "acronyms" ){
        acro_desc[NR] = $1
        next
        }
for ( name in acro_desc )
        for (i = 1; i <= NF; i++)
                if ($i == acro_desc[name]) {
                        print $0
                }
}' acronyms $*
```

The current filename is stored in the system variable FILENAME. The procedure within the first conditional statement is only performed while input is taken from acronyms. The next statement ends this procedure by reading the next line of input from the file. Thus, the program does not advance beyond this procedure until input is taken from a different file.

The purpose of the first procedure is to assign each acronym ($1) to an element of the array acro_desc; the record number (NR) indexes the array.

In the second half of the program, we start comparing each element in the array to each field of every record. This requires two for loops, one to cycle through the array for each input line, and one to read each field on that line for as many times as there are elements in the array. An if statement compares the current field to the current element of the array; if they are equal, then the line is printed.

The line is printed each time an acronym is found. In our test example, because there were two acronyms on a single line, the one line is duplicated. To change this, we could add next after the print statement.

What if we changed awkronym so that it not only scanned the file for the acronym, but printed the acronym with the description as well? If a line refers to *BASIC*, we'd like to add the description (*Beginner's All-Purpose Symbolic Instruction Code*). We can design such a program for use as a *filter* that prints all lines, regardless of whether or not a change has been made. To change the previous version, we simply move the print statement outside the conditional statement. However, there are other changes we must make as well. Here's the first part of the new version.

```
awk ' {
        if ( FILENAME == "acronyms" ){
        split($0,fields,"|————|")
        acro_desc[fields[1]]=fields[2]
        next
        }
```

The records in acronyms use a tab as a field separator. Rather than change the field separator, we use the split function (we'll look at the syntax of this function later on) to give us an array named fields that has two elements, the name of the acronym and its description. This numeric array is then used in creating an associative array named acro_desc. An associative array lets us use a string as a subscript to the elements of an array. That is, given the name of the acronym, we can locate the element corresponding to the description. Thus the expression `acro_desc[GIGO]` will access `Garbage In, Garbage Out`.

Now let's look at the second half of the program:

```
for ( name in acro_desc )
        for (i = 1;  i <= NF;  i++)
             if ($i == name) {
                     $i = $i " ("acro_desc[name]")"
                }
print $0
```

Just like the previous version, we loop through the elements of the array and the fields for each record. At the heart of this section is the conditional statement that tests if the current field (`$i`) is equal to the subscript of the array (`name`). If the value of the field and the subscript are equal, we concatenate the field and the array element. In addition, we place the description in parentheses.

It should be clear why we make the comparison between `$i` and `name`, and not `acro_desc[name]`; the latter refers to an element, while the former refers to the subscript, the name of the acronym.

If the current field (`$i`) equals `BASIC` and the index of the array (`name`) is the string *BASIC*, then the value of the field is set to:

```
BASIC (Beginner's All-Purpose Symbolic Instruction Code)
```

For this program to be practical, the description should be inserted for the first occurrence of an acronym, not each time. (After we've inserted the description of the acronym, we don't need the description any more.) We could redefine that element in the array after we've used it:

```
acro_desc[name]  = name
```

In this instance, we simply make the element equal to the subscript. Thus, `acro_desc[BASIC]` is equal to *Beginner's All-Purpose Symbolic Instruction Code* at the beginning of the procedure, and equal to *BASIC* if a match has been made. There are two places where we test the element against the subscript with the expression `"(acro_desc[name] != name)."` The first place is after the `for` loop has read in a new element from `acro_desc`; a conditional statement ensures that we don't scan the next input record for an acronym that has already been found. The second place is when we test `$i` to see if it matches `name`; this test ensures that we don't make another match for the same acronym on that line.

```
if ($i == name && acro_desc[name] != name)
```

This conditional statement evaluates a compound expression. The `&&` (and) boolean operator states a condition that both expressions have to be true for the compound expression to be true.

Another problem that we can anticipate is that we might produce lines that exceed 80 characters. After all, the descriptions are quite long. We can find out how many characters are in a string, using a built-in `awk` function, `length`. For instance, to evaluate the length of the current input record, we specify:

```
length($0)
```

The value of a function can be assigned to a variable or put inside an expression and evaluated.

```
if (length($0) > 70){
        if (i > 2)
                $i = "\n" $i
        if (i+1 < NF )
                $(i+1) = "\n" $(i+1)
        }
```

The length of the current input record is evaluated after the description has been concatenated. If it is greater than 70 characters, then two conditions test where to put the newline. The first procedure concatenates a newline and the current field; thus we only want to perform this action when we are not near the beginning of a line (field greater than 2). The second procedure concatenates the newline and the next field (i+1) so that we check that we are not near the end of the line. The newline precedes the field in each of these operations. Putting it at the end of the field would result in a new line that begins with a space output with the next field.

Another way to handle the line break, perhaps more efficiently, is to use the length function to return a value for each field. By accumulating that value, we could specify a line break when a new field causes the total to exceed a certain number. We'll look at arithmetic operations in a later section.

Here's the full version of awkronyms:

```
awk '   {
   if ( FILENAME == "acronyms" ){
   split($0,fields,"|———|")
   acro_desc[fields[1]]=fields[2]
   next
   }
for ( name in acro_desc )
   if (acro_desc[name] != name)
      for (i = 1; i <= NF; i++)
         if ($i == name && acro_desc[name] != name) {
            $i =  $i " ("acro_desc[name]")"
            acro_desc[name] = name
            if (length($0) > 70){
               if (i > 2)
                  $i = "\n" $i
               if (i+1 < NF)
                  $(i+1) = "\n" $(i+1)
            }
         }
print $0
}' acronyms $*
```

And here's one proof that it works:

```
$ cat sect1
Most users of microcomputers have had some
exposure to BASIC programming.
Many data-processing applications are written
in COBOL and take advantage of a DBMS environment.
C, the language of the UNIX environment,
is used by systems programmers.
Of the high-level languages, BASIC is probably
the easiest to learn, and C is the most difficult.
Nonetheless, you will find the fundamental programming
constructs common to most languages.

$ awkronym sect1
Most users of microcomputers have had some
exposure to
BASIC (Beginner's All-Purpose Symbolic Instruction Code)
programming.  Many data-processing applications are
written in COBOL (Common Business Orientated Language)
and take advantage of a
DBMS (Data Base Management System) environment.
C, the language of the UNIX environment,
is used by systems programmers.
Of the high-level languages, BASIC is probably
the easiest to learn, and C is the most difficult.
Nonetheless, you will find the fundamental programming
constructs common to most languages.
```

Notice that the second reference to BASIC has not been changed. There are other features we might add to this program. For instance, we could use awk's pattern-matching capabilities so that we don't make the change on lines containing macros, or on lines within pairs of certain macros, such as .DS/.DE.

Another version of this program could trademark certain terms or phrases in a document. For instance, you'd want to locate the first occurrence of UNIX and place \(rg after it.

▪ awk Applications ▪

A shell program is an excellent way to gather data interactively and write it into a file in a format that can be read by awk. We're going to be looking at a series of programs for maintaining a project log. A shell script collects the name of a project and the number of hours worked on the project. An awk program totals the hours for each project and prints a report.

The file day is the shell script for collecting information and appending it to a file named daily in the user's home directory.

```
$ cat /usr/local/bin/day
case $# in
0) echo "Project: \c";read proj;echo "Hours: \c";read hrs;;
1) proj=$1; echo "Hours: \c"; read hrs;;
2) proj=$1;hrs=$2;;
esac
set `who am i`; name=$1; month=$3; day=$4;
echo $name"\t"$month $day"\t"$hrs"\t"$proj>>$HOME/daily
```

The case statement checks how many arguments are entered on the command line. If an argument is missing, the user is prompted to enter a value. Prompting is done through a pair of statements: echo and read. The echo command displays the prompt on the user's terminal; \c suppresses the carriage return at the end of the prompt. The read command waits for user input, terminated by a carriage return, and assigns it to a variable. Thus, the variables proj and hrs are defined by the end of the case statement.

The set command can be used to divide the output of a command into separate arguments ($1, $2, $3...). By executing the command who am i from within set, we supply the user's name and the day's date automatically. The echo command is used to write the information to the file. There are four fields, separated by tabs. (In the Bourne shell, the escape sequence \t produces a tab; you must use quotation marks to keep the backslash from being stripped off by the shell.)

Here's what daily contains for one user at the end of a week:

```
$ cat /usr/fred/daily
fred    Aug 4 7     Course Development
fred    Aug 5 4     Training class
fred    Aug 5 4     Programmer's Guide
fred    Aug 6 2     Administrative
fred    Aug 6 6     Text-processing book
fred    Aug 7 4     Course Development
fred    Aug 7 4     Text-processing book
fred    Aug 8 4     Training class
fred    Aug 8 3     Programmer's Guide
```

There are nine records in this file. Obviously, our input program does not enforce consistency in naming projects by the user.

Given this input, we'd like an awk program that reports the total number of hours for the week and gives us a breakdown of hours by project. At first pass, we need only be concerned with reading fields three and four. We can total the number of hours by accumulating the value of the third field.

```
total += $3
```

The += operator performs two functions: it adds $3 to the current value of total and then assigns this value to total. It is the same as the statement:

```
total = total + $3
```

We can use an associative array to accumulate hours ($3) by project ($4).

```
hours[$4] += $3
```

Each time a record is read, the value of the third field is added to the accumulated value of `project[$4]`.

We don't want to print anything until all input records have been read. An END procedure prints the accumulated results. Here's the first version of `tot`:

```
awk '
        BEGIN { FS="|———|" }
{
                total += $3
                hours[$4] += $3
}
        END    {
                for (project in hours)
                print project, hours[project]
                print
                print "Total Hours:", total
} ' $HOME/daily
```

Let's test the program:

```
$ tot
Course Development 11
Administrative 2
Programmer's Guide 7
Training class 8
Text-processing book 10

Total Hours: 38
```

The program performs the arithmetic tasks well, but the report lacks an orderly format. It would help to change the output field separator (OFS) to a tab. But the variable lengths of the project names prevent the project hours from being aligned in a single column. The awk program offers an alternative print statement, `printf`, which is borrowed from the C programming language.

Formatted Print Statements

The `printf` statement has two parts: the first is a quoted expression that describes the format specifications; the second is a sequence of arguments such as variable names. The two main format specifications are `%s` for strings and `%d` for decimals. (There are additional specifications for octal, hexadecimal, and noninteger numbers.) Unlike the regular print statement, `printf` does not automatically supply a newline. This can be specified as `\n`. A tab is specified as `\t`.

A simple `printf` statement containing string and decimal specifications is:

```
printf "%s\t%d\n", project, hours[project]
```

First `project` is output, then a tab (\t), the number of hours, and a newline (\n). For each format specification, you must supply a corresponding argument.

Unfortunately, such a simple statement does not solve our formatting problem. Here are sample lines that it produces:

```
Course Development 11
Administrative   2
Programmer's Guide 7
```

We need to specify a minimum field width so that the tab begins at the same position. The `printf` statement allows you to place this specification between the `%` and the conversion specification. You would use `%-20s` to specify a minimum field width of 20 characters in which the value is left justified. Without the minus sign, the value would be right justified, which is what we want for a decimal value.

```
END     {
        for (project in hours)
        printf "%-20s\t%2d\n", project, hours[project]
        printf "\n\tTotal Hours:\t%2d\n", total
        }
```

Notice that literals, such as the string `Total Hours`, are placed in the first part, with the format specification.

Just as we use the `END` procedure to print the report, we can include a `BEGIN` procedure to print a header for the report:

```
BEGIN { FS="|————|"
        printf "%20s%s\n\n","PROJECT     ", " HOURS"
        }
```

This shows an alternative way to handle strings. The following formatted report is displayed:

```
        PROJECT         HOURS

Course Development      11
Administrative          2
Programmer's Guide      7
Training class          8
Text-processing book    10

        Total Hours:    38
```

Defensive Techniques

After you have accomplished the basic task of a program—and the code at this point is fairly easy to understand—it is often a good idea to surround this core with "defensive" procedures designed to trap inconsistent input records and prevent the program from failing. For instance, in the `tot` program, we might want to check that the number of hours is greater than 0 and that the project description is not null for each input record. We can use a conditional expression, using the logical operator `&&`.

```
$3 > 0 && $4 != ""{

                procedure

        }
```

Both conditions must be true for the procedure to be executed. The logical operator `&&` signifies that if both conditions are true, the expression is true.

Another aspect of incorporating defensive techniques is error handling. In other words, what do we want to have happen after the program detects an error? The previous condition is set up so that if the procedure is not executed, the next line of input is read. In this example the program keeps going, but in other cases you might want the program to print an error message and halt if such an error is encountered.

However, a distinction between "professional" and "amateur" programmers might be useful. We are definitely in the latter camp, and we do not always feel compelled to write 100% user-proof programs. For one thing, defensive programming is quite time consuming and frequently tedious. Second, an amateur is at liberty to write programs that perform the way he or she expects them to; a professional has to write for an audience and must account for their expectations. Consider the possible uses and users of any program you write.

awk and nroff/troff

It is fairly easy to have an `awk` program generate the necessary codes for form reports. For instance, we enhanced the `tot` program to produce a `troff`-formatted report:

```
awk ' BEGIN { FS = "|———|"
print ".ce"
print ".B "
print "PROJECT ACTIVITY REPORT"
print ".R"
print ".sp 2"
        }
NR == 1 {
        begday = $2
        }
$3 > 0 && $4 != "" {
                hours[$4] += $3
                total += $3
                endday = $2
                logname = $1
        }
```

```
        END   {
printf "Writer: %s\n", logname
print ".sp"
printf "Period: %s to %s\n",begday, endday
print ".sp"
printf "%20s%s\n\n","PROJECT      ", " HOURS"
print ".sp"
print ".nf"
print ".na"
        for (project in hours)
printf "%-20s\t%2d\n", project, hours[project]
print ".sp"
printf "Total Hours:\t %2d\n", total
print ".sp"
}' $HOME/daily
```

We incorporated one additional procedure in this version to determine the weekly period. The start date of the week is taken from the first record (NR == 1). The last record provides the final day of the week.

As you can see, awk doesn't mind if you mix print and printf statements. The regular print command is more convenient for specifying literals, such as formatting codes, because the newline is automatically provided. Because this program writes to standard output, you could pipe the output directly to nroff/troff.

You can use awk to generate input to tbl and other troff preprocessors such as pic.

Multiline Records

In this section, we are going to take a look at a set of programs for order tracking. We developed these programs to help operate a small, mail-order publishing business. These programs could be easily adapted to track documents in a technical publications department.

Once again, we used a shell program, take.orders, for data entry. The program has two purposes: The first is to enter the customer's name and mailing address for later use in building a mailing list. The second is to display seven titles and prompt the user to enter the title number, the number of copies, and the price per copy. The data collected for the mailing list and the customer order are written to separate files.

Two sample customer order records follow:

```
Charlotte Smith
P.O  N61331 87 Y 045      Date: 03/14/87
#1 3  7.50
#2 3  7.50
#3 1  7.50
#4 1  7.50
#7 1  7.50
```

```
Martin S. Rossi
P.O  NONE     Date: 03/14/87
#1 2   7.50
#2 5   6.75
```

These are multiline records, that is, a newline is used as the field separator. A blank line separates individual records. For most programs, this will require that we redefine the default field separator and record separator. The field separator becomes a newline, and the record separator is null.

```
BEGIN { FS = "\n"; RS = "" }
```

Let's write a simple program that multiplies the number of copies by the price. We want to ignore the first two lines of each record, which supply the customer's name, a purchase order number, and the date of the order. We only want to read the lines that specify a title. There are a few ways to do this. With awk's pattern-matching capabilities, we could select lines beginning with a hash (#) and treat them as individual records, with fields separated by spaces.

```
awk '/^#/ {
                amount = $2 * $3
                printf "%s %6.2f\n", $0, amount
                next
        }
{print}' $*
```

The main procedure only affects lines that match the pattern. It multiplies the second field by the third field, assigning the value to the variable amount. The printf conversion %f prints a floating-point number; 2 specifies a minimum field width of 6 and a precision of 2. Precision is the number of digits to the right of the decimal point; the default for %f is 6. We print the current record along with the value of the variable amount. If a line is printed within this procedure, the next line is read from standard input. Lines not matching the pattern are simply passed through. Let's look at how addem works:

```
$ addem orders
Charlotte Smith
P.O  N61331 87 Y 045     Date: 03/14/87
#1 3   7.50   22.50
#2 3   7.50   22.50
#3 1   7.50    7.50
#4 1   7.50    7.50
#7 1   7.50    7.50

Martin S. Rossi
P.O  NONE    Date: 03/14/87
#1 2   7.50   15.00
#2 5   6.75   33.75
```

Now, let's design a program that reads multiline records and accumulates order information for a report. This report should display the total number of copies and the total amount for each title. We also want totals reflecting all copies ordered and the sum of all orders.

We know that we will not be using the information in the first two fields of each record. However, each record has a variable number of fields, depending upon how many titles have been ordered. First, we check that the input record has at least three fields. Then a `for` loop reads all of the fields beginning with the third field:

```
NF >= 3 {
    for (i = 3; i <= NF; ++i)
```

In database terms, each field has a value and each value can be further broken up into subvalues. That is, if the value of a field in a multiline record is a single line, subvalues are the words on that line. You have already seen the `split` function used to break up an input record; now we'll see it used to subdivide a field. The `split` function loads any *string* into an *array*, using a specified character as the subvalue separator.

```
split (string, array, separator)
```

The default subvalue separator is a blank. The `split` function returns the number of elements loaded into the array. The *string* can be a literal (in quotation marks) or a variable. For instance, let's digress a minute and look at an isolated use of `split`. Here's a person's name and title with each part separated by a comma:

```
title="George Travers, Research/Development, Alcuin Inc."
```

We can use `split` to divide this string and print it on three lines.

```
need = split(title, name, ",")
    print ".ne ", need
    for ( part in name)
        print name[part]
```

This procedure prints each part on a separate line. The number of elements in the array (3) is saved in the variable `need`. This variable is passed as an argument to an `.ne` request, which tells `troff` to make sure there are at least three lines available at the bottom of the page before outputting the first line.

The `awk` program has twelve built-in functions, as shown in Table 13-2. Four of these are specialized arithmetic functions for cosine, sine, logarithm, and square root. The rest of these functions manipulate strings. (You have already seen how the `length` function works.) See Appendix A for the syntax of these functions.

Going back to our report generator, we need to split each field into subvalues. The variable `$i` will supply the value of the current field, subdivided as elements in the array `order`.

```
sv = split($i, order)
    if (sv == 3) {
            procedure
    }
    else print "Incomplete Record"
```

TABLE 13-2. awk Built-in Functions

Function	Description
cos	Cosine
exp	Exponent
getline	Read input line
index	Return position of substring in string
int	Integer
length	Length of string
log	Logarithm
sin	Sine
split	Subdivide string into array
sprintf	Format string like printf
sqrt	Square root
substr	Substring extraction

The number of elements returned by the function is saved in the sv variable. This allows us to test that there are three subvalues. If there are not, the else statement is executed, printing the error message to the screen.

Next, we assign the individual elements of the array to a specific variable. This is mainly to make it easier to remember what each element represents.

```
title = order[1]
copies = order[2]
price = order[3]
```

Then a group of arithmetic operations are performed on these values.

```
amount = copies * price
total_vol += copies
total_amt += amount
vol[title] += copies
amt[title] += amount
```

These values are accumulated until the last input record is read. The END procedure prints the report.

Here's the complete program:

```
awk ' BEGIN { FS = "\n"; RS = "" }
NF >= 3 {
for (i = 3; i <= NF; ++i) {
   sv = split($i, order)
     if (sv == 3) {
        title = order[1]
        copies = order[2]
        price = order[3]
        amount = copies * price
        total_vol += copies
```

```
        total_amt += amount
        vol[title] += copies
        amt[title] += amount
        }
    else print "Incomplete Record"
    }
}
    END {
      printf "%5s\t%10s\t%6s\n\n", "TITLE", \
      "COPIES SOLD", "TOTAL"
      for (title in vol)
    printf "%5s\t%10d\t$%7.2f\n", title, vol[title],\
      amt[title]
      "printf" " "%s\n", "-------------"
    printf "\t%s%4d\t$%7.2f\n","Total ",total_vol,total_amt}'
    $*
```

In awk, arrays are one dimensional; a two-dimensional array stores two elements indexed by the same subscript. You can get a pseudo two-dimensional array in awk by defining two arrays that have the same subscript. We only need one for loop to read both arrays.

The addemup file, an order report generator, produces the following output:

```
$ addemup orders.today
TITLE COPIES SOLD    TOTAL

  #1          5   $   37.50
  #2          8   $   56.25
  #3          1   $    7.50
  #4          1   $    7.50
  #7          1   $    7.50
------------
      Total  16   $  116.25
```

After you solve a programming problem, you will find that you can re-use that approach in other programs. For instance, the method used in the awkronym program to load acronyms into an array could be applied in the current example to read the book titles from a file and print them in the report. Similarly, you can use variations of the same program to print different reports. The construction of the next program is similar to the previous program. Yet the content of the report is quite different.

```
awk ' BEGIN { FS = "\n"; RS = ""
printf "%-15s\t%10s\t%6s\n\n", "CUSTOMER", "COPIES SOLD", \
  "TOTAL"
  }
NF >= 3 {
customer = $1
  total_vol = 0
  total_amt = 0
```

```
   for (i = 3;  i <= NF;  ++i) {
      split($i, order)
      title = order[1]
      copies = order[2]
      price = order[3]
      amount = copies * price
      total_vol += copies
      total_amt += amount
   }
   printf "\t%s%4d\t$%7.2f\n","Total ",total_vol,total_amt}'
   }' $*
```

In this program, named `summary`, we print totals for each customer order. Notice that the variables `total_vol` and `total_amt` are reset to 0 whenever a new record is read. In the previous program, these values accumulated from one record to the next.

The `summary` program, reading a multiline record, produces a report that lists each record on a single line:

```
$ summary orders
CUSTOMER        COPIES SOLD     TOTAL

J. Andrews                7 $   52.50
John Peterson             4 $   30.00
Charlotte Miller         11 $   82.50
Dan Aspromonte          105 $  787.50
Valerie S. Rossi          4 $   30.00
Timothy P. Justice        4 $   30.00
Emma  Fleming            25 $  187.50
Antonio Pollan            5 $   37.50
Hugh Blair               15 $  112.50
```

▪ Testing Programs ▪

Part of writing a program is designing one or more test cases. Usually this means creating a sample input file. It is a good idea to test a program at various stages of development. Each time you add a function, test it. For instance, if you implement a conditional procedure, test that the procedure is executed when the expression is true; test what happens when it is false. Program testing involves making sure that the syntax is correct *and* that the problem has been solved.

When `awk` encounters syntax errors it will tell you that it is "bailing out." Usually it will print the line number associated with the error. Syntax errors can be caused by a variety of mistakes, such as forgetting to quote strings or to close a procedure with a brace. Sometimes, it can be as minor as an extra blank space. The `awk` program's error messages are seldom helpful, and a persistent effort is often required to uncover the fault.

You might even see a UNIX system error message, such as the dreadful declaration:

```
Segmentation fault—core dumped.
```

Not to worry. Although your program has failed badly, you have not caused an earthquake or a meltdown. An image of "core" memory at the time of the error is saved or dumped in a file named `core`. Advanced programmers can use a debugging program to examine this image and determine where in memory the fault occurred. We just delete `core` and re-examine our code.

Again, check each construct as you add it to the program. If you wait until you have a large program, and it fails, you will often have difficulty finding the error. Not only that, but you are likely to make unnecessary changes, fixing what's not broken in an attempt to find out what is.

Checking that you have solved the problem you set out to tackle is a much larger issue. After you begin testing your program on larger samples, you will undoubtedly uncover "exceptions," otherwise known as *bugs*. In testing the `awkronym` program, we discovered an exception where an acronym appeared as the last word in the sentence. It was not "found" because of the period ending the sentence. That is, `awk` found that *BASIC* and *BASIC.* were not equal. This would not be a problem if we could test the search string as a regular expression but we have to test the array variable as a literal string.

Programming is chiefly pragmatic in its aims. You must judge whether or not specific problems merit writing a program or if certain exceptions are important enough to adapt the general program to account for them. Sometimes, in large public programs as well as small private ones, bugs just become part of the program's known behavior, which the user is left to cope with as best as he or she can. The bug found in `awkronym` is a common enough problem, so it is necessary to implement a fix.

The fix for the `awkronym` bug does not involve `awk` at all. We run a a sed script before the `awkronym` program to separate punctuation marks from any word. It converts a punctuation mark to a field containing garbage characters. Another script processes the `awkronym` output and strips out these garbage characters. The example below shows how both scripts are used as bookends for the `awkronym` program.

```
sed 's/\(..*\)\([.,!;]\)/\1 @@@\2/g' $* |
awk ' {
        program lines
}' acronyms - |
sed 's/ @@@\([.,!;]\)/\1/g'
```

14

Writing `nroff` and `troff` Macros

The `nroff` and `troff` formatters include a powerful macro definition and substitution capability. As we suggested when macros were first discussed in Chapter 4, they are a good way to combine frequently used sequences of formatting requests into a single instruction. But after working with the `ms` and `mm` macro packages, you must know that macros are more than that.

Macros are an essential part of `nroff` and `troff`—you cannot escape them if you want to make serious use of the formatter. Precisely because macros are so essential, many users never learn to fully use them. The most obviously useful macros are already included in the existing macro packages, whose complex internal control structures make them difficult to understand and modify.

The purpose of this chapter is to introduce the fundamental `nroff` and `troff` requests that are used for creating macros. You'll learn the basics in this chapter. Then, in later chapters we can examine how to write macros for specific purposes, without having to make continual asides to introduce a new request.

Chapter 15 describes additional requests for creating special effects (such as pictures) with your macros, and Chapters 16 through 18 discuss how to go beyond writing individual macros and how to develop or extend an entire macro package.

· Comments ·

Before we start, we'll introduce the syntax for inserting comments into your macro definitions. Macros can get quite confusing, so we advise you to put in comments that explain what you are doing. This will help immensely when you go back weeks or months later to modify a macro you have written.

A line beginning with the sequence:

```
.\"
```

will not be interpreted or printed by the formatter. Any part of a line following the sequence `\"` will be treated the same way. For example:

```
.\" O'Reilly & Associates, Inc. custom macro set
.\" Last modified 4/25/87
.de IZ \" Initialization macro
        .
        .
        .
```

Note that there is an important difference between:

```
.\" A full line comment
```

and:

```
\" A partial line comment
```

If you simply start the sequence `\"` at the margin, the formatter will insert a blank line into the output, because this sequence by itself does not suppress newline generation.

(Note that comments can be used at any time, not just in macros. You can write notes to yourself in your input file and they will never appear in the output. But if you accidentally type the sequence `\"` in your file, the remainder of the line on which it appears will disappear from the output.)

▪ Defining Macros ▪

As we've already discussed, use the `.de` request to define a macro:

```
.de AB        \" Define macro AB
Requests and/or text of macro here
..
```

There are also requests to remove or add to existing macros. The `.rm` request removes a macro:

```
.rm PQ  \" Remove macro PQ
```

You may sometimes want to define a macro for local use, and remove it when you are done. In general, though, this is an advanced request you will not use often.

The `.am` request appends to the end of an existing macro. It works just like `.de` but does not overwrite the existing contents:

```
.am DS  \" Append to the existing definition of DS
.ft CW
..
```

At first, you may think that this request has only limited usefulness. However, as you work more with macros, you will find unexpected uses for it. We'll mention a few of these in later chapters.

▪ Macro Names ▪

A macro name can be one or two characters, and can consist of any character(s), not just alphanumeric characters. For example:

```
.de ^(    \" Macro used internally whose name, we hope,
          \" never has to be remembered
```

You can even use control characters in macro names. Names can be uppercase or lowercase, or any combination of the two, and uppercase and lowercase are distinct. For example, the four names `.gm`, `.GM`, `.gM`, and `.Gm` can all be used without conflict.

If you are starting from scratch, you can use whatever macro or number register names you like except for the names of existing formatter requests. However, if you are adding macros to an existing package, you have to work around the existing names, because creating a new macro with the same name as an old one will discard the previously read-in definition.

This is not as easy as it sounds, because macro packages include internal macro, string, and number register definitions that are not visible to the casual user. You may be surprised when your new macro makes some other part of the package go haywire. (In an attempt to forestall this problem, most macro developers give odd, unmnemonic names to internally called macros. However, collisions still can and do occur.)

Finding the Names of Existing Macros

Before you start adding macros to an existing package, it's a good idea to print the names of all existing macros.

There are two ways to do this. The `.pm` request will print (in blocks of 128 characters) the names and sizes of all macros defined in a given run of the formatter. So, for example, creating a file containing the single request:

```
.pm
```

and formatting it like this:

```
$ nroff -ms pmfile
```

will print on the screen a list of all the macros defined in the ms macro package. (The output could also be redirected to a file or printer.)

However, macro names are drawn from the same pool as string names (see the next example), so it might be better to search for macro or string definitions using `grep` *et al*, like this:

```
$ grep '^\.d[esia]' macrofiles | cut -f1,2 -d' ' | sort | uniq
```

(grep will select all lines beginning with either `.de`, `.ds`, `.di`, or `.da`; cut will select only the first two space-separated fields on each of those lines; `sort` and `uniq` together will produce a sorted list consisting of only one copy of each line. Note that for -mm, which does not use a space before the macro name, you would need to specify `cut -f1` only. You will also need to substitute for *macrofiles* the actual filenames containing the macros of interest.)

You should do the same for number registers:

$ **sed −n −e** '**s/.*.nr *\\(..\\).*/\\1/p**' *macrofiles* **| sort | uniq**

here, because we can't rely on number registers being set at the start of a line, as we can with macro definitions. The one-line `sed` script included here saves the first two nonspace characters (`..`) following the string `.nr`, and substitutes them for the rest of the line (i.e., it throws away the rest of the line).

You could also just `grep` for an individual macro, string, or number register name before you use it! Or you could take the easy way, and check Appendix B, where we've listed all the names in each of the packages.

In addition to looking for conflicting names, you may also need to look for conflicting usage, or to understand in detail the operation of a macro you are intending to call within a new macro you are writing.

To do this, you can simply read in the entire macro definition file with the editor and search for what you want. However, to make things easier, we use the `getmac` shell script described in Chapter 12 to print out the definition of the desired macro. The script prints the result on standard output, which can easily be redirected into a file, where it can become the basis for your own redefinition.

Renaming a Macro

If you do find a conflict, you can rename macros that have already been defined. The `.rn` macro renames an existing macro:

```
.rn ^( H1    \" Rename ^( to H1; easier to remember
```

The old name will no longer work. You must use the new name to invoke the macro.

A good trick that you can *sometimes* pull off with `.rn` is to temporarily redefine a macro (without ever modifying its contents). For example, the `ms` macros include a macro to draw a box around a paragraph; however, these macros do not leave any space above or below the box. We can add some like this:

```
.rn B1 b1     \" Rename B1 to b1
.de B1        \" Now redefine B1
.sp .5        \" Add some space before the box is drawn
.b1           \" Execute the old definition
..
.rn B2 b2     \" Rename B2 to b2
.de B2        \" Now redefine B2
.b2           \" Execute the old definition
.sp .5        \" Add some space after the box is drawn
..
```

This only works for adding extra control lines before or after the current contents of the macro. Remember it, though, because this trick may come in handy if you don't want to (or can't) directly modify a macro in one of the existing packages, but do want a slightly different effect.

▪ **Macro Arguments** ▪

The simplest kind of macro is a sequence of stored commands, starting with a `.de` request and ending with the two dots (..) at the beginning of a line.

However, as you've seen when you've used `mm` and `ms`, macros can take arguments, and can act differently depending on various conditions. It's also possible for a macro to save information and pass it to other macros to affect their operation. An understanding of how to do these things is essential if you plan any serious macro design.

A macro can take up to nine arguments and can use them in any way. Arguments are described positionally by the character sequences `\\$1` through `\\$9`[*].

For example, we could define a very simple `.B` macro to boldface a single argument:

```
.de B              \"  Macro to boldface first argument
\fB\\$1\fP
..
```

Or, we could write a simple paragraph macro that, instead of having a fixed indent, might take a numeric argument to specify the depth of the indent:

```
.de PI             \"  Simple paragraph macro
.sp
.ne 2              \"  Prevent widows
.ti \\$1           \"  Indent to the depth specified by first
..                 \"  argument
```

As you can see in the first example, you can print an argument in your text. Or, shown in the second example, you can use it inside the macro as an argument to one or more of the requests that make up the macro.

Notice that there is nothing intrinsic about a macro that causes a break. The `.B` macro, for instance, can be placed in the input file as in the following example:

```
There are a number of ways to
.B embolden
text.
```

As long as filling is in effect, it will produce exactly the same output as:

```
There are a number of ways to \fBembolden\fP text.
```

Macro arguments are separated by spaces. If you want to include an explicit space in an argument, you should enclose the entire string in quotation marks, like this:

---

[*]Actually, the sequences are `\$1` through `\$9`, with only a single backslash. But for reasons to be described shortly, you always need at least two backslashes.

```
There are a number of ways to
.B "make text stand out."
```

If you didn't enclose the phrase *make text stand out* in quotation marks, a single word, *make*, would have been interpreted as the first argument, the next word, *text*, as the second argument, and so on. This wouldn't cause a program error—there is no requirement that arguments to a macro be used by that macro—but the unused arguments would simply disappear from the output. As shown here, the entire phrase is treated as a single argument.

To actually print a quotation mark inside a macro argument, double it. For example:

```
.B "The Quote ("") Character"
```

will produce:

The Quote (") Character

You've probably recognized that the syntax for specifying arguments by position is very similar to that used with shell scripts. You might wonder, though, about backslashes, which are used in the shell to prevent interpretation of a special character. In fact, they serve the same function in troff.

The nroff and troff formatters always read a macro at least twice: once when they read the definition (and store it away for later use), and once when they encounter it in the text. At the time the macro is defined, *there are no arguments*, so it is essential to prevent the formatter from doing any argument substitution.

When the macro definition is read, the formatter operates in what is referred to (in the *Nroff/Troff User's Manual*) as *copy mode*. That is, none of the requests are executed; they are simply copied (in this case, presumably into memory) without interpretation. The exception is that various escape sequences that may have a different value at macro definition time than at macro execution time (most notably \n, for interpolating number registers, *, for interpolating strings, and \$, for interpolating arguments) are executed, unless you suppress interpretation with a preceding backslash. (Other escape sequences are also interpreted, but because they have fixed values, this makes no difference to the action of the macro.)

A backslash prevents interpretation of the character that follows it by sacrificing itself. The backslash tells the formatter: "Take me but let the next guy go." Each time the character sequence is read, the backslash is stripped off—that is, \\ is actually stored as \. (You can think of \ as saying "I really mean...." So in the shell, for example, if you want to use an asterisk literally, rather than as a filename expansion metacharacter, you write *—that is, "I really mean *." In a similar way, \\ says "I really mean backslash.")

When macro definitions are nested inside one another, you will need to add additional backslashes to get what you want. The true argument interpolation escape sequence is \$n, rather than \\$n; the extra backslash is needed because the first one is stripped when the macro is interpreted in copy mode. The same rule applies when you want to interpolate the value of a number register or a string in a macro definition. Think through the number of times the definition will be read before it is executed, and specify the appropriate number of backslashes, so that you get the actual value used at the point where you need it. A failure to understand this will cause more frustration than almost any other error when you are writing macros.

In the example of the .B macro, the sequences \fB and \fP did not need to be escaped, because troff could just as easily interpret them at the time the macro is defined. However, the macro would also work if they were specified with double backslashes—it is just that the interpretation of the codes would take place when the macro was used.

▪ Nested Macro Definitions ▪

We said previously that a macro definition begins with a .de request and ends with two dots (..). This is a simplification. The .de request takes an alternate terminator as an optional second argument. This feature allows you to create nested macro definitions.

```
.de M1              \"  Start first macro
.de M2 !!           \"  Start second macro
.!!                 \"  End second macro
..                  \"  End first macro
```

You can also nest macros by delaying interpretation of the .. on the second macro:

```
.de M1              \"  Start first macro
.de M2              \"  Start second macro
\\..                \"  End second macro
...                 \"  End first macro
```

For example, a group of related macros for producing a certain type of document might be nested inside a "master" macro. A user would have to invoke the master macro, indicating document type, to make the other macros available for use. Nested macros could be used to provide alternate versions of the same set of macros within a single macro package.

▪ Conditional Execution ▪

One of the most powerful features of nroff and troff's macro programming language is its facility for conditional execution. There are three conditional execution requests: .if, .ie (*if else*), and .el (*else*). The .if request is used for a single condition. ("If the condition is met, do this; otherwise, simply go to the next line.") The .ie and .el requests are used as a pair, testing a condition and then performing either one action or the other. ("If the condition is met, do this; otherwise, do that.")

Predefined Conditions

There are a number of different conditions that can be tested with `.if` and `.ie`. The simplest looks to see if a predefined condition is true or false. There are four predefined conditions, as listed in Table 14-1.

TABLE 14-1. Built-in Conditions

Condition	True if
o	Current page number is odd
e	Current page number is even
n	The file is being formatted by `nroff`
t	The file is being formatted by `troff`

For example, in a page bottom macro, to print the page number in the outside corner, you might write:

```
.if o .tl '''%' \" If odd, put page number in right corner
.if e .tl '%''' \" If even, put page number in left corner
```

(The `.tl` request prints three-part titles, at the left, center, and right of the page. And, within this request, the `%` character always prints the current page number. We'll explain these two items in detail later, when we look at how to write a complete page transition macro. For right now, we just want to understand how the conditions themselves work.)

Because the two conditions, odd and even, are mutually exclusive, you could also write:

```
.ie o .tl '''%' \" If odd, put page number in right corner
.el .tl '%'''    \" Otherwise, put it in left corner
```

Notice that you do not specify a condition to be tested in the `.el` request.

Arithmetic and Logical Expressions

A closely related condition simply tests for a nonzero number or a true arithmetic expression. This is generally used with number registers, but it could also be used to test the value of numeric arguments to a macro. For example, we could write a paragraph macro that was either indented or flush left, depending on the value of its argument:

```
.de P
.sp
.ne 2
.if \\$1 .ti \\$1  \" If there is an arg, use it for indent
..
```

That is, if there is a nonzero numeric argument, do a temporary indent to the distance specified by the value of the argument.

Rather than using the simple presence of a numeric argument to satisfy the condition, you could also use an arithmetic expression to test for a value. Used in this way, the argument can simply be a *flag* telling the macro what to do.

```
.de P
.sp
.ne 2
.if \\$1=1 .ti 5n      \" If first arg = 1, indent 5 ens
..
```

The operators shown in Table 14-2 can be used in constructing an expression.

TABLE 14-2. Expression Operators

Operator	Description
+, -, /, *	Standard arithmetic operators
%	Modulo
>, <	Greater than, less than
>=, <=	Greater than or equal, less than or equal
=, ==	Equal
&	AND
:	OR

Expressions are evaluated from left to right, except where indicated otherwise by the presence of parentheses. There is no precedence of operators.

Frequently, you will see numeric conditions involving number registers. Here are a few simple examples:

```
.if \\nb
.if \\nb>1
.if \\nb<\\nc
.if \\nb+\\nc>1
```

(Be sure to note the double backslash before each number register invocation: we are assuming that these requests are made within a macro definition. If they were made outside a macro, you would use only a single backslash.) The first of these conditions is commonly used in the existing macro packages. It takes a little getting used to—it is not always obvious to new users what is being tested in an expression like:

```
.if \\nb
```

A condition of this form simply tests that the specified expression (the number register b in this case) has a value greater than 0. A more complex expression that does the same thing might be:

```
.if \\nb-1
```

Comparing Strings

Another frequent test that you can use as the basis of a condition is whether or not two strings are equal—for example, whether an argument contains a particular string. The syntax is simply:

.if "*string1*"*string2*"

(Note that there are a total of three quotation marks—either single or double will do—and no equals sign. A frequent error among beginners is to use an equals sign to compare string arguments, which will not work.)

For example, suppose you are writing a macro to center the output if the second argument is the letter *C*. You could write:

```
.if "\\$2"C" .ce  \" If 2nd arg is C, center the next line
```

You can also test for a null argument in this way:

.if "\\$1"" *do something*

Use of this condition or its inverse, the test for a non-null argument (described in the next section), allows the user to skip over an argument by supplying a null string (`""`).

Executing Multiple Requests as a Result of a Condition

All of the examples we've shown so far consist of a single request executed on the basis of a condition. But often you'll want to execute more than one command when a condition is met. To do so, you enclose the sequence to be executed in backslashes and braces, as in this example:

```
.if o \{\
.po +.25i
.tl '''%'\}
```

The initial sequence is terminated with an additional backslash to "hide the newline." You could also type:

```
.if o \{ .po +.25i
.tl '''%'\}
```

However, the syntax shown in the first example is almost always used, because it is easier to read. There is one caveat! You can't put any other characters, even a comment, following the slash. For example, if you type:

```
.if o \{\    \" If odd...
```

you won't be escaping the newline, you'll be escaping the spaces that precede the comment. If you want to include a comment on a condition like this, use the alternate syntax, and follow the brace with a dot, just like you would if the comment started on a line of its own:

```
.if o \{.    \" If odd...
```

The concluding \} can appear on the same line as most requests. However, we have found a problem when it immediately follows a string definition or a .tm request. For some reason:

```
.ds string \}
```

appends a ^Q character to the end of the string, at least in our version of troff. The concluding \} should be put on the next line, after an initial . to suppress newline generation in the output:

```
.\}
```

Another convention followed in multiple-line execution is to separate the initial request control character (. or ') from the body of the request with a tab. This greatly enhances readability, and can be used to show nesting of conditions:

```
.if o \{\
.       po +.25i
.       tl '''\\n%'\}
```

Conditions can be nested within each other using this syntax. However, you might wonder if a nested condition could instead be expressed using one of the logical operators & or : in an expression. Suppose, as described previously, you want to put page numbers on the outside corners of each page, except on the first page, where you want it in the center. You might put the following requests in the page bottom macro:

```
.ie \\n%>1 \{\             \"If pageno > 1
.       if o .tl '''%'
.       if e .tl '%'''\}
.el .tl ''%''
```

You might think to achieve the same result with the following requests:

```
.if \\n%>1&o .tl '''%'    \"If pageno > 1 and odd
.if \\n%>1&e .tl '%'''    \"If pageno > 1 and even
.if \\n%=1 .tl ''%''      \"If pageno = 1
```

Unfortunately, however, this example will not work. The & and : operators can only be used to construct arithmetic expressions. For example, in the case of:

```
.if \\nX&\\nY do something
```

something will be done only if both register X and register Y are non-zero. (Notice that there are no spaces surrounding the & operator.)

You can construct an else if clause by following an .el with another .if, and then the request to be executed if the condition is met.

```
.ie condition          do something
.el .if condition      do something else if
```

Inverse Conditions

The meaning of any of the condition types described can be reversed by preceding them with an exclamation point (!). For example:

```
.if !e        \" If the page number is not even
.if !\\nc=1   \" If number register c is not equal to 1
.if !"\\$1""  \" If the first argument is non-null
```

It may not be immediately obvious what this adds to your repertoire. However, we will encounter many cases in which it is easier to detect when a condition is not met than when it is. In particular, negative conditions can be more comprehensive than equivalent positive conditions. For example, the condition:

```
.if !\\nc=1
```

tests not only for the cases in which number register c has been set to some number larger than 0, or explicitly to 0, but the case in which it has never been set at all.

    The test for a non-null argument is also useful. For example, in the sequence:

```
.if !"\\$3"" \{\  \"  If there is a third argument
.ce               \"  center it
\\$3\}
```

you only want the `.ce` request to be executed if there is an argument to be centered. Otherwise, the request will cause unexpected results, perhaps centering the line of text following the macro. Saying ''If the third argument is non-null, then it exists'' may be the inverse of the way you think, and will take some getting used to.

    If you are reading through the definitions for the ms or mm macros, you may also encounter a construct like this:

```
.if \\n(.$-2
```

The `.$` is a special predefined number register (more on this topic in a moment) that contains the number of arguments that have been given to a macro. If there are two or fewer arguments, the value of the conditional expression shown will be 0. However, it will evaluate true if there are more than two arguments. It is used in mm's `.SM` macro because a different action is taken on the second argument if there are three arguments instead of two.

```
.if \\n(.$-3 \\$1\s-2\\$2\s+2\\$3
.if \\n(.$-2 \s-2\\$1\s+2\\$2
```

▪ Interrupted Lines ▪

Occasionally, when writing a complex macro—especially one with multiple conditions—you may find yourself writing a request that is too long to fit on a single 80-character line.

    You could simply let the line wrap on your screen—UNIX recognizes lines much longer than the 80 columns usually available on a terminal screen. However, you need not do this. Simply putting a backslash at the end of a line will "hide the newline" and cause the next line to be interpreted as a continuation of the first.

• Number Registers •

To set a number register, you use the .nr request. Like macros, number registers can have either one- or two-character names consisting of any character(s), not just alphanumeric characters. For example:

```
.nr ^( 1
```

sets a number register called ^(to 1. Number register names are stored separately from macro names, so there is no conflict in having a number register with the same name as a macro. Thus, you can create mnemonic number register names, which helps to make macros that use those number registers more readable.

(If you are writing your own macro package, you can name registers from scratch. If you are adding to an existing package, check the number registers used by that package.)

To use the value stored in a number register, use the escape sequence $\ln x$ for a one-character number register name, and $\ln(xx$ for a two-character name. (In the standard nroff and troff documentation, this is referred to as "interpolating" the value of the number register.) The point made previously, about using backslashes to delay the interpretation of an argument, applies equally to number registers. In macros, you will usually see the invocation of number registers preceded by a double backslash, because you don't want to interpolate the value until the macro is executed.

The values stored in number registers can be literal numeric values (with or without scaling indicators), values from other number registers (whose value can be interpolated at a later time), or expressions. You can also increment or decrement the value placed in a number register by preceding the value with a plus or minus sign. For example:

```
.nr PN 1     \" Set number register PN to 1
.nr PN +1    \" Add 1 to the contents of number register PN
```

When you add scaling indicators to the value supplied to a number register, be aware that values are converted to basic units before they are stored, and that when you increment the value of a number register, it is incremented in basic units. So, in the previous example, in which no units were specified, the value of PN after incrementing is 2, but in the following case:

```
.nr LL 6.5i
.nr LL +1
```

the value initially stored into LL is converted into units (i.e., for a 300 dpi output device, it contains the value 1950); after incrementing, it contains the value 1951 (again, assuming a 300 dpi device). If you want to increment LL by 1 inch, append the proper scaling indicator. Likewise, when interpolating the value of a number register, specify that the value is in units. For example, the construct:

```
.nr IN 1i
.in \\n(IN
```

will produce unexpected results. What you are really writing is:

```
.in 300m
```

(assuming a 300 dpi device) because the default scaling for an indent request is ems. The proper usage is:

```
.in \\n(INu
```

Number Registers as Global Variables

Number registers can be used in different ways. First, and probably most important, they can generalize a macro package. For example, in `ms`, the default line length is stored in a number register called `LL`.

Periodically, macros in the package may muck with the line length, and then reset it to its default state. Requests to reset the line length to its default value thus have the form:

```
.ll \n(LLu    \" Single backslash within the body of text
```

or

```
.ll \\n(LLu   \" Double backslash within a macro definition
```

Because the line length is not "hard coded" in the document, users can change the line length throughout simply by changing the default value stored in the number register.

You might wonder why this is necessary. After all, you can simply set an initial line length, and then increment it or decrement it as necessary. And many macros take this approach. But there are other cases where the line length is a factor in another calculation.

For example, the output text can be centered horizontally on the physical page regardless of the line length if the page offset is set not absolutely, but in terms of the line length:

```
.po (8.5i-\n(LLu)/2u
```

In general, it is good programming practice to place values that are used at many different places in a program into globally accessible variables. To change the action of the program, it is only necessary to change the value of the variable. It is the same in `nroff` and `troff`. When we look at the overall design of a macro package in Chapter 16, we'll return to this subject in more detail.

Number Registers as Flags

In the chapters on the existing macro packages, you've also seen number registers used as flags—signals to a macro to act in a certain way. For example, in `mm`, paragraphs are flush left by default, but if the user sets the `Pt` number register to 1, all paragraphs will be indented.

Within the paragraph macro, there is a line that tests the Pt register, and acts accordingly:

```
.if \\n(Pt=1 .ti +\\n(Pin
```

This line actually uses number registers in both ways. If the number register Pt is set to 1, the macro indents by the value stored in another register, Pi.

One-character number register names can also be set from the command line, with nroff or troff's −r option. This gives you the ability to construct macros that will act differently depending on command-line options. We'll show some examples of this in Chapter 16, when we discuss how to print a document on either an 8½-by-11 inch or a 6-by-9 inch page, simply by specifying a single command-line switch.

Predefined Number Register Names

In addition to number registers set by the various macro packages, or set by macros you write, there are quite a few number registers whose usage is predefined by the formatter. You've already seen one of these—%, which always contains the current page number. Table 14-3 (and Table 14-4) list some of the most important preset registers, and Appendix B includes a complete listing. Not all of these registers will be meaningful at this point, but we'll tell you more about them as we go on.

TABLE 14-3. Predefined Number Registers

Register	Contents
%	Current page number
dl	Width (maximum) of the last completed diversion
dn	Height (vertical size) of the last completed diversion
dw	Current day of the week (1 to 7)
dy	Current day of the month (1 to 31)
hp	Current horizontal place on the *input* line
ln	Output line number
mo	Current month (1 to 12)
nl	Vertical position of the last printed text baseline
yr	Last two digits of the current year

The registers in Table 14-3 can be reset. For example, if you want to arbitrarily reset the page number to 1, you can type:

```
.nr % 1
```

The formatter will keep incrementing the register on each new page, but will count from the new baseline. (You might want to do this, for example, if you are following the convention used in many technical manuals, which number pages on a chapter-by-chapter basis, with a number made up of both the chapter number and the page number. In this case, the page number is reset to 1 at the start of each new chapter.)

Note that `%` is a true number register name, and don't let the special use of the `%` character in the `.tl` request confuse you. In `.tl`, `%` alone will interpolate the current page number; however, in any other place, you must specify the full number register interpolation `\n%`.

The set of registers in Table 14-4 cannot be modified. In reading their names, be sure to note that they are two-character names beginning with `.` (dot). If you are reading through one of the existing macro packages, it is easy either to confuse them with macros or requests, because they begin with a period, or to miss the period and read them as one-character names.

TABLE 14-4. Read-Only Number Registers

Register	Contents
`.$`	Number of arguments available in the current macro
`.c`	Number of lines read from the current input file
`.d`	Current vertical place in current diversion; equal to `nl` if no diversion
`.f`	Current font position (1 to 4 in `otroff`)
`.H`	Available horizontal resolution in machine units
`.i`	Current indent
`.j`	Current adjustment mode (0 = `.ad` `l` or `.na`; 1 = `.ad` `b`; 3 = `.ad` `c`; 5 = `.ad` `r`)
`.L`	Line spacing set with `.ls`
`.l`	Current line length
`.n`	Length of text on previous line
`.o`	Current page offset
`.p`	Current page length
`.s`	Current point size
`.t`	Distance to the next trap (usually the page bottom)
`.u`	Equal to 1 in fill mode and 0 in no-fill mode
`.V`	Available vertical resolution in machine units
`.v`	Current vertical line spacing
`.w`	Width of previous character
`.z`	Name of current diversion

The registers in Table 14-4 are particularly useful when you want to temporarily change some value (for example, the font) and then restore it, without having to know what was there before.

For example, if you print an italicized footer on each page, you might include the following requests in your page bottom macro:

```
.nr FT \\n(.f
.ft I
        .

        .

        .
.ft \\n(FT
```

This is safer than simply using the `.ft` request without an argument to restore the previous font, which can create havoc if a user makes a font change within a definition of the footer string.

Be aware that registers with scaled values (e.g., `.l` for the line lengths or `.v` for the current vertical spacing) contain those values as basic machine units (as do all number registers containing scaled values). As described previously, this means you should append a `u` whenever you want to use the contents of one of these registers as an argument to a request.

Autoincrementing Registers

We've described how to increment the value stored in a register by prefixing the value you supply to the `.nr` request with a plus sign (+), and how to decrement it by specifying a minus sign (-).

You can also *autoincrement* or *autodecrement* a register whenever you interpolate its value. To make this work, you must supply two values to an initial `.nr` request: the starting value and the increment value. For example:

```
.nr TE 1 1
.nr ST 10 3
```

Then, when you interpolate the contents of the register, instead of using the standard `\nx` or `\n (xx`, specify a plus or a minus after the `\n` and before the register name. The value that is interpolated will be the original contents of the number register plus (or minus) the increment (or decrement) value. At the same time, the value in the register will be updated by the increment value. For example, assuming the initial definitions in the previous example:

```
\n+(TE \" Increment TE by 1, and interpolate the new value
\n-(ST \" Decrement ST by 3, and interpolate the new value
```

Number register interpolations of the normal sort can still be used and will, as always, simply give you the value currently stored in the register.

Altering the Output Format

As we've seen, sometimes number registers are simply used to supply values to requests, or to pass information between macros. But there are many cases in which the value of a number register is actually interpolated into the formatter output and printed. The page number register `%` is a good example. Although it might be used as the basis to test conditions in macros, it is usually printed as well.

The `.af` (*alter format*) request allows you to specify the format in which to express the value of a number register. This request takes two arguments, the name of the register to be affected and the format:

```
.af register format
```

The *format* codes are given in Table 14-5.

TABLE 14-5. Format Codes

Format	Description	Numbering Sequence
1	Arabic	0, 1, 2, 3, 4, 5, ...
i	Lowercase roman	0, i, ii, iii, iv, v, ...
I	Uppercase roman	0, I, II, III, IV, V, ...
a	Lowercase alphabetic	0, a, b, c, ... z, aa, ab, ... zz, aaa, ...
A	Uppercase alphabetic	0, A, B, C, ... Z, AA, AB, ... ZZ, AAA, ...

In addition to the numbering sequences in Table 14-5, an arabic format having additional digits (e.g., 001) will result in a numbering sequence with at least that many digits (e.g., 001, 002, 003, ...).

For example, to change to lowercase roman page numbering in the front matter of a book, you could write:

```
.af % i
```

(Note that, depending on exactly how a macro package implements page numbering, this may or may not work exactly as shown. Some macro packages interpolate % into another register and print the contents of that register. For example, ms stores the page number in the register PN and the request would be `.af PN i`.)

Alphabetic formats are generally used in macros for automatically numbered (or lettered) lists. We'll take a close look at some of these macros in Chapter 17.

Removing Registers

With the very large number of possible register names (nearly 10,000 names are possible, given all one- and two-character combinations of the printing character set), it is unlikely that you will run out of number register names.

However, if your macros create a very large number of registers, the formatter can run out of internal storage space. For this reason, it may occasionally be necessary (or at least wise) to remove temporary registers that you no longer need, using the `.rr` request. For example:

```
.rr TE        \" Remove register TE
```


▪ Defining Strings ▪

In addition to macros and number registers, `nroff` and `troff` allow you to define character strings that will be stored and can be re-invoked at will. This is not intended as a general-purpose abbreviation function, although in certain cases it can be used that way. Rather, it is designed to allow you to store global string variables for use throughout a package, in much the same way that number registers provide numeric variables.

For example, in both ms and mm, you can define headers, footers, or both that will be printed on every page. To do this, the header or footer macro contains a reference to a predefined string. All the user has to do is give the string a value. The user doesn't have to modify the macro itself.

As we've already seen, to define a string, use the .ds (*define string*) request. For example:

```
.ds RH Tools for Building Macros  \" Define right header
```

String names, like macro and number register names, can have either one or two characters. However, unlike number registers, string names are drawn from the same pool as macro and request names, so you have to be careful not to conflict with existing names.

To interpolate the value of a string, use the escape sequence *x for a one-character name, or *(xx for a two-character name. For example, our page top macro might include the lines:

```
.if o .tl '\\*(RH''%'    \" Print header string then page #
.if e .tl '%''\\*(RH'    \" Print page # then header string
```

Another good example of how to use this request (as well as how to use predefined number registers) is given by the technique used in ms and mm to build a date string.

The troff program reads in the date from the system clock into the predefined number registers mo (*month*), dy (*day*), and yr (*year*). To set a complete date string that users can easily reference, we might write the following requests in our macro package:

```
.if \n(mo=1 .ds MO January
.if \n(mo=2 .ds MO February
.if \n(mo=3 .ds MO March
.if \n(mo=4 .ds MO April
.if \n(mo=5 .ds MO May
.if \n(mo=6 .ds MO June
.if \n(mo=7 .ds MO July
.if \n(mo=8 .ds MO August
.if \n(mo=9 .ds MO September
.if \n(mo=10 .ds MO October
.if \n(mo=11 .ds MO November
.if \n(mo=12 .ds MO December
.ds DY \*(MO \n(dy, 19\n(yr
```

(Note that these requests do not need to be executed from within a macro. The register values can be interpolated when the macro package is first read in. For this reason, the string and number register interpolations shown here are not escaped with an additional backslash.)

Another request, .as (*append [to] string*), also allows you to add to the contents of an existing string. The last line of the previous sequence could also have been written:

```
.as MO \n(dy, 19\n(yr
```

to append the day and year to whatever value had been stored into MO. Here, this is a little contrived—it is better to maintain the month and the date as a whole in separate strings. However, the technique of appending to a string is used appropriately in the definition of a macro to produce numbered section headers, as we'll see in Chapter 17.

▪ Diversions ▪

So far, we have discussed macros that you define in advance as a sequence of stored requests. There is also another class of macros that are created by a process called *diversion.*

A diversion consists of temporary storage of text into a macro, which can be saved and output at a later time. In reading the chapters on ms or mm, you might have wondered how troff manages to move footnotes embedded anywhere in the text to the bottom of the page, or how it "floats" a figure, table, or block of text to the top of a succeeding page, after filling the current page with text that comes later in the input file.

The answer is simple: the formatter stores the text (or other output) in a macro created by diversion. (Such a macro is often called simply a diversion.) The size of the diversion is stored into number registers that you (your macros, that is) can test to see if the diversion will fit on the current page, and how much space you need to allocate for it. The macro package can then make decisions about how and where to place the contents of the diversion.

To create a diversion, use the .di (*divert*) request. This request takes as an argument the name of a macro. All subsequent text, requests, etc. will be processed normally, but instead of being output, they will be stored into the named macro. A .di request without an argument ends the diversion.

The output that has been stored in the diversion can now be output wherever you like, simply by invoking the macro named in the initial .di request. For many purposes, this invocation will be performed automatically by a page transition macro. We will look at this in more detail in succeeding chapters, but just to get the idea, let's look at a simple definition for a pair of keep macros.

(In general, diversions are handled by pairs of macros—one to start the diversion, the other to end it. However, there are other cases in which we will see that this is not necessary.)

Both ms and mm use diversions in their display macros. In ms, the display macros handle text positioning, and call lower-level macros called keep macros to make sure the text in the display stays on the same page.

The purpose of the keep macros, in case you are not familiar with this concept from earlier chapters, is to make sure that a block of text is not split across two pages. A typical example of a block that should not be split is a figure—whether it is reserved space for a figure, or an actual picture created with pic or some other graphics tool.

A simple macro to start a keep might look like this:

```
.de KS              \" Keep Start
.br
.di KK
..
```

A simple macro to end a keep might look like this:

```
.de KE              \" Keep End
.br
.di
.ne \\n(dnu
.nr fI \\n(.u
.nf
.KK
.if \\n(fI .fi
..
```

In both macros, the .br requests are extremely important; they flush any partial lines that have not yet been output. In the .KS macro, the break makes sure that the keep begins with the text following the macro; in .KE, it makes sure that the last partial line is included in the diversion.

It is also important to output the diversion in no-fill mode. If you don't, the text contained in the diversion will be filled and adjusted a second time, with unpredictable results. (Consider, for example, when the diversion includes an already formatted table. The table would be scrambled by a second pass.)

You can't just switch back to fill mode after you output the diversion, though. What if the body of the text was meant to be in no-fill mode? To get around this problem, you should save the value of troff's read-only register .u, and test the saved value to see whether or not filling should be restored.

There are a few times when you might not want to follow this rule. For example, what should you do if there is a chance that the diversion will be output on a page where the line length is different? You still want to avoid processing the text twice. You can put the text into the diversion in no-fill mode, and can embed any formatting requests into the diversion by preceding them with a backslash (e.g., \.in 5n). Any requests treated in this way will be acted on when the diversion is output.

As always, it is important to specify the correct units. In the previous example, the value in dn is stored using basic device units (as is the case with all scaled values stored in a number register), so you *must* add a u on the end of the interpolation. For example, on a 300 dpi device, after a diversion 2 inches high, dn will contain the value 600. The request:

```
.ne \\n(dn
```

will always result in a page break because (in this example) what you are really writing is:

```
.ne 600
```

What you want to write is:

```
.ne \\n(dnu
```

Any text and requests that are issued between the initial `.KS` and the terminating `.KE` will be stored in the macro called `.KK`. The height of the last-completed diversion is always stored in the number register `dn`. We can simply say that we need (`.ne`) at least that much space. If the size of the diversion is greater than the distance to the bottom of the page, we simply start a new page. Otherwise, we output the text and continue as if the diversion had never happened.

The case of a floating keep, in which text that follows the keep in the source file floats ahead of it in the output, and fills up the current page, is more difficult to handle than the simple example just shown. However, this example should give you an idea of how to use diversions.

There is also a `.da` (*divert append*) request that adds output to an existing diversion. (A second `.di` given the same macro name as the first will overwrite the diversion's previous contents, but `.da` will add the new material to the end.)

The `.da` request has numerous applications. For example, consider footnotes. To calculate where to place the first footnote, you need to calculate the size of all the footnotes you want to put on the page. That's easy—just append them to the same diversion.

However, there are other far less obvious applications for appended diversions. For example, you can divert and append section headings or index entries to macros that will be processed at the end of the file to produce a table of contents or an index.

▪ Environment Switching ▪

The `nroff` and `troff` formatters allow you to issue many requests that globally affect the format of a document. The formatter is generally quite thorough in providing ways to change and restore the value of various parameters. This makes it relatively easy to change values such as the line length or fill/no-fill mode in order to treat certain blocks of text differently and then restore the original values.

Nonetheless, if you want to make major changes to a number of values, it can be awkward to save and restore them all individually. For this reason, `nroff` and `troff` provide a mechanism called *environment switching*. By default, text processing takes place in what is considered to be environment 0. The `.ev` request allows you to switch to either of two additional environments, referred to as environment 1 and environment 2.

For example, to change to environment 2, you would enter

```
.ev 2
```

To restore a previous environment, you simply issue an `.ev` request without an argument. Environments are stored in a "push down stack." So if you are using multiple environment switches, a sequence of `.ev` requests without arguments won't toggle you between two environments, but will actually backtrack the specified number of environment switches. That is:

```
.ev 1
```
do something
```
.ev 2
```
do something
```
.ev                     \" Go back to ev 1
.ev                     \" Go back to ev 0
```

If you use `.ev` with an argument, you will not pop the stack. For example, the requests:

```
.ev 2
.ev 0
```

will leave both environments on the stack. You might get away with this on one occasion, but if you do this in a macro that is used with any frequency, your stack will keep getting deeper until it overflows and the formatter fails with the message ''Cannot do ev.''

Within each environment, settings made with the following requests are remembered separately:

```
.c2 .cc .ce .cu .fi .ft .hc .hy .in .it .lc .ll .ls .lt
.mc .nf .nh .nm .nn .ps .sp .ss .ta .tc .ti .ul .vs
```

Number registers, macros, and strings are common to all environments. However, any partially collected lines are part of a given environment. If you switch environments without causing a break, these partial lines will be held till the environment that contains them is restored.

What this means is best shown by example:

```
.               \"  Set parameters for environment 0
.ll 4.5i
.ad b
.ev 1           \" Switch to environment 1
.ll -10n        \" Set parameters for environment 1
.in +10n
.ad l
.ev             \" Restore previous environment (ev 0)
This text will be formatted using the parameters for
environment 0.  Notice that part of the last input
line appears to be lost when we switch environments.
It reappears when the environment is restored.
.ev 1
.sp             \" The break caused by this request is in ev 1
Now we've switched to environment 1.  Notice how the text
is now formatted using the parameters for environment 1.
Also notice that this time, we're going to issue an .sp
request after this sentence to cause a break and make sure
the last partial line is output before we leave this
environment.
.sp
```

```
.ev              \" Back once more to environment 0
This sentence will be preceded by the remainder of input
left over from the last time we were in this environment.
```

Here's the resulting output (from `nroff`):

```
This  text  will  be  formatted   using   the
parameters  for environment 0.  You'll notice
that part of the last input line  appears  to
be   lost  when  we  switch  environments.  It


        Now we've switched to environment 1.  Notice
        how the text is now formatted using the
        parameters for environment 1.  Also notice
        that this time, we're going to issue an .sp
        request after this sentence to cause a break
        and make sure the last partial line is output
        before we leave this environment.


reappears when the environment  is  restored.
This   sentence   will   be  preceded  by  the
remainder of the input  left  over  from  the
last time we were in this environment.
```

Environments are very powerful and versatile. The example given previously could have been handled more appropriately with a macro. However, as you will find, there are tasks that are best handled by an environment switch.

Printing footnotes is a primary example. Footnotes are usually collected in a diversion, which must be output at the bottom of the page without causing a break or other interference with the text.

Unfortunately, you must use environment switching with caution if you are working within one of the existing macro packages, because they may use different environments internally, and changing parameters in an environment may affect the operation of the package. For example, it was necessary to process the preceding example independently with `nroff`, and then read the resulting output into the source file, because the use of environments by the macro package that produced this book was incompatible with what we were trying to show.

▪ Redefining Control and Escape Characters ▪

There are special requests to reset the control characters that begin requests (`.` and `'`) and the escape character:

```
.eo          \"Turn escape character off except for comments
.ec !        !" Set escape character to !
.ec \        \" Set escape character back to \
.cc #        \" Change control character from . to #
.c2 ^        \" Change no-break control character from ' to ^
```

As far as we can tell by experiment, turning the escape character off entirely with .eo
does not affect the comment sequence \"; however, if you change the escape character
with .ec, comments must be introduced by the new escape character.

We have not found a significant use for these requests in our own work, or in
macros we've studied, although there are no doubt cases where they are precisely what
is needed.

One application that immediately suggests itself is the representation of control
and escape characters in the examples shown in this book. However, in practice there
are many problems.

For example, if you use these requests in a pair of macros to frame examples, the
closing macro must be invoked with the appropriate control character, creating inconsistencies for the user. Even more seriously, if control character translations are in
effect during a page transition (something that is difficult to control) or other macro
invoked by a trap, they will render that macro inoperable, unless it has been designed
with the same control and escape characters.

Our preferred solution to this problem is to use the .tr request, which is discussed in the next chapter.

▪ Debugging Your Macros ▪

When using a markup language as complex as that provided by nroff and troff,
it is easy to make mistakes, particularly when you are designing complex macros.

To limit the number of mistakes you make, you can take lessons from programmers in more general-purpose languages:

- Start by writing and testing small pieces of a complex macro. Then, after you
  know the pieces work, put them together. It is much easier to find a problem
  in a simple macro than in one that is already very complex.

- Be aware of interactions between the macro you are writing and other macros
  in the package. Initialize variables (number registers and strings) that might
  also be used by other macros.

- Include extensive comments, so you can reconstruct what you were trying to
  do when you go back to the macro later. (Errors often arise unexpectedly after
  the macro has been in use for a while, and you have a chance to exercise it
  fully. Be sure you can follow what you originally wrote.)

- Test each macro thoroughly before you put it into general use.

However, even with the best of intentions, you are likely to make mistakes. This short section is intended to give you a few pointers on how to track them down.

The term debugging is familiar even to nonprogrammers. In general, it refers to the process of finding errors in programs. I would like to suggest an alternate definition that may give you better insight into how to go about this process: *Debugging is the process of finding out what your macro really does, instead of what you thought it should do.*[*]

When you write a program or a macro, you have an idea in your mind of what you want to accomplish. When it doesn't do what you expect, you consider it an error.

But as we all know, computers are very literal. They generally do just what they are told. (The exception being when there is an error in some underlying layer of software that causes problems on a higher layer.) Therefore, the essence of debugging is to compare, on a step-by-step basis, exactly what the program or macro is actually doing with what you expect it to do.

There are several tools that you can use in debugging macros. First, and most obviously, you can look carefully at the output. Try to reconstruct the sequence of instructions and text that have been executed to produce the (presumably) undesirable result. Often, this will be all you need to do—think like a text formatter, and go through the requests that have been executed, in the order that they are executed.

You will often find that problems are due to an incorrect understanding of the action of one of the requests or escape sequences, so it may be advisable to consult the bible of macro programming, Joseph Osanna's extraordinarily dense but thorough *Nroff/Troff User's Guide*.

Secondly, you can use `nroff` or `troff` interactively. If you simply type:

```
$ nroff
```

or:

```
$ troff -a
```

the program will take standard input from the keyboard and send its results to standard output (the screen). The `troff -a` command creates an ASCII approximation of what the `troff` output would be; if you are using `ditroff`, you can also save the normal output in a file and look directly at the output. However, this output is in an obscure format and takes considerable time to learn.

With `troff -a`, special characters (such as underlines) are represented by their special character names. For example, underlining will show up as a sequence of \(uls. Because proportional type is considerably more compact than the characters that appear on a terminal screen, lines will appear too long, and will wrap around on the screen. However, what you see does represent how `troff` will break the lines.

---

[*]I am indebted to Andrew Singer of Think Technologies for this definition. Andrew used similar words in describing to me the debugging philosophy of his company's innovative Pascal compiler for the Macintosh, Lightspeed Pascal.

Now, by typing in your macros (or reading them in from existing files with the `.so` request), you can reproduce the environment of the formatter, and watch the results as you type in text. As each line is completed in the input buffer, the formatted result will be output. You can force output of a partially completed line with the `.fl` (*flush*) request, which was designed for this purpose.

This method has definite limits, but has just as definite a place in pinning down what the commands you type are doing.

Another debugging tool that you may find useful is the `.ig` (*ignore*) request. It tells the formatter to ignore subsequent input, up to a specified terminator (`..` by default). The `.ig` request acts like `.de`, only the input is discarded. (The only exception to this is that autoincremented registers whose values are interpolated within the ignored block will still be incremented or decremented.)

This request is useful when you are trying to pin down exactly where in an input file (or a long macro definition) a fatal error (one that causes the formatter to stop processing) occurs. By successively isolating parts of the file with `.ig`, you can locate the problem more closely.

This request is also useful for "commenting out" extensive blocks of macro definition or input text that you don't want in your output. It is much easier to bracket a large block of input in this way than it is to insert comment characters at the beginning of each line.

Because you may want to "ignore" more than one macro definition, you may want to get in the habit of specifying a special delimiter for the `.ig` request, so that the "ignore" is not accidentally terminated by the end of the first macro definition. This will also make it much easier to find the end of the ignored section. For example, if you insert the line:

```
.ig ++
```

anywhere in your input, the formatter will ignore the input until it sees the request:

```
.++
```

The final tool provided for debugging is the `.tm` (*terminal message*) request, which prints a message on standard error. This is particularly useful for tracking down errors involving number registers. For example, if you have set a condition based on the value of a number register, and the condition never seems to be satisfied, you might want to insert `.tm` messages to print out the value of the number register at certain points in your file. For example:

```
.tm Before calling B1, the value of BC is \n(BC
.B1
.tm After calling B1, the value of BC is \n(BC
```

(Note that there are no double backslashes before the number register interpolations, because these requests are not made while you're inside a macro definition. From inside a macro, be sure to double the backslashes, or you will get the value of the number register at the time the macro was defined.)

A read-only number register that is useful in this regard is `.c`, which contains the number of lines read from the current input file. This allows you to create messages that will help you (or the user of your macros) find out where in the input file an error (or other event) occurs:

```
.tm  On input line \\n(.c, the value of BC was \\n(BC
```

(Here, there are double backslashes, because this example is intended to be inside a macro definition.) Sometimes it is helpful to follow just how far the formatter has gotten in a file. The most difficult errors to track are those that cause the formatter to quit without producing a block of output. A series of messages of the form:

```
.tm At top of page \\n%, I've processed \\n(.c input lines
```

inserted into the page top macro will help you determine how far the formatter has gotten, and can thus help locate an error. If the formatter is processing standard input rather than an individual file, the `.c` register will be empty.

Another register that you may find useful in printing error messages is `.F`, which contains the name of the current file. (Yes, the filename is a string, even though it's stored in a number register.)

The `.R` register is also useful. It contains the number of free number registers. You can print its value to see if you are running out of number registers or coming close to the limit. (`tbl` and `eqn` use many dynamic number registers, and it is possible to run out if you use a lot in your macros as well.)

Although we use the tools described here to debug our macros, we know that they don't always help you deal with the complexity of a macro package. The relationships among different macros are not always apparent. For instance, you can usually tell from looking at your output what macro is causing a problem; however, when you look at the macro definition, you might find that this macro is calling several other macros or testing registers that have been set elsewhere in the macro package. It soon leads to the wish for a debugging tool that traced the interpretation and execution of macro definitions.

At least one version of `troff` does support a *trace* facility. Users of SoftQuad's `SQtroff` can enable a trace mode to show the invocation of each request, diversion, trap, and macro call. For instance, suppose that a macro tests the value of a number register to determine whether a request should be executed. In trace mode, you can see at what point the `.if` request was invoked, whether it was evaluated as true or false, and determine the actual value of the number register at that point. SoftQuad has also taken another step to make debugging easier by improving `troff`'s obscure error messages. In general, SoftQuad has enhanced standard `troff` in other ways that aid the process of macro writing and debugging, such as allowing longer names (up to 14 characters) for macros, requests, strings, registers, and fonts.

▪ Error Handling ▪

There are many different ways that users can get into trouble while coding documents, and your macros can help them identify and recover from problems. The three most common classes we have encountered are:

- A user fails to properly understand the action of the formatter itself. For example, he or she begins a text line with a single quote or period, or defines a special character (such as %) as an eqn delimiter. This problem becomes more pronounced as users try out more advanced capabilities without really understanding them.

- A user fails to properly understand the macro package. For example, he or she gives the wrong argument to a macro or specifies the wrong units.

- A user temporarily resets some condition, either directly or by failing to close a set of paired macros. This causes undesirable effects to propagate through the document.

The mm macros attempt to solve the first problem by creating so comprehensive a macro package that users never need use many low-level formatter requests. However, in doing so, its developers have created an environment that is in many ways more complex than the raw formatter environment itself. And in our opinion, no macro package is comprehensive enough to meet all user needs. Over time, users come up with formatting problems that they need to know how to solve on their own. There is no solution to this problem except better user education.

To some extent, you can compensate for the second problem by testing for arguments and printing error messages if a macro is misused. For example, if a macro requires an argument, consider printing a message if the user fails to supply it:

```
.if "\\$1"" .tm Line \\n(.c: .Se requires section \
number as first argument
```

Of course, by the time the user sees the error message, he or she has already formatted the document, and it is too late to do anything else but repair the damage and reprint. However, messages can sometimes make it easier for users to find errors and can give them warning to look more closely at their printout.

The .ab request takes things one step further—it lets you terminate processing if the formatter encounters a condition you don't like. For example, you could write a macro that aborts if it is called without a necessary argument:

```
.if !\\n(.$ .ab You forgot the argument!
```

The .ab request prints its argument as an error message, just like .tm. It just takes the further, definite step of quitting on the spot.

Probably more suitable, though, is a separate tool for checking macro syntax. Such a tool exists for mm in the mmcheck program. A program like this checks the syntax of macros and requests used in a document and reports possible errors.

This kind of approach is especially suitable for the third kind of error—the failure to close a set of paired macros.

▪ Macro Style ▪

As you develop more of your own macros, you might begin thinking about overall macro style. Developing macros that behave in a consistent, reliable way becomes all the more important as the number of new macros you have increases along with the number of people using them. Recognizing different styles of macro writing helps to suggest alternatives and improvements in the way a macro works.

If you have read the chapters on ms and mm in detail, or if you are already familiar with both of these packages, you have probably noticed that they embody somewhat different text-processing philosophies.

For example, ms generally attempts to recover and continue when it encounters a serious error, but mm aborts the formatting run. And although ms allows a certain amount of user customization (generally by providing a few number registers and strings that the user is expected to modify), it has nowhere near the complexity of mm in this regard. An mm user is expected to set up various number registers that affect the operation of many different macros.

In writing your own macros (especially ones that will be integrated with one of the existing packages), you should take some time to think about style, and how you want users to interact with your macros. This is most easily shown by comparing several different paragraph macros:

```
.de P            \" A very simple paragraph macro
.br
.ne 2v
.ti 2P
..


.de LP           \" An ms style flush left paragraph
.RT
.ne 1.1
.sp \\n(PDu
.ti \\n(.iu
..


.de PP           \" An ms style indented paragraph
.RT
.ne 1.1
.sp \\n(PDu
.ti +\\n(PIu
..


.deP             \" An mm style variable paragraph
.br              \" Note that this is much
.sp (\\n(Ps*.5)u \" simplified from true mm code
.ne 1.5v
```

```
.if\\n(.$>0&(0\\$1)  .ti+\\n(Pin
.if\\n(.$=0  .if\\n(Pt=1  .ti+\\n(Pin
..
```

The first example shows a very simple paragraph macro using a fixed indent value.

The second and third examples are adapted from ms. They show the use of an embedded reset macro (discussed in Chapter 16) and the specification of values such as indents and interparagraph spacing by means of number registers so that users can change them without rewriting the macro. The different types of paragraphs (flush left or indented) are handled by defining two different macros.

The fourth example is adapted from mm. It shows how a macro can be controlled in a number of different ways. First of all, the size of the paragraph indent can be controlled by the user, as in ms. Second, though, users can specify whether they want an indent for a particular paragraph by specifying an argument to the macro. Finally, they can specify whether all paragraphs are to be indented or flush left by setting the Pt (*paragraph type*) register.

Although you may not want to go as far as mm in giving different ways to affect the action of a macro, it is good to realize that all of these options are available and to draw on them as necessary.

However, it does make sense to be consistent in the mechanisms you use. For example, suppose you create macros to put captions on figures, tables, and examples. If you allow the user to control the amount of space before the caption with an optional argument, you ought to do so in all three analogous macros.

As much as possible, a user should be able to infer the action of a macro from its name, and should be able to guess at its arguments by analogy to other, similar macros in the same package. If you are capricious in your design, other users will have a much greater burden to shoulder when it comes time for them to learn your macros. Even if you are the only user of macros you develop, consistency will help you keep out of trouble as you gradually extend your package.

The issue of macro style really comes up as you begin to develop your own custom macro package, as you will see when we examine the elements of a macro package in Chapters 16 and 17.

Figures and Special Effects

This chapter discusses a variety of formatter requests that you can use to draw figures and achieve special effects like overstriking and vertically stacked text. It also dissects some of the most complex macros we've seen so far, so it should advance your knowledge of how to write macros as well as your knowledge of its explicit subject matter.

· Formatter Escape Sequences ·

Preprocessors like `tbl` and `pic` draw boxes, lines, and simple figures using an underlying library of formatter escape sequences that you can also use directly. The `eqn` preprocessor also uses many of these escape sequences, as well as others that are more appropriate for creating special effects with text characters.

The escape sequences are listed in Table 15-1. As you can see, there are quite a few! Fortunately, many of these need not be learned by the average user. The various preprocessors often allow a user to achieve the same effect more easily. Although `tbl` or `eqn` might seem difficult to learn, they are far simpler than the formatter commands they replace. For example, an `eqn` construct like `10% sup 5%` is easier to learn and type than an equivalent `troff` construct like:

```
10\s-3\v'-3p'5\v'3p'\s0
```

When it comes to drawing lines and figures, things get even more complex.

For this reason, many of the escape sequences we are about to discuss are not often used by the average person trying to achieve special effects. However, they are extremely useful to a developer of macros.

In this chapter, we'll cover the sequences for local vertical and horizontal motions and line drawing, because these requests are most commonly used in macros. In addition, we will show several large macros that do line drawing in order to demonstrate both the use of escape sequences and techniques for writing complex macros.

TABLE 15-1. Formatter Escape Sequences

Escape	Description
\v'*distance*'	Move *distance* vertically down the page. Precede *distance* with a minus sign to move back up the page.
\h'*distance*'	Move *distance* horizontally to the right. Precede *distance* with a minus sign to move back to the left.
\u	Move ½ em up (½ line in nroff).
\d	Move ½ em down (½ line in nroff).
\r	Move 1 em up (1 line in nroff).
\c	Join next line to current output line, even across a break.
\p	Cause a break, and adjust current partial output line.
\x'*distance*'	Add extra line space for oversize characters.
\(space)	Move right one space (distance determined by .ss).
\0	Move right the width of a digit in the current font and size.
|	Move right 1/6 em (ignored in nroff).
\^	Move right 1/12 em (ignored in nroff).
\w'*string*'	Interpolate width of *string*.
\k$x$	Mark current horizontal place in register x.
\o'*xy*'	Overstrike characters x and y.
\z$c$	Output character c without spacing over it.
\b'string'	Pile up characters vertically (used to construct large brackets, hence its name).
\l'*Nc*'	Draw a horizontal line consisting of repeated character c for distance N. If c isn't specified, use _.
\L'*Nc*'	Draw a vertical line consisting of repeated character c for distance N. If c isn't specified, use |.
\D'l *x,y*'	Draw a line from the current position to coordinates x,y (ditroff only).
\D'c *d*'	Draw a circle of diameter d with left edge at current position (ditroff only).
\D'e *d1 d2*'	Draw an ellipse with horizontal diameter $d1$ and vertical diameter $d2$, with the left edge at the current position (ditroff only).
\D'a *x1 y1 x2 y2*'	Draw an arc counterclockwise from current position, with center at $x1,y1$ and endpoint at $x1+x2,y1+y2$ (ditroff only).
\D'~ *x1 y1 x2 y2*...'	Draw a spline from current position through the specified coordinates (ditroff only).
\H'*n*'	Set character height to n points, without changing the width (ditroff only).
\S'*n*'	Slant output n degrees to the right. Negative values slant to the left. A value of zero turns off slanting (ditroff only).

Many of the escape sequences in Table 15-1 take arguments that must be delimited from any following text. The delimiter character is most often ′ or ^G (*CTRL-G*), but it can be any character. The first character following the escape sequence will be taken as the delimiter, and the argument list will be terminated when that same character is encountered a second time.

▪ Local Vertical Motions ▪

There are a number of escape sequences for *local* vertical motions. They are so called because they take place within a line, without causing a break or otherwise interrupting the filling and justification process.

However, this is not to say that the motions they cause are limited. For example, you can use \v, the vertical motion escape sequence, to move anywhere on the page, just as you can with the .sp request. However, the remainder of the line that has been collected in the formatter's internal buffers will be output in the new location just as if the motion had never taken place.

To make this point clearer, let's look at three examples of input text that use different types of vertical motion.

What happens with .sp:

Input lines:

```
Especially in troff, it is sometimes  uncanny  the  way  that
vertical motions can occur
.sp 12p
independently from the output of the text.
```

Output lines:

Especially in troff, it is sometimes uncanny the way that vertical motions
can occur

independently from the output of the text.

What happens with ′sp:

Input lines:

```
Especially in troff, it is sometimes  uncanny  the  way  that
vertical motions can occur
′sp 12p
independently from the output of the text.
```

Output lines:

> Especially in `troff`, it is sometimes uncanny the way that vertical motions
>
> can occur independently from the output of the text.

What happens with `\v'12p'`:

Input lines:

```
Especially in troff, it is sometimes uncanny the way that
vertical motions can occur \v'12p'
independently from the output of the text.
```

Output lines:

> Especially in `troff`, it is sometimes uncanny the way that vertical motions
> can occur
>   independently from the output of the text.

As you can see, `.sp` causes a break as well as a downward movement on the page. The partially collected line is output before the movement takes place. With `'sp`, the line currently being collected is completely filled and output before the spacing takes place. With `\v`, the motion is completely independent of the process of filling and justification.

It is also independent of traps, as we discovered once when trying to put a pointing finger (☞) at the bottom of a page to indicate that the subject was continued on the overleaf. We used a macro invoked by the page bottom trap to print the finger. At first, we made the mistake of using `.sp -1` to move back up the page to place the finger. Unfortunately, this put `troff` into an endless loop around the trap position. The `\v` escape sequence, on the other hand, did the trick nicely. Since it does not change the current baseline spacing, it will not trigger a trap.

Long-winded examples aside, that is why `\v` is considered a local motion. In general, `\v` escape sequences are used in pairs to go away from, and then back to, the current vertical position.

A superscript is a good example of vertical motion using `\v`. For example, you could create a simple superscript macro like this:

```
.de SU
\\$1\s-2\v'-3p'\\$2\v'3p'\s0\\$3
..
```

This macro

- prints its first argument;

- reduces the point size;

- makes a 3-point reverse vertical motion;

- prints the second argument;

- makes a 3-point vertical motion to return to the original baseline;

- restores the original size;

- prints an optional third argument immediately following. (This allows punctuation to be introduced immediately following the superscript, rather than on the next line. If no third argument is supplied, this argument interpolation will be ignored.)

This macro could also be implemented using the \u (*up*) and \d (*down*) escape sequences, which use a fixed ½-em distance. If you did this—or if you specified the distance for the \v escape sequence in a relative unit like ems, instead of a fixed unit like points—it would be essential to have both of the vertical motions either inside or outside the font size change. For example, assuming that the current font size was 10 points:

```
.de SU
\\$1\u\s-2\\$2\d\s0\\$3
..
```

would produce an unbalanced effect, because the upward motion would be 5 points (½ em at 10 points), while the downward motion would be only 4 points (½ em at 8 points). This caution holds true whenever you mix font and size changes with local motions.

• Local Horizontal Motions •

Much of what has been said about local vertical motions is true for local horizontal motions. They take place independently of the process of filling and justification, and so, if improperly used, can result in horrors like:

Look what happensyouwhenmake a mistake with \h!

which was produced by the line:

```
Look what happens when \h'-3m'you make a mistake with \h!
```

Horizontal motions are not as likely to take place in pairs as vertical motions. For example, there are cases where you want to close up the space between two special characters, or open up additional space on a line. For example, >>, produced by >\h'-1p'>, looks better than >>.

In addition to \h, there are a number of escape sequences that affect horizontal motion in specific ways.

For example, ``\ '' (it's quoted so you can see the blank space following the backslash) will space over to the right by *exactly* one space. That sounds trivial, but it isn't. When it justifies a line, troff feels free to expand the spaces between words. (The default space size is normally 12/36 of an em, but can be reset with the .ss

request using units of 36ths of an em). The "\ " escape sequence makes sure that you
get exactly one space. This is generally thought of as the unpaddable space character
and is used when you want to keep two words together. However, it can also be used
simply as a horizontal motion sequence.

Another useful sequence is \0. It provides exactly the width of a digit in the
current font and size. (Unlike alphabetic characters, all digits are always the same
width on the standard fonts, to allow them to line up properly in numeric displays.)
The \0 sequence is most useful when you want to line up spaces and digits manually.

The two escape sequences \| and \^, which give, respectively, a 1/6 em and
1/12 em space, are useful when you want to create just a little bit of fixed space
between two characters. (The normal space size created by an actual space character is
1/3 em, so these two characters give you, respectively, one-half and one-quarter of the
normal interword spacing.) You may remember that we used \^ in Chapter 12 to
create a little bit of space before and after the em dashes we were introducing into our
files with sed.

▪ Absolute Motions ▪

As you've probably gathered from the preceding discussion, you can specify the distance for a horizontal or vertical motion using any of the units discussed in Chapter 4.
The values can be given explicitly, or by interpolating the value of a number register.
In addition, as discussed in Chapter 4, you can use a vertical bar (|) to indicate absolute
motion relative to the top of the page or the left margin.

This is not as simple as it first appears. For vertical motions, you pretty much get
what you expect. For example, .sp |2i, \v'|2i' will move you to a position 2
inches from the top of the page. Depending on where you are on the page before you
issue the command, the generated motion will be either positive or negative.

For horizontal motions, things are a little more ambiguous. The absolute position
indicator doesn't move you to an absolute position based on the output line, but on the
input line. For example:

```
This is a test of absolute horizontal motion\h'|1i'_
```

produces:

```
    This is a test of absolute horizontal motion
```

But:

```
This is a test of
absolute horizontal motion\h'|1i'_
```

produces:

```
    This is a test of absolute horizontal motion
```

What is really supplied as an argument to \h when you use the absolute position indicator is the *distance* from the current position on the input line to the specified position. Even though it looks the same, the argument will have a different value, depending on the length of the input line. And again, as with vertical motions, the actual movement may be positive (to the right) or negative (to the left), depending on the relationship between the current position and the absolute position specified.

It may appear odd to have these motions relative to the input line. However, as we will see (especially in line drawing), there is a method to the madness.

▪ Line Drawing ▪

Now we come to the fun part. Moving around on the page is of little use unless you plan to write something at the point you've moved to. Superscripts, subscripts, and overprinting provide some application of local motion, but local motions are most useful with the escape sequences for drawing lines and curves.

Applications range from underlining words in troff, to boxing single words (if you are writing computer manuals, this is very useful for showing the names of keys to be pressed), to drawing boxes around whole blocks of text, just like tbl does.

The \l sequence draws a horizontal line; \L draws a vertical line. Both escape sequences take two arguments, the second of which is optional. Both arguments should be enclosed together in a single pair of delimiters.

The first argument is the distance to draw the line. A positive value means to draw a horizontal line to the right, or a vertical line downward (depending on whether \l or \L is used). A negative value means to draw a line back to the left, or back up the page.

When you draw a line back to the left, either by explicitly specifying a negative value, or by specifying an absolute value (such as | 0) that results in a negative movement, troff first moves back to the specified position, then draws the line from left to right. It is as if the line is drawn *from* the specified distance to the current position.

For example:

\l'3i'	draws a line 3 inches to the right
\l'-3i'	draws a line from a position 3 inches to the left
\L'3i'	draws a line 3 inches down
\L'-3i'	draws a line 3 inches up
\L'|3i'	draws a line to a position 3 inches from the top of the page

The optional second argument is the character with which to draw the line. By default, a horizontal line is drawn with the baseline rule—a horizontal line that is aligned with the bottom of the other characters on a line. However, if you want to underline text, be sure to use the underscore, which is printed in the space allotted for characters that descend below the line:

```
These_words_are_separated_by_baseline_rules.
These_words_are_separated_by_underscores.
```

The underscore is usually generated by the underscore character that appears above the hyphen on most keyboards. However, to be on the safe side, you should refer to it by its special character name in troff—\(ul. (The baseline rule can be specified with the sequence \(ru.)

Vertical lines are drawn by default with a character called the box rule (which can be generated by the \(br escape sequence or the vertical bar character on most keyboards). The box rule is a zero-width character—that is, when troff draws the box rule, it does not space over as it does with other characters. This allows troff to form exact corners with horizontal lines drawn with underrules. However, as you will see, it may therefore require you to manually specify additional space to keep it from crowding previous or succeeding characters.

Except in the case where you draw a line to the left, as described previously, the current position at which text output will continue is changed to the endpoint of the line. In drawing a box, you will naturally find yourself returning to the starting point. However, if you are drawing a single line, you may need to use \v or \h to adjust the position either before or after the line is drawn.

Let's look at a couple of examples. A simple macro to underline a word in troff might look like this:

```
.de UL
\\$1\l'|0\(ul'\\$2
..
```

This example prints its argument, backs up a distance equal to the length of the argument *on the input line*, then draws a line from that point to the current position. The optional second argument allows you to specify punctuation without separating it with the space that is required if it were entered on the next input line. (This reverse motion is implicit in the negative value generated by the absolute position request |0—that is, the distance from the end of the word to the beginning of the line. Lines drawn with \l and a negative distance generate a negative horizontal motion for the specified distance. The line is then drawn in a positive direction back to the current position.)

That is:

```
.UL Hello ,
```

produces:

Hello,

and:

```
.UL Hello
,
```

produces:

Hello ,

(In nroff, you can underline simply by using an italic font switch, or the .ul request, because italics are represented in nroff by underlines.)

A macro to enclose a word (like the name of a key) in a box might look like this:

```
.de BX
\(br\|\\$1\|\(br\l'|0\(rn'\l'|0\(ul'\^\\$2
..
```

For example, the input text:

```
Press the
.BX RETURN
key.
```

will produce the line:

Press the $\boxed{\text{RETURN}}$ key.

This macro prints a single box rule (\(br), spaces over 1/6 em (\|), prints the argument, spaces over another 1/6 em space, and prints a concluding box rule. Then it draws two horizontal lines back to 0 (the beginning of the input line—that is, the width of the argument plus the two requested 1/6-em spaces).

The first horizontal line is drawn not with \(ul but with another special character, the *root en* (\(rn). This character is used when drawing equations to produce the top bar in a square root symbol, but it is just as useful when you want to draw a line over the top of some text without moving back up the page. The second horizontal line is drawn, as usual, with \(ul.

Both lines can be drawn back to zero without compensating horizontal motions because, as we have already noted, horizontal lines drawn backwards actually generate a reverse horizontal motion followed by a line drawn back to the current position.

The macro concludes with an additional 1/12-em space (\^) and an optional second argument, designed to allow you to specify punctuation following the box.

A macro to box multiple lines of text (like this paragraph) is more complex. It requires the use of a diversion to capture the text to be boxed. The diversion can then be measured, and the lines drawn to fit. And when you are using diversions, you need two macros, one to start the diversion, and one to finish it, as in the following macros:

```
.de BS              \" Box Start
.br                 \" Space down one line; cause break
.di bX              \" Start diverting input to macro bX
..
.de BE              \" Box End
.br                 \" Ensure partial line is in bX
.nr bI 1n           \" Set "box indent"--space between
.                   \" box and text
.di                 \" End diversion
.nr bW \\n(dlu      \" Set "box width" to diversion width
.nr bH \\n(dnu      \" Set "box height" to diversion height
.ne \\n(bHu+\\n(.Vu \" Make sure bH plus one line is
.                   \" left on page
```

```
.nr fI \\n(.u          \" Set fI to 1 if text is filled
.nf                    \" Specify no-fill before printing bX
.ti 0
.in +\\n(bIu           \" Add "box indent" to any other indent
.bX                    \" Output the text stored in macro bX
.in -\\n(bIu           \" Subtract bI to restore prev indent
.nr bW +2*\\n(b        \" Add 2x "box indent" to "box width"
.sp -1                 \" Compensate for baseline spacing
\l'\\n(bWu\(ul'\L'-\\n(bHu'\l'|0\(ul'\h'|0'\L'\\n(bHu'
.                      \" Draw box
.if \\n(fI .fi         \" Restore fill if prev text was filled
.sp                    \" Space down 1 line after box is drawn
..
```

There are a number of interesting things about these macros. First, they provide a good illustration of the use of diversions. Note that the macro causes a break (with either .br or .sp) before the diversion is started and before it is terminated. Note also how the predefined read-only registers dn and dl are used to measure the height and width of the diversion and therefore set the dimensions of the box. (The contents of these registers are not used directly when the lines are drawn because the registers are read-only, and the width needs to be adjusted to account for a small amount of spacing between the box rule and the text contained in the box.)

Second, because these macros are complex, they use quite a few number registers. We want to use register names that are mnemonic, but not use up names that might be useful for user-level macros. We get around this problem by using names that combine lowercase and uppercase letters. This is entirely a matter of convention, but one that we find preferable to mm's use of completely obscure internal register names like ;p.

Third, there is the actual line drawing—the point of this presentation. Let's look at this aspect of these macros in detail.

As we've discussed, bH and bW have been set to the height and width, respectively, of the diversion. Because the box rule is a zero-width character, however, the macro needs to allow a small amount of space between the sides of the box and the text it encloses. It does this by specifying a 1-en indent (which is added to any existing indent, in case the box occurs in a block of text that is already indented). When the diversion is output, it will thus be indented 1 en.

After the diversion is output, the indent is reset to its previous value. However, twice the value of the indent is added to the box width. The box will thus be drawn 2 ens wider than the text it encloses. The text will start in 1 en; the right side of the box will be drawn 1 en beyond the right margin.

The actual line to draw the box:

```
\l'\\n(BWu\(ul'\L'-\\n(BHu'\l'|0\(ul'\h'|0'\L'\\n(BHu'
```

draws a horizontal line using \(ul from the left margin to the distance specified by bW (*box width*), which, as we have seen, now includes a small extra margin. It then draws a line back up the page to the height specified by bH, and back across the page to the left margin again.

At this point, even though we have drawn the bottom, right, and top sides of the box, we are still at the top right corner of the box. The macro needs to move horizontally back to the left margin, because horizontal lines to the left are actually drawn *from* the left, and leave the current position the same as it was before the line was drawn. In this case we actually want to move to the left as well. Therefore, we must do so explicitly, by following the \l'|0\(ul' request with a \h'|0'. Finally, the box is closed by drawing a vertical line back down the left side.

The current position is now at the start of the last line of the contents of the box, so the macro issues an .sp request to move down one line. Alternatively, you could write this macro in such a way that it leaves no additional space above and below the box, but lets the user leave space by issuing some kind of spacing or paragraph request.

By default, the box is drawn just long enough to surround the text it contains. (The number register dl, which is used to set the box width, contains the width of the text in the diversion.) For short lines in no-fill mode, the box will also be shorter:

> Here are some short lines of text in no-fill mode.
> Let's see how they come out.

This raises the idea that it might be nice to center a box that is shorter. A more complete set of box macros will do this, as well as let the user change the default box indent (the distance between the text and the edge of the box):

```
.de BS                    \" Box Start
.sp
.di bX
.nr bC 0                  \" Clear centering flag
.nr bI 0                  \" Clear box indent
.if "\\$1"C" .nr bC 1     \" Set flag if user wants centered
.if !"\\$2"" .nr bI \\$2n\" Set box indent if specified
..
.de BE                    \" Box End
.br
.if !\\n(bI .nr bI 1n     \" Set bI if not already set
.di
.nr bW \\n(dlu
.nr bH \\n(dnu
.ne \\n(bHu+\\n(.Vu
.nr fI \\n(.u
.nf
.ti 0
.nr iN \\n(.iu            \" Save current indent
.if \\n(bC .in +(\\n(.lu-\\n(bWu)/2u
.                         \" If centering, adjust indent
.in +\\n(bIu
.bX
.in -\\n(bIu
.nr bW +2*\\n(bIu
```

```
.sp -1
\l'\\n(bWu\(ul'\L'-\\n(bHu'\l'|0\(ul'\h'|0'\L'\\n(bHu'
.if \\n(fI .fi
.in \\n(iNu                   \" Restore original indent
.sp
..
```

Using the full macro, and specifying `.BS C 5n`, the box now looks like this:

> Here are some short lines of text in no-fill mode.
> Let's see how they come out with `.BS C 5n`.

These macros also provide insight into how to use number registers. For example, B1 takes C as a possible argument to indicate that the box should be centered. Because the B2 macro controls the output, there must be some way to communicate the user request for centering between B1 and B2. The B1 macro sets number register BC to 1 as a signal, or flag, to B2 to do the centering. (Note that BC is first zeroed, to make sure that centering is not propagated into the current environment from a previous invocation of the box macros.)

Likewise, BQ is set as a flag to indicate whether justification is enabled. The box is drawn in no-fill mode, but the macro must reset filling if it was previously enabled. The read-only number register `.u` is nonzero if filling is in effect, so the lines:

```
.nr BQ \\n(.u
        .
        .
        .
.if \\n(BQ .fi
```

will execute the `.fi` request only if justification was previously in effect.

Changing Line Weight

You may occasionally want to change the weight of a line you are drawing. The way to do this is simple: change the point size with either the `.ps` request or the `\s` escape sequence before drawing the line. For example:

```
\l'3i'
```

will produce:

_____

and:

```
\s20\l'3i'\s0
```

will produce:

_____

(This trick only works with \l and \L. It will not change the weight of lines drawn with any of the \D escape sequences.) You might also want to consider the text size when you are drawing boxes around text. For example, if you are using a macro like .BX (shown previously) to draw boxes around the names of keys, you might want to set the text 2 points smaller, either by specifying the font-switch codes as part of the argument:

```
.BX "\s-2RETURN\s0"
```

or by modifying the macro so that they are built right in:

```
.de BX
\(br\|\s-2\\$1\s0\|\(br\l'|0\(rn'\l'|0\(ul'\^\\$2
..
```

If either of these things were done, our earlier example would look like this, which is even better:

Press the RETURN key.

Drawing Curves

The previous line drawing escape sequences work in nroff and otroff as well as ditroff. There are also additional drawing sequences that only work in ditroff. These escape sequences allow you to draw circles, arcs, ellipses, splines (curved lines between a series of coordinates), and straight lines.

Table 15-2 summarizes these sequences. The syntax of the escape sequences is familiar—an initial escape code is followed by a series of arguments enclosed in single quotation marks or some other user-supplied delimiter. In this case, though, all of the escape sequences begin with the same code—\D—with the type of item to be drawn (circle, arc, ellipse, spline, or straight line) given by the first argument.

TABLE 15-2. ditroff Escape Sequences for Drawing

Escape	Description
\D'l *x,y*'	Draw a line from the current position to coordinates *x,y*.
\D'c *d*'	Draw a circle of diameter *d* with left edge at the current position.
\D'e *d1 d2*'	Draw an ellipse with horizontal diameter *d1* and vertical diameter *d2*, with the left edge at the current position.
\D'a *x1 y1 x2 y2*'	Draw an arc counterclockwise from the current position, with center at *x1,y1* and endpoint at *x1+x2,y1+y2*.
\D'~ *x1 y1 x2 y2...*'	Draw a spline from the current position through the specified coordinates.

Learning the geometry used by these escape sequences is best accomplished by example. Although we have shown the arguments to the line, arc, and spline sequences as if they were *x, y* coordinates, they are in fact troff's usual vertical and horizontal distances. Read *x* as *horizontal* distance, and *y* as *vertical distance*. You can get very confused if you treat them as a true coordinate system.

Let's start simple, with individual fixed-size figures. The following input will produce the output shown in Figure 15-1:

```
.sp 1i
.in .5i
The circle starts here\D'c 1i'and ends here.
.sp 1i
The line starts here\D'l 1i -1i'and ends here.
.sp 1i
The ellipse starts here\D'e 2i 1i'and ends here.
.sp 1i
The arc starts here\D'a .5i 0 0 .5i'and ends here.
.sp 1i
The spline starts here
\D'~ .5i -.5i .5i .5i .5i .5i .5i -.5i'and ends here.
.sp .5i
.in 0
```

As you can see, arcs and splines are the most difficult figures to construct. Instinct cries out for the ability to draw an arc between two endpoints with the current position as the center of the arc. Instead, for consistency with the other figures, drawing begins at the current position, and the first set of values specify the center of the arc. This takes a little getting used to.

With splines, the problem is that distances are additive, and relative to the previous position, rather than to the initial position. Our familiarity with *x, y* coordinate systems leads us to think that the spline should be produced by a request like this:

```
\D'~ .5i -.5i 1i 0 1.5i .5i 2i 0'
```

(in which the *x* value increases relative to the origin rather than to the previous point) instead of by the request shown previously.

You may also have noticed something rather odd. Text continues right after the endpoint of the figure, yet the .sp 1i requests seem to give us 1 inch of space from the original baseline, regardless of the endpoint of the figure. This is most obvious with the line, which clearly moves back up the page. Yet the next figure is also spaced down 1 inch. This fact becomes even more obvious if we do this:

```
.sp 1i
The line starts here\D'l 1i -.5i'and ends here.
What happens to text that wraps and continues in fill mode?
```

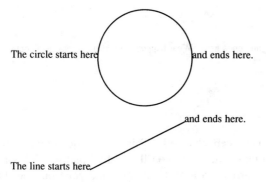

The circle starts here   and ends here.

and ends here.

The line starts here

The ellipse starts here   and ends here.

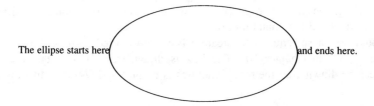

The arc starts here

and ends here.

The spline starts here   and ends here.

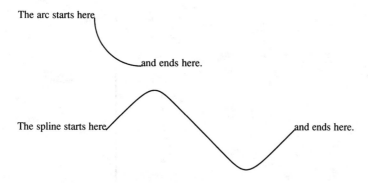

Fig. 15-1. Some Simple Figures

Here's the result:

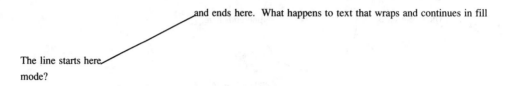

and ends here. What happens to text that wraps and continues in fill

The line starts here

mode?

The current baseline has not been changed. This is a major contrast to lines drawn with \L or \l. As you play with lines, you'll also find that lines drawn to the left with \D really do move the current position to the left, and you don't need to add a compensating horizontal motion if you are drawing a complex figure.

You'll have to experiment to get accustomed to drawing figures. One other problem is to get figures to start where you want. For example, to get the endpoints of arcs with various orientations in the right place, you may need to combine arc drawing requests with vertical and horizontal motions.

You could use these requests to create a box with curved corners similar to the one done with pic in Chapter 10. The box is drawn starting with the lower left corner (so it can be drawn after the text it encloses is output) and will look like this:

The box was drawn using the following drawing commands. These commands are shown on separate lines for ease of reading. To make them draw continuously, we need to add the \c escape sequence to the end of each line. This escape sequence joins succeeding lines as if the line feed were not there. Warning: using fill mode will not achieve the same result, because the formatter will introduce spaces between each drawing command as if it were a separate word.

`\v'-.25i'\c`	Go back up the page 1/4 inch
`\D'a .25i 0 0 .25i'\c`	Draw bottom left arc 1/4 inch down and to the right
`\D'l 3i 0'\c`	Draw horizontal line 3 inches to the right
`\D'a 0 -.25i .25i 0'\c`	Draw bottom right arc 1/4 inch up and to the right
`\D'l 0 -2i'\c`	Draw vertical line 2 inches back up the page
`\D'a -.25i 0 0 -.25i'\c`	Draw top right arc 1/4 inch up and to the left
`\D'l -3i 0'\c`	Draw horizontal line 3 inches to the left
`\D'a 0 .25i -.25i 0'\c`	Draw top left arc 1/4 inch down and to the left
`\D'l 0 2i'\c`	Draw vertical line 2 inches down the page
`\v'.25i'`	Restore original baseline position

To build a complete macro to enclose examples in a simulated computer screen, we can adapt the `.B1` and `.B2` macros shown previously:

```
.de SS                      \" Start Screen with
.                           \" Curved Corners
.sp .5v
.ie !"\\$1"" .nr BW \\$1\" Get width from first arg
.el .nr BW 4i               \" or set default if not specified
.ie !"\\$2"" .nr BH \\$2\" Get height from second arg
.el .nr BH 2.5i             \" or set default if not specified
.br
.di BB
..
.de SE \" Screen End
.br
.nr BI 1n
.if \\n(.$>0 .nr BI \\$1n
.di
.ne \\n(BHu+\\n(.Vu
.nr BQ \\n(.j
.nf
.ti 0
.in +\\n(BIu
.in +(\\n(.lu-\\n(BWu)/2u
.sp .5
.BB
.sp +(\\n(BHu-\\n(dnu)
.in -\\n(BIu
.nr BH -.5i
.nr BW +2*\\n(BIu
.nr BW -.5i
\v'-.25i'\c
\D'a .25i 0 0 .25i'\c
\D'l \\n(BWu 0'\c
\D'a 0 -.25i .25i 0'\c
\D'l 0 -\\n(BHu'\c
```

```
\D'a -.25i 0 0 -.25i'\c
\D'l -\\n(BWu 0'\c
\D'a 0 .25i -.25i 0'\c
\D'l 0 \\n(BHu'\c
\v'.25i'
.sp -1.5
.if \\n(BQ .fi
.br
.sp .5v
..
```

Because a screen has a fixed aspect ratio, we don't want the box to be proportional to the text it encloses. Hence, we give the user of the macro the ability to set the box width and height. If no arguments are specified, we provide default values.

Because the box size is fixed, there are some additional steps necessary in the closing macro. First, we must decrement the specified box width and height by the distance used in drawing the curves, so that the user gets the expected size. Second, because the box is drawn from the lower left corner back up the page, we must make sure that the lower left corner is correctly positioned before we start drawing.

To do this, we again need to use a diversion. We measure the height of the diversion, then add enough additional space (.sp +(\\n(BHu-\\n(dnu)) to bring the starting point for drawing low enough so that the box is not drawn back over the text that precedes the invocation of .SS. (If you don't understand why this was done, delete this line from the macro, and watch the results.)

We've also centered the screen by default, and added a half-line of vertical spacing above and below the box. (As an exercise, modify the .BX macro to produce a key-cap with curved corners.)

▪ Talking Directly to the Printer ▪

Depending on the output device and postprocessor you are using, you may be able to send specialized control commands directly to your printer. For example, you may be able to embed raster graphics images (such as a file created on an Apple Macintosh with MacPaint) directly in your output. Or if you are using a PostScript-driven printer, you can integrate figures done with MacDraw, or issue PostScript commands to print grey screens over your text.

These capabilities are provided by the two requests \! and .cf, *copy filename [to standard output]* (ditroff only).

The \! request is the *transparent output* indicator. Any text following this escape sequence on a line is placed directly into the output stream, without any processing by troff. This makes it possible to insert control lines that will be interpreted by a postprocessor or an output device. (As mentioned in the last chapter, transparent output is also useful for embedding control lines in a diversion, to be executed when the text in the diversion is output.)

Likewise, the contents of the file specified as an argument to `.cf` are placed directly on standard output, without processing by `ditroff`.

Unfortunately, there is a catch! PostScript is a page-description language that resides in the printer. Before you can talk directly to the printer, you must get through the postprocessor that translates `ditroff` output into PostScript. If the postprocessor mucks with the data you send out, all bets are off.

As of this writing, TranScript, Adobe Systems' own `troff`-PostScript converter, does not allow you to use `\!`. However, with Pipeline Associates' `devps`, any lines beginning with `!` are ignored by the postprocessor, and go directly to the printer. This allows you to use transparent output by entering the sequence `\!!` followed by the appropriate PostScript commands. Or, if you are sending a PostScript file created on the Mac, use an editor to insert an exclamation point at the beginning of each line.

In any event, this is not a job for the novice, since you must learn PostScript as well as `troff`. Experiment with your printer and postprocessor, or ask around to see if other users have solutions you can adapt to your situation.

▪ **Marking a Vertical Position** ▪

There are many cases, both in macros and in the body of your text, where you may want to mark a spot and then return to it to lay down additional characters or draw lines.

The `.mk` request marks the current vertical position on the page; `.rt` returns to that position. This is useful for two-column processing. To give a simple example:

```
Two columns are useful when you have a linear list
of information that you want to put side-by-side, but don't
want to bother rearranging with the cut-and-paste programs.
.sp .5
.ll 2.5i
.nf
.mk
Item 1
Item 2
Item 3
.ll 5i
.in 2.75i
.rt
Item 4
Item 5
.in 0
.sp
```

This example produces the following output:

```
Two columns are useful when you have a linear list of
information that you want to put side-by-side, but
don't want to bother rearranging with the cut-and-paste
programs.

Item 1                              Item 4
Item 2                              Item 5
Item 3
```

Notice that it is entirely your responsibility to make sure that the second column doesn't overprint the first. In this example, we did this by manually adjusting the indent and the line length. In addition, because the second column is shorter than the first, a concluding `.sp` is necessary to return to the original position on the page. If this had not been done, subsequent text would overprint the last line of the first column.

Proper two-column processing for an entire document requires a much more complex setup, which must in part be handled by the page bottom macro. We'll look at that in detail in Chapter 16, but this example should be enough to give you the idea.

The `.mk` request can take as an argument the name of a number register in which to store the vertical position. This allows you to mark multiple positions on a page, and return to them by name. The `.rt` request always returns to the last position marked, but you can go to a position marked in a register using the `.sp` request:

```
.mk Q
.sp |\nQu
```

or (more to the point of the current discussion) with `\v`:

```
\v'|\nQu'
```

In addition, `.rt` can take as an argument a distance from the top of the page. That is:

```
.rt 3i
```

will return to a point 3 inches from the top of the page. The `.mk` request need not be used in this case.

· Overstriking Words or Characters ·

There are a number of escape sequences that allow you to overstrike words or characters to create special effects. These include

- boldfacing an entire font by overstriking;

- marking and returning to a specific horizontal position;

- calculating the width of a word and backing up over it;

- centering two characters on top of each other;

- stacking characters vertically.

Boldfacing a Font by Overstriking

The `.bd` request specifies that a font should be artificially boldfaced by overstriking. The request has two forms, one for ordinary fonts and one for the special font.

A request of the form:

```
.bd font offset
```

will overstrike all characters printed in *font* by overprinting them, with the second strike offset from the first by *offset*-1 basic units. The following:

```
.bd S font offset
```

will overstrike characters printed in the special font, while *font* is in effect. And:

```
.bd font
.bd S font
```

will restore the normal treatment of the font.

This request is particularly useful when you are boldfacing headings and want to account for special characters or italics in arguments supplied by the user. (This assumes that you don't have an explicit bold italic font.) Especially at sizes larger than 10 points, the stroke weights of bold and italic fonts can be quite different.

For example, assume that you had a macro that produced a boldface heading for a table:

```
.de Th   \" Table Heading
.ft B
.ce
Table \\$1: \\$2
.ft P
..
```

If the user supplied italics or special characters in the arguments to the macro, the contrast between the different character weights might not be as pleasing as it could be. For example:

```
.Th "3-1" "Special Uses for \(sr in \fItroff\fP"
```

would produce:

Table 3-1: Special Uses for √ in *troff*

If the macro had `.bd` requests added like this:

```
.de Th   \" Table Heading
.ft B
.bd I 3
.bd S B 3
.ce
Table \\$1: \\$2
.ft R
```

```
.bd I
.bd S
..
```

the output would look like this:

Table 3-1: Special Uses for √ in *troff*

Another example is provided by the constant-width (CW) font used in this book. Because the font is optimized for the LaserWriter, where the ink bleeds slightly into the paper, the font is very light on the typesetter. Throughout this book, we have emboldened this font slightly, with the requests:

```
.bd CW 4
.bd S CW 4
```

This sentence shows how the `constant width` font looks without these requests.

Marking and Returning to a Horizontal Position

Just as you can mark a vertical position, you can also mark and move to a specific horizontal position. This is chiefly useful for overstriking characters.

Just as you use a value stored into a register with the `.mk` request to indicate a fixed vertical location on the page, you mark a horizontal location with `\k`. Then, you can use the absolute position indicator `|` to specify the distance for `\h`.

To borrow an example from Kernighan's *Troff Tutorial*:

```
\kxword\h'|\nxu+2u'word
```

will artificially embolden *word* by backing up almost to its beginning, and then overprinting it. (At the start of *word*, `\k` stores the current horizontal position in register x. The `\h'|\nxu+2u'` sequence returns to that absolute position, plus 2 units—a very small offset. When *word* is printed a second time, an overstriking effect is created.)

This sequence might be useful if you were using a font that had no bold equivalent, and in circumstances where the `.bd` request could not be used because the special effect was not desired for all instances of that font on the same line. And, to be really useful, the sequence should probably be saved into a macro.

The Width Function

The `\w` escape sequence returns the length of a string in units. For example:

```
\w'Hi there'
```

will tell you the length of the string *Hi there*.

This sequence returned by \w can be used as an argument with \h or with any horizontally oriented request (such as .in). This has many uses, which we'll introduce as we need them.

To give you an idea of how to use \w, though, we can rewrite the example used with \k as follows, to produce the same effect:

```
.de BD        \" Artificially embolden word
\\$1\h'-\w'\\$1'-2u'\\$1
..
```

This macro prints its first argument, then backs up the width of that argument, less two units. Then it prints the argument a second time— at a two-unit offset from the first. Hint: to avoid awkward constructions involving nested \w sequences, first read the width into a number register. For example, the previous macro could be rewritten like this:

```
.de BD        \" Artificially embolden word
.nr WI (\w'\\$1'-2u)
\\$1\h'-\\n(WIu'\\$1
..
```

In this case, the difference isn't so great; however, at other times the sequence can become too confusing to read easily.

Overstriking Single Characters

Although \k provides a good method for overstriking an entire word, there are also more specialized functions for overstriking a single character.

The \o sequence takes up to nine characters and prints one on top of the other. This is most useful for producing accents, and so forth. For example, \o'e^' produces ê.

You can also produce other interesting character combinations, although you may need to tinker with the output to get it to look just right. For example, we once tried to simulate a checkmark in a box with the sequence: \o'\(sq\(sr'. (Note that the special character escape sequences are treated as single characters for the purpose of overstriking.) This example produced the following output:

The square root symbol is too low in the box, so we tried to introduce some local motions to improve the effect, like this:

```
\o'\(sq\v'-4p'\(sr\v'4p''
```

Unfortunately, this didn't work. Although you can nest most escape sequences inside each other (as long as you use the correct number and order of delimiting quotation marks), local motions do not work with \o. However, there was a solution.

The \z sequence also allows overstriking, but in a different way. The \o sequence knows the width of each character, and centers them on top of each other. The \z sequence simply outputs the following character, *but does not space over it*. That means the current position after printing the character is the same as it was before the character was printed. A subsequent character will have its left edge at the same point as the character immediately following the escape sequence. Because \z does allow you to mix vertical motions with overstriking, it solved our problem.

Because all these escape sequences can be a bit much to type, we defined the checkmark in a box as a string:

```
.ds CK \z\(sq\\v'-4p'\(sr\\v'4p'
```

After we did that, simply typing *(CK will produce ☑.

Stacking up Characters

The \b sequence also does a kind of overstriking—it stacks the characters in the following string. It was designed for use with eqn. There are special bracket-building characters that are meant to stack up on top of each other. See Table 15-3.

TABLE 15-3. Bracket-Building Characters

Character	Name	Description
⌠	\(lt	Left top of big curly bracket
⌡	\(lb	Left bottom
⌠	\(rt	Right top
⌡	\(rb	Right bottom
{	\(lk	Left center of big curly bracket
}	\(rk	Right center of big curly bracket
|	\(bv	Bold vertical
⌊	\(lf	Left floor (left bottom of big square bracket)
⌋	\(rf	Right floor (right bottom)
⌈	\(lc	Left ceiling (left top)
⌉	\(rc	Right ceiling (right top)

A typical invocation looks like this:

```
\b'\(lt\(lk\(lb'
```

which produces:

{

When you're creating a tall construct like this, you need to allow space so that it doesn't overprint preceding lines. You can create space above or below the line with .sp requests. However, this will cause breaks. Although 'sp might do the trick, it is sometimes hard to predict just where the break will fall.

The troff program has a special construct designed to solve just this problem of a tall construct in the middle of filled text. The \x request allows you to associate extra interline spacing with a word. A positive value specifies space above the line; a negative value specifies space below the line. So, when illustrating the previous bracket-building function, we could have shown the results inline, like this $\Big\{$, rather than in an example broken out by blank lines. Typing the sequence:

```
\b'\(lt\(lk\(lb'\x'9p'\x'-9p'
```

gives us the result we want.

The \x sequence is also useful when you want to allow extra space for an over-sized letter at the start of a paragraph. (You've probably seen this technique used in some books on the first paragraph of a new chapter. It was commonly used in illuminated manuscripts.)

An application of \b that you might find useful is to create vertically stacked labels. For example, consider the following macro, which will put such a label in the outside margin of a book:

```
.de SL
.mk         \" Mark current vertical position
.ft B       \" Change to bold font
.cs B 24    \" We'll explain this later
.po -.25i   \" Shorten the page offset by 1/4 inch
.lt +.5i    \" Extend the title length used by .tl
.           \"  This request will be explained later
.if e .tl '\b:\\$1:''  \" Use .tl to put stacked label
.if o .tl '''\b:\\$1:'  \"    in the margins
.lt -.5i    \" Restore original title length
.po +.25i   \" Restore original page offset
.cs B       \" We'll explain this later
.ft         \" Restore original font
.rt         \" Return to original vertical position
..
```

So, for example:

```
.SL "Clever Trick!"
```

will produce the effect shown in the margin.

· Tabs, Leaders, and Fields ·

We discussed tabs in Chapter 4. However, there are a couple of additional points that need to be covered. When you enter a tab on a typewriter, the typing position shifts over to a predefined *position*, or tab stop. In nroff and troff, what is actually generated is the *distance* from the current position *on the input line* to the next tab stop.

What this means is best illustrated by an example that will *not* work. Suppose you want to create a table of contents in which one entry (the page number) is all the way over to the right margin, and the other (the heading) is indented from the left, like this:

C
l
e
v
e
r

T
r
i
c
k
!

Getting Started   1-1

        Turning On the Power 1-2

        Inserting Diskettes 1-3

You might be tempted to code the example as follows (where a tab is shown by the symbol |——|):

```
.ta 6.5iR
Getting Started|——|1-1
.in .5i
Turning On the Power|——|1-2
Inserting Diskettes|——|1-3
```

This will not work. Indents cannot be combined with tabs. A tab character generates the distance from the current position on the input line to the tab stop. Therefore, the page number will be indented an additional half-inch—extending out into the right margin—instead of staying where you put it.

    The way to achieve this effect (in no-fill mode) is to use either spaces or tabs to manually indent the first text string.

    When you use right or center-adjusted tabs, the text to be aligned on the tab is the entire string (including spaces) from one tab to the next, or from the tab to the end of the line. Text is aligned on a right-adjusted tab stop by subtracting the length of the text from the distance to the next tab stop; text is aligned on a center-adjusted tab stop by subtracting half the length of the text from the distance.

Using Leaders

A leader works like a tab; however, it produces a character string instead of horizontal motion. A single character is repeated until a specific horizontal position is reached. There is actually a leader character, just as there is a tab character. But there is no key for it on most keyboards, so it is not obvious how to generate it. The magic character is ^A (*CTRL-A*), and you can insert it into a file with vi by typing ^V^A (*CTRL-V, CTRL-A*).

    If you insert a ^A into your file where you would normally insert a tab (incidentally, the tab itself is equivalent to ^I, and will show up as such if you display a line with ex's :l command), you will generate a string of dots. For example:

```
.nf
.ta 1i 2.5i 3.5i
|——|First^ASecond^AThird
.fi
```

will produce:

First ....Second ....Third

You can change the leader character from a period to any other single character with the
.lc request. For example, you could create a fill-in-the-blanks form like this:

```
.nf
.ta 1i 3iR
.lc _
Signature:|————|^A
Date:|————|^A
.fi
```

This example would produce the following output in troff:

```
┌────────────                                                      ───────────┐
│
│    Signature:        _____
│    Date:             _____
│
```

As you can see from the example, tabs and leaders can be combined effectively to line
up both ends of the underlines.

A second way to create leaders is to redefine the output of the tab character with
.tc. This request works just like .lc, only it redefines what will be output in
response to a tab character. For example, if you issue the request:

```
.tc .
```

a tab character (^I) generates a string of repeated dots, just like a leader (^A). However,
you will then lose the ability to intermix tabs and leaders on the same line, as in the
previous example.

Issuing a .tc request without an argument will restore the default value, which
generates motion only. (Incidentally, the same is true of .lc—that is, .lc without
an argument will cause leaders to generate motion only, just like tabs. To reset the
leader character to its default value, you need to request .lc .).

Using Fields

In addition to tabs and leaders, nroff and troff support *fields*, which are blocks
of text centered between the current position on the input line and the next, or between
two tab stops.

The .fc request allows you to specify a delimiter that indicates the boundaries
of the field, and a second character (called the *pad* character) that divides the contents
of the field into subfields. A blank space is the default pad character. The .fc
request without any arguments turns off the field mechanism. This request is a little
difficult to explain, but easy to illustrate. The requests:

```
.nf
.ta 1i 3i
.fc #
|————|#Hi there#
|————|#Hi how are you#
.fc
.fi
```

will produce the following output:

```
               Hi                        there
               Hi       how      are     you
```

Within the field, the pad character (a space by default) is expanded so that the text evenly fills the field. The first line contains only a single space, so the two words are adjusted at either end of the field. The second line contains three spaces, so the words are evenly spaced across the field.

By specifying a pad character other than a space, you can achieve fine control over spacing within the field. For example, if we modify the input like this:

```
.fc # ^
|———|#Hi^how are^you#
.fc
```

we'll get this result:

```
                Hi        how are        you
```

What's this good for? To return to our *fill-in-the-blanks* example, the construction:

```
.nf
.ta .5i 2i 2.5i 4i
.fc # ^
.lc _
|———|^A|———|^A
.sp .5
|———|#^Signature^#|———|#^Date^#
.fc
.lc .
.fi
```

would produce the following output:

```
        _____            _____
            Signature                   Date
```

You should also know that `.fc`, like many other advanced formatter requests, is used by the `tbl` preprocessor to create complex tables. It is wise to avoid using it inside a table.

Using Tabs and Leaders in Macros

Within a macro definition, tabs and leader characters are not interpreted. They will take effect when the macro is used, not when it is defined. Within a macro definition, you can also specify tabs and leaders with the escape sequences `\t` and `\a`. These sequences are also not interpreted until the macro is used, and can be substituted for the actual tab or leader characters whenever interpretation is to be delayed.

▪ Constant Spacing ▪

One font that you may frequently encounter, especially in the `ditroff` environment, is called `CW` (*constant width*). It is the font used in this book for examples. It has become something of a convention in computer books to print all "computer voice" examples—input from the keyboard, the contents of a file, or output on the screen—in a constant-width font. (This convention is based on the fact that in many computer languages, precise indentation is syntactically or at least semantically significant, and the variable-width typesetting fonts cannot preserve the alignment of the original text.) When you use a constant-width font, you are essentially asking `troff` to act like `nroff`—to work in a realm where all characters, and all spaces, are of identical width.

To use the constant-width font in `ditroff`, request it like any other font, using either the request `.ft CW` or the escape sequence `\f(CW`. In `otroff`, depending on the output device, you could use constant width by using a preprocessor called `cw`, which got around the four font `troff` limit by handling the constant-width font in a separate pass. See the description of `cw` in your *UNIX Reference Manual* if you are interested in the details. (There are other ways to do this as well, depending on the output device and the postprocessor you are using to drive it. For example, we used `otroff` with TextWare International's `tplus` postprocessor and the HP LaserJet. To get around the font limit, we set a convention *in the postprocessor* that 11-point type was actually constant width, and then used the `.cs` and `.ss` requests to give `troff` the correct spacing.)

There is also a request that allows you to simulate the effect of a constant-width font even when you are using a variable-width font. The `.cs` request tells `troff`: "Use the spacing I give you, even if it doesn't match what you've got in your width tables." The request takes up to three arguments. The first two arguments are the most commonly used. They are the font to be so treated and the width to be used, in 36ths of an em. By default, the em is relative to the current type size. By using the optional third argument, you can use the em width of a different type size. So, for example:

```
.cs B 21
Space the bold font at 21/36 of an em.
.cs B 21 12
Space the bold font at 21/36 of a 12-point em.
```

Let's see what we get with these requests:

Space the bold font at 21/36 of an em.
Space   the   bold   font   at   21/36   of   a   12-point   em.

To return to normal spacing for the font, use `.cs` without a width argument. For example:

```
.cs B
```

will return control of spacing for the bold font to `troff`'s width tables.

Although the results are not always aesthetically pleasing, it may be necessary to use this request if you have a real need to represent constant-width text. It is also useful for special effects. For example, you may have noticed that in the headings of each chapter of this book, the word *Chapter* is broadly and evenly spaced, and the boxes underneath align with the letters. This was done with the `.cs` request.

The `.cs` request is also useful when you are creating vertically stacked labels, as shown earlier in this chapter. Normally, characters are positioned with their left edge at the current position on the output line. When constant spacing with `.cs` is in effect, the left corner of the *character box* is placed at that position, and the character itself is centered in the box. You can see the difference between this graphically in the following example:

```
.sp .7i
.ft B
.in 1i
.mk
\b'Variable'
.in 3i
.rt
.cs B 24
\b'Constant'
.br
.cs B
.ft
.in 0
.sp .7i
```

which produces:

<pre>
          V   C
          a   o
          r   n
          i   s
          a   t
          b   a
          l   n
          e   t
</pre>

The `.ss` request is a closely related request that sets the space size. The default size of an interword space in `troff` is 12/36 of an em; for true constant-width effects, you should set it to the same size as the font spacing you have set with `.cs`.

▪ **Pseudo-Fonts** ▪

Using the `.bd` request to create a bold italic is not the only way to simulate a nonstandard font, at least in `ditroff`. In `ditroff`, there are two new escape sequences, `\S` and `\H`. The `\S` sequence slants characters by a specified number of degrees. (Positive values slant characters to the right; negative values slant characters back to the left.) For example:

    \S'15'

will slant characters 15 degrees to the right. This can be used to create a pseudo-italic font. The `\S` sequence without an argument turns off slanting.

The `\H` sequence sets the character height to a specified point size without changing the width. For example, if type is currently being set at 10 point, the construct:

    \H'12'

will create characters that are 12 points high, but only 10 points wide (assuming you are at the default 10-point size). A height value of 0 turns off the function.

These escape sequences will only work on certain output devices. You'll have to experiment to find whether or not they'll work in the setup you're using.

▪ **Character Output Translations** ▪

"Garbage in, garbage out" is a truism of computer science. You get out of a computer what you put in. However, there are cases in `nroff` and `troff` in which what you put in is not the same as what you get out.

The first of these cases is only true for `troff`. It involves a special class of characters called *ligatures*. As we've previously discussed, typeset characters have different widths. Even so, when two narrow characters are printed together, such as a pair of *f*'s, or an *f* and an *i*, there is excess space between the characters.

To get around this problem, there are special characters called ligatures, which are really single characters designed so that they appear the same as a pair of narrow characters. (These are truly single characters, defined as such in `troff`'s character set.)

The ligature characters and the equivalent individual characters are:

Input	Ligature	Equivalent Characters
\(fi	fi	fi
\(fl	fl	fl
\(ff	ff	ff
\(Fi	ffi	ffi
\(Fl	ffl	ffl

The `troff` formatter automatically converts any of these groups of characters to the equivalent ligature, although all ligatures are not supported by every output device.

(For example, *fi* and *fl* are the only ones in the standard PostScript fonts.) You can turn this conversion off with the request:

```
.lg 0
```

and restore it with:

```
.lg
```

Normally, you won't need to do this, but there are special cases in which it may hang you up, and you'll need to know what to do. We'll get to one of them in a moment.

The `.tr` (*translate*) request provides a more general facility for controlling output character conversions. It takes one or more pairs of characters as an argument. After such a translation list has been defined, `troff` will always substitute the second character in each pair for the first, whenever it appears in the input.

Let's look at some examples. First, consider the case encountered throughout this book, in which we illustrate the syntax of various requests without actually executing them. For example, we want to show a period at the start of a line or the backslash that starts an escape sequence, without actually having them executed.

We could simply insulate the special characters from execution. For example, we can put the zero-width character `\&` in front of a period that begins a request, and we can double all backslashes (`\\` will appear as `\` in the output) or use the `\e` escape sequence, to print `\`.

However, this grows tedious and hard to read in the input file. Another approach is to do a character translation:

```
.tr #.%\\          \" Translate # to ., % to \
```

(As usual, we have to double the backslash.) Now, whenever `#` appears in the input, `.` appears in the output, and whenever `%` appears in the input, `\` appears in the output. So, in our examples, we can actually type:

```
#sp 1i            %" Space down one inch
```

But what appears on the page of this book is:

```
.sp 1i            \" Space down one inch
```

The translations are built into the example start and end macros. (The end macro resets the characters to their normal values.)

If you translate characters with `.tr`, be sure to restore their original values correctly when you are done. To reset the previous translation to the normal character values, the request is:

```
.tr ##%%          \" Translate # to #, % to %
```

In addition, the translation must be in effect at the time the line is output. If you translate characters without first causing a break, any partially filled line will be affected by the translation.

It is also possible (and recommended in some of the `troff` documentation) to use `.tr` to substitute some other character (usually `~`) for a space. This creates an equivalent to the unpaddable space.

```
.tr ~
```

This will allow you to type single characters for unpaddable spaces; your input text will be more readable and will line up properly on the screen.

Yet another application of `.tr`, and one that you will find useful in designing macros for chapter headings and so on, is to translate lowercase input into uppercase, and then back again:

```
.de UC  \" Translate input to uppercase
.tr aAbBcCdDeEfFgGhHiIjJkKlLmMnNoOpPqQrRsStTuUvVwWxXyYzZ
\\$1
.br
.tr aabbccddeeffgghhiijjkkllmmnnooppqqrrssttuuvvwwxxyyzz
..
```

(The break is important. These character translations must be in effect at the time the line is output, not when it is read into the buffer.)

It is in this last case that you may have trouble with ligatures. If the `.UC` macro were defined as shown in the previous example, the line:

```
.UC troff
```

might produce the following output:

TROﬀ

To have the macro work correctly, we would need to turn ligatures off (`.lg  0`) for the duration of the translation.

▪ Output Line Numbering ▪

Do you remember the treatment of the `proof` shell script in Chapter 12? It was such a long example that it required line numbers that could be referred to later in the text. The `nroff` and `troff` programs provide requests that allow you to automatically number output lines as was done in that example.

The `.nm` (*number*) request turns numbering on or off. The request:

```
.nm [±]N
```

will turn numbering on, with the next line numbered *N*. For example, the next paragraph is numbered with `.nm 1`.

1 A 3-digit arabic number followed by a space is placed at the start of each line.
2 (Blank lines and lines containing formatter requests do not count.) The line length is
3 not changed, so this results in a protruding right column, as in this paragraph. You may
4 need to decrease the line length (by `\w'000 'u`) if you are numbering filled text
5 rather than an example in no-fill mode. (Be sure to notice the space following the three
6 zeroes.) We'll do that from now on, so only the current paragraph will protrude.

There are several optional arguments as well: a step value, the separation

2 between the number and the beginning of the line, and an indent that will be added
to the line. By default, the step value is 1, the separation is 1, and the indent is 0.

4 For example, if you specified:

```
.nm 1 2
```

6 every second line would be numbered, as was done at the start of this paragraph.

The `.nn` (*not numbered*) request allows you to temporarily suspend numbering for a specified number of lines, as was done for this paragraph using the request
`.nn 4`. The specified number of lines is not counted. This could be useful if you
were interspersing numbered lines of code with a textual discussion.

To turn numbering off entirely, use `.nm` without any arguments. We'll do

8 that now.

The last line number used by `.nm` is saved in the register `ln`, and it is possible
to restart numbering relative to that number by preceding the initial line number you
give to `.nm` with a + or a −. For example, to restart numbering at exactly the point
it was turned off, you can use this request:

```
.nm +0
```

Let's do that now. As you can see, numbering resumes just where it left off, with

10 the same step value and indent, as if no intervening lines had been present. After
this line, we'll turn numbering off entirely.

When using `.nm` in fill mode, you have to watch for breaks. Because `.nm` itself
does not cause a break, it make take effect on the output line above where you expect it.
You may need to force an explicit break before `.nm` to make sure numbering starts on
the next line.

• Change Bars •

The `.mc` (*margin character*) request allows you to print "change bars" or other marks |
in the margin, as was done with this paragraph. This is especially useful if you are |
revising a document, and want to indicate to reviewers which sections have changed.

You can specify any single character as the margin character—so don't restrict
yourself to change bars when thinking up uses for this request. For example, you could
use an arrow, or the left-hand character (\ (lh) to draw attention to a particular point in
the text, like this. (These characters are oddly named. The right-hand character ☞
(\ (rh) is a left-hand that points to the right (☞); the left-hand character (\ (lh) is a
right hand that points to the left (☜). These characters are mapped onto arrows on
some output devices.)

You can control the distance the mark character appears from the margin with an
optional second argument. If no argument is given, the previous value is used; if there
is no previous value, the default distance is `0.2i` in `nroff` and `1m` in `troff`.

Incidentally, on many UNIX systems, there is a version of `diff`, called `diffmk`, that will compare two versions of a file, and produce a third file containing `.mc` requests to mark the differences. Additions and changes are marked with a bar in the margin, as shown previously. Deletions are marked with an asterisk.

In our business, we find this very useful for producing interim drafts of technical manuals. We archive the first draft of the manual, as it was turned in to our client. Then, after review changes have been incorporated, we use `diffmk` to produce an annotated version for second draft review:

```
$ diffmk draft1 draft2 marked_draft
$ ditroff ... marked_draft
```

This could also be done by manually inserting `.mc` requests as the edits were made. But, as stated in Chapter 12, why not let the computer do the dirty work?

▪ Form Letters ▪

No formatter would be complete without the ability to create form letters that merge existing text with externally supplied data. The `nroff` and `troff` programs are no exception in providing requests to handle this type of problem.

The `.rd` (*read*) request allows you to read from standard input. This request prints a prompt on standard error (the user's terminal) and reads input up to a pair of newlines. For example, you could have a form letter constructed like this:

```
.nf
.rd Enter_the_person's_name
.rd Enter_the_company
.rd Enter_the_street
.rd Enter_the_city,_state,_and_zip
.sp
.fi
Dear
.rd Enter_the_salutation
.sp
       .
       .
       .
```

Unfortunately, `.rd` terminates the prompt at the first space, and does not recognize quotation marks to delimit an entire string as the prompt. As a result, for a wordy prompt, you must tie the string together using an unobtrusive character like an underscore, as was done here.

Here's what would happen when this letter is formatted:

```
$ nroff letter | lp
```

```
Enter_the_person's_name:  Tim O'Reilly
```

```
Enter_the_company:   O'Reilly & Associates, Inc.
```

```
Enter_the_street:   981 Chestnut Street

Enter_the_city,_state,_and_zip:   Newton, MA 02164

Enter_the_salutation:   Tim:
```

Note that a colon is appended to the prompt, and that the *RETURN* key must be pressed twice after each response. If no prompt is specified, `.rd` will ring the terminal bell when it expects input.

In addition, the input need not come from the keyboard. It can come from a pipe or from a file. There are two other requests that come in handy to create a true form letter generation capability.

The `.nx` (*next*) request causes the formatter to switch to the specified file to continue processing. Unlike the `.so` request discussed in Chapter 4, it doesn't return to the current file. The `.ex` request tells the formatter to quit.

You can put these requests together with `.rd`. First, create a list of variable data (like names and addresses) either in a file or as the output of a database program. Then pipe this file to the formatter while it is processing a letter constructed like this:

```
.nf
.rd
.rd
.rd
.sp
.fi
Dear
.rd
```

Body of letter here

```
Sincerely,



Jane Doe
.bp
.nx letter
```

The `.nx` request at the end of the form letter causes the file to reinvoke itself when formatting is complete. Assuming that the standard input contains a sequence of name, street, city (*et al*), and salutation lines, one line for each `.rd` request, and address block, in the data file, that are each separated by pairs of newlines, you can generate an endless sequence of letters.

However, be warned that formatting will continue in an endless loop, even when the standard input has run out of data, unless you terminate processing. This is where `.ex` comes in. By putting it at the end of the list of names coming from standard input, you tell the formatter to quit when all the data has been used.

The command line to produce this marvel (assuming a form letter in a file called `letter` and a list of names followed by an `.ex` request in a file called `names`) would be:

```
$ cat names | nroff letter | lp
```

or:

```
$ nroff < names | lp
```

It is possible to imagine a more extensive data entry facility, in which a variety of blank forms are constructed using `troff`, and filled in with the help of a data entry front end.* To generalize the facility, you could associate the various fields on the form with number register or string names, and then interpolate the number or string registers to actually fill in the form.

This approach would allow you to reuse repeated data items without having to query for them again. Even more to the point, it would allow you to construct the data entry facility with a program other than `troff` (which would allow features such as data entry validation and editing, as well as increased speed). The data entry front end would simply need to create as output a data file containing string and number register definitions.

▪ Reading in Other Files or Program Output ▪

In addition to `.nx`, don't forget the `.so` (*source*) request, which allows you to read in the contents of another file, and then return to the current file.

We've mentioned this request briefly in the context of reading in macro definitions. However, you can also use it to read in additional text. In our business, we've found it very useful in certain types of manuals to break the document into many separate files read in by `.so`. For example, we often need to write alphabetically-ordered reference sections in programming manuals. Unfortunately, the developers often haven't finalized their procedure names. If the section consists of a list of `.so` requests:

```
.so  BEGIN_MODULE
.so  BUFFER
.so  CONFIGURE
        .
        .
        .
```

the job of reorganization is trivial—all you need to do is change the filenames and real-phabetize the list.

---

*For this idea, I am indebted to a posting on Usenet, the UNIX bulletin board network, by Mark Wallen of the Institute for Cognitive Science at UC San Diego (Usenet Message-ID: <203@sdics.UUCP>, dated June 13, 1986).

The only caution, which was mentioned previously in Chapter 8, is that you can't include data that must be handled by a preprocessor, such as tables and equations. A quick look at the command line:

$ **tbl** *file* | **nroff**

will show you that the preprocessor is done with the file before the formatter ever has a chance to read in the files called for by the `.so` request. Some systems have a command called `soelim` that reads in the files called for by `.so`. If you use `soelim` to start the file into the pipeline, there is no problem.

One useful tip: if you are using `soelim`, but for some reason you *don't* want `soelim` to read in a file because you would rather it were read in by `troff`, use `'so` rather than `.so` to read in the file. The `soelim` command will ignore the `'so` request.

Another interesting request is `.sy`. This request executes a specified system command. If the command has output, it is not interpolated into the `troff` output stream, nor is it saved. However, you can redirect it into a file, and read that file into `troff` with `.cf` (or with `.so`, if you want it processed by `troff` instead of sent directly to the output stream).

What's in a Macro Package?

In Chapters 4, 14, and 15, you've seen almost all of the individual formatting requests that `nroff` and `troff` provide, and many examples of groups of requests working together in macros. However, writing individual macros is still a far cry from putting together a complete package.

In Chapters 5 and 6, you've seen the features built into the `ms` and `mm` macro packages, so you can imagine the amount and complexity of macro definitions. Perhaps you have even looked at a macro package and determined that it was impossible to decipher. Nonetheless, it is possible even as a beginner to write your own macro package or to make extensions to one of the existing packages.

In this chapter, we'll look at the structure of a macro package—the essentials that allow you to handle basic page formatting. Then, in the next chapter, we'll look at a macro package with extensions for formatting large technical manuals or books. Even if you have no plans to write a new macro package, this chapter will help you understand and work with existing packages.

· Just What Is a Macro Package, Revisited ·

When considering what a macro package is, you might think only of the visible features provided by macros in existing macro packages. But a macro package is more than a collection of user macros that implement various features. Failing to understand this fact might cause someone to import an `mm` macro into an `ms`-based macro package, and never understand why this macro fails to work.

Individual macros are dependent upon other elements of the macro package, which sometimes makes it hard to isolate a particular macro, even for purposes of understanding what it does. These interdependencies also make it difficult to understand what a macro package is doing. That is why we want to look at the underlying structure of a macro package, and not just the obvious features it provides. We want to look first at what a macro package *must* do before we look at what it *can* do.

A macro package is a structure for producing *paged* documents. The `nroff` and `troff` formatters do the actual collecting and formatting of lines of text, as steadily as a bricklayer placing bricks in a row. But they do not define the structure that is so obvious by the end result. Fundamentally, it is the macro package that defines the placement of lines on a page. At a minimum, a macro package must set traps and create macros to handle page transitions. It usually also defines the layout of the physical page.

A macro package may also provide a way to arrange the parts of a documents and affect their appearance. Remember the distinction we made earlier between *formatting* and *formats*. A format reflects the type of document being produced, just as a floor plan reflects the functions of rooms in a building. For instance, a technical manual might consist of chapters and sections that require headings. Other elements might be bulleted lists and numbered lists, a table of contents, and an index. These elements help readers to identify and to locate important parts of the document. But these features—so obviously important to users—are really not the essential elements in a macro package.

Page formatting is the foundation of a macro package, and this foundation must be solid before you can build a variety of custom document formats.

New or Extended?

The first question to ask when you contemplate writing a whole new package is whether you need to do it all yourself or can simply build on an existing package.

There are benefits to either approach. The existing macro packages are quite complex (especially mm). It can be easier to start over, writing only the macros you need, than to learn the intricate internals of ms or mm. A custom macro package can be quite small, including only macros for page transition (which can be minimal, as we shall see) and whatever other macros you want. This is the best approach if you have something specific in mind.

As with all programming projects, though, you may find your package growing larger than intended, as your needs and understanding grow and you start to add features. A macro package begun haphazardly can also end that way, without any consistent structure.

If you do find yourself wanting to create an entire macro package, rather than just a few macros, you should think about modular programming techniques. Modular programming suggests that you break the tasks to be performed by a program into the smallest possible functional units, then build up larger tasks with each of these smaller units. This not only helps with debugging and testing of new macros, but also makes it much easier to write macros, because you end up with a library of low-level general-purpose macros that perform important functions. You don't have to reinvent the wheel for each new macro.

There are numerous advantages to building on the existing packages, especially if you want to have a general-purpose package:

- They already contain a wide range of useful macros that you not only can use directly, but can call on within new macros.

- They are tested and proven. Unless you are very experienced at text processing, it is difficult to foresee all of the kinds of problems that can arise. When you write your own package, you may be surprised by the kinds of errors that are filtered out by the design of ms or mm.

- If you are familiar with ms or mm, adding a few extended macros to your repertoire is easier than learning an entire new package.

- It can be easier than you expect to modify or add to them.

In our own work, we have chosen to extend the ms macro package rather than to build an entirely new package. In this chapter, though, we're going to take a hybrid approach. We'll build a minimal ms-like package that illustrates the essentials of a macro package and allows users who don't have access to the full ms package to make use of some of the extensions described in this and later chapters.

In this "mini-ms" package, we have sometimes pared down complex macros so it is easier to understand what they are doing. We try to uncover the basic mechanism of a macro (what it *must* do). As a caveat to this approach, we realize that simplifying a macro package can reduce its functionality. However, we see it as part of the learning process, to recognize that a macro in a certain situation fails to work and understand the additional code needed to make it work.

Implementing a Macro Package

As discussed in Chapter 4, the actual option to nroff and troff to invoke a macro package is −m*x*, which tells the program to look in the directory /usr/lib/tmac for a file with a name of the form tmac.*x*. This means you can invoke your own macro package from the command line simply by storing the macro definitions in a file with the appropriate pathname. This file will be added to any other files in the formatting run.

If you don't have write privileges for /usr/lib/tmac, you can't create the tmac.*x* file (although your system administrator might be willing to do it for you). But you can still create a macro package. You will simply have to read it into the formatter some other way. You can either

- include it at the start of each file with the .so request:

  ```
  .so /usr/fred/newmacros
  ```

- or list it on the command line as the first file to be formatted:

  ```
  $ nroff /usr/fred/newmacros myfile
  ```

Nor do the macros need to be stored in a single file. Especially if you are using a package as you develop it, you may want to build it as a series of small files that are called in by a single master file. You may also want to have different versions of some macros for `nroff` and `troff`. So, for example, the mh (Hayden) macros used to format this book are contained in many different files, which are all read in by `.so` requests in `/usr/lib/tmac/tmac.h`:

```
.so /work/macros/hayden/startup
.so /work/macros/hayden/hidden
.so /work/macros/hayden/ch.heads.par
.so /work/macros/hayden/display
.so /work/macros/hayden/ex.figs
.so /work/macros/hayden/vimacs
.so /work/macros/hayden/lists
.so /work/macros/hayden/stuff
.so /work/macros/hayden/index
.so /work/macros/hayden/cols
```

Or, like mm, you might have two large files, one for `nroff` and one for `troff`. In `/usr/lib/tmac/tmac.m`, you find:

```
.if n .so /usr/lib/macros/mmn
.if t .so /usr/lib/macros/mmt
```

In extending an existing macro package, you are not restricted to creating a few local macro definitions that must be read into each file. You can make a complete copy of one of the existing packages, which you can then edit and add to. Or even better, you can read the existing package into your own package with `.so`, and then make additions, deletions, and changes. For example, you might create a superset of ms as follows:

```
.\" /usr/lib/tmac/tmac.S - superset of ms - invoke as -mS
.so /usr/lib/tmac/tmac.s      \" Read in existing package
.so /usr/macros/S.headings
.so /usr/macros/S.examples
.so /usr/macros/S.toc
      .
      .
      .
```

▪ Building a Consistent Framework ▪

One of the chief factors that distinguishes a macro package from a random collection of macros is that the package builds a consistent framework in which the user can work.

This consistent framework includes:

▪ Setting traps to define the top and bottom of each page. This is the one essential element of a macro package, because it is the one thing `nroff` and `troff` do not do.

- Setting default values for other aspects of page layout, such as the page offset (left margin) and line length. (The default page offset in `nroff` is 0, which is not likely to be a useful value, and `troff`'s default line length of 6.5 inches is really too long for a typeset line.)

- Setting default values for typographical elements in `troff` such as which fonts are mounted, the point size and vertical spacing of body copy and footnotes, adjustment type, and hyphenation.

- Giving the user a method to globally modify the default values set in the macro package, or temporarily modify them and then return to the defaults.

In a very simple macro package, we might set up default values for `troff` like this:

```
.po 1i       \" Set page offset to one inch
.ll 6i       \" Set line length to six inches
.ad l        \" Adjust left margin only
.hy 14       \" Hyphenate, using all hyphenation rules
.wh 0 NP     \" Set new page trap at the top of the page
.            \" (see below for details)
.wh -1i FO \" Set footer trap
```

(We are assuming here that `troff`'s default values for point size and vertical spacing are acceptable. In `otroff`, we also need to mount the default fonts with `.fp`, as described in Chapter 4; in `ditroff`, a default set of fonts is already mounted.)

Simply setting up explicit default values like this will do the trick, but for a more effective and flexible macro package, you should take the further step of storing default values into number registers. This has numerous advantages, as we'll see in a moment.

Using Number Registers to Increase Flexibility

Writing `troff` macros is essentially a kind of programming. If you pay heed to the principles learned by programmers, you will find that your macros are more effective, if at first somewhat more complex to write and read.

One important lesson from programming is not to use explicit (so called "hard-coded") values. For example, if you supply the indent in a paragraph macro with an explicit value, such as:

```
.in 5n
```

you make it difficult for users to change this value at a later time. But if you write:

```
.in \\n(INu
```

the user can change the indent of all paragraphs simply by changing the value stored in number register `IN`. Of course, for this to work, you must give a default value to the `IN` register.

In programming, the process of setting variables to a predefined starting value is called *initialization*. To give you an idea of the kinds of variables you might want to initialize, Table 16-1 lists the values stored into number registers by the `ms` macros.

TABLE 16-1. Number Registers Used in ms

Description	Name	Value	
		troff	nroff
Top (header) margin	HM	1i	1i
Bottom (footer) margin	FM	1i	1i
Point size	PS	10p	1P
Vertical spacing	VS	12p	1P
Page offset	PO	26/27i	0
Line length	LL	6i	6i
Title length	LT	6i	6i
Footnote line length	FL	\\n(LLu*11/12	\\n(LLu*11/12
Paragraph indent	PI	5n	5n
Quoted paragraph indent	QI	5n	5n
Interparagraph spacing	PD	0.3v	1v

The mm package uses *many* more number registers—in particular, it uses number registers as flags to globally control the operation of macros. For example, in addition to registers similar to those shown for ms in Table 16-1, there are registers for paragraph type, numbering style in headings, hyphenation, spacing between footnotes, as well as counters for automatic numbering of figures, examples, equations, tables, and section headings. (See Appendix B for a complete listing.) However, the registers used in ms should give you a sufficient idea of the kinds of values that can and should be stored in registers.

An Initialization Sequence

In the ms macro package, a major part of the initialization sequence is performed by the .IZ macro.* This macro is executed at the start of a formatting run; then it is removed. Let's take a look at a *much* simplified version of the initialization sequence for an ms-like package:

```
.de IZ            \" Initialization macro
.                 \" Initialize Number Registers
.nr HM 1i         \" Heading Margin
.nr FM 1i         \" Footing Margin
.nr PS 10         \" Point Size
.nr VS 12         \" Vertical Spacing
.nr PO 1i         \" Page Offset
.nr LL 6i         \" Line Length
```

---

*There's no real reason why this sequence needs to be put in a macro at all, other than the consistency of putting two backslashes before number registers when they are read in.

```
.nr LT 6i                    \" Length of Titles for .tl
.nr FL \\n(LLu*11/12         \" Footnote Length
.nr PI 5n                    \" Paragraph Indent
.nr QI 5n                    \" Quoted Paragraph Indent
.nr PD 0.3v                  \" Interparagraph Spacing
.                  \" Set Page Dimensions through requests
.ps \\n(PS
.vs \\n(VS
.po \\n(POu
.ll \\n(LLu
.lt \\n(LTu
.hy 14        \" Specify hyphenation rules
.             \" Set Page Transition Traps
.wh 0 NP
.wh -\\n(FMu FO
.wh -\\n(FMu/2u BT
..
.IZ                    \" Execute IZ
.rm IZ                 \" Remove IZ
```

As you can see, the initialization sequence stores default values into registers, then actually puts them into effect with individual formatting requests.

A number of the points shown in this initialization sequence will be a bit obscure, particularly those relating to trap positions for top and bottom margins. We'll return to the topic of page transitions shortly.

A Reset Macro

After you have initialized number registers, the next question is how to make use of the default values in coding. Some registers, like a paragraph indent, will be used in a paragraph macro. But where, for example, might you use the LL register?

First of all, as suggested, putting default values into number registers allows users to change values without modifying the macro package itself. For instance, a user can globally change the interparagraph spacing just by putting a new value into the PD register.

However, the package itself can use these registers to periodically *reset* the default state of various formatting characteristics.

The ms package defines a macro called .RT (*reset*), which is invoked from within every paragraph macro. The .RT macro

- turns off centering—.ce 0;

- turns off underlining—.ul 0;

- restores the original line length—.ll \\n(LLu;

- restores the original point size and vertical spacing—`.ps \\n(PS` and `.vs \\n(VS`;

- restores the indent that was in effect before any `.IP`, `.RS`, or `.RE` macros were called (too complex to show here);

- changes back to the font in position 1—`.ft 1`;

- turns off emboldening for font 1—`.bd 1`;

- sets tab stops every 5n—`.ta 5n 10n 15n 20n...`;

- turns on fill mode—`.fi`.

This is part of the ms error recovery scheme. Rather than aborting when it encounters an error, ms frequently invokes the `.RT` macro to restore reasonable values for many common parameters.

If you have used ms for a while, and then switch to another package, you may find all kinds of errors cropping up, because you've come to rely on this mechanism to keep unwanted changes from propagating throughout a document. For example, suppose you create a macro that decrements the line length:

```
.ll -5n
```

but you forget to increment it again. You may never notice the fact, because ms will restore the line length at the next paragraph macro. Other packages are far less forgiving.

Unless you plan to explicitly test for and terminate on error conditions, it is wise to implement a reset facility like that used by ms.

A simple ms-like reset macro follows:

```
.de RT \" Reset
.ce 0           \" Turn off centering, if in effect
.ul 0           \" Turn off underlining, if in effect
.ll \\n(LLu     \" Restore default line length
.ps \\n(PS      \" Restore default point size
.vs \\n(VS      \" Restore default vertical spacing
.ft 1           \" Return to font in position 1
.ta 5n 10n 15n 20n 25n 30n 35n 40n 45n 50n 55n 60n 65n 70n
.fi             \" Restore fill mode
..
```

The ms version of `.RT` also ends any diversion invoked outside of the standard ms macros that create diversions. Thus, a reset may occur within a keep (`.KS`, `.KE`), footnotes (`.FS`, `.FE`), boxed material (`.B1`, `.B2`), and tables (`.TS`, `.TE`) without ending the diversion.

If you look at the actual ms reset macro, you will see that it calls another macro, named `.BG`, the very first time it is itself called. The `.BG` macro removes the macros associated with the unused Bell Labs technical memorandum formats (because the format has already been determined at that point). Like `.IZ`, the `.BG` macro is only called once during a formatting run. In our emulation, we don't make use of the

Technical Memorandum macros so we have not implemented the `.BG` macro. However, one could easily apply the idea behind the `.BG` macro: to execute a macro before we begin processing the body of a document. This can be useful if a format requires a number of preliminary or header macros that supply information about the document.

▪ Page Transitions ▪

A single page transition macro is the only macro that *must* be implemented for `nroff` and `troff` to produce paged output. An example of this simplest of all possible macro packages follows.*

```
.de NP      \" New Page
'bp
'sp 1i
'ns
..
.wh -1.25i NP
.br
.rs
.sp |1i
```

The page transition is triggered by a *trap* set 1.25 inches from the bottom of the page. When output text reaches the trap, the `.NP` macro is executed, which breaks the page (but not the line), spaces down 1 inch, and enters no-space mode. The three lines following the macro and trap definition take care of the special case of the first page, for which the `.NP` macro is not invoked.

The `.wh` request, which sets the location of the traps used for page transition, interprets the value 0 as the top of the page. Negative values are interpreted relative to the bottom of the page. So, for example, assuming that the page length is 11 inches, the requests:

```
.wh 10i BT \" Bottom Title Macro
```

and:

```
.wh -1i BT \" Bottom Title Macro
```

are equivalent. The second form is the most common.

This simple ''package'' provides only one macro for page transition. The bottom margin of the text portion of the page is determined by the trap location; the top margin by a spacing request in the macro executed at the trap. However, it is far more common to work with at least two page transition macros: one for the page top and one for the bottom.

---

*This ''package'' was contributed by Will Hopkins of VenturCom, Inc.

An example of a two-trap, two-macro macro package is given below:

```
.wh 0 NP
.wh -1i FO
.de NP                          \"New Page
'sp 1i
.tl 'Top of Page \\n%'''  \".tl does not cause break
'sp |2i
'ns
..
.de FO                          \"Page Footer
'sp .25i
.tl ''Page Bottom''
'bp
..
```

A trap is set at the top of the page (.wh 0) to execute the .NP macro. This macro provides a top margin and outputs a title in that space. The formatter begins processing lines of text until the bottom of the page trap is encountered. It invokes the .FO macro, which supplies a footer margin and outputs a centered title. The .FO macro then causes a page break, which in turn invokes .NP at the top of the new page. It is important that both of these macros avoid causing a break, so that text in fill mode will continue smoothly onto the next page.

By setting traps for both the top and bottom of a page you have more control over the size of the bottom and top margins, the placement of headers and footers, and advanced features like footnotes and multiple-column processing.

Take some time to experiment with this bare bones macro package. If you place it in a file, such as pagemacs, you can use it to format text files, as in the following example:

```
$ nroff pagemacs text
```

No-Space Mode in Page Transitions

No-space mode is often used in a page transition macro to keep space from being output at the top of a page. It is standard page makeup for the top line of each page to begin at the same point. Without no-space mode, a spacing request (such as prespacing in a paragraph macro) that falls just before the page transition would result in space being output at the top of the page, causing uneven positioning of the top line of the page.

Any output text lines restore space mode, so you don't have to explicitly turn it back on. However, if you explicitly want to put space at the top of the page (to paste in a figure, for example), use .rs (*restore spacing*) before the spacing request. The following sequence can be used to start a new page and space down 2 inches below the top margin:

```
'bp
.rs
'sp 2i
```

This works in all cases, except on the first page. You must force a break on the first page before you can restore spacing. An `.fl` request will do the trick:

```
.fl
.rs
.sp 3i
.ce
A Title on a Title Page
.bp
```

The `.fl` request is useful when you want to flush the line buffer and cause a break.

The First Page

As you might expect from the previous example, the first page is unlike others that follow it. That is because there is no automatic transition to the first page. To get around this, the formatter causes a "pseudo-page transition" when it first encounters a break or begins processing text outside a diversion.

For the top of page trap to be executed on the first page, you must set the trap and define the top of page macro before specifying any request that causes a break or initiates processing. You can test this with the sample macros by putting an explicit `.br` request before the `.NP` macro definition. After that test, try replacing `.br` with a `.tl` request. Even though this request does not cause a break, it does initiate processing of text, and so the `.NP` macro is not executed.

▪ Page Transitions in ms ▪

Let's take a closer look now at the trap positions we set in the initialization sequence for our ms-like package, together with the definitions of the macros placed at those positions:

```
.de IZ
    .
    .
    .
.                       \" Set Page Transition Traps
.wh 0 NP
.wh -\\n(FMu FO
.wh -\\n(FMu/2u BT
.                       \" Define Page Transition Macros
..
.de NP                  \"      New Page Macro
'sp \\n(HMu/2u
.PT
```

```
'sp |\\n(HMu
'ns
..
.de FO                  \"       Footer Macro
'bp
..
.de PT                  \"       Page Top Title Macro
.tl '\\*(LH'\\*(CH'\\*(RH'
..
.de BT                  \"       Bottom Title Macro
.tl '\\*(LF'\\*(CF'\\*(RF'
'sp .5i
..
```

You'll notice a couple of differences from our earlier example. Instead of specifying "hard-coded" values for trap locations, we have set up a top margin value in the register HM (*header margin*) and a bottom margin value in FM (*footer margin*).

Now we have three trap locations and four page transition macros. In the simplified form shown here, you may wonder why so many macros are used for this simple task. We'll look at that later, as we show some of the additional things that are done in these macros. But for the moment, let's focus on what these macros are. Their trap locations are shown in Figure 16-1.

- .NP (*new page*) is invoked by a trap at the top of each page (.wh 0 NP). It spaces down ½ the distance specified in the HM register, calls the PT macro, and then spaces down the full distance specified by the header margin.

- .PT (*page title*) prints out a three-part title consisting of user-definable strings LH, CH, and RH (*left header*, *center header*, and *right header*).

- .FO (*footer*) is invoked by a trap at the distance from the bottom of the page specified by the FM register (.wh −\\n(FMu FO). This macro causes a break to a new page. Note the use of 'bp rather than .bp so that any partially filled line is not output, but is held till the next page.

- .BT (*bottom title*) is invoked by a trap at ½ the distance from the bottom of the page specified by the FM register (.wh −\\n(FMu/2u BT).

Although this sequence is different than our earlier example, it is about as easy to understand. The main difference, however, is that there are two traps at the bottom of the page. The first (FO) causes a page break, and the second (BT) places the footer. Even though the first trap caused a page break, *the formatter keeps going till it reaches the true bottom of the page specified by the page length*. On its way, it passes the second trap that invokes .BT.

The use of the four page transition macros is slightly inconsistent in ms; .PT is invoked from .NP, but .BT, which could just as well be invoked by .FO, is instead invoked by a trap.

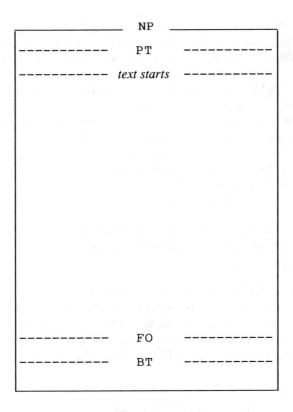

Fig. 16-1. Top and Bottom Margins

Headers and Footers

Most books, and many shorter documents, include headers and footers. In books, headers often include the title of the book on the left-hand page, and the title of the chapter on the right. The footer typically includes the page number, either centered or in the lower outside corner, alternating from left to right. (Although all three elements are usually present, they can be in different positions depending on the book design.)

As previously mentioned, the `.tl` request was designed specifically for producing the three-part titles used in headers and footers. The `ms` package uses this request in both the `PT` and `BT` macros, filling the three fields with symmetrically named string invocations. If the string is undefined, the field is blank.

The macro package itself may define one or more of the fields. The `.IZ` macro from `ms` contains this piece of code:

```
.if "\\*(CH"" .ds CH "- \\\\n(PN -
.if n .ds CF "\\*(DY
```

The `ms` macros define the center header as the page number set off by hyphens. For `nroff` only, the center footer is set to the current date. (An `nroff`-formatted document is assumed to be a draft, but a `troff`-formatted document is assumed to be final camera-ready copy.)

The `ms` macros transfer the page number from the `%` register to one called `PN`. Note the number of backslashes required to get the page number output at the proper time—not in the string definition, nor in the macro definition, but at the time the title is output.

If you don't like this arrangement, you can simply redefine the strings (including redefining them to nothing if you want nothing to be printed). As a developer of macros built on top of `ms`, you could, for example, have a chapter heading macro automatically set the chapter title into one of these strings. (More on this later.)

Headers and footers are often set in a different type and size than the body of the book. If you are using a standard macro package, font and size changes can simply be embedded in the header or footer strings:

```
.ds LH "\fIAn Introduction to Text Processing\fP
```

Or, if you are writing your own macros or redefining an underlying package like `ms`, you can embed the changes directly into the `.tl` request:

```
.tl '\s-2\\*(LF'\\*(CF'\\*(RF\s0'
```

Another point: it is often desirable to alternate headers and footers on odd and even pages. For example, if you want to put a book title at the outside upper corner of a left-hand (even) page, and the chapter title at the outside upper corner of a right-hand (odd) page, you can't really work within the structure `ms` provides.

To do this properly, you could use a construct like the following within your `.PT` macro:

```
.if e .tl '\\*(TI''
.if o .if \\n%-1 .tl '''\\*(CH'
```

where the string `TI` holds the title of the book, and `CH` holds the title of the chapter. If it's an odd page, we also test that it's not the first page. By invoking specific strings, you do lose the generality of the mechanism provided by `ms`.

Page Numbers in Three-Part Titles

Inasmuch as the chief application of three-part titles is in producing header and footer lines from within page transition macros, there is a special syntax for including page numbers. A `%` character anywhere in a title will be replaced with the current page number. This saves the trouble of having to do a proper number register interpolation and makes it easier for unsophisticated users of `ms` or `mm` to include page numbers in header and footer strings.

Whenever `nroff` or `troff` makes use of a character in a special way, you can be sure there is a back door that allows you to change that character. The `.pc` (*page character*) request allows you to specify that some other character than `%` should perform this function:

```
.pc ^        \" Use ^ instead of % to print page # in .tl
```

This does not change the name of the `%` number register, which also contains the page number.

Title Length

The other thing you can adjust is the length of the three-part title produced by .tl. Usually it is set to the same length as a text line, but this need not be so. Title length is specified independently of line length with the .lt (*length [of] title*) request. For example:

```
.lt 6.5i
```

The title length is *not* independent of the page offset, so if you want a title that is longer than the line length, yet centered on the page, you will need to muck with the page offset as well. (Note that this is most likely to occur within a page transition macro.)

```
.po 1i                          \" Page Layout Defaults
.ll 6.5i
   .

   .

   .
.lt 7i
.tl 'Alcuin User's Guide''%'   \" Title will extend 1/2 inch
   .                            \" past right margin

   .

   .
.po -.25i
.lt 7i
.tl 'Alcuin User's Guide''%'   \" Title will extend 1/4 inch
.po +.25i                       \" on either side
```

An .lt request without an argument will restore the previous title length.

▪ Some Extensions to the Basic Package ▪

Thus far, we've looked at what it will take to implement a small ms-like macro package. Now let's look at some extensions to the basic structure of the package that will make it more flexible. These extensions could be added to the minimal package shown earlier in this chapter, or they could be added to a full ms package, as we have done at our own site.

Changing Page Size

As mentioned earlier, the initialization sequence usually sets up default values for line length, page offset, and the placement of the top and bottom traps. In the standard ms package, all of these values are set up to produce an $8^1/2$-by-11 inch page.

This is fine for nroff, but with troff, one might well want to produce a different page size. For example, many books are typeset for a $5^1/2$-by-$8^1/2$ inch page.

The most obvious move is to change the page length:

```
.pl 8.5i
```

and then reset the line length, title length, and page offset using the standard registers
ms provides.

This may not work if your output device uses continuous-roll paper, such as a
typesetter. However, in nroff, or when using troff with a sheet-fed laser printer,
this may split your formatted output pages across physical sheets of paper. (Some devices translate a .bp into a page eject code or *formfeed*; others simply add blank lines
to push text onto the next physical page. For this reason, it is perhaps preferable to
think of .pl as the *paper length* rather than the *page length*.)

In addition, when you are printing a small page, it is nice to print cut marks to
show the location of the page boundaries. If you change the page length, any cut marks
you place will be off the page that troff knows about, and will not be printed.

For both of these reasons, we took a different approach. We modified the ms
.IZ macro so that changing the header and footer margins would effectively change
the page size, instead of just the margins. (In standard ms, you can change the size of
the top and bottom margins, but this doesn't change the page size, because the placement of the footers is fixed after the initialization macro has been called. The trap position for FO is reset at the top of every page, thus taking into account changes in the
value of the FM register. But the trap position for BT is never touched after .IZ has
been executed.)

In our package, we decided to set up some standard page sizes as part of .IZ.
In our business, writing and producing technical manuals, we often print books in both
sizes. Early drafts are printed on the laser printer in 8½ by 11 format; later drafts and
final camera-ready copy are produced in 5½ by 8½ format. We also produce quick-
reference documents in a narrow 6-panel card or pamphlet. The user selects the size by
specifying a command-line switch. This approach has the advantage of letting the user
change all of the parameters associated with a given size with one easy command.

The .IZ macro in our mini-ms package now looks like this:

```
.de IZ                    \" Initialization macro
.                         \" Initialize Number Registers
.                         \" Quick Reference Card size
.if \\nS=2 \{\
.         nr pW 3.5i      \" Page Width
.         nr tH 1.25i     \" Trim Height adjustment
.         nr LL 2.8i      \" Line Length
.         nr LT 2.8i\}    \" Title Length
.                         \" 5 1/2 by 8 1/2 size
.ie \\nS=1 \{\
.         nr pW 5.5i      \" Page Width
.         nr tH 1.25i     \" Trim Height adjustment
.         nr LL 4.25i     \" Line Length
.         nr LT 4.25i\}   \" Title Length
.                         \" 8 1/2 by 11 size
.el \{\
.         nr pW 0         \" Page Width
```

```
.          nr tH 0              \" Trim Height adjustment
.          nr LL 6i             \" Line Length
.          nr LT 6i\}           \" Title Length
.                       \"Values independent of page size
.nr FM 1i                       \" Footer Margin
.nr HM 1i                       \" Header Margin
.nr PO 1i                       \" Page Offset
.nr PS 10                       \" Point Size
.nr VS 12                       \" Vertical Spacing
.nr FL \\n(LLu*11/12            \" Footnote Length
.nr PI 5n                       \" Paragraph Indent
.nr QI 5n                       \" Quoted Paragraph Indent
.nr PD 0.3v                     \" Interparagraph Spacing
.               \" Set Page Dimensions through requests
.ps \\n(PS
.vs \\n(VS
.po \\n(POu
.ll \\n(LLu
.lt \\n(LTu
.ft 1
.hy 14                          \" Specify hyphenation rules
.                               \" Set Page Transition Traps
.wh 0 NP                        \" Top of page
.wh -(\\n(FMu+\\n(tHu) FO       \" Footer
.wh -((\\n(FMu/2u)+\\n(tHu) BT \" Bottom titles
.if \\nS .wh -\\n(tHu CM        \" Position of bottom mark
..
```

The .NP macro has been modified as follows:

```
.de NP                       \" New Page Macro
'sp \\n(tHu                  \" Space down by trim height
.ie \\nS \{\
.       CM                   \" If small format, print cut mark
'       sp \\n(HMu/2u-1v\}\" Correct baseline spacing
.el 'sp \\n(HMu/2u           \" Space down by half HM
.PT
'sp |\\n(HMu+\\n(tHu         \" Space to HM plus adjustment
'ns
..
```

By simply setting the S (*size*) register from the command line, the user can choose from one of three different sizes. For example:

    $ **ditroff -Tps -rS1** *textfile* **| devps | lp**

will choose the $5^1/_2$-by-$8^1/_2$ page size.

What we've done here is to assume that the paper size is still 8½ by 11. We've defined a fudge factor, which we've called the *trim height adjustment*, and stored it in a register called `tH`. If the user has set the size register from the command line, we use this adjustment factor to:

- shift the location of the footer trap:

```
.wh -(\\n(FMu+\\n(tHu)  FO
```

- shift the location of the bottom title trap:

```
.wh -((\\n(FMu/2u)+\\n(tHu)  BT
```

- place a new trap to print cut marks at the true bottom of the page:

```
.if \\nS .wh -\\n(tHu CM
```

- space down at the start of the `.NP` macro:

```
'sp \\n(tHu
.ie \\nS \{\
.        CM
'        sp \\n(HMu/2u-1v\}
.el 'sp \\n(HMu/2u
.PT
'sp |\\n(HMu+\\n(tHu
```

Note that in `.NP` we need to adjust for the extra line spacing that occurs as a result of printing the cut marks. Otherwise, the `.PT` macro would be invoked one line lower on a page with cut marks than on one without.

Cut Marks

We've mentioned that if you are producing typeset or laser-printed copy on less than an 8½ by 11 page, it is usually desirable to place marks showing the actual page boundary. The paper is then cut on these marks in preparation for pasteup on camera-ready boards.

As you've seen in the preceding discussion, we print the cut mark at the top of the page from the `.NP` macro, after spacing down by the desired trim height. The cut marks at the bottom of the page are printed by calling the cut mark macro with a trap placed at the trim height from the bottom of the page.

As you'll notice, the execution of the cut mark macro is conditioned on the presence of the `S` register, which indicates that the user has requested a small page.

Here's a simple version of the actual cut mark macro:

```
.de CM                      \" Cut Mark macro
'po -(\\n(pWu-\\n(LLu/2u)   \" Center cut mark around text
.lt \\n(pWu                 \" Set title length for cut mark
'tl '+''+'                  \" Print cut mark
```

```
.lt \\n(LTu                 \" Reset title length
'po +(\\n(pWu-\\n(LLu/2u)   \" Reset page offset
..
```

As with all activity that takes place during the page transition, it is very important that nothing in the cut mark macro causes a break. For this reason, all break causing requests are started with the no-break control character (′), and the cut marks them-selves are printed with `.tl`, which doesn't cause a break. (The other way to avoid breaks is to do all of your page transition work in a different environment, but doing this uses up one of the environments, which might be better used for another purpose.)

We've specified the width of the page in the `pW` register. To center the cut marks around the text, we adjust the page offset by the difference between the page width and half the line length. Then we set the title length to the page width, and actu-ally print the cut marks with `.tl`. Then, of course, we reset the original page offset and title length.

In the implementation shown, we use simple plus signs to create the cut marks. This creates a slight inaccuracy, because the page width will be from end to end of the plus signs, and the height from baseline to baseline, rather from the center of the plus as we'd like.

There are two ways that we could deal with this. One is to fudge the height and the width to account for the character widths. The other is to use a specially drawn mark that will put the actual cut lines at the edge rather than the center of the figure.

A very simple way to do this is to use the box rule, the root-en, and the underrule. Because the cut marks are no longer symmetrical, though, we'll need to give the cut mark macro an argument to specify whether we're at the top or the bottom of the page:

```
.de CM                      \" Cut Mark macro
'po -(\\n(pWu-\\n(LLu/2u)   \" Center cut mark around text
'lt \\n(pWu                 \" Set title length for cut mark
.ie "\\$1"T" 'tl '\(br\(rn''\(rn\(br'   \" Print cut mark
.el 'tl '\(br\(ul''\(ul\(br'
'lt \\n(LTu                 \" Reset title length
'po +(\\n(pWu-\\n(LLu/2u)   \" Reset page offset
..
```

When we invoke `.CM` from within `.NP`, we'll just have to add the argument `T` to specify we're at the top.

The cut marks will look like this:

· Other Exercises in Page Transition ·

We've looked at the basic mechanism for page transition, and shown one way to extend
that mechanism to allow the user to select different page sizes. We have not exhausted
the topic of page transition, however. Before we begin to discuss the development of
macros that prescribe document formats, rather than basic page formatting, we will
briefly consider these topics:

- Footnotes
- Multicolumn processing
- Page top resets
- Handling widows and orphans

Footnotes

Footnotes make page transition an even more complex exercise. Anyone who has typed
footnotes on a typewriter knows the problem. Because the presence of a footnote shor-
tens the space available on the page for regular text, you need to know the size of the
footnote before you know if its reference will fit on the bottom of the current page, or
will be pushed to the top of the next. There is always the possibility of a classic
Catch-22: a footnote whose reference falls at the bottom of the page only if the footnote itself isn't printed there.

Let's look first at a very simple footnote mechanism—one that has a reasonable
chance of failure in the face of heavy demand, but nonetheless illustrates the basic
mechanism at work.

The first thing we need to know is the position of the page bottom trap for a normal page—one without any footnotes. For example, in ms, we know that its location
is -\\n(FMu. (Now ms has a perfectly good footnote mechanism, but for purposes
of argument, we're going to pretend we need to add one.)

All we really need to do, on the simplest level, is to save footnotes in a diversion,
measure them, then move the footer trap back up the page by a distance equal to the
size of the diversion.

In the new page macro, we initialize (reset to 0) a counter (fC) that will tell us if
there are any footnotes on the page and how many. (We want to handle the first footnote differently than others on that page.) We also initialize a bottom position for printing footnotes (Fb) and initialize it with the value of the standard footer margin. (This
will be the starting point that will be decremented as footnotes are encountered.) Last,
we provide a reset that restores the page footer trap at the standard footer margin if it
has been changed because of footnotes on a previous page.

```
.                           \" Add to .NP
.nr fC 0 1                  \" Initialize footnote counter
.nr Fb 0-\\n(FMu            \" Initialize footnote position
.ch FO -\\n(FMu             \" Reset normal footer location
```

Now, a pair of footnote macros are required to open and close a diversion:

```
.de FS              \" Footnote Start
.nr fC 1            \" Set flag that there are footnotes
.ev 1               \" Use environment 1
.da FN              \" Divert text of footnote
.if \\n(fC=1 \{\ \" If first footnote
\l'1i'              \" Print 1 inch line before it
.br\}
..
.de FE              \" Footnote End
.br
.di                 \" End diversion
.ev                 \" Restore environment
.nr Fb -\\n(dn      \" Decrement footnote position by
.                   \" size of diversion;
.                   \" note that Fb is already negative.
.                   \" Reset footer trap
.ie (\\n(nl+1v)>(\\n(.p+\\n(Fb) .ch F0 \\n(nlu+1vu
.el .ch F0 -\\n(Fb
..
```

The footnotes are processed in a separate environment. This environment needs to be initialized, perhaps as part of the `.IZ` macro, or as part of the `.FS` macro the very first time it is called. The latter method makes it easier for users to change settings for this environment. It is recommended that you preserve a separate environment (either 1 or 2) for footnote processing. Here is a sample initialization sequence:

```
.ev 1       \" Initialize first environment for footnotes
.ps 8
.vs 10
.ll \\n(FLu \" FL was initialized to 11/12 of LL
.ev
```

The `.FS` macro opens a diversion (`.da FN`) into which we append the text of the footnote. Before the first footnote on a page, the `.FS` macro adds a one-inch reference line to mark the beginning of footnotes. After we have closed the diversion in the `.FE` macro, we obtain the size of it from the read-write register `.dn`. This amount is used to increase `Fb` (two negatives amounts are added together) and change the location of the footer trap further up the page.

Before changing that trap, the footnote end macro has to find out if the new footer trap will be placed above or below the current location. If the new trap location is below where we are, all is well; the page trap is moved up to that location. However, if the current footnote places the location above the current position, there's going to be trouble. In this case, we need to execute the footer macro immediately.

The `troff` formatter keeps the current page position in the `nl` register, and the page length in the register `.p`. As a result, we can set the trap position based on a conditional:

```
.ie (\\n(nl+1v)>(\\n(.p+\\n(Fb) .ch FO \\n(nlu+1vu
.el .ch FO -\\n(Fb
```

If the footnote won't fit, this code puts the trap one line below the current position; otherwise, the footer trap location is moved up the page.

Now we'll have to redefine the footer macro to print the diverted footnotes, if there are any:

```
.de FO              \" Redefine FO
.if \\n(fC\{\
.ev1                \" Invoke first environment
.nf                 \" Good practice when outputting diversions
.FN                 \" Print diversion
.rm FN              \" Remove printed diversion
.ev\}
'bp                 \" Now break page
..
```

Because the footnote macros are complicated, it might be a useful aside to look at the process of debugging these macros. We used several .tm requests to report (to standard error) on the sequence of events during a formatting run of a file that included footnotes. What we wanted to know was the location of the footer trap and when it was sprung. Inside the .FE macro, we inserted .tm requests to show which of the conditional .ch requests were executed.

```
.ie (\\n(nl+1v)>(\\n(.p+\\n(Fb) \{\
.tm !!!!!! FE: Change trap to current location (\\n(nl+1v)
.ch FO \\n(nlu+1vu \}
.el \{\
.tm !!!!!! FE: Move trap up the page (\\n(Fbu)
.ch FO -\\n(Fb \}
```

Then, inside the .FO macro, we inserted messages to locate two positions on the page: where the footer macro is invoked by the trap and where the footnotes have been output.

```
.de FO
.tm !!!! FO: position is \\n(nl (\\n(.p+\\n(Fb) BEFORE
.
.
.
.tm !!!! FO: position is \\n(nl AFTER footnotes
'bp
..
```

To see these terminal messages without the formatted text, we invoke nroff and redirect output to /dev/null. (tmacpack is a small macro package used for testing these macros.)

```
$ nroff tmacpack textfile > /dev/null
!!!!!! FE: Move trap up the page (-360u)
!!!!!! FE: Move trap up the page (-440u)
!!!!!! FE: Move trap up the page (-520u)
!!!!!! FE: Move trap up the page (-680u)
!!!! FO: position is 1980 (2640+-680) BEFORE
!!!! FO: position is 2420 AFTER footnotes
!!!!!! FE: Move trap up the page (-360u)
!!!!!! FE: Move trap up the page (-440u)
!!!!!! FE: Move trap up the page (-520u)
!!!!!! FE: Change trap to current location (2100+1v)
!!!! FO: position is 2140 (2640+-640) BEFORE
!!!! FO: position is 2580 AFTER footnotes
!!!!!! FE: Move trap up the page (-320u)
!!!! FO: position is 2320 (2640+-320) BEFORE
!!!! FO: position is 2400 AFTER footnotes
```

Part of the reason for making this aside is the difficulty of writing effective footnote macros. It requires a fair amount of testing to make sure they work in all cases. When we spring the footer trap for the second time, the messages alert us to a problem—the Catch-22 we mentioned earlier. The formatter encountered a footnote on the last input line. The only way to fit both the footnote reference and the footnote on the same page was to ignore the footer margin and let the footnote run into it.

Standard ms provides a better way of handling this overflow. In addition, the *Nroff/Troff User's Manual* describes a similar mechanism. Our simplified version, adequate only for demonstration of this mechanism, will borrow from both of these sources. (It might be said that a "working" version requires several empirically discovered fudge factors or, as Joseph Ossanna called them, "uncertainty corrections".)

The problem is how to split the footnote overflow if it extends beyond where we want the bottom of the page to be. The solution is to put *two* trap-invoked macros at the original (standard) page bottom location. The trap mechanism in troff allows only one macro to be executed by a trap at a given location. If you write:

```
.wh -\\n(FMu M1    \"Place first macro
.wh -\\n(FMu M2    \"Overwrite first macro at this location
```

all you will succeed in doing is wiping out the first placement with the second.

However, you can *move* a trap location to an occupied position. The second trap "hides" the first and renders it ineffective, but the first is still in place and is restored if the second subsequently moves off the spot.

So here's what we do in our trap initialization:

```
.wh 16i FO          \" Put regular footer out of the way
.                   \" (way off the page)
.wh -\\n(FMu FX     \" Place footnote overflow macro
.ch FO -\\n(FMu     \" Hide footnote overflow macro
```

The .FX (*footnote overflow*) macro will be invoked only if the FO trap is moved (as it will be whenever there are footnotes on the page). In .FX, all we do is start another diversion, so that excess footnote text that would overflow at the bottom of the page is saved for the next:

```
.de FX                  \" Footnote overflow
.if \\n(fC .di eF      \" Divert extra footnote
..
```

(We'll explain the reason for the test in a moment.)

Odd as it may seem, this diversion can be terminated from the footer macro .FO, even though that macro is invoked before the footnote overflow macro! Because the .FN diversion inside the .FO macros springs the footnote overflow trap and starts the overflow diversion, we can close that diversion by a request in .FO following the diversion.

The code in .FO now looks like this:

```
.nr dn 0                \" Reset diversion size register
.if \\n(fC \{\          \" If there are footnotes
.ev 1
.nf
.FN
.rm FN
.if'\\n(.z'eF'.di       \" End diversion opened by FX
.ev
.nr fC 0 \}             \" Done with footnotes
'bp
```

There are several things here that need further explanation. The number register .z always contains the name of the last completed diversion. (Don't ask us how they manage to put a string into a number register!) If our overflow diversion was this last completed diversion, we terminate it:

```
.if '\\n(.z'eF'.di
```

Then, we must take care of another eventuality. If we get this far *without* triggering the overflow trap—that is, if .FN did fit on the page—we want to disable the overflow macro, which we can do by zeroing our count register fC.

Now on the next page we have to handle any footnote overflow. We write a new macro that invokes .FS and .FE to output the overflow diversion (.eF) into the normal footnote diversion (.FN).

```
.de Fx          \" Process extra footnote
.FS
.nf             \" No-fill mode
.eF             \" Overflow diversion
.fi
.FE
.rm eF
..
```

In the new page macro, we add a test to check if the last diversion amounted to anything, and if it did, we invoke the .Fx macro.

```
.
                             \" added to .NP
.if \\n(dn .Fx
.
```

To test this new feature, we might add messages inside `.FX`, the macro invoked by a hidden trap to open a diversion that collects any footnote overflow, and inside `.Fx`, the macro that redirects the overflow back into the normal footnote diversion. You should be able to accomplish this part on your own, as well as to venture into areas that we did not cover (such as automatic numbering or marking of footnotes.) Before implementing a footnote mechanism, we urge you to study the mechanisms in one of the existing macro packages. However, following the chain of events from when a footnote is encountered to when it is output in the footer macro—on the current page or on the next—may seem like a `troff` exercise equivalent to what Alfred Hitchcock called a MacGuffin: a hopelessly complicated plot not meant to be figured out but that supplies a reason for many entertaining scenes.

Multicolumn Processing

While we're still on the subject of page transition, we should look briefly at how multi-column processing works.

Multiple columns are generally produced by using the mark and return mechanism—`.mk` and `.rt`—and by manipulating the line length and page offset for each successive column. The basic trick is to have the page bottom macro check if multiple columns are in effect, and if so, whether or not the current column is the last one.

A simple macro to initiate two-column processing might look like this*:

```
.de 2C
.mk                          \" Mark top position
.nr CL 0 1                   \" Initialize column count flag
.ie \\$1 .nr CW \\$1         \" Test arg 1 for Column Width
.el .nr CW 2.75i             \" or set default CW
.ie \\$2 .nr GW \\$2         \" Test arg 2 for Gutter Width
.el .nr GW .5i               \" or set default GW
.                            \" Save current one-column settings
.nr pO \\n(.o                \" Save current page offset
.nr lL \\n(LLu               \" Save original line length
.nr LL \\n(CWu               \" Set line length to Column Width
.ll \\n(LLu                  \" Set line length to Column Width
..
```

---

*Despite similar macro and number register names, this is *not* the two-column macro used in ms. The ms package provides a more general multiple column macro, `.MC`, of which `.2C` is a specialized call.

(We must save the default line length in a new register and redefine LL, or else a paragraph macro, or any other macro that calls .RT, will interfere with two-column processing.)

The page footer needs to include the following requests:

```
.de FO                      \" New footer macro
.ie \\n+(CL<2\{\            \" If incremental column count < 2
'po+(\\n(CWu+\\n(GWu)       \" then increase page offset
'rt                         \" Return to mark
'ns \}                      \" Enter no-space mode
.el \{\                     \" Otherwise
'po \\n(pOu                 \" Restore original page offset
'bp \}                      \" Start a new page
..
```

Because two-column processing is likely to continue beyond a single page, we need to modify the page top macro to mark the top of the page and initialize (set to zero) the column count register. The two requests at the bottom of the definition have been added:

```
.de NP                      \"New Page Macro
'sp \\n(HMu/2u
.PT
'sp |\\n(HMu
'ns
'mk                         \"Mark top of page
.if \\n(CL .nr CL 0 1 \"Reset autoincrementing column count
..
```

After the CL register has been created by .2C, it can also be used as a flag that two-column processing is in effect. The page top resets it to 0 to start the first column on a new page.

The macro to return to single-column processing looks like this:

```
.de 1C
.rr CL              \" Remove column count register
.po \\n(POu         \" Reset original page offset
.nr LL \\n(lLu
.ll \\n(LLu         \" and line length
.bp                 \" Start a new page
..
```

The column count register is removed, and the original page offset and line length are restored. Unfortunately, using this mechanism, you cannot return to single-column mode on the same page, without resorting to extensive use of diversions. If the first column has already gone to the bottom of the page, there is no way for a prematurely terminated second column to "go back" and fit the text into two even-sized columns on the same page.

Page Top Resets

We've already discussed the use of a reset macro from within paragraphs to deal with common errors. Page transitions are also a convenient place to put some different kinds of resets. Like paragraphs, you can rely on their regular occurrence and can therefore trap certain conditions.

In particular, you can use them when you want an effect to take place for only one page and then stop. For example, in our business, we are often required to produce not just complete manuals, but replacement pages to be inserted into an existing manual. Sometimes the update page will be exactly the same size as the original, but often it is longer, and requires additional space.

To avoid changing the numbering on subsequent pages, additional full or partial pages are inserted with a special numbering scheme. For example, if a page is numbered 3-4 (section 3, page 4), and changes to that page run on to an additional page, the new page will be numbered 3-4a.

In this situation, we need to temporarily change the way page numbers are handled, then change back when the page is done. We've defined a macro called .UN, which looks like this:

```
.de UN                   \" Update page numbering macro
.nr Un 1                 \" Set flag to test on page break
.nr % -1
.ie !"\\$1"" .as NN \\$1
.el .as NN a
..
```

Our extended ms macro package normally puts the section number (sE) and the page number (PN), separated by a hyphen, into the string NN. In this macro, we simply append a letter to that string. By default we add the letter *a*, but we give the user the option to specify another letter as an argument to the macro, so pages can be numbered 3-4, 3-4a, 3-4b, and so on. To use the macro, the user simply enters it anywhere on the update page. Voilá! The page number now has an *a* on the end.

Notice that the original page number register (%) was first decremented, so that this new page will have the same number as the previous one. More to the point of this discussion, notice that the macro sets the Un number register to 1 as a flag that update numbering is in effect.

This flag is tested in the page top macro for the next page, and if it is set, the original page numbering scheme is restored as follows:

```
.if \\n(Un=1 \{\
.       ds NN \\\\n(sE-\\\\n(PN
.       nr Un 0\}
```

(Note that four backslashes are required in the number register interpolations used in defining NN because the string definition will be interpreted twice, once when the macro is defined, and once when it is executed.)

Keep this trick in mind because there are many cases in which you can use the page bottom or page top macro to reset conditions that you don't want to carry across more than one page. We'll see another in just a moment.

Handling Widows and Orphans

Widows and orphans are the bane of any markup language—the one real advantage of current *wysiwyg* systems. A widow is a single or partial line from the end of a paragraph left over at the start of the next page. An orphan is a single line from the start of a paragraph left alone at the bottom of a page. Both of these are considered poor page layout.

As we've discussed, a macro package can take care of orphans simply by including an `.ne` request in the paragraph macro. Widows are much harder to take care of, because you don't know where the end of the paragraph will fall until you reach it.

In `nroff` and `troff`, the only way you can handle this problem is to process each paragraph in a diversion, find out how long it was, then go back and break it up if necessary. This greatly increases processing time, and is probably not worth the effort.

You could limit the extra work by testing the position on the page and only diverting paragraphs that occur within range of the page bottom. However, even so, this is a difficult problem you may not want to attempt.

It may be satisfactory to give users an increased capability for dealing with widows when they do occur. Normally, the solution is to print out the document, find any offending widow lines, then go back and manually break the pages a line earlier. However, sometimes it is inconvenient to break the paragraph earlier—it would be better to add the line to the bottom of the current page.

In standard `ms`, the location of the footer trap is reset to `-\n(FMu` in the `.NP` macro at the top of every page. The user can get extra length on a page just by changing the value of `FM` on the preceding page.

We could also write a macro that would let the user make the change on the offending page. For example, in `ms`:

```
.de EL                \" Extra Line macro
.nr eL 1              \" Set flag
.ch FO -(\\n(FMu-1v)u \" Put trap one line lower
..
```

All the user has to do is to introduce this macro anywhere on the page to be affected. It is your job as macro developer to reset the normal page length—and the most likely place is in the page top macro for the next page:

```
.if \\n(eL=1 \{\
.ch FO -\\n(FMu       \" Reset to normal location for ms
.nr eL 0\}            \" Clear flag
```

17

An Extended ms Macro Package

In the previous chapter, we've looked at some of the essential elements of a macro package—the innards that make it tick. However, few people will write a macro package just because they think they can do a better job at the basics than ms or mm. More often, users who need specific formatting effects will build a macro set to achieve those effects.

The macros used to produce this book are a good example of a custom macro package. They were developed to create a distinctive and consistent style for a series of books on UNIX by different authors. Although this macro package must of course do all of the basics we've talked about, many of its macros provide solutions to more specific problems. For example, there are macros for showing side-by-side before and after screens for vi and macros for inserting italicized commentary in examples.

To illustrate more concretely the issues that force you to create or significantly extend a macro package, this chapter will look at a set of extended ms macros for typesetting technical manuals. Extensions built into this package fall into two major categories:

- Extensions that make it easier to control the appearance of a document, particularly the page size (described in the last chapter) and the style of section headings, tables, and figures.

- Extensions that address needs of books, manuals, and other documents larger than the technical papers that ms and mm were originally designed for. These extensions include improved methods for handling tables of contents and indexes.

One of the chief weaknesses of the ms and mm packages is that they were designed for smaller documents. For example, ms does not provide table of contents generation, and the approach used by mm is suitable only for short documents. Neither package supports automatic index generation. In this chapter and the next, we will also look at ways to redress these problems.

▪ Creating a Custom Macro Package ▪

In this chapter, we will present an extended macro package designed for technical documentation. Based on the ms macro package, these extensions were originally developed by Steve Talbott of Masscomp; they have been extended and altered during several years of use in our technical writing and consulting business. Because we needed to produce technical manuals for a number of different clients, we needed a macro package that allowed us the flexibility to achieve a variety of document formats.

An important step in implementing this package was to establish the relation of new and redefined macros to the original ms package. We wanted to read in the standard tmac.s package, and then simply overwrite or remove unwanted macros. Then we organized our extensions into three groups: redefinitions of standard ms macros, common macros we added to provide specific features or capabilities for all documents, and format macros that were most often used to control the appearance or structure of a document.

The format macros can be modified for the specifications of a unique document format. Each format design has its own file, and the user only needs to specify which of these formats are to be read in during the formatting run.

Following is a summary of the steps we followed to implement our mS macro package. While describing this implementation, we don't pretend that it is unique or right for all uses; we do hope that it suggests ways to set up your own custom package.

1. Create a new directory to store the macro files.

2. Make a working copy of tmac.s and any subordinate files it reads in, moving them to a new directory.

3. Create the tmac.Sredefs file to contain definitions of standard ms macros that we've redefined, such as .IZ.

4. Create the tmac.Scommon file to contain utility and feature macros available in all formats. The list macros described in this chapter are kept here.

5. Create separate files containing definitions for unique document formats.

6. Set up tmac.S to control which files are read in and to handle certain parameters that might be set from the command line.

7. Put tmac.S in /usr/lib/tmac, either by placing the file in that directory or by creating a tmac.S file that sources the tmac.S file in the macro directory.

The master file of this package is tmac.S, although it does not contain any macro definitions. It allows users to set some parameters from the command line, and then it reads in the standard ms macro package and the two files that contain redefinitions and common macros. Last, it checks the value of a number register (v) to determine which group of format macros are to be read in.

Here's what our `tmac.S` file looks like:

```
.\"  tmac.S - the main format macro package
.
.so /work/macros/tmac.s         \" Read in standard ms
.so /work/macros/tmac.Sredefs   \" Redefinitions of macros
.so /work/macros/tmac.Scommon   \" Common utility macros
.                               \" Check register v for version
.                               \"  and read in special format macros
.ie \nv \{\
.if \nv=9 .so /work/macros/tmac.Stest
.if \nv=8 .so /work/macros/tmac.Squickref
.if \nv=7 .so /work/macros/tmac.Slarge
.if \nv=6 .so /work/macros/overheads
.if \nv=5 .so /work/macros/tmac.Straining
.if \nv=4 .so /work/macros/tmac.Sprime
.if \nv=3 .so /work/macros/tmac.Scogx
.if \nv=2 .so /work/macros/tmac.Smanuals
.if \nv=1 .so /work/macros/tmac.Snutshell\}
.el .so /work/macros/tmac.Sstandard
```

The −r option to `nroff` and `troff` is used to select a particular version of the format macros. For instance, the first set of format macros is designed for producing our Nutshell Handbooks. To format a document using the macros defined in `tmac.Snutshell`, a user would enter:

$ ditroff −Tps −mS −rv1 ch01 | devps | lp

One of the files, `tmac.Stest`, is available for use during the development and testing of new versions of the macros. We'll look at some of the different formats later in this chapter.

A few other details about this implementation may help you customize a package. Both ms and mm include a number of Bell-specific macros that are not very useful for users outside of AT&T. For example, it is unlikely that you will require the various styles of technical memoranda used internally at Bell Labs. Unused macro definitions need not get in your way, but they do use up possible names and number registers that may conflict with what you want to do. The `.rn` macro allows you to rename a macro; `.rm` will remove the definition of a macro.

You may want to remove selected macros. For example, you might want to start the modifications to a macro package built on ms with the following request:

```
.rm TM IM MF MR EG OK RP TR S2 S3 SG IE [] ][ [. .] [o \
    [c [5 [4 [3 [2 [1 [0 [< ]< [> ]> [- ]-
```

(Note the use of the backslash to make this apparent two-line request into a single long line.)

There is a slight performance loss in reading in a large macro package, and then removing a number of the macros. For efficiency, you'd be better off removing the undesirable macros from your copy of the ms source file.

Reading in `tmac.Sredefs` after `tmac.s` overwrites some of the standard ms macros with our own definitions. The standard versions are thus not available. If you want to retain a standard macro definition, you can make it available under a different name. Use the `.rn` request to rename the standard macro before overwriting its definition.

As discussed in the previous chapter, we redefined the `.IZ` macro to allow the setting of various page sizes. Because the standard `.IZ` macro is invoked from `tmac.s` at the start of the formatting run, we can't simply overwrite its definition. We must either delete the standard `.IZ` macro definition or comment out its invocation. Then the new `.IZ` macro in `tmac.Sredefs` will be executed.

As you develop your own set of extensions, you will undoubtedly consider additional modifications. Appendix F lists the set of extended macros that we use. You may not need many of the specialized macros provided in this package. But it wil! show you how to build on an existing package and how easy it is to modify the appearance of a document.

▪ Structured Technical Documents ▪

The ms and mm packages provide a number of macros to produce title pages, abstracts, and so on for technical memoranda. Subsections can be numbered or unnumbered.

Anyone who has used the *UNIX Programmers' Manual* is familiar with the output of these packages. The technical papers collected in that volume bear superficial resemblance to the chapters of a book. However, they lack continuity—section, figure, and table numbers, where present, are relative only to the current section, not to the entire volume.

A macro package designed for producing technical books or manuals may need at least some modification to produce section headings. Chapter and section headings should make the structure of a document visible. In a nontechnical book, chapters are often the only major structural element. They divide the book into major topics, and give readers stopping points to digest what they have read.

Chapters are usually distinguished from a formatting point of view by a page break and some kind of nonstandard typesetting. For example, a chapter number and title may be set in large type, and the text may begin lower on the page.

In technical books and manuals, which are often not read straight through as much as they are used for reference, frequent section headings within a chapter give the reader guideposts. There are often several levels of heading—more or less depending on whether the book is intended primarily for reading or for reference. This book uses three levels of headings within a chapter, one for major changes in topic, the others for less significant changes.

Section headings can be distinguished merely by type font and size changes, as in this book, or by section numbering as well. Properly used, section numbers can be very helpful in a technical manual. They allow detailed cross references to different parts of the book without using page numbers. Referencing by page numbers can result in errors because page numbers are not fixed until the book is done.

Detailed breakdown of a chapter into subsections can also help the writer of a technical manual. Because a manual (unlike an essay or other free-form work of non-fiction) has definite material that must be covered, it can be written successfully from an outline. It is often possible to write technical material by entering the outline in the form of section and subsection headings and then filling in the details.

In this approach, numbered sections also have a place because they make the outline structure of the document more visible. In reviewing technical manuals, we can often identify many weaknesses simply by looking at the table of contents. Sections in a technical manual should be hierarchical, and the table of contents should look effective *as an outline*. For example, a chapter in our hypothetical *Alcuin User's Guide* might look like this:

```
Chapter Two:  Getting Started with Alcuin


2.1      Objectives of this Session

2.2      Starting Up the System
2.2.1       Power-up Procedure
2.2.2       Software Initialization

2.3      Creating Simple Glyphs
2.3.1       Opening Font Files
2.3.2       Using the Bit Pad
2.3.2.1       The Cell Coordinate System
2.3.2.2       Pointing and Clicking
                     .
                     .
                     .
```

How much easier it is to see the structure than in a case where the proper hierarchical arrangement of topics has not been observed. How often have you seen a "flat" table of contents like this?

```
Chapter Two:  Using Alcuin


2.0      Starting Up the System
2.1      Power-up Procedure
2.2      Software Initialization
2.3      Creating Simple Glyphs
2.4      Opening Font Files
2.5      Using the Bit Pad
2.6      The Cell Coordinate System
2.7      Pointing and Clicking
                 .
                 .
                 .
```

Even when numbered section headings are not appropriate, they can be a useful tool for a writer during the draft stage, because they indicate where the organization has not been properly thought through. For example, we often see manuals that start with a general topic and then describe details, without a transitional overview.

A macro package should allow the writer to switch between numbered and unnumbered headings easily. Both mm and ms do provide this capability, and we want to include it in our macros. However, we also want to include more flexibility than either of these packages to define the format of headings.

Because headings are the signposts to the book's structure, changing their appearance can make a big difference in how the book is read. Different levels of headings need to stand out from the text to a greater or lesser degree, so that readers can easily scan the text and find the topic that they want.

The mechanisms for emphasis (in troff) are font and size changes, and the amount of space before and after a heading. Underlining and capitalization can also be used (especially in nroff but also in troff) for alternate or additional emphasis.

In our package, we include five levels of heading: a chapter-level heading and four levels of numbered or unnumbered subsection headings.

As described in the previous section, our custom macro package incorporates several different versions of the basic macros required to produce technical documents. In each version, the name of the heading macro is the same, but its definition is modified slightly to produce a different appearance. These different versions help us conform to the document styles used by our clients. Whenever we have a client who needs a new format, we customize the macro definitions, rather than add new macros.

The beauty of this approach is that the input macros the user needs to enter in a document are identical, or nearly so. Thus, we don't increase the number of new macros that our users must learn, and it eliminates the recoding of existing documents to achieve a new format.

This approach is also useful when you support different types of output devices. Originally, our designs were developed for the HP LaserJet printer, which supports a limited set of fonts and sizes. When we purchased an Apple LaserWriter and Linotronic L100 typesetter, our formatting options increased, making available multiple fonts and variable point sizes. In an environment supporting multiple types of printers, you might want to adapt formats for specific printers.

The Chapter Heading

The chapter heading is in a class by itself, because it requires more emphasis than subsection headings, and because the macro that produces it may need to initialize or reset certain registers used within the chapter (such as section, figure, or table numbers).

In an arbitrary reversal of terminology, we call our chapter macro .Se (*section*). It could just as well be called .CH for chapter, but we use .Ch for a subsection heading (as we'll see in a moment) and want to avoid confusion. In addition, this macro can be used for appendices as well as chapters, so the more general name seems appropriate.

The chapter heading has three major parts:

- chapter-specific register initialization, including registers for section numbering, table and figure numbering, and page numbering

- appearance of the actual chapter break

- table of contents processing

Because this is a long macro definition, let's look at it in sections.

```
.de Se                  \" section; $1 = number; $2 = name;
.                       \" $3 = type (Chapter, Appendix, etc)
.                       \"
.                       \" 1. Number Register Initialization
.                       \"
.ie !"\\$1"" \{.                 \" Test for sect number
.       nr sE \\$1                \" Assign to register sE
.       if !\\n(sE \{.            \" Test if not a numeric
.           .af sE A             \"  Handle appendices
.           if "\\$1"A" .nr sE 1
.           if "\\$1"B" .nr sE 2
.           if "\\$1"C" .nr sE 3
.           if "\\$1"D" .nr sE 4
.           if "\\$1"E" .nr sE 5
.           if "\\$1"F" .nr sE 6
.           if "\\$1"G" .nr sE 7
.           if "\\$1"H" .nr sE 8
.           if "\\$1"I" .nr sE 9
.           if "\\$1"J" .nr sE 10\}\}
.                               \" Only go as far as J
.el \{\
.       nr sE 0
.       tm Preface or if Appendix past letter J:
.       tm      Set number register sE to position
.       tm      of that letter in the alphabet
.       tm      and alter register format:
.       tm       For Appendix K, enter:
.       tm        .Se K "Title"
.       tm        .nr sE 11
.       tm        .af sE A
.\}
.if \\n%>1 .bp          \" Check if consecutive sections
.                       \"  in same file and break page
.nr % 1                 \" Now reset page number
.nr PN 1
.af PN 1
.ie !"\\$1"" \{.        \" Test for sect number
.                       \"  to set page number type
```

```
.        ds NN \\\\n(sE-\\\\n(PN
.        ds H1 \\n(sE          \" Set for subsection numbering
.        \}
.el \{
.        ds NN \\\\n(PN
.        nr sE 0\}
.ds RF \\\\*(NN              \" Assign page number to footer
.nr fG 0                     \" Initialize figure counter
.nr tB 0                     \" Initialize table counter
```

The macro first initializes a number of registers. Chapters are usually numbered on the first page, along with the title. If subsections are to be numbered, the chapter number is the root number for all headings. We need to take this number as an argument, and store it into a register for later use.

Because appendices are usually lettered rather than numbered, we also need to consider the special case of appendices. (This could be done with a separate macro; however, this package uses a single multipurpose macro.) The code for this is quite cumbersome, but works nonetheless: if the first argument to the macro is non-numeric, it is tested to see if it is one of the first ten letters in the alphabet. If so, a number is stored into the register, but the output format is changed to alphabetic.

If the argument is not a letter between A and J, a message is printed. This message is more verbose than you would generally want to use, but it is included to make the point that you can include detailed messages.

The macro next sets up the special page numbering scheme used in many computer manuals—the chapter number is followed by a hyphen and the page number (e.g., 1-1). This numbering scheme makes it easier to make last minute changes without renumbering and reprinting the entire book.

Finally, the macro initializes counters for automatically numbering figures and tables. We'll see how these are used in a few pages.

The next portion of the macro is the part that is most variable—it controls the actual appearance of the chapter heading. This is the part of the macro that has led us to develop several different versions.

In designing chapter headings, let your imagination be your guide. Look at books whose design you like, and work from there. Three different designs we used on the HP LaserJet are shown in Figure 17-1. (These designs are a compromise between aesthetics and the capabilities of the output device.) This book is another model.

The macro for the first heading in Figure 17-1 is used as follows:

```
.Se 2 "Getting Started with Alcuin"
```

or:

```
.Se A "Summary of Alcuin Drawing Primitives" "Appendix"
```

The heading starts on a new page. If a third argument is not present, it is assumed that the section type is *Chapter*, and the section is labeled accordingly. An alternate section type can be specified in the optional third argument. This argument is usually *Appendix* but can be any string the user wants printed before the section number.

**CHAPTER 2
GETTING STARTED WITH ALCUIN**

2

Getting Started with Alcuin

Chapter 2
Getting Started with Alcuin

Fig. 17-1. Some Different Styles of Chapter Heading

The portion of the macro definition that creates the first heading in Figure 17-1 follows:

```
.\" Part 2 of Se Macro: Output chapter heading
.RT
.in 0
.lg 0                     \" Disable ligature before .tr
.                         \" Translate title to uppercase
.tr aAbBcCdDeEfFgGhHiIjJkKlLmMnNoOpPqQrRsStTuUvVwWxXyYzZ
.sp
.na
.                         \" Test for section type argument
.ie !"\\$3"" .ds cH \\$3
.el .ds cH Chapter        \" Default is chapter
.                         \" If section number supplied
.                         \" output section number and type
.                         \" in 14 pt. bold.
.if !"\\$1"" \{\
\s14\f3\\*(cH \\$1\f1\s0
\}
.                         \" If no section number but
.                         \" there is a type (i.e., Preface)
.                         \" then output section type
.if "\\$1"" .if !"\\$3"" \{\
\s14\f3\\*(cH\f1\s0
\}
.sp 5p
.                         \" Test for section title
.                         \" Print it in 14 pt. bold
.if !"\\$2"" \{\
\s14\f3\\$2\f1\s0
\}
.sp 6p
.ad b
.Hl                       \" Draw line
.                         \" Retranslate arguments
.tr aabbccddeeffgghhiijjkkllmmnnooppqqrrssttuuvvwwxxyyzz
.sp 3
.ns                       \" Enable no-space mode
```

There are a couple of points you may want to note about this code:

- The actual section title, as specified in the second argument, is forced to all uppercase using the `.tr` request.

- The horizontal line under the title is drawn using a utility macro called `.Hl` (*horizontal line*), which simply draws a line the width of the page, less any indent that is in effect:

```
.de Hl   \" Horizontal line.   $1 = underline char
.br
\l'\\n(.lu-\\n(.iu\&\\$1'
.br
..
```

- No-space mode is turned on at the end of the macro, to inhibit inconsistent spacing caused by users placing spacing requests or paragraph macros after the .Se macro. All of the heading macros use this technique because inconsistent spacing around headings will give the page an uneven look.

An alternate definition for this section of the macro follows. This code produces the second heading shown in Figure 17-1.

```
.\" Part 2 of Se Macro (Alternate):
.ad r              \" Right justified
.fl
.rs
.sp .75i           \" Move down from top
.                  \" Section number in 24 pt. bold
.if !"\\$1"" \{\
\s24\f3\\$1\f1\s0\}
.sp 12p
.                  \" Section title in 20 pt. bold
.if !"\\$2"" \s20\f3\\$2\fP\s10
.sp 12p
.                  \" Optional 2nd line of title
.if !"\\$3"" \s20\f3\\$3\fP\s10
.sp 3
.ad b
.ns
```

This version is much simpler; it doesn't print the section type at all, just the number or letter. However, because it prints a right-justified title, we have given the user the option of splitting a long title into two parts.

The final part of the macro (in either version) adds the section title to the table of contents. As was the case with .Hl, this is done by an internal utility routine that is defined elsewhere. We'll discuss how this works later.

```
.                  \" Last Part of Se Macro
.                  \" Now do toc
.tC \\$1 \\$2 \\$3
..
```

A Mechanism for Numbered Headings

Before we describe the lower-level headings used within a chapter, we need to explore how to generate automatically numbered sections. We have defined a version of the ms .NH macro that is called internally by our own heading macros. It has the same name and uses the same internal registers as the ms macro, but the font and spacing requests specified in the ms .NH macro are removed. All that this macro now does is generate the section number string.

```
.de NH                        \" redefine from -MS
.nr NS \\$1                    \" Set NS to arg 1
.if !\\n(.$ .nr NS 1   \" Set NS to 1 if no arg
.if !\\n(NS .nr NS 1   \"  or NS is null or negative
.nr H\\n(NS +1                \" Increment Heading level register
.                             \" Test which level is in effect
.if !\\n(NS-4 .nr H5 0   \" then reset lower levels to 0
.if !\\n(NS-3 .nr H4 0
.if !\\n(NS-2 .nr H3 0
.if !\\n(NS-1 .nr H2 0
.                             \" Put together section number
.if !\\$1 .if \\n(.$ .nr H1 1   \" Set first level
.ds SN \\n(H1                 \" Begin building SN
.ie \\n(NS-1 .as SN .\\n(H2    \" == 1.1 2nd level
.el .as SN .                  \"   or == 1.
.if \\n(NS-2 .as SN .\\n(H3    \" == 1.1.1     3rd
.if \\n(NS-3 .as SN .\\n(H4    \" == 1.1.1.1   4th
.if \\n(NS-4 .as SN .\\n(H5    \" == 1.1.1.1.1 5th
'ti \\n(.iu
\\*(SN                        \" Output SN string
..
```

This macro repays study, because it shows several clever ways to use number registers. First, the argument to the macro is placed into a number register. This register is then used to select which of a series of further registers will be incremented:

```
.nr NS \\$1
       .
       .
       .
.nr H\\n(NS +1
```

If the macro is called as .NH 1, register H1 will be incremented; if the call is .NH 2, register H2 will be incremented, and so on. Then, depending on the value of that same NS register, the appropriate register value will be appended to the section number string SN.

Subsection Headings

In our package, we allow four levels of subsection headings, created by macros called
`.Ah` (*A head*) through `.Dh` (*D head*). The macros for all four levels have the same
essential structure; they differ only in the appearance of the printed text. Again, we
have different styles for different clients.

The distinction between levels of headings in one of those styles is as follows:

- The A head prints the heading in 14-point bold type, all uppercase, with 26
  points of space above the heading and 18 points below.

- The B head prints the heading in 14-point bold type, mixed case, with 23
  points of space above the heading and 15.5 points below.

- The C head prints the heading in 12-point bold type, mixed case, with 18
  points of space above the heading and 12 points below.

- The D head prints the heading in 10-point bold type, mixed case, with 18
  points of space above the heading and none below. The heading actually runs
  into the text and is separated from it only by a period.

All levels of headings can be either numbered or unnumbered, depending on the state of
a number register called `nH`. If `nH` is 0, headings are unnumbered; if it is 1, they are
numbered.

Here is one version of the `.Ah` macro. From this example, you should be able to
build the lower-level headings as well.

```
.de Ah              \" A-heading ; $1 = title
.sp 26p
.RT
.ne 8               \" Need room on page
.ps 14              \" 14 pt. on 16 pt. heading
.vs 16
.lg 0
.tr aAbBcCdDeEfFgGhHiIjJkKlLmMnNoOpPqQrRsStTuUvVwWxXyYzZ
.bd I 4             \" Embolden italic font (optional)
\f3\c               \" Bold font; concatenate next input
.if \\n(nH \{.      \" if producing numbered heads
.       ie \\n(sE .NH 2     \" If chapter (Se macro) is
.                           \" numbered, then 2nd level
.          el .NH 1\}       \" If not, 1st level head
\&\\$1\f1           \" Output title
.LP 0               \" Paragraph reset; (0 = no space)
.                   \"   RT resets default point size
.bd I               \" Turn off emboldening
.tr aabbccddeeffgghhiijjkkllmmnnooppqqrrssttuuvvwwxxyyzz
.lg
.sp 18p
.ns
```

```
.tC \\*(SN \\$1 Ah     \" Output TOC info
..
```

Some pointers: First, whenever you force capitalization with `.tr`, be sure to turn off ligatures, because they do not capitalize. Second, when you boldface a user-supplied string, it is wise to artificially embolden italics as well, in case the user embeds an italic font switch in the heading. Third, don't forget to enter no-space mode to ensure consistent spacing following the heading.

As you can see, the `.NH` macro is called to generate a section heading only if the nH register has been set. In addition, the macro checks to make sure that a major section number has been specified by the `.Se` macro. As you may recall, `.Se` sets the first number in the numbered heading string (H1). If `.Se` has been called, the subsection headings start at level 2, otherwise they start from the top.

To make it very easy for even novice users to specify whether they want numbered or unnumbered headings, the package includes a macro called `.Nh` (*numbered headings*) that turns numbering on or off:

```
.de Nh     \" Numbered headings; $1 = turn on (1) or off (0)
.          \" $1 = 2 will cause only A heads to be numbered
.nr nH \\$1
..
```

This is a matter of macro package style, as mentioned earlier. Steve Talbott's style, when he initially developed this package, was to code everything as macros, even where the macro simply sets a number register or defines a string. This makes the package very easy to learn, because you can give a new user a concise, unambiguous list of macros to enter into a file.

Other examples of this style include the `.Ti` and `.St` (*title* and *subtitle*) macros, described in Appendix F, which simply define the `ms` `RF` and `LF` strings for running footers. Because of the mnemonically named macros, new users don't have to remember whether the title goes in the right footer or the left, and so on. They simply enter the title of the book and chapter as arguments to the respective macros. The disadvantage is that users are insulated from an understanding of what is really going on, which may be an obstacle to learning more advanced skills.

An Alternate Definition

To give you an idea of how easy it is to change the look of a document by redefining a few macros, let's look at how we could redefine the heading for this section. One popular layout style in technical manuals uses a very wide left margin in which only the headings are printed, as follows.

| An Alternate Definition | To give you an idea of how easy it is to change the look of a document... |

Here's the modified macro to produce this heading:

```
.de Ah                  \" A-heading; alternate version
.                       \" Requires resetting default page
.                       \" (PO) to allow for extra offset.
.                       \" .nr PO 2.5i for 1.5 extra offset
.nr Po 1.5i             \" Set amount of extra offset
.nr Gw .2i              \" Set width of gutter
.mk                     \" Mark vertical position
.po -1.5i               \" Set new page offset
.ll \\n(Pou-\\nGwu
.ps 12                  \" Set 12 pt. on 14 pt.
.vs 14
\&\f3\\$1\f1            \" Output header in bold
.rt                     \" Return to vertical position
.po \\n(POu             \" Reset default page offset
.LP 0                   \" Reset point size and line length
.ns
.tC \\*(SN \\$1 Ah      \" Output TOC info
..
```

▪ Figure and Table Headings ▪

In technical manuals, it is common to number and title all figures and tables, both for easy reference from within the text, and for collection into lists of figures and tables that will appear in the table of contents.

These macros are easy to construct and, apart from whatever appearance you decide to give them, nearly identical in content. There is a "start" macro and an "end" macro:

```
.de Fs                  \" Start figure; $1= reserved space;
.                       \"                $2= F, floating figure
.RT
.if "\\$2"F" \{.        \" Figure can float
.       nr kF 1
.       KF\}
.if \\$1 \{.            \" Specify amount of space
.       ne \\$1         \"  required for paste-up
.       fl
.       rs
.       sp \\$1\}
..
.de Fe                  \" Figure end; $1 = title
.sp
.bd I 3
.nr fG +1               \" Increment Figure counter
```

```
.                     \" then determine format
.ie \\n(Se .ds fG \\*(H1-\\n(fG
.el .ds fG \\n(fG
.ce                   \" Output centered figure
\f3Figure \\*(fG.  \\$1\f1
.tC "\\*(fG" "\\$1" "Figure"
.bd I
.sp
.if \\n(kF=1 .KE     \" End keep if in effect
.tC "\\*(fG" "\\$1" "Figure"  \" Output TOC info
..
```

As you can see, the .Fs (*figure start*) macro allows the user to reserve space for a figure to be pasted in, and for it to float to a new page, using the ms "floating keep"
mechanism.

Neither of these options are necessary. The macro can simply bracket a figure
created with pic, for example, in which case all that the macro provides is a consistent amount of space before the figure starts.

The .Fe (*figure end*) macro does most of the work. If a keep is in effect, .Fe
terminates it. In addition, it prints the figure caption below the figure and adds a consistent amount of space below the caption. The figure is automatically numbered with
the section number, and a figure number that is incremented each time the macro is
called. As you may remember, this figure number register, fG, was initialized to 0 in
.Se.

To give the user some options with figure numbering, a second argument allows
the user to turn it off entirely. In addition, if the section is unnumbered, the section
number and hyphen will be omitted. To accomplish this involves a little juggling of
strings and number registers (which is something you should plan to get used to when
you write macros). Notice that we use the string H1 for the section number rather than
the section number register itself (sE), because we went to some trouble in the .Se
macro to handle lettered appendices as well as numbered chapters.

You could easily add optional appearance features to this macro. For example, in
one implementation, we draw a horizontal line above and below the figure, and print the
caption left justified and in italics below the bottom line.

The figure end macro also calls the table of contents macro, which will be
described later.

The macros for labeling tables are very simple, because the standard .TS and
.TE macros do everything necessary except providing consistent pre- and post-spacing
and printing the caption. In this case, the caption is at the top:

```
.de Ts                      \" Table start; $1 = title
.nr tB +1                   \" Increment Table counter
.                           \"   Determine format
.ie \\n(Se .ds tB \\*(H1-\\n(tB \" Section Table
.el .ds tB \\n(tB
.sp
.ce 2                       \" Output label and
```

```
\f3Table \\*(tB.              \" title on 2 lines
\&\\$1\f1
.tC "\\*(tB" "\\$1" "Table"  \" Output TOC info
.bd I
.LP                          \" Paragraph reset
..
.de Te    \" Table end -- no arguments
.RT                          \" Reset
.sp
..
```

▪ Lists, Lists, and More Lists ▪

One of the significant features lacking in the ms macros is the ability to generate automatically numbered or lettered lists. You can use the .IP macro and number or letter a list yourself—but what good is a computer if it can't handle a task like this?

One of the nicest features of Steve Talbott's extended ms package is its set of comprehensive, general-purpose list generation macros. There are three macros: .Ls (*list start*), .Li (*list item*), and .Le (*list end*). Unlike mm, in which different types of lists must be specified using different macros, here you request a different type of list by giving an argument to the .Ls macro. You can request any of the types of lists in Table 17-1.

TABLE 17-1. List Types

Argument	List Type
A	Alphabetic with uppercase letters
a	Alphabetic with lowercase letters
B	Bulleted with • by default
N	Numbered with arabic numerals
R	Numbered with uppercase roman numerals
r	Numbered with lowercase roman numerals

The bulleted list uses the bullet character (•) by default. However, as you will see, the macro allows you to specify an alternate bullet using an optional third argument. This "bullet" could be a dash, a box (\(sq), a checkmark (\(sr), or any other character.

Lists can be nested, and there is a default list type for each level of nesting, so the type argument does not really need to be specified.

Here's the list start macro:

```
.nr 10 0 1        \" Initialize nested list level counter
.de Ls
.\" list start; $1 = A(LPHA), a(alpha), B(ullet), N(umeric),
.\"               R(oman), r(oman);   $2 = indent
.\"               $3 = alternate bullet character
.br
.if !"\\$1"A" .if !"\\$1"B" .if !"\\$1"N" .if !"\\$1"R" \
.      if !"\\$1"r" .if !"\\$1"a" .if !"\\$1"" \
.      tm Ls: Need A a B N R r or null as list type
.nr 1\\n+(10 0 1
.ie "\\$1"" \{\                          \"Set defaults
.      if "\\n(10"1" .af 1\\n(10 1     \"Numeric at 1st level
.      if "\\n(10"2" .af 1\\n(10 a     \"lc alpha at 2nd level
.      if "\\n(10"3" .af 1\\n(10 i     \"lc roman at 3rd level
.      if "\\n(10"4" .ds 1\\n(10 \(bu\"Bullet at 4th level
.      if "\\n(10"5" .ds 1\\n(10 \f3\-\f1\"Dash at 5th level
.      if \\n(10-5 .ds 1\\n(10\(bu   \"Bullet above 5th level
.      if \\n(10-3 .nr 1\\n(10 0-1 \}
.el \{\
.      if "\\$1"A" .af 1\\n(10 A
.      if "\\$1"a" .af 1\\n(10 a
.      if "\\$1"B"\{\
.            if "\\$3"" .ds 1\\n(10 \(bu
.            if !"\\$3"" .ds 1\\n(10 \\$3
.            nr 1\\n(10 0-1\}
.      if "\\$1"R" .af 1\\n(10 I
.      if "\\$1"r" .af 1\\n(10 i \}
.ie !"\\$2"" .nr i\\n(10 \\$2     \" List indent
.el .nr i\\n(10 5                 \" Default indent
.RS
..
```

When you first look at this macro, you may be a little overwhelmed by the complex number register names. In fact, there is not much to it.

One number register, 10, is used as a counter for nested lists. As you can see, this register is initialized to 0 outside of the list macro definition itself. Then, when the .Ls macro is called, this register is autoincremented at the same time as it is used to define the *name* of another number register:

```
.nr 1\\n+(10 0 1
```

It is this second number register interpolation—1\\n+(10—that is actually used to number the list. This is a technique we promised to show you back when we were first describing number registers. We create a series of related number register names by interpolating the value of another register as one character in the name.

Think this through for a moment. The first time .Ls is called, the request:

call a reset macro to restore the default state—but this may not actually be the state that was in effect at the time.

In addition, you shouldn't rely on troff's ability to return to the previous setting by making a request like .ll without any argument. If you do so, an error might result if the user has himself made an .ll request in the interim.

In short, you should either save registers or use a different environment whenever you change formatting parameters in the opening macro of a macro pair. Then restore them in the closing macro of the pair.

• Notes, Cautions, and Warnings •

Another important macro for technical manuals is one that gives a consistent way of handling notes, cautions, and warnings. (Traditionally, a note gives users important information that they should not miss, but will not cause harm if they do. A caution is used for information that, if missed or disregarded, could lead to loss of data or damage to equipment. A warning is used for information that is critical to the user's life or limb.)

Obviously, this is a simple macro—all that is required is some way of making the note, caution, or warning stand out from the body of the text. You could redefine the macro shown here in any number of ways depending on the style of your publications.

```
.de Ns \" note/caution/warning; $1 = type "N", "C", "W"
.sp 2
.ne 5
.ce
.if !"\\$1"N" .if !"\\$1"C" .if !"\\$1"W" \{\
.	tm "Need N, C, or W as argument for Ns macro—using N"
\f3NOTE\f1\}
.if "\\$1"N" \f3NOTE\f1
.if "\\$1"C" \f3CAUTION\f1
.if "\\$1"W" \f3WARNING\f1
.sp
.ns
.nr nI \\n(.iu        \" Save current indent, if any
.nr nL \\n(.lu        \" Save current line length
.ie \\nS>0 .nr IN 5n\" Make indent less if in small format
.el .nr IN 10n        \" Larger indent for full-size page
.in +\\n(INu          \" Indent specified amount
.ll -\\n(INu          \" Decrement line length same amount
..
.de Ne \" "note end"; no args
.in \\n(nIu           \" Restore previous indent
.ll \\n(nLu           \" Restore previous line length
.rr nI                \" Remove temporary registers
.rr nL
.sp 2
```

```
.nr l\\n+(l0 0 1
```

defines a number register that is actually called l1 (the letter *l* followed by the value of number register l0—which is 1). A second call to .Ls without closing the first list (which, as we shall see, bumps the counter back one) will define number register l2, and so on.

In a similar way, another series of number registers (i\\n(l0) allows a different indent to be specified for each nested level, if the user so desires.

With the exception of the bulleted list, all of the different list types are numbered using the same number register (l*n*, where *n* is the nesting depth). The different types of lists are created simply by changing the output format of this register using the .af request.

Here's the .Li macro:

```
.de Li  \" List item;  $1 = 0 no blank line before item
.br
.if "\\$1"0" .ns
.ie "\\n(l\\n(l0"-1" .IP "\\*(l\\n(l0" "\\n(i\\n(l0"
.el \{\
.nr l\\n(l0 +1
.IP "\\n(l\\n(l0." "\\n(i\\n(l0" \}
..
```

The actual list counter itself (as opposed to the nesting counter) is incremented, and the appropriate value printed.

The number and the associated text is positioned with the standard ms .IP macro. If you don't have access to the ms macros, you could simulate the action of the .IP macro as follows:

```
.de IP
.nr Ip 1
.sp \\n(PDu
.in \\$2u
.ti -\\$2u
.ta \\$2u
\\$1\t\c
..
```

However, there is one drawback to using an .IP-style macro as the basis of the list.

- The .IP macro puts its argument at the left margin, as was done with this sentence.

- Instead, we'd like something that puts the mark in the middle of the indent, as was done with this sentence.

Here's the macro that produced the second example:

```
.de IP
.nr Ip 1
.sp \\n(PDu
.in \\$2u
.nr i1 \\$2/2u+\w'\\$1'    \" Amount to move left
.nr i2 \\$2-\w'\\$1'       \" Amount to move back
.ta \\n(i2u
.ti -\\n(i1u
\\$1\t\c
..
```

This version of the macro places the mark not just at a position half the depth of the indent, but exactly in the middle of the indent by adjusting the indent by the width of the mark argument. Number registers are used for clarity, to avoid nesting the various constructs too deeply.

(Note that this simplified .IP macro lacks some of the functionality of the ms .IP macro, which saves the current indent and therefore allows you to nest indents by using the .RS and .RE macros.)

If you are using ms, and you want to create a macro that puts the mark in the center of the indent, be sure to name this macro something other than .IP, so that you don't conflict with the existing macro of that name.

Here's the list end:

```
.de Le  \" List end; $1=0 no blank line following last item
.br
.rr l\\n(l0
.rr i\\n(l0
.rm l\\n(l0
.nr l0 -1
.RE
.ie !\\n(l0 \{\
.       ie "\\$1"0" .LP 0
.       el .LP\}
.el .if !"\\$1"0" .sp \\n(PDu
..
```

This macro removes the list numbering registers and strings, decrements the nested list counter, and calls the ms .RE macro to "retreat" back to the left (if necessary because of a nested loop). Finally, it leaves a blank line following the end of the list. (As you might remember, PD is the ms register containing the *paragraph distance*—0.3v by default.)

▪ Source Code and Other Examples ▪

In a technical manual, there are often further issues brought out by the need to show program source code or other material that loses essential formatting if it is set with proportional rather than monospaced type.

As previously discussed, the basic trick in ditroff is to use the (you are using otroff, you will need to use the cw preprocessor (see manual for details) or some other type of workaround. (When we otroff, our print driver allowed font substitutions based on size. We to to use the printer's constant-width font whenever troff used a poin Then, we wrote a macro that changed the point size to 11, but used character spacing to the actual size for the printer's constant-width font. very elegant solution, but it worked—so if you are stuck with otroff Put your ingenuity to work and you should come up with something.)

Besides the change to the CW font, though, there are several (like to see in a macro to handle printouts of examples. We'd like ex sistently indented, set off by a consistent amount of pre- and post-lir in no-fill mode.

Here's an example of a pair of macros to handle this situation:

```
.de Ps \" Printout start; $1 = indent (defaul
.br
.sp \\n(PDu
.ns
.nr pS \\n(.s  \" Save current point size
.nr vS \\n(.v  \" Save current vertical sp
.nr pF \\n(.f  \" Save current font
.nr pI \\n(.i  \" Save current indent
.ps 8
.vs 10
.ft CW
.ie !"\\$1"" .in +\\$1n
.el .in +5n
.nf
..
.de Pe  \" Printout end; $1 non-null,
.br
.if "\\$1"" .sp \\n(PDu
.ps \\n(pSu
.vs \\n(vSu
.ft \\n(pF
.in \\n(pIu
.rr pS
.rr vS
.rr pF
.rr pI
.fi
..
```

The trick of saving the current environment in t alternative is to use a separate environment fo available environments are not already in use

A warning looks like this:

WARNING

You should be careful when reading books on `troff`, because they can be damaging to your health. Although escape sequences are allowed, they are not exactly high adventure.

A different version of a caution macro is shown below. It uses a graphic symbol to mark a caution statement.

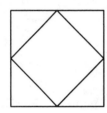

CAUTION

One client had a convention of marking a caution statement with a large diamond in a square. These diamonds will appear in a second color in the printed book.

To produce the escape sequences to draw the symbol, we used `pic`, processing the description and capturing it in a file. Then we read it into our macro definition. (We could also have produced the escape sequences to draw the symbol without `pic`'s help; this would result in much more compact code.) The drawing of the symbol does take up most of the `.Gc` macro definition. Before we actually output the symbol, the current vertical position is marked. After it is output, we mark its bottom position. Then we return to the top before placing the warning label and processing the text. After the caution statement is output, the closing macro, `.GE`, checks the current vertical position against the bottom position of the symbol.

```
.de Gc \"Graphic Caution Macro
.ne 10
.mk a                    \" Mark current top position
.br                      \" pic output belongs here
\v'720u'\D'l0u -720u'
.sp -1
\D'l720u 0u'
.sp -1
\h'720u'\D'l0u 720u'
.sp -1
\h'720u'\v'720u'\D'l-720u 0u'
.sp -1
\h'360u'\D'l360u 360u'
.sp -1
```

```
\h'720u'\v'360u'\D'l-360u 360u'
.sp -1
\h'360u'\v'720u'\D'l-360u -360u'
.sp -1
\v'360u'\D'l360u -360u'
.sp -1
.sp 1+720u             \" End of pic output
.sp
.mk q                  \" Mark bottom of symbol
.sp |\\nau             \" Move back to top (.mk a)
.in +1.5i              \" Indent to right of symbol
.ll -.5i               \" Reduce line length
.sp .5v
.ce
\f3CAUTION\f1          \" Output Caution label
.sp .3v
.
.de GE                 \" Graphic Caution end
.br
.sp
.in                    \" Reset previous settings
.ll
.                      \" If bottom of symbol (.mk q)
.                      \" is below current vertical position
.                      \" then move to that position
.if \\nqu>\\n(nlu+\\n(.vu .sp |\\nqu
.sp .3v
..
```

▪ Table of Contents, Index, and Other End Lists ▪

Here's the part you've all been waiting for. One of the nicest things a formatter can do for a writer is automatically generate lists such as a table of contents and an index. These are very time consuming to produce manually, and subject to error. There are basically two ways to do the trick, and both apply to an index as well as a table of contents, endnotes, and other collected lists.

The technique used by mm, which generates an automatic table of contents at the end of each formatting run, is to collect headings into a diversion using the .da request. This diversion is then output from within a special macro called the "end macro," which we have yet to discuss.

The second technique is to use the .tm request to write the desired information to standard error output. Then that output is redirected to capture the messages in a file, where they can be edited manually or automatically processed by other programs.

The advantage of the first approach is that it is clean and simple, and entirely internal to the formatter. However, it is really suitable only for short documents. A long document such as a book is not normally formatted in a single pass, but chapter by chapter. It is not desirable to format it all at once just to get the table of contents at the end. In addition, a large document generally will end up creating a large diversion—often one that is too large for `troff` to handle.

The second approach, on the other hand, opens up all kinds of possibilities for integration with other tools in the UNIX environment. The output can be saved, edited, and processed in a variety of ways. As you can imagine from our philosophy of letting the computer do the dirty work, this is the approach we prefer.

However, there is still a place for diversions, so we'll take a close look at both approaches in the sections that follow.

Diverting to the End

Although we prefer to create our major end lists—the table of contents and index—by writing to `stderr`, we find it very useful to use diversions for another type of list.

We've added a couple of special macros that allow a writer to insert remarks intended specifically for the reviewers of a draft document or for personal use. Because technical reviewers frequently miss questions embedded in the text, we designed the `.Rn` macro to highlight notes. This macro makes these remarks stand out in the text and then collects them for output again at the end of the document.

```
.de Rn    \" Note to reviewers : $1 = Note
.         \" Print note in text and at end
.                        \" Output note first
.sp
\f3Note to reviewers:\fP \\$1
.sp
.ev 2
.da rN                   \" Then append into diversion
.sp 0.2v
.in 0
.ie "\\*(NN"" \(sq Page \\n(PN: \\$1
.el \(sq Page \\*(NN: \\$1
.br
.da
.nr RN 1                 \" Flag it for EM
.ev
..
```

Another macro, `.Pn`, is used to collect a list of personal notes or reminders and output them on a page at the end. These notes do not appear in the body of the text.

```
.de Pn     \" Personal Note; $1= note
.          \" Note listed at end, but not in text
.ev2
.if \\n(Pn<1 .nr Pn 0 1   \" Set up autoincrement counter
```

```
.da pN
.br
.IP "\\n+(Pn." 5n
\\$1
.ie "\\*(NN"" (Page \\n(PN)
.el (Page \\*(NN)
.br
.da
.nr pN 1                    \" Flag it for EM
.ev
..
```

Only the `.Rn` macro produces output in the body of the document, but both macros append the notes into a diversion that we can process at the end of the document. The *divert and append* (`.da`) macro creates a list of notes that can be output by invoking the macro created by the diversion.

For each macro, we format the lists slightly differently. In the `.Rn` macro, we print a box character (□) (to give the feeling of a checklist), then the page number on which the review note occurred. This allows the reviewer or the writer to easily go back and find the note in context. In the `.Pn` macro, we use an autoincrementing counter to number personal notes; this number is output through `.IP`. It is followed by the note and the page reference in parentheses.

The formatting of text inside a diversion can be tricky. The text could be formatted twice: when it is read into the diversion, and when the diversion is output. The one thing to keep in mind is that you don't want line filling to be in effect both times. If line filling is in effect when the text is read into the diversion, you should turn it off when the diversion is output. You can also use transparent output (`\!`) to hide macros or requests so that they will be executed only at the time the diversion is output. We have also taken the precaution of processing the diversion in a separate environment.

Now what about printing the list at the end? Well, as it turns out, `nroff` and `troff` include a special request called `.em` that allows you to supply the name of a macro that will be executed at the very end of the processing run, after everything else is finished.

The `.em` request allows you to define the name of a macro that will be executed when all other input has been processed. For example, the line:

```
.em EM
```

placed anywhere in a file or macro package, will request that the macro `.EM` be executed after everything else has been done. The definition of `.EM` is up to you.

The `ms` macros already have specified the name of this macro as `.EM`, the *end macro*. In its usual obscure way, `mm` calls its end macro `.)q`. If you are writing your own package, you can call it anything you like. You can either edit the existing end macro, or simply add to it using the `.am` (*append to macro*) request.

All that `ms` does with this macro is to process and output any diversions that have not been properly closed. (This might happen, for example, if you requested a floating keep, but its contents had not yet been printed out.)

The end macro is a good place to output our own special diversions that we've saved for the end. What we need to do now is to add some code for processing our list of review notes:

```
.de EM
.br
.if \\n(RN=1 \{\
\&\c
'bp
.


.ce
\f3NOTES TO REVIEWERS\f1
.sp 2
Reviewers, please address the following questions:
.sp
.ev 2
.nf
.rN
.ev
.\}
.if \\n(pN=1 \{\
.br
\&\c
'bp
.
.ce
\f3Notes To Myself:\f1
.sp 2
.ev 2
.nf
.pN
.ev
.\}
..
```

(Note: we have found that to print anything from the .EM macro in the standard ms package, it is necessary to invoke .NP explicitly following a page break. However, when using our simplified version of this package as shown in the last chapter, our .EM does not need a .NP.) The list collected by the .Rn macro is printed on a new page, looking something like this:

NOTES TO REVIEWERS

Reviewers, please address the following questions:

□ Page 3-1: Why can't I activate the bit pad before opening a font file?

□ Page 3-7: Is there a size restriction on illuminated letters?

A Diverted Table of Contents

Given the preceding discussion, it should be easy for you to design a diverted table of contents. The magic `.tC` macro we kept invoking from our headings might look something like this:

```
.de tC  \" table of contents; $1=sect number;
.                             $2=title; $3=type
.if "\\$3"\\*(cH"\{\
.da sL           \" Divert and append to section list
.sp 3
\\*(cH \\$1:    \\$2
.sp 1.5
.da
.\}
.if "\\$3"Ah"\{\
.da sL           \" Divert and append to section list
.br
\\$1       \\$2\\a\\t\\*(NN
.br
.da
.\}
.if "\\$3"Bh"\{\
.da sL           \" Divert and append to section list
.br
\\$1     \\$2\\a\\t\\*(NN
.br
.da
.\}
.if "\\$3"Figure" \{\
.da fL           \" Divert and append to figure list
\\$1  \\$2\\a\\t\\*(NN
.da
.\}
.if "\\$3"Table" \{\
.da tL           \" Divert and append to table list
\\$1  \\$2\\a\\t\\*(NN
```

```
.da
.\}
..
```

The diversion `sL` is set up to handle the main heading (chapter, appendix, unit, or section) and two levels of subheadings (A-heads or B-heads). The diversions `fL` and `tL` are set up to compile lists of figures and tables, respectively.

In the end macro, to print the table of contents, you have to cause a break to a new page, print: introductory captions, and so on, and then follow by outputting the collected diversion of each type. The following example shows the code to print:

```
.br                    \" Automatically invoke diverted toc
\&\c                   \" by including these lines in EM macro
'bp                    \" Or place in own macro
.ta  \\n(LLu-5n \\n(LLuR
.ce
\f3Table of Contents\fR
.sp 2
.nf                    \" Process in no-fill mode
\\t\f3Page\fP
.sL
.rm sL                 \" Clear diversion
.                      \" Add code here to output figure
.                      \" and table list diversions
```

We set two tab stops based on the default line length (`\n(LLu`). The second tab stop is used to set a right-adjusted page number in the right margin. The first tab stop is used to run a leader from the entry to the page number. The escape sequences that output the leader and tab (`\a` and `\t`) were specified in the `.tC` macros. (And to protect the escape sequence inside a diversion an extra backslash was required.)

Now we can obtain a table of contents each time we format the document. The format of the table of contents shows the hierarchical structure of the document:

Table of Contents

Page

Chapter Two: Getting Started with Alcuin

2.1	Objectives of this Session	2-1
2.2	Starting Up the System	2-2
2.2.1	Power-up Procedure	2-2
2.2.2	Software Initialization	2-3
2.3	Creating Simple Glyphs	2-4

When Diversions Get Too Big

One of the major problems with collecting a table of contents in a diversion is that, with a large document, the diversions quickly grow too large for the formatter to handle. It will abort with a message like "Out of temp file space."

The solution is to break up your diversions based on the number of entries they contain. One way to do this is to base the name of the diversion on a number register, and do some arithmetic to increment the name when the diversion has been added to a certain number of times.

For example, instead of just diverting to a macro called `.sL`, we could divert to one called `xn`, where *n* is a number register interpolation generated as follows:

```
.de tC
        .
        .
        .
.nr xX +1
.nr x0 \\n(xX/100+1
.da x\\n(x0
        .
        .
        .
```

Each time `.tC` is called, register `xX` is incremented by 1, and its value, divided by 100, is placed into another register, `x0`. Until the value of register `xX` exceeds 100—that is, until `.tC` has been called 99 times—`x0` will be equal to 1. From 100 to 199, `x0` will be equal to 2, and so on.

Accordingly, the actual macro into which output is diverted—represented as `x\\n(x0`—will first be `x1`, then `x2`, and so on.

When it comes time to output the collected entries, instead of calling a single diversion, we call the entire series:

```
.x1
.x2
.x3
.x4
```

Here, we are assuming that we will have no more than 400 entries. If there are fewer entries, one or more of these diverted macros may be empty, but there's no harm in that. If there are more than 400, the contents of `.x5` (*et al*) would still have been collected, but we would have failed to print them out. We have the option of adding another in the series of calls in the end macro, or rebuking the user for having such a large table of contents!

Writing to Standard Error

Although we've answered one of the objections to a diverted table of contents by the register arithmetic just shown, there is another, more compelling reason for not using this approach for large documents: there is no way to save or edit the table of contents.

It is produced on the fly as part of the processing run and must be recreated each time you print the document.

For a very large document, such as a book, this means you must format the entire book, just to get the table of contents. It would be far preferable to produce the table of contents in some form that could be saved, so the tables from each chapter could be assembled into a single large table of contents for the entire book.

(Incidentally, producing a table of contents for a large document introduces some other issues as well. For example, you may want to have an overall table of contents that shows only top-level headings, and individual chapter table of contents that give more detail. Working out the macros for this approach is left as an exercise for the reader.)

The best way to produce a table of contents for a large book is simply to write the entries to standard error using .tm, and rely on an external program to capture and process the entries.

In ditroff, you can instead use the .sy request to execute the echo command and redirect the entries to a file. An example of this method might be:

```
.sy echo \\$1 \\$2\a\t\\*(NN >> toc$$
```

However, this approach causes additional system overhead because it spawns echo subprocesses. Also, because it does not work with otroff, we have used the more general approach provided by .tm.

Our .tC macro might look like this:

```
.de tC  \" Standard error; table of contents;
.       \" $1=sect number; $2=title; $3=type
.if "\\$3"\\*(cH"\{\
.tm ><CONTENTS:.sp 3
.tm ><CONTENTS:\\*(cH \\$1\\$2
.tm ><CONTENTS:.sp 1.5
.\}
.if "\\$3"Ah" .tm ><CONTENTS:\\$1   \\$2\a\t\\*(NN
.if "\\$3"Bh" .tm ><CONTENTS:\\$1      \\$2\a\t\\*(NN
.if "\\$3"Figure" .tm ><FIGURE:\\$1   \\$2\a\t\\*(NN
.if "\\$3"Table" .tm ><Table:\\$1   \\$2\a\t\\*(NN
..
```

Instead of diverting the section lists to separate macros from the lists of figures and tables, we send all entries out to standard error.

To capture this output in a file, we simply need to redirect the error output:

```
$ ditroff -Tps ... 2> toc
```

To do this, we will use our format shell script, which was introduced in Chapter 12, and will be revisited in the next (and final) chapter.

Because actual error messages might be present in the output, we prefix a label indicating the type of entry, for example:

```
><CONTENTS:
><FIGURE:
><TABLE:
```

It will be up to some outside program to separate the different groups of entries and subject them to further processing. We'll use a `sed` script to separate the entries in the table of contents from the figure lists, table lists, and index entries. (In the next chapter, we'll look at the post-processing of these entries.) Now let's look at a macro to generate index entries that will also be written to standard error.

Indexes

A simple index can be handled in much the same way as a table of contents. A macro for a simple index might look like this:

```
.de XX
.                       \"  Section-page number set up
.                       \"  by Se macro in string NN
.tm INDEX:\\$1\t\\*(NN
..
```

You might also want to have a macro that doesn't print the page number, but is just used for a cross-reference:

```
.de XN  \" Cross-reference Index entry, no page number
.tm INDEX:\\$1
..
```

You might also want a macro pair that will index over several different pages:

```
.de IS                  \"  Index macro
.                       \"  Interpolate % for page number
.ie \\n(.$=1 .tm INDEX:\\$1, \\n%
.el \{\
.nr X\\$2 \\n%
.ds Y\\$2 \\$1 \}
.if \\n(.t<=1P .tm *\\$1* near end of page
.if \\n(nl<1.2i .tm *\\$1* near top of page
..
.de IE                  \"  Index end macro
.ie !\\n(.$=1 .tm IE needs an argument!
.el .tm INDEX:\\*(Y\\$1, \\n(X\\$1-\\n%
.if \\n(.t<=1P .tm *\\*(Y\\$1* near end of page
.if \\n(nl<1.2i .tm *\\*(Y\\$1* near top of page
..
```

The `.IS` macro prints out an entry, just like `.XX`. However, in addition, it saves the argument into a string, and takes a letter or digit as an optional second argument. This second argument is used to define a number register and string that will be saved, and not printed until the index and macro is called with the same argument. The index and macro print the starting number, followed by a hyphen and the current page number.

All of this discussion still avoids one major issue. The real trick of indexing is what you do with the raw output after you have it, because a great deal of sorting, concatenation, and reorganization is required to rearrange the entries into a meaningful order. Fortunately or unfortunately, this topic will have to wait until the next chapter.

18

Putting It All Together

Before returning to the topic of table of contents and index processing, using shell tools that we will build, let's review what we've covered so far.

We started with a promise to show you how the UNIX environment could support and enhance the writing process. To do that, we've had to delve into many details and may have lost the big picture.

Let's return to that big picture here. First, UNIX provides what any computer with even rudimentary word-processing capabilities provides: the ability to save and edit text. Few of us write it perfectly the first time, so the ability to rewrite the parts of a document we don't like without retyping the parts we want to keep is a major step forward.

However, no one will argue that UNIX offers better tools at this simple level than those available in other environments. The vi editor is a good editor, but it is not the easiest to learn and lacks many standard word-processing capabilities.

Where UNIX's editing tools excel is in performing complex or repetitive edits. A beginner may have little use for pattern matching, but an advanced user cannot do without it. Few, if any, microcomputer-based or standalone word processors can boast the sophisticated capabilities for global changes that UNIX provides in even its most primitive editors.

When you go beyond vi, and begin to use programs such as ex, sed, and awk, you have unmatched text-editing capabilities—power, if you will, at the expense of user friendliness.

Second, UNIX's hierarchical file system, multiuser capabilities, and ample disk storage capacity make it easy to organize large and complex writing jobs—especially ones involving the efforts of more than one person. This can be a major advantage of UNIX over microcomputer-based or dedicated word processors.

Anyone who has tried to write a multiauthor work on a floppy-based system knows how easy it is to lose track of the latest version of a file, and to get lost among a multitude of disks. UNIX makes it easy to share files, and to set up a consistent framework for managing them.

In addition to storing multiple versions of documents on line, you can use the file system to set up specific environments for writing. For example, a separate `.exrc` file in each directory can define abbreviations and command maps specific to a book or section.

Third, UNIX provides a wide range of formatting tools. Using `troff`, `pic`, `tbl`, and `eqn`, you can easily typeset books. This is not as unique and powerful a capability as it was even two or three years ago. The advent of low-cost laser printers and *wysiwyg* "desktop publishing" tools like Microsoft WORD, MacWrite, and Aldus Pagemaker allow PC users to do typesetting as well.

However, despite the glamor of desktop publishing, and the easy-to-use appeal of products for the Macintosh, the UNIX typesetting facilities offer many advantages. Chief among these advantages is the very feature in which `troff` at first seems much weaker than its low-end competitors, namely, the use of embedded codes to control formatting.

Wysiwyg systems are easy for beginners to use, and they are very satisfying because you can immediately see what you are going to get on the printed page. But have you ever tried to make a global font change in MacWrite? Or had to make a change to a document after it was "pasted up" with Pagemaker? Or had to wait endlessly while Microsoft WORD reformats an entire document after you change the margins?

Because `troff` codes can be edited, just like any other text in a file, it is very easy to change your mind about formatting and make global changes. And after you have mastered the art of writing macros, it is even easier to change formats simply by changing macro definitions. And because the editing and formatting functions are separate, you don't have to wait for the computer while you are making those changes—that happens while you print.

This is not to say that `troff` is superior to the best possible *wysiwyg* system. High-end systems from companies like Interleaf, Xyvision, and Texet offer power, speed, and ease of use all at once. Unfortunately, the software is costly, and requires the use of high-cost bit-mapped workstations. This can lead to a bottleneck in document production unless you have enough money to spend on hardware. Because `troff` requires only a standard alphanumeric terminal, it provides much more "bang for the buck."

There is no question that the publishing system of the future will be a *wysiwyg* system. But for now, a low-cost UNIX system with `vi` and `troff` is still one of the most cost-effective publishing systems around.

This brings us to the final strength of UNIX—its extensibility. More than an operating system or a collection of programs, UNIX is a philosophy of computing. Let's consider an analogy. The Volkswagen beetle was a unique automobile of the sixties and seventies. Its simple design was one of the reasons that made it popular; the "bug" was user-maintainable. VW owners ("users") could tinker with their cars, performing such tasks as changing spark plugs by hand. They scoffed at owners of other cars who depended upon mechanics. It is perhaps this same feeling of independence— let me do it myself—that the UNIX environment fosters in its users. There are many quite capable software environments that are packaged to keep users out. In some ways, the secret of UNIX is that its working parts are visible. The UNIX environment, like the VW beetle, is designed so that users can take it apart and put it back together. UNIX is a philosophy of computing. As we've stressed again and again, UNIX provides general-purpose tools, all of which are designed to work together.

No single program, however well thought out, will solve every problem. There is always a special case, a special need, a situation that runs counter to the expected. But UNIX is not a single program: it is a collection of hundreds. And with these basic tools, a clever or dedicated person can devise a way to meet just about any text-processing need.

Like the fruits of any advanced system, these capabilities don't fall unbidden into the hands of new users. But they are there for the reaching. And over time, even writers who want a word processor they don't have to think about will gradually reach out for these capabilities. Faced with a choice between an hour spent on a boring, repetitive task and an hour putting together a tool that will do the task in a flash, most of us will choose to tinker.

The index and table of contents mechanism in this chapter is a good example of putting together individual UNIX tools to do a job that no one of them can easily do alone. Its explanation is a fitting end to this book, which has tried throughout to put the UNIX text-processing tools in a wider context.

▪ Saving an External Table of Contents ▪

As discussed in the last chapter, `troff` does provide a mechanism (namely diversions) to collect and process a table of contents directly within the formatter. However, this approach is best suited to short documents, because it requires that the entire document be reformatted to produce the table of contents.

Likewise, you could even produce and sort an index entirely within `troff`, though the effort required would be large. (In fact, a recent article on Usenet, the on-line UNIX news network, described an implementation of a sort algorithm using `troff` macros. It is painfully slow—it was done just to prove that it could be done, rather than for practical application.)

The beauty of UNIX, though, is that you don't have to stretch the limits of `troff` to do everything necessary to produce a book. Just as editing is separated from formatting, you can separate processing the table of contents and the index from formatting the rest of the text.

The `troff` formatter provides the basic mechanisms for producing the raw material—the lists of headings or index terms, accompanied by the page numbers on which they occur. However, the actual saving and processing of the raw material is done with `make`, `sed`, `awk`, `sort`, and the shell.

In Chapter 12, we began to look at how a shell script (which we called `format`) could manage the formatting process. We used the programming power of the shell not only to save the user the trouble of remembering command-line options and complicated postprocessor names, but also to apply the power of `sed` to various ancillary formatting tasks.

The collection of a table of contents and index requires that we first return to this script. As we left Chapter 17, both the table of contents and the index macros simply write data to standard error.

A Bourne shell user can redirect this error output to a file using the following syntax:

$ **ditroff** *file* **2>** *tocfile*

The problem is that the table of contents, index entries, and potential formatter error messages are all captured in the same file. We need a mechanism for parsing this file into its separate elements. The user could do this manually, but it is far better to let a program do it.

The first step is to redirect all of the error output from the formatter to a temporary file. After formatting is done, we can use sed to search for the identifying strings that we introduced as part of the ''error message'' and output the matching lines into separate files. True error messages should be sent back to the screen, and the temporary file removed.

The trick here is naming the files into which the saved data is stored by sed. It is not appropriate simply to append table of contents data to one file, because we are likely to reformat a document many times while rewriting and revising it. Instead, we want to have a unique table of contents file and a unique index file for each source file that we format. The best way to do this without cluttering up the current directory is to create a subdirectory for each type of data we want to save—toc, index, and so on.

Let's look at how we did these things in the format script:

```
roff="ditroff -Tps"; files=""; options="-mS"
pre="| ditbl"; post="| devps "
sed="| sed -f /work/macros/new/cleanup.sed"
pages=""; toc="2>/tmp$$"; lp="| lp -s"
if [ ! -d index a ! -d toc ]; then
    echo "No index and toc. Use the buildmake command."
    toc="2>/dev/null"
fi
while [ "$#" != "0" ]; do
  case $1 in
    -?) echo "Format Options are:"
        echo "-m*    Specify other macro package (-mm)"
        echo "-s     Use small format (5-1/2 by 8-1/2)"
        echo "-o     Print selected pages"
        echo "-cg    Format for Compugraphic typesetter"
        echo "-E     Invoke EQN preprocessor"
        echo "-P     Invoke PIC preprocessor"
        echo "-G     Invoke GRAP & PIC preprocessors"
        echo "-x     Redirect output to /dev/null"
        echo "-y     Invoke nroff; pipe output to screen";
        echo "-a     Set interactive troff -a option"
        echo "-*     Any troff option"; exit;;
    -m*) options="$1";;
```

```
      -s) options="$options -rS1 -rv1";;
      -o) pages="$pages -o$1";toc="2>/dev/null";;
      -cg) roff="ditroff -Tcg86"; post="| ditplus -dtcg86";;
      -E) pre="$pre | dieqn";;
      -P) pre="| pic -T720 -D $pre";;
      -G) pre="| grap | pic -T720 -D $pre";;
      -x) options="$options -z"; post=""; lp="";;
      -y) roff="nroff"; post=""; lp="| col | pg";;
      -a) post=""; options="$options -a";;
      -*) options="$options $1";;
       *) if [ -f $1 ]; then
             files="$files $1"
             txfile="$1"
             if [ -d /print ]; then touch /print/$txfile
          else
             echo "USAGE: format (options) files"
             echo "To list options, type format -? "; exit
          fi;;
   esac
   shift
done
if [ -n "$files" -o ! -t 0 ]; then
# Use soelim to expand .so's in input files
#    otherwise use cat to send files down pipe.
 eval "cat $files $sed $pre |
       $roff $options - $toc $post $pages $toc $lp"
else echo "fmt:  no files specified"; exit
fi
if [ -f tmp$$ ]; then
   if [ -d toc ]; then
   sed -n -e "s/^><CONTENTS:\(.*\)/\1/p" tmp$$ > toc/$txfile
   fi
   if [ -d index ]; then
   sed -n -e "s/^><INDEX:\(.*\)/\1/p" tmp$$ > index/$txfile
   fi
   if [ -d figlist ]; then
   sed -n -e "s/^><FIGURE:\(.*\)/\1/p" tmp$$ > figlist/$txfile
   fi
   if [ -d tablist ]; then
   sed -n -e "s/^><TABLE:\(.*\)/\1/p" tmp$$ > tablist/$txfile
   fi
   sed -n "/^></!p"
   rm /tmp$$
fi
exit
```

Now, for example, when we format a file called `ch01`, a file of the same name will be written in each of the four subdirectories `toc`, `index`, `figlist`, and `tablist`. Each time we reformat the same file, the output will overwrite the previous contents of each accessory file, giving us the most up-to-date version. When we use the `−o` option for only partial formatting, writing out of these files is disabled by redirecting error output to `/dev/null`, so that we don't end up with a partial table of contents file.

There's also a `−x` option, to allow us to format a file to produce the table of contents and index without producing any regular output. This option uses `troff`'s `−z` option to suppress formatted output, and sets the `post` and `lp` shell variables to the null string.

(You may also notice the `−cg` option, which specifies a different device to both `troff` and the postprocessor—in this case, a Compugraphic typesetter instead of an Apple LaserWriter. This is included as an aside, to give you an idea of how this is done.)

The contents of the `toc`, `figlist`, and `tablist` directories can be assembled into a complete table of contents, or formatted on the spot for a chapter-level table of contents. We can use the following simple sequence of commands (which could be saved into a shell script):

```
echo .ta \n(LLu-5n \n(LLuR  > book.toc
echo .ce >> book.toc
echo \f3TABLE OF CONTENTS\fP >> book.toc
echo .sp 2 >> book.toc
echo "\t\f3Page\fP" >> book.toc
cat  /toc/ch?? /toc/app?  >> book.toc
echo .bp >> book.toc
cat  /figlist/ch?? /figlist/app? >> book.toc
echo .bp >> book.toc
cat  /tablist/ch?? /tablist/app? >> book.toc
```

The resulting `book.toc` source file looks like this:

```
.ta \n(LLu-5n \n(LLuR
.ce
\f3TABLE OF CONTENTS\fP
.sp 2
|————|\f3Page\fP
.sp 3
Chapter 1  Introduction to Alcuin
.sp 1.5
1.1    A Tradition of Calligraphic Excellence\a\t1-2
1.2    Illuminated Bit-Mapped Manuscripts\a\t1-4
.sp 3
Chapter 2  Getting Started with Alcuin
.sp 1.5
2.1    Objectives of this Session\a\t2-1
2.2    Starting Up the System\a\t2-2
```

```
2.2.1        Power-up Procedure\a\t2-2
  .
  .
  .
```

The index will require more serious postprocessing.

▪ **Index Processing** ▪

It is relatively simple to assemble the components of a table of contents into sequential order, but it is much more difficult to process the index entries, because they must be sorted and manipulated in a variety of ways.

This is one of the most complex tasks presented in this book. So let's start at the beginning, with the raw data that is output by `troff`, and directed to our index subdirectory by the `format` shell script. For illustration, we'll assume a sparse index for a short book containing only three chapters.

As you may recall, the user creates the index simply by entering macro calls of the form:

```
.XX "input devices"
```

or:

```
.XX "input devices, mouse"
```

or:

```
.XR "mouse (see input devices)"
```

throughout the text. Both macros write their arguments to standard output; the `.XX` macro adds the current page number, but the `.XR` (*cross reference*) macro does not. The user is responsible for using consistent terminology, capitalization, and spelling. A comma separates optional subordinate entries from the major term.

An index term should be entered on any page that the user wants indexed—at the start and end of a major topic, at least, and perhaps several in between if the discussion spans several pages.

In our example, entries are saved into the three files `ch01`, `ch02`, and `ch03` in the order in which they appear in the respective input files. The indexing term entered by the user is printed, separated from the current page number by a tab. Certain cross reference entries do not have a page number. The content of the raw index files after chapters 1 through 3 have been formatted follows. (Here, and in the following discussion, a tab is represented by the symbol |———|.)

```
$ cat index/ch??
Alcuin, overview of|———|1-1
illuminated manuscripts|———|1-1
fonts, designing|———|1-2
Alcuin, supported input devices|———|1-2
input devices|———|1-2
input devices, mouse|———|1-2
input devices|———|1-2
mouse (see input devices)
```

```
input devices, bit pad|————|1-3
bit pad (see input devices)
input devices|————|1-3
startup, of system|————|2-1
power, location of main switch|————|2-1
power, for graphics display|————|2-1
startup, of system|————|2-2
input devices, mouse|————|2-2
input devices, bit pad|————|2-3
fonts, selecting|————|3-1
glyphs, designing|————|3-2
extra line space|————|3-3
symbolic names|————|3-3
@ operator|————|3-4
```

To create a presentable index from this raw data, we need to do the following:

- Sort the entries into dictionary order, and remove duplicates, if any. (Duplicate entries occur whenever the user enters `.XX` macros with the same argument over several input pages, and two or more of those entries fall on the same output page.)

- Combine multiple occurrences of the same term, appending a complete list of page numbers and properly subordinating secondary terms.

- Introduce formatting codes, so that the resulting file will have a pleasing, consistent appearance.

Just how complex a task this is may not be immediately apparent, but rest assured that it takes the combined operation of `sort`, `uniq`, and several different `awk` and `sed` scripts to do the job properly.

Fortunately, we can hide all of this complexity within a single shell program, so that all the user needs to type is:

```
$ cat index/files | indexprog > book.ndx
```

Sorting the Raw Index

The first part of `indexprog` processes the index entries before they are passed to `awk`. The `sort` program prepares a list of alphabetical index entries; `uniq` removes duplicate entries.

```
sort -t\|————| -bf +0 -1 +1n | uniq
```

The options to the `sort` command specify primary and secondary sort operations, affecting the first and second fields separately. The `-t` option specifies that a tab character separates fields. The primary sort is alphabetic and performed on the indexing term; the secondary sort is numeric and performed on the page number. The primary sort is also controlled by the following options: the `-b` option (ignore leading blanks in making comparisons) is a safety feature; the −f (fold uppercase and lowercase letters) is more important because the default sort order places all uppercase letters before all lowercase ones; and +0 −1 ensures that the alphabetic sort considers only the first field. The secondary sort that is performed on the second field (+1n) is numeric and ensures that page numbers will appear in sequence.

Now let's look at the index entries after they have been sorted:

```
@ operator|———|3-4
Alcuin, overview of|———|1-1
Alcuin, supported input devices|———|1-2
bit pad (see input devices)
extra line space|———|3-3
fonts, designing 1-2
fonts, selecting|———|3-1
glyphs, designing|———|3-2
illuminated manuscripts|———|1-1
input devices|———|1-2
input devices|———|1-3
input devices, bit pad|———|1-3
input devices, bit pad|———|2-3
input devices, mouse|———|1-2
input devices, mouse|———|2-2
mouse (see input devices)
power, for graphics display|———|2-1
power, location of main switch|———|2-1
startup, of system|———|2-1
startup, of system|———|2-2
symbolic names|———|3-3
```

Multiple entries that differ only in their page number are now arranged one after the other.

The sort command is a simple way to obtain a sorted list of entries. However, sorting can actually be a complicated process. For instance, the simple sort command that we showed above obviously works fine on our limited sample of entries. And while it is designed to process entries with section-page numbering (*4-1, 4-2, 4-3*), this command also works fine when sorting entries with continuous page numbering (*1, 2, 3*).

However, section page numbering does present a few additional problems that we did not encounter here. Two-digit section numbers and page numbers, as well as appendices (*A-1, A-2, A-3*) will not be sorted correctly. For instance, this might cause the indexing program to produce the following entry:

```
Alcuin, software   A-2, 1-1, 1-10, 1-3, 11-5, 2-1
```

There are two ways to handle this problem. One is to change the indexing macro in troff so that it produces three fields. Then the sorting command can sort on the section number independent of the page number. (Because our awk portion of the indexing program is set up to operate on entries with one or two fields, you'd have to change the program or use a `sed` script to reduce the number of fields.)

The second method uses `sed` to replace the hyphen with a tab, creating three fields. Actually, we run a `sed` script *before* the entries are sorted and another one *after* that operation to restore the entry. Then `sort` will treat section numbers and page numbers separately in secondary numeric sort operations, and get them in the right order.

The only remaining problem is how to handle appendices. What happens is that when a numeric sort is performed on section numbers, lettered appendices are sorted to the top of the list. This requires cloaking the letter in a numeric disguise. Presuming that we won't have section numbers greater than 99, our `sed` script prepends the number 100 to each letter; this number is also removed afterwards.

```
sed '
    s/|————|\([0-9][0-9]*\)-/|————|\1|————|/
    s/|————|\([A-Z]\)-/|————|100\1|————|/' |
sort -t\      -bf +0 -1 +1n +2n | uniq |
sed '
    s/|————|100\([A-Z]\)|————|/|————|\1-/
    s/\(|————|.*\)|————|/\1-/'
```

Now the sorting operation of our index program handles a wider range of entries.

Building the Page Number List

The next step is more complex. We must now combine multiple occurrences of each term that differ only in the page number, and combine all of the page numbers into a single list. The `awk` program is the tool of choice. We can use a script for comparing and manipulating successive lines similar to the one described in Chapter 13. We begin by building the page number list for each entry.

```
awk '
BEGIN { ORS = ""; FS = "|————|" }
NF == 1 { if (NR == 1) printf ("%s", $0);
          else printf ("\n%s", $0) }
NF > 1 {
  if ($1 == curr)
    printf (",%s", $2)
  else  {
    if (NR == 1) printf ("%s", $0)
    else printf ("\n%s", $0)
    curr = $1
    }
}'
```

First, the program sets the output record separator (ORS) to the null string, rather than the default newline. This means that output records will be appended to the same line, unless we specify an explicit newline.

Second, it sets the field separator (FS) to the tab character. This divides each index entry into two fields: one containing the text, the other containing the page number. (As you may recall, the page number is separated from the text of the entry by a tab when it is output from troff.)

Then, if the number of fields (NF) is 1 (that is, if there is no tab-separated page number, as is the case with cross reference entries generated with .XR), the program prints out the entire record ($0). If this is not the first line in the file (NR = 1), it precedes the record with an explicit newline (\n).

If the number of fields is greater than 1 (which is the case for each line containing a tab followed by a page number), the program compares the text of the entry in the first field ($1) with its previous value, as stored into the variable curr.

The next few lines might be easier to understand if the condition were written in reverse order:

```
if ($1 != curr)
{ if (NR == 1) printf ("%s", $0)
  else printf ("\n%s", $0)
  curr = $1
}
else printf (",%s", $2)
```

If the first field is not equal to curr, then this is a new entry, so the program prints out the entire record (again preceding it with an explicit newline if this is not the first line of the file). The value of curr is updated to form the basis of comparison for the next record.

Otherwise (if the first field in the current record is the same as the contents of the variable curr), the program appends a comma followed by the value of the second field ($2) to the current record.

The output after this stage of the program looks like this:

```
@ operator|———|3-4
Alcuin, overview of|———|1-1
Alcuin, supported input devices|———|1-2
bit pad (see input devices)
extra line space|———|3-3
fonts, designing 1-2
fonts, selecting|———|3-1
glyphs, designing|———|3-2
illuminated manuscripts|———|1-1
input devices|———|1-2,1-3
input devices, bit pad|———|1-3,2-3
input devices, mouse|———|1-2,2-2
mouse (see input devices)
power, for graphics display|———|2-1
power, location of main switch|———|2-1
startup, of system|———|2-1,2-2
symbolic names|———|3-3
```

Subordinating Secondary Entries

The next trick is to subordinate secondary entries under the main entry, without reprinting the text of the main entry. In addition, we want to represent consecutive page numbers as a range separated by two dots (..) rather than as a list of individual pages. We'll show this script in two sections:

```
1   awk '
2   BEGIN   { FS = "|————|"; }
3   {
4   n = split ($1, curentry, ",")
5   if (curentry[1] == lastentry[1])
6     printf ("  %s", curentry[2])
7   else {
8     if (n > 1) printf ("%s\n  %s", curentry[1], curentry[2])
9     else printf ("%s", $1)
10    lastentry[1] = curentry[1]
11    }
12  }
```

This section of the script uses awk's split function to break the first field into two parts, using a comma as a separator.

There are several cases that the program has to consider:

- The text of the entry does not contain a comma, in which case we can just print the entire first field. See line 9: printf ("%s", $1).

- The entry does contain a comma, in which case we want to see if we have a new primary term (curentry[1]) or just a new secondary one (curentry[2]).

- If the primary term is the same as the last primary term encountered (and saved into the variable lastentry), we only need to print out the secondary term. See line 6: printf ("%s", curentry[2]).

- Otherwise, we want to print out both the primary and secondary terms: See line 8: printf ("%s\n %s", curentry[1], curentry[2]).

For example:

```
@ operator|————|3-4
Alcuin, overview of|————|1-1
Alcuin, supported input devices|————|1-2
```

When the first line is processed, the split will return a value of 0, so the entire line will be output.

When the second line is processed, lastentry contains the string @ *operator*, curentry[1] contains *Alcuin*, and curentry[2] contains *overview of*. Because lastentry is not the same as curentry[1], the program prints out both curentry[1] and curentry[2].

When the third line is processed, curentry[1] again contains the word *Alcuin*, but curentry[2] contains the words *supported input devices*. In this case, only curentry[2] is printed.

The next part of the script, which follows, looks considerably more complicated, but uses essentially the same mechanism. It splits the second field on the line (the page number list) on the hyphens that separate section number from page number. Then, it compares the various sections it has split to determine whether or not it is dealing with a range of consecutive pages. If so, it prints only the first and last members of the series, separating them with the range notation (. .).

If you were able to follow the previous portion of the script, you should be able to piece this one together as well:

```
NF == 1{ printf ("\n") }
(NF > 1) && ($2 !~ /.*_.*/) {
  printf ("\t")
  n = split ($2, arr, ",")
  printf ("%s", arr[1])
  split (arr[1], last, "-")
  for (i = 2; i <= n; ++i) {
  split (arr[i], curr, "-")
  if ((curr[1] == last[1])&&(curr[2]/1 == last[2]/1+1)) {
    if (i != n) {
      split (arr[i+1], follow, "-")
      if ((curr[1] != follow[1])||(curr[2]/1+1 != follow[2]/1))
        printf ("..%s", arr[i])
    } else printf ("..%s", arr[i])
  } else printf (", %s", arr[i])
  last[1] = curr[1]; last[2] = curr[2]
}
printf ("\n")
}'
```

The output from this awk program (in sequence with the previous ones) now looks like this:

```
@ operator|———|3-4
Alcuin
    overview of|———|1-1
    supported input devices|———|1-2
bit pad (see input devices)
extra line space|———|3-3
fonts
    designing 1-2
    selecting|———|3-1
glyphs
    designing|———|3-2
illuminated manuscripts|———|1-1
input devices|———|1-2..1-3
    bit pad|———|1-3, 2-3
    mouse|———|1-2, 2-2
mouse (see input devices)
```

```
power
    for graphics display|————|2-1
    location of main switch|————|2-1
startup
    of system|————|2-1..2-2
symbolic names|————|3-3
```

That's starting to look like an index!

Adding Formatting Codes

We could simply quit here, and let the user finish formatting the index. However, awk can continue the job and insert formatting codes.

We'd like awk to put in headings and divide the index into alphabetic sections. In addition, it would be nice to insert indentation requests, so that we can format the index source file in fill mode so that any long lines will wrap correctly.

Let's look at the coded output before we look at the script that produces it. Only the beginning of the output is shown:

```
.ti -4n
@ operator|————|3-4
.br

.ne 4
.ti -2n
\fBA\fR
.br
.ne 2
.ti -4n
Alcuin
.br
.ti -4n
  overview of|————|1-1
.br
.ti -4n
  supported input devices|————|1-2
.br

.ne 4
.ti -2n
\fBB\fR
.br
.ne 2
.ti -4n
bit pad (see input devices)
.br
```

```
.ne 4
.ti -2n
\fBE\fR
.br
.ne 2
.ti -4n
extra line space|————|3-3
.br
```

Here's a script that does this part of the job:

```
awk '
BEGIN   {OFS = ""
  lower = "abcdefghijklmnopqrstuvwxyz"
  upper = "ABCDEFGHIJKLMNOPQRSTUVWXYZ"
}
NF > 0 {
  if ($0 !~ /^ .*/) {
    n = 1
    while ((newchar = substr($1,n,1)) !~ /[A-Za-z]/) {
      n = n + 1
      if (n == 100) {# bad line
        newchar = oldchar
        break
      }
    }
    if (newchar ~ /[a-z]/) {
      for (i = 1; i <= 26; ++i) {
        if (newchar == substr (lower, i, 1)) {
          newchar = substr (upper, i, 1)
          break
        }
      }
    }
    if (substr($1,1,1) ~ /[0-9]/)
      newchar = ""
    if (newchar != oldchar) {
      printf ("\n\n%s\n", ".ne 4")
      printf ("%s\n", ".ti -2n")
      printf ("%s%s%s\n", "\\fB", newchar, "\\fR")
      printf ("%s\n", ".br")
      oldchar = newchar }
    printf ("%s\n", ".ne 2")
  }
  printf ("%s\n", ".ti -4n")
  printf ("%s\n", $0)
```

```
   printf ("%s\n", ".br")
}'
```

Every line in the input (NF > 1) will be subjected to the last three lines in the program. It will be surrounded by formatting codes and printed out.

```
        printf ("%s\n", ".ti -4n")
        printf ("%s\n", $0)
        printf ("%s\n", ".br")
```

The rest of the script checks when the initial character of a primary entry changes and prints a heading.

As you may have noticed, in the output of the previous script, secondary entries were indented by three leading spaces. They can be excluded from consideration at the outset by the condition:

```
    if ($0 !~ /^ .*/) {
```

All other lines are checked to determine their initial character. The awk program's substr function extracts the first letter of each line. Then, much as it did before, the program compares each entry with the previous until it detects a change.

The program is basically looking for alphabetic characters, but must test (especially in computer manuals) for strings that begin with nonalphabetic characters. (If it doesn't do this, it will loop endlessly when it comes to a string that doesn't begin with an alphabetic character.) If the program loops 100 times on a single line, it assumes that the character is nonalphabetic, breaks out of the loop, and goes on to the next line.

When the program finds a change in the initial alphabetic character, it prints a heading consisting of a single capital letter and associated formatting requests.

Primary terms beginning with nonalphabetic characters are output without causing a change of heading. (Because they are already sorted to the beginning of the file, they will all be listed at the head of the output, before the A's.)

Final Formatting Touches

Having come this far, it hardly seems fair not to finish the job, and put in the final formatting codes that will allow us to format and print the index without ever looking at the source file (although we should save it to allow manual fine-tuning if necessary).

A simple sed script can be used for these final touches:

```
sed "1i\\
.Se \"\" \"Index\"\\
.in +4n\\
.MC 3.15i 0.2i\\
.ds RF Index - \\\\\\\\\n(PN\\
.ds CF\\
.ds LF\\
.na
s/|————|/  /"
```

Assuming that we're using our extended ms macros, these initial macros will create the
section heading *Index*, print the index in two columns, and use a page number of the
form Index − *n*. (Note how many backslashes are necessary before the number
register invocation for PN. Backslashes must be protected from the shell, sed, and
troff. This line will be processed quite a few times, by different programs, before it
is output.)

Finally, the script converts the tab separating the index entry from the first page
number into a pair of spaces.

Special Cases

But our indexing script is not complete. There are a number of special cases still to
consider. For example, what about font changes within index entries? In a computer
manual, it may be desirable to carry through ''computer voice'' or italics into the index.

However, the troff font-switch codes will interfere with the proper sorting of
the index. There is a way around this—awkward, but effective. As you may recall, we
use a sed script named cleanup.sed called from within format. This script
changes double quotation marks to pairs of matched single quotation marks for typesetting, and changes double hyphens to em dashes. We can also use it to solve our current
problem.

First, we add the following lines to cleanup.sed:

```
/^\.X[XR]/{
        s/\\\(fP\)/%%~/g
        s/\\\(fS\)/%%~~/g
        s/\\\(fB\)/%%~~~/g
        s/\\\(fI\)/%%~~~~/g
        s/\\\(fR\)/%%~~~~~/g
        s/\\\(f(CW\)/%%~~~~~~/g
}
```

Within an .XX or .XR macro, the script will change the standard troff font-
switch codes into an arbitrary string of nonalphabetic characters.

Then we add the −d option (*dictionary order*) to our initial sort command in
the index program. This option causes sort to ignore nonalphabetic characters when
making comparisons. (The exception will be lines like @ *operator*, which contain no
alphabetic characters in the first field. Such lines will still be sorted to the front of the
list.)

Finally, we use the concluding sed script in the indexing sequence to restore the
proper font-switch codes in the final index source file:

```
s/%%~~~~~~/\\\\f(CW/g
s/%%~~~~~/\\\\fR/g
s/%%~~~~/\\\\fI/g
s/%%~~~/\\\\fB/g
s/%%~~/\\\\fS/g
s/%%~/\\\\fP/g
```

We might also want to consider the case in which a leading period (as might occur if we were indexing `troff` formatting requests) appears in an index entry. Inserting the following line one line from the end of the last `awk` script we created will do the trick. These lines insulate `troff` codes in index entries from the formatter when the index source file is processed by `troff` for final printing:

```
if ($0 ~ /^\..*/) printf ("\\&")
if ($0 ~ /^%%~~*\./) printf ("\\&")
```

Lines beginning with a `.` will be preceded with a `troff` zero-width character (`\&`).

The Entire Index Program

We have broken the indexing process into stages to make it easier to understand. However, there is no need to keep individual `awk` and `sed` scripts; they can be combined into a single shell program simply by piping the output of one portion to another, within the shell program.

Here's the whole program, as finally assembled:

```
sed '
    s/|———|\([0-9][0-9]*\)-/|———|\1|———|/
    s/|———|\([A-Z]\)-/|———|100\1|———|/' |
sort -t\|———| -bdf +0 -1 +1n +2n | uniq |
sed '
    s/|———|100\([A-Z]\)|———|/|———|\1-/
    s/\(|———|.*\)|———|/\1-/' |
awk '
BEGIN { ORS = ""; FS = "|———|" }
NF == 1 { if (NR == 1) printf ("%s", $0);
          else printf ("\n%s", $0) }
NF > 1 {
  if ($1 == curr)
    printf (",%s", $2)
  else   {
    if (NR == 1) printf ("%s", $0)
    else printf ("\n%s", $0)
    curr = $1
    }
}' | awk '
BEGIN { FS = "|———|"; }
{
n = split ($1, curentry, ",")
if (curentry[1] == lastentry[1])
  printf (" %s", curentry[2])
else {
  if (n > 1) printf ("%s\n  %s", curentry[1], curentry[2])
```

```
        else printf ("%s", $1)
        lastentry[1] = curentry[1]
        }
}
NF == 1{ printf ("\n") }
(NF > 1) && ($2 !~ /.*_.*/) {
    printf ("\t")
    n = split ($2, arr, ",")
    printf ("%s", arr[1])
    split (arr[1], last, "-")
    for (i = 2; i <= n; ++i) {
    split (arr[i], curr, "-")
    if ((curr[1] == last[1]) && (curr[2]/1 == last[2]/1+1)) {
        if (i != n) {
            split (arr[i+1], follow, "-")
            if ((curr[1] != follow[1])||(curr[2]/1+1 != follow[2]/1))
                printf ("..%s", arr[i])
        } else printf ("..%s", arr[i])
    } else printf (", %s", arr[i])
    last[1] = curr[1]; last[2] = curr[2]
}
printf ("\n")
}' | awk '
BEGIN  {OFS = ""
    lower = "abcdefghijklmnopqrstuvwxyz"
    upper = "ABCDEFGHIJKLMNOPQRSTUVWXYZ"
}
NF > 0 {
    if ($0 !~ /^ .*/) {
        n = 1
        while ((newchar = substr($1,n,1)) !~ /[A-Za-z]/) {
            n = n + 1
            if (n == 100) {# bad line
                newchar = oldchar
                break
            }
        }
        if (newchar ~ /[a-z]/) {
            for (i = 1; i <= 26; ++i) {
                if (newchar == substr (lower, i, 1)) {
                    newchar = substr (upper, i, 1)
                    break
                }
            }
        }
```

```
     if (substr($1,1,1) ~ /[0-9]/)
        newchar = ""
     if (newchar != oldchar) {
        printf ("\n\n%s\n", ".ne 4")
        printf ("%s\n", ".ti -2n")
        printf ("%s%s%s\n", "\\fB", newchar, "\\fR")
        printf ("%s\n", ".br")
        oldchar = newchar
     }
     printf ("%s\n", ".ne 2")
   }
   printf ("%s\n", ".ti -4n")
   if ($0 ~ /^\..*/) printf ("\\&")
        if ($0 ~ /^%%~~*\./) printf ("\\&")
   printf ("%s\n", $0)
   printf ("%s\n", ".br")
}' | sed "1i\\
.Se \"\" \"Index\"\\
.in +4n\\
.MC 3.4i 0.2i\\
.ds RF Index - \\\\\\\\n(PN\\
.ds CF\\
.ds LF\\
.na
s/%%~~~~~~/\\\\\f(CW/g
s/%%~~~~~/\\\\\fR/g
s/%%~~~~/\\\\\fI/g
s/%%~~~/\\\\\fB/g
s/%%~~/\\\\\fS/g
s/%%~/\\\\\fP/g"
```

The result of all this processing is source text that can be piped directly to the formatter, saved in a file for later formatting (or perhaps minor editing), or both (using tee to "split" standard output into two streams, one of which is saved in a file).

Assuming that the various raw source files produced by troff are stored in a subdirectory called indexfiles, and that the index script is called indexprog, we can format and print the index as follows:

```
$ cat indexfiles/* | indexprog | ditroff -mS | ... | lp
```

The result will look something like this:

INDEX

@ operator 3-4

A

Alcuin
  overview of 1-1
  supported input devices 1-2

B

bit pad (see input devices)

P

power
  for graphics display 2-1
  location of main switch 2-1

S

startup
  of system 2-1—2-2
symbolic names 3-3

.
.
.

▪ Let make Remember the Details ▪

Even though we've hidden the really complex details of index processing inside a shell script, and the format shell script itself handles a lot of the dirty work, there is still a lot for the user to keep track of. The make utility introduced in Chapter 11 can take us a long way towards making sure that everything that needs to happen for final production of the finished book comes together without a hitch.

Here are some of the things we want to make sure have been done:

- All of the relevant sections have been printed in their most up-to-date form. Odd as it may seem, it is possible to have last minute changes to a file that never make it into the printed book.

- The book has been proofed using whatever automatic tools we have provided, including the proof and double shell scripts (or wwb if you have it). All ''review notes'' embedded in the text must also be satisfied and removed.

- An updated table of contents and index have been printed.

You can probably think of others as well.

The `make` utility is the perfect tool for this job. We've already seen in Chapter 11 how it can be used to specify the files (and the formatting options) required for each section of the book. Unfortunately, this part of the job requires that you keep formatted output files, which are quite large. If disk space is a problem, this drawback might lead you to think that `make` isn't worth the bother.

However, with a little thought, you can get around this restriction. Instead of keeping the formatted output file, you can keep a zero-length file that you `touch` whenever you format the source file. You could add the following line to the end of the `format` script:

```
touch print/$file
```

Or, if you use `make` itself to print your document, you could put the `touch` command into the makefile. Your makefile might look like this:

```
book : print/ch01 print/ch02 print/ch03...

print/ch01 : ch01
    sh /usr/local/bin/format -mS -rv1 -rS2 ch01
    touch print/ch01

print/ch02 : ch02
    sh /usr/local/bin/format -mS -P -rv1 -rS2 ch02
    touch print/ch02
                    .
                    .
                    .
```

Notice that in order to execute the local formatting shell script, it is necessary to execute `sh` and specify the complete pathname. The options specified with the `format` shell script can be specific to each file that is formatted. However, generally you want to use the same options to format all the files that make up a particular document. Using variables, you can create a more generalized makefile that is easier to change.

```
FORMAT: sh /usr/local/bin/format
OPTIONS: -mS -P -rv1 -rS2

book : print/ch01 print/ch02 print/ch03...

print/ch01 : ch01
    $(FORMAT) $(OPTIONS) ch01
    touch print/ch01

print/ch02 : ch02
    $(FORMAT) $(OPTIONS) ch02
    touch print/ch02
                    .
                    .
                    .
```

The variables used by make are set like shell variables. But when they are referenced, the name of the variable must be enclosed in parentheses in addition to being prefixed with a dollar sign.

A user can now easily edit the OPTIONS variable to add or remove options. You could also place additional options on the command for a particular file. This is not necessary, though, just because some of the files have tables, equations, or pictures and others don't. Other than the small bit of extra processing it requires, there's no reason not to run the preprocessors on all files.

Our makefile can be further expanded. To make sure that our index and table of contents are up-to-date (and to automate the process of creating them out of the individual raw output files that the format script creates), we can add the following dependencies and creation instructions:

```
book: print/ch01 ... proof/ch01 ... book.index book.toc
                        .
                        .
                        .


print/ch01 : ch01
                        .
                        .
                        .


book.index : index/ch01 index/ch02 ...
    cat index/* | sh /usr/local/bin/indexprog > book.index

book.toc : toc/ch01...figlist/ch01...tablist/ch01...
        echo .ta \n(LLu-5n \n(LLuR > book.toc
        echo .ce >> book.toc
        echo \f3TABLE OF CONTENTS\fP >> book.toc
        echo .sp 2 >> book.toc
        echo "\t\f3Page\fP" >> book.toc
    cat toc/ch01...toc/appz >> book.toc
    echo '.bp' >> book.toc
    cat figlist/ch01...figlist/appz >> book.toc
    echo '.bp' >> book.toc
    cat tablist/ch01...tablist/appz >> book.toc

toc/ch01 : ch01
  $(FORMAT) $(OPTIONS) -x ch01
toc/ch02 : ch02
  $(FORMAT) $(OPTIONS) -x ch02
                        .
                        .
                        .


index/ch01 : ch01
  $(FORMAT) $(OPTIONS) -x ch01
                        .
```

```
      ⋅
      ⋅
      ⋅
figlist/ch01 : ch01
  $(FORMAT) $(OPTIONS) -x ch01
      ⋅
      ⋅
      ⋅

tablist/ch01 : ch01
  $(FORMAT) $(OPTIONS) -x ch01
      ⋅
      ⋅
      ⋅
```

Because we have directories named `toc` and `index`, we give our source files names such as `book.toc` and `book.index`.

We can therefore enter:

$ **make book.toc**

and the table of contents will be compiled automatically. When you enter the above command, the `make` program recognizes `book.toc` as a *target*. It evaluates the following line that specifies several dependent components.

```
book.toc: toc/ch01 toc/ch02 toc/ch03
```

In turn, each of these components are targets dependent on a source file.

```
toc/ch02: ch02
$(FORMAT) $(OPTIONS) -x ch02
```

What this basically means is that if changes have been made to to `ch02` since the file `book.toc` was compiled, the source file will be formatted again, producing new toc entries. The other files, assuming that they have not been changed, will not be re-formatted as their entries are up-to-date.

We can add other "targets", for instance, to check whether or not every chapter in the book has been proofed since it was last edited. Based on when the dependent components were last updated, you could invoke the `proof` program on the associated file, `grep` for Review Note macros, or just print a message to the user reminding him or her to proof the file.

To do this, we create a pseudo-target. If no file with the name `proof` exists, it can never be up-to-date, so typing:

$ **make proof**

will automatically force proofing of the document according to the rules you have specified in the makefile.

The `print` directory also serves as a pseudo-target, useful for printing individual chapters. Users don't have to remember the formatting options that must be specified for a particular file.

And if all these reasons don't convince you to learn `make` and begin constructing makefiles for large documents, perhaps this next benefit will. It gives you a simple two-word command to print an entire book and its apparatus.

```
$ make book
```

When you enter this command, each formatting command as it is being executed will
be displayed on the screen. If you wish to suppress these messages while you do other
work, invoke make with the −s option or place the line .SILENT: at the top of
the makefile.

Building the Makefile

You are limited only by your imagination and ingenuity in organizing your work with a
makefile. However, the more complex the makefile, the longer it gets, and the more
difficult for inexperienced users to create.

    You can get around this problem too—just write a shell script to build the
makefile, taking as arguments the files that make up the document. Here's such a
script, called buildmake, that will produce a makefile similar to the one just
described. (The make utility requires that the actions to be performed for each target
begin with a tab. Such explicit tabs are shown in the following script by the symbol
|———|.)

```
if [ $# -eq 0 ]; then
    echo "USAGE: buildmake files"
    echo "(You must specify the files that make up the book)"
    exit
fi
if [ ! -d print ]; then
    mkdir print
    mkdir proof
fi
if [ ! -d index ]; then
    mkdir index
fi
if [ ! -d toc ]; then
    mkdir toc
    mkdir figlist
    mkdir tablist
fi
for x
do
    prifiles="$prifiles print/$x"
    profiles="$profiles proof/$x"
    tcfiles="$tcfiles toc/$x"
    xfiles="$xfiles index/$x"
    fgfiles="$fgfiles figlist/$x"
    tbfiles="$tbfiles toc/$x"
done
echo ".SILENT:" > makefile
```

```
echo "FORMAT = sh /usr/local/bin/format" >> makefile
echo "OPTIONS = -mS" >> makefile
echo "INDEXPROG = sh /usr/local/bin/indexprog">>makefile
echo "book : $prifiles $profiles book.toc book.index">>makefile
echo "book.index : $xfiles/" >> makefile
echo "|———|cat $xfiles | $(INDEXPROG) > book.index">>makefile
echo "|———|$(FORMAT) $(OPTIONS) book.index" >> makefile
echo "book.toc : $tcfiles" >> makefile
echo "|———|echo .ta \n(LLu-5n \n(LLuR  > book.toc">>makefile
echo "|———|echo .ce >> book.toc" >> makefile
echo "|———|echo \f3TABLE OF CONTENTS\fP >> book.toc">>makefile
echo "|———|echo .sp 2 >> book.toc" >> makefile
echo "|———|echo "\t\f3Page\fP" >> book.toc" >> makefile
echo "|———|cat /work/lib/toc_top > book.toc" >> makefile
echo "|———|cat $tcfiles >> book.toc" >> makefile
echo "|———|echo .bp >> book.toc" >> makefile
echo "|———|cat $fgfiles >> book.toc" >> makefile
echo "|———|echo .bp >> book.toc" >> makefile
echo "|———|cat $tbfiles >> book.toc" >> makefile
echo "|———|$(FORMAT) $(OPTIONS) book.toc" >> makefile
for x
do
    echo "print/$x : $x" >> makefile
    echo "|———|$(FORMAT) $(OPTIONS) $x" >> makefile
    echo "proof/$x : $x" >> makefile
    echo "|———|echo $x has not been proofed" >> makefile
    echo "toc/$x : $x" >> makefile
    echo "|———|$(FORMAT) $(OPTIONS) -x $x" >> makefile
    echo "index/$x : $x" >> makefile
    echo "|———|$(FORMAT) $(OPTIONS) -x $x" >> makefile
done
```

To create a complex makefile, all the user needs to do is type:

> $ **buildmake** *files*

In addition, the user may want to manually edit the first line of the makefile, which specifies formatter options.

· **Where to Go from Here** ·

Large as this book is, it is far from comprehensive. We have covered the basic editing and formatting tools in some detail, but even there, topics have been glossed over. And when it comes to the more advanced tools, programs not explicitly designed for text processing, much has been left out.

The sheer size and complexity of UNIX is one of its fascinations. To a beginner, it can be daunting, but to an advanced user, the unknown has an appeal all its own. Particularly to a technical writer, for whom the computer is a subject as well as a tool, the challenge of taking more control over the process of book production can be endlessly fascinating. The subject and the method of inquiry become ever more intertwined, until, in Yeats's immortal phrase:

How can you know the dancer from the dance?

A

Editor Command Summary

This section is divided into five major parts, describing the commands in the text editors vi, ex, sed, and awk, and the pattern-matching syntax common to all of them.

· Pattern-Matching Syntax ·

A number of UNIX text-processing programs, including ed, ex, vi, sed, and grep, allow you to perform searches, and in some cases make changes, by searching for text patterns rather than fixed strings. These text patterns (also called regular expressions) are formed by combining normal characters with a number of special characters. The special characters and their use are as follows:

.   Matches any single character except newline.

*   Matches any number (including zero) of the single character (including a character specified by a regular expression) that immediately precedes it. For example, because . means "any character," .* means "match any number of any characters."

[...]   Matches any one of the characters enclosed between the brackets. For example, [AB] matches either A or B. A range of consecutive characters can be specified by separating the first and last characters in the range with a hyphen. For example, [A-Z] matches any uppercase letter from A to Z, and [0-9] matches any digit from 0 to 9. If a caret (^) is the first character in the brackets, the comparison is inverted: the pattern will match any characters *except* those enclosed in the brackets.

\{*n,m*\}   Matches a range of occurrences of the single character (including a character specified by a regular expression) that immediately precedes it. *n* and *m* are integers between 0 and 256 that specify how many occurrences to match. \{*n*\} matches exactly *n* occurrences, \{*n*,\} matches at least *n* occurrences, and \{*n,m*\} matches any number of occurrences between *n* and *m*. For example, A\{2,3\} matches either AA (as in AARDVARK) or AAA (as in AAA Travel Agency) but will not match the single letter A. This feature is not supported in all versions of vi.

^   Requires that the following regular expression be found at the beginning of the line.

$ Requires that the preceding regular expression be found at the end of the line.

\   Treats the following special character as an ordinary character. For example, \. stands for a period and * for an asterisk.

\(\)   Saves the pattern enclosed between \(and \) in a special holding space. Up to nine patterns can be saved in this way on a single line. They can be "replayed" in substitutions by the escape sequences \1 to \9. This feature is not used in grep and egrep.

n   Matches the *n*th pattern previously saved by \(and \), where *n* is a number from 0 to 9 and previously saved patterns are counted from the left on the line. This feature is not used in grep and egrep.

The egrep and awk programs use an extended set of metacharacters:

regexp+   Matches one or more occurrences of the regular expression (*regexp*).

regexp?   Matches zero or one occurrences of the regular expression.

regexp | *regexp*   Matches lines containing either *regexp*.

(*regexp*)   Used for grouping in complex regular expressions (e.g., with | above).

Regular expressions in ex (: commands from vi) offer some different extensions:

\<   Constrains the following pattern to be matched only at the beginning of a word.

\>   Constrains the following pattern to be matched only at the end of a word.

\u   Appended to the *replacement* string of a substitute command, converts first character of replacement string to uppercase.

\U   Appended to the *replacement* string of a substitute command, converts entire replacement string to uppercase.

\l   Appended to the *replacement* string of a substitute command, converts first character of replacement string to lowercase.

\L   Appended to the *replacement* string of a substitute command, converts entire replacement string to uppercase.

▪ The **vi** Editor ▪

Command-Line Syntax

There are two commands to invoke the **vi** editor:

> **vi** [*options*] [*file(s)*]

or:

> **view** [*file(s)*]

If a file is not named, **vi** will open a file that can be given a name with the **:f** command or when it is saved using the **:w** command. If more than one file is named, the first file is opened for editing and **:n** is used to open the next file. The **view** command opens the first *file* for read-only use; changes cannot be saved.

Options:

-l	Open file for editing LISP programs
-r	Recover file
-R	Open file in read-only mode; same as using **view**
-t*tag*	Start at *tag*
-x	Open encrypted file
+	Open file at last line
+ *n*	Open file at line *n*
+/*pattern*	Open file at first occurrence of *pattern*
-w*n*	Set window to *n* lines

Operating Modes

After the file is opened, you are in command mode. From command mode, you can invoke insert mode, issue editing commands, move the cursor to a different position in the file, invoke ex commands or a UNIX shell, and save or exit the current version of the file.

The following commands invoke insert mode:

```
a A i I o O R s S
```

While in insert mode, you can enter new text in the file. Press the *ESCAPE* key to exit insert mode and return to command mode.

Command Syntax

The syntax for editing commands is:

    [n] operator [n] object

The commands that position the cursor in the file represent objects that the basic editing operators can take as arguments. Objects represent all characters up to (or back to) the designated object. The cursor movement keys and pattern-matching commands can be used as objects. Some basic editing operators are:

c	Change
d	Delete
y	Yank or copy

If the current line is the object of the operation, then the operator is the same as the object: cc, dd, yy. *n* is the number of times the operation is performed or the number of objects the operation is performed on. If both *n*'s are specified, the effect is *n* times *n*.

The following text objects are represented:

word	Includes characters up to a space or punctuation mark. Capitalized object is variant form that recognizes only blank spaces.
sentence	Up to . ! ? followed by two spaces.
paragraph	Up to next blank line or paragraph macro defined by para= option.
section	Up to next section heading defined by sect= option.

Examples:

2cw	Change the next two words
d}	Delete up to the next paragraph
d^	Delete back to the beginning of the line

5yy	Copy the next five lines
3dl	Delete three characters to the right of the cursor

Status Line Commands

Most commands are not echoed on the screen as you input them. However, the status line at the bottom of the screen is used to echo input for the following commands:

/ ?	Start pattern-matching search forward (/) or backwards (?)
:	Invoke an ex command
!	Invoke a UNIX command that takes as its input an object in the buffer and replaces it with output from the command

Commands that are input on the status line must be entered by pressing the *RETURN* key. In addition, error messages and output from the ^G command are displayed on the status line.

Summary of vi Commands

.	Repeat last command (insert, change, or delete).
^@	Repeat last command.
@*buffer*	Execute command stored in *buffer*.
a	Append text after cursor.
A	Append text at end of line.
^A	Unused.
b	Back up to beginning of word in current line.
B	Back up to word, ignoring punctuation.
^B	Scroll backward one window.
c	Change operator.
C	Change to end of current line.
^C	Unused.
d	Delete operator.
D	Delete to end of current line.
^D	Scroll down half-window.
e	Move to end of word.
E	Move to end of word, ignoring punctuation.
^E	Show one more line at bottom of window.
f	Find next character typed forward on current line.
F	Find next character typed back on current line.

^F	Scroll forward one window.
g	Unused.
G	Go to specified line or end of file.
^G	Print information about file on status line.
h	Left arrow cursor key.
H	Move cursor to home position.
^H	Left arrow cursor key; *BACKSPACE* key in insert mode.
i	Insert text before cursor.
I	Insert text at beginning of line.
^I	Unused in command mode; in insert mode, same as *TAB* key.
j	Down arrow cursor key.
J	Join two lines.
^J	Down arrow cursor key.
k	Up arrow cursor key.
K	Unused.
^K	Unused.
l	Right arrow cursor key.
L	Move cursor to last position in window.
^L	Redraw screen.
m	Mark the current cursor position in register (a-z).
M	Move cursor to middle position in window.
^M	Carriage return.
n	Repeat the last search command.
N	Repeat the last search command in reverse direction.
^N	Down arrow cursor key.
o	Open line below current line.
O	Open line above current line.
^O	Unused.
p	Put yanked or deleted text after or below cursor.
P	Put yanked or deleted text before or above cursor.
^P	Up arrow cursor key.
q	Unused.
Q	Quit `vi` and invoke `ex`
^Q	Unused in command mode; in input mode, quote next character.
r	Replace character at cursor with the next character you type.
R	Replace characters.
^R	Redraw the screen.
s	Change the character under the cursor to typed characters.
S	Change entire line.
^S	Unused.
t	Move cursor forward to character before next character typed.
T	Move cursor back to character after next character typed.
^T	Unused in command mode; in insert mode, used with *autoindent* option set.

u	Undo the last change made.
U	Restore current line, discarding changes.
^U	Scroll the screen upward half-window.
v	Unused.
V	Unused.
^V	Unused in command mode; in insert mode, quote next character.
w	Move to beginning of next word.
W	Move to beginning of next word, ignoring punctuation.
^W	Unused in command mode; in insert mode, back up to beginning of word.
x	Delete character under the cursor.
X	Delete character before cursor.
^X	Unused.
y	Yank or copy operator.
Y	Make copy of current line.
^Y	Show one more line at top of window.
z	Redraw the screen, repositioning cursor when followed by CR at the top, . at the middle, and − at the bottom of screen.
ZZ	Exit the editor, saving changes.
^Z	Unused.

Characters Not Used in Command Mode

The following characters are unused in command mode and can be mapped as user-defined commands.

^A	g	K	^K
^O	q	^T	v
V	^W	^X	^Z
*	\	_ (underscore)	

vi set Options

The following options can be specified with the :set command.

Option (Abbreviation)	Default	Description
autoindent (ai)	noai	Indents each line to the same level as the line above. Use with shiftwidth option.

autoprint (ap)	ap	Changes are displayed after each editor command. (For global replacement, last replacement displayed.)
autowrite (aw)	noaw	Automatically writes (saves) file if changed before opening another file with :n or before giving UNIX command with :!.
beautify (bf)	nobf	Ignores all control characters during input (except tab, newline, or formfeed).
directory (dir)	=tmp	Names directory in which ex stores buffer files. (Directory must be writable.)
edcompatible	noed- compatible	Uses ed-like features on substitute commands.
errorbells (eb)	errorbells	Error messages ring bell.
hardtabs (ht)	=8	Defines boundaries for terminal hardware tabs.
ignorecase (ic)	noic	Disregards case during a search.
lisp	nolisp	Indents are inserted in appropriate LISP format. () {} [[and]] are modified to have meaning for *lisp*.
list	nolist	Tabs print as ^I; ends of lines are marked with $. (Used to tell if end character is a tab or a space.)
magic	magic	Wildcard characters . * [are special in *patterns*.
mesg	mesg	Permits messages to display on terminal while editing in vi.
number (nu)	nonu	Displays line numbers on left of screen during editing session.
open	open	Allows entry to *open* or *visual* mode from ex.

optimize (opt)	noopt	Deletes carriage returns at the end of lines when printing multiple lines; speeds output on dumb terminals when printing lines with leading white space (blanks or tabs).
paragraphs (para)	=IPLPPPQP LIpplpipbp	Defines paragraph delimiters for movement by { or }. The pairs of characters in the value are the names of nroff/troff macros that begin paragraphs.
prompt	prompt	Sets ex prompt (:).
readonly (ro)	noro	Any writes (saves) of a file will fail unless you use ! after the write (works with w, ZZ, or autowrite).
redraw (re)	noredraw	Terminal will redraw the screen whenever edits are made (insert mode pushes over existing characters; deleted lines immediately close up). Default depends on line speed and terminal type. noredraw is useful at slow speeds on a dumb terminal; deleted lines show up as @, and inserted text appears to overwrite existing text until you press *ESC*.
remap	remap	Allows nested map sequences.
report	=5	Size of a large edit (i.e., number of lines affected by a single edit) that will trigger a warning message on bottom line of screen.
scroll	=[½ window]	Amount of screen to scroll.
sections	=SHNHH HU	Defines section delimiters for { } movement. The pairs of characters in the value are the names of nroff/troff macros that begin sections.
shell (sh)	=/bin/sh	Pathname of shell used for shell escape (:!) and shell command (:sh). Value is derived from shell environment.

shiftwidth (sw)	sw=8	Defines number of spaces to indent when using the >> or << commands in the autoindent option.
showmatch (sm)	nosm	In vi, when) or } is entered, cursor moves briefly to matching (or {. (If match is not on the screen, rings the error message bell.) Very useful for programming.
showmode (smd)	nosmd	(System V, Release 2 vi only). The string *Input Mode* is printed on the command line whenever input mode is entered.
slowopen (slow)		Holds off display during insert. Default depends on line speed and terminal type.
tabstop (ts)	=8	Sets number of spaces that a *TAB* indents during editing session. (Printer still uses system tab of 8.)
taglength (H)	=0	Defines the number of characters that are significant for tags. Default (zero) means that all characters are significant.
tags	=tags /usr/lib/tags	Pathname of files containing tags. (See the tag(1) command.) By default, system searches /usr/lib/tags and the file tags in the current directory.
term		Terminal type.
terse	noterse	Displays briefer error messages.
timeout	timeout	Macros "time out" after 1 second.
ttytype		Terminal type.
warn	warn	Displays *No write since last change* as warning.
window (w)		Shows a certain number of lines of the file on the screen. Default depends on line speed and terminal type.
wrapscan (ws)	ws	Searches wraparound end of file.

wrapmargin (wm)	=0	Defines right margin. If greater than zero, automatically inserts carriage returns to break lines.
writeany (wa)	nowa	Allows saving to any file.

▪ The ex Editor ▪

The ex editor is a line editor that serves as the foundation for the screen editor, vi. All ex commands work on the current line or a range of lines in a file. In vi, ex commands are preceded by a colon and entered by pressing *RETURN*. In ex itself, the colon is supplied as the prompt at which you enter commands.

The ex editor can also be used on its own. To enter ex from the UNIX prompt:

ex *filename*

Any of the options described for invoking vi may also be used with ex. In addition, the vi command Q can be used to quit the vi editor and enter ex.

To exit ex:

x	Exit, saving changes
q!	Quit, without saving changes
vi	Enter vi from ex

To enter an ex command from vi:

:*address* command *options*

The colon (:) indicates an ex command. The *address* is a line number or range of lines that are the object of the *command*.

The following options can be used with commands:

!	Indicates a variant form of the command.
parameters	Indicates that additional information can be supplied. A parameter can be the name of a file.
count	Is the number of times the command is to be repeated.
flag	#, p, and l indicate print format.

Unlike vi commands, the *count* cannot precede the command as it will be taken for the *address*. d3 deletes three lines beginning with the current line; 3d deletes line 3.

As you type the address and command, it is echoed on the status line. Enter the command by pressing the *RETURN* key.

Addresses

If no address is given, the current line is the object of the command. If the address specifies a range of lines, the format is:

x, y

where x and y are the first and last addressed lines. x must precede y in the buffer. x and y may be line numbers or primitives. Using ; instead of , sets the current line to x before interpreting y (that is, the current position will be at x at the completion of the command). 1, $ addresses all lines in the file.

The following address symbols can be used:

.	Current line
n	Absolute line *n*umber
$	Last line
%	All lines, same as 1, $
$x-$ | $+n$	n line before or after x
-[n]	One or n lines previous
+ [n]	One or n lines ahead
'x	Line marked with x
' '	Previous context
/*pat*/ or ?*pat*?	Ahead or back to line matching *pat*

ex Commands

abbrev   ab [*string text*]
Define *string* when typed to be translated into *text*. If *string* and *text* are not specified, list all current abbreviations.

append   [*address*]a[!]
                     text

                     .

Append *text* at specified *address*, or at present address if none is specified. With the ! flag, toggle the autoindent setting during the input of *text*.

args

ar
Print the members of the argument list, with the current argument printed within brackets ([ ]).

change

[*address*]c[!]
text

.

Replace the specified lines with *text*. With the ! flag, toggle the `autoindent` setting during the input of *text*.

copy

[*address*]co*destination*
Copy the lines included in *address* to the specified *destination* address. The command t is a synonym for `copy`.

delete

[*address*]d[*buffer*]
Delete the lines included in *address*. If *buffer* is specified, save or append the text to the named buffer.

edit

e[!] [+*n*] *file*
Begin editing on *file*. If the ! flag is used, do not warn if the present file has not been saved since the last change. If the +*n* argument is used, begin editing on line *n*.

file

f [*filename*]
Change the name of the current file to *filename*, which is considered "not edited." If no *filename* is specified, print the current status of the file.

global

[*address*]g[!]/*pattern*/[*commands*]
Execute *commands* on all lines that contain *pattern*. If *commands* are not specified, print all such lines. If the ! flag is used, execute *commands* on all lines not containing *pattern*.

insert

[*address*]i[!]
text

.

Insert *text* at line before the specified *address*, or at present address if none is specified. With the ! flag, toggle the `autoindent` setting during the input of *text*.

join

[*address*]j[*count*]
Place the text in the specified range on one line, with white space adjusted to provide two blank characters after a (.), no blank characters if a) follows, and one blank character otherwise.

k

[*address*]k*char*
Mark the given *address* with *char*.

list   [*address*]l[*count*]
Print the specified lines in an unambiguous manner.

map   map *char commands*
Define a macro named *char* in visual mode with the specified sequence of *commands*. *char* may be a single character, or the sequence #*n*, representing a function key on the keyboard.

mark   [*address*]ma*char*
Mark the specified line with *char*, a single lowercase letter. Return later to the line with ' x.

move   [*address*]m*destination*
Move the lines specified by *address* to the *destination* address.

next   n[!][[+*command*] *filelist*]
Edit the next file in the command-line argument list. Use args for a listing of arguments. If *filelist* is provided, replace the current argument list with *filelist* and begin editing on the first file; if *command* is given (containing no spaces), execute *command* after editing the first such file.

number   [*address*]nu[*count*]
Print each line specified by *address* preceded by its buffer line number. # may be used as an abbreviation for number as well as nu.

open   [*address*]o[/*pattern*/]
Enter open mode at the lines specified by *address*, or lines matching *pattern*. Exit open mode with Q.

preserve   pre
Save the current editor buffer as though the system had crashed.

print   [*address*]p[*count*]
Print the lines specified by *address* with nonprinting characters printed. P may also be used as an abbreviation.

put   [*address*]pu[*char*]
Restore previously deleted or yanked lines from named buffer specified by *char* to the line specified by *address*; if *char* is not specified, the last deleted or yanked text is restored.

quit   q[!]
Terminate current editing session. If the file was not saved since the last change, or if there are files in the argument list that have not yet be accessed, you will not be able to quit without the ! flag.

read   [*address*]r[!] [*file*]
Copy the text of *file* at the specified *address*. If *file* is not specified, the current filename is used.

read   [*address*]r !*command*
Read in the output of *command* into the text after the line specified by *address*.

recover   rec [*file*]
Recover *file* from system save area.

rewind   rew[!]
Rewind argument list and begin editing the first file in the list. The ! flag rewinds without warning if the file has not been saved since the last change.

set   se *parameter parameter2* ...
Set a value to an option with each *parameter*, or if no *parameter* is supplied, print all options that have been changed from their defaults. For Boolean-valued options, each *parameter* can be phrased as *option* or n*option*; other options can be assigned with the syntax, *option=value*.

shell   sh
Create a new shell. Resume editing when the shell is terminated.

source   so *file*
Read and execute commands from *file*.

substitute   [*address*]s[[/*pattern*/*repl*/]*options*][*count*]
Replace each instance of *pattern* on the specified lines with *repl*. If *pattern* and *repl* are omitted, repeat last substitution. The following options are supported:
         g   Substitute all instances of *pattern*
         c   Prompt for confirmation before each change

t   [*address*]t*destination*
Copy the lines included in *address* to the specified *destination* address.

ta   [*address*]ta *tag*
Switch the focus of editing to *tag*.

unabbreviate una *word*
Remove *word* from the list of abbreviations.

undo   u
Reverse the changes made by the last editing command.

unmap   unm *char*
Remove *char* from the list of macros.

v   [*address*]v /*pattern* / [*commands*]
Execute *commands* on all lines not containing *pattern*. If *commands* are not specified, print all such lines.

version   ve
Print the current version number of the editor and the date the editor was last changed.

visual   [*address*]vi [*type*] [*count*]
Enter visual mode at the line specified by *address*. Exit with Q. *type* is either −, ^, or . (see the z command). *count* specifies an initial window size.

write   [*address*]w[!] [[>>] *file*]
Write lines specified by *address* to *file*, or full contents of buffer if *address* is not specified. If *file* is also omitted, save the contents of the buffer to the current filename. If >> *file* is used, write contents to the end of the specified *file*. The ! flag forces the editor to write over any current contents of *file*.

write   [*address*]w !*command*
Write lines specified by *address* to *command* through a pipe.

wq   wq[!]
Write and quit the file in one movement.

xit   x
Write file if changes have been made to the buffer since last write, then quit.

yank   [*address*]ya[*char*][*count*]
Place lines specified by *address* in named buffer indicated by *char*. If no *char* is specified, place in general buffer.

z   [*address*]z[*type*][*count*]
Print a window of text with line specified by *address* at the top. *type* is as follows:
     +   Place specified line at the top of the window (default)
     -      Place specified line at bottom of the window
     ^   Print the window before the window associated with type −
     =   Place specified line in the center of the window and leave the current line at this line
count specifies the number of lines to be displayed.

!

    [address] ! *command*
Execute *command* in a shell. If *address* is specified, apply the lines contained in *address* as standard input to *command*, and replace the lines with the output.

=

    [address]=
Print the line number of the line indicated by *address*.

< >

    [address]<*[count]*
or *[address]* > *[count]*
Shift lines specified by *address* in specified direction. Only blanks and tabs are shifted in a left shift (<).

address

    address
Print the lines specified in *address*.

RETURN

    RETURN
Print the next line in the file.

&

    [address]&*[options]**[count]*
Repeat the previous substitute command.

~

    [address]~*[count]*
Replace the previous regular expression with the previous replacement pattern from a `substitute` command.

▪ The `sed` Editor ▪

> `sed` *[options]* *file(s)*

The following options are recognized:

    `-n`   Only print lines specified with the p command, or the p flag of the s command

    `-e` *cmd*   Next argument is an editing command

    `-f` *file*   Next argument is a file containing editing commands

All `sed` commands have the general form:

> *[address]*[, *address*][!]*command* *[arguments]*

The `sed` editor copies each line of input into a pattern space. `sed` instructions consist of addresses and editing commands. If the address of the command matches the line in the pattern space, then the command is applied to that line. If a command has no address, then it is applied to each input line. It is important to note that a command affects the contents of the space; subsequent command addresses attempt to match the line in the pattern space, not the original input line.

Pattern Addressing

In a sed command, an *address* can either be a line number or a *pattern*, enclosed in slashes (*/pattern/*). Address types cannot be mixed when specifying two addresses. Patterns can make use of regular expressions, as described at the beginning of this appendix. Additionally, \n can be used to match any newline in the pattern space (resulting from the N command), but not the newline at the end of the pattern space. If no pattern is specified, *command* will be applied to all lines. If only one address is specified, the command will be applied to all lines between the first and second addresses, inclusively. Some commands can only accept one address.

The ! operator following a pattern causes sed to apply the command to all lines that do not contain the pattern.

A series of commands can be grouped after one pattern by enclosing the command list in curly braces:

[*/pattern/*][*, /pattern/*]{
command1
command2
  }

Alphabetical List of Commands

:   **:** *label*
Specify a label to be branched to by b or t. *label* may contain up to eight characters.

=   [*/pattern/*]=
Write to standard output the line number of each line addressed by *pattern*.

a   [*address*]a\
text
Append *text* following each line matched by *address*. If *text* goes over more than one line, newlines must be "hidden" by preceding them with a backslash. The insertion will be terminated by the first newline that is not hidden in this way. The results of this command are read into the pattern space (creating a multiline pattern space) and sent to standard output when the list of editing is finished or a command explicitly prints the pattern space.

b   [*address1*][*, address2*]b[*label*]
Branch to *label* placed with : command. If no *label*, branch to the end of the script. That is, skip all subsequent editing commands (up to *label*) for each addressed line.

c

[*address1*][*, address2*]c\
text
Replace pattern space with *text*. (See a for details on *text*.)

d

[*address1*][*, address2*]d
Delete line in pattern space. Thus, line is not passed to standard output and a new line of input is read; editing resumes with first command in list.

D

[*address1*][*address2*]D
Delete first part (up to embedded newline) of multiline pattern created by N command and begin editing. Same as d if N has not been applied to a line.

g

[*address1*][*, address2*]g
Copy contents of hold space (see h or H command) into pattern space, wiping out previous contents.

G

[*address1*][*, address2*]G
Append contents of hold space (see h or H command) to contents of the pattern space.

h

[*address1*][*, address2*]h
Copy pattern space into hold space, a special buffer. Previous contents of hold space are obliterated.

H

[*address1*][*, address2*]H
Append pattern space to contents of the hold space. Previous and new contents are separated by a newline.

i

[*address1*]i\
text
Insert *text* before each line matched by *address*. (See a for details on *text*.)

n

[*address1*][*, address2*]n
Read next line of input into pattern space. Current line is output but control passes to next editing command instead of beginning at the top of the list.

N

[*address1*][*, address2*]N
Append next input line to contents of pattern space; the two lines are separated by an embedded newline. (This command is designed to allow pattern matches across two lines.)

p

[*address1*][*, address2*]p
Print the addressed line(s). Unless the −n command-line option is used, this command will cause duplication of the line in the output. Also used when commands change flow control (d, N, b).

P

[*address1*][*, address2*]P
Print first part (up to embedded newline) of multiline pattern created by N command. Same as p if N has not been applied to a line.

q

[*address*]q
Quit when *address* is encountered. The addressed line is first written to output, along with any text appended to it by previous a or r commands.

r

[*address*]r *file*
Read contents of *file* and append after the contents of the pattern space. Exactly one space must separate the r and the filename.

s

[*address1*][*, address2*]s/*pattern*/*replacement*/[*flags*]
Substitute *replacement* for *pattern* on each addressed line. If pattern addresses are used, the pattern // represents the last pattern address specified. The following flags can be specified:
- g Replace all instances of /*pattern*/ on each addressed line, not just the first instance.
- p Print the line if a successful substitution is done. If several successful substitutions are done, multiple copies of the line will be printed.
- w *file* Write the line to a *file* if a replacement was done. A maximum of ten different *files* can be opened.

t

[*address1*][*, address2*]t [*label*]
Test if successful substitutions have been made on addressed lines, and if so, branch to *label*. (See b and :.) If label is not specified, drop to bottom of list of editing commands.

w

[*address1*][*, address2*]w *file*
Write contents of pattern space to *file*. This action occurs when the command is encountered rather than when the pattern space is output. Exactly one space must separate the w and the filename. A maximum of ten different files can be opened.

x

[*address1*][*, address2*]x
Exchange contents of the pattern space with the contents of the hold space.

▪ **awk** ▪

An awk program consists of patterns and procedures:

pattern {*procedure*}

Both are optional. If *pattern* is missing, {*procedure*} will be applied to all lines. If {*procedure*} is missing, the line will be passed unaffected to standard output (i.e., it will be printed as is).

Each input line, or record, is divided into fields by white space (blanks or tabs) or by some other user-definable record separator. Fields are referred to by the variables $1, $2,..., $*n*. $0 refers to the entire record.

Patterns

Patterns can be specified using regular expressions as described at the beginning of this appendix.

pattern {*procedure*}
The following additional pattern rules can be used in awk:

- The special pattern BEGIN allows you to specify procedures that will take place before the first input line is processed. (Generally, you set global variables here.)

- Interrupt place after the last input line is processed.

- ^ and $ can be used to refer to the beginning and end of a field, respectively, rather than the beginning and end of a line.

- A pattern can be a relational expression using any of the operators <, <=, ==, !=, >=, and >. For example, $2 > $1 selects lines for which the second field is greater than the first. Comparisons can be either string or numeric.

- Patterns can be combined with the Boolean operators || (or), && (and), and ! (not).

- Patterns can include any of the following predefined variables. For example, NF > 1 selects records with more than one field.

Special Variables

FS	Field separator (blank and tab by default)
RS	Record separator (newline by default)
OFS	Output field separator (blank by default)
ORS	Output record separator (newline by default)
NR	Number of current record
NF	Number of fields in current record
$0	Entire input record

$1, $2, ..., $n   First, second, ...*n*th field in current record, where
                    fields are separated by FS

Procedures

Procedures consist of one or more commands, functions, or variable assignments,
separated by newlines or semicolons, and contained within curly braces. Commands
fall into four groups:

- variable or array assignments

- printing commands

- built-in functions

- control flow commands

Variables and Array Assignments

Variables can be assigned a value with an = sign. For example:

    FS = ``,''

Expressions using the operators +, −, /, and % (modulo) can be assigned to variables.

Arrays can be created with the split function (see following awk commands)
or can be simply named in an assignment statement.   ++, +=, and −= are used to
increment or decrement an array, as in the C language. Array elements can be subscripted with numbers (*array*[1],...,*array*[*n*]) or with names. (For example, to count
the number of occurrences of a pattern, you could use the following program:

    /pattern/ {*n*["*/pattern/*"]++}
    END {print *n*["*/pattern/*"] }

awk Commands

for

                for (*i=lower*;*i<=upper*;*i++*)
                    command
                While the value of variable *i* is in the range between *lower* and
                upper, do *command*. A series of commands must be put within
                braces. <= or any relational operator can be used; ++ or −− can
                be used to decrement variable.

for	`for` *i* in *array*
	command
	For each occurrence of variable *i* in *array*, do *command*. A series of commands must be put inside braces.
if	`if` (*condition*)
	command
	`[else]`
	[*command*]
	If *condition* is true, do *command(s)*, otherwise do *command* in `else` clause. *condition* can be an expression using any of the relational operators `<`, `<=`, `==`, `!=`, `>=`, or `>`, as well as the pattern-matching operator `~` (e.g., `if $1 ~ /[Aa].*/`). A series of commands must be put within braces.
length	*x* = `length` (*arg*)
	Return the length of *arg*. If *arg* is not supplied, `$0` is assumed.
log	*x*=`log` (*arg*)
	Return logarithm of *arg*.
print	`print` [*args*]
	Print *args* on output. *args* is usually one or more fields, but may also be one or more of the predefined variables. Literal strings must be surrounded by quotation marks. Fields are printed in the order they are listed. If separated by commas in the argument list, they are separated in the output by the character specified by `OFS`. If separated by spaces, they are concatenated in the output.
printf	`printf` "*format*," *expression(s)*
	Formatted print statement. Fields or variables can be formatted according to instructions in the *format* argument. The number of arguments must correspond to the number specified in the format sections.

Format follows the conventions of the C language's `printf` statement. Here are a few of the most common formats:

    `%`*n.m*`d`   a floating point number;

                n = total number of digits.

                m = number of digits after decimal point.

    `%`[`-`]*nc*   *n* specifies minimum field length for

                format type *c*. `-` justifies value in

                field; otherwise value is right justified.

Format can also contain embedded escape sequences: `\n` (newline) or `\t` (tab) are the most common.

Spaces and literal text can be placed in the *format* argument by surrounding the entire argument with quotation marks. If there are multiple expressions to be printed, you should specify multiple formats. An example is worth a thousand words. For an input file containing only the line:

```
5  5
```

The program:

```
{printf (''The sum on line %s is %d \n'', NR, $1+$2)}
```

will produce:

```
The sum on line 1 is 10.
```

followed by a newline.

split   *x* = split (*string*, *array* [, *sep*])
Split *string* into elements of array array[1], . . ., array[*n*]. *string* is split at each occurrence of separator *sep*. If *sep* is not specified, FS is used. The number of array elements created is returned.

sprintf   *x* = sprintf("*format*", *expression*)
Return the value of *expression(s)*, using the specified *format* (see printf).

sqrt   *x* = sqrt(*arg*)
Return square root of *arg*.

substr   *x* = substr (*string*, *m*, [*n*])
Return substring of *string* beginning at character position *m* and consisting of the next *n* characters. If *n* is omitted, include all characters to the end of *string*.

while   while (*condition*)
     command
Do *command* while *condition* is true (see if for a description of allowable conditions). A series of commands must be put within braces.

B

Formatter Command Summary

This appendix is divided into ten subsections, each covering a different facet of the `nroff/troff` formatting system. These sections are:

- `nroff/troff` command-line syntax
- `nroff/troff` requests
- escape sequences
- predefined number registers
- special characters
- the `ms` macro package
- the `mm` macro package
- the `tbl` preprocessor
- the `eqn` preprocessor
- the `pic` preprocessor

In the following sections, italics are used for values that you supply. Optional arguments to requests or macros are enclosed in brackets.

▪ **nroff/troff** Command-Line Syntax ▪

nroff [*options*] [*files*]

−c*name*	Prepend /usr/lib/macros/cmp.n.[dt].*name* to *files* (old versions of nroff only).
−e	Space words equally on the line instead of in full multiples of the space character.
−h	Use tabs in large spaces.
−i	Read standard input after *files* are processed.
−k*name*	Compact macros and output to [dt].*name* (old versions of nroff only).
−m*name*	Prepend /usr/lib/tmac/tmac.*name* to *files*.
−n*n*	Number first page *n*.
−o*list*	Print only pages contained in *list*. Individual pages in *list* should be separated by commas; a page range is specified by *n–m*; *n*– indicates from page *n* to the end.
−q	Invoke simultaneous input/output of .rd requests.
−r*an*	Set register *a* to *n*.
−s*n*	Stop every *n* pages.
−T*name*	Output is for device type *name*. Values are shown in Table B-1. (Check your manual for other devices, especially those supported by the mm command.)
−u*n*	Embolden characters by overstriking *n* times.
−z	Throw away output except messages from .tm request.

TABLE B-1. Device Names for nroff

Abbreviation	Used for
37	TELETYPE Model 37 terminal (default for nroff)
450	DASI 450 terminal (default for mm)
tn300	GE TermiNet 300 printer
300	DASI 300 terminal
832	Anderson Jacobson 832 printer
2631	Hewlett-Packard 2631
4000a	Trendata 4000a
8510	C. Itoh printer
lp	ASCII line printer
X	EBCDIC line printer

`troff` Options

`troff` [*options*] [*files*]

`-a`	Send printable ASCII approximation to standard output. `otroff` sends its output directly to a connected typesetter unless the `-t` or `-a` option is specified, in which case it is sent to standard output. `ditroff` always writes to standard output.
`-b`	Report phototypesetter status (`otroff` only).
`-c`*name*	Prepend `/usr/lib/macros/cmp.t.[dt]`.*name* to *files* (`otroff` only).
`-f`	Do not stop the phototypesetter when the formatting run is done (`otroff` only).
`-F`*dir*	Format output for device name using the font tables in directory *dir* instead of `/usr/lib/font` (`ditroff` only).
`-i`	Read standard input after files.
`-k`*name*	Compact macros and output to [dt].*name* (`otroff` only).
`-m`*name*	Prepend `/usr/lib/tmac/tmac`.*name* to *files*.
`-n`*n*	Number first page *n*.
`-o`*list*	Print only pages contained in *list*. Individual pages in *list* should be separated by commas. A page range is specified by *n–m*; *n–* indicates from page *n* to the end.
`-p`*n*	Print all characters in point size *n*, but retain motions for sizes specified in document (`otroff` only).
`-q`	Do not echo `.rd` requests.
`-r`*an*	Assign value *n* to register *a*.
`-s`*n*	Stop every *n* pages.
`-t`	Send output to standard output instead of directly to the phototypesetter (`otroff` only).
`-T`*name*	Format output for device *name* using the device description and font width tables in `/usr/lib/font/dev`*name* (`ditroff` only).
`-w`	If the phototypesetter is busy, wait until it is free (`otroff` only).

▪ `nroff`/`troff` Requests ▪

`.ab` [*text*]	Abort and print *text* as message. If *text* is not specified, the message *User Abort* is printed.
`.ad` [*c*]	Adjust one or both margins if filling is in effect (see `.fi`). *c* can be:

                  b or n   Adjust both margins

                  c   Center all lines

	l	Adjust left margin only
	r	Adjust right margin only
.af *r c*	Assign format *c* to register *r*. *c* can be:	
	1	0, 1, 2, etc.
	001	000, 001, 002, etc.
	i	Lowercase roman
	I	Uppercase roman
	a	Lowercase alphabetic
	A	Uppercase alphabetic

.am *xx yy*   Append to macro *xx*; end append at call of *yy* (default *yy* = ..).

.as *xx string*   Append to *string xx*.

.bd *f n*   Overstrike characters in font *f*, *n* times.

.bd *f s n*   Overstrike special font *s*, *n* times when font *f* is in effect.

.bp [*n*]   Begin new page. Number next page *n*.

.br   Break to a new line (output partial lines).

.c2 *c*   Set no-break control character to *c* (default ′).

.cc *c*   Set control character to *c* (default .).

.cf *file*   Copy contents of *file* into output, uninterpreted (ditroff only).

.ce [*n*]   Center next *n* lines; if *n* is 0, stop centering (default *n* = 1).

.ch *xx* [*n*]   Change trap position for macro *xx* to *n*. If *n* is absent, remove the trap.

.cs *f n m*   Use constant character spacing for font *f* of *n*/36 ems. If *m* is given, the em is taken to be *m* points.

.cu [*n*]   Continuous underline (including interword spaces) on next *n* lines. If *n* is 0, stop underlining. Italicize in troff. (See .ul.)

.da [*xx*]   Divert following text, appending it to macro *xx*. If no argument, end diversion.

.de *xx* [*yy*]   Define macro *xx*. End definition at .*yy* (default .yy = ..).

.di [*xx*]   Divert following text to newly defined macro *xx*. If no argument, end diversion.

.ds *xx string*   Define *xx* to contain *string*.

.dt *n xx*   Install diversion trap to invoke macro *xx* at position *n*.

.ec [*c*]   Set escape character to *c* (default \).

.el *anything*   Else portion of if-else. See .ie.

.em *xx*   Set end macro to *xx*.

.eo   Turn escape character mechanism off. See .ec.

.ev [*n*]   Change environment to *n*. If no argument, restore previous environment ($0 \leq n \leq 2$ = initial value 0).

.ex   Exit from formatter.

.fc *a b*   Set field delimiter to *a* and pad character to *b*.

`.fi`	Turn on fill mode (default: fill is on).
`.fl`	Flush output buffer.
`.fp` *n f*	Assign font *f* to position *n*.
`.ft` *f*	Change font to *f*.
`.hc[c]`	Change hyphenation-indication character used with `.hw` to *c* (default −).
`.hw` *words*	Specify hyphenation points for *words* (e.g., `.hw spe-ci-fy`).
`.hy` *n*	Turn hyphenation on (*n*≥1) or off (*n*=0).

n=1	Hyphenate whenever necessary
n=2	Don't hyphenate last word in page or diversion
n=4	Don't split off first two characters of word
n=8	Don't split off last two characters of word
n=14	Use all three restrictions

`.ie` *c anything*	If portion of `if-else`. See `.el`.
`.if` *!c anything*	If condition *c* is false, do *anything*.
`.if` *n anything*	If expression *n* >0, do *anything*.
`.if` *!n anything*	If expression *n* ≤0, do *anything*.
`.if` *' string1' string2' anything*	
	If *string1* and *string2* are identical, do *anything*.
`.if` *!' string1' string2' anything*	
	If *string1* and *string2* are not identical, do *anything*.
`.ig` *yy*	Ignore following text, up to line beginning with `.yy`.
`.in` *[±][n]*	Set indent to *n* or increment indent by ±*n*. If no argument, restore previous indent.
`.it` *n xx*	Set input line count trap to invoke macro *xx* after *n* lines of input text have been read.
`.lc` *c*	Set leader repetition character to *c*. (See `.tc`.) Leaders are invoked by `\a`.
`.lg` *n*	Turn ligature mode on if *n* is absent or nonzero.
`.ll` *[±][n]*	Set line length to *n* or increment line length by ±*n*. If no argument, restore previous line length (default 6.5 inches).
`.ls` *n*	Set line spacing to *n*. If no argument, restore previous line spacing (initial value 1).
`.lt` *n*	Set title length to *n*. If no argument, restore previous value.
`.mc` *[c] [n]*	Set margin character to *c*, and place it *n* spaces to the right of margin. If *c* is missing, turn margin character off. Default for *n* is 0.2 inches in `nroff` and 1 em in `troff`.
`.mk` *[r]*	Mark current vertical place in register *r*. Return to mark with `.rt`, or `.sp|\nr`.
`.na`	Do not adjust margins. (See `.ad`.)
`.ne` *n*	If *n* lines do not remain on this page, start new page.
`.nf`	No filling or adjusting of output lines. (See `.ad` and `.fi`.)

.nh	Turn hyphenation off. (See .hy.)
.nm [n m s i]	Number output lines ($n \geq 0$) or turn numbering off ($n=0$). $\pm n$ sets initial line number; m sets numbering interval; s sets separation of numbers and text; i sets indent of text.
.nn n	Do not number next n lines, but keep track of numbering sequence, which can be resumed with .nm+0.
.nr r n [m]	Assign the value n to number register r and optionally set autoincrement to m.
.ns	Turn no-space mode on. (See .rs.)
.nx file	Switch to file and do not return to current file. (See .so.)
.os	Output saved space specified in previous .sv request.
.pc c	Set page number character to c.
.pi cmd	Pipe output of troff to cmd instead of to standard output.
.pl [±][n]	Set page length to n or increment page length by $\pm n$. If no argument, restore default (default 11 inches).
.pm	Print names and sizes of all defined macros.
.pn [±][n]	Set next page number to n, or increment page number by $\pm n$.
.po [±][n]	Offset text a distance of n from left edge of page, or increment the current offset by $\pm n$. If no argument, restore previous offset.
.ps n	Set point size to n (troff only). (Default 10 points.)
.rd [prompt]	Read input from terminal, after printing optional prompt.
.rm xx	Remove macro or string xx.
.rn xx yy	Rename request, macro, or string xx to yy.
.rr r	Remove register r.
.rs xx yy	Restore spacing. (Turn no-space mode off; see .ns.)
.rt [±n]	Return (upward only) to marked vertical place, or to $\pm n$ from top of page or diversion. (See .mk.)
.so file	Switch out to file, then return to current file. (See .nx.)
.sp n	Leave n blank lines (default 1).
.ss n	Space character size set to n/36 em (no effect in nroff).
.sv n	Save n lines of space; output such space with .os.
.sy cmd [args]	Execute UNIX command cmd with optional arguments (ditroff only).
.ta n[t] m[t]	Set tab stop at positions n, m, etc. If t is not given, tab is left adjusting; if t is:
	R Right adjust
	C Center
.tc c	Define tab character as c (e.g., .tc . will draw a string of dots to tab position).
.ti [±][n]	Indent next output line n spaces, or increment the current indent by $\pm n$ for the next output line.

`.tl 'l'c'r'`	Specify left (*l*), centered (*c*), right (*r*) title.
`.tm` *text*	Terminal message. (Print *text* on standard error.)
`.tr` *ab*	Translate character *a* to *b*.
`.uf` *f*	Underline font set to *f* (to be switched to by `.ul`).
`.ul` [*n*]	Underline (italicize in `troff`) next *n* input lines. Do not underline interword spaces.
`.vs` [*n*]	Set vertical line spacing to *n*. If no argument, restore previous spacing (default 1/6 inch in `nroff`, 12 points in `troff`).
`.wh` *n xx*	When position *n* is reached, execute macro *xx*; negative values of *n* are with respect to page bottom.

▪ Escape Sequences ▪

`\`	To prevent or delay the interpretation of `\`.
`\e`	Printable version of the *current* escape character.
`\´`	´ (acute accent); equivalent to `\(aa`.
`` \` ``	` (grave accent); equivalent to `\(ga`.
`\-`	− Minus sign in the *current* font.
`\.`	Period (dot). (See `de`.)
`\` (space)	Unpaddable space-size space character.
`\0`	Digit width space.
`|`	1/6-em narrow space character (zero width in `nroff`).
`\^`	1/12-em half-narrow space character (zero width in `nroff`).
`\&`	Nonprinting, zero-width character.
`\!`	Transparent line indicator.
`\"`	Beginning of comment.
`\\$N`	Interpolate argument $1 \leq N \leq 9$.
`\%`	Default optional hyphenation character.
`\(xx`	Character named *xx*.
`\*x, \*(xx`	Interpolate string *x* or *xx*.
`\a`	Noninterpreted leader character for use in macros.
`\b´abc...´`	Bracket building function—stack *abc*... vertically.
`\c`	Interrupt text processing.
`\d`	Downward 1/2-em vertical motion (1/2 line in `nroff`).
`\D´l x,y´`	Draw a line from current position to coordinates *x,y* (`ditroff` only).
`\D´c d´`	Draw circle of diameter *d* with left edge at current position (`ditroff` only).

\D´e *d1 d2*´	Draw ellipse with horizontal diameter *d1* and vertical diameter *d2*, with left edge at current position (ditroff only).
\D´a *x1 y1 x2 y2*´	Draw arc counterclockwise from current position, with center at *x1,y1* and endpoint at *x1+x2,y1+y2* (ditroff only).
\D´~ *x1 y1 x2 yx*...´	Draw spline from current position through the specified coordinates (ditroff only).
\f*x*,\f (*xx*,\f*N*	Change to font named *x* or *xx* or to position *N*.
\h´*N*´	Local horizontal motion; move right *N* (negative left).
\H´*n*´	Set character height to *n* points, without changing width (ditroff only).
\j*x*	Mark horizontal place on output line in register *x*.
\k*x*	Mark horizontal place on input line in register *x*.
\l´*Nc*´	Horizontal line drawing function (optionally with *c*, default _).
\L´*Nc*´	Vertical line drawing function (optionally with *c*, default ⏐).
\n*x*,\n (*xx*	Interpolate number register *x* or *xx*.
\o´*abc*...´	Overstrike characters *a*, *b*, *c*...
\p	Break and spread output line.
\r	Reverse 1-em vertical motion (reverse line in nroff).
\s*N*,\s±*N*	Point-size change function.
\S´*n*´	Slant output *n* degrees to the right (ditroff only). Negative values slant to the left. A value of zero turns off slanting.
\t	Noninterpreted horizontal tab.
\u	Reverse (up) 1/2-em vertical motion (1/2 line in nroff).
\v´*N*´	Local vertical motion; move down *N* (negative up).
\w´*string*´	Interpolate width of *string*.
\x´*N*´	Extra line-space function (negative before, positive after).
\z*c*	Print *c* with zero width (without spacing).
\{	Begin conditional input.
\}	End conditional input.
\(newline)	Concealed (ignored) newline.
X	*X*, any character *not* listed above.

▪ Predefined Number Registers ▪

Read-Only Registers

.$	Number of arguments available at the current macro level.
.$$	Process ID of troff process (ditroff only).
.A	Set to 1 in troff, if −a option used; always 1 in nroff.
.H	Available horizontal resolution in basic units.
.T	In nroff, set to 1 if −T option used; in troff, always 0; in ditroff, you can print the value of −T with the string *(.T.
.V	Available vertical resolution in basic units.
.a	Extra line space most recently utilized using \x´N´.
.c	Number of *lines* read from current input file.
.d	Current vertical place in current diversion; equal to nl if no diversion.
.f	Current font as physical quadrant (1 to 4 in otroff; no limit in ditroff).
.h	Text baseline high-water mark on current page or diversion.
.i	Current indent.
.j	Current adjustment type (0=.adl or .na; 1=.adb; 3=.adc; 5=.adr).
.l	Current line length.
.n	Length of text portion on previous output line.
.o	Current page offset.
.p	Current page length.
.s	Current point size.
.t	Distance to the next trap.
.u	Equal to 1 in fill mode and 0 in no-fill mode.
.v	Current vertical line spacing.
.w	Width of previous character.
.x	Reserved version-dependent register.
.y	Reserved version-dependent register.
.z	Name of current diversion.

Read/Write Registers

%	Current page number.
ct	Character type (set by width function).
dl	Width (maximum) of last completed diversion.
dn	Height (vertical size) of last completed diversion.
dw	Current day of the week (1 to 7).

dy	Current day of the month (1 to 31).	
hp	Current horizontal place on input line.	
ln	Output line number.	
mo	Current month (1 to 12).	
nl	Vertical position of last printed text baseline.	
sb	Depth of string below baseline (generated by `width` function).	
st	Height of string above baseline (generated by `width` function).	
yr	Last two digits of current year.	

▪ Special Characters ▪

On the Standard Fonts

The following special characters are usually found on the standard fonts:

'	'	close quote	fi	\(fi	fi ligature
'	`	open quote	fl	\(fl	fl ligature
—	\(em	3/4 em dash	ff	\(ff	ff ligature
-	-	hyphen	ffi	\(Fi	ffi ligature
-	\(hy	hyphen	ffl	\(Fl	ffl ligature
—	\-	current font minus sign	°	\(de	degree
•	\(bu	bullet	†	\(dg	dagger
□	\(sq	square	′	\(fm	foot mark
_	\(ru	rule	¢	\(ct	cent sign
¼	\(14	1/4	®	\(rg	registered trademark
½	\(12	1/2	©	\(co	copyright
¾	\(34	3/4			

On the Special Font

The following characters are usually found on the special font except for the uppercase Greek letter names followed by † which are mapped into uppercase English letters in whatever font is mounted on font position one (default is Times Roman).

Miscellaneous Characters

§	\ (sc	section	↓	\ (da	down arrow
´	\ (aa	acute accent	|	\ (br	box rule
`	\ (ga	grave accent	‡	\ (dd	double dagger
_	\ (ul	underrule	☞	\ (rh	right hand
→	\ (->	right arrow	☜	\ (lh	left hand
←	\ (<-	left arrow	○	\ (ci	circle
↑	\ (ua	up arrow			

Mathematic Symbols

+	\ (pl	math plus	∪	\ (cu	cup (union)
−	\ (mi	math minus	∩	\ (ca	cap (intersection)
=	\ (eq	math equals	⊂	\ (sb	subset of
*	\ (**	math star	⊃	\ (sp	superset of
/	\ (sl	slash (matching backslash)	⊆	\ (ib	improper subset
√	\ (sr	square root	⊇	\ (ip	improper superset
‾	\ (rn	root en extender	∞	\ (if	infinity
≥	\ (>=	greater than or equal to	∂	\ (pd	partial derivative
≤	\ (<=	less than or equal to	∇	\ (gr	gradient
≡	\ (==	identically equal	¬	\ (no	not
≠	\ (~=	approx equal	∫	\ (is	integral sign
~	\ (ap	approximates	∝	\ (pt	proportional to
≠	\ (!=	not equal	∅	\ (es	empty set
×	\ (mu	multiply	∈	\ (mo	member of
÷	\ (di	divide	|	\ (or	or
±	\ (+-	plus-minus			

Bracket Building Symbols

⌈	\ (lt	left top of large curly bracket
{	\ (lk	left center of large curly bracket
⌊	\ (lb	left bottom of large curly bracket
⌉	\ (rt	right top of large curly bracket
}	\ (rk	right center of large curly bracket
⌋	\ (rb	right bottom of large curly bracket
⌈	\ (lc	left ceiling (top) of large square bracket
|	\ (bv	bold vertical
⌊	\ (lf	left floor (bottom) of large square bracket
⌉	\ (rc	right ceiling (top) of large square bracket
⌋	\ (rf	right floor (bottom) of large square bracket

Greek Characters

α	\(*a	alpha	A	\(*A	Alpha†
β	\(*b	beta	B	\(*B	Beta†
γ	\(*g	gamma	Γ	\(*G	Gamma
δ	\(*d	delta	Δ	\(*D	Delta
ε	\(*e	epsilon	E	\(*E	Epsilon†
ζ	\(*z	zeta	Z	\(*Z	Zeta†
η	\(*y	eta	H	\(*Y	Eta†
θ	\(*h	theta	Θ	\(*H	Theta
ι	\(*i	iota	I	\(*I	Iota†
κ	\(*k	kappa	K	\(*K	Kappa†
λ	\(*l	lambda	Λ	\(*L	Lambda
μ	\(*m	mu	M	\(*M	Mu†
ν	\(*n	nu	N	\(*N	Nu†
ξ	\(*c	xi	Ξ	\(*C	Xi
o	\(*o	omicron	O	\(*O	Omicron†
π	\(*p	pi	Π	\(*P	Pi
ρ	\(*r	rho	P	\(*R	Rho†
σ	\(*s	sigma	Σ	\(*S	Sigma
ς	\(ts	terminal sigma			
τ	\(*t	tau	T	\(*T	Tau†
υ	\(*u	upsilon	Y	\(*U	Upsilon
φ	\(*f	phi	Φ	\(*F	Phi
χ	\(*x	chi	X	\(*X	Chi†
ψ	\(*q	psi	Ψ	\(*Q	Psi
ω	\(*w	omega	Ω	\(*W	Omega

▪ The ms Macros ▪

Summary of ms Macros

.1C	Return to single-column format.
.2C	Start two-column format.
.AB	Begin abstract.
.AE	End abstract.
.AI *name*	Name of author's institution (used in cover sheet).
.AU *name*	Author's name (used in cover sheet).
.B [*text*]	Print *text* in boldface. If *text* is missing, equivalent to .ft 3.

`.B1`	Enclose following text in a box.
`.B2`	End boxed text.
`.BX` *word*	Surround *word* in a box.
`.DA`	Print date on each page.
`.DS`	Start displayed text.
`.DSB`	Start left-justified block, centered.
`.DSC`	Start centered display.
`.DSL`	Start left-centered display.
`.DE`	End displayed text.
`.EQ`	Begin equation.
`.EN`	End equation.
`.FS`	Start footnote.
`.FE`	End footnote.
`.I` [*text*]	Print *text* in italics. If *text* is missing, equivalent to `.ft 2`.
`.IP` *label n*	Indent paragraph *n* spaces with hanging *label*.
`.KS`	Start keep.
`.KE`	End of keep or floating keep.
`.KF`	Begin floating keep.
`.LG`	Increase type size by two points (`troff` only).
`.LP`	Start block paragraph.
`.ND`	Change or omit date.
`.NH` *n*	Numbered section heading, level *n*.
`.NL`	Restore default type size (`troff` only).
`.PP`	Start indented paragraph.
`.R` [*text*]	Print *text* in roman. If *text* is missing, equivalent to `.ft 1`.
`.RP`	Initiate title page for a "released paper."
`.RS`	Increase relative indent one level. Use with `.IP`.
`.RE`	End one level of relative indent.
`.SG`	Signature line.
`.SH`	Unnumbered section heading.
`.SM`	Decrease type size by two points (`troff` only).
`.TL`	Title line.
`.TS` [H]	Start table. H will put table header on all pages. Use this option with following `.TH`.
`.TH`	Table header ends. Must be used with `.TS H`.
`.TE`	End table.
`.UL`	Underline following text, even in `troff`.

Internal Macros Worth Knowing About

`.IZ`	Basic initialization; executed automatically before any text is processed. It is then removed, and cannot be invoked again.
`.RT`	Reset. Invoked by all paragraph macros, plus `.RS`, `.RE`, `.TS`, `.TE`, `.SH`, and `.NH`. Resets various values to defaults stored in number registers listed below.
`.BG`	Prints cover sheet, if any. Also performs some special first page initialization. Invoked once by the very first `.RT` in a document.
`.NP`	New page. Invoked at the top of each page. Performs various page top resets, and calls `.PT`.
`.PT`	Page titles. Contains running headers. Can be redefined. Invoked by `.NP` at `\n(HMu` from the top of the page.
`.BT`	Bottom titles. Continuous running footers. Invoked by trap at `\n(FMu/2u` from the bottom of the page.
`.FO`	Footer. The bottom of the text on the page. Invoked by trap at `\n(FMu`.

Number Registers Containing Page Layout Defaults

`CW`	Column width (default 7/15 of line length).
`FL`	Footnote length (default 11/12 of line length).
`FM`	Bottom margin (default 1 inch).
`GW`	Intercolumn gap width for multiple columns (default 1/15 of line length).
`HM`	Top margin (default 1 inch).
`LL`	Line length (default 6 inches).
`LT`	Title length (default 6 inches).
`PD`	Paragraph spacing (default 0.3 of vertical spacing).
`PI`	Paragraph indent (default 5 ens).
`PO`	Page offset (default 26/27 inches).
`PS`	Point size (default 10 points).
`VS`	Vertical line spacing (default 12 points).

Predefined and User-Definable Strings

DY	The current date.
LH	Left header, printed by `.tl '\\*(LH'\\*CH'\\*(RH'` in PT macro. Null unless user-defined.
CH	Center header, printed by `.tl '\\*(LH'\\*CH'\\*(RH'` in PT macro. Null unless user-defined.
RH	Right header, printed by `.tl '\\*(LH'\\*CH'\\*(RH'` in PT macro. Null unless user-defined.
LF	Left footer, printed by `.tl '\\*(LH'\\*CH'\\(RH'` in BT macro. Null unless user-defined.
CF	Center footer, printed by `.tl '\\*(LH'\\*CH'\\RH'` in BT macro. Contains PN by default.
RF	Right footer, printed by `.tl '\\*(LH'\\*CH'\\RH'` in BT macro. Contains PN by default.

Reserved Macro and String Names

The following macro and string names are used by the ms package. Avoid using these names for compatibility with the existing macros. An italicized *n* means that the name contains a numeral (generally the interpolated value of a number register).

'	AX	DA	FL	KJ	OD	RT	TR
.]	B	DW	FN	KS	OK	S0	TS
:	B1	DY	FO	LB	PP	S2	TT
[.	B2	EE	FS	LG	PT	S3	TX
[c	BB	EG	FV	LP	PY	SG	UL
[o	BG	EL	FX	LT	QE	SH	US
^	BT	EM	FY	MC	QF	SM	UX
`	BX	EN	HO	ME	QP	SN	WB
~	C	E*n*	I	MF	QS	SY	WH
1C	C1	EQ	IE	MH	R	TA	WT
2C	C2	EZ	IH	MN	R3	TC	XF
AB	CA	FA	IM	MO	RA	TD	XK
AE	CC	FE	I*n*	MR	RC	TE	XP
AI	CF	FF	IP	ND	RE	TH	
A*n*	CH	FG	IZ	NH	R*n*	TL	
AT	CM	FJ	KD	NL	RP	TM	
AU	CT	FK	KF	NP	RS	TQ	

The following number register names are used by the ms package. An italicized *n* means that the name contains a numeral (generally the interpolated value of another number register).

#T	EF	H5	IX	MF	OJ	QP	TV
AJ	FC	HM	I#	MG	PD	RO	TY
AV	FL	HT	J#	ML	PE	SJ	TZ
BC	FM	I0	KG	MM	PF	ST	VS
BD	FP	IF	KI	MN	PI	T.	WF
BE	GA	IK	KM	NA	PN	TB	XX
BH	GW	IM	L1	NC	PO	TC	YE
BI	H1	IP	LE	ND	PQ	TD	YY
BQ	H2	IR	LL	NQ	PS	TK	ZN
BW	H3	IS	LT	NS	PX	TN	
CW	H4	IT	MC	NX	QI	TQ	

Note that with the exception of [c and [o, none of the number register, macro, or string names contain lowercase letters, so lowercase or mixed case names are a safe bet when you're writing your own macros.

· The mm Macros ·

Summary of mm Macros

.1C — Return to single-column format.

.2C — Start two-column format.

.AS [*x*][*n*] — Start abstract type *x*, indent *n* spaces. (Used with .TM and .RP only.) (Types: 1=abstract on cover sheet and first page; 2=abstract only on cover sheet; 3=abstract only on Memorandum for File cover sheet.) End with .AE.

.AE — End abstract. Begin with .AS.

.AF [*company name*] — Alternate format for first page. Change first page "Subject/Date/From" format. If argument is given, other headings are not affected. No argument suppresses company name and headings.

.AL [*x*][*n*] — Start list type *x* (1, A, a, I, or i), indent *n* spaces. If third argument is 1, don't put a blank line between items. Default is numbered listing, indented 5 spaces.

.AT *title* — Author's *title* follows.

.AU *name* — Author's *name* and other information follows.

.AV *name* — Approval signature line for *name*.

.B [*w*] [*x*]... — Set *w* in bold (underline in nroff) and *x* in previous font; up to six arguments.

.BS — Begin block of text to be printed at bottom of page, after footnotes (if any), but before footer.

`.BE`	End bottom block and print after footnotes (if any), but before footer.
`.BI` [*w*] [*x*]	Set *w* in bold (underline in `nroff`) and *x* in italics; up to 6 arguments.
`.BL` [*n*] [*1*]	Start bullet list and indent text *n* spaces. If second argument is 1, don't put a blank line between items.
`.BR` [*w*] [*x*]	Set *w* in bold (underline in `nroff`) and *x* in roman; up to six arguments.
`.CS` [*pgs*] [*other*] [*tot*] [*figs*] [*tbls*] [*ref*]	
	Cover sheet numbering information.
`.DF` [*x*] [*y*]	Start floating display of type *x* and mode *y*, with indent *n*. (Default is no indent, no-fill mode.) End with `.DE`. *x* is: L (no indent), I (indent standard amount), C (center each line individually), or CB (center as a block). *y* is: N (no-fill mode) or F (fill mode).
`.DS`	Start floating or static display of type *x* and mode *y*, with indent *n*. Type and mode are as in `.DF`. End with `.DE`.
`.DE`	End floating or static display started with `.DS` or `.DF`.
`.DL` [*n*] [*1*]	Start dashed list and indent text *n* spaces. If second argument is 1, no space between items.
`.EC` [*caption*] [*n*] [*f*]	
	Equation *caption*. Arguments optionally override default numbering, where flag *f* determines use of number *n*. If *f*=0 (default), *n* is a prefix to number; if *f*=1, *n* is a suffix; if *f*=2, *n* replaces number.
`.EF` [*text*]	Print *text* as the footer on all even pages. *text* has the format: 'left' center 'right'.
`.EH` [*text*]	Print *text* as the heading on all even pages. *text* has the format: 'left' center 'right'.
`.EQ` [*text*]	Start equation display using *text* as label.
`.EN`	End equation display.
`.EX` [*caption*] [*n*] [*f*]	
	Exhibit *caption*. Arguments optionally override default numbering, where flag *f* determines use of number *n*. If *f*=0 (default), *n* is a prefix to number; if *f*=1, *n* is a suffix; if *f*=2, *n* replaces number.
`.FC` [*text*]	Use *text* for formal closing.
`.FD` [*0-11*]	Setup default footnote format.
`.FS` [*c*]	Start footnote using *c* for indicator. Default is numbered footnote.
`.FE`	End footnote.
`.FG` [*title*]	Figure *title* follows.
`.H`*n* [*heading*]	Numbered *heading* level *n* follows.
`.HC` [*c*]	Use *c* as hyphenation indicator.

.HM [*mark*]   Heading *mark* style follows arabic (1 or 001), roman (i or I),
                    or alphabetic (a or A).

.HU *heading*   Unnumbered *heading* follows.

.HX   User-supplied exit macro before printing heading.

.HY   User-supplied exit macro in middle of printing heading.

.HZ   User-supplied macro after heading.

.I [*w*] [*x*]   Set *w* in italics (underline in nroff) and *x* in previous font.
                    Up to six arguments.

.IB [*w*] [*x*]   Set *w* in italics (underline in nroff) and *x* in bold. Up to
                    six arguments.

.IR [*w*] [*x*]   Set *w* in italics (underline in nroff) and *x* in roman.

.LB *n m pad type* [*mark*] [LI-*space*] [LB-*space*]

    List beginning. Allows complete control over list format. It takes the following arguments:

        n — Text indent.

        m — Mark indent.

        pad — Padding associated with mark.

        type — If 0, use the specified *mark*. If nonzero, and *mark* is 1, A, a, I, i, list will be automatically numbered or alphabetically numbered or alphabetically sequenced. In this case, *type* controls how the *mark* will be displayed. For example, if *mark* is 1, *type* will have the following results:

Type	Format
1	1.
2	1)
3	(1)
4	[1]
5	<1>
6	{1}

        mark — The symbol or text that will be used to start each list entry. *mark* can be null (creates hanging indent), a text string, or 1, A, a, I, or i to create an automatically numbered or lettered list. Format of the *mark* will be affected by *type*.

        LI-*space* — The number of blank lines to be output between each following .LI macro (default 1).

        LB-*space* — The number of blank lines to be output by the LB macro itself (default 0).

.LC [*n*]   Clear list level *n*.

.LE   End list.

.LI [*mark*]   Item in list and specify *mark*.

.ML *mark* [*n*] [*1*]

    Start marked list, indent *n* spaces. If third argument is 1, no space between items in list.

.MT [*type*] [*title*]
    Specify memorandum *type* and *title*. *type* is:
      " " = No type
      0 = No type
      1 = Memorandum for file (default)
      2 = Programmer's notes
      3 = Engineer's notes
      4 = Released paper
      5 = External letter
      string = *string* is printed.
    title is user-supplied text prefixed to page number.

.ND *date*
    New date. Change date to *date*.

.nP
    Double-line indent on paragraph start.

.NS [*type*]
    Notation start. Specify notation *type*. *type* is:
      " " = Copy to
      0 = Copy to
      1 = Copy (with att.) to
      2 = Copy (no att.) to
      3 = Att.
      4 = Atts.
      5 = Enc.
      6 = Encs.
      7 = Under Separate Cover
      8 = Letter to
      9 = Memorandum to
      10 = Copy (with atts.) to
      11 = Copy (without atts.) to
      12 = Abstract Only to
      13 = Complete Memorandum to
      string = Copy *string* to

.NE
    Notation end.

.OF [*text*]
    Print *text* as the footer on all odd pages. *text* has the format: 'left' center 'right'.

.OH [*text*]
    Print *text* as the heading on all odd pages. *text* has the format: 'left' center 'right'.

.OK [*topic*]
    Other keywords. Specify *topic* for TM cover sheet.

.OP
    Force an odd page.

.P [*type*]
    Start paragraph type. *type* is: 0 = left justified (default), 1 = indented, 2 = indented except after .H, .LC, .DE.

.PF [*text*]
    Print *text* as the page footer on all pages. *text* has the format: 'left' center 'right'.

.PH [*text*]
    Print *text* as the page heading on all pages. *text* has the format: 'left' center 'right'.

.PM [*type*]
    Proprietary marking on each page (*type*: P=PRIVATE; N=NOTICE).

`.PX`	Page-heading user exit.
`.R`	Return to roman font (end underlining in `nroff`).
`.RB [w] [x]`	Set *w* in roman and *x* in bold.
`.RD [input]`	Read *input* from terminal.
`.RI [w] [x]`	Set *w* in roman and *x* in italics.
`.RS [arg]`	Start automatically numbered reference. *arg* manually specified reference number.
`.RF`	End of reference text.
`.RL [n] [1]`	Start reference listing, indent text *n* spaces. If second argument is 1, no space between list items.
`.RP`	Produce reference page.
`.S [n] [m]`	Set point size to *n* and vertical spacing to *m* (`troff` only) (defaults: 10 or 12). Alternatively, either argument can be specified as ±*n/m* to increment/decrement current value, D to use default, C to use current value, P to use previous value.
`.SA [n]`	Set right margin justification to *n*. *n* is: 0 = no justification or 1 = justification. (Defaults: no justification for `nroff`, justification for `troff`.)
`.SG [name]`	Use *name* for signature line.
`.SK n`	Skip *n* pages.
`.SM x[y][z]`	Reduce string *x* by one point. If strings *x*, *y*, and *z* are specified, *y* is reduced by one point.
`.SP [n]`	Leave *n* blank vertical spaces.
`.TB [title][n][f]`	Supply table *title*. Arguments optionally override default numbering, where flag *f* determines use of number *n*. If *f*=0 (default), *n* is a prefix to number; if *f*=1, *n* is a suffix; if *f*=2, *n* replaces number.
`.TS [H]`	Start table. H will put table header on all pages. Use this option with following `.TH`.
`.TH N`	Table header ends. Must be used with `.TS H`. N = only print table headers on new page.
`.TE`	End table.
`.TC [level] [level] [tab] [head1] ...`	Generate table of contents.
`.TL`	Title of memorandum follows on next line.
`.TM [n]`	Number a technical memorandum *n*. (Up to nine may be specified.)
`.TP`	Top-of-page macro.
`.TX`	User-supplied exit for table-of-contents titles.
`.TY`	User-supplied exit for table-of-contents header.
`.VL n [m] [1]`	Start variable item list. Indent text *n* spaces and mark *m* spaces. If third argument is 1, no space between list items.
`.VM [n] [m]`	Add *n* lines to top margin and *m* lines to bottom.

`.WC [x]`	Change column or footnote width to *x*. *x* is:	
	`FF`	All footnotes same as first
	`-FF`	Turn off `FF` mode
	`N`	Normal default mode
	`WD`	Wide displays
	`-WD`	Use default column mode
	`WF`	Wide footnotes
	`-WF`	Turn off `WF` mode

Predefined String Names

`BU`	Bullet; same as `\(bu`.
`Ci`	List of indents for table of contents levels.
`DT`	Current date, unless overridden. Month, day, year (e.g., July 28, 1986).
`EM`	Em dash string (em dash in `troff` and a double hyphen in `nroff`).
`F`	Footnote number generator.
`HF`	Fonts used for each level of heading (1=roman, 2=italic, 3=bold).
`HP`	Point size used for each level of heading.
`Le`	Title set for *List Of Equations*.
`Lf`	Title set for *List Of Figures*.
`Lt`	Title set for *List Of Tables*.
`Lx`	Title set for *List Of Exhibits*.
`RE`	SCCS Release and Level of mm.
`Rf`	Reference number generator.
`Rp`	Title for references.
`TM`	Trademark string. Places the letters *TM* one-half line above the text that it follows.

Number Registers Used in mm

A dagger (†) next to a register name indicates that the register can *only* be set from the command line or before the mm macro definitions are read by the formatter. Any register that has a single-character name can be set from the command line.

A†	If set to 1, omits technical memorandum headings and provides spaces appropriate for letterhead. See .AF macro.
Au	Inhibits author information on first page. See .AU macro.
C†	Flag indicating type of copy (original, draft, etc.).
Cl	Level of headings saved for table of contents (default 2). See .TC macro.
Cp	If set to 1, list of figures and tables appear on same page as table of contents. Otherwise, they start on a new page. (Default is 1.)
D†	If set to 1, sets debug mode (default 0). If set, mm will continue even when it encounters normally fatal errors.
De	If set to 1, ejects page after each floating display. (Default is 0.)
Df	Format of floating displays. See .DF macro.
Ds	Sets the pre- and post-space used for static displays.
E†	Font for the Subject/Date/From: 0=bold; 1=roman. (Default is 0.)
Ec	Equation counter, incremented for each .EC macro.
Ej	Heading level for page eject before headings. (Default is 0, no eject.)
Eq	If set to 1, places equation label at left margin. (Default is 0.)
Ex	Exhibit counter, incremented for each .EX macro.
Fg	Figure counter, incremented for each .FG macro.
Fs	Vertical spacing between footnotes.
H1–H7	Heading counters for levels 1-7, incremented by the .H macro of corresponding level or the .HU macro if at level given by the Hu register. The H2–H7 registers are reset to 0 by any .H (or .HU) macro at a lower-numbered level.
Hb	Level of heading for which break occurs before output of body text (default 2 lines).
Hc	Level of heading for which centering occurs (default 0).
Hi	Indent type after heading. (Default 1=paragraph indent.) Legal values are: 0 left justified, 1 indented, 2 indented except after .H, .LC, .DE. (Default is 0.)
Hs	Level of heading for which space after heading occurs. (Default = 2; .H2.)
Ht	Numbering type of heading: single (1) or concatenated (0). (Default is 0.)
Hu	Sets level of numbered heading that unnumbered heading resembles. (Default = 2; .H2.)
Hy	Sets hyphenation. If set to 1, Hy enables hyphenation. (Default is 0.)
L†	Sets length of page. (Default is 66v.)
Le	Flag for list of equations following table of contents. 0 = do not print; 1 = print. (Default is 0.)

Lf	Flag for list of figures following table of contents. 0 = do not print; 1 = print. (Default is 0.)
Li	Default indent of lists. (Default is 5.)
Ls	List spacing between items by level. (Default = 6, spacing between all levels of list.)
Lt	Flag for list of tables following table of contents. 0 = do not print; 1 = print (Default is 0.)
Lx	Flag for list of exhibits following table of contents. 0 = do not print; 1 = print (Default is 0.)
N†	Page numbering style. 0=header on all pages; 1=header printed as footer on page 1; 2=no header on page 1; 3=section page as footer; 4=no header unless .PH defined; 5=section page and section figure as footer. (Default is 0.)
Np	Numbering style for paragraphs. 0 = unnumbered; 1 = numbered.
O	Offset of page. For nroff, this value is an unscaled number representing character positions. Default is 9 (7.5i). For troff, this value is scaled. Default is .5i.
Oc	Table of contents page numbering style. 0=lowercase roman; 1=arabic. (Default is 0.)
Of	Figure caption style. 0=period separator; 1=hyphen separator. (Default is 0.)
P	Current page number.
Pi	Amount of indent for paragraph. (Default is 5 for nroff, 3 for troff.)
Ps	Amount of spacing between paragraphs. (Default is 3v.)
Pt	Paragraph type. Legal values are: 0 left justified, 1 indented, 2 indented except after .H, .LC, .DE. (Default is 0.)
Pv	Inhibits "PRIVATE" header. See .PV macro for values.
Rf	Reference counter, incremented for each .RS.
S†	Default point size for troff. Default is 10. (Vertical spacing is \n5+2.)
Si	Standard indent for displays. (Default is 5 for nroff, 3 for troff.)
T†	Type of nroff output device. Causes register settings for specific devices.
Tb	Table counter, incremented for each .TB.
U*	Underlying style (nroff) for .H and .HU. If not set, use continuous underline; otherwise, don't underline punctuation and white space. (Default is 0.)
W†	Width of page (line and title length). (Default is 6i.)

Other Reserved Macro and String Names

In mm, the only macro and string names you can safely use are names consisting of a single lowercase letter, or two character names whose first character is a lowercase letter and whose second character is *anything but* a lowercase letter. Of these, c2 and nP are already used.

▪ **tbl** Command Characters and Words ▪

.TS	Start table.
.TE	End table.
.TS H	Used when the table will continue onto more than one page. Used with .TH to define a header that will print on every page.
.TH	With .TS H, ends the header portion of the table.
.T&	Continue table after changing format line.

Options

Options affect the entire table. The options should be separated by commas, and the option line must be terminated by a semicolon.

center	Center with current margins.
expand	Flush with current right and left margins.
(*blank*)	Flush with current left margin (default).
box	Enclose table in a box.
doublebox	Enclose table in two boxes.
allbox	Enclose each table entry in a box.
tab (*x*)	Define the tab symbol as *x*.
linesize (*n*)	Set lines or rules (e.g., from box) to *n* point type.
delim (*xy*)	Recognize *x* and *y* as the eqn delimiters.

Format

The format line affects the layout of individual columns and rows of the table. Each line contains a key letter for each column of the table. The column entries should be separated by spaces, and the format section must be terminated by a period. Each line of format corresponds to one line of the table, except for the last, which corresponds to all following lines up to the next `.T&`, if any.

Key letters

c	Center.
l	Left justify.
r	Right justify.
n	Align numerical entries.
a	Align alphabetic subcolumns.
s	Horizontally span previous column entry across this column.
^	Vertically continue entry from previous row down through this row.

Other choices (must follow a key letter)

b	Boldface. Must be followed by a space.
i	Italics. Must be followed by a space.
p*n*	Point size *n*.
t	Begin any corresponding vertically spanned table entry at the top line of its range.
e	Equal width columns.
w (*n*)	Minimum column width. Also used with text blocks. *n* can be given in any acceptable `troff` units.
v*n*	Vertical line spacing. Used only with text blocks.
n	Amount of separation between columns (default is 3n).
|	Single vertical line. Typed between key letters.
| |	Double vertical line. Typed between key letters.
_	Single horizontal line. Used in place of a key letter.
=	Double horizontal line. Used in place of a key letter.

Data

The data portion includes both the heading and text of the table. Each table entry must be separated by a tab symbol.

`.xx`	`troff` commands may be used (such as `.sp #` and `.ce #`). Do not use macros, unless you know what you're doing.
`\`	As last character in a line, combine following line with current line (\ is hidden).
`\^`	Vertically spanned table entry. Span table entry immediately above over this row.
`_` or `=`	As the only character in a line, extend a single or double horizontal line the full width of the table.
`\$_` or `\$=`	Extend a single or double horizontal line the full width of the column.
`\_`	Extend a single horizontal line the width of the contents of the column.
`\Rx`	Print x's as wide as the contents of the column.
`...T{`	Start text block as a table entry. Must be used with wn, column width option.
`...T}`	End text block.

▪ eqn Command Characters ▪

`.EQ`	Start typesetting mathematics
`.EN`	End typesetting mathematics

Character Translations

The following character sequences are recognized and translated as shown.

`>=`	$\geq$	`approx`	$\approx$
`<=`	$\leq$	`nothing`	
`==`	$\equiv$	`cdot`	$\cdot$
`!=`	$\neq$	`times`	$\times$
`+-`	$\pm$	`del`	∇
`->`	$\rightarrow$	`grad`	∇
`<-`	$\leftarrow$	`. . .`	$\ldots$
`<<`	$\ll$	`,...,`	$,\ldots,$
`>>`	$\gg$	`sum`	$\sum$
`inf`	∞	`int`	$\int$
`partial`	∂	`prod`	$\prod$
`half`	$\frac{1}{2}$	`union`	$\cup$
`prime`	$'$	`inter`	$\cap$

Digits, parentheses, brackets, punctuation marks, and the following words are converted to roman font when encountered:

```
sin cos tan sinh cosh tanh arc
max min lin log ln exp
Re Im and if for det
```

Greek letters can be printed in uppercase or lowercase. To obtain Greek letters, simply spell them out in the case you want:

`alpha`	α	`sigma`	σ
`beta`	β	`tau`	τ
`gamma`	γ	`upsilon`	υ
`delta`	δ	`phi`	ϕ
`epsilon`	ε	`chi`	χ
`zeta`	ζ	`psi`	ψ
`eta`	η	`omega`	ω
`theta`	θ	`GAMMA`	Γ
`iota`	ι	`DELTA`	Δ
`kappa`	κ	`THETA`	Θ
`lambda`	λ	`LAMBDA`	Λ
`mu`	μ	`XI`	Ξ
`nu`	ν	`PI`	Π
`xi`	ξ	`SIGMA`	Σ
`omicron`	o	`UPSILON`	Υ
`pi`	π	`PHI`	Φ
`rho`	ρ	`PSI`	Ψ
		`OMEGA`	Ω

The following words translate to marks on the tops of characters.

x dot	$\dot{x}$	x vec	$\vec{x}$
x dotdot	$\ddot{x}$	x dyad	$\overset{\leftrightarrow}{x}$
x hat	$\hat{x}$	x bar	$\bar{x}$
x tilde	$\tilde{x}$	x under	$\underline{x}$

Words Recognized By `eqn`

above	Separate the pieces of a pile or matrix column.
back *n*	Move backwards horizontally *n* 1/100's of an em.
bold	Change to bold font.
ccol	Center a column of a matrix.
col???	Used with a preceding l or r to left or right adjust the columns of the matrix.
cpile	Make a centered pile (same as pile).
define	Create name for a frequently used string.
delim	Define two characters to mark the left and right ends of an `eqn` equation to be printed in line.
down *n*	Move down *n* 1/100's of an em.
fat	Widen the current font by overstriking it.
font *x*	Change to font *x*, where *x* is the one-character name or the number of a font.
from	Used in summations, integrals, and similar constructions to signify the lower limit.
fwd *n*	Move forward horizontally *n* 1/100's of an em.
gfont *x*	Set a global font *x* for all equations.
gsize *n*	Set a global size for all equations.
up *n*	Move up *n* 1/100's of an em.
italic	Change to italic font.
lcol	Left justify a column of a matrix.
left	Create large brackets, braces, bars, etc.
lineup	Line up marks in equations on different lines.
lpile	Left justify the elements of a pile.
mark	Remember the horizontal position in an equation. Used with lineup.
matrix	Create a matrix.
ndefine	Create a definition which only takes effect when `neqn` is running.
over	Make a fraction.
pile	Make a vertical pile with elements centered above one another.
rcol	Right adjust a column of a matrix.
right	Create large brackets, braces, bars, etc.
roman	Change to roman font.

`rpile`	Right justify the elements of a pile.
`size` *n*	Change the size of the font to *n*.
`sqrt`	Draw a square root sign.
`sub`	Start a subscript.
`sup`	Start a superscript.
`tdefine`	Make a definition that will apply only for `eqn`.
`to`	Used in summations, integrals, and similar constructions to signify the upper limit.
`~`	Force extra space into the output.
`^`	Force a space one half the size of the space forced by `~`.
`{ }`	Force `eqn` to treat an element as a unit.
`' . . . '`	A string within quotation marks is not subject to alterations by `eqn`.

Precedence

If you don't use braces, `eqn` will do operations in the order shown in the following list.

```
dyad vec under bar tilde hat dot dotdot
fwd   back  down   up
fat   roman  italic  bold   size
sub   sup  sqrt  over
from  to
```

These operations group to the left:

```
over   sqrt   left   right
```

All others group to the right.

▪ The `pic` Preprocessor ▪

In `pic` there are often dozens of ways to draw a picture, not only because of the many permissible abbreviations, but because `pic` combines the language of geometry with English. You can specify a line, for example, with direction, magnitude, and starting point, yet often achieve the same effect by simply stating, "from *there* to *there*."

Full descriptions of primitive objects in `pic` can be ended by starting another line, or by the semicolon character (;). A single primitive description can be continued on the next line, however, by ending the first with a backslash character (\). Comments may be placed on lines beginning with #.

pic Macros

The following macros are used to delimit pic input from the body of the source file. Only text within these macros will be processed by pic.

.PS [*h* [*w*]]   Start pic description. *h* and *w*, if specified, are the desired height and width of the picture; the full picture will expand or contract to fill this space.

.PS *<file*   Read contents of *file* in place of current line.

.PE   End pic description.

.PF   End pic description and return to vertical position before matching PS.

Declarations

At the beginning of a pic description, you may declare a new scale, and declare any number of variables.

pic assumes you want a 1-to-1 scale, with 1 = one inch. You can declare a different scale, say 1 = one-*n*th of an inch, by declaring, scale = *n*.

pic takes variable substitutions for numbers used in the description. Instead of specifying, line right *n*, you may use a lowercase character as a variable, for example, a, by declaring at the top of the description:

a = *n*

You may then write line right a.

Primitives

Primitives may be followed by relevant options. Options are discussed later in this section.

arc [cw] [*options*] [``*text*'']
> A fraction of a circle. (Default = 1/4 of a circle.) The cw option specifies a clockwise arc; default is counterclockwise.

arrow [*options*] [``*text*''] [then . . .]
> Draw an arrow. Essentially the same as line −>.

box [*options*] [``*text*'']
> Draw a box.

circle [*options*] [``*text*'']
> Draw a circle.

`ellipse` [*options*] [` ``text`` `]
>   Draw an ellipse.

`line` [*options*] [` ``text`` `] [`then . . .`]
>   Draw a line.

`move` [*options*] [` ``text`` `]
>   A move of position in the drawing. (Essentially, an invisible line.)

`spline` [*options*] [` ``text`` `] [`then . . .`]
>   A line, with the feature that a "then" results in a gradual (sloped) change in direction.

` ``text`` `
>   Text centered at current point.

Options

`right` [*n*] `left` [*n*] `up` [*n*] `down` [*n*]	Specifies direction of primitive; default is direction in which the previous description had been heading. Diagonals result by using two directions on the option line. Each direction can be followed by a specified length *n*.
`rad` *n* `diam` *n*	Specifies a primitive to have radius *n* (or diameter *n*).
`ht` *n* `wid` *n*	Specifies the height or width of the primitive to be *n*. For an arrow, line, or spline, refers to size of arrowhead.
`same`	Specifies a primitive of the same dimensions of the most recent matching primitive.
`at` *point*	Specifies primitive to be centered at *point*.
`with` *.position* `at` *point*	Specifies the designated *position* of the primitive to be at *point*.
`from` *point1* `to` *point2*	Specifies the primitive to be drawn from *point1* to *point2*. Points may be expressed as Cartesian coordinates or in respect to previous objects.
`->`	Specify the arrowhead to be directed forwards.
`<-`	Specify the arrowhead to be directed backwards.
`<->`	Specify the arrowhead to be directed both ways.
`chop` *n m*	Chop off *n* from beginning of primitive, and *m* from end. With only one argument, the same value will be chopped from both ends.

`dotted`	Specifies the primitive to be drawn dotted, dashed, or to be
`dashed`	invisible. Default is solid line.
`invis`	

`then...`	Continue primitive in a new direction. Relevant only to lines, splines, moves, and arrows.

Text

Place text within quotation marks. To break the line, break into two (or more) sets of quotation marks. Text always appears centered within the object, unless given one of the following arguments:

`ljust`	Text appears left justified to the center.
`rjust`	Text appears right justified to the center.
`above`	Text appears above the center.
`below`	Text appears below the center.

Object Blocks

A complex object that is the combination of several primitives (for example, an octagon) can be treated as a single object by declaring it as a block:

```
Object:[
  description
    .
    .
    .
  ]
```

Brackets are used as delimiters. Note that the object is declared as a proper noun, hence it should begin with a capital letter.

Macros

The same sequence of commands can be repeated by using macros. The syntax is:

```
define sequence %
  description
    .
    .
    .
  %
```

In this example, we have used the percent sign (%) as the delimiter, but any character that is not in the description may be used.

Macros can take variables, expressed in the definition as "$1" through "$9". Invoke the macro with the syntax: *sequence(value1,value2,...)*

Positioning

In a `pic` description, the first action will begin at (0,0), unless otherwise specified with coordinates. Thus, the point (0,0) will move down and right on the drawing, as objects are placed above and to the left of the first object.

All points are ultimately translated by the formatter into x- and y-coordinates. You may therefore refer to a specific point in the picture by incrementing or decrementing by coordinates, i.e., `2nd ellipse - (3,1)`.

You may refer to the x- and y-coordinates of an object by placing `.x` or `.y` at the end. For example, `last box.x` will refer to the x-coordinate of the most recent box drawn. Some of the physical attributes of the object may also be referred to similarly, as follows:

`.x`	X-coordinate of object's center.
`.y`	Y-coordinate of object's center.
`.ht`	Height of object.
`.wid`	Width of object.
`.rad`	Radius of object.

Unless otherwise positioned, each object will begin at the point where the last object left off. If a command (or sequence of commands) is set off by braces ({ }), however, `pic` will then return to the point before the first brace.

Positioning between Objects

When referring to a previous object, you must use proper names. This can be done two ways:

- By referring to it by order, e.g., `1st box`, `3rd box`, `last box`, `2nd last box`, etc.

- By declaring it with a name, in initial caps, on its declaration line, e.g., `Line1: line 1.5 right from last box.sw`

To refer to a point between two objects, or between two points on the same object, you may write: *fraction* `of the way between` *first.position* `and` *second.position* or (abbreviated) *fraction<first.position, second.position>*

Corners

When you refer to a previous object, pic will assume that you mean the *center* of the object, unless you use a *corner* to specify a particular point on the object. The syntax is:

> .*corner* of *object*

for example, .sw of last box. You can also use an abbreviated syntax:

> *object*.*corner*

for example, last box.sw.

These *corners* may be:

n	North (same as t)
s	South (same as b)
e	East (same as r)
w	West (same as l)
ne	Northeast
nw	Northwest
se	Southeast
sw	Southwest
t	Top (same as n)
b	Bottom (same as s)
r	Right (same as e)
l	Left (same as w)
start	Point where drawing of object began
end	Point where drawing of object ended

You may also refer to the upper right, upper left, lower right, and lower left of an object.

Numerical Operators

Several operators are functional in pic. These are:

+	Addition
−	Subtraction
*	Multiplication
/	Division
%	Modulo

Default Values

arcrad	0.25	ellipsewid	0.75
arrowwid	0.05	linewid	0.5
arrowht	0.1	lineht	0.5
boxwid	0.75	movewid	0.5
boxht	0.5	moveht	0.5
circlerad	0.25	scale	1
dashwid	0.05	textht	0
ellipseht	0.5	textwid	0

A P P E N D I X
C

Shell Command Summary

This section describes the syntax of the Bourne Shell. It lists special characters, variables, and built-in programming commands used by the shell.

Special Files

$HOME/.profile   Executed at shell startup.

Special Characters for Filename Generation

`*`	Match any string of characters.
`?`	Match any single character.
`[ ... ]`	Match any of the enclosed characters. A pair of characters separated by a minus will match any character lexically between the pair.

Special Characters for Control Flow

`|`	Perform pipeline (use output of preceding command as input of following command, e.g., `cat file | lpr`).
`;`	Separate sequential commands on the same line.
`&`	Run command in background (e.g., `lpr` *file*`&`).
`&&`	Execute command if previous command was successful (e.g., `grep` *string file* `&&` `lpr` *file*).

‖	Execute command if previous command was unsuccessful (e.g., `grep` *string1 file* ‖ `grep` *string2 file*).
( )	Execute commands enclosed in ( ) in a subshell; output from the entire set can then be redirected as a unit or placed in the background.
' ... '	Take all characters between single quotation marks literally. (Don't allow special character meaning.)
\	Take following character literally.
" ... "	Take enclosed characters literally but allow variable and command substitution.
'*cmd*'	Use output of *cmd* as argument to another command.
#	Begin a comment in a shell file.
<*file*	Take input from *file*.
<<*string*	Read standard input up to a line identical to *string*.
>*file*	Redirect output to *file* (overwrite).
>>*file*	Redirect output to end of *file* (append).
>&*digit*	Duplicate standard input from *digit* e.g., `2>&1`.
<&−	Close standard input.
>&−	Close standard output.

Variable Substitution

variable=value	Set *variable* to *value*.
$*variable*	Use value of *variable*.
$*variable-value* $*variable*[:]-*value*	Use *variable* if set; otherwise set to *value*. For example: `TERM=${1:-$TERM}` will set the TERM variable to the value of the first argument to a shell script, if given, or else to the existing (default) value of TERM.
$*variable=value* $*variable*[:]=*value*	Use *variable* if not set; otherwise set to *value*.
$*variable?value* $*variable*[:]?*value*	Use *variable* if set; otherwise print *value* then exit.
$*variable+value* $*variable*[:]+*value*	Use *value* if *variable* is set; otherwise nothing.

If the colon (:) is included in these expressions, a test is performed to see if the variable is non-null as well as set.

Shell Parameters Set by the Shell under Execution

$#	Number of command-line arguments.
$−	Options supplied in invocation or by the set command.
$?	Return value of last executed command.
$$	Return process number of current process.
$!	Return process number of last background command.

Shell Variables Initially Set By profile

$HOME	Default (home directory) value for the cd command.
$IFS	Internal field separators.
$MAIL	Default mail file.
$PATH	Default search path for commands.
$PS1	Primary prompt string; default is $.
$PS2	Secondary prompt string; default is >.
$TERM	Specifies the type of terminal.

Shell Functions

name ( ) {*command1*; ...; *commandn*}
> Create a function called *name* that consists of the commands enclosed in braces. The function can be invoked by name within the current script.

Built-in Commands

file
> *file*
> Execute contents of *file*.

break
> break [*n*]
> Exit from a for, while, or until loop in *n* levels.

case	`case` *value* `in`
	    pattern1) *commands* `;` `;`
	        .
	        .
	        .
	    patternn) *commands* `;` `;`
	`esac`
	For each item in *list* that matches *pattern*, execute *command*.

cd	`cd` [*dir*] Change current directory to *dir*.
continue	`continue` [*n*] Resume *n*th iteration of a `for`, `while`, or `until` loop.
echo	`echo` *args* Print *args* on standard output.
eval	`eval` [*arg* ...] Evaluate arguments, then execute results.
exec	`exec` [*cmd*] Execute *cmd* in place of current shell.
exit	`exit` [*n*] Exit the shell with exit status *n*, e.g., `exit 1`.
export	`export` [*var* ...] Export variable *var* to environment.

for	`for` *variable* [`in` *list* ...]
	`do`
	    commands
	`done`
	For variable *x* (in optional *list*) do *commands*.

if	`if` *condition*
	    `then` *commands*
	    [`elif` *condition2*
	    `then` *commands2*] ...
	    [`else` *commands3*]
	`fi`
	If *condition* is met, do list of *commands*, or else if *condition2* is met, do *commands2*, otherwise do *commands3*. (See `test` for a list of conditions.)

hash	`hash` *cmds* Temporarily add *cmds* to search path.

login   `login` [*user* ...]
Log in as another user.

newgrp   `newgrp` [*group* ...]
Change your group ID to *group*; if no argument, change back to your default group.

pwd   `pwd`
Print current working directory.

read   `read` [*var* ...]
Read value of *var* from standard input.

readonly   `readonly` [*var* ...]
Mark variable *var* as read only.

return   `return`
Stop execution of current shell function and return to calling level.

set   `set` [*t*] [options]   [*arg* ...]
With no arguments, `set` prints the values of all variables known to the current shell. The following options can be enabled (-option) or disabled (+option).

     −−   Don't treat subsequent arguments beginning with − as options.
     −a   Automatically export all subsequently defined variables.
     −e   Exit shell if any command has a nonzero exit status.
     −k   Put keywords in an environment for a command.
     −n   Read but do not execute commands.
     −t   Exit after one command is executed.
     −u   Treat unset variables as an error.
     −v   Print commands as they are executed.
     −x   Turn on `trace` mode in current shell (echo commands in scripts as they are executed).
     arg ...   Assigned in order to `$1`, `$2`, ... `$9`.

shift   `shift`
Perform a shift for arguments, e.g., `$2` becomes `$1`.

test   `test` *exp* | [*exp*]
Evaluate the expression *exp*. An alternate form of the command uses [ ] rather than the word *test*. The following primitives are used to construct *expression*.

     −b *file*   True if *file* exists and is a block special file.
     −c *file*   True if *file* exists and is a character special file.

−d *file*	True if *file* exists and is a directory.
−f *file*	True if *file* exists and is a regular file.
−g *file*	True if *file* exists and its set-group-id bit is set.
−k *file*	True if *file* exists and its sticky bit is set.
−n *s1*	True if the length of string *s1* is nonzero.
−r *file*	True if *file* exists and is readable.
−s *file*	True if *file* exists and has a size greater than zero.
−t [*n*]	True if the open file whose file descriptor number is *n* (default is 1) is associated with a terminal device.
−u *file*	True if *file* exists and its set-user-id bit is set.
−w *file*	True if *file* exists and is writable.
−x *file*	True if *file* exists and is executable.
−z *s1*	True if the length of string *s1* is zero.
s1 = *s2*	True if strings *s1* and *s2* are identical.
s1 != *s2*	True if strings *s1* and *s2* are not identical.
s1	True if string *s1* is not the null string.
n1 -eq *n2*	True if the integers *n1* and *n2* are algebraically equal. Any of the comparisons −ne, −gt, −ge, −lt, and −le may be used in place of −eq.

times	**times** Print accumulated process times.

trap	**trap** [*cmd*] [*n*]
	Execute *cmd* if signal *n* is received. Useful signals include:
	    0 Successful exit of command.
	    1 Hangup of terminal line.
	    2 Interrupt.
	   15 Process is killed.

type	**type** *commands* Print information about *commands*.
until	**until** *condition* [do *commands*] **done** Until *condition* is met, do *commands* (see test for conditions).
ulimit	**ulimit** [*size*] Set maximum size of file that can be created to *size*; if no arguments, print current limit.
umask	**umask** [*nnn*] Set file creation mask to octal value *nnn*.

unset   unset *vars* ...
                 Remove definitions for variable *var*.

wait   wait [*n*]
                 Wait for specified process with identification number (*n*) to terminate
                 and report its status.

while   while *condition*
                    [do *commands*]
                 done
                 While *condition* is met, do *commands* (see test for conditions).

filename   *filename*
                 Read and execute commands from executable file *filename*.

D

Format of `troff` Width Tables

As discussed in Chapter 4, `troff` uses width tables stored in the directory `/usr/lib/font` to determine how to place text on the page. To do this, it needs to know how wide each character is.

For each type of `troff` output device supported by your system, there should be a directory called `/usr/lib/font/dev`*xx*, where *xx* is the name of the device. For example, on our system:

```
$ ls -F /usr/lib/font
devlj/
devps/
```

Within each of these directories resides an overall device description file, called `DESC`, and individual font files for the fonts on your system. These files exist both in ASCII and binary form. The binary files are created from the ASCII versions using a utility called `makedev`, and have the suffix `.out`.

On our system, here's what the font directory for the HP Laserjet contains:

```
$ ls /usr/lib/font/devl
B          DESC        I          S
B.out      DESC.outI.out          S.out
CW         HB          R          TY
CW.out     HB.out      R.out      TY.out
```

· The DESC File ·

The `DESC` file contains an overall description of the output device, including its resolution in dots per inch, the paper size, the fonts that will be mounted by default, the available point sizes, and a complete list of all the `troff` special character names supported on that device.

A DESC file might look something like the following example:

```
# HP LaserJet
fonts 6 R I B HB CW S
sizes 7 8 10 12 14 17 22 27 0
res 300
hor 1
vert 1
unitwidth 12
paperwidth 2400
paperlength 3300

charset
\|  \^  \-
fi fl ff Fi Fl
br vr ul ru
bu sq em hy 14 12 34 aa ga
        .
        .
        .
sc gr no is pt es mo
dd rh lh bs or ci
lt lb rt rb lk rk bv lf rf lc rc
```

The following keywords are used in the DESC file:

fonts
: The number of fonts to be mounted for the device, followed by a list of the font names (maximum is ten). The user can request other fonts from within a document. However, the fonts listed here will be "mounted" (by analogy with the CAT typesetter), and can by referenced by position (\f1, \f2...) as well as by name.

sizes
: The sizes in which the various fonts are available.

res
: The resolution of the output device, in dots per inch.

hor
: The minimum number of units of resolution that the device can move in a horizontal direction.

vert
: The minimum number of units of resolution that the device can move in a vertical direction.

unitwidth
: The point size at which character widths are specified in the other files.

paperwidth
: The width of the page in units of resolution (e.g., 8 inches x 300 = 2400, the width for the LaserJet, because it forces a $1/2$-inch margin).

`paperlength`   The length of the page in units of resolution (e.g., 11 inches x 300 = 3300, the length for the LaserJet).

`biggestfont`   The maximum number of characters in a font.

`charset`   The list of character names that are supported on this output device. The keyword should be on a line by itself; the list of characters starts on the next line.

`#`   Begins a comment.

▪ Font Description Files ▪

For each font listed on the `fonts` line of the `DESC` file, there should be a font file with the same name. The font file contains a list of all the characters in the font, along with the width and other associated information.

A font file looks like this:

```
name R
internalname Roman

charset
        4       0       0
        8       0       0
vr      0       3       13
ru      25      0       17
                .
                .
                .

A       42      2       65
B       35      2       66
C       37      2       67
                .
                .
                .

w       40      0       119
x       28      0       120
y       28      1       121
z       25      0       122
                .
                .
                .
```

Four columns, separated by tabs, are listed for each character.

The first column lists the character name—either the letter, digit, or symbol, or a two-character `troff` special character name defined in the `charset` section of `DESC`.

The second column contains the width of the character in output device units. The width is the width of the character at the point size specified by the `unitwidth` keyword in `DESC`. For example, if `unitwidth` is 12, then from the portion of the table just shown, we know that a 12-point A in the roman font is 42 units wide. The `troff` formatter determines the width at other point sizes by scaling the `unitwidth` size.

The third column describes the character type—that is, whether it is an descender (1), ascender (2), both (3), or neither (0).

The fourth column contains the typeset code for the character. This code is the value that the output device will recognize to generate the character. This information is obtained from the typesetter or laser printer vendor. The code can be in decimal or octal form. (Octal is specified by a leading zero.)

In general, whomever supplied the driver for the output device will provide you with appropriate width tables for the supported fonts. However, you may have access to other public domain fonts for output devices that support downloadable raster fonts. In this case, you may need to build your own tables.

In addition, you may want to "tune" tables by adjusting the widths slightly if you find that the character spacing is poor. Creating a font table from scratch requires a magnifying glass, a micrometer, a good eye, and a lot of patience.

▪ Compiling Font Files ▪

After you are satisfied with your width tables, they need to be compiled using the `makedev` utility:

```
$ makedev DESC          Compile all fonts in DESC
```

Running `makedev` on `DESC` will compile all of the fonts listed on the `fonts` line in that file. You can compile a font that is not included in `DESC` by specifying its name on the command line:

```
$ makedev B             Compile the bold font
```

▪ Font Usage Limitations ▪

The user is not restricted to using the "mounted" fonts that have been listed in `DESC`. Any font supported by the output device, and for which a compiled width table exists, can be referred to from within a document. For example, if you had a Palatino font family named `PA`, `PB`, and `PI`, there should be files called:

```
PA.out      PB.out      PI.out
```

One problem that is sometimes encountered is that `troff` has problems if a font that is used in this way is larger (in absolute file size) than the largest of the mounted fonts specified in DESC. The `troff` formatter only allocates enough memory for the largest font in DESC. If you encounter this problem, you can either strip unneeded characters out of the font, pad a font in DESC, or add the large font that is giving you trouble to DESC.

E

Comparing mm and ms

If you have both ms and mm on your system, you may be interested in looking at both packages, perhaps evaluating features. In general, ms has many of the same capabilities as mm. However, it lacks some essential features, such as automatically numbered lists and table of contents generation. On the other hand, it is much easier to learn the internals of ms, and therefore easier to extend it with your own macros.

· Paragraphs ·

The basic paragraph types are block and indented.

ms	mm	Description
.P	.LP	Begin a block paragraph.
.P 1	.PP	Begin a paragraph with indented first line.

In mm, the default paragraph type can be changed from block to indented by setting the number register Pt to 1 or 2. The ms macros lack this generalizing mechanism.

· Justification ·

When using the nroff formatter, mm does not justify the right margin. .SA 1 turns on justification for both formatters. .SA 0 turns it off.

The ms macros do not provide a macro for inhibiting the normal justification of paragraphs. However, the .na request can be used to do this.

▪ Displays ▪

Displays are produced in a very similar way in both macro packages, using the DS/DE pair of macros. In mm, display are left justified; in ms, displays are indented. The options that allow you to change the placement of the display are basically the same.

The mm macros provide for static and floating displays (.DF). In ms, this is done with a separate pair of keep macros (KS/KF and KE).

In mm, you can turn on fill mode within the display and specify an indent from the right margin. This is used for quoted material and has its equivalent in ms with the QP or the QS/QE pair.

In addition, the same set of delimiter pairs for tbl, eqn, and pic are available in both packages.

▪ Formatting Lists ▪

The mm macros have sophisticated list formatting macros that are lacking in ms. The .IP macro in ms produces the equivalent of a variable-item list in mm. In other words, you can get a numbered list by specifying the number as a label to an indented paragraph, but you cannot get an automatically numbered list.

▪ Change Font ▪

The .B (change to bold), .I (change to italic), and .R (change to roman) macros used for changing fonts are the same. The mm macros allow up to seven arguments for alternating with the previous font, but ms is limited to two.

▪ Change Point Size ▪

Both packages allow you to change point size. In mm, .S specifies a new point size and .SM reduces point size relative to the current size.

When you change the point size using ms macros, it is always done relative to the current point size. The .LG and .SM macros increase and decrease the current point size by 2 points. The .NL macro restores the default point size.

▪ **Headers and Footers** ▪

The mm macros provide macros for specifying a delimited string that will appear left justified, centered, and right justified in a page header or footer. The `.PH` macro defines a page header and `.PF` defines a page footer. In addition, mm provides variations of these macros for specifying headers and footers for odd and even pages.

The ms macros handle this through setting individual strings. To define a string that appears left justified in a header, use:

`.ds LH` *string*

The other strings for the header are CH and RH; other strings for the footer are LF, CF, and RF.

▪ **Section Headings** ▪

Numbered and unnumbered section headings are available in both packages. The `.SH` and `.NH` macros are used in ms. The `.H` and `.HU` macros are used in mm. The main difference is where you specify the heading string. In mm, it is the first argument on the line with the macro. In ms, it follows on the line after the macro and continues up to the first paragraph macro.

▪ **Footnotes** ▪

The pair of macros used for footnotes is the same (`.FS` and `.FE`), although automatic numbering of footnotes is provided in mm. One difference is that in mm the footnote at the bottom of the page is printed in 8 points. The mm macros also provide a pair of macros (`.RF` and `.RE`) for collecting a page of references.

F

The format Macros

Throughout this book, we've made extensive references to portions of the extended ms macro package that we use in our technical writing business. These macros are used in conjunction with the format shell script to provide a complete document formatting environment.

This package was originally developed by Steve Talbott of Massachusetts Computer Corp. (MASSCOMP). We have extended and generalized it to meet the document design needs of many different clients.

The purpose of this appendix is to summarize, in one place, the function of the macros that the package contains. We have found that this set of macros covers the basic needs of people involved in the development of technical books and manuals.

The package relies on the existence of the underlying ms macros. In this sense, it is not a complete package. However, it is possible to define a simple subset of the ms macros to cover the basics if the full implementation of ms is not available.

For more information on the full implementation of these macros, please feel free to contact us in care of the publisher.

▪ Summary of the Macros ▪

The following list summarizes the user-callable macros in the format macro package.

.[ABCD]h	A-level head, B-level head, and so on.
.Dr	Specify whether the current version is a draft. (Drafts are dated.)
.Fs	Start a figure.

.Fe *title*	Figure end. Figures are automatically numbered, and given the specified *title*.
.Hl [*c*]	Print a horizontal line the width of the page, using character *c*. (Default is underscore.)
.IOC [*strings*]	Start an interoffice memo.
.TO	List of names following .TO "" will be placed in separate distribution list.
.TO *name*	*name* is addressee. Maximum of five such .TO lines.
.DA *date*	*date* is date of the memo; will be included in page footer.
.ND *date*	*date* is date of the memo; will be omitted from page footer.
.FR *name*	*name* is sender. Maximum of five such .FR lines.
.CC *name*	*name* is person to receive copy of memo. Maximum of five .CC lines.
.SU *subject*	*subject* is subject of the memo.
.IP *label indent* [0]	Begin paragraph with "hanging indent." Following text is indented, while *label* remains at the margin.
.LP [0]	Start a (left-justified) paragraph. 0 suppresses blank line.
.Ls [*type*] [*indent*] [*bullet*]	
	Start a (possibly nested) list. *type* is N (number), A (alphabetical uppercase), a (alphabetical lowercase), I (Roman numeral uppercase), i (Roman numeral lowercase), B (bullet). Default indent is 5. *bullet* is alternative bullet string (null string is acceptable).
.Li [0]	List item. 0 suppresses preceding blank line.
.Le [0]	End of innermost list. 0 suppresses preceding blank line.
.Lt [1 | 2]	Enter address blocks and date (1), and salutation (2) of a letter.
.Nd *n*	Need *n* lines. If *n* lines do not remain on the page, eject new page. Unlike .ne, .Nd causes a break.
.Nh [1 | 0]	Enable/disable numbered headings (enabled by default).
.Ns *type*	Start a NOTE of type N (Note), C (Caution), W (Warning), R (Review Note), or P (Private Note). Review notes are printed in the text and summarized in a list at the end. Private notes appear only in the end list.

.Ne   End a note.

.OB *string*   Print an overbar (over a string).

.Ps [*indent*]   Start a "printout" (display). Text is printed in the CW font and preserved as is—there is no filling.

.Pe   End a printout. See .Ps.

.Rh [0 | 1] [*desc*] *head*...
                          Create reference page header.

.Se [*number*] [*title*] Start a section (chapter). This sets up many defaults, and is desirable to use for most documents.

.SE   Screen end. End a computer screen illustration begun with .SS.

.SS [*width*] [*height*] Start a screen illustration (box with curved corners). If width and height are not specified, scale to size of contents.

.Tc *level*   Specify what level of heading will be saved in the table of contents (Ah to Dh)

.Ti *text*   Title—goes in left page footer.

.St *text*   Subtitle—goes in right page footer.

.Ts *title*   Start a table with given caption. Tables are automatically numbered.

.Te   End a table. (Output a blank line.)

.XX *text*   Make an index entry out of *text*, with automatic addition of a page number.

.XN *text*   Make an index cross-reference out of *text* (no page number).

G

Selected Readings

The following books may be helpful either when you're starting out, or when you're ready to go on to more advanced topics.

· Introductory UNIX Texts ·

Kochan, Steven G. and Patrick H. Wood. *Exploring the UNIX System*, Hasbrouck Heights, NJ: Hayden Book Co., 1984. A comprehensive introduction to the UNIX system. (371 pp.)

Todino, Grace. *Learning the UNIX Operating System*, Newton, MA: O'Reilly and Associates, Inc., Nutshell Handbooks, 1985. A brief introduction to essential UNIX skills, designed to be read and mastered in one or two sessions. (73 pp.)

· Advanced Topics ·

Kernighan, Brian and Rob Pike. *The UNIX Programming Environment*, Englewood Cliffs, NJ: Prentice-Hall, 1984. The best introduction to the practical philosophy of UNIX programming. (240 pp.)

Kochan Steven G. and Patrick H. Wood. *UNIX Shell Programming*, Hasbrouck Heights, NJ: Hayden Book Co., 1985. A comprehensive and readable discussion of shell programming. (422 pp.)

Talbott, Steve. *Managing Projects with Make*, Newton, MA: O'Reilly and Associates Inc., Nutshell Handbooks, 1985. A concise but thorough description of the UNIX `make` utility. (63 pp.)

I N D E X

.1C macro (ms) 125-126
.2C macro (ms) 125-126

A

.AB macro (ms) 122-123
.ab request 440
absolute motions 448, 464
.ad request 71-72, 485
.AE macro (ms) 122-123
.AI macro (ms) 122-123
.AL macro (mm) 156-158
alias command 294
alphabetic lists
   mm macros 156-158
.am request 413, 534
arguments
   in macros 416
   in shell scripts 23
   to UNIX commands 13
arithmetic expressions
   in troff 419
.as request 430
.AU macro (ms) 122-123
autoincrementing number registers 428
awk 342, 387-411, 551-557
   arrays 395, 409, 589

awkronym script 390, 392-393, 396-397,
   399-400
basic operations 387
BEGIN procedures 392
built-in functions 408
capabilities of 387
changing the field separator 391
command summary 587, 589, 591
conditional statements 394
debugging 410-411
dividing input into records and fields 389
error handling in 404
for loops 393, 409
for loops with arrays 396
formatted print statement 402
invoking 388-389
passing parameters from a shell script 390
pattern matching 388, 588
scripts for order tracking 405
similarities to sed 387
subdividing a field 407, 553
substr function 557
syntax of procedures 589
system variables 392, 588
testing fields 390
used for indexing 551-557
variables 395, 589
while loops 393

B

.B macro (mm) 141-142
.B macro (ms) 114-115
.B1 macro (ms) 124
.B2 macro (ms) 124
background processing 20
backing up files 336-338
baseline spacing 98-99
.BD macro (ms) 119
.bd request 463
bdiff command 319
.BG macro (ms) 488
.BI macro (mm) 143
.BL macro (mm) 151, 154-155
boldfacing
    by overstriking 463
Bourne shell 13-14, 343-354
    background processing 20
    breaking out of a script (exit) 352
    cancelling commands 13
    CDPATH environment variable 294
    command summary 625-634
    conditional execution 347-349
    discarding and shifting arguments 349
    export command 352, 51
    HOME variable 17
    interrupting commands 13
    long command lines 22
    PATH variable 344
    prompt 13
    repetitive execution 350, 355
    resuming commands 13
    secondary prompt 22
    shell functions 630
    special characters 629
    test options 347
    variable substitution 17, 629
    variables set by .profile 630
    variables set by shell under execution 630
.bp request 86, 89-91
.BR macro (mm) 143

.br request 432, 69
bracket-building characters 466, 603
breaks
    importance of 432, 72
    no-break control character 73
    troff requests which cause 73
.BT macro ms) 492
.BX macro (ms) 123

C

C shell 13-14, 294, 343
.c2 request 435
case shell command 347-349
cat command 129, 14-15, 298
C/A/T typesetter 64, 66, 76
.cc request 435
cd command 16
.CD macro (ms) 117, 119
CDPATH environment variable 294
.ce request 80-82
.cf request 460
.ch request 503
change bars 476
change pages 507
checkeq command 251
checkmm command 154
chmod command 19, 23, 298
chown command 298
col command 86
comm command 327-328
commands
    cancelling 13
    interrupting 13
    resuming 13
comments
    in troff 412
conditional execution
    in shell scripts 347-349
    in troff 418-423
    in awk 394

constant spacing 471, 529

copy mode 417

core dumps 411

cover sheet macros 122-123, 127

cp command 17

cpio command 336-338, 340
   using with find 337-338

crypt command 335

.cs request 471

csh command 343

.cshrc file 294

csplit command 333-335

CTRL key 42

cu command 339

.cu request 83-84

cursor movement 28

customizing vi 51

cut command 328, 331

cut marks 498-499

D

.da request 433, 534

date command 13

DDL 67

.DE macro (mm) 138

.DE macro (ms) 117-120

.de request 99, 413

debugging
   in awk 410-411
   in pic 281
   in troff 436-438

deroff command 322-323

DESC file 635-636

devps postprocessor 66-67, 460

.DF macro (mm) 147-148

.di request 431, 451

dial-up line 339

diff command 312-314, 316-317, 357

diff3 command 314, 317-318

diffmk command 477

directories
   changing 16
   creating 17
   home 16
   listing contents of 16
   printing current 16
   public 339
   root 15
   sub- 15

displays
   fill options (mm) 146
   floating (mm) 147
   floating (ms) 119
   in mm macros 145-146
   in ms macros 117-120
   labels (mm) 148
   mm vs. ms 640
   static (mm) 147
   static (ms) 119

diversions 431, 451, 533, 536-538
   appending to 433
   closing 431
   creating 431
   naming by number register interpolation 538
   splitting 538
   table of contents 532
   used for footnotes 504

.DL macro (mm) 154-155

Documenter's Workbench 64

dot-matrix printers 8

drawing (see also pic preprocessor)
   boxes 123, 451
   changing line weight 454
   curves 455
   including Macintosh illustrations 460
   lines 449
   sample figures 455

.DS macro (mm) 138, 145-146

.DS macro (ms) 117-120

.ds request 101, 429

E

.EC macro (mm) 133, 148-150
.ec request 435
echo command 14
.EF macro (mm) 133
egrep command 303
.EH macro (mm) 133
.el request 418-423
elif shell command 348
em (defined) 76
em dash 364
.em request 534
emacs editor 5, 24
en (defined) 76
end macro 534-536
environment variables
   EXINIT 51
   HOME 17
   PATH 344
   path 345
   setting 20-21
   TERM 20
environments 433, 529
.eo request 435
eqn preprocessor 86, 232-252
   abbreviating a string 247
   arrays 244
   braces and brackets 243
   diacritical marks 232, 246
   displayed equations 234
   fonts 232, 249
   fractions 244
   Greek alphabet 232, 239
   grouping items 250
   horizontal spacing 232
   inline expressions 235
   integrals 242
   invoking 233
   limits 242
   lining up equations 248
   matrices 244
   point sizes 232, 249
   precedence of operations 250, 621

   problem checklist 251
   problems with .so request 480
   quotation marks 237, 242, 248
   simple example 233
   spaces in equations 236
   special character names 232, 239, 241
   square root signs 242
   subscripts 237-238
   summary of command characters 618-621
   summations 242
   superscripts 237-238
   syntax 233
   tabs within equations 237
   using braces for grouping 238
   using mm with 235
   using nroff with 234
   using tbl with 205, 234
   vertical piles (columns) 245
   vertical spacing 232, 250
errors
   in mm 130
   in ms 105
   in troff macros 439
   messages from UNIX commands 14
escape sequences
   in troff 443-444
.ev request 433
ex editor 177-202, 342-346, 355-357
   @ functions 201
   : prompt 27
   abbreviating recurring phrases 198
   address symbols 579
   appending to existing file 191
   command mode 179
   command summary 578-584
   confirming replacements 182
   copying lines 180
   creating a subshell 192
   current line 178
   deleting lines 180
   differences from sed 361
   editing multiple files 195
   executing from vi 180, 27
   executing UNIX commands from 192

`EXINIT` variable 51
exiting 190, 578
`.exrc` file 50, 52
filtering text through a UNIX command 193
global search and replace 183, 186
insert mode 179
invoking 178, 578
leaving insert mode 179
limiting search to complete words 186
line addressing in 181, 579
mapping commands to keys 198, 200
moving lines 180
moving text blocks by patterns 187
pattern matching 184, 188
printing line(s) 178
quitting without saving edits 191
range of lines 179
reading in a file 192
reading in result of UNIX command 192
renaming the buffer 191
saving files 190
saving part of a file 191
scripts 342-346, 355-357
search and replace 181-182
search for general classes of words 186
substitute command 179-181
switching files 196
syntax of commands 178, 342
using current and alternate filenames 197
yanking text from one file to another 197
`.EX` macro (mm) 133, 148-150, 169-170
`.ex` request 478
ex scripts 354-355
    built by `diff` 357
    executing with `:so` 354
`EXINIT` variable 51
`exit` shell command 352
`export` command 51
`expr` command 388
expression operators
    in `awk` 393
    in `pic` 625
    in `troff` 420

`.exrc` file 50, 52
extended `ms` macros 509-541, 643-645
    chapter headings 514, 518-519
    drawing horizontal lines 518
    figure numbering 523
    headers and footers 522
    invoking 511
    lists 525-528
    notes 530-531
    numbered headings 520
    section headings 521-522
    structure of 511
    summary of 643-645
    table numbering 523
    table of contents 532

F

`.FC` macro (mm) 133
`.fc` request 469
`.FD` macro (mm) 132, 171
`.FE` macro (mm) 170-171
`.FE` macro (ms) 124-125
`.FG` macro (mm) 148-150, 169-170
`fgrep` command 303
`.fi` request 69
fields
    in `awk` 389-392
    in `cut` and `paste` 328
    in `sort` 325-326
    in `troff` 469
file management 3
file system 15
files
    backing up 336-338
    characteristics 298
    copying 17
    counting characters in 21
    date and time last modified 298
    editing multiple 195
    locating 296
    metacharacters 13, 19, 295, 627
    moving 17

naming restrictions 25
organizing 293
permissions 18-19, 298
renaming 17
searching within (see also `grep`) 301
size in bytes 298
tracking changes to (SCCS) 319
transferring to other systems 340
viewing contents 298
filling (definition of) 60
filters 21-22, 298, 360
final book production 562
`find` command 296-298, 302
    using with `cpio` 337-338
`.fl` request 127, 438, 491
flushing output buffer (see `.fl`)
`.FO` macro 490, 492
fonts 62, 66
    boldfacing by overstriking 463
    changing 92-94
    changing (`eqn`) 249
    changing (`ms`) 114-115
    changing (`tbl`) 216
    constant width 471, 529
    contents of font files 66, 635-639
    downloadable 66
    four standard 64
    mounted 92, 636
    special 64, 96
footers 126, 133, 493
footnotes 500-501, 641
    mm macros 170-171
    ms macros 124-125
`for` shell command 355
form letters 477
`format` shell script 364-365, 369, 539, 542, 545, 559
formatting
    with a markup language 6
    with a word processor 6
formatting defaults
    mm (see also mm macros) 130
    ms (see also ms macros) 106

`.fp` request 92, 95
`.FS` macro (mm) 170-171
`.FS` macro (ms) 124-125
`.ft` request 92, 95
function keys (mapping) 199

G

`getopt` command 349
graphics (see also `pic` preprocessor) 253
Greek characters 232, 239, 604
`grep` command 22, 301-302
    using with `find` 302

H

`.H` macro (mm) 162-166
hanging indents 79-80, 110-111
`head` command 300
headers 126, 133, 493
headings
    in extended ms 514-522
    in mm 160-168
    in ms 120-122
    in wide margin 522
here documents 357
`.HM` macro (mm) 167-168
home directory 16
HOME variable 17
`.HU` macro (mm) 162-166
`.hw` request 73-74
`.hy` request 74-75, 485
`hyphen` command 307, 74
hyphenation 61
    checking for correctness 74
    enabling in `troff` 74
    in mm 101, 137
    rules for 73

I

.I macro (mm) 141-142
.I macro (ms) 114-115
.IB macro (mm) 143
.ID macro (ms) 117, 119
.ie request 418-423
.if request 418-423
if shell command 347-349
.ig request 438
.in request 79
indents 79-80, 135
indexing 540, 548
    adding formatting codes 555
    building the page number list 551
    final formatting codes 557
    form of user entries 548
    sorting raw entries 549
    special formatting problems 558
    subordinating secondary entries 553
integrals (see eqn) 242
Interpress 67
interrupted lines (in troff 423

inverse conditions 423
.IP macro 527
.IP macro (ms) 106, 110-113
.IR macro (mm) 143
.IZ macro 486

J

join command 325-327
justification 60, 73, 137
    definition of 60
    mm macros 137
    ms macros 107
    nroff vs. troff 61
    types of 71-72

K

.KE macro (ms) 120
keep and release (see also displays) 120, 431
Kernighan and Pike
    UNIX Programming Environment 11, 395
kerning 61
.KS macro (ms) 120

L

laser printers 9
.lc request 468
.LD macro (ms) 117, 119
.LE macro (mm) 151-152
leaders 468-469
leading 98
letter-quality printers 8
.LG macro (ms) 116-117
.lg request 474-475
.LI macro (mm) 151-152
ligatures 473, 475, 522
line numbers (in vi) 47
lists
    alphabetic (mm) 156-158
    alphabetic (mS) 525-526
    bulleted (mS) 525-526
    extended in mS 525, 528
    in ms 113
    marked (mm) 154
    mm macros 150-151
    mm vs. ms 640
    nested (mm) 153
    nested (mS) 525-526
    numbered (mm) 156-158
    numbered (mS) 525-526
    reference (mm) 158
    user-supplied marks (mm) 156
    variable-item (mm) 158, 161-162
.ll request 78, 485
local horizontal motions 447

local vertical motions 445
.login file 343
lp command 129
.LP macro (ms) 106-107, 121
ls command 13, 16
.ls request 86, 99
.lt request 495

M

Macintosh
    illustrations 460
    word processing on 9
macros (see also mm and ms)
    appending to 413
    arguments 416
    comparing mm and ms 640-642
    copy mode in 417
    defining 127, 173, 413
    developing a package 481
    initializing 486
    listing existing names 414
    naming conventions 414
    nested 418
    new or extended? 482
    page transition 489
    removing 413
    renaming 415
    reset 487
    setting default values 485
    structure of package 481, 483
    style 441, 522
    tabs and leaders in 470
    /usr/lib/tmac 483
mail command 21
make command 320-321
    coordinating final book production with 562
    building makefile with a shell script 566
makedev command 637
man macros 88
mapping function keys 199

marking a horizontal position 464
marking a position
    in troff 461
    in vi 57
.MC macro (ms) 125-126
.mc request 476
me macros 88, 104
.mk request 461, 505
mkdir command 17
.ML macro (mm) 154, 156
mm command 129
mm macros 88
    .AL macro 156-158
    alphabetic lists 156-158
    altering heading style 164-168
    .B macro 141-142
    .BI macro 143
    .BL macro 151, 154-155
    bold font 141
    bottom-of-page processing 176
    .BR macro 143
    changing fonts 141
    changing point sizes 143-144
    changing reference defaults 172
    changing the heading mark 167-168
    compared to ms 640-642
    .DE macro 138
    default formatting 130
    .DF macro 147-148
    display fill options 146
    display formatting options 145
    display labels 148
    displays 138, 145-146, 148
    .DL macro 154-155
    .DS macro 138, 145-146
    .EC macro 133, 148-150
    .EF macro 133
    .EH macro 133
    errors 130
    .EX macro 133, 148-150, 169-170
    extensions to 173
    .FC macro 133
    .FD macro 132, 171
    .FE macro 170-171

.FG macro 148-150, 169-170
floating displays 147
footers 133
footnotes 170-171
.FS macro 170-171
.H macro 162-166
headers 133
heading number registers 165
heading strings 165
headings 165, 176
.HM macro 167-168
.HU macro 162-166
hyphenation 101, 137
.I macro 141-142
.IB macro 143
indented paragraphs 135
invoking 129
.IR macro 143
italic font 141
justification 137
.LE macro 151-152
.LI macro 151-152
lists 150-156
marked lists 154
.ML macro 154, 156
modifying 173
nested lists 153
number registers 174
numbered headings 162-166
numbered lists 156-158
.P macro 135-136
page break 150
page layout 132, 134
page numbering styles 132
page transition 91, 176
paragraphs 135
paragraphs indented with exceptions 136
.PF macro 133
.PH macro 133
predefined string names 612
.R macro 141-142
.RB macro 143
reference lists 158
references 171-172

reserved macro and string names 615
.RF macro 171-172
.RI macro 143
.RL macro 158
roman font 141
.RP macro 132, 172-173
.RS macro 171-172
.S macro 143-144
.SA macro 137
.SK macro 150
.SM macro 144-145
.SP macro 136-137
spacing between paragraphs 136
static displays 147
strings 175
summary of macros 608-613
summary of number registers 613
table of contents 168-170, 176
.TB macro 133, 169-170
.TC macro 168
top-of-page processing 176
unnumbered headings 162-166
user exit 176
user-supplied list marks 156
variable-item lists 158, 161-162
vertical margins 176
vertical spacing 136-137, 143-144
.VL macro 158, 161-162
mmt command 129
modem 339
more command 129, 298
mptx macros 88
mS macros (see extended ms macros)
ms macros 104-127
.1C macro 125
.AB macro 122
.AE macro 122
.AI macro 122
.AU macro 122
.B macro 114-115
.B1 macro 124
.B2 macro 124
.BD macro 119
.BG macro 488

.BT macro 492
.BX macro 123
.CD macro 117, 119
changing bottom margin 508
compared to mm 640-642
date string 126
.DE macro 117-120
displays 117-118
drawing a box 123
.DS macro 117-120
error handling 105
extensions to (see extended ms macros)
.FE macro 124-125
.FO macro 490, 492
fonts 114-115
footers 126, 493
footnotes 124-125, 500
.FS macro 124-125
headers 126, 493
headings 120-122
.I macro 114-115
.ID macro 117, 119
indented paragraphs 110
initialization sequence 486
internal macros 606
internal number register names 606
invoking 105
.IP macro 106, 110-113, 527
.KE macro 120
.KS macro 120
labeled item lists 110
.LD macro 117, 119
.LG macro 116-117
.LP macro 106-107, 121
.MC macro 125-126
multi-column processing 125-126, 505-506
.NH macro 120-122, 520
.NL macro 116-117
.NP macro 127, 490, 492
numbered lists 113
number register default values 485
page layout 106, 606
page layout defaults 106
page size 495

page transition 91, 483-508
paragraphs 106-110
point size 116-117
.PP macro 106-107, 121
predefined and user-definable strings 607
problems on first page 127
.PT macro 492
.QE macro 110
.QP macro 106-107, 110
.QS macro 110
quoted paragraphs 107
.R macro 114-115
.RE macro 111
redefining header or footer 494
reserved macro and string names 607
reset macro 106, 487-488
.RS macro 111
.RT macro 106, 487-488
.SH macro 120-122
.SM macro 116-117
spacing between paragraphs 107
summary of macros 604-606
.TL macro 122-123
two-column processing 125-126, 505
.UL macro 116
underlining 116
vertical spacing 107
multi-column processing 125-126, 505-506
mv command 17

N

.na request 71
.ne request 90, 508
.nf request 69
.NH macro (ms) 120-122, 520
.NL macro (ms) 116-117
.nm request 475
.nn request 476
no-break control character 73
no-fill mode 60, 69, 83, 146

no-space mode 490, 519

notes, cautions and warnings 530-531

.NP macro (ms) 127, 490, 492

.nr request 101, 419-424

nroff formatter (see also troff)

    command line options 593, 63

    default line length 78

    device units 76

    inability to use pic with 253

    interword spacing 62

    invoking 593, 63

    sample output from 68

    submitting documents coded for troff 67

    summary of requests 594-598

    units of measure 76

    using eqn with 234

.ns request 127, 490, 90-91

number registers 100-101, 419-425, 485, 526, 529

    altering output format 428

    as global variables 425

    as nested list counter 526

    autoincrementing 428, 526

    finding names of existing 415

    in ms 100

    interpolating 424

    mm 174

    ms default values 485

    naming 424

    naming by interpolation 526

    predefined 426

    read-only 427

    removing 429

    scaled units 424

    setting default values with 485

    setting from command line 101

    substituting for environment switch 529

    used as flags 425

    used to generalize macros 425

numbered headings 514

numbered lists

    mm macros 156-158

    mS macros 525-528

.nx request 478

O

options to UNIX commands 13

.os request 90-91

output redirection 14-15, 21, 298

    appending to a file 15

overstriking 462, 465

P

.P macro (mm) 135-136

pack command 338

page breaks 508

    mm macros 150

    without line breaks 89

page description languages 67

page layout 492

    in mm 132, 134

    in ms 106

page number

    in mm 130, 132-133

    in three-part titles 494

    setting from command line 133

page offset 78, 485, 523

page size 495

page top resets 507

page transition 91, 176, 483-508

paragraphs

    indented (mm) 135

    indented (ms) 110

    indented with exceptions (mm) 136

    mm macros 135

    ms macros 106

    quoted (ms) 107

    spacing between (mm) 136

    spacing between (ms) 107

paste command 328, 331

PATH variable 344

pathname 16
.pc request 494
pcat command 338
.PF macro (mm) 133
pg command 129, 298-299
    help screens 299
.PH macro (mm) 133
pic preprocessor 253-292, 531
    adjusting drawing motion 260
    adjusting label placement 257
    arc 263, 283
    arrow 262
    as a programming language 281, 291
    automatic scaling 279
    basic figures (graphics primitives) 255
    changing direction of drawing 260
    controlling the dimensions of a drawing 279
    copy facility 289
    debugging 281
    declarations 622
    default dimensions of standard objects 278
    defining macros 285, 624
    defining object blocks 276, 624
    delimiters 622
    describing single objects 255
    diagonal lines 262
    dimension variables 278
    double-headed arrow 267
    drawing in clockwise direction 263
    drawing motion 258
    enhancements to 291
    executing UNIX commands from 291
    expressions 284, 626
    for loops 291
    functions 284
    height of object 256
    if conditional statements 291
    inability to use with nroff 253
    invisible reference object 268
    labeling objects 257, 624
    language of 253
    leaving space between objects 259
    library of frequently used objects 289
    line 257

locating objects using Cartesian coordinates 282
locating specific points 266
macros 289-290
movement from a referenced object 265
naming an object 273
place and position notations 272
placing objects 264
placing text in a drawing 270, 274
positioning object blocks 277, 625
problems with .so request 480
programming drawings 281
reading description from remote file 289
redefining standard dimensions 278
relational operators for if statements 292
reusing dimensions 256
scaling 282
specifying dimensions 255
specifying size of graphics primitives 255
spline 263
spline 283
start and end macros 253
start and end of an object 261, 267
summary of graphics primitives 622
turning a corner 266
typical figure description 254
units of measure 255
use of object blocks 277
used with troff 253, 257
user-defined variables 285
using bit-mapped input 292
pica (defined) 76
pipes 21-22
.pl request 86, 88, 496
.pm request 414
.pn request 91
.po request 78, 485
point size 62, 76, 97-98, 116-117
    changing (eqn) 249
    changing (mm) 143-144
    changing (ms) 116-117
    changing (tbl) 216

postprocessors 460
PostScript 67, 460, 474
.PP macro (ms) 106-107, 121
pr command 299
predefined conditions
   in troff 419
printers (types of) 8-9
problems on first page (ms) 127
.profile 343
proof shell script 304, 380-386
proofreading
   double awk script 395
   shell script for 380-386
.ps request 97, 99
pseudo-page transition 491
.PT macro (ms) 492
pwd command 16

Q

.QE macro (ms) 110
.QP macro (ms) 106-107, 110
.QS macro (ms) 110

R

.R macro (mm) 141-142
.R macro (ms) 114-115
.RB macro (mm) 143
.rd request 477
.RE macro (ms) 111
read shell command 400
recommended readings 646
records (in awk) 389
redefining control and escape characters 435
reference lists (mm macros) 158
regular expressions 184-188, 568
reset macro 106, 487
returning to a horizontal position 464
returning to a marked position
   in troff 461
   in vi 57

.RF macro (mm) 171-172
.RI macro (mm) 143
.RL macro (mm) 158
.rm request 413, 511
.rn request 415, 512
root directory 15
.RP macro (mm) 132, 172-173
.RS macro (mm) 171-172
.RS macro (ms) 111
.rs request 90, 127, 490
.RT macro (ms) 106, 487
.rt request 461, 505

S

.S macro (mm) 143-144
.SA macro (mm) 137
SCCS (Source Code Control System) 319
script command 341
scrolling 4, 42-43
sdiff command 312, 315-316, 318-319
search (see also grep) 22, 45, 181, 301
search path 344
section headings 512, 521
sed editor 5, 342, 360-380, 585-587
   addressing 361-362, 585
   branching to parts of script 366, 369
   command summary 585-587
   command syntax 360, 584
   differences from ex 361
   excluding lines from editing 365-366
   hold space 375-379
   in format script 364
   inserting lines of text 369
   invoking 360-361, 584
   matching patterns across 2 lines 374-379
   pattern space 375-379
   print command 370
   quit command 373
   script for extracting information from a file
      370
   substitute command 363
   used in for loop 363

used in indexing script 557-558
set command 20
sh command 343
.SH macro (ms) 120-122
shell scripts 23, 343-346, 354
    breaking out of 352
    conditional execution 347-349
    discarding and shifting arguments 349
    looping 355
    number of arguments ($#) 350
    repetitive execution 350, 355
    arguments to 23
    C shell search path 345
    definition of 343
    export command 352
    initializing variables 352
    making executable 344
    passing arguments to 345-346
    proofreading script 380, 386
    putting in path 344
    reading data interactively 400
    setting default values 352
    test command in 347-349
shift shell command 349
.SK macro (mm) 150
.SM macro (mm) 144-145
.SM macro (ms) 116-117
.so request 103, 438, 479, 484
soelim command 480
sort command 22, 323, 325, 549
.SP macro (mm) 136-137
.sp request 73, 84-85
space at top of page 490
spell command 296, 304, 380
split command 333
SQtroff 439
square root signs (see eqn)
.ss request 471-472
standard error 14, 538
standard input 21
standard output 14, 21
strings
    appending to 430
    comparing 421

    defining 429
    in troff 101
    interpolating 102, 430
    mm 175
    multiline 102
    naming 430
subdirectory 15
subscripts (see also eqn) 237
superscripts (see also eqn) 237, 446
super-user 298
.sv request 90-91
.sy request 480, 539

T

.ta request 467, 82-83
table of contents 532, 544
    created by diversion 532, 536
    mm macros 168-170
    written to standard error 532, 538
tabs (in troff) 82-83, 467
tail command 300
tar command 341
.TB macro (mm) 133, 169-170
tbl preprocessor 203-231
    alphabetic data columns 212
    breaking up long tables 224
    changing format within table 219
    column format options 209, 617
    column width 217, 219
    complex table example 227
    data 205-206, 618
    describing column formats 209
    drawing lines within tables 214
    equations within tables 212
    fonts 216
    format options 205-207
    global format options 205-208, 616
    headers 210
    horizontally spanning headers 211
    invoking 204
    numeric data columns 212
    point sizes 216

problems with `.so` request 480
putting text blocks in a column 221
repeating table headers 224
simple table example 206
spacing within tables 211
staggered columns 218
summary of commands 616-618
table end macro 205
table formatting checklist 226
table specifications 204
table start macro 205
titling tables 225
using `eqn` with 205, 234
vertical spacing within data blocks 218
vertically spanned columns 213
`.TC` macro (mm) 168
`.tc` request 469
`TERM` variable 20, 27
terminal messages from `troff` 438, 440
terminal type 20, 27, 33
`test` command 347-349
`.ti` request 79
`tip` command 339
title length 495
`.TL` macro (ms) 122-123
`.tl` request 493
`.tm` request 438, 440, 502, 532, 539
`tplus` postprocessor 471
`tr` command 332
`.tr` request 436, 473-474
transparent output 460, 534
traps 89, 485, 489, 491-492, 495, 503
`troff` formatter 58-103, 412-480
    `.ab` request 440
    aborting 440
    absolute motions 448, 464
    `.ad` request 485, 71-72
    adjusting title length 495
    aligning numeric data 83
    `.am` request 413
    appending to a diversion 433
    appending to a macro 413
    appending to a string 430
    arithmetic expressions 419

`.as` request 430
autoincrementing number registers 428
basic assumptions 59
`.bd` request 463
boldfacing fonts by overstriking 463
`.bp` request 86, 89-91
`.br` request 432, 69
bracket-building characters 466, 602
`.c2` request 435
`.cc` request 435
`.ce` request 80-82
`.cf` request 460
`.ch` request 503
change bars 476
changing page size 495
character output translations 473
command line options 594
comments 412
comparing strings 421
compiling font files 638
conditional execution 418
constant spacing 471
copy mode 417
`.cs` request 471
`.cu` request 83-84
cut marks 498-499
`.da` request 433, 534
`.de` request 413, 99
debugging 436-438
default units 77
defining macros 413, 87, 99
defining strings 429
device units 76
`.di` request 431, 451
diversions 451
double or triple spacing 86
downloadable fonts 66
drawing 449-455
`.ds` request 101, 429
`.ec` request 435
`.el` request 418-423
`.em` request 534
environment switching 433
`.eo` request 435

error handling 439

escape sequences 67, 444, 598-599

.ev request 433

.ex request 478

executing system commands from 480

expression operators 420

.fc request 469

.fi request 69

fields 469

.fl request 127, 438, 491

flushing output buffer 438

fonts 65, 92-93

footnotes 500-501

form letters 477

.fp request 92, 95

.ft request 92, 95

Greek characters 604

headers and footers 493

horizontal spacing 76

.hw request 73-74

.hy request 74-75, 485

hyphenation 73-75, 485

.ie request 418-423

.if request 418-423

.ig request 438

ignoring input 438

.in request 79

including Macintosh illustrations 460

interactive use 437

interrupted lines 423

interword spacing 62

inverse conditions 423

invoking 66, 594

justification using mm 137

keeping text block together 431

.lc request 468

leaders 468-469

.lg request 474-475

ligatures 473, 475

line drawing 449

line weight 454

.ll request 78, 485

local horizontal motions 447

local vertical motions 445

.ls request 86, 99

.lt request 495

macro arguments 100, 416

macro names 414

macro style 441

marking a horizontal position 464

marking a vertical position 461

mathematic symbols 602

.mc request 476

.mk request 461, 505

multi-column processing 461, 505-506

multiline conditions 421

.na request 71

names of existing macros 414

names of existing number registers 415

.ne request 508, 90

negative vertical motions 85

nested macros 418

.nf request 69

.nm request 475

.nn request 476

.nr request 101, 424

.ns request 127, 490, 90-91

number registers 100-101, 419-425, 485, 526, 529

numeric expressions 77

.nx request 478

.os request 90-91

output line numbering 475

overstriking 462, 465

page breaks 508

page breaks without line breaks 89

page layout 75, 492

page length 86, 88

page numbering 91

page numbers 494

page offset 523

page top resets 507

page transition 86-87, 483-508

.pc request 494

.pl request 496, 86, 88

.pm request 414

.pn request 91

.po request 485, 78

point size 65, 97-98

postprocessors 460, 66-67

predefined conditions 419

predefined number register names 426, 599-
     600

`.ps` request 97, 99

pseudo-page transition 491

`.rd` request 477

reading standard input 477

read-only number registers 427, 599

redefining control and escape characters 435

removing macros 413

removing number registers 429

renaming macros 415

returning to a horizontal position 464

returning to a vertical position 461

`.rm` request 413, 511

`.rn` request 415, 512

`.rs` request 127, 490, 90

`.rt` request 461, 505

selecting output pages from command line
     92

setting page number from command line 91

`.so` request 103, 438, 479, 484

`.sp` request 73, 84-85

space at top of page 490

space size 472

spacing to an absolute position 85

special characters 96, 602-604

`.ss` request 471-472

stacking up characters 466

summary of requests 594-598

superscripts 446

suspending line numbering 476

`.sv` request 90-91

`.sy` request 480

syntax of requests 67

`.ta` request 82-83, 467

tabs and leaders 467

tabs in macros 470

`.tc` request 469

terminal messages 438

three-part titles 494

`.ti` request 79

`.tl` request 493

`.tm` request 438, 440, 502, 532

`.tr` request 436, 473-474

transparent output 460

traps 87, 485, 489, 491-492, 495, 503

two-column processing 461

`.ul` request 83-84

underlining 449-450

units of measure 76-77

used with laser printers 9

using with ms 105

using pic with 253, 257

versions of 64, 66

vertical spacing 65, 76, 84, 98

vertically stacked labels 467

`.vs` request 98-99

`.wh` request 485, 489, 503, 87

widows and orphans 508

width function 464

two-column processing,
     ms macros 125-126
     simple macro for 505-506

U

`.UL` macro (ms) 116

`.ul` request 83-84

underlining 115
     in troff 449-450
     ms macros 116

uniq command 323, 325

UNIX
     syntax of commands 13
     system fundamentals 12
     version used for this book 12

unpack command 338

unpaddable space 112-113, 474, 73

user exit macros (mm) 176

/usr/lib/font 63, 65, 93, 635-639
     DESC file 635-637
     font description files 637-638

/usr/lib/tmac 103
uucp command 339
uuname command 339

V

variable-item lists
    mm macros 158, 161-162
vertical spacing 76, 84, 98, 107, 136, 143
vertically stacked labels 467
vi editor 24-54, 177-202
    abbreviations 198
    alternative insert commands 54
    append text 54
    appending text 54
    appending to named buffers 56
    changing text 34-35
    characters not used in command mode 574
    command line options 49
    command mode 27
    command summary 572, 578
    command syntax 27, 571
    copying text 39, 54
    current and alternate filenames 197
    cursor movement 28, 30
    cursor movement by line numbers 47
    cursor movement by text blocks 44
    cursor movement with numeric argument 45
    cursor movement within lines 44
    cursor movement within screen 43
    deleting single characters 37-38
    deleting text 32, 35-37
    displaying line numbers 31, 48
    editing multiple files 195
    errors when opening 27
    ex commands in (see also ex) 180
    filtering text through a UNIX command 193
    ignoring case during searches 51
    insert mode 24, 27
    inserting text 27, 32
    joining lines 41
    leaving insert mode 27, 33
    mapping command sequences 198

    marking place in file 57
    movement by line number 48
    moving by screenfuls 42
    moving cursor by single lines 30
    moving cursor by spaces 30
    moving cursor by text blocks 31
    moving text 32, 38, 54
    named buffers 55-56
    numbered buffers 54-55
    numeric arguments to commands 30
    numeric prefixes to commands 53
    on a dumb terminal 33, 37
    opening a file 25-26
    opening a file to a specific place 49
    opening a new line for insertion 54
    pattern matching characters 222
    prompt line 26
    quitting 27
    quitting without saving edits 41
    read-only mode 50
    recovering a buffer 50
    recovering deletions 55
    repeat last search 46
    repeating last command 40
    replacing characters 35, 54
    returning to a position 48
    saving a file 28
    screen lines vs. logical lines 30
    scrolling 42-43
    search for pattern 45-47
    search options 53
    search within current line 47
    setting options 50-51, 53, 574
    shiftwidth 53
    showing contents of numbered buffers 55
    size of window 51
    status line 572
    summary of options 570
    undoing last change 40, 55
    view mode 50
    wrapmargin 28, 53
view command (see vi editor) 50

`.VL` macro (mm) 158, 161-162
`.vs` request 98-99

W

`wc` command 21
`.wh` request 485, 489, 503, 87
`while` shell command 350
`who` command 22
widows and orphans 508
width function 464
word processors
    characteristics of 2-5
    command mode vs. insert mode 4
    influence on writing process 1-2
    limitations of 3, 7
    vs. text editors 3
Writer's Workbench 308
    analyze style/readability (`style`) 308
    explain `diction` errors (`explain`) 311
    miscellaneous programs 311
    search for poor phrasing (`diction`) 309
wysiwyg defined 6

X

`xargs` command 303